Microeconomics
Individual Choice and Its Consequences
Second Edition

Microeconomics
Individual Choice and Its Consequences
Second Edition

Neil T. Skaggs

J. Lon Carlson

First published 1996

Blackwell Publishers, Inc.
238 Main Street
Cambridge, Massachusetts 02142

Blackwell Publishers Ltd.
108 Cowley Road
Oxford OX4 1JF
UK

Library of Congress Cataloging-in-Publication Data
Skaggs, Neil T. (Neil Thomas). 1953–
    Microeconomics / Neil T. Skaggs. J. Lon Carlson. --2nd ed.
        p. cm.
    Rev. ed. of the "Microeconomics" section of: Economics / Alan E. Dillingham. c1992.
        Includes bibliographical references and index.
        ISBN 1-55786-926-X (pb)
        1. Microeconomics.   I. Carlson, J. Lon.   II. Dillingham, Alan E. Economics.   III. Title.
    HB172-S567   1996
    338.5--dc20   96-4125
                                                                 CIP

British Library Cataloguing in Publication Data

A CIP catalogue record for this book is available from the British Library.

Commissioning Editor: Rolf Janke
Production Manager: Jan Leahy
Text Design: Benchmark Productions, Inc.
Typesetting: Benchmark Productions, Inc.

Typeset in Bodoni on 11 pt. by Benchmark Productions, Inc.

Printed in the United States of America

This book is printed on acid-free paper

To Barb and the girls, Caroline, Becky Jo, Meridith, and Lindsey, for sharing me with "the book."

To Brenda, for all her patience, encouragement, and support.

Preface

Unlike macroeconomic theory, which has undergone significant changes in recent years, the fundamental elements of microeconomic theory have gone unchanged. This characteristic of microeconomic theory has both a good and a bad side. On the one hand, there is a fair amount of agreement on basic issues. On the other hand, insofar as the theory is concerned, there is little to distinguish one text from another.

Because the basic principles of microeconomics are well established, the content of *Microeconomics: Individual Choice and Its Consequences*, *Second Edition* is similar to that of other texts. However, we believe that we have improved on the standard approach in several ways. A central theme of *Microeconomics* is purposeful decision making in the face of constraints. We emphasize this theme throughout the text. The theory of consumer behavior repeatedly emphasizes the effect of the budget constraint on the individual's efforts to maximize the benefits from consumption. In a similar manner, the production decisions of firms are constrained by the consumers' willingness to pay and the firm's production costs. In resource markets, wages are constrained by the interaction of supply and demand.

Microeconomics is also distinguished from other texts by its organization. In particular, the section on market structures and the behavior of the firm is organized to help students more readily retain the basic concepts. We present the basic principles of production cost theory and profit maximization that are independent of the market in which a firm operates before developing the individual market structures. Students thus see that the profit-maximizing condition does not depend on market structure.

The content of *Microeconomics* also differs from other texts in its treatment of regulation and deregulation. The presentation is balanced, giving attention both to the theory and practice of regulation and to the continuing trend to deregulation. The deregulation section is filled with examples that illustrate the successes and failures of deregulation.

Our experience with the first edition, and in particular, the reactions we received from adopters confirmed in our minds that this is a solid approach to microeconomics at the principles level. Thus, we have continued it in the second edition and, where appropriate, have extended it.

Goals of Microeconomics

The first edition of *Microeconomics* was innovative in both content and pedagogy. All the major features of the first edition discussed in this section have been carried over into the second edition.

Content

The content of a textbook encompasses the topics covered, the order of the discussion, and the emphasis placed on the various topics. The content of *Microeconomics* is innovative on all three scores. *Microeconomics* provides a careful analysis of the decision-making process of consumers, firms, and resource demanders and suppliers, as well as selected topics, such as income distribution and environmental quality, that are critically important to society's well being. The order of our discussion is designed to be logical and to emphasize what we believe are the fundamental concepts relevant to an understanding of basic microeconomic issues.

Part I: Basic Economic Principles Chapters 1 through 5 provide students with all the tools needed to assemble and use the microeconomic model. The distinct approach of *Microeconomics* emerges in Chapter 2, in which students encounter a discussion of the gains from trade and the principle of comparative advantage, using examples ranging from simple individual exchanges to international trade. This provides a solid foundation for the theories of demand and supply. All the basic elements of demand and supply analysis, including the basis of supply in marginal cost, are covered in Chapter 3. In Chapter 4 we present an extended discussion of efficiency under conditions of perfect competition in order to highlight the importance of economic efficiency in all economic decision and policy making. We close Part I with a discussion of how and why market outcomes can fail to be efficient and of the possibility of government intervention to improve efficiency or to achieve other goals. Instructors who prefer to omit Chapters 4 and 5 can do so without loss of continuity.

Part II: The Basic Economic Model In Part II, the innovations in content and pedagogical technique show through clearly. We develop the theory of consumer behavior by building on a set of basic assumptions and then using these assumptions to predict the consumer's response to a change in relative prices. Most notably, the theory of consumer behavior does not rely on such concepts as the law of diminishing marginal utility or cardinal utility to develop the consumers' decision rule. Rather, we present an approach to the subject that is consistent with modern theory.

The theory of the firm is organized around the concepts of price-taking and price-searching firms. The model of a perfectly competitive market provides a benchmark against which more common market structures can be judged. Unlike the traditional approach, which emphasizes the differences among the three types of price-searching firms: monopolistic competitors, oligopolists, and monopolists, we emphasize the effects of the size of the price-searching firms relative to the market. Consequently, monopoly and oligopoly are presented in a single chapter to emphasize the similarities of the behavior of firms in these types of markets. The contrast between the behavior of price-taking and price-searching firms is carried through to the discussion price determination in resource markets.

Part III: Factor Markets The analysis of the behavior of factor markets begins with an overview of the determinants of resource demand and the determination of equilibrium price and quantity in competitive resource markets. Subsequent chapters examine the labor market in greater detail, including a separate chapter on the effects of unions in labor markets. A separate chapter is also devoted to the capital market.

Part IV: Applications of the Microeconomic Model This section of the text uses the basic principles of microeconomic theory developed in the preceding chapters to explore the issues of income distribution and poverty (Chapter 19) and the problems associated with externalities, public goods, and common property resources (Chapter 20). Attention is devoted to both the outcomes that can arise in the absence of intervention in the market, and policies that can be employed to address these issues.

Pedagogy

Content and pedagogy go hand-in-hand. In the first edition, we sought to present microeconomics in a way that

1. highlights the core of economic reasoning – constrained decision making.

2. shows how all areas of economics are related.

3. leads students to understand the basic methods of economists by practicing them repeatedly.

4. applies economic theories to real-world events to show students the relevance of economics.

5. focuses on the process of change – which goes on continually around us – rather than solely on the position of equilibria.

In doing this, we sought to repeatedly use relatively few fundamental principles so as not to overwhelm students with theoretical tools, to draw on the students' own experiences, and to be logically ordered. We continue these emphases in the second edition.

By focusing on microeconomic decision-making throughout the text, we are able to accomplish our first two goals.

With regard to economic methods, we continue to practice rather than preach by demonstrating how economists approach their subject.

1. The assumptions of theories are made explicit.

2. Model construction proceeds logically.

3. Models sufficient to analyze specific issues, e.g., the impacts of minimum-wage legislation, are constructed before the issue is discussed.

The first edition had a "real-world" flavor because of all the examples appearing throughout the text. In addition to extended applications of theory to the real world in the body of the text, we include in each chapter *Why the Disagreement?* and *Does It Make Economic Sense?* boxes in which we consider issues of interest to economists and noneconomists alike. Finally, since we live in a dynamic world, we spend a lot of time discussing how the economy gets from one static equilibrium point to another. How people act when confronted with changed circumstances is the focus of many discussions.

New Features of the Second Edition

While the basic framework of *Microeconomics* has not changed, the second edition goes beyond the first in a number of ways to more fully implement our philosophy. Major changes to the second edition include the following:

1. A complete overhaul of Chapter 7: The Theory of Consumer Behavior. Although the law of diminishing marginal utility and the notion of cardinally measurable utility have long been dismissed by microeconomists, both continue to appear in principles texts on a regular basis. In the second edition, we have chosen to discard this traditional approach to the introduction of the theory of consumer behavior. Instead, the chapter presents a largely intuitive discussion of the theory of utility maximization, focusing on

   • the assumptions that underlie the theory of utility maximization, i.e., nonsatiation, the substitution principle, and a declining marginal rate of substitution between two goods,

   • the rule for utility maximization emphasizing the concept of exchange value,

   • the substitution and income effects as explanations of downward-sloping demand curves, and

   • a "stand alone" presentation of the theory of utility maximization based on the concepts of indifference curves and a budget constraint (this is the appendix material in the first edition of Chapter 7).

   The new appendix presents an example of utility maximization based on an assumption of cardinally measurable utility.

2. Reorganization of the chapters on costs, revenues, and profit maximization. In the first edition, Chapters 8, 9, and 10 addressed, among other things, the various ways firms can be categorized for analytical purposes, the distinction between economic and accounting profits, the theory of short-run and long-run costs, firm revenues, profit maximization, how to determine profits or losses, and the firm's shutdown

and breakeven points. The material in these chapters has been reorganized to emphasize the individual elements that go into the determination of firm profits or losses and those characteristics of costs, revenues and profit maximization that are common to all firms.

- Chapter 8: Entrepreneurial Behavior has been updated and streamlined. In particular, the discussions of explicit versus implicit costs and the short run versus the long run have been moved to the beginning of Chapter 9. In addition, the discussion of economic versus accounting profit has been moved to a new Chapter 10.

- Chapter 9: Production Costs (old title: Production Costs, Revenues, and Profit Maximization) was too long in its previous form and attempted to accomplish too much. Consequently, the section on revenues and profit maximization for price-taking and price-searching firms has been moved to a new Chapter 10.

- Chapter 10: Revenues and Profit Maximization. This new chapter combines material previously found in Chapters 8, 9, and 10. The major sections of the chapter include:

  1. a discussion of the distinction between economic and accounting profit,

  2. the revenue functions for price-taking and price-searching firms,

  3. the rule any firm must follow if it wishes to maximize profits,

  4. the algebraic and graphical measurement of profits or losses, and

  5. identification of the firm's breakeven and shutdown points for both price-taking and price-searching firms.

Learning Aids

We believe that the most important learning aid in the *Microeconomics* package is the organization of the text itself. As in the first edition, the following features reinforce the organizational structure of the text:

1. **Chapter overviews** give a bird's eye view of what is coming in each chapter.

2. **Learning objectives** follow each chapter overview and highlight the most important themes in that chapter.

3. **Extended examples** demonstrate the relevance of economic theory to real-world events.

4. **Why the Disagreement?** boxes in every chapter present opposing views on current hot topics of economic policy. The economic interests of both parties are explained by showing the underlying economic model and how it applies to the point of disagreement.

5. **Does It Make Economic Sense?** boxes in every chapter illustrate how economic theory, applied properly, can explain what on the surface appears to be behavior that contradicts economic principles.

6. **The Economist's Tool Kit** boxes appear in selected chapters and discuss specialized economic techniques or data.

7. **Margin definitions** of key terms run throughout every chapter.

8. **Section Recaps** summarize the major points of each section of the text.

9. **Chapter summaries** briefly recount each chapter's main arguments.

10. **Questions for Thought** conclude each chapter and are arranged in three categories: knowledge questions, application questions, and synthesis questions. They are designed to test understanding of the material and to prepare for exams.

11. **Glossary** of key terms at the end of the text provides a quick and handy reference for review.

12. **Carefully selected and designed graphs** appear throughout the text. Three features of the graphs are especially useful:

   • Pedagogical use of color: Successive curves are shown in a lighter shade than preceding curves, making shifts of curves easy to follow.

   • Highlight boxes within graphs concisely explain the concept of the graph right next to the graph itself.

   • A complete caption for each graph helps interpret and explain the graph in clear and simple terms.

Supplements

Our supplements package includes a(n):

Instructor's Manual containing a transition guide, annotated outlines, chapter focuses, learning objectives, lecture suggestions, graph suggestions, and answers to questions for thought.

Test Bank containing multiple-choice questions for each chapter.

Computerized Test Bank (IBM format) offers instructors the ability to produce and customize tests based on the questions in the printed Test Bank.

Transparency Masters feature 134 graphs and tables selected from the text.

Study Guide provides students with chapter overviews, key graphs and terms, exercises ranging from fill-in-the-blank to applications involving graphical and numerical analysis, review questions in multiple-choice format to serve as a self-test, and answers to exercise and review questions.

Graph Notes are note-taking templates featuring the key graphs and tables covered in the text and are designed to improve student note-taking ability.

Acknowledgments

The number of people who contributed to the first edition of the text in various capacities was large, and we cannot recognize them again here. However, their contributions to the project are reflected in this edition of the text, as well as in the first. In particular, we want to note the contribution to the text made by Alan Dillingham, who co-authored the first edition. Since that time, Alan has become Associate Vice President of Instruction and Dean of Undergraduate Students at Illinois State University, a position with as many responsibilities as words in its title. Consequently, Alan is no longer working on the text, but his influence remains strong. We also wish to acknowledge the contributions to this edition by the following people, many of whom also aided in the development of the first edition:

Doug Brown, Northern Arizona University
Ray Cohn, Illinois State University
Sarah Culver, University of Alabama
Larry Gwinn, Wittenberg University
Dean Hiebert, Illinois State University
David Martin, Davidson College
Mat Morey, Illinois State University
Mike Nelson, Illinois State University

Eliot Orton, New Mexico State University
Tony Ostrosky, Illinois State University
David Plant, University of Utah
Dipankar Purkayastha, California State University
Chuck Smith, Illinois State University
Mark Walbert, Illinois State University
Mark Wohar, University of Nebraska

Production of the text has been handled with skill and good humor by the editorial staff at Blackwell Publishers and the production personnel at Benchmark Productions. Editorial Director Rolf Janke has shepherded the book quickly through the production process, with the assistance of the production manager, Jan Leahy, the senior project editor, Mary Riso, and the assistant editor, Mary Beckwith. At Benchmark, Andrea Mulligan and Andrew Williams have seen to it that production has proceeded smoothly. We owe all of them a debt of gratitude.

Contents

Part I: Basic Economic Principles   1

Chapter 1:
Economic Thinking   2

    Introduction   4
    Basic Economic Choices   6
    The Fundamental Premise of Economics   8
    Economics as Science   9
    An Introduction to Modeling:
    Budget Constraints and the Production Possibilities Frontier   14
    Summary   22
    Questions for Thought   23
    Appendix to Chapter 1   25
    End Notes   31

Chapter 2:
Mutually Beneficial Exchange   32

    Choice and Value   34
    Economic Efficiency   35
    Gains from Exchange   37
    Costs of Exchange   46
    Summary   50
    Questions for Thought   51
    End Notes   53

Chapter 3:
The Market Mechanism: Supply and Demand   54

    The Market as a Rationing Device   56
    Consumption Decisions: Demand   59
    Production Decisions: Supply   66
    The Market Mechanism at Work: Equilibrium   72
    Summary   88
    Questions for Thought   89
    End Notes   90

Chapter 4:
Economic Efficiency:
A Measure of Market Performance   92

Gains from Trade   94
Economic Efficiency of Market Equilibrium   94
Market Disequilibrium Generates Market Inefficiency   104
Price Controls Introduce Economic Inefficiencies   106
Why Would Society Choose to Be Inefficient?   111
Summary   116
Questions for Thought   117
End Notes   119

Chapter 5:
Decision Making in an Imperfect World   120

The Market Mechanism Is a Decision-Making Device   122
Problems for the Market   124
Opportunities for Collective Action   133
Summary   140
Questions for Thought   141
End Notes   142

Part II: The Basic Economic Model   143

Chapter 6:
The Elasticity of Demand   144

Changes in Price and Quantity Demanded   146
Determinants of Price Elasticity of Demand   160
Other Measures of Elasticity   165
Summary   168
Questions for Thought   169
End Notes   170

Chapter 7:
The Theory of Consumer Behavior   172

Consumer Utility   175
Derivation of the Demand Curve   181
Consumer Decision Making in Practice   185
Indifference Curves Analysis   190
Summary   197
Questions for Thought   198
Appendix to Chapter 7   200
End Notes   205

Chapter 8:
Entrepreneurial Behavior   206

The Entrepreneurial Challenge   208
Ways to Categorize Firms   210
The Firm's Objective: Profit   217
Summary   220
Questions for Thought   221
End Notes   222

Chapter 9:
Production Costs   224
   Explicit versus Implicit Costs   226
   Short Run versus Long Run   227
   The Short Run Production Process   228
   Long Run Production Costs   242
   Technology and Production Costs   250
   Isoquants, Input Prices, and Least-Cost Production   250
   Summary   256
   Questions for Thought   257
   End Notes   259

Chapter 10:
Revenues and Profit Maximization   260
   Economic Profit   262
   The Firm's Output and Revenue   265
   Short Run Profit Maximization   269
   Determination of Profit...Or Loss   272
   Supply Decisions in a Dynamic Economy   279
   Summary   279
   Questions For Thought   281
   End Notes   282

Chapter 11:
The Perfect Competition Model   284
   Characteristics of a Perfectly Competitive Market   286
   Short Run Equilibrium for the Perfectly Competitive Firm 287
   Short Run Supply Curve for the Price-Taking Firm   289
   Perfect Competition and Rational Behavior   290
   The Dynamics of the Market Mechanism: Long Run Equilibrium 291
   Production Costs and Efficiency   297
   General Equilibrium in the Economy   304
   Costs and Benefits Again: The Invisible Hand of the Market 307
   The Perfectly Competitive Market Model in the Science of Economics 308
   Summary   312
   Questions for Thought   313
   End Notes   315

Chapter 12:
Small Firm Behavior:
The Imperfect Competition Model   316
   Real People, Space, and Time   318
   Monopolistic Competition   319
   Long Run Equilibrium Position   322
   Competitive Pressure   327
   Summary   332
   Questions for Thought   334
   End Notes   335

Chapter 13:
Large Firm Behavior: The Imperfect
Competition Model — 336

Resource Immobility and Competitive Pressure — 338
Monopoly — 342
Oligopoly — 353
Alternatives to Competition — 358
Oligopoly: Economic Profits and Efficiency — 364
Summary — 366
Questions for Thought — 367
End Notes — 369

Chapter 14:
The Regulation of Business Behavior:
Policy in Transition — 370

Lack of Competition and Inefficient Outcomes — 372
Collective Decision-Making Options — 373
The Deregulation of Business Behavior — 383
The Case for Deregulation — 386
Airline Deregulation: A Case Study — 391
The Market Mechanism in Action — 394
Summary — 395
Questions for Thought — 396
End Notes — 397

Part III: Factor Markets — 399

Chapter 15:
The Theory of Resource Markets — 400

Determinants of Resource Prices — 402
The Firm's Demand for Resources — 402
Market Demand for Resources — 407
Price Elasticity of Demand for Resources — 411
Determinants of Resource Price Elasticity — 412
Supply of Resources — 414
Equilibrium in the Resource Market — 421
Summary — 423
Questions for Thought — 424
End Notes — 426

Chapter 16:
The Labor Market — 428

Significance of Labor in the Economy — 430
The Labor Market as an Abstraction — 431
The Aggregate Labor Market: Wage and Employment Determination — 432
Explaining Observed Wage Differences — 434
Investment in Education: Costs and Benefits...Again — 442
Discrimination in the Labor Market — 445
Noncompetitive Labor Markets — 446

The Minimum Wage Controversy ... 448
Long-Term Employment Contracts ... 450
Summary ... 452
Questions for Thought ... 453
End Notes ... 455

Chapter 17:
Trade Unions And Collective Bargaining ... 456

The Purpose of Labor Unions ... 458
American Unionism: Structure and Membership ... 461
Union Membership in the United States: Growth and Decline ... 463
The Goals of Labor Unions ... 468
A Model of Unions' Impact on Wages and Employment ... 471
Policies to Increase Union Power ... 473
Unions and Wages: The Evidence ... 475
The Effects of Unions: Monopsony ... 475
Unions and Economic Welfare: A Broader View ... 477
Summary ... 477
Questions for Thought ... 478
End Notes ... 479

Chapter 18:
The Capital Market ... 480

Consumption or Investment: Costs and Benefits ... Again ... 482
The Investment Decision ... 483
Demand for Capital ... 484
Investment Benefits ... 488
Investment Costs: The Interest Rate ... 492
Summary ... 499
Questions for Thought ... 500
End Notes ... 501

Part IV: Applications of the Microeconomic Model ... 503

Chapter 19:
Income Inequality and Poverty ... 504

The Distribution of Income in the United States ... 506
Poverty in the United States ... 518
Income Redistribution and Antipoverty Policy ... 525
Summary ... 530
Questions for Thought ... 531
End Notes ... 532

Chapter 20:
Externalities, Public Goods, And
Common-Property Resources:
Problems For The Market Mechanism ... 534

Conditions That Lead to Inefficient Market Outcomes ... 536
Externalities ... 539
External Costs and Environmental Pollution ... 544

Contents

Public Goods 552
Common-Property Resources 556
Cost of Information 559
Opportunities for Collective Action 561
Summary 562
Questions for Thought 563
End Notes 564

Chapter 21:
International Trade 566

Theory of Trade 568
Changing the Terms of Trade 577
Exports, Imports, and the Balance of Trade 585
Summary 590
Questions for Thought 592
End Notes 593

Index 595

Part I: Basic Economic Principles

2

Economic Thinking

Overview

Our civilization is founded on the accomplishments of our ancestors. Through hard work, determination, and sacrifice, generations of ordinary people built quite an extraordinary social system. They literally constructed society, at no small cost to themselves. As we go about our daily affairs, we seldom pause to consider this basic human enterprise. We are caught up in educating ourselves, raising our families, pursuing careers, and generally enjoying the fruits of our labors and those of generations that preceded us. Much of the world's population enjoys a higher standard of material well-being than ever before. We have developed mechanisms of social cooperation that reconcile the rights and goals of individuals with those of societies.

We have gained a measure of control over our environment. We have succeeded in extending the time one can expect to spend on earth. We are even capable of exploring the universe.

This impressive record of human accomplishment, which has given us life as we know and enjoy it today, has not altered the fundamental nature of human existence: *achievement requires sacrifice*. Economics focuses on this fact. Economics is concerned with the decision-making process confronting people who are forced to make costly choices. This chapter introduces the subject of economics, identifies the basic nature of economics, and presents the economic decision-making framework.

Learning Objectives

After reading and studying this chapter, you will be able to

1. Define economics

2. Use the basic economic problem of scarcity to explain the Fundamental Premise of Economics

CHAPTER 1

3. Identify the economic dimension of decisions, problems, or policies

4. Explain the basic process of science, a process shared by economics

5. Use the production possibilities frontier model to illustrate the concepts of scarcity, choice, and opportunity cost by applying the model to individual and social choice problems

Introduction

The 1990s have been characterized by vigorous debate over a variety of issues. Health care reform dominated President Clinton's first two years in office. Welfare reform was one of the major elements of the Republican Party's 1994 "Contract with America." Issues related to environmental quality, such as the Clean Air Act Amendments of 1990 and the emerging debate over reauthorization of the Clean Water Act, are a continuing source of disagreement among affected parties. The North American Free Trade Agreement and the General Agreement on Tariffs and Trade generated heated arguments between proponents and opponents of free trade. While these examples cover a diverse range of topics, they nonetheless share a common characteristic – they all have an economic dimension. Thus, economic analysis can shed light on each of these issues and help inform policymakers, as the following discussion illustrates.

Americans spent $931 billion on health care in 1993, about 14.3 percent of the total value of all goods and services produced in the economy. This level of health care spending amounts to $3,605 per person annually. Accompanying this level of expenditure on health care is a rapidly advancing medical technology by which more and more lives are saved than would have been possible in earlier years. Average life expectancy is increasing because we are learning the causes of and developing treatments for more and more diseases. Yet health care is a major social problem in the United States.

The cost of health care has risen rapidly, about 8.5 percent a year over the last twenty years. This rate of growth is much faster than the rate at which prices in general and income have been rising over the same time period. Health care cost increases are occurring in spite of rapid technological advance. At the same time, over 36 million people have no insurance coverage. Many of these people cannot afford simple medical procedures. It is estimated that by the year 2020, health care expenditures could consume as much as a third of the value of all goods and services produced in the economy.

The extent of these problems has made health care reform one of the leading social issues in the United States in the 1990s. During the 1992 presidential campaign, candidate Bill Clinton stated that reforming the health care system would be one of his administration's top priorities. Shortly after taking office, President Clinton appointed a task force to examine the options for health care reform. The task force presented a report of its findings to the President in late summer 1993, and in September 1993, the Clinton Administration released its proposal for health care reform. Thus began a process that is sure to entail a huge effort on the part of a great many people. No health care reform legislation was passed in 1994, and when this text was being written policymakers were still debating what form such legislation should take.

The amount of work that will be required to implement some form of health care reform reflects the enormity of the problems facing the Administration and the Congress. It is an extremely difficult and complex task to create a system that will make health care less expensive, more accessible, and more efficient. At the heart of the problem is the fact that society has limited resources available to meet its health care needs. Rapidly rising health care costs force society to give up more and more other goods and services in order to continue to provide health care. Yet society wants good health care. Many people feel that access to basic health care is, in a sense, a right that should be extended to all individuals. But how do we provide adequate health care to all without giving up more and more other goods and services?

Negotiation of the North American Free Trade Agreement (NAFTA) with Canada and Mexico and the more recent debate over whether the Congress should approve the General Agreement on Tariffs and Trade (GATT) highlighted the controversial issue of foreign import competition. Proponents of NAFTA and GATT argued that these agreements would lower the cost of goods produced in foreign countries to consumers in the United States and would increase employment in U.S. exporting industries. Opponents responded that such agreements would lead to job losses in the United States as foreign suppliers gain larger shares of some U.S. markets and as some U.S. firms move domestic production outside the United States.

When the potential loss of jobs caused by deliberate government policy is placed in the context of thousands of lost jobs due to industrial restructuring, people have legitimate concerns about the ability of the economy to provide employment and income that will permit a stable or growing standard of living. In fact, consumers buy foreign goods because they are cheaper or of better quality than domestically produced goods. Consumers get more for their money. This motivation accounts for the volume of Japanese imports in the automobile and consumer electronics markets. Increased imports do reduce domestic employment. How do we balance the desire for more and better goods and services against the social disruption that accompanies job loss in specific sectors of the economy?

Environmental quality also continues to receive a great deal of attention in the United States. The debate over survival of the spotted owl versus logging jobs in the Northwest spurred a great deal of controversy that is sure to continue into the foreseeable future. The debate over the effects of acid rain and what to do about it continues to rage. Among the many issues involved is the adverse effects of acid rain on aquatic life versus the jobs of coal miners in the East and Midwest. Concerns about ozone depletion and global warming have also spurred many groups to demand actions by the federal and state governments. Ever since the Love Canal incident, people have become increasingly concerned about the problems of waste management. These problems, and a host of other environmental issues, have led to demands for actions to protect the environment and improve the overall level of environmental quality.

These three social controversies share a common element: An economic problem is at the heart of the dilemma. Individuals have limited incomes, but seek the most goods and services from that income. They must make costly tradeoffs. They can have more of something, but only by forgoing something else of value to them. They feel a sense of progress or gain when their income rises or they can obtain more with a fixed income. On the other hand, they feel worse when changes in employment, income, or prices reduce their access to goods and services. Of course, society faces the same problem: limited means with which to achieve the best possible standard of living for its members. In its decision making, society must make costly tradeoffs too. There is an important additional dimension to society's decisions. Often society must make decisions that make one group better off at the expense of others.

Nearly everyone recognizes that issues such as the rising cost of health care, competition from foreign imports, deterioration of environmental quality, unemployment, slow economic growth, and government deficits are economic problems. However, fewer people are able to pinpoint the common element in these diverse problems. The common element is the desire to use one's limited resources to their fullest effect. The economic problem is limited means to satisfy unlimited wants.

Defining Economics

Most people can tell you that economists work in banks, corporations, academia, or for the government. The public even turns some economists into media figures who receive the kind of attention usually reserved for heads of state, artists, and movie and TV stars. If you ask people to identify economic problems, they inevitably name such social problems as those discussed in the preceding section. However, this familiarity with economic issues and the economist's profession does not extend to an understanding of the discipline itself. This book explains the nature of economic problems and demonstrates the widespread usefulness of economic analysis by developing the basic principles of economics and applying them to a variety of individual and social problems.

Economics:

The study of how people decide to use scarce resources to produce goods and services and distribute them for consumption.

We begin with a definition of economics, one found in dictionaries and in most economics textbooks: **Economics** is the study of how individuals and societies decide to use scarce resources to produce goods and services and distribute them for consumption. Note that the word "decide" is as important to the definition as the "economic" terms "resources" and "consumption." The focus of economics is choice when resources are scarce. Thus, we will focus on the process of making choices throughout the text. We want to stress that the end goal of economic decision making is current or future consumption.

Basic Economic Choices

Resource:

A raw material or produced good available for use in the production of other goods and services.

Factor of production (input):

A resource used in production.

We satisfy our wants by consuming goods and services. We are nourished by food and water. We clothe ourselves and seek shelter. Human wants extend far beyond these basic survival needs, but regardless of the specific want, consumption is the act of satisfying a want. The amount of goods and services we can have depends, in large part, on the amount of resources available to us.

A productive **resource** is a raw material (a natural substance) or a man-made good that is used in the production of other goods or services. Such resources are also called **factors of production**, since they are used as **inputs** into the production process. Factors of production include land (defined broadly to include all natural resources), labor, capital (man-made tools of production and the technology embodied in them) and *human capital* (the skills and knowledge embodied in a person), and entrepreneurial ability (the ability to organize and plan production and develop new products). Resources are required to produce the goods and services with which wants are satisfied.

Resources are *scarce* in the sense that they are available in limited quantities, while human wants tend to be unlimited. Since not all wants can be satisfied with existing resources, choice is necessary: Individuals and societies must decide how limited resources will be used. It is not possible for all people to satisfy all their wants. *In a world of scarce resources, it is impossible to avoid making choices.*

Scarcity necessitates choices of many different types. As individuals, we must decide how to use the resources that we have: our intellectual and physical assets, our material wealth, and our time. Do I want to be a concert pianist or a chemical engineer? As a student, do I want to maintain a perfect 4.0 grade point average or do I want a more active social and extracurricular life? Should I buy a car? Should I save more and spend less?

Businesses face choices because of limited resources as well. Should a new product line be added? How many units should be produced this month? Should workers be hired or laid off? Should the firm invest in a new production technology? Should one firm buy another company it has been watching, or agree to be purchased by an interested third company?

Societies are faced with innumerable complex social choices. How much of society's resources should be devoted to national defense? Should government spending be increased or decreased? How much individual liberty will be permitted? Should the government try to control the economy? How will society choose which goods to produce? What criteria will be used to distribute the goods produced?

Such decisions as these – about what to produce, how to produce it, and how to distribute the goods produced – are made every day by individuals in their roles as consumers, producers, resource owners, and citizens. The nature of the decisions varies widely, but they all have a common element: The decisions are required because resources are scarce; each choice entails an **opportunity cost**. Choosing one alternative means forgoing another. The true cost of a decision is the value of the next best opportunity given up because of the decision.

Opportunity cost:
The value of the most desirable alternative given up when choosing an option.

The opportunity cost of becoming a concert pianist is the value of the opportunities given up to become a skilled pianist. The years of training devoted to piano and the money spent on lessons could have been used to do other things. The opportunity cost of buying a car is the value of other goods and services that cannot be purchased because one's income and savings go to pay for the car. The opportunity cost of saving is the satisfaction forgone by consuming less now. The opportunity cost of attending an economics lecture is the highest-valued alternative use of the time that one spends in class.

What is the opportunity cost incurred by a business when it adds a new product? When an automobile company develops a new model, it spends some of its profits developing the new car rather than using them to improve current models or paying higher dividends to stockholders. The firm's engineers spend time developing and refining the new model rather than working on making existing models safer, more fuel efficient, or more durable. Introducing a new model may mean the company cannot afford to refit factories producing other models with robotics technology that would lower production costs. The firm forgoes a number of alternatives when it chooses to introduce a new car line.

Social choices also have opportunity costs. The opportunity cost of national defense is the nonmilitary production forgone to provide a defense for the country. The opportunity cost of a war is the highest-valued alternative uses of the human and nonhuman resources expended in the war effort. The cost to society of redistributing income (taking income from one group of individuals and giving it to another) includes both the resources that must be devoted to managing the redistribution program (resources that have alternative uses) and any output that might be lost if taxing one group and providing income grants to another causes either group to work less.

In a world of scarcity, the ability to identify true opportunity costs is very valuable. One of the most important objectives of studying economics is to acquire this skill. The chapters that follow repeatedly raise the question of what the true costs of choosing an alternative are. The next section develops a proposition based on the basic concepts of scarcity, choice, and opportunity cost.

The Fundamental Premise of Economics

Rational decision maker:
Someone capable of setting goals and acting purposefully toward achieving those goals.

How do people go about making necessary, but costly, choices? Economics is based on the assumption that people behave rationally, that is, that individuals are **rational decision makers**. This assumption implies that people can and do make choices that they believe will make them better off. The assumption of rationality does not imply that people never behave emotionally or act on a whim. Sometimes people buy things on the spur of the moment and later regret they made the purchase. Such an action may be irrational, but most people learn from such disappointments. Economists believe that rational decisions predominate, and the assumption of rationality enables us to explain a great deal of human behavior.

Going one step further, the assumption of rationality implies nothing about what an individual likes or dislikes. A person's preference for heavy metal rock music over Mozart, or for hot dogs over prime rib, implies nothing about rationality. A person who prefers hot dogs to prime rib behaves rationally by purchasing hot dogs. *Rationality means that people are capable of establishing goals and of acting in a manner consistent with the achievement of those goals.* People are purposeful, making decisions that benefit themselves. Goals vary from person to person and across societies, but people act in ways they believe are beneficial to themselves.

Fundamental Premise of Economics:
In all decision making, individuals choose the alternative for which they believe the net gains to be the greatest.

Combining the fact that scarcity implies costly choice with the assumption of rationality enables us to formulate a proposition that we shall call the **Fundamental Premise of Economics**: *In all decision making, individuals choose the alternative for which they believe* *the net gains to be the greatest.* Virtually all economic theory and analysis is built upon this premise. The conclusions of every chapter in this book are based on it.

An extremely important implication follows from the Fundamental Premise: When decisions are costly, *incentives matter.* The Fundamental Premise asserts that people attempt to obtain the maximum benefit possible from the choices they make. This is equivalent to saying that they seek to achieve their goals at the minimum cost. To accomplish this they must pay attention to costs and benefits. Changes in costs and benefits alter the incentives for people to make particular choices by altering the gains from different alternatives. When the benefits of an alternative increase and its costs remain the same, the incentive to choose that alternative increases. The alternative becomes more attractive because the net gain from choosing it has increased. When the perceived benefits of a college education increase, more people go to college. On the other hand, as the costs of a particular alternative increase, fewer people choose the now-less-attractive alternative. The number of drivers who exceed the speed limit depends upon the cost of speeding. When the law is enforced by radar monitoring, fewer drivers speed. The use of radar raises the expected cost of speeding. In short, in attempting to achieve the greatest gain possible from a set of alternatives, *individuals economize.*

The Fundamental Premise of Economics is a powerful tool for understanding, predicting, and even altering human behavior. We demonstrate its power throughout this text by applying it to diverse individual and social problems.

Economics as Science

Science is the systematic study of how the world works. It represents an attempt to determine cause and effect – to understand the likely consequences of particular events. Nobel laureate George Stigler classified economics as a science when he said, "The central task of an empirical science such as economics is to provide general understanding of events in the real world."[1] Economists seek to understand how the world works just as physicists or biologists do, though the particular objects of study differ markedly among these scientific disciplines.

Science:
The systematic study of how the world works.

Science develops when people interested in a particular set of problems interact with one another in an attempt to solve those problems. Once again quoting Professor Stigler, "A science requires for its very existence a set of fundamental and durable problems."[2] Only when problems persist for extended periods can they be addressed systematically. Clearly, one enduring problem for every society is how to organize societal decision making and institutions in order to satisfy as many of the unlimited economic wants of its citizens as possible with its limited resources.

Adam Smith, one of the first scientific economists, addressed this basic problem over two hundred years ago. The basic theory of markets developed by Smith still exists today, though in a modified form. Modern economic theory addresses issues Smith would never have thought about tackling, but the basic insight into the economic process is the same now as in 1776 when Smith published *An Inquiry into the Nature and Causes of the Wealth of Nations.* Smith noted that rational, self-interested behavior, instead of producing chaos, usually produces social coordination. Economists are still concerned with how this process of social coordination works and why it sometimes breaks down. Because many basic economic problems have never changed, progress in understanding economic behavior can take place. One generation of economists can learn from the mistakes and successes of preceding generations.

This learning process parallels ordinary life. We behave "scientifically" in response to problems with which we are familiar by reacting in the ways that have proven successful in the past. For example, from previous experience we react to driving on icy streets by slowing down, braking gently, and turning gradually. However, drivers in northern regions who face icy streets every winter tend to respond much more systematically than drivers in southern states who rarely encounter ice. So it is with science. When enduring problems are addressed systematically, the probability of better solutions increases as experience grows.

Scientific Process

The manner in which science proceeds is not difficult to understand. The development of a particular science begins with the observation of regularities. Observers attempt to explain the regularities by developing generalizations – called **theories** – about the causes of the observed regularities. The theories link cause and effect. From theories, testable implications – called **hypotheses** – can be developed. If the theory is correct, then certain patterns must occur. Scientific experiments are efforts to identify and control all causal factors that might lead to a specific effect in order to identify the cause-and-effect relationship. The many laws of chemistry and physics were established this way. Hypotheses were developed from theories and then tested through experimental means. Those causal relationships that were verified by many replicable experiments became accepted relationships, or laws.

Economics is a science in that its purpose is to establish generalizations about economic relationships and use these generalizations to explain the economic performance of economies. What conditions, or causal factors, lead to more rapid economic growth or lower rates of inflation or higher levels of unemployment? What causes consumers to buy more of a good or producers to produce less of a good? Does more education cause higher lifetime income? Do income redistribution policies improve economic efficiency? These are some of the many questions that economists attempt to answer by developing theories of economic relationships and testing hypotheses derived from the theories by scientific methods.

Scientific Models Scientific theories are usually expressed in terms of **models**. A model is a simplified representation of reality designed to abstract from nonessential features while concentrating on essential features. Models come in all forms, many of which are familiar. Department stores use mannequins to display clothes, thus enabling us to imagine how good the clothes would look on us. The mannequins are models of

Theory:
A set of generalizations purporting to explain observed regularities.

Hypothesis:
An implication of a theory that can (in principle) be shown to be true or false.

Model:
A simplified representation of reality that focuses attention on the issues the scientist wishes to examine.

real people, though they lack any of the internal organs necessary to life. To carry out their purpose, it is only necessary that mannequins look like humans on the outside.

Scientists study the effect of automobile crashes on passengers by placing crash dummies in cars and running the cars into concrete block walls. The crash dummies are also models of people, though they have few if any external features. For their purpose, looking "real" is unnecessary. What is important is that they measure the effect of an auto crash on the human body.

Scientific models come in many forms: maps, graphs, pictures, mathematical equations. Each model is an attempt to represent the problem being addressed in as simple and manageable a way as possible. Reality is too complex to be understood without simplification. Scientists, including economists, use models as aids in locating the important linkages producing observed behavior.

Social Goals and the Progress of Science

As noted, science is based on the existence of a set of durable problems. However, over time, society's ideas about what constitutes important problems change. Thus, the basic attitudes and goals of society affect the progress of science. Science is not only affected by social values, however; it also affects them by raising new issues or concerns that alter the way we think about our world.

Some examples are instructive. Scientists working with the theory of atomic physics developed nuclear fission. This discovery was first used in atomic bombs, and today a number of countries have arsenals of nuclear weapons. Concern that these weapons might some day be used changed the face of politics in the United States. Presidential, senatorial, and congressional candidates were forced to develop positions on nuclear weapons control. More recently, with the dissolution of the Soviet Union, attention has turned to determining the extent of resources that should be allocated away from military goods and toward meeting other needs. Similarly, but more positively, developments in the treatment of cancer and other diseases have altered the way we react to these diseases. Government faces political pressure from groups who think more should be spent on research and prevention of cancer. In both examples, scientific progress – *increased understanding of how the world works* – has led to a change in social attitudes.

Social goals also affect science. The rapid spread of the AIDS virus has led to a surge of research in that area. A major social goal is finding a cure for the disease, and science is being enlisted in the service of this social goal. The poor performance of American school children in comparison to those in other countries has led to research on how students learn. This increased emphasis on education reflects, in part, the increasing level of competition in the world economy.

Positive and Normative Issues The scientists seeking an antibody to the AIDS virus are practicing **positive science**. Positive science is the study of how the world works. Either an antibody fights the AIDS virus, or it does not. It is a question of

Positive science: The study of how the world works; an examination of what is (rather than what should be).

Why the DISAGREEMENT?

Would You Donate a Kidney for $1,000?

Since the early 1980s organ transplants have become almost a routine practice to extend the lives of those with failing vital organs. The most common organ transplants are for lungs, pancreas, heart, kidney, and heart-lung. Transplant success rates for these procedures are quite high today, reaching 97 percent for some kinds of kidney transplants. Over the history of organ transplant procedures, there has been general agreement that donors should not receive compensation for generously volunteering to give up their organs at death in order to save the lives of others. The medical community and legislators believe that one's conscience should govern these decisions. Now, however, some individuals – physicians, educators, medical ethicists – are proposing a radically new policy: the use of incentives to encourage the donation of organs, thereby increasing the supply of organs available for transplant. One suggestion is for the families of organ donors to receive a fixed fee, such as $1,000. Another proposal suggests that the donor's burial expenses be paid. Another proposes a contract which, in the event of a potential donor's death, would pay $5,000 to a designated beneficiary for each organ that is transplanted. Why the disagreement over the means by which society obtains organs for transplantation?

Even though organ transplants are commonplace surgical procedures today, they are a relatively new viable alternative for individuals experiencing vital organ failure. The advances in medical technology provide new opportunities to save many lives, but this new area of medicine raises some difficult ethical issues surrounding the notion of living and dying. We are all familiar with the most difficult situations. A successful transplant requires that the organ be removed from the donor soon after death. When is an individual dead? What is the medical definition of death? Does this definition conflict with the wishes of the donor's family?

Normative position:
Based on a set of values; expresses what should be (rather than what is).

fact. On the other hand, the belief that society should use more of its scarce resources to find a cure for AIDS is a **normative position**. In the past fifteen years, breast cancer has claimed more lives than AIDS, so it is not obvious to everyone that scarce medical research dollars should be allocated to AIDS research rather than to research on causes of breast cancer. Similarly, determining how children learn is a positive issue; deciding what they should be taught is normative. Normative issues are not questions of fact but of values or beliefs. Such issues cannot be settled by positive scientific analysis, although the consequences of normative decisions can be analyzed.

Although positive and normative issues are conceptually distinct, the two often tend to blend together. Scientists study important problems, but what is considered important is a normative issue. AIDS research is being expanded because many people believe it *should* be. Limits are placed on biogenetic engineering because some people fear the unknown consequences of altering genes and believe we *should* be very cautious in such research.

Economics is as subject to the overlapping of positive and normative issues as any other science. Major economic problems have arisen that have caused the course of economic research to change. The Great Depression of the 1930s, when over one-fourth

Medical practitioners can save lives with donated organs, but they must not devalue life by appearing too eager to take organs from potential donors. This ethical concern is compounded by a related legal one for physicians and hospitals. Donors and their families must give approval for organ donations. Medical-care providers want to ensure that proper approvals have been voluntarily obtained from the donor or family in order to avoid legal liability. Furthermore, even in states, such as Texas, where there is legal protection for taking organs from a body whose family cannot be identified in a timely fashion, physicians are reluctant to use the law. They recognize that families have a cherished moral and legal right to make all the decisions associated with the death of a family member. By appearing not to recognize this valued right, the medical community might lose the existing trust of the public and have even fewer volunteer organ donors.

The calls for incentives to increase the number of organ donors arise from a very large imbalance in the number of organs available for transplant and the number of prospective donor recipients. As transplant technology has advanced and transplant success rates have improved, the number of prospective recipients has increased much faster than the supply of organ donors. For example, in 1991 there were almost 30,000 prospective recipients of kidney transplants, but only about 6,500 available kidney donors. In the same year, over 5,000 people were awaiting heart transplants, but only 2,000 donor organs were available. Consequently, people are dying because there are not enough donated organs to meet the needs, given existing medical technology. Those proposing incentives for organ donation do so out of a desire to save lives; all such proposals have tried to take into account the extremely sensitive ethical issues involved.

The opponents of incentives for organ donation base their position on normative values and, in so doing, avoid the economic dimension of the issue. They believe this is a practice that society should not allow for ethical or moral reasons. Proponents of incentives acknowledge their sensitivity to the issue of social values, but they accept the proposition that individuals alter their behavior in response to economic incentives. They believe that properly and carefully structured financial incentives will solve an acknowledged social problem: loss of life from organ failure. Like most social problems, the issues in this instance are complex and involve social, ethical, cultural, and political, as well as economic, elements. We will focus on the economic dimensions of the social and political problems discussed in this book. However, we should not lose sight of these other questions in the process of carrying out our economic analysis.

of all American workers were without jobs, caused a shift in the focus of economic research. Previously, little attention had been paid to analyzing how unemployment might be overcome. In the 1930s this became a major problem to be addressed and remains so to this day. The inflation of the 1970s similarly affected economic thinking, spurring research into the causes and consequences of rapid price increases.

Despite the overlapping of normative and positive issues, the two often are separable. Many economic issues are matters of fact: Does or does not a particular consequence result from a particular cause? As is the case in other sciences, however, many hypotheses are difficult, if not impossible, to test. Economists attempt to resolve issues that cannot be directly tested by examining the predictions of theoretical models, statistically estimating how one thing affects another, and examining the historical record for clues to the relationship between economic variables. Even then, many issues are not resolvable, so that one's *beliefs* about how the world works are important in determining how one interprets economic behavior.

Science progresses as people systematically study a set of durable problems. Science progresses through the development of theories and the testing of hypotheses implied by the theories. The questions studied by scientists are shaped by the values of society, just as the results of scientific research shape society's values.

Section Recap

An Introduction to Modeling: Budget Constraints and the Production Possibilities Frontier

Scarce resources limit the extent to which individuals or societies can satisfy their wants and achieve their goals. In this section we illustrate constrained choice making and the opportunity costs associated with such choices. We develop models to illustrate the concepts of scarcity, choice, and opportunity cost. Before plunging into the analysis of these issues, however, a brief word of advice and encouragement about graphical analysis is in order.

Make Graphs Work for You

Economists use graphical analysis extensively in their courses and books; this book is no exception. It is full of graphs, for very good reasons. We use graphical analysis to help explain the principles of economics. Graphs are intended to be an aid to learning. This book uses a combination of approaches to convey information. For instance, the concept of a production possibilities frontier is developed in writing and illustrated with graphs. You should concentrate on understanding the connection between the graphs and the written explanation, avoiding the tendency to memorize graphs. If you understand a concept well enough, you should also understand the graphical illustration. Try to develop graphical illustrations of concepts on your own. Working with graphs is a good way to *practice* economics.

Graphs serve a dual purpose in economics. First, they convey a large amount of information at a glance. Graphs conveniently illustrate the relationships between variables. Second, graphs serve as an aid to economic reasoning. By correctly shifting the lines in a graph, a student can produce the outcome that results from a change in an economic variable. Understanding how to work with graphs is not a substitute for thinking correctly about the problem at hand, but such understanding can guide correct thinking.

Graphs are expressions of mathematical relationships. The benefits of using graphs are increased by a sound understanding of basic algebra. An appendix on graphical analysis appears at the end of this chapter. It serves as a review and refresher for readers who are uncomfortable with graphs or who want to review the basic mathematics of graphical analysis. *If, in reading the remainder of the chapter, you feel unsure about what a graph means or how it is used, you should read the appendix before continuing.*

Individual Choice: The Budget Constraint

Consider a problem that all individuals face: the allocation of time. People have only twenty-four hours a day at their disposal. People must eat, sleep, study, and possibly work. They also spend time in various social and extracurricular activities. Assume that a student named Kim spends eight hours each day in such activities as eating, sleeping, and bathing. She is left with sixteen hours a day to either study or participate in other college activities.

Here is the basic economic problem: Kim has limited resources. This example considers only one resource: time. Because time is limited, Kim cannot do all she would like to do. She has sixteen hours a day to allocate to various activities of value to her. She must make some choices. Lumping her time use into two categories simplifies the problem: Kim either studies or participates in other activities. The daily time that she spends studying cannot be spent doing something else and *vice versa*. Kim faces a tradeoff.

Graphing her **resource constraint** illustrates Kim's problem – how to allocate her time between studying, on one hand, and all other activities, on the other. In Figure 1.1, hours of study time are measured along the vertical axis and hours of other activities are measured along the horizontal axis. Only sixteen hours are available each day for both activities. Kim could choose to spend all sixteen hours a day studying. If she did, no time would be left for other activities, and she would be at point A. Or, she could spend all sixteen hours on other activities and no time studying. She would then be at point D. If she chose to spend some time on both activities, she would be at some point between A and D.

The line AD connects all combinations of hours that total sixteen. Kim could choose any combination of points (or hours) on the line AD, but because she has exactly sixteen hours available, no combination of hours off the line AD is possible. Kim is constrained by her sixteen hours a day. If Kim chooses to study ten hours a day, she will have available only six hours for other activities (point B). She can increase the time available for other activities only if she reduces the time devoted to studying. If Kim spends ten hours a day in other activities, she can devote only six hours to study. The opportunity cost of four more hours of other activities (moving from point B to point C) is the value she attaches to four hours of study time.

Resource constraint:
Maximum quantity of resources available for use in production or consumption.

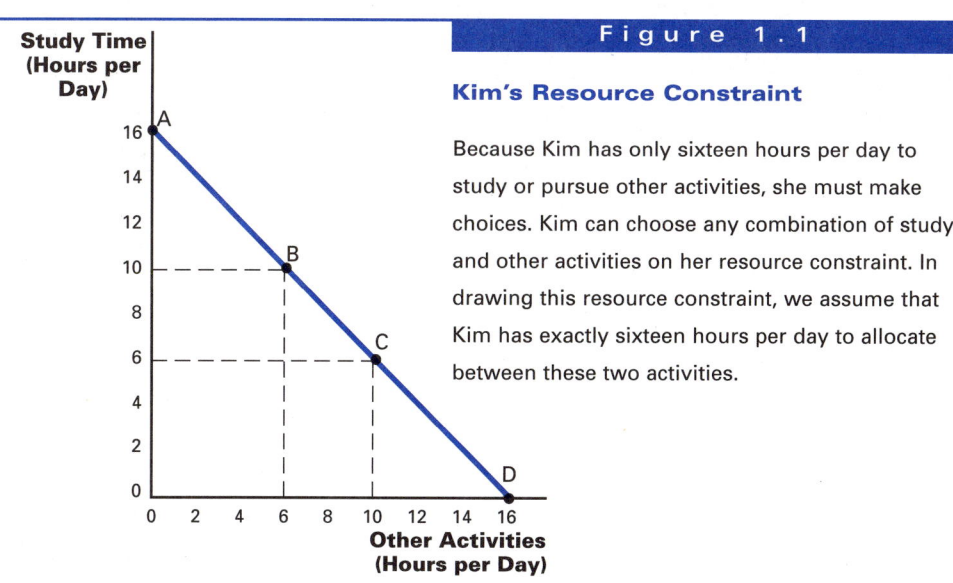

Study Time (Hours per Day) / **Other Activities (Hours per Day)**

Figure 1.1

Kim's Resource Constraint

Because Kim has only sixteen hours per day to study or pursue other activities, she must make choices. Kim can choose any combination of study and other activities on her resource constraint. In drawing this resource constraint, we assume that Kim has exactly sixteen hours per day to allocate between these two activities.

This simplified example of the allocation decisions caused by a scarce resource demonstrates that choices caused by scarcity have opportunity costs associated with them. The assumption that Kim devotes exactly sixteen hours to two particular kinds of activities simplified the problem. However, other sacrifices are open to Kim if she decides to study more without eliminating any of her other activities. By reducing the time she spends sleeping and eating, Kim would have more than sixteen hours to devote to study or other activities. Graphically, the resource constraint would shift outward. Total time devoted to studying and other activities would increase. (Lack of sleep and proper nourishment might also prove costly, however.)

Social Choice: The Production Possibilities Frontier

Each day people make literally hundreds of decisions like the one just described. Although many decisions are not very complicated or significant, many are extremely important. The impact of scarce resources and the cost of choices forced on people by scarcity are great.

Every society must decide what goods and services it will produce. An important choice facing the U.S. economy is determining the share of national resources to devote to the production of health care. Because resources are limited, the more resources we devote to health care, the fewer we have available for non-health care goods. Some countries devote a relatively large amount of their resources to health care; other countries spend very little on health care.

Production possibilities frontier (PPF):

All the maximum possible combinations of two goods that can be produced with available resources.

With a given stock of resources, the output – goods and services – an economy can produce in a period of time is limited. The limit can be represented by a **production possibilities frontier (PPF)**. A PPF shows all the possible combinations of two goods that can be produced if currently available resources are fully employed using the available technology. The PPF for the United States when it chooses between health care and all other goods and services is illustrated in Figure 1.2. The production of health care is measured on the vertical axis; the production of all other goods is measured on the horizontal axis. Note that, while Figure 1.1 showed a *resource constraint*, Figure 1.2 shows *production possibilities*. The focus has shifted from the resources themselves to what can be produced with the resources.

The output of health care and other goods is limited to the quantity combinations lying on or beneath the production possibilities frontier AG. 0A health care can be produced if no other goods are produced. If no health care is produced, 0G other goods can be produced. With the existing stock of resources and level of technology, combinations of health care and other goods beyond the frontier, such as point U, are unattainable.

The first thing you might have noticed about the production possibilities frontier in Figure 1.2 is its shape. While the resource constraint in Figure 1.1 was a straight line (linear), the PPF in Figure 1.2 is concave from below (bowed away from the origin between A and G). There are sound economic reasons for these shapes. When Kim spent one more hour studying, she automatically spent one less hour on other activities. When we focus on resources, a one-to-one tradeoff exists. This tradeoff never varies, so the resource constraint is linear.

The PPF is drawn concave because not all resources are equally useful in producing health care and other goods. Some resources have rather specialized uses. They are not very productive when transferred to other uses. For example, suppose the United States was at point A in Figure 1.2. All resources are devoted to producing health care. How much would production of health care fall if some resources were transferred to the production of other goods? The answer depends on *what* resources are used. If the resources that contribute least to the production of health care, such as the labor of skilled furniture makers or clothing designers, were transferred to the production of those goods, production of health care would fall very little. However, these resources would contribute greatly to consumer goods production. In moving from point A to point B on the PPF, very little health care is given up to acquire a substantial quantity of furniture and clothing. The shape of the PPF is implied by the Fundamental Premise of Economics: To be on the PPF, society must produce health care and other goods in a manner yielding the greatest net gains.

If additional quantities of other goods equal in size to $0F_1$ are desired, their opportunity cost increases. The quantity of health care given up to acquire more of other goods increases as production of other goods rises, because resources less specialized to production of such goods are now being transferred away from the production of health care. As production of other goods expands, skills that are well suited to providing health care services are used to produce other types of goods and services such as houses and banking. The farther out along the other-goods axis we move, the greater the opportunity cost of additional units of other goods. More and more health care must be forgone, because resources better suited to the production of health care are now being used to produce

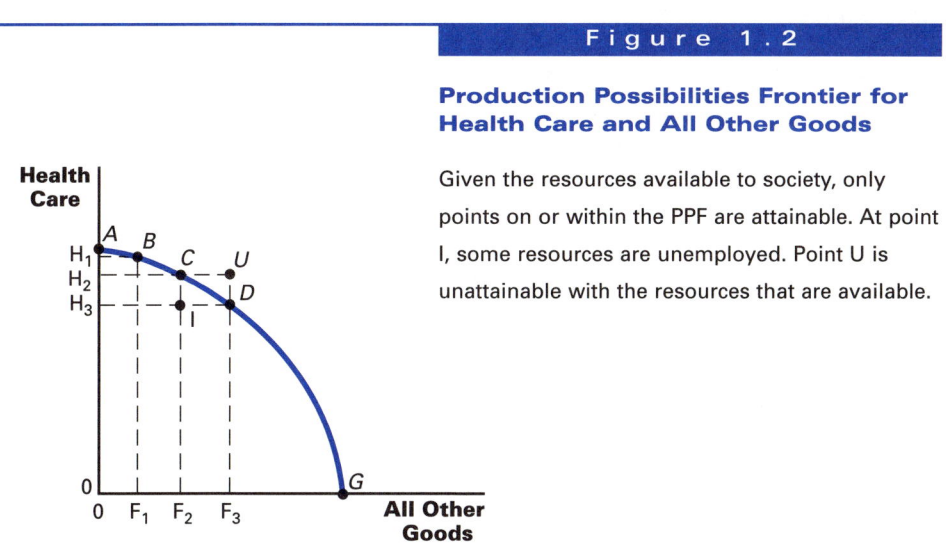

Figure 1.2

Production Possibilities Frontier for Health Care and All Other Goods

Given the resources available to society, only points on or within the PPF are attainable. At point I, some resources are unemployed. Point U is unattainable with the resources that are available.

Does It Make ECONOMIC SENSE?

Putting a Price On a Human Life

Technological advance has enabled economies to grow rapidly over the past century and has contributed to an increase in the standard of living in many countries. However, in addition to numerous benefits, advances such as the introduction of thousands of new chemicals and the development of new modes of transportation have also entailed various costs, including the imposition of new risks of death on people. Consequently, policymakers have passed a variety of laws and regulations to reduce such risks. However, when the costs of these policies are compared to their benefits, measured by the number of lives expected to be saved, an interesting result emerges: the

implied value of a human life varies considerably depending on the risk in question. For example, the costs associated with safety standards that have been imposed on X-ray equipment suggest that each life saved is worth a minimum of $400,000.[3] In contrast, the costs of regulations governing radiation from uranium mine tailings imply that each life saved is worth a minimum of $190 million. Does this make economic sense?

To answer this question, we need to understand how estimates of the value of a life are derived. Assume a new safety regulation would reduce the risk of an accidental death by one in one million. If one million people are affected by the regulation, then it is expected that one life will be saved.

Suppose we assume that the cost of the regulation is $5 per person. Then the regulation costs $5 million ($5 x 1 million people). Thus, the implied value of the life saved is at least $5 million.

In fact, most economists would argue that using the value of a small change in the risk of death to infer the value of a human life is incorrect. Talking about a small change in a risk of death as opposed to certainty of death (that is, the value of a life) are two very different matters. Thus, trying to make too strong a connection between the two is risky business. Nonetheless, it is still true that people (policymakers and average citizens) appear to attach very different values to a given change in

other goods. By the time we reach point G, very few additional other goods are being produced with the last resources shifted from health care to non–health care production. The tendency for the opportunity cost of producing a good to rise as more and more of the good is produced is known as the *law of increasing opportunity cost*.

If the economy's resources are fully employed, some combination of health care and other goods on the production possibilities frontier will be produced. In this case, a decision to have more health care or more of other goods is costly. Suppose the economy is producing at point C, and society decides to produce more non–health care goods. It must sacrifice some health care production. Because of its resource constraint, it cannot move to point U; it must reduce its production of health care, moving along the frontier to a new combination such as point D. Production of other goods increases from $0F_2$ to $0F_3$, but this increased output is paid for by a reduction in health care production from $0H_2$ to $0H_3$. The opportunity cost of more non–health care goods is less health care.

Note that if resources are not fully employed, that is, if society is not producing on the frontier, output of either health care or other goods can be increased without giving up any of the other type of goods. If society is initially at point I inside the frontier, unemployed resources exist. Some valuable resources are not being utilized in any type of production. By employing these idle resources, the production of health care or other goods or both can be increased without reducing the output of any goods.

the probability of death, depending on the situation.

There are a number of possible explanations for this seeming inconsistency. First, economists and other experts (such as psychologists and sociologists) who have considered this problem have noted that people tend to behave quite differently depending on whether a risk is voluntarily or involuntarily assumed. For example, people who drive small cars rather than large cars to save on fuel costs know that there is a higher probability of injury (and death) should they be involved in an accident, all else held constant. Nonetheless they are willing to assume this increased risk even though the costs of avoiding it are relatively small (increased fuel expenses). On the other hand, people routinely indicate that they would be willing to pay relatively large amounts of money to reduce or eliminate involuntarily assumed risks, such as the risks imposed by locating a nuclear power plant close to a population center, or the adverse effects of groundwater contamination from a waste disposal site. Thus, a change in an involuntarily assumed risk will usually produce an implied value of life that is larger than the same change in a voluntarily assumed risk.

A second explanation for the observed differences is that policymakers are responding to political pressures. In this case, it is quite possible that the opportunity costs are not given much, if any, consideration when safety standards are being set. The cleanup of so-called "Superfund" sites, which include a large number of abandoned hazardous waste disposal facilities, is a good example. Beginning in the 1970s, the public became increasingly aware of the potential risks posed by the disposal of hazardous wastes. People demanded that something be done to alleviate these risks. The result was the passage of federal legislation (the Comprehensive Environmental Response, Compensation, and Liability Act) that calls for the identification and cleanup of such sites throughout the country. Recent estimates of the average cost of a cleanup have been put at $20 million. However, it is not clear what the accompanying reduction in risk is in certain instances. While it could be argued that this is just another example of an involuntarily assumed risk, it is also quite evident that costs have been much less important than total cleanup of the sites.

We conclude that variations in the value of reductions in risk may or may not make economic sense. To the extent that variations reflect differences in peoples' preferences, such variations are consistent with the fundamental premise. However, in some situations, considerations other than economic factors (costs and benefits) may dominate the decision-making process.

Recall our earlier discussion of positive versus normative analysis. The relationship between the level of resource utilization and where we are relative to the PPF is a positive issue. The question of how idle resources should be employed involves normative considerations.

Economic choice is costly. If the economy is operating on its PPF, acquiring more of one good means giving up more of another good. A PPF illustrates this tradeoff. A PPF shows the maximum quantities of two goods that an economy can produce at any particular time.

The Drive to Satisfy More Wants

The production possibilities frontier presents a vivid illustration of the constraint imposed by scarce resources. Since not all wants can be satisfied, people attempt to use available resources to their best advantage. The Fundamental Premise of Economics embodies this human reaction to resource constraints. People seek to get as much as they can from their limited resources.

Production possibilities frontier analysis illustrates the costliness of unemployed resources. Even when resources – factories, machines, people – are not idle, not all wants can be satisfied. Some goals must be sacrificed to achieve others. When resources are underutilized, some wants that could be satisfied are not. Opportunities are wasted. Full employment of resources is an important economic goal.

The drive to satisfy more individual or social wants extends beyond attempting to operate on the production possibilities frontier. If the PPF can be pushed outward, more wants can be satisfied. By obtaining more resources or by using existing resources to produce more goods and services, societies can push their production possibilities frontiers outward.

Increasing the Stock of Resources Societies obtain additional future resources by using existing resources to produce them. This process is called **investment**. Some resources that could be used to satisfy current wants instead are used to produce more factories or machines or training facilities or to explore for more mineral deposits in order to expand the society's future resource base. The factories, machines, transportation systems, and other produced goods that are used to produce other goods and services are called the **capital stock**. Thus, investment is often referred to as **capital formation**. Resources are also devoted to education and training designed to increase the intellectual and technical capabilities of the population. The quality of the labor force depends on society's investment in human capital.

When a society increases its resources, its production possibilities rise. Investment in productive resources loosens the resource constraint, enabling people to enjoy more of all goods. Investment is not a costless activity, however. Resources devoted to the production of hydraulic drill presses or the planting of pine forests or the training of engineers are unavailable to satisfy consumer wants. The opportunity cost of an investment good is the highest-valued collection of consumption goods forgone when resources are devoted to investment. Increasing future resources requires society to give up some current consumption.

Figure 1.3 illustrates the investment decision for the United States. At the present time we face a choice. We can devote our resources to two alternative uses, either current consumption or investment (capital formation). Consider two different points, A and B, on the PPF. If we choose to operate at point A, we will forgo a large amount of current consumption to devote a relatively large share of our resources to capital formation. On the other hand, production at point B would result in the consumption of most of our current resource stock; only a small fraction of resources is devoted to investment.

Figure 1.3 (b) shows the future outcome of this consumption versus investment decision. Because production at point A commits more of existing resources to the creation of capital equipment, the economy's future resource base is larger than it would be with production at point B. The PPF associated with production at point A lies to the right of the PPF associated with production at point B. In the future, when faced with the consumption versus investment decision, society has the luxury of both consuming and investing more than it could had it chosen production at point B. This is possible only because production at point A resulted in a larger sacrifice in terms of forgone consumption in an earlier period. Note, once again, the positive and normative dimensions of this example. The effect of production at point A versus point B is a positive issue. The question of which point society should choose is a normative issue.

Investment:
The use of existing resources to create additional future resources.

Capital stock:
The factories, machines, and other goods used to produce more goods and services.

Capital formation:
Investment in productive capital stock.

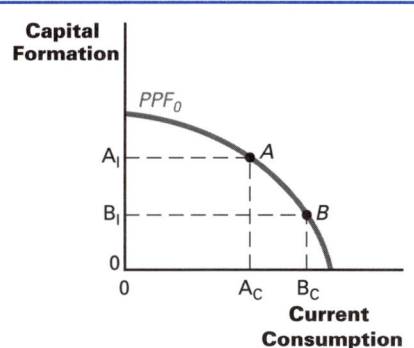

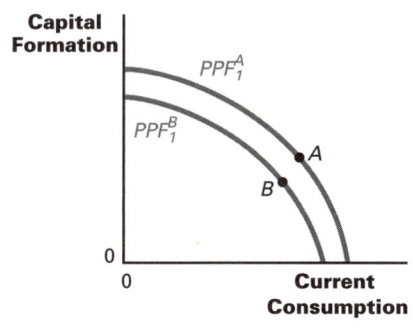

Figure 1.3

The Investment Decision

(a) The Present (b) The Future. Investment in capital formation enables a society to produce and consume more in the future. Operating at point A will entail forgoing a large amount of current consumption to devote a relatively large share of our resources to capital formation. With production at point B this outcome is reversed (a). However, the future PPF associated with production at point A, PPF_1^A, lies to the right of the future PPF associated with production at point B, PPF_1^B, (b).

Investment is the primary way societies increase their stocks of resources and satisfy more wants over time. Investment takes many forms. A firm uses its existing resources to build new plants and add new equipment. Individuals forgo current consumption to educate themselves. Nations forgo current governmental services to build more infrastructure, such as highways, for the future. Both firms and governments use resources in an effort to develop ways to produce more goods and services with the existing stock of resources. Improved technology enables societies to make better use of resources.

Getting More Through Technological Change Technology is an important determinant of the output that can be produced with a given stock of resources. **Technology** is the application of knowledge about the physical and natural world to the production of goods and services. It determines the kind and quantity of inputs necessary to produce a good or service as well as the kind and quality of goods available. Technological advances permit economies to produce both higher-quality new products and old products at lower cost. Thus, an improvement in technology shifts the PPF out to the right just as an increase in the stock of resources does.

The benefits of technological change have been readily apparent since the Middle Ages. Improved technologies are in large part responsible for the remarkable increases in the standard of living experienced by much of the world's population. Many new ideas arise quite by accident, the fruit of someone's imagination and creativity. However, the benefits of such advances are so great that most societies devote significant quantities of resources to the pursuit of technological advancement. People give up some current con-

Technology:

The application of knowledge about the world to the production of goods and services.

sumption to support the research, experimentation, exploration, and development that can lead to technological change.

Escaping the Frontier Through Specialization and Trade Individuals and nations have different **resource endowments** (stocks of resources). Individuals vary in terms of intelligence, physical skills, imagination, and interpersonal skills. Nations have different endowments of natural resources. Some countries have a great deal of land relative to other inputs. Other countries have rich mineral resources and little farm land. Resource differences mean that the opportunity cost of performing certain services or producing certain kinds of goods varies across individuals and countries.

Differences in resource endowments generate opportunities for individuals and countries to escape their resource constraints by specializing in low opportunity cost activities and trading for other goods and services that are relatively costly for them to produce. If two countries have different resource endowments and agree to trade, each can escape its production possibilities frontier by specializing and trading.

Chapter 2 discusses the principle of mutually beneficial trade in detail. Trade is treated at length in a separate chapter because it is such an important vehicle for escaping individual resource constraints and satisfying more wants with the limited resources available.

> **Resource endowment:**
> The stock of resources available to a person or nation.

Section Recap

The desire to acquire more goods and services leads societies to invest in capital goods and technological development in an attempt to push their PPFs outward. It also leads to specialization and trade, which enables individuals and economies to escape their PPFs.

Summary

Economics is the study of how individuals and societies **decide** to use **scarce resources** to produce goods and services and **distribute** them for **consumption**. The **basic economic problem** is the scarcity of resources relative to human wants. Since all individuals, groups, and societies face this constraint, their decision making is similar in that they all attempt to achieve as much as possible with their available resources. We call this notion the **Fundamental Premise of Economics**: In all decision making, individuals choose the alternative for which they believe the net gains to be the greatest.

Scarcity necessitates choice. If resources were not scarce, we could all have everything we want. Since we cannot have everything, we must make choices. The costs of a choice are forgone opportunities. The true cost of a decision is the value of the best opportunity given up because of the decision. The key to good decision making is the ability to identify the true **opportunity costs** of a choice.

Economics is a (social) **science**. Economists seek to develop generalizations about observed economic phenomena in order to explain, predict, and possibly influence the economic environment. Science develops when people systematically study fundamental and durable problems. One generation of scientists builds on the knowledge of the preceding generation. Social values affect and are affected by scientific research. What society believes is important, a **normative** value, becomes the subject of scientific research. This research attempts to determine how the world works – a **positive** question, a question of fact.

Scientific theories are usually presented as **models** – simplifications of the relationships among a set of variables. Models are built for specific purposes, omitting aspects of the real world irrelevant for those purposes.

The basic concepts of scarcity, choice, and opportunity cost are illustrated with a **production possibilities frontier** model. The model reveals the costs of choices made when resources are fully employed. The model also separates all attainable choices from those that are unattainable because of resource constraints.

The shape of the production possibilities frontier reflects the nature of the opportunity costs in a decision. When opportunity costs are constant, regardless of the quantities of goods produced, the PPF is linear. When opportunity costs increase as additional units of a good are produced, the PPF is concave – bowed out from the origin.

A society can increase its stock of resources by (1) investing current resources in capital formation, (2) achieving technological progress, which increases output from a stock of resources, and (3) trading with others on the basis of least cost production.

Questions for Thought

Knowledge Questions

1. What is the opportunity cost of your college education?

2. Is it rational to get a college education? Do the benefits outweigh the costs? How are benefits and costs calculated?

3. What is a scientific model?

4. Think of the decisions you have made in the last week. Which ones were economic decisions? What made them economic decisions? Explain.

Application Questions

5. Consider the production possibilities for the country New Coolidge. Its citizens produce two goods, garlic and wool, according to the following production possibilities schedule:

Garlic	0	150	300	450	600	750	900
Wool	450	375	300	225	150	75	0

What is the opportunity cost of a unit of wool (in terms of garlic)? Is the opportunity cost of producing wool constant or increasing? If the economy is initially producing and consuming 450 units of garlic and 225 units of wool, what will be the cost of increasing wool production to 375 units? Why would New Coolidge decide to make such a change?

6. Choose a recent article from the *Wall Street Journal* (or other newspaper) on an economic policy or problem. Identify the different viewpoints and disagreements. Which ones are positive? Normative?

7. What is the opportunity cost of consuming: (1) a cup of coffee; (2) a cigarette; (3) a marijuana cigarette? What is the opportunity cost of an hour of work for a college student? What determines the cost?

8. Roger has been placed on a strict diet: 1,500 calories per day. Without exceeding his calorie limit, Roger must eat a balanced diet. Demonstrate that Roger's problem is essentially an economic problem.

Synthesis Questions

9. List at least three ways that society can reduce the litter of drink cans and bottles. Which alternative would be most effective? Are there any disadvantages with this scheme? Which alternative would be least effective? Does this alternative have any advantages?

10. Think of some models that you use to anticipate the events of a day. Which ones explain why the events occur? Which ones help you control events?

11. We all own things that break or malfunction. What factors influence our decision to repair something ourselves or to hire someone to fix it?

12. Suppose you are thinking of becoming a distance runner. What economic decision must you first make? Explain. What must you know and do to become a successful distance runner?

Appendix to Chapter 1

Graphs present numerical or mathematical information in a convenient, readable form – for those who know how to read them. This appendix provides a brief review of a few of the basics of graphical analysis.

When confronting a graph, the first thing you should ask is, What's measured along the axes? Economists use graphs to display all sorts of relationships. A huge variety of variables can be measured along the axes. Be sure you know what is being measured. Next, note the units of measurement. Economic variables may be measured in dollars, or physical units, or percentage points, or other ways. Some of these variables may have a time dimension. For example, a graph might plot *annual* expenditures on color television sets on one axis. It is important to recognize the time dimension involved.

The graphs in this book are either one or two dimensional. A one-dimensional graph plots data in one direction only. The most common form of a one-dimensional graph is a *bar chart*. Figure 1.4 is an example of a bar chart. It shows the level of spending in the United States on gasoline and oil for the years 1983 through 1986. Expenditures, measured in dollars, are plotted along the vertical (y) axis. Nothing is measured along the horizontal (x) axis; the spending bars are simply lined up side by side.

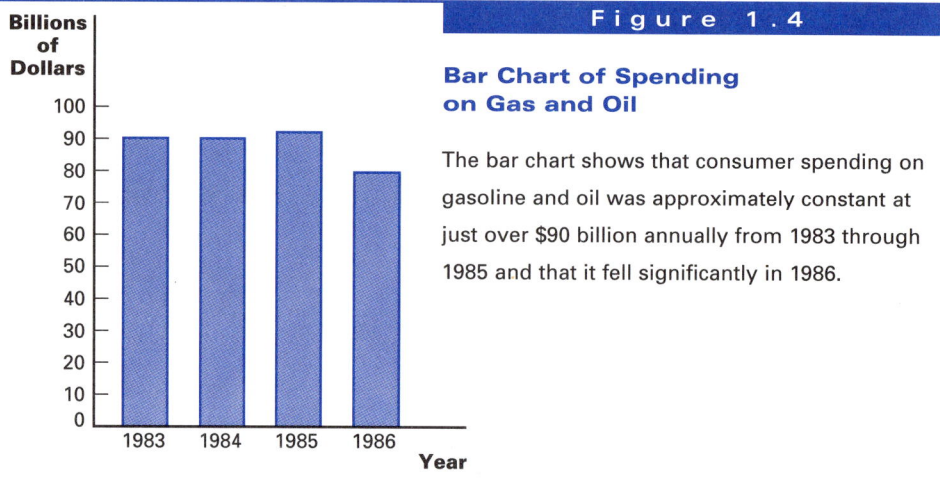

Figure 1.4

Bar Chart of Spending on Gas and Oil

The bar chart shows that consumer spending on gasoline and oil was approximately constant at just over $90 billion annually from 1983 through 1985 and that it fell significantly in 1986.

Source: *Economic Report of the President, 1986,* Table B-14.

Most of the graphs in this book are two-dimensional; they measure variables along two axes. The simplest form of a two-dimensional graph is a *scatter diagram*. It is used to show the relationship between two variables. Figure 1.5 provides an example of a scatter diagram. It shows the inflation rate–unemployment rate combinations for each year during the 1970s. The inflation rate is measured in percentage points along the *y*-axis. The unemployment rate is measured in percentage points along the *x*-axis.

Note that each point on a scatter diagram conveys two bits of information. Consider the point labelled "1975" in Figure 1.5. It tells us that the inflation rate in 1975 was 9.8 percent, while the unemployment rate was 8.5 percent. The other nine points on the diagram provide the same information for the other nine years in the decade. Scatter diagrams provide a convenient way to display the relationship between two variables.

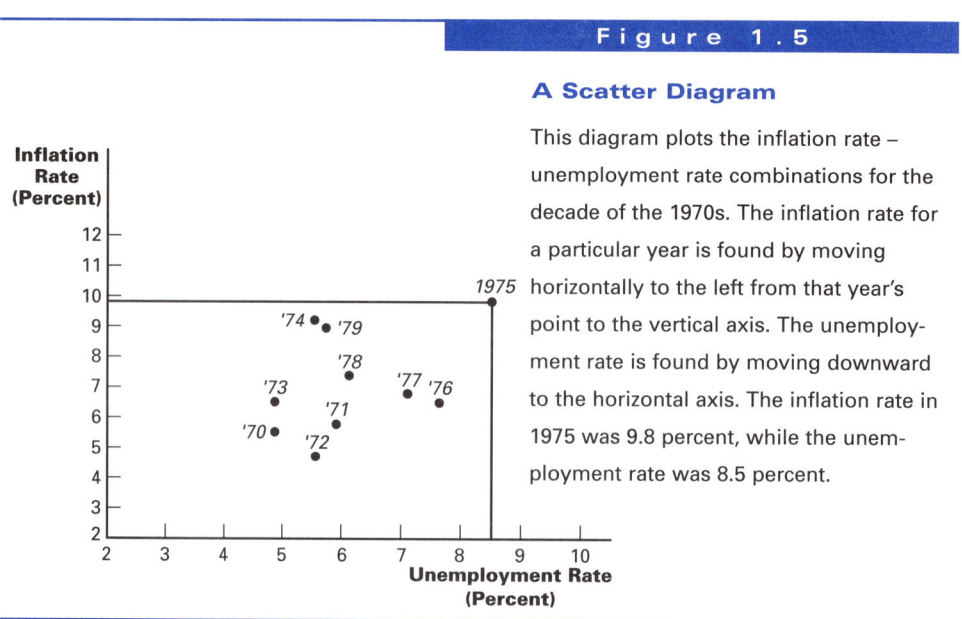

Figure 1.5

A Scatter Diagram

This diagram plots the inflation rate – unemployment rate combinations for the decade of the 1970s. The inflation rate for a particular year is found by moving horizontally to the left from that year's point to the vertical axis. The unemployment rate is found by moving downward to the horizontal axis. The inflation rate in 1975 was 9.8 percent, while the unemployment rate was 8.5 percent.

Source: *Economic Report of the President, 1986,* Tables B-3 and B-35.

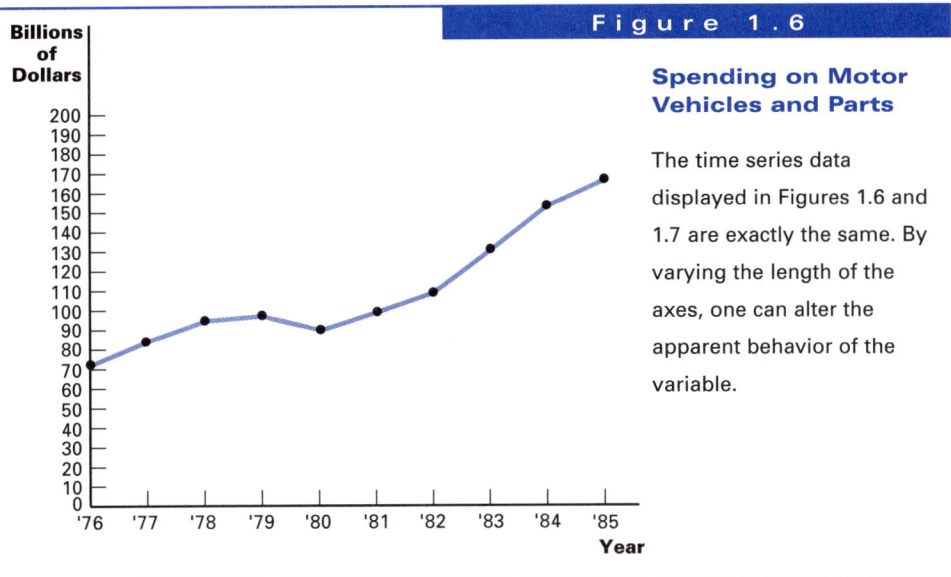

Figure 1.6

Spending on Motor Vehicles and Parts

The time series data displayed in Figures 1.6 and 1.7 are exactly the same. By varying the length of the axes, one can alter the apparent behavior of the variable.

Source: *Economic Report of the President, 1986,* Table B-14.

Time series graphs are a convenient way to show the behavior of a variable over time. In a time series graph, time is plotted along the *x*-axis and the variable (or variables) of interest along the *y*-axis. Figure 1.6 shows how a time series graph can be used to present information. It plots the behavior of consumer spending on motor vehicles and parts for the decade 1976-1985. Spending is measured in billions of dollars *per year*. Each point tells us how much was spent in a particular year.

While time series graphs seem straightforward, they can be deceptive. You must be careful to note the units in which the plotted variable is measured. By varying the units of measurement, or by shrinking or stretching the units along the axes, the time series behavior of a variable can be made to appear to change. Figure 1.7 illustrates this. It duplicates the plot of spending on motor vehicles and parts shown in Figure 1.6. However, in Figure 1.7 we stretch the units of measurement by focusing on the range of spending values actually experienced during the 1976-1985 period.

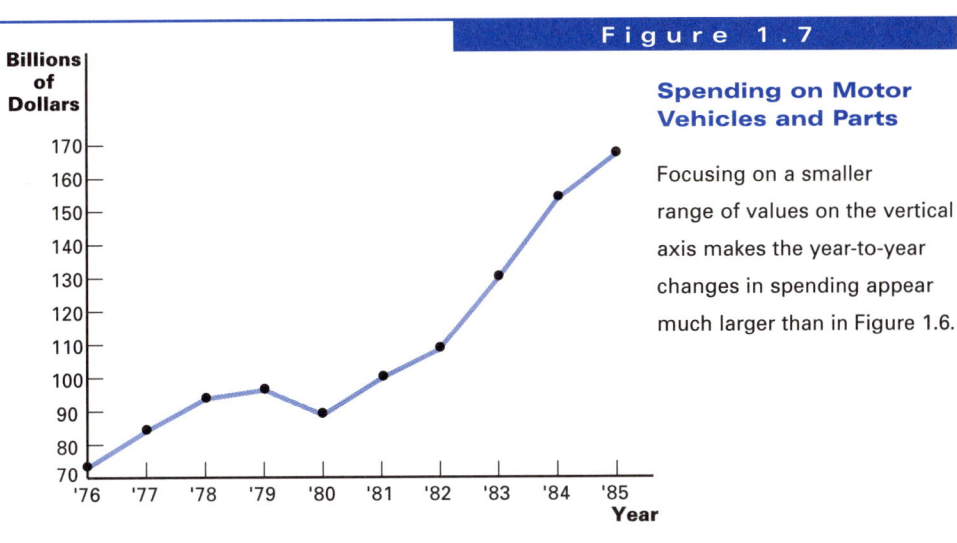

Figure 1.7

Spending on Motor Vehicles and Parts

Focusing on a smaller range of values on the vertical axis makes the year-to-year changes in spending appear much larger than in Figure 1.6.

Many of the graphs in this book – indeed, most of them – do not plot actual data. Rather, they illustrate theoretical relationships. It is the *relationship between variables* that is important in such graphs. This relationship is mathematical; the graph summarizes it in simple form.

Chapter 1 develops one graph of this type – the production possibilities frontier (PPF). PPFs illustrate the maximum quantity of two goods that can be produced from a given stock of resources. Since a linear PPF is simpler mathematically than a curved PPF, we will examine a linear PPF first. Consider PPF_1 in Figure 1.8. It shows the tradeoff facing a farmer who can produce corn or soybeans on his land. Both corn and beans are measured in bushels per year. PPF_1 shows that by devoting all his cropland (and other resources) to corn production, he can produce a maximum of 6000 bushels in a year. If he devotes all his resources to soybean production, he can grow 2000 bushels of beans. By allocating some land to the production of corn and some to beans, he can trade off corn for beans along the PPF.

This PPF illustrates an algebraic relationship. The equation of PPF_1 can be derived easily. Suppose soybean production is zero. Then the farmer produces 6000 bushels of corn. If soybean production rises to 1000 bushels, corn production *falls* by 3000 bushels. For every bushel of beans produced, corn production declines by three bushels. Thus, the equation for PPF_1 can be written as:

CORN = 6000 − (3 × BEANS).

In terms of conventional xs and ys, it would read,

$y = 6000 - 3x$.

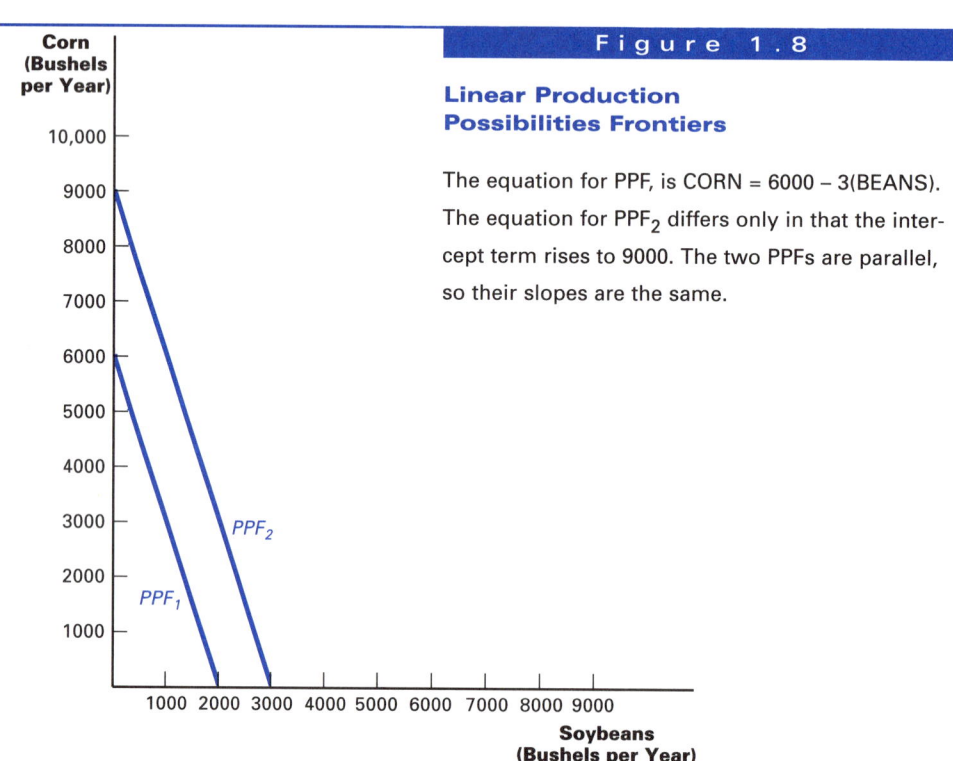

Corn
(Bushels
per Year)

Figure 1.8

Linear Production Possibilities Frontiers

The equation for PPF, is CORN = 6000 – 3(BEANS). The equation for PPF_2 differs only in that the intercept term rises to 9000. The two PPFs are parallel, so their slopes are the same.

PPF_2

PPF_1

Soybeans
(Bushels per Year)

The *y*-intercept of the equation (obtained by setting *x* to zero) is 6000. The *slope* of PPF$_1$ is -3. Slope measures the change in the *y* variable per one unit increase in the *x* variable. In this case, *y falls* by three units when *x rises* by one unit, so the slope is negative.

Suppose the farmer was given some additional land and equipment. Then he could produce more of both corn and soybeans. His PPF would shift outward to PPF$_2$. The equation describing PPF$_2$ differs from the equation for PPF$_1$ in only one respect: Its intercept term is larger. The rate at which corn can be traded off for beans (represented by the slope) does not change. The equation for PPF$_2$ is $y = 9000 - 3x$.

The slope of a straight line is constant. The slope of a curved line changes as one moves along the line. Figure 1.9 shows a curved production possibilities frontier. We can see immediately that the slope of the PPF is negative everywhere; when soybean production rises (along the *x*-axis), corn production falls (along the *y*-axis). But the *amount* by which corn production declines when soybean production rises by one bushel depends upon where on the PPF the farmer is operating.

Consider the movement from point A to point B. The slope of a *straight line* drawn from A to B is $-750/675 = -1.11$. (Corn production falls by 750 bushels, while soybean production rises by 675.) The slope of a straight line from C to D is $-750/225 = -3.33$. As noted, the slope changes as we move along a curve.

We find the slope of a curve at a particular point by drawing a straight line *tangent to the curve* at the relevant point. Then we measure the slope of the straight line. A tangent line touches the curve *only* at one point. The slope of the line tangent to point A in Figure 1.9 is -0.77. The slope of the tangent to point B (not shown) is -1.8.

Figure 1.10 illustrates a positively sloped curve. As in the case of the concave PPF, as one moves along the curve its slope changes. The slope between points A and B is smaller than the slope between points C and D, because the change in *y* between A and B is

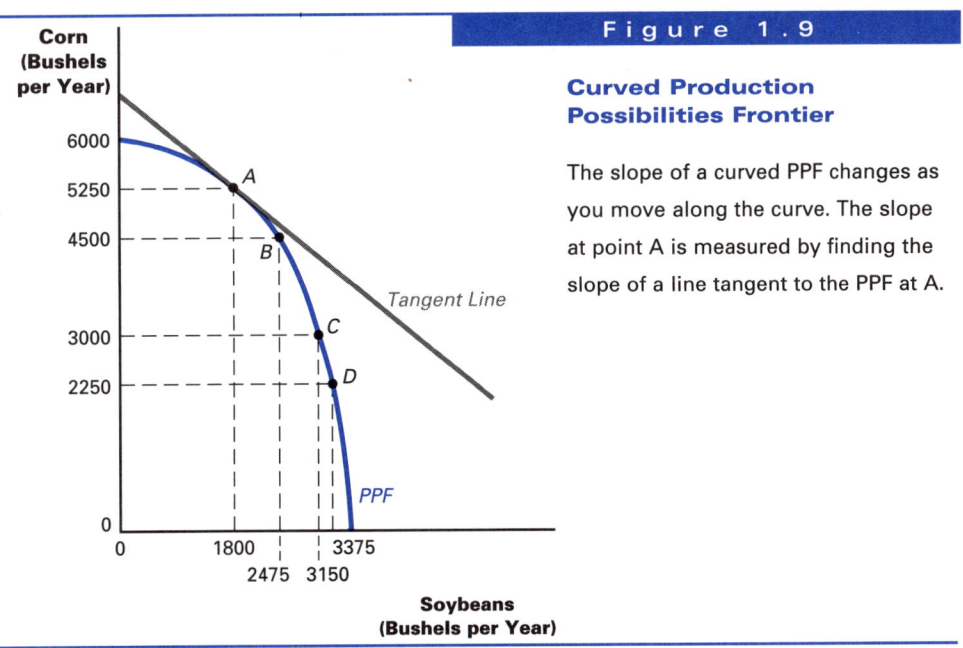

Figure 1.9

Curved Production Possibilities Frontier

The slope of a curved PPF changes as you move along the curve. The slope at point A is measured by finding the slope of a line tangent to the PPF at A.

Figure 1.10

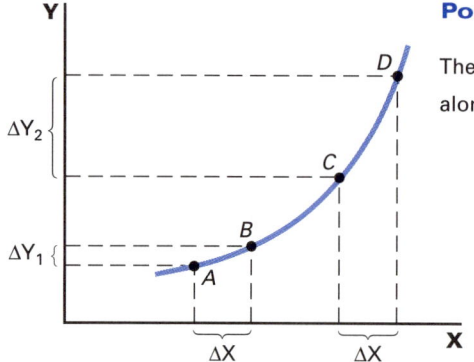

Positively Sloped Curve

The slope increases as we move up to the right along the curve.

smaller than the change in y between C and D, although the change in x is the same between each pair of points.

The area under a curve is sometimes of interest in economic analysis. Deriving the area under a linear curve is not difficult. Suppose we want to determine the area under the curve in Figure 1.11. Since the area is a triangle, we apply the equation for the area of a triangle: 1/2(length × width). Measuring the length along the x-axis and the width along the y-axis, we calculate the area to be $1/2(50 \times 10) = 250$.

Another calculation frequently called for in microeconomics is even simpler. Suppose we want to calculate the area under the curve in Figure 1.12 up to $x = 20$ and $y = 6$. This area is a rectangle, the area of which is calculated according to the formula $A = $ length × width. In this case, the area is $20 \times 6 = 120$. Many times the size of an irregularly shaped area can be calculated by dividing the area into triangles and rectangles, calculating the area of each, and summing the areas.

Sometimes the minimum or maximum value on a curve is important. Figure 1.13 illustrates the relationship between the average cost of producing a bushel of corn and the quantity of corn being produced. At $Q = 12,000$ bushels the average cost of producing

Figure 1.11

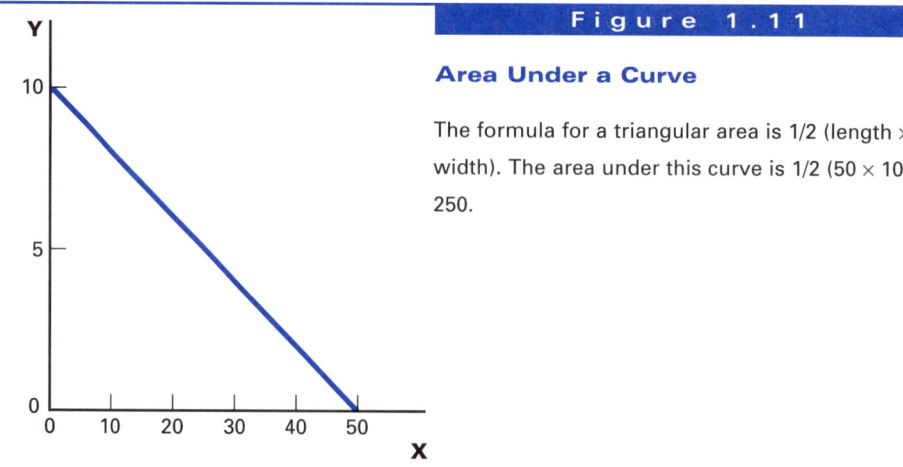

Area Under a Curve

The formula for a triangular area is 1/2 (length × width). The area under this curve is 1/2 (50 × 10) = 250.

Figure 1.12

Rectangular Area

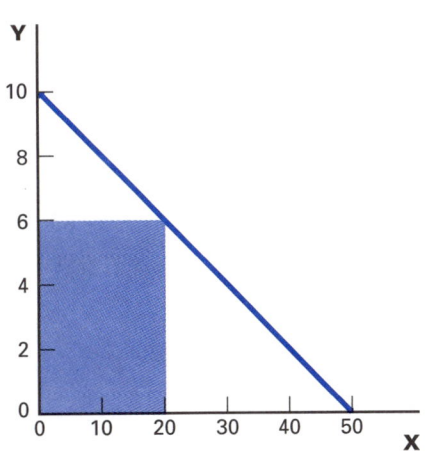

The formula for this area of a rectangle is length ×
width. The shaded rectangle has an area of
20 × 6 = 120.

a bushel of corn reaches its minimum. A curve turned upside down relative to the cost
curve in Figure 1.13 could be used to show the maximum value attained by a variable.

You will learn more about graphs as you work your way through this book. These
basics should help you get started. The most important thing to remember is that all the
graphs in the text convey information. Concentrate on understanding their message,
rather than just remembering what they look like.

Figure 1.13

Minimum Average Cost

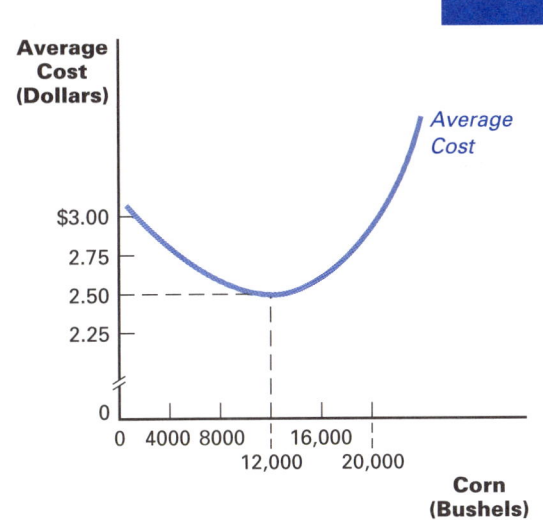

The minimum average cost of
producing corn is reached at the
low point on the curve showing the
average cost of producing a bushel
of corn.

End Notes

[1] George Stigler, "Nobel Lecture: The Process and Progress of Economics," *Journal of
Political Economy*, 91 (August 1983), p. 533.

[2] "Nobel Lecture," p. 533.

[3] Passell, Peter, "How Much for a Life? Try $3 Million to $5 Million," *The New York
Times*, January 29, 1995, p. F3.

Mutually Beneficial Exchange

Overview

Chapter 1 introduced the discipline of economics by identifying a simple, basic proposition upon which all economic theory is based: People make choices in a manner consistent with improvement of their well-being. We discussed the behavioral implications of this fundamental premise, as well as the scope of the economics discipline. Chapter 2 extends this introductory discussion of economics by illustrating the notion of value and how it influences decisions. We consider more formally the concept of efficiency and its relationship to value. Finally, we illustrate these concepts with two examples of voluntary exchange. The purpose of the examples is to show how the Fundamental Premise of Economics is applied in a variety of contexts and to demonstrate the motivation for exchange between people and between economies.

Learning Objectives

After reading and studying this chapter, you will be able to

1. Define the notion of value

2. Define *economic efficiency* and explain how it is related to *productive efficiency*

CHAPTER 2

3. Explain how the concept of economic efficiency is related to the Fundamental Premise of Economics

4. Explain the principle of comparative advantage

5. Use the production possibilities frontier model to explain a country's gains from specialization and trade

6. Identify and explain the costs of trade and exchange

7. Distinguish between the individual and social perspectives on a problem

Choice and Value

People seek to satisfy as many wants as their scarce resources will permit. This is true even though the preferences of different people differ widely. Social customs, ethnic traditions, and religious values all affect people's preferences, though the individuality of people from similar backgrounds is often obvious. Different people also differ greatly in their resource endowments: physical and financial assets, labor skills, and intellectual and physical abilities. Similarly, income varies widely. In 1992 per capita (per person) income was $23,400 in the United States, but only $380 in China and $780 in Senegal.

Despite the variety of wants and resource constraints, all individuals seek to maximize the net benefits, or value, they derive from their incomes. However, differences in preferences and resources imply that the specific ways in which individuals go about maximizing the value of their resources vary greatly. The following example illustrates this phenomenon.

Individual Choice

Consider a person named Henry, who has retired to the isolated countryside to live simply and in solitude, much like Henry Thoreau did at Walden Pond. The production possibilities frontier in Figure 2.1 belongs to Henry. It illustrates the maximum quantities of fish and vegetables that he can produce with the total stock of resources – primarily labor and some basic tools – available to him. The resources are valuable to Henry only because he can use them to produce and consume something of value to him: food. The value of the resources derives from the uses to which they can be put. Given the amount of resources available and the production conditions that determine how much fish and vegetables can be produced with those resources, Henry can have any combination of fish and vegetables on PPF_1. He could choose to be at A or B, for example. If Henry chooses to produce and consume at point A, his choice indicates that that combination of fish and vegetables is more satisfying to him than any other combination of fish and vegetables on PPF_1. That is, Henry prefers point A to any other point on PPF_1.

Another person with the same resource constraint might prefer the combination at point B in Figure 2.1. The fact that this person prefers more vegetables and less fish than Henry implies that he or she values fish and vegetables differently than Henry does. The valuation of goods and services is subjective; it reflects differences in tastes and goals. This notion of valuation is normative; we cannot appeal to other facts or objective criteria to argue that one person is somehow right and the other is wrong.

An individual's valuation of a good is reflected in his actions. Henry could choose to produce and consume at point B, but he opts for A because he prefers that combination. Since the other person prefers B to A, he or she uses resources differently than Henry uses his.

This example illustrates an important point. Satisfaction is achieved not by possessing resources, but by consuming the goods or services produced with them. The value an individual attaches to a stock of resources depends on the satisfaction derived from them. Individuals seek to make themselves as well off as they can by using resources to satisfy

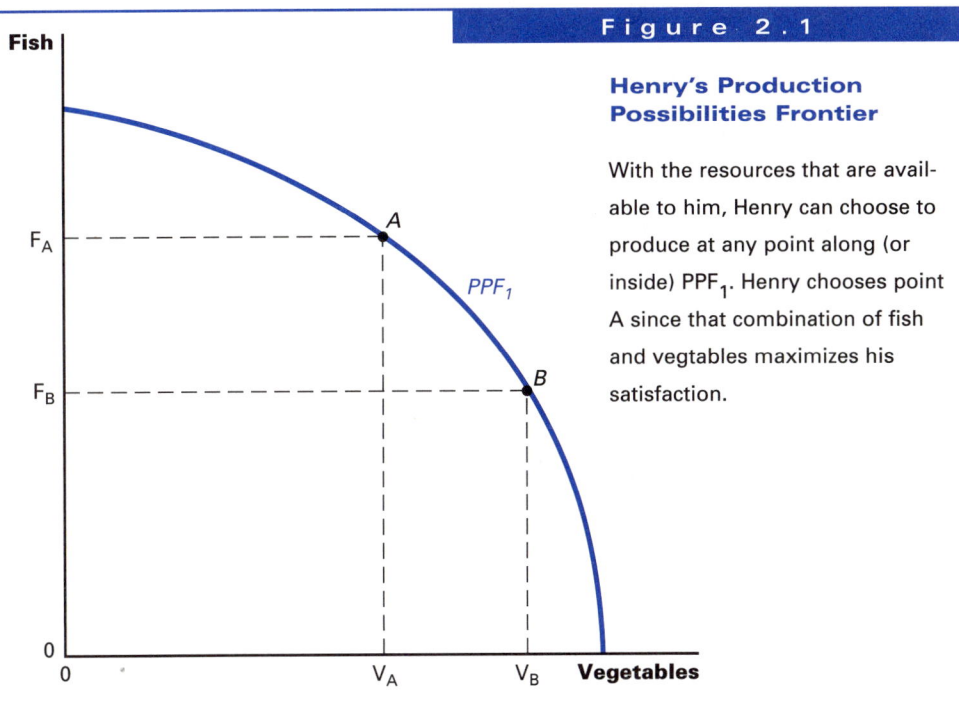

Figure 2.1

Henry's Production Possibilities Frontier

With the resources that are available to him, Henry can choose to produce at any point along (or inside) PPF₁. Henry chooses point A since that combination of fish and vegtables maximizes his satisfaction.

their particular wants. Resources are valuable only to the extent that they can be used to achieve an objective. If possessing resources were the end of economic behavior, everyone would be indifferent between points on the same PPF, because a PPF represents what can be produced with a *given* resource endowment.

Costs and Benefits

As we emphasized in Chapter 1, the fact that resources are limited implies that choices are costly. A decision to have more of one good is a decision to have less of another. The preferences and goals of individuals determine the values associated with alternatives and therefore influence the economic decisions individuals make. Thus, the benefits and costs of an alternative are specific to individuals or groups and are, to some extent, determined subjectively.

Economic Efficiency

Early in Chapter 1 we defined the Fundamental Premise of Economics: In all decision making, individuals choose the alternatives which they believe will produce the greatest net gains. The **net gain** of an action is the difference between the benefits received and the costs incurred. Benefits and costs reflect the subjective valuations of individual decision makers. An economically efficient choice is one that maximizes net gain. **Economic efficiency** means obtaining the maximum benefits for a given cost or minimizing the cost of a given benefit. In other words, economic efficiency is getting the most satisfaction out of available resources.

Net gain:
Difference between benefits received and costs incurred.

Economic efficiency:
Obtaining the maximum net gain from an action.

Productive efficiency:

Operating on the production possibilities frontier; producing without wasting resources.

Allocative efficiency:

Using resources to produce goods with the highest possible value.

We can illustrate the concept of economic efficiency by referring to the choice of a point on a production possibilities frontier. PPF_1, in Figure 2.1, illustrates the maximum combinations of fish and vegetables Henry can produce with a given stock of resources. If Henry utilizes his resources as productively as possible, not wasting any of them, he can produce any combination of fish and vegetables on PPF_1. Operating on the production possibilities frontier requires **productive efficiency**. No resources are wasted; the maximum amount of output is obtained from the available inputs.

However, not all points on PPF_1 are equally satisfactory to Henry. Although the resource cost to Henry of all combinations on PPF_1 is the same, his satisfaction is maximized at point A. If Henry were to use his resources to produce and consume at any point other than point A, such as at point B, he would not maximize his benefits. Thus, *economic efficiency requires not only productive efficiency (no waste) but also* **allocative efficiency** *– the allocation of resources to their highest-valued uses.* Only at point A does Henry maximize the difference between the benefits and costs of production and consumption.

Efficiency as a Goal

Individuals and societies have many different goals. The unhampered pursuit of individual satisfaction may not be compatible with some other goals. For example, society may choose to guarantee a minimum income level for all members of society. To do this, it may have to redistribute income from wealthier members of society to poorer ones through government taxation and spending programs. Such redistribution may reduce the level of satisfaction wealthy people are able to attain (while increasing the satisfaction of poorer people), and may even reduce the level of production in the economy, moving the economy inside its production possibilities frontier to a point such as E in Figure 2.2. In such a case, the goal of social equity dominates the goal of economic efficiency.

However, *within the constraints imposed by other social goals,* such as concern for equity, liberty, or economic growth, individuals and societies attempt to achieve economic

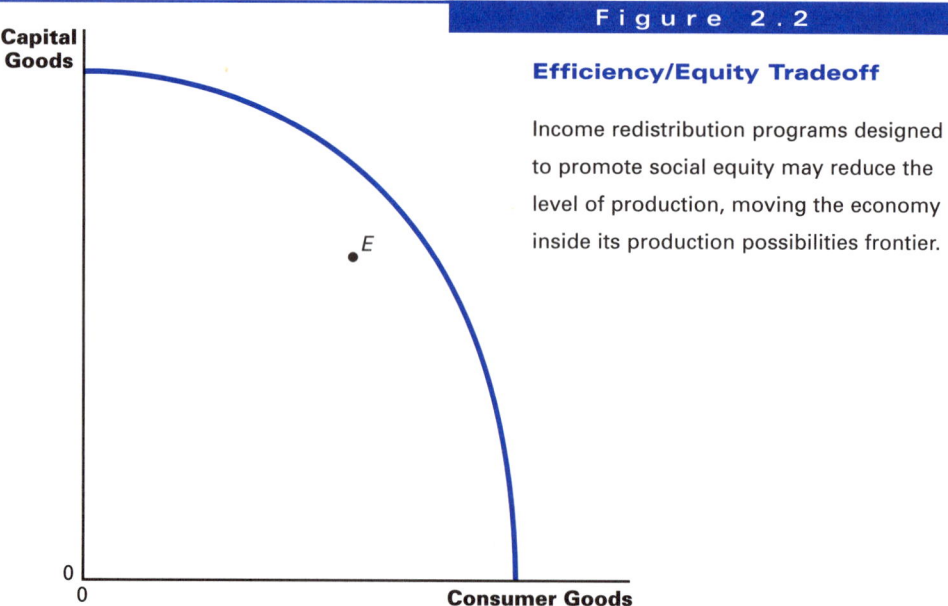

Figure 2.2

Efficiency/Equity Tradeoff

Income redistribution programs designed to promote social equity may reduce the level of production, moving the economy inside its production possibilities frontier.

efficiency. To do otherwise would be to waste scarce resources. Since economics contributes greatly to our understanding of how economic efficiency can be achieved, discussions of efficiency absorb most of our attention in this book. To a large extent, the job of an economist is to determine how specified goals can be achieved as efficiently as possible.

Economic efficiency combines both productive efficiency (producing without waste, on the PPF) with allocative efficiency (allocating resources to their most highly valued uses).

Section Recap

Gains from Exchange

Within the constraints imposed by other individual or social goals, people attempt to act in an economically efficient manner, that is, to obtain the greatest satisfaction possible out of available resources. This was Henry's objective in his individual production and consumption of food and is the objective of all those people who interact with large numbers of other people in their daily economic activities. The large majority of people in the world fit into the latter category; very few people are, or want to be, totally self-sufficient.

Why are so few people self-sufficient? The Fundamental Premise of Economics asserts that people choose to do what is most beneficial for themselves. If the Premise is true (and we believe it is), then most people must believe that economic interaction, specifically the voluntary exchange of goods and services, makes them better off than they could be without trading. Refer back to Figure 2.1. Henry maximizes his benefits, subject to the amount of resources available to him, by producing and consuming at point A. He cannot do as well producing and consuming at any other point on PPF$_1$. If he wants to be better off, then he must move to a point *beyond* his production possibilities frontier. This is exactly what voluntary exchange enables individuals – or societies – to do. By specializing in production and trading for other desired goods, individuals are able to push their *joint* production possibilities outward.

The remainder of the chapter investigates the nature of voluntary trade. It shows how trade can result in mutual gain for the traders by developing two different examples of trade and exchange. Each example demonstrates that an individual (or a society) can make himself (itself) better off by consuming at a point beyond his (or its) *individual* production possibilities frontier, by engaging in mutually beneficial trade. The examples illustrate different ways in which exchange can improve economic welfare. In the first example, an exchange allows two people to produce the same output with less effort. In the second example, two countries are able to increase the quantity of goods available for consumption by specializing and trading with one another.

Comparative Advantage at "Walden Pond"

The first illustration of the benefits of exchange involves two individuals, Henry and Kim. We've already met Henry. And Kim is, in fact, our student from Chapter 1. Kim has decided to take a break from school and, like Henry, move to the countryside to live simply and in solitude. Henry and Kim use their time for thinking, writing, and communing with nature. Each has a cabin on the edge of a large stream at the base of a small wooded hill, which separates the cabins. They spend their days fishing, foraging for wild vegetables, and enjoying quiet contemplation. Neither of them enjoys fishing or foraging as activities; rather, they fish and forage to provide themselves with food.

Henry and Kim discover one another one day at the stream, where both are fishing. Evening visits and conversations reveal the following interesting patterns. Henry spends much of his day foraging and fishing. It takes him four hours a day to catch enough fish for his daily diet; he also spends two hours a day searching for wild vegetables. Although Kim has exactly the same daily diet, it takes her only one and a half hours each in foraging and fishing to get the same daily foodstuffs for which Henry works six hours a day. Kim is better at both fishing and foraging than Henry; she has an **absolute advantage** in both activities.

These productivity differences cause Kim and Henry to wonder if there is a way for them to trade tasks and get the same work done in less time. In fact, there is. Suppose Kim fishes for both of them, while Henry forages for both. Then the total time spent on fishing and foraging is reduced from nine hours a day to seven. Kim spends three hours each day catching fish, and Henry spends four hours foraging for wild vegetables. This time-saving trade raises several questions, the first of which is how the trade reduces total work time.

Henry and Kim are able to reduce the time it takes to produce their vegetables and fish by *specializing* in activities for which each is the least-cost producer and then *trading* the fruits of their labors. In what sense is Kim the least-cost producer of fish? *Cost must be measured in terms of alternatives forgone.* In the time it takes for Kim to catch her desired quantity of fish, she could have found and picked her daily vegetables. The opportunity cost to Kim of her daily diet of fish is one daily serving of vegetables. It takes her one and a half hours to complete either activity. Henry must give up two daily servings of vegetables to catch his daily provision of fish. He requires four hours to catch his daily fish, but only two hours to gather his vegetables. Thus, Kim gives up less than Henry to get a day's fish. Figure 2.3 and Table 2.1 present the opportunity cost data in convenient form.

While Kim is the least-cost producer of fish, Henry is the least-cost forager; he gives up only half a day's serving of fish to gather his vegetables. Kim gives up one day's serving of vegetables to catch her fish. Kim is the least-cost fish producer relative to Henry, and Henry is the least-cost producer of vegetables relative to Kim.

Absolute advantage:

Ability to produce a good at a lower resource cost than other producers.

Table 2.1

"Walden Pond" Opportunity Costs

Relative Costs of Activity	Henry	Kim
Opportunity cost of one day's fish in terms of servings of vegetables	2.0	1.0
Opportunity cost of one day's vegetables in terms of servings of fish	0.5	1.0

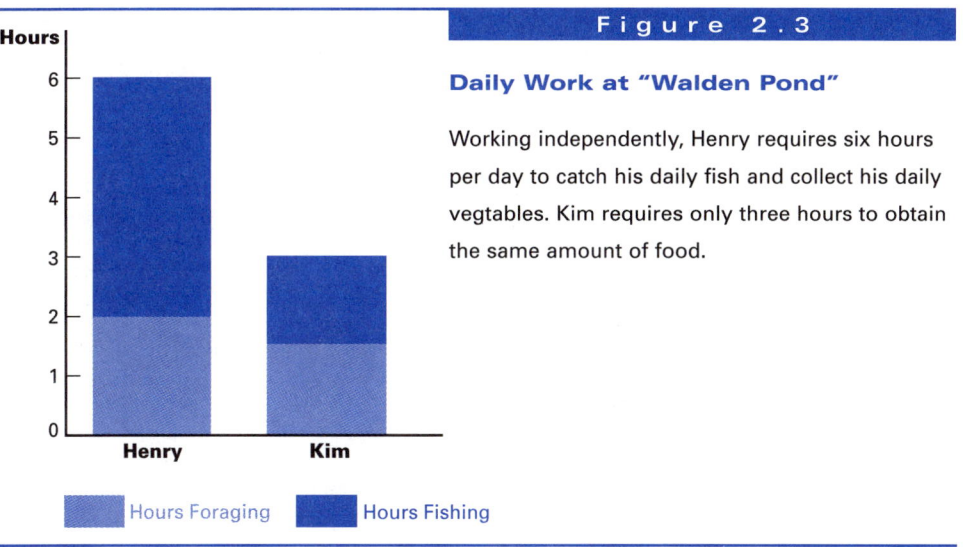

Figure 2.3

Daily Work at "Walden Pond"

Working independently, Henry requires six hours per day to catch his daily fish and collect his daily vegtables. Kim requires only three hours to obtain the same amount of food.

Suppose the two agree to specialize in production and trade goods. Kim catches fish for both, while Henry gathers vegetables for both. By specializing and trading, they are able to reduce the total time required to produce two daily servings of fish and two daily servings of vegetables. Figure 2.4 shows the time spent fishing and foraging with and without trade. If each person both fishes and forages, the total daily time required to complete the activities is nine hours (six for Henry plus three for Kim). If Kim specializes in fishing, while Henry forages, the total time requirement falls to seven hours. If they attempted to specialize in the "wrong" goods, producing their relatively high–opportunity-cost goods, the total time required to complete their daily activities would rise to eleven hours.

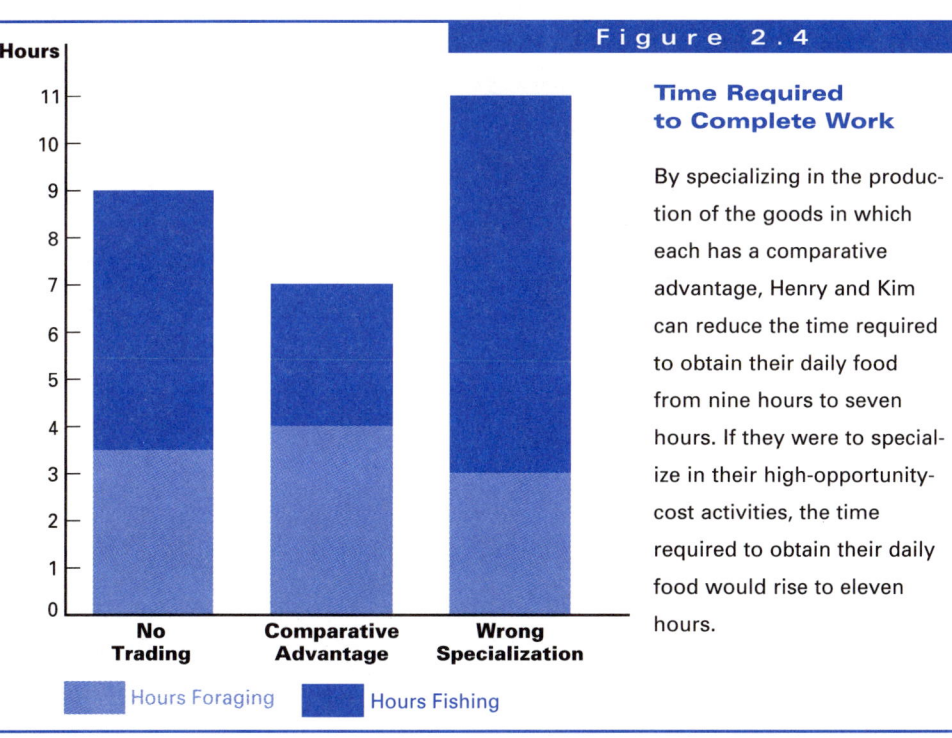

Figure 2.4

Time Required to Complete Work

By specializing in the production of the goods in which each has a comparative advantage, Henry and Kim can reduce the time required to obtain their daily food from nine hours to seven hours. If they were to specialize in their high-opportunity-cost activities, the time required to obtain their daily food would rise to eleven hours.

Paying for
the Right to Pollute

Acid rain, which is attributed to excessive amounts of sulfur dioxide (SO_2) in the atmosphere, has been blamed for a number of problems, including adverse effects on aquatic life, decreased yields of certain agricultural crops, and more rapid deterioration of building materials such as stone and metal. The source of much of the excess atmospheric SO_2 has been traced to the use of high-sulfur coal in coal-fired electric utility plants. Unless this coal is pretreated or the resulting exhaust fumes are somehow "cleaned," the sulfur is transformed into SO_2, which is then emitted into the atmosphere. This SO_2 eventually makes its way back to the earth's surface where it contributes to the problems described.

The Clean Air Act Amendments of 1990 included a number of provisions designed to reduce the amount of SO_2 emitted into the atmosphere. Among these provisions is a program that allows coal-fired electric utilities to purchase permits that allow them to emit a specified amount of SO_2 into the atmosphere each year. In effect, utilities can purchase the right to pollute.

When the Clean Air Act Amendments were being drafted, the permits program generated a great deal of controversy. Opponents argued, among other things, that the creation of permits would, in effect, legitimize air pollution. Supporters responded that such a program could help speed the process of addressing the problem of acid rain. In light of the amount of debate this program generated, it is worth asking: Does selling the right to pollute make economic sense?

To begin, it is important to recognize that eliminating the SO_2 that is emitted from existing coal-fired electric utilities would require that these plants either switch to a different, non-sulfur fuel or shut down. Such a move would cause the price of electricity to increase by a substantial amount in many parts of the country. In addition, it would increase reliance on other forms of energy, such as natural gas, hydro power, and nuclear fuel. While conservation could offset some of the loss of coal-fired

**Comparative
advantage:**

Ability to produce a good at a lower opportunity cost than other producers.

When each one specializes in that activity for which he or she is the least-cost producer, Henry and Kim are able to minimize the total cost of a day's worth of food for each of them. By specializing and trading they have reduced the opportunity cost of a day's food, even though Kim has an absolute advantage in both activities (she can complete either activity in less time than Henry). The gains come from exploiting comparative advantage. The **principle of comparative advantage** says that *total output is greatest when each good is produced by its least-opportunity-cost producer*. This principle applies to groups of individuals, to nations, and to the world economy.

How the gains from an exchange are distributed is another important issue. Notice that the specialization and exchange required to reduce the total time requirement to seven hours also distributes the entire two hour savings to Henry, who now works four hours rather than six, while Kim continues to work three hours as she did before specializing. What kind of exchange would save time for both Henry and Kim? Henry would have to forage for both and do some fishing. For example, Henry might gather vegetables for both and then catch a third of his daily fish. That would leave Kim with responsibility for one and two-thirds servings of fish. Henry would spend four hours foraging and an hour and a third fishing. Kim would spend two and a half hours fishing. To get both tasks done, trading one day's serving of vegetables for two-thirds of a serving of fish, they would spend a total of seven hours and fifty minutes, saving over an hour in total, with the savings split roughly equally.

electric power, this also would force people to incur tradeoffs. Since completely eliminating the use of coal to produce electricity does not appear to be feasible in the near future, the question becomes, "What is the most efficient way to reduce the rate of SO_2 emissions?"

Historically, the dominant approach to pollution control has been to impose some form of standards on polluters. For example, regulations have been passed that limit the amount of certain pollutants that firms can emit. Under this approach, firms are treated equally; each firm must reduce its pollution by the same amount, or to the same maximum allowable level. However, a problem with this approach is that not all firms are alike. In many situations, the costs of controlling additional units of pollution tend to increase with the amount of pollution controlled. In addition, the costs of controlling pollution vary across firms. Thus, some firms can control more

pollution than other firms for the same total cost. Since costs represent the amount of resources used, resource use would be minimized by having the more efficient firms control more pollution.

A permits market can result in the type of outcome just described. To see why, assume that it is decided that SO_2 emissions should be reduced to fifty units per year. To keep things simple, assume also that there are only two affected firms, Firm 1 and Firm 2, and each firm currently is emitting forty units of SO_2. Twenty-five permits (one permit equals one unit of SO_2) are given to each firm (it can be shown that the initial distribution of permits does not affect the final outcome). Thus, if no permits are traded, each firm must reduce its SO_2 emissions by fifteen units. However, so long as one firm can control SO_2 more cheaply than the other, it will be worthwhile for the more efficient firm to sell some of its permits to the less efficient firm. For example, assume Firm 1 can

control its 16th unit of SO_2 for $50, and it costs Firm 2 $70 to control its 15th unit of SO_2. Firm 2 could buy one of Firm 1's permits for a price between $50 and $70, for example, $60. Firm 1 would use the revenue from the sale of the permit to control the 16th unit of SO_2 (it would now emit 24 units of SO_2) and still have $10 left over. Firm 2 would use the permit to emit a 26th unit of SO_2 and save $10 – the difference between the cost of control ($70) and the price of the permit ($60). The total amount of SO_2 is still held to 50 units, but control costs have been reduced by $20.

As this example illustrates, once the level of pollution is set, allowing firms to exchange permits to pollute makes economic sense. The pollution target is met with the more efficient firms controlling more pollution, and total costs of control are minimized. The market for tradeable pollution permits is simply another illustration of the gains that follow from mutually beneficial exchange.

Specializing in low-opportunity-cost production activities and trading with others reduces the total cost of producing a given quantity of goods.

Section Recap

Comparative Advantage and International Trade

The second example of comparative advantage and exchange examines trade between countries. Such trade is motivated by the same kind of gains that motivated Henry and Kim to cooperate for time savings. Countries trade when they can make themselves better off. This basis for trade may seem strange to you, since news reports frequently suggest that a country is harmed, rather than helped, by trade with other countries. Congress regularly considers measures to "protect" domestic firms from foreign competition. A variety of protectionist measures restricts the quantity of imports that can enter the United States. Does trade really improve an economy's well-being?

The basis for international trade is the principle of comparative advantage. Trade between two countries arises when it is mutually beneficial. International trade permits countries to consume more goods and services than they could without trade. That is, it permits countries to "escape" their individual resource constraints.

Let's consider a simple example of trade in two goods, shoes and wheat, between two countries, the United States and South Korea. Each country can produce both shoes and wheat, and initially they do not trade. Both countries produce wheat and shoes and consume what they produce. The production and consumption options for each country are given by their respective production possibilities frontiers, depicted in Figure 2.5 and Table 2.2. South Korea can produce 150,000 pairs of shoes and no wheat or 50,000 tons of wheat and no shoes, or any (linear) combination of the two goods on its PPF. The United States can produce 150,000 pairs of shoes and no wheat or 150,000 tons of wheat and no shoes. (Linear PPFs are used for simplicity.)

Several possible production-consumption combinations are identified in Table 2.2. For example, Koreans could choose to produce and consume 150,000 pairs of shoes and no wheat or 120,000 pairs of shoes and 10,000 tons of wheat, or any of the other combinations shown. Assume that in the absence of trade, Koreans choose to annually produce and consume the combination of 50,000 pairs of shoes and 33,333 tons of wheat. The United States, on the other hand, can produce 150,000 pairs of shoes and no wheat or 150,000 tons of wheat and no shoes, or any linear combination therof. Before trade the United States chooses to produce and consume 50,000 pairs of shoes and 100,000 tons of wheat.

South Korea and the United States can both benefit from trade because of their different resource endowments and consequent differences in relative opportunity costs. Table 2.3 identifies these costs. To produce an additional 1,000 tons of wheat, South Koreans must give up 3,000 pairs of shoes. For example, in moving from the combination of 150,000 pairs of shoes and no wheat to the combination of 120,000 pairs of shoes and 10,000 tons of wheat, the Koreans must give up 3,000 pairs of shoes for each 1,000 tons of wheat produced. The United States gives up only 1,000 pairs of shoes per 1,000 tons of wheat. Therefore, the United States is the least-cost producer of wheat: It gives up less than South Korea to get additional wheat.

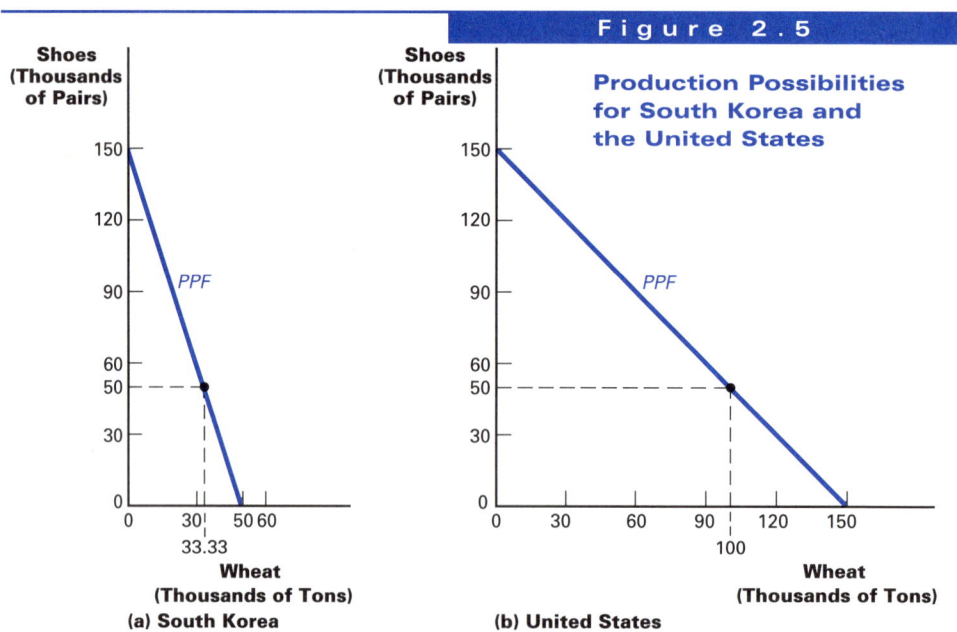

Figure 2.5

Production Possibilities for South Korea and the United States

(a) South Korea

(b) United States

The production possibilities frontier for South Korea shows that three pairs of shoes must be given up to produce one ton of wheat. The U.S. production possibilities frontier shows that only one pair of shoes must be given up to produce one ton of wheat.

Table 2.2

South Korean and U.S. Production Possibilities

South Korea		United States	
Shoes	Wheat	Shoes	Wheat
150	0	150	0
120	10	120	30
90	20	90	60
60	30	60	90
*50	33.33	*50	100
30	40	30	120
0	50	0	150

Shoes are measured in thousands of pairs, wheat in thousands of tons.

Note: * indicates pre-trade positions of the two countries.

To obtain an additional 1,000 pairs of shoes, Korea only gives up 333 tons of wheat (10,000 tons of wheat for 30,000 pairs of shoes), while the United States must sacrifice 1,000 tons of wheat for a thousand pairs of shoes. Thus, Korea is the least-cost producer of shoes relative to the United States. South Korea has a comparative advantage in shoes, and the United States has a comparative advantage in wheat. South Korea and the United States can gain from trade.

Americans are willing to trade wheat for shoes any time they can obtain 1,000 pairs for less than 1,000 tons of wheat. For instance, a trade of 500 tons of wheat for 1,000 pairs of shoes would make U.S. consumers better off. On the other hand, Koreans would trade 1,000 pairs of shoes anytime they could get more than 333 tons of wheat for them. Thus, an exchange of 1,000 pairs of shoes for 500 tons of wheat also would benefit Korean consumers.

If the United States specializes in the production of the good in which it has a comparative advantage (wheat) and South Korea specializes in the production of the good in which it has a comparative advantage (shoes), the two countries can trade and make themselves better off. By specializing in production and trading at a ratio between one ton of wheat for one pair of shoes and one ton of wheat for three pairs of shoes, both South Korea and the United States could achieve wheat and shoe consumption levels beyond their respective production possibilities frontiers. At a ratio of, for example, one ton of wheat for two pairs of shoes, both nations benefit from trading.

Table 2.3

Opportunity Cost of Producing Wheat and Shoes

	South Korea	United States
Cost of 1,000 tons of wheat (thousands of pairs of shoes given up)	3	1
Cost of 1,000 pairs of shoes (thousands of tons of wheat given up)	1/3	1

Figure 2.6 illustrates graphically the result of specialization and trade. South Korea specializes in shoe production, producing 150,000 pairs of shoes and no wheat, point A on its PPF. The United States specializes in wheat production, producing 150,000 tons of wheat and no shoes, point A′ on its PPF. South Korea continues to consume 50,000 pairs of shoes annually, so it has 100,000 pairs to trade to the United States for wheat. The United States continues to consume 100,000 tons of wheat, so it has 50,000 tons available for trade.

The two nations exchange goods at a ratio of two pairs of shoes for a ton of wheat. South Korea obtains 50,000 tons of wheat in exchange for its 100,000 pairs of shoes. After trade South Korea consumes 50,000 pairs of shoes and 50,000 tons of wheat annually, a net increase of 16,667 tons of wheat. This is represented by point B, a point beyond the South Korean production possibilities frontier. The United States consumes 100,000 tons of wheat and 100,000 pairs of shoes, a net increase of 50,000 pairs of shoes. Point B′ lies beyond the U.S. production possibilities frontier. Without sacrificing more shoes, Koreans are able to consume more wheat. Likewise, Americans are able to consume more shoes without sacrificing more wheat.

Specialization and trade allows each nation to reduce the opportunity cost of the good it acquires in trade. By trading, South Korea is able to acquire one ton of wheat for two pairs of shoes; producing its own wheat requires giving up three pairs of shoes. The United States gains by reducing the opportunity cost of shoe consumption from one ton of wheat per pair of shoes to one-half ton of wheat per pair. In fact, South Koreans would gain by trading at any ratio lower than three pairs of shoes per ton of wheat. Americans would gain at any ratio higher than one pair of shoes per ton of wheat. Thus, any trading ratio between one pair of shoes per ton of wheat and three pairs of shoes per ton of wheat benefits both countries. *For trade to be mutually beneficial, the trading ratio (commonly called the **terms of trade**) need only to lie between the two countries' individual opportunity cost ratios.*

Terms of trade:
The ratio at which two goods are traded for one another.

After trade, South Korea no longer produces wheat, nor does the United States produce shoes. Specialization eliminated one industry – and its employment opportunities – in each country. However, the other industry expanded – increasing employment – because of trade. It is this aspect of trade, the specialization of production, that prompts calls for protection. Although shoe firms go out of business in the United States, and shoe industry jobs vanish, the wheat industry expands, and new jobs are created. In the process, total output in South Korea and the United States increases. Trade based on comparative advantage allows more output to be produced from the stock of resources in the two countries. Greater economic efficiency is achieved.

Resource reallocations and employment changes can cause problems in an economy, at least in the short run. In addition, complete specialization makes South Korea and the United States dependent upon one another, a situation that carries some risks for both countries. Both of these important issues are considered in detail in Chapter 20 on international trade.

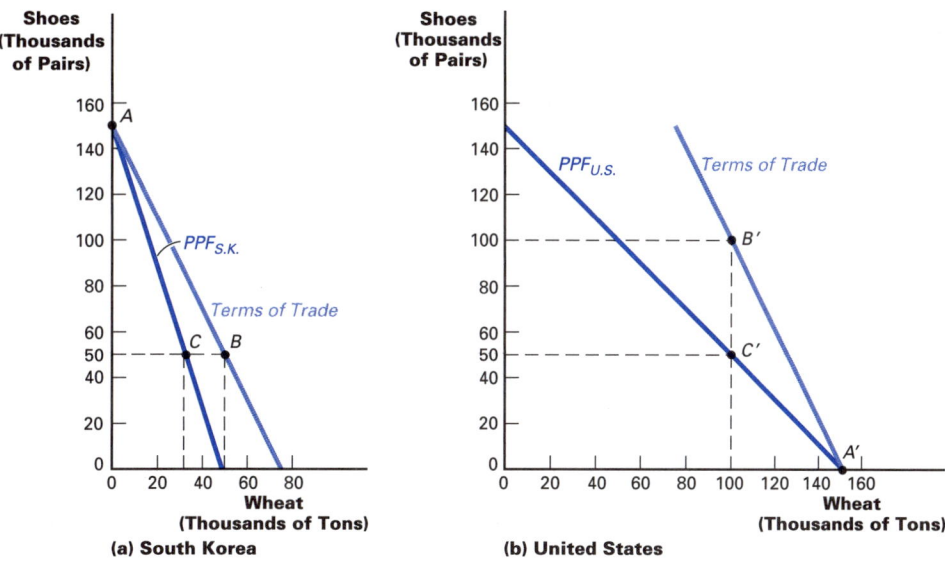

Figure 2.6

Gains from Trade Between South Korea and the United States

(a) South Korea

(b) United States

Before trade, South Korea and the United States consume at points C and C′. After trade they consume B and B′, points which lie outside their individual production possibilities frontiers.

By specializing in the production of goods in which a nation has a comparative advantage and trading with other nations, a nation can escape its production possibilities frontier.

Section Recap

Gains from Trade: Costs and Benefits . . . Again

Both of the preceding examples of exchange demonstrated that both parties to voluntary trade gain. In the case of individual exchange we saw that individuals pursuing their self-interest were able to make themselves better off – without making anyone worse off. Henry and Kim were able to reduce the time required for a given amount of production. In the case of international trade, the total production and consumption of the two trading nations increased. If the gains from international trade were allocated properly, no one in either South Korea or the United States need consume less, and some (or all) could consume more.

The principle of comparative advantage lies behind these gains. This principle presents a simple, yet powerful rule for achieving the objective of welfare maximization: Give up that which is less valuable in return for something that is more valuable. Specialize in producing those goods for which you have a comparative advantage, and trade for other goods of value to you. Doing so enables individuals or nations to use their resources in a way that increases their value.

DISAGREEMENT?

Just How Free Is a Free-Trade Agreement?

In the summer of 1992, negotiators representing the United States, Canada, and Mexico reached agreement on the general principles of the North American Free Trade Agreement (NAFTA). All three countries ratified the treaty shortly thereafter. The primary effect of NAFTA will be to significantly lower the barriers to trade among the three countries. Business leaders in the United States were generally in favor of NAFTA. In addition to opening up new markets for the products produced by U.S. firms, business leaders pointed out that NAFTA would result in lower prices for a variety of goods and services purchased in each country. In spite of the expected benefits to consumers, however, considerable opposition to the treaty arose, especially in the United States. The U.S. Congress was also split over the question of the relative merits of the agreement. Many Democrats were opposed to ratification, while the majority of Republicans favored it. In light of the gains promised by freer trade, it is worth asking, Why the disagreement?

The proponents of NAFTA argued that reduced barriers to trade would enable them to enter new markets and increase their levels of output. This would result in increased employment opportunities in industries that export a portion of the goods they produce. The benefits to consumers are the result of exploiting the comparative advantage(s) that different countries possess with respect to the production of certain goods and the effects of increased competition on

Alternatives play a very important role in the nature and extent of trade and exchange. Alternatives determine the gains from trade. What matters are relative benefits and costs. For instance, Kim was an efficient fisherman relative to Henry. Or to put it another way, Kim specialized in fishing because Henry was relatively bad at it. If by chance Henry could have caught the daily requirement of fish in one hour rather than four, Kim would have been the relatively inefficient fisherman. In the second example, the United States is a relatively inefficient shoe producer but an efficient wheat producer. The actions taken to improve one's welfare depend upon the alternatives available. When alternatives change, relative costs and benefits change, and other actions may become more beneficial.

Costs of Exchange

Our discussion of the benefits of specialization and exchange raises several important issues. We have emphasized the benefits of voluntary exchange because these gains are the motivation for much of the economic activity that occurs throughout the world. However, the emphasis on gains from exchange is not intended to ignore problems that can accompany trade and exchange.

Transactions Costs

Transactions costs:
Costs of trading, including costs of acquiring information, working out trade agreements, and transporting goods.

Trade cannot be carried out without cost. Resources are consumed in acquiring information about trading opportunities, working out trade agreements, and transporting goods. Such **transactions costs** reduce or possibly eliminate the gains that could be real-price. (Increased competition tends to push product prices lower.)

NAFTA's critics argued that rather than producing benefits for the U.S. economy, the treaty was likely to result in the loss of American jobs and adverse environmental effects. With respect to jobs, they argued that because the wages of foreign workers tend to be lower than the wages paid to their U.S. counterparts, U.S. firms would have an incentive to move their operations to foreign countries. In the case of the environment, critics argued that environmental standards, especially those in Mexico, are less restrictive than those in the United States and are weakly enforced. Consequently, U.S. firms would have a further incentive to relocate where the costs of environmental compliance, and therefore overall production costs, would be lower. The result would be further degradation of the environment and all of the costs that go with it.

The extent to which the claims of each side are correct is subject to some debate. For example, one study estimated that although approximately 145,000 U.S. jobs would be lost to Mexico as a result of NAFTA, an additional 316,000 new jobs would be created over a ten-year period. Thus, while it may be true that, on net, additional jobs would be created, it is also true that some currently employed people are likely to lose their jobs, and in fact, this has happened to a limited extent. With respect to concerns about cheap foreign labor, it is worth noting that the wages of U.S. workers are higher, at least in part, because of the relatively higher productivity of U.S. labor. Thus, there is only an incentive for firms to relocate if costs per unit of output are actually lower elsewhere. Finally, concerns about adverse effects on environmental quality were addressed separately. Provisions that require strict enforcement of existing and new standards could go a long way toward avoiding the potential adverse consequences suggested by some of NAFTA's opponents.

How the benefits and costs of NAFTA will be distributed within and across the three countries remains to be seen. There is little doubt that certain individuals in all three countries have been adversely affected. However, the evidence that has been collected thus far, as well as economic theory, suggests that the overall benefits should far outweigh the costs incurred.

ized if trade was costless. If transactions costs are equal to or greater than the gains from trading, trade will not take place.

Because transactions costs reduce the gains from trading, society benefits when people discover ways to reduce transactions costs. The development of the internal combustion engine and its use in motor vehicles reduced transportation costs tremendously and enabled exchange to expand. Nearly a century before the automobile, the development of steam locomotives and the technology to make steel rails reduced costs in a similar fashion. Modern computer technology has revolutionized the financial sector of the economy. Information – and money – moves from place to place in seconds, enabling exchange to proceed in a manner unimagined fifty years ago.

Transactions costs represent a use of society's resources, just as production costs do. When transactions costs are lowered, more resources are available for other uses. The production possibilities frontier moves outward.

Potential Costs of Specialization

When we think of specialization, assembly line jobs often come to mind. Tasks are broken down into different steps, and workers are assigned only one repetitive task. Such jobs are often monotonous, requiring a machine-controlled work pace and offering little or no opportunity to exercise initiative. An example of such a job is that of "boiled-egg peeler." Restaurants often find it less costly to buy boiled, peeled eggs from a supplier than to cook and prepare the eggs themselves. Firms specializing in the sale of pre-cooked, peeled eggs employ workers to peel the eggs by hand.[1] A peeler peels the egg, inspects it, and sorts it into one of several categories. Workers are expected to peel at least twenty eggs a minute.

Such specialization reduces the cost of producing goods and services. However, specialized jobs can generate boredom, alienation, and "emptiness" in the lives of workers. Do individuals really benefit from this kind of work?

The gains from specialization and trade cannot be measured by some narrowly defined, objective measure, such as increased output. The gains from an exchange are measured in terms of value to the parties to the exchange. Workers who voluntarily accept a job, such as that of egg-peeler, are trading their time and effort, and their willingness to put up with possibly unattractive working conditions, for the benefits of employment, such as wages and fringe benefits. For many people, the costs of the job would be greater than the benefits, since they have alternative opportunities that are more attractive. For other workers, this job may be the best opportunity available. Higher output is the reward for specialization, but the cost of this reward might be negative effects on the individual. In general, an exchange is based on all factors that matter to individuals, either as benefits or costs.

Trade Can Make Some People Worse Off

We have stressed the gains that accrue to those participating in voluntary exchange. According to the principle of comparative advantage, economic efficiency is achieved when goods and services are produced by the people with the lowest opportunity costs. Specialization and trade on the basis of comparative advantage do not always make *everyone* better off, however. Following the principle of comparative advantage can quickly make some people worse off.

The pressure put on many locally owned stores in small towns by the opening of a Wal-Mart store provides an excellent example of how changing trade patterns – based on changes in comparative advantage – can impose costs on some. Because of its large volume purchases, Wal-Mart can buy most goods at a lower price than can small stores. The savings are then passed along to consumers. Inability to compete causes many small stores to lose business and eventually close. Thus, although the opening of a Wal-Mart store benefits consumers in small towns and rural areas, it usually harms the owners of small stores. It is not surprising that such business people often band together to oppose the opening of a Wal-Mart in their town.

Individual Versus Group Well-Being

The Wal-Mart example poses an important question for society. When one individual or group is harmed and another benefits by an action, how are the benefits and costs to be weighed? An international trade example illustrates the general problem. Over the quarter century from 1965 to 1989 the share of U.S. auto sales accounted for by foreign cars rose from six percent to about thirty-three percent. This trend caused the domestic auto manufacturing industry to reduce employment by about fifteen percent. The auto industry and its workers argued that the foreign competition was unfair and that they should be protected from it by restrictions on imports. Although millions of consumers gained by being able to buy the cars they liked best at lower prices – foreign cars – thousands of autoworkers lost their jobs. Should society have "protected" them?

In answering this question we must recognize that two views always exist on such an issue: an individual view and a social perspective. Although we cannot ignore the individual view, it is the social perspective to which we must pay attention if we are interested in society's overall welfare. The individual view of this problem varies depending upon the individuals concerned. Consumers were better off as a result of the foreign competition; they got cheaper, and often better, automobiles. Displaced autoworkers were clearly worse off. Unemployed autoworkers lost good jobs and the attractive lifestyles built around them. With the arrival of lower-cost foreign producers, a valuable employment opportunity disappeared. Was society better or worse off?

The social perspective acknowledges that some individuals were better off and others worse off as a result of the imports. What was the net gain to society from the foreign trade in automobiles? Did the benefits outweigh the costs? The evidence suggests that trade was indeed beneficial. Two major studies of the impact of foreign competition on the auto industry and the restrictions placed on such competition found that the cost to consumers of protecting the domestic automobile industry in the 1980s was three to four times as great as the benefits to autoworkers, as measured by worker compensation. Put another way, if society had wanted to protect autoworker incomes, it would have been only one-fourth to one-third as costly to consumers to have simply paid higher taxes to support displaced autoworkers at their previous income levels, rather than paying the higher automobile prices resulting from restricting trade.[2]

Society is composed of many people. Taking the social perspective amounts to making a decision about what is best for these people, not just in the present, but also over long periods of time. Individuals acting in concert as society must determine the limits of both individual and social rights. For example, society might determine that no individual has the right to take another's property by force or coercion but that it is perfectly acceptable to reduce another person's income by performing better than that person in the marketplace. In such a case, society determines whether the *processes* by which individuals seek to maximize their satisfaction are acceptable, without determining the *outcomes* of those processes. In other cases, the people of a society, acting through government, may choose to determine outcomes, as when a minimum standard of living is guaranteed by the government (acting on behalf of society).

The people of a society must also determine the limits of social rights. The more rights granted to government, the fewer rights left for individuals. For example, when society chooses to use government to make a high level of services available to all citizens, it also chooses to limit the rights of individuals to the enjoyment of the income produced by their own labor. Government services must be financed, so individual incomes will be taxed. The higher the level of government services, the higher the level of taxation. Individual actions to maximize satisfaction thus are limited by social goals.

Both individual and social perspectives exist on almost all issues. Efficient social decisions are made within the constraints imposed by the social perspective, which in democratic societies reflects the values and goals of the people comprising society. Costs and benefits are associated with almost every decision in a world of limited resources. Although we cannot avoid some costs, we want to avoid making decisions that generate costs greater than the accompanying benefits. In making social decisions the individuals who incur the costs are often different from those who reap the benefits. Only if we choose alternatives that generate net benefits do we have the opportunity and the resources to help those who bear the burden of an efficient decision.

Section Recap

Specialization and trade can harm producers who do not have a comparative advantage. Therefore, individuals often oppose free trade, even when the net gains to society from such trade are large.

Summary

Scarcity forces individuals and societies to make choices to maximize the consumption value of their resources. The preferences, goals, and resource endowments of people and societies vary widely. This diversity leads to a wide variety of choices by individuals attempting to maximize the value of their resources.

A "valuable" use of resources is defined by the individual; it reflects the preferences and goals of the individual. **Value** is determined subjectively. **Economic efficiency** implies getting the most satisfaction from available resources – maximizing the difference between the benefits and costs of alternatives. This general notion of efficiency pervades economic analysis. Specific applications appear throughout the remainder of the text.

Economic efficiency is enhanced when individuals engage in **mutually beneficial exchange**. The basis for these exchanges is the principle of **comparative advantage**. Since tastes and resource endowments differ across individuals and societies, two individuals can gain by exchanging lesser-valued goods or resources for more highly valued goods or resources. What one person values highly may be of little value to another person.

Comparative advantage is concerned with **relative opportunity costs**. Output is maximized and economic efficiency is achieved when each good is produced by the low-opportunity-cost producer. Gains from specialization and trade exist when resource endowments differ. The pattern of trade and exchange based on comparative advantage depends fundamentally on the alternatives available to individuals and nations. Available alternatives determine the low-opportunity-cost options. When alternatives change, the pattern of specialization and trade changes.

Society must reconcile patterns of exchange that impose costs on some and confer benefits on others. The interaction among people and nations motivated by the principle of comparative advantage requires individuals and groups to choose appropriate decision-making techniques. The people comprising society must decide what limits to place on individual rights, as well as what limits to impose on government acting as society's agent. Such decisions determine which exchanges and what terms of trade are permitted.

Two perspectives exist on virtually every issue: an individual perspective and a social one. Individuals are assumed to follow their own self-interest. That which makes an individual better off does not necessarily make everyone in society better off. If society decides to prohibit some economic activities, the decision itself makes some individuals better off and others worse off. A social decision is efficient when the value of the benefits generated exceeds the value of the costs imposed. A significant attribute of economic analysis is that it focuses on the social perspective.

Chapter 3 begins to consider in some detail the issues just raised. We give particular attention to the identification and analysis of decision-making techniques that reconcile the pursuit of individual economic efficiency with economic efficiency for society.

Questions for Thought

Knowledge Questions

1. What is the difference between productive efficiency and economic efficiency?

2. What is the *principle of comparative advantage*? How is economic efficiency improved by following this principle?

3. Under what circumstances is a trading ratio beneficial to both parties to a potential exchange?

4. Before the 1970s, houses in the Midwest were built with very little insulation, a construction method considered efficient at the time. By 1980, it was considered inefficient. Why?

Application Questions

5. Explain the difference between a linear (straight line) production possibilities frontier and a production possibilities frontier that is concave to the origin (bowed out). In particular, what assumption is made regarding opportunity costs in each case?

6. It takes 2.5 hours to travel by bus to Chicago's O'Hare Airport from Bloomington, Illinois, but only thirty minutes by plane. The bus fare is $20.00 and the air fare is $50.00. If the value of your time is $10.00 an hour, would you travel by bus or plane? At $15.00 an hour? At $20.00 an hour?

7. Professor Anderson is a respected economist who runs a thriving research and consulting firm whose services are demanded throughout the state. Because of his abilities, Professor Anderson commands a wage rate of $40.00 an hour for his services. He is also an excellent computer programmer. In fact, he can program twice as fast as the graduate student programmers he hires for $7.50 an hour. Should he do his own programming? Explain.

8. The average size of a farm in the United States is about 450 acres and is worked by two or three people. The same number of people work a farm of less than an acre

in parts of Asia. What role do relative prices play in determining the land/labor mix for agricultural production? Which of these two farm sizes is more efficient?

9. When repairs on a car are necessary, some people do the work themselves. Others who know just as much about automobiles hire an auto mechanic to do the work. What factors influence this decision?

10. Idaho and California produce oranges and potatoes. The production possibilities frontiers for both states are given below. What is the opportunity cost of potatoes in California? In Idaho? What is the opportunity cost of oranges in California? In Idaho? Who has the comparative advantage in orange growing? In potato growing? Would they both gain from trade with one another if they traded at a ratio of 100 pounds of potatoes for 300 pounds of oranges?

California		Idaho	
Oranges	Potatoes	Oranges	Potatoes
0	60	0	150
50	50	50	125
100	40	100	100
150	30	150	75
200	20	200	50
250	10	250	25
300	0	300	0

Quantities are in hundreds of pounds

Synthesis Questions

11. Meredith and Lindsey have much in common. Each is married, their husbands both have the same income, they each have two children whose ages are the same. However, Meredith has a full-time job, while Lindsey works at home, devoting her time and effort to "home" work. What would cause them to choose these different careers? Explain.

12. During the energy crisis of the 1970s, the federal government gave much thought to rationing gasoline usage. Economists argued that the efficiency of a gasoline rationing plan allotting an equal number of gasoline coupons to each private automobile would be enhanced if auto owners were permitted to buy and sell the coupons from one another. Explain why the opportunity to trade coupons would improve economic efficiency.

13. Consumers trade part of their incomes for agricultural products like flour and milk. These exchanges are motivated by the drive for economic efficiency. How does a government program that raises the price of wheat and milk affect these trades between consumers and farmers (through retailers)?

14. Should a society permit unrestricted mutually beneficial trading in the following goods and services? Explain.

- Medical care
- Drinking water
- Land
- Public transportation
- Private transportation
- Liquor
- Marijuana

End Notes

[1] The job is explained in "Boiled-Egg Peelers Aim for Perfection, and That's No Yolk," *The Wall Street Journal*, July 9, 1985.

[2] Similar conclusions are reached by Robert W. Crandall, "Import Quotas and the Automobile Industry: The Costs of Protectionism," *The Brookings Review* 2, No. 4 (Summer 1984), pp. 8-16; and Charles Collyns and Steve Dunaway, "The Cost of Trade Restraints: The Case of Japanese Automobile Exports to the United States," *IMF Staff Papers* 34, No. 1 (March 1987), pp. 150-175.

The Market Mechanism: Supply and Demand

Overview

The scarcity of resources, and of the goods and services produced with resources, forces every society to adopt some mechanism to ration goods and services to uses and users. Many possible rationing mechanisms exist. Some rationing mechanisms rely on a few people following a plan, to make economic choices for society, while others give wide latitude to individual choice in allocating resources and goods and services. If individual choices are not to produce economic chaos, however, they must be reconciled to one another in some manner. The market mechanism provides a means of reconciling millions of individual choices when these choices are constrained by scarce resources.

Since the U.S. economy relies heavily on markets to coordinate economic activity, we deal with market behavior in every chapter. We use the market model to address a wide variety of problems, all having a common element: people making choices under resource constraints. Thus, it is important to understand the basic market model presented in this chapter.

We begin the chapter with a discussion of the general rationing problem caused by scarce resources. A number of potential decision-making criteria are discussed. We then proceed to the definition of a market, the development of the concepts of demand and supply, and an exploration of the process by which demand and supply interact to determine equilibrium in the market. We then consider how market forces work to re-establish market equilibrium in response to a change in market conditions.

Learning Objectives

After reading and studying this chapter, you will be able to

1. Distinguish between centralized and decentralized decision making

2. Understand how markets ration goods to consumers and producers

CHAPTER 3

3. Explain why the laws of demand and supply are important to economists

4. Distinguish between a change in demand (or supply) and a change in quantity demanded (or quantity supplied)

5. Describe how market clearing is achieved in a free market economy

6. Explain how a specific change in demand or supply alters prices and amounts produced and consumed

The Market as a Rationing Device

Many, if not most, of the purchases we make depend upon, among other things, the price of the good or service we're considering buying. From the buyer's perspective, the price is taken as a given. With a few exceptions – the purchase of a car or a house, for example – we rarely haggle over price. But how are prices determined? Our intuition suggests that sellers will set prices as high as they can to earn as much income as possible. Buyers, on the other hand, are looking for the best bargain, comparing the prices of different goods. In Chapter 1 we identified the fundamental economic problem – scarcity. Resource scarcity implies that not all wants can be satisfied. Thus, societies must develop ways of reconciling the competing claims of individuals and groups. In this chapter we explore the nature of this basic social problem and analyze in depth one particular mechanism for reconciling competing claims – the market.

The *market* is a term applied to the processes that coordinate the wishes of consumers who demand goods and services and producers who supply goods and services. By affecting the prices of goods and services, the forces of consumer demand and producer supply interact to bring order to an economic system that is controlled by no single planner. Individuals pursuing their own interests also serve the interests of society by helping to satisfy the wants of others.

Scarcity Implies Choices

Every economy must answer three basic questions:

1. What will be produced?

2. How will it be produced?

3. For whom will it be produced?

Since most resources can be used to produce a variety of goods or services, the economy must somehow determine which of the many possible goods and services will actually be produced. For example, consider the many possible uses of steel. Somehow the economy must determine how much steel to produce and how to use that quantity. Should the steel go into automobiles, or bridges, or metal buildings, or industrial machines? The economy must have a mechanism to determine which goods will be produced and to allocate resources to the production of the goods and services people actually prefer. An economy that produces lots of goods nobody wants has failed to properly allocate its resources.

The allocation decision is closely related to the decisions of how to produce goods and how to distribute the goods produced. Most goods can be produced in more than one way. An economy that uses its resources efficiently (that is, doesn't waste resources) can produce more goods and services than an economy that produces inefficiently. Once produced, the goods must be distributed in some manner to the people who ultimately consume them.

The rules an economy uses to ration goods to ultimate consumers heavily influence how resources are allocated. Different economic systems have vastly different rationing mechanisms. Some economies ration resources and products by relying almost entirely on markets to reconcile individual choices. In such **market economies** individuals own most property and have the freedom to make decisions concerning how to use their property. Although not a pure market economy, the U.S. economy is dominated by market activity. At the opposite extreme are **command economies**, in which decision making is centralized in the hands of a few powerful planners, and individuals have limited economic choices. The North Korean economy is of this type, as to a large extent is the Chinese economy, although the use of markets is increasing. The economy of the former Soviet Union was also, by and large, a command economy.

Most economies lie between the extremes of free markets and complete government direction. Sweden is an example of a **mixed economy** – an economy in which economic decision making is shared by market participants and government. Even in the United States the government plays an important role in the economy. However, the market is used to a much greater extent in the United States than in Sweden, where the government provides most basic economic services, such as housing, health care, and education. To finance these services, the Swedish government claims more than half the income of Swedish citizens through various forms of taxation, while total taxes in the United States claim about one-third of total income.

In a democratic society, the economic decision-making system is based on the people's values and goals, which are shaped by the society's particular history and its political and moral philosophy. Social differences lead to economic differences. Thus, it is not surprising that even in democratic societies we see a wide variety of economic arrangements.

Market economy:
An economy in which individuals own most property and make most decisions about its use; decisions are coordinated through markets.

Command economy:
An economy in which decision making is centralized in the hands of a few planners.

Mixed economy:
An economy in which economic decision making is shared by individuals and government.

Rationing Mechanisms and Behavior

Since scarce goods must be rationed, *some* rationing mechanism is always in use. The rationing mechanism actually chosen may reflect either philosophical, social, or cultural values, or the views of a powerful ruling elite. However they are chosen, once in place, rationing mechanisms affect the behavior of members of society. Competition for goods and services exists in every society, since competition results from scarcity. However, the form competition takes depends to a large extent on the rationing mechanism used by a society.

The rationing mechanism used in market economies is *price*, or willingness to pay. Goods are rationed to those who are willing (and able) to pay the most. In a market economy, competition largely takes the form of attempting to acquire wealth, because wealth enhances a person's ability to acquire goods and services on the basis of willingness to pay. Income becomes an important measure of one's power and position in a market economy.

Other rationing mechanisms produce different types of competitive behavior. One simple rationing device used in some economies is *rationing by queue*. People line up to buy meat or bread or tickets to sporting events. Competition takes a different form when goods are rationed to those who stand in line. People who are best able or most willing to wait in line the longest are able to obtain the most resources, having outbid other individuals who are unwilling to pay as much in terms of time spent in line.

Political criteria are often used to ration goods. Political leaders may attempt to effect a desired income distribution or may simply override the market to achieve other aims, such as military conquest. Sets of rules, some quite arbitrary, are used to allocate resources. The rules reflect the power of some individual or group or society's values. For instance, racial or ethnic preference or membership in a party can be a rationing criterion. When affiliation with a political party is an important rationing criterion, people compete for goods by attempting to advance politically.

Often a combination of rationing mechanisms is used in a single economy. Access to a college education in the United States is based in part on willingness to pay and academic performance, and students bid to enter college on these bases. Market exchanges often require waiting in line as well as willingness to pay the market price. Employers hire new employees on the basis of past performance, general knowledge, and even appearance, and job seekers compete on these criteria. To borrow money one must demonstrate credit worthiness and some financial security. Potential borrowers compete for borrowed funds by establishing good credit ratings, sources of collateral with which a loan can be secured, and an income stream that will enable the borrower to repay the loan.

When analyzing the strengths and weaknesses of the market as a rationing device, it is important to remember that *some rationing device is always in use*. The fact that the market does not perform as well as one might hope in a particular instance is not grounds for replacing it unless some other rationing mechanism is likely to produce better results.

The Market Mechanism: Mutually Beneficial Exchange

When decision making is left to individuals, the basic economic questions (what? how? for whom?) are answered by the free interaction of individuals in society. People are free to arrange and negotiate mutually beneficial exchanges. Of course, society defines property ownership rights and the kinds of exchanges that are allowed through some social decision-making process. The government establishes the rules of the game and allows individuals to make their own decisions within the framework of those rules. Since the decisions made by individuals reflect the rules governing market exchange, the particular set of rules adopted by government is important.

As we argued in Chapter 2, all voluntary trades reflect the attempt to trade something of lesser value for something of greater value. Markets arise in response to this desire. If individuals are to obtain the maximum benefit from exchanging goods and services, they must know what their alternatives are. They seek to make the best trade they can, but they are able to do this only if they know the available trading opportunities: who has goods for trade, what kind of goods are being offered, and what terms of trade are acceptable. Acquiring such information is costly. To make a beneficial trade decision, one must commit time, effort, and resources to the task. Markets have developed to economize on such transactions costs.

Although a market can be a physical location, not all markets operate in one place. People buy vegetables at a produce market, brokers sell common stocks on the New York Stock Exchange, feedlot owners buy cattle at an auction barn, and people borrow (buy) and lend (sell) loanable funds at banks and thrift institutions. In each of these examples a market exists in both a physical and an abstract sense. Buyers and sellers meet at a specific geographic location to interact, establish a **market price**, and determine the quantity of the good exchanged. However, a market need not have a specific geographic location. The *market* is the *process* by which buyers and sellers determine the terms of trade. Although purchases of new cars or fast food take place at specific locations, the markets for new cars and fast food – as well as the markets for cattle and loanable funds – encompass transactions occurring in many places at once. Market participants are aware of market prices, trends in prices, and other market-related information, and they tie geographically separated markets together by searching for the most beneficial trades.

The precise manner in which the market mechanism operates to establish a market price and determine the quantity exchanged is very important for understanding the benefits and limitations of market decision making. The remainder of the chapter explores the functioning of the market mechanism.

Market price:
Price established by the interaction of consumers demanding a good and producers supplying the good.

Scarce resources force societies to ration goods. Some rationing mechanism is always in use. The market rations goods by allocating them to those who are able and willing to pay the most for them.

Section Recap

Consumption Decisions: Demand

People satisfy wants by purchasing and consuming goods and services. The decisions that individuals and families make as consumers have an important impact not only on their own welfare but also on the economic well-being of others.

Budget-Constrained Choice

Limited incomes force consumers to make choices. Choosing one good or service forces them to give up other desirable goods and services. Thus, consumers attempt to acquire the goods and services that provide them with the maximum benefits. This is the Fundamental Premise of Economics applied to consumption decisions.

How does an individual decide which goods to buy and which to give up? A consumer cannot simply buy those goods that yield the most benefits, because different goods have different opportunity costs. A new car yields much more benefits than a candy bar, but its opportunity cost is thousands of times higher. A consumer must pay attention not only to the benefits of a good, but also to the opportunity cost of the good.

Changes in the market price of a good alter the opportunity cost of consuming the good. When the price of a good increases, a consumer must make a greater sacrifice to obtain the good. The increased cost makes the good less attractive to consumers, who *economize* on the now more costly good by reducing their purchases of the good and switching to other less costly ways of satisfying their wants.

Negatively Sloped Demand Curve

Law of demand:

The quantity demanded of a good is negatively related to its price, holding constant other factors that affect demand.

Ceteris paribus:

A Latin phrase meaning, "other things being equal."

Marginal benefit:

The benefits derived from consuming an additional unit of a good.

The relationship between the consumption of a good and its price is so predictable that economists have dubbed it the **law of demand**: The quantity of a good consumed is negatively related to the price of the good, holding constant other factors that influence consumers' willingness or ability to pay for the good. A higher price reduces consumption, and a lower price encourages consumption.

Consider a teenager's demand for flavored iced tea (such as Snapple). The law of demand says that as the price of a can of flavored iced tea rises, the number of cans Shane (the teenager) will purchase falls. That is, *holding other factors besides price constant*, the quantity of flavored iced tea demanded by Shane at any particular price falls as the price rises. The Latin phrase **ceteris paribus**, meaning "other things being equal," is usually substituted in economic writing for the phrase *other factors held constant*.

Table 3.1 shows Shane's *demand schedule* for flavored iced tea. The demand schedule shows the maximum quantity of cans demanded per week at various prices, assuming all other factors affecting Shane's demand for flavored iced tea to be constant. The demand schedule is graphed in Figure 3.1.

Shane's demand schedule displays the negative relationship between price and quantity demanded, summarized by the law of demand. This negative relationship exists because Shane experiences *declining marginal benefits* from consuming flavored iced tea. The **marginal benefit** of a can of flavored iced tea is the added benefit Shane derives from consuming *one additional* can. As Shane acquires more cans of iced tea, the marginal benefit of each *additional* can falls. Shane values the first few cans of flavored iced tea more highly than additional cans. He is willing to pay 90¢ per can to consume four cans each week. However, the benefit he receives from drinking flavored iced tea declines with each additional can he drinks, so the price of a can would have to fall to induce him to buy more than four cans. Should the price decline to 85¢ per can, Shane would be willing to buy an additional three cans (for a total of seven) per week. *Shane's demand schedule for flavored iced tea is a marginal benefit schedule.*

Table 3.1	

Shane's Demand for Flavored Iced Tea

Price	Quantity Demanded (cans per week)	
$0.50	28	€14 .
0.55	25	€13 75
0.60	22	€13 2
0.65	19	12·35
0.70	16	11·2
0.75	13	9·75
0.80	10	8·00
0.85	7	5·95
0.90	4	36
0.95	1	5·95

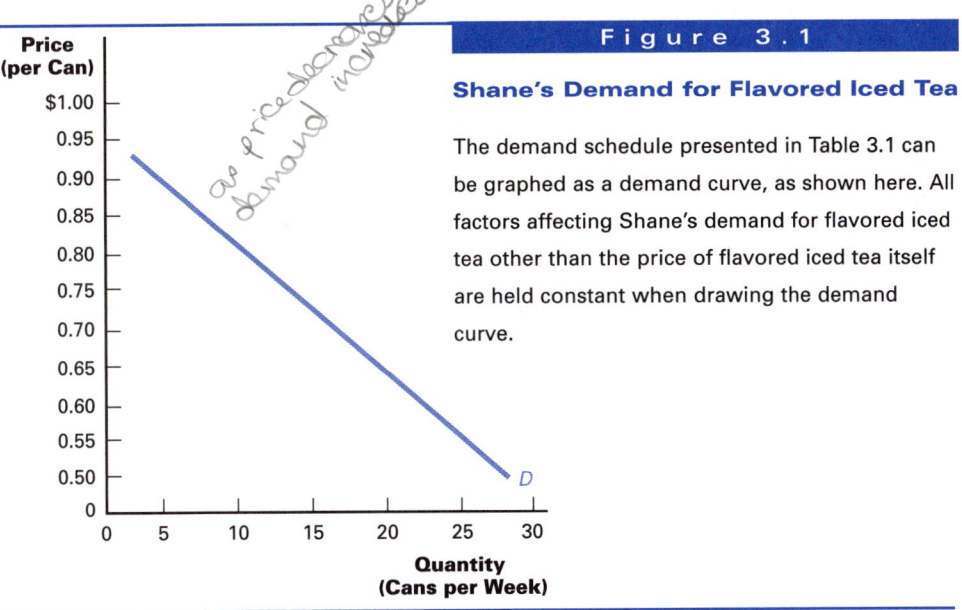

Figure 3.1

Shane's Demand for Flavored Iced Tea

The demand schedule presented in Table 3.1 can be graphed as a demand curve, as shown here. All factors affecting Shane's demand for flavored iced tea other than the price of flavored iced tea itself are held constant when drawing the demand curve.

Note the terminology used in this example. The term *demand* applies to the entire demand schedule or to the demand curve that depicts the schedule. *Demand* refers to a relationship between price and quantity demanded. The entire schedule of prices and quantities demanded listed in Table 3.1 represents Shane's demand for flavored iced tea. The term *quantity demanded* refers to a particular number of cans demanded at a particular price. Given a price, quantity demanded can be read from the demand schedule or curve. At a price of 85¢ per can, Shane's quantity demanded is seven cans per week. Since the popular media often misuse these terms, referring to particular quantities as "the demand for good X," you should be aware of the precise definitions.

Factors Shifting the Demand Curve

The demand schedule in Table 3.1 and the demand curve in Figure 3.1 illustrate the importance of opportunity cost (price) as a determinant of the quantity of a good demanded (willingly consumed). However, the demand for goods and services is also influenced by factors other than price. These factors include

- Consumer income

- Prices of other goods and services

- Consumer tastes

- Consumer expectations

When we draw a demand curve we assume that all factors affecting quantity demanded, except price, remain constant. Only the good's own price is allowed to vary: *Demand is the relationship between quantity demanded and market price, ceteris paribus. When one of the other factors changes, the quantity demanded at any particular price changes, and the demand schedule (curve) shifts.*

Income Income changes alter the budget constraint facing consumers, causing them to change their demands for goods and services. An increase in income usually causes demand for a good to increase. For instance, people tend to eat out more often as their income increases. An increase in income causes the demand for restaurant meals to increase, *ceteris paribus*. Returning to our previous example, an increase in income might cause Shane to increase his demand for flavored iced tea. With a higher income, Shane might be willing to buy more cans of flavored iced tea at every market price. Table 3.2 illustrates the impact of increased income on Shane's demand for flavored iced tea: The demand schedule shifts from D_1 to D_2. Figure 3.2 (a) illustrates the rightward shift in demand. Goods whose demand increases when income increases are called *normal goods*.

An increase in income causes the demand for some goods to decrease. Consumers often substitute more expensive but more preferred goods for less expensive, less attractive goods as their incomes increase. For example, Shane might decrease his demand for peanut butter sandwiches as his income rises, choosing to substitute hamburgers and pizza for peanut butter sandwiches. The demand for hamburgers and pizza increases and the demand for peanut butter sandwiches decreases as income rises. In this case peanut butter is an *inferior good*. If an increase in income were to cause the demand for peanut butter sandwiches to decrease, we would observe a reduction in the quantity demanded at every market price. Table 3.2 and Figure 3.2 (b) illustrate a decrease in demand for peanut butter sandwiches; the demand curve shifts to the left, from D_1 to D_3.

Prices of Other Goods The demand for a good such as flavored iced tea is influenced by the prices of other goods as well as its own price. Often consumers can choose among several alternatives – or **substitutes** – to satisfy a particular want. People switch from chicken or pork to beef when beef prices fall relative to poultry and pork prices. They rent more movie videos as movie theater prices rise. They fly instead of taking the bus or train when air fares fall relative to bus and train fares.

Substitutes:

Goods that are alternatives to one another in consumption.

Table 3.2

Effect of a Change in Income on Shane's Demand

Flavored Iced Tea			Peanut Butter Sandwiches		
Price	Quantity Demanded (Original Income)	Quantity Demanded (Higher Income)	Price	Quantity Demanded (Original Income)	Quantity Demanded (Higher Income)
$0.50	28	31	$0.20	14	11
0.55	25	28	0.25	11	8
0.60	22	25	0.30	8	5
0.65	19	22	0.35	6	3
0.70	16	19	0.40	4	1
0.75	13	16	0.45	2	0
0.80	10	13	0.50	1	0
0.85	7	10	0.55	0	0
0.90	4	7			
0.95	1	4			

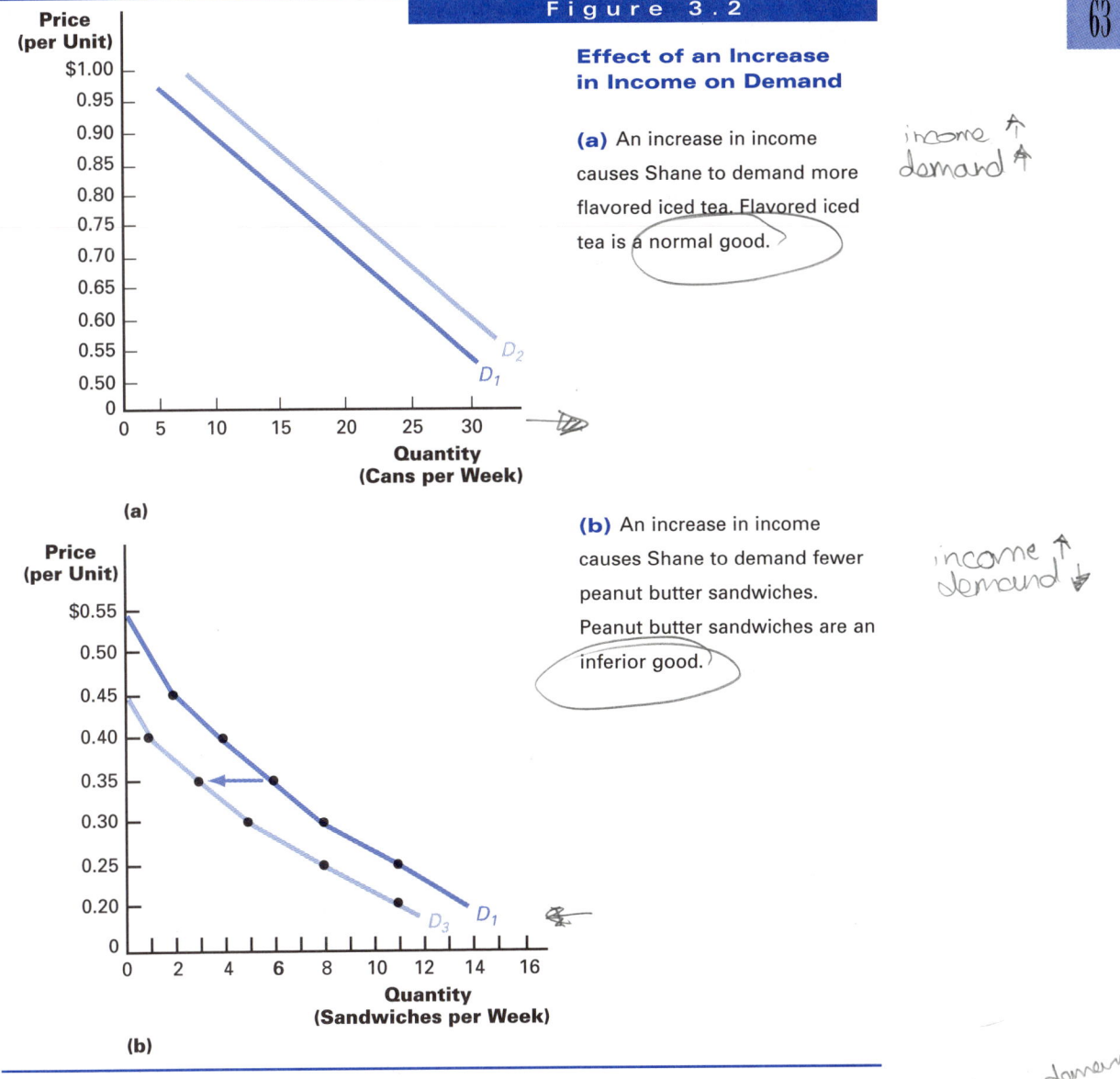

Figure 3.2

Effect of an Increase in Income on Demand

(a) An increase in income causes Shane to demand more flavored iced tea. Flavored iced tea is a normal good.

income ↑ demand ↑

(b) An increase in income causes Shane to demand fewer peanut butter sandwiches. Peanut butter sandwiches are an inferior good.

income ↑ demand ↓

more Pepsi demanded

The demand for a good decreases when the price of a substitute falls and increases when the price of a substitute rises. Thus, a decrease in Pepsi-Cola prices causes a decrease in the demand for flavored iced tea, and an increase in movie theater prices causes an increase in demand for movie videos. The demand for a good is positively related to the prices of substitute goods: The demand for the good (flavored iced tea) increases as the substitute good (Pepsi) becomes more expensive. At every price, a larger quantity of flavored iced tea is demanded.

Consumers value some goods more highly when they are consumed along with other **complementary goods**. Examples include bread and butter, automobiles and gasoline, and compact disc players and compact discs (CDs). The demand change caused by an increase in the price of a complementary good is the opposite of the change caused

Complementary goods:
Goods that produce more consumer satisfaction when consumed together than when consumed separately.

by an increase in the price of a substitute. When the price of CD players rises, the demand for CDs decreases. Fewer consumers purchase CD players, so fewer CDs are demanded at any CD price. When the price of a complementary good (CD players) rises, the demand for a good (CDs) falls.

Consumer Tastes A demand schedule tells us the maximum amount consumers are willing to give up to acquire various quantities of a good. The willingness to sacrifice to consume a good is determined by consumer tastes. Any change in consumer tastes causes demand to change. Tastes are revealed by what we consume. Today, U.S. consumers purchase more whole wheat bread and less white bread than twenty years ago. People eat less beef and more chicken now. Flavored iced tea drinks have made inroads into the soft drink market. Since such changes in tastes change the quantities of goods consumers are willing to buy at any market price, changes in tastes cause demands to increase and decrease. Increased preferences for flavored iced tea cause the demand for flavored iced tea to increase, and the corresponding shift in tastes away from carbonated soft drinks causes a decrease in demand for them.

Expectations The decision to buy goods today is influenced both by current prices and incomes and by expected future prices and incomes. An early freeze in Brazil that destroys the coffee crop causes consumers to anticipate increased coffee prices. As a result, some coffee drinkers buy more coffee today than they would in the absence of the expected price increase. (Today's demand for coffee increases.) Similarly, an expected income increase can cause a family's *current* demand for furniture to increase. Altered expectations cause the current relationship between quantity demanded and market price to change.

From Individual Demand to Market Demand

The total market demand for a good depends on the factors influencing individual demand and on the number of consumers in the market. Market demand reflects the demand of many individuals. A *market demand curve* is the horizontal sum of all individual demand curves for a good. Table 3.3 derives the market demand for flavored iced tea under the assumption that only two consumers exist. The market demand schedule is the summation of the individual quantities demanded by Shane and Blythe (Shane's friend) at every price. For example, at a price of 50¢ per can, Blythe demands eighteen cans of flavored iced tea per week, while Shane demands twenty-eight cans per week. Market quantity demanded equals the sum of the individual quantities demanded: 46 = 18 + 28. The market demand curve is shown in Figure 3.3, along with the individual demand curves.

This example helps to explain the role of advertising in the business world. If the makers of Snapple iced tea can persuade more consumers to drink their product, the quantity of Snapple demanded will increase at every price. Advertising attempts to affect consumer tastes, persuading people to try a product they don't use or to consume more of products they already use. By influencing the preferences of current consumers and by attracting new consumers, advertising shifts the market demand curve to the right. At every price a larger quantity of the good is demanded.

Table 3.3

Deriving Market Demand

Price	Shane's Quantity Demanded	+	Blythe's Quantity Demanded	=	Market Quantity Demanded
$0.50	28		18		46
0.55	25		16		41
0.60	22		14		36
0.65	19		12		31
0.70	16		10		26
0.75	13		8		21
0.80	10		6		16
0.85	7		4		11
0.90	4		2		6
0.95	1		0		1

Market demand depends on the same factors as individual demand (price, income, other prices, tastes, and expectations). An increase in a good's price moves us up along the market demand curve. Changes in consumer income, the prices of substitutes or complements, tastes, and expectations affect market demand just as they affect individual demand. In addition, market demand is affected by the number of buyers in the market.

A demand curve shows the maximum quantities of a good consumers are willing to purchase at various prices at a point in time. All factors affecting demand except the good's own price are held constant when deriving a demand curve. A change in the good's price alters quantity demanded, causing a movement along the demand curve. A change in any factor affecting demand other than the good's price causes the demand curve to shift.

Section Recap

Figure 3.3

Market Demand for Flavored Iced tea

The market demand curve is derived by adding individual quantities demanded at each price.

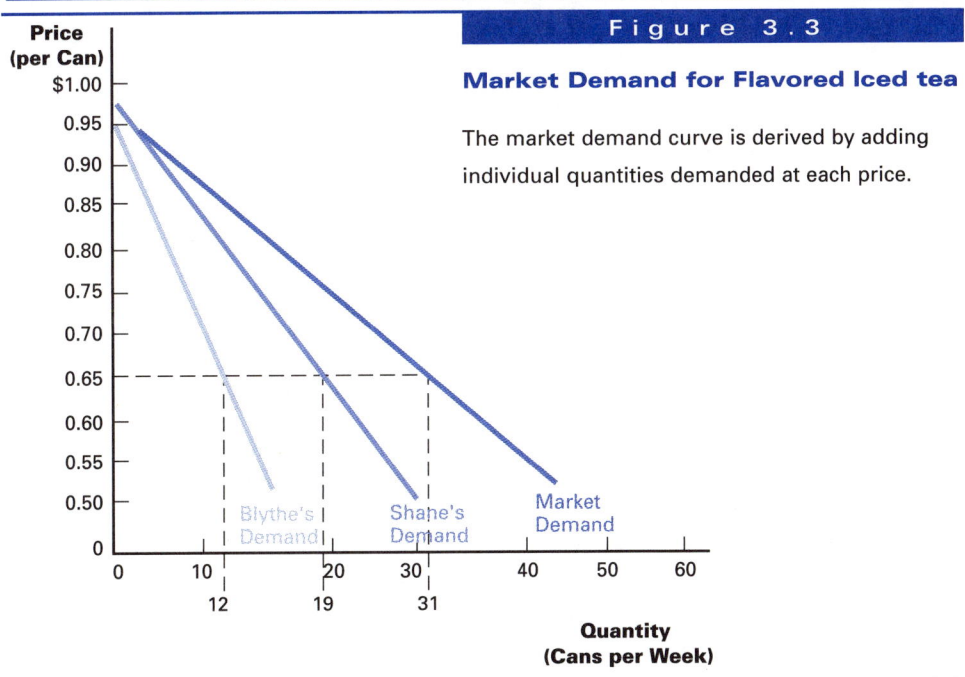

Production Decisions: Supply

This section considers the decisions of firms, or producers, and develops the law of supply. When considering the consumer side of the market we emphasized the relationship between quantities demanded and the opportunity cost of consumption, market price. Consumers compare the benefits they obtain from consumption to the price of the good (determined in the market) in making decisions about the kinds and quantities of goods to consume. We now turn to production or supply decisions. How do producers decide which goods to produce and in what quantities to produce them? Market price also plays an important role in these decisions.

Firms Are Profit Seekers

Business enterprises – *firms* – are formed by entrepreneurs seeking to maximize income by producing and selling goods or services. In many ways firms are as unique as individuals. They produce different kinds of products and have different management philosophies. However, all firms are alike in that they have one primary objective: They are in business to make a profit. **Profit** is the difference between revenue and the opportunity cost of production. Producers attempt to earn a profit by purchasing factors of production – *inputs* – and using them to produce a good or service for sale to consumers. The opportunity cost of production is composed of two elements: (1) the total cost of inputs used in production, and (2) the profits forgone when firms choose not to produce other products (that is, the value of the best alternatives given up).

Profit:

Difference between revenue and the opportunity cost of production.

Positively Sloped Supply Curve

Just as demand curves reflect the marginal benefits consumers derive from consuming goods and services, so supply curves reflect the marginal costs incurred by firms in the production of goods and services. Firms are willing to supply goods and services to the market only if they expect to receive a price that covers the marginal cost of production. The cost in question is opportunity cost. **Marginal cost** is the highest-valued opportunity forgone by a firm to produce an *additional* unit of output.

Marginal cost:

The value of the best alternative given up to produce an additional unit of a good.

A firm producing with a *fixed capital stock* – a fixed amount of factory or office space and a fixed number of machines – typically experiences an increase in marginal cost as production expands. Additional units of output are more costly to produce than previously produced units. Marginal cost rises as firms expand production under conditions of fixed capital because additional inputs are less productive. Firms will produce at higher output levels (and at higher marginal cost levels) only if they receive a higher price for their products. Firms will only produce quantities of output for which price equals or exceeds marginal cost.

Consider the example of flavored iced tea production. Factories must use special machines to fill and seal the cans and bottles of flavored iced tea and then package them in six-packs, twelve-packs, and cases. The finished, packaged, flavored iced tea must then be shipped by truck to buyers. To expand production, the firm must purchase more inputs and either require workers to work overtime or hire more workers. If overtime is required, workers must perform their tasks for ten or twelve hours per day rather than eight. The firm must pay the workers a higher wage rate for overtime work, thus increasing the labor cost of the additional output. Furthermore, since the workers are tired after eight hours of work, they may make more mistakes during the overtime period, thus ruining more materials than usual. This raises the input cost of additional output.

If the production level is increased further, the firm must hire more workers. Adding additional workers to a fixed number of machines and factory space usually reduces worker productivity. Workers get in each other's way, production bottlenecks force some workers to waste time waiting for other workers to catch up, and more workers are needed for such tasks as inventory control and moving supplies around the factory. If firms choose to circumvent such overcrowding problems by establishing a second or third work shift, they usually must pay workers more to work odd hours. Furthermore, running machines "around the clock" leaves no time for maintenance, so that production has to be shut down just to service the machines.

Finally, if output is greater than the shipping capacity of the producing firms' trucks, firms will be forced to find alternative means of transporting the flavored iced tea to their buyers. These alternatives will be costlier than using the firm's trucks. (If they were not costlier, firms would be using them instead of operating their own trucks.) Hence, higher transportation costs also affect the marginal opportunity cost of output.

Under such conditions, firms will produce additional units of output only if the price of output covers the marginal cost of production. Consider Table 3.4 and Figure 3.4, which display the marginal cost schedule and marginal cost curve for the flavored iced tea firm. The marginal cost of the two-millionth can produced during a week is 60¢. The firm is willing to produce two million cans of flavored iced tea each week only if the price offered for flavored iced tea is at least 60¢ per can. The marginal cost of the three-millionth can is 62¢. Only if the price offered is at least 62¢ will the firm expand its production from two million to three million cans per week. As the price of flavored iced tea rises, the firm is willing to produce additional units. Given the price of flavored iced tea we can see how many cans the firm is willing to produce by looking at the firm's marginal cost schedule. When the market price equals the firm's marginal cost of production for a particular output level, the firm will supply that output level to the market. Since a supply curve tells us the maximum quantity a firm is willing to supply at various prices, *the firm's marginal cost curve is its supply curve.*

Table 3.4

Flavored Iced Tea Firm's Supply Curve

Quantity Supplied (Millions of cans)	Marginal Cost (Dollars per can)
2	$0.60
3	0.62
4	0.66
5	0.72
6	0.80
7	0.90
8	1.02
9	1.22

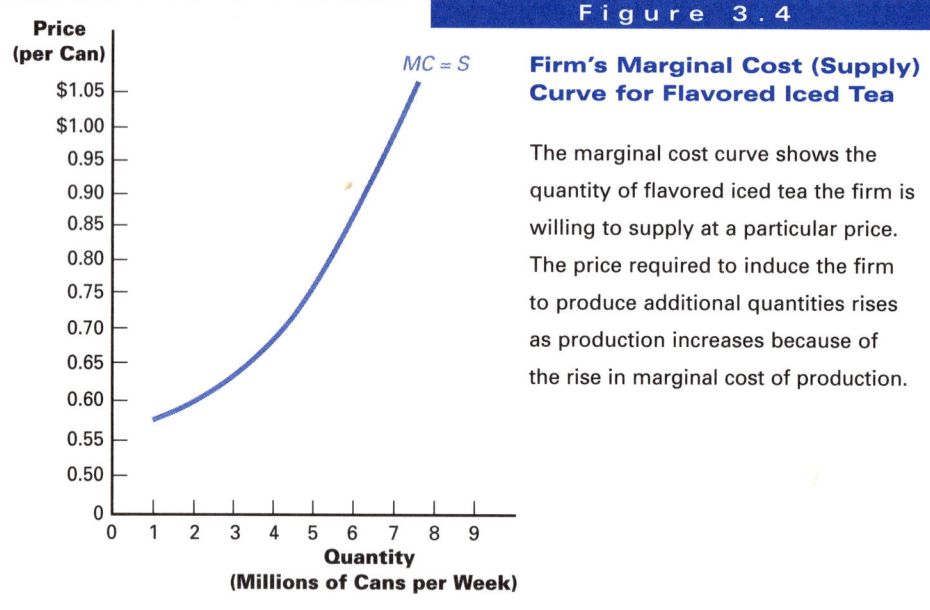

Figure 3.4

Firm's Marginal Cost (Supply) Curve for Flavored Iced Tea

The marginal cost curve shows the quantity of flavored iced tea the firm is willing to supply at a particular price. The price required to induce the firm to produce additional quantities rises as production increases because of the rise in marginal cost of production.

Law of supply:

The quantity supplied of a good is positively related to its price, holding constant other factors that affect supply.

Short run:

The period of time during which at least one factor of production is fixed in quantity.

Long run:

A period of time sufficient for a firm to vary the quantities of all factors of production.

Since marginal cost typically rises with output when capital is fixed, we can state the **law of supply** under conditions of fixed capital as follows: The quantity willingly supplied during a specified period of time is positively related to market price, *ceteris paribus*. A higher price gives producers the incentive to increase production.

The period during which a firm's capital stock is fixed is called the **short run**. During the short run, firms can buy more material inputs and hire more labor, but they do not have time to expand their plant (factory or office space) and equipment. The length of the short run varies depending upon what firms are producing. The time required for an accounting firm to acquire new office space, computers, and file cabinets may be very short, while the time needed to construct a new electrical power plant may be several years. Whatever the length of time required to expand its capital stock, most firms can produce larger outputs more efficiently with more capital. Thus, in the **long run** when firms have time to adjust the amount of capital used in production, production costs may fall. The discussion in the remainder of this chapter focuses on production in the short run (when capital is fixed).

Factors Shifting the Supply Curve

Although price is a powerful influence on the firm's output, it is not the only factor influencing production decisions. Even in the short run, the quantity supplied is affected by a number of other factors, including

- Input prices

- Technology

- Prices of other goods

Input Prices Input prices are the prices firms pay to obtain factors of production. Wages and payments for fringe benefits constitute the price of labor. Rent is the payment for the use of land and equipment that is not purchased. Firms pay interest on borrowed financial capital. An increase in input prices increases the cost of production, shifting the marginal cost (supply) curve up and to the left from S_1 to S_2 in Table 3.5 and Figure 3.5 (a). Since at every market price the firm is now willing to produce fewer cans of flavored iced tea, an increase in input prices decreases supply. A decline in input prices lowers marginal cost and increases supply, as illustrated by the shift from S_1 to S_3 in Figure 3.5 (b).

Technology The state of technology determines the kind and quantity of inputs necessary to produce a given quantity of a good or service. When a firm uses the best available technology, it can produce a unit of a good at the lowest possible cost (productive efficiency). An advance or improvement in technology is the development of new means of producing a good using a smaller quantity of inputs than was previously possible. For example, advances in the technology of computer chip manufacturing have led to drastic reductions in the cost of producing computers. Technological innovation also results in the development of new products that are less costly to produce than the products they replace. Thus, technological change lowers production costs and increases supply. If a technological improvement were to lower the cost of producing flavored iced tea, the flavored iced tea supply curve would shift to the right, as shown in Figure 3.5 (b).

Other Output Prices Firms are not permanently committed to the production of particular goods. Rising prices for other goods may cause firms to switch to the production of different goods. For example, if the price of carbonated soft drinks were to rise sharply, flavored iced tea bottlers might switch from bottling iced tea to bottling carbonated soft drinks. The increased price of carbonated soft drinks increases the bottlers' opportunity cost of bottling flavored iced tea – more potential profit is given up by continuing to bottle flavored iced tea. Thus, an increase in carbonated soft drink prices could lead to a reduction in the supply of flavored iced tea as bottlers switch from producing flavored iced tea to producing carbonated soft drinks.

Other output prices can affect the supply of certain products in another way. Some products can be produced only in combination with other products. For example, an increase in the price of beef, which increases the quantity of beef supplied to the market,

Table 3.5

Effect of Changes in Input Prices on Supply

Marginal Cost, Price	Quantity Supplied (Millions of Units)		
	Original	After Input Price Increase	After Input Price Decrease
$0.60	2	1	3
0.62	3	2	4
0.66	4	3	5
0.72	5	4	6
0.80	6	5	7
0.90	7	6	8
1.02	8	7	9
1.22	9	8	10

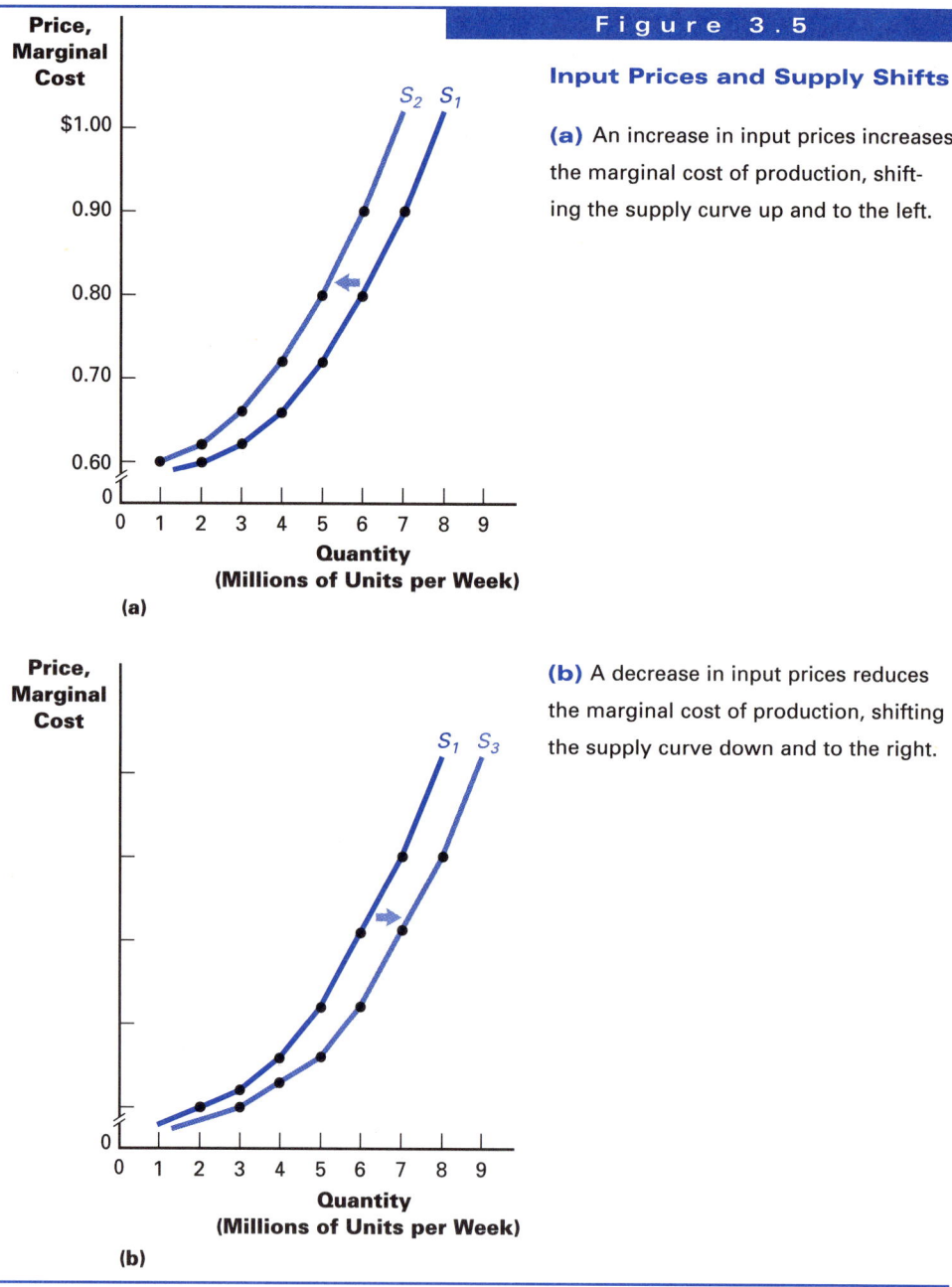

Figure 3.5

Input Prices and Supply Shifts

(a) An increase in input prices increases the marginal cost of production, shifting the supply curve up and to the left.

(b) A decrease in input prices reduces the marginal cost of production, shifting the supply curve down and to the right.

automatically increases the supply of hides, from which leather products are made. That is, increased beef prices cause the supply curve for leather to shift to the right.

From Individual Firm Supply to Market Supply

The number of suppliers affects supply just as the number of consumers affects demand. The *market supply curve* is the horizontal sum of all individual firm supply curves. A market supply curve is constructed by adding up the quantities that each firm willingly supplies at each market price. This exercise is illustrated in Table 3.6 and Figure 3.6.

Table 3.6

Deriving Market Supply

Price	Sweet Tooth, Inc. Quantity Supplied +	Tingle Flavored Iced Tea, Ltd. Quantity Supplied =	Market Quantity Supplied
$0.60	2	0.5	2.5
0.62	3	2.0	5.0
0.66	4	3.25	7.25
0.72	5	4.25	9.25
0.80	6	5.0	11.0
0.90	7	5.75	12.75
1.02	8	6.5	14.5
1.22	9	7.0	16.0

All quantities are in millions of cans.

In this simple example only two firms, Sweet Tooth, Inc. and Tingle Flavored Iced Tea, Ltd., produce and sell flavored iced tea in a particular area. Their supply schedules are given in Table 3.6, and the corresponding supply curves are shown in Figure 3.6. To derive the market supply curve, add the quantities that the two firms are willing to supply at each market price and plot them against various prices, as in Figure 3.6. For example, if the price of flavored iced tea were 80¢ per can, Tingle would produce five million cans per week and Sweet Tooth, Inc. would produce six million cans per week, jointly supplying the market with 11 million cans per week. If other suppliers were to enter the market, the market supply curve would shift further to the right. Additional quantities would be supplied at every market price. If the number of suppliers were to decrease, because, for

Figure 3.6

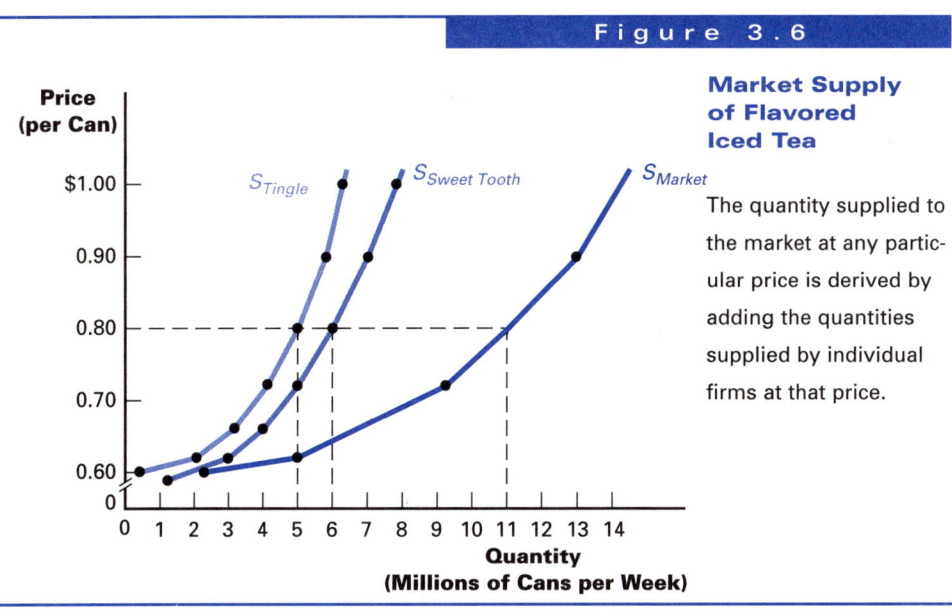

Market Supply of Flavored Iced Tea

The quantity supplied to the market at any particular price is derived by adding the quantities supplied by individual firms at that price.

example, a firm goes out of business, market supply would decrease. A smaller quantity would be available at every market price.

In summary, an increase in input prices or in the prices of alternative outputs causes the supply of a good to decrease. The supply curve shifts to the left as marginal (opportunity) costs rise. An improvement in technology or an increase in the number of suppliers producing a good increases supply, shifting the supply curve to the right.

Section Recap

A supply curve shows the maximum quantities of a good firms are willing to supply at various prices at a point in time. A supply curve slopes positively because marginal cost increases as output increases in the short run. All factors affecting supply decisions except product price are held constant when deriving a supply curve. A change in a good's price alters quantity supplied, causing a movement along the supply curve. A change in any other factor affecting supply causes the supply curve to shift.

The Market Mechanism at Work: Equilibrium

The market mechanism is the process by which buyers and sellers, acting in their own interests, establish a market price and determine the quantity of a good exchanged in a market.

Individual Choice and Competition

Buyers and sellers voluntarily engage in market transactions. Buyers (consumers) attempt to improve their well-being by obtaining goods and services for consumption at the lowest possible prices. Sellers (producers) seek to earn profits by selling goods and services at the highest possible prices. However, in a competitive market, neither buyers nor sellers can control the market price. Furthermore, both buyers and sellers must have good information about relevant alternatives, and they must be able to purchase or sell in a variety of geographically separated markets if the market outcome is to be efficient. If buyers or sellers do not possess good information about product quality or the existence of other traders, potentially beneficial exchanges will not be made. If buyers are unable to shop outside a particular geographic area, sellers in that area may be able to raise prices above their competitive levels, to the detriment of consumers. A market that satisfies these characteristics – many buyers and sellers, good information, and trader mobility – and in which relatively homogeneous (identical or nearly identical) goods are traded is said to be *competitive*. In such a market, price is determined by the interaction of buyers and sellers, and the competitive process of price determination establishes market equilibrium.

Equilibrium:
A price-output combination at which there is no pressure for either price or output to change.

Market Equilibrium

Demand and supply determine price and quantity exchanged in the market. A price-output **equilibrium** is established in a market when demand and supply factors are balanced so that there is no pressure for the outcome to change. An *equilibrium price* is a market price from which there is no tendency to change. So long as the forces affecting supply and demand remain the same, the equilibrium price remains unchanged.

Given the laws of demand and supply, only one equilibrium price-output combination exists. All other price-output combinations are **disequilibrium** combinations; they cannot be maintained because forces in the market push price and output toward the equilibrium combination. These forces originate in the competition among buyers and sellers. The process by which market equilibrium is established can be illustrated using the flavored iced tea market example.

Figures 3.7 (a) and 3.7 (b) show demand and supply schedules for flavored iced tea. The demand curve was derived by adding up the individual demand curves of all of the consumers in the flavored iced tea market (Shane, Blythe, and all the other flavored iced tea drinkers). The supply curve is taken from Figure 3.6. The demand and supply curves in Figures 3.7 (a) and 3.7 (b) are combined in Figure 3.7 (c). Notice that the demand and supply curves intersect at only one point, where price equals 80¢ per can and output equals eleven million cans. Eighty cents is an equilibrium price, because at this price the quantity willingly demanded each week by consumers just equals the quantity willingly supplied by producers (eleven million cans). At a price of 80¢ per can, market forces do not push the price higher or lower.

If the price of flavored iced tea were not equal to 80¢ a can, market forces would push the market price toward the equilibrium level. Consider Figure 3.8 (a), which reproduces Figure 3.7 (c). If the market price of flavored iced tea were 70¢ per can, the quantity of flavored iced tea demanded by consumers would exceed the quantity supplied by producers. The demand schedule shows that consumers are willing to purchase fifteen million cans weekly at 70¢ per can. The supply curve shows that producers are willing to supply only 8.6 million cans at this price. Consumers are not able to purchase all the flavored iced tea they want at a price of 70¢ per can. A **shortage** or **excess demand** exists *at a price of 70¢ per can.*

In this situation consumers will quickly purchase the available quantity of flavored iced tea. Those consumers who shop a day or two after the flavored iced tea has been delivered to stores will find the shelves empty, all the flavored iced tea having been purchased by shoppers who arrived earlier. Retailers, noticing that their stocks of flavored iced tea are being purchased faster than they are being delivered, will increase their orders from producers. As their stocks are depleted, producers will ration flavored iced tea to stores by increasing the price at which they sell the drinks. They also will increase production.

Retailers will raise the price they charge for flavored iced tea because they are paying a higher price. At the higher price, consumers reduce the quantity they demand. For example, at a price of 75¢ a can, quantity supplied increases to 10 million cans per week, while quantity demanded falls to 13 million. Increasing the price to 75¢ reduces but does not eliminate the shortage. Since quantity demanded still exceeds quantity supplied, consumers will continue to bid up the price of flavored iced tea by purchasing all that is available. Stores will continue to increase their orders for flavored iced tea, and suppliers will respond to the signal that consumers want more by increasing quantity supplied *at a higher price.* So long as quantity demanded exceeds quantity supplied, the price will continue to rise. When the price reaches the point at which quantity demanded and supplied are

Disequilibrium:
Any price-output combination at which market forces are acting to change price or quantity.

Shortage (excess demand):
Quantity demanded exceeds quantity supplied at a particular price.

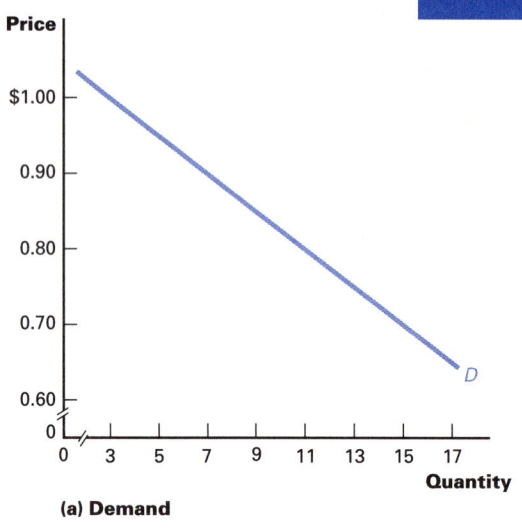

Figure 3.7

Flavored Iced Tea Market Equilibrium

(a) The demand for flavored iced tea.

(a) Demand

(b) The supply of flavored iced tea.

(b) Supply

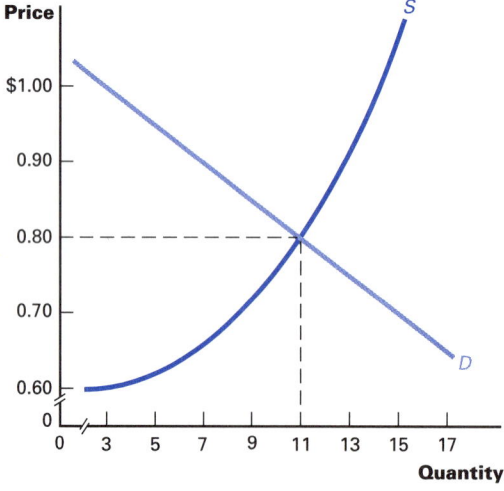

(c) Quantity demanded equals quantity supplied at a price of $0.80 per can. At this price the market is in equilibrium.

(c) Equilibrium

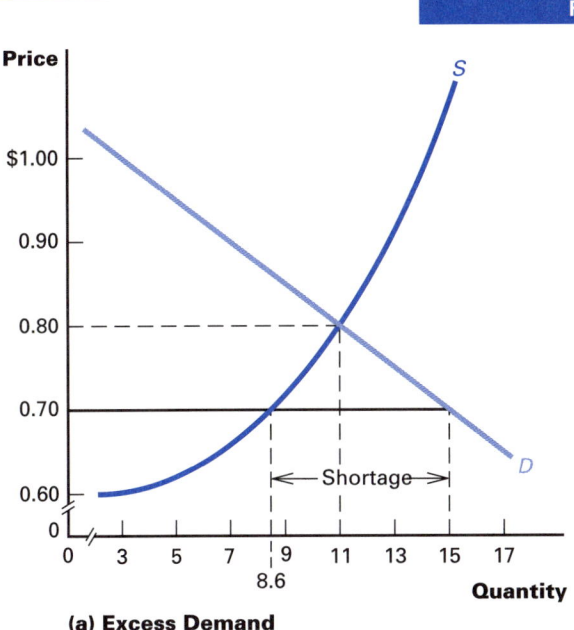

Figure 3.8

Excess Demand and Excess Supply

(a) *Excess Demand.* A price below the equilibrium level generates excess demand. At a price of $0.70 per can, the quantity demanded (15 million cans) exceeds the quantity supplied (8.6 million cans), creating a shortage.

(a) Excess Demand

(b) *Excess Supply.* A price above the equilibrium level generates excess supply. At a price of $0.90 per can, the quantity supplied (12.75 million cans) exceeds the quantity demanded (7 million cans), creating a surplus.

(b) Excess Supply

equal, a price of 80¢ in this case, the shortage is eliminated, as is the pressure for producers to increase the price.

While a price below the equilibrium price causes a shortage and sets in motion forces
that push the price up, a price above equilibrium causes a **surplus** or **excess supply** that
pushes the price down. A surplus exists when the quantity willingly supplied at a particular
price exceeds the quantity willingly demanded. Figure 3.8 (b) illustrates the effect of a
surplus. At a price of 90¢ per can, the quantity of flavored iced tea demanded is less than
the quantity supplied. In particular, a price of 90¢ causes a surplus of 5.75 million cans.
Retailers find their flavored iced tea inventories growing, and they reduce the size of their

Surplus (excess supply):
Quantity supplied exceeds quantity demanded at a particular price.

orders from producers. Producers, competing against one another to sell flavored iced tea, begin to lower their prices to encourage purchases. They produce and sell less at the lower prices, and consumers increase quantities consumed at the lower price. The surplus shrinks, but so long as quantity supplied exceeds quantity demanded, downward pressure on the price exists. At lower prices, retailers notice that consumers are increasing their purchases so that store inventories of flavored iced tea are shrinking. Competition among producers drives the price down to the equilibrium level, where quantity supplied equals quantity demanded.

Price as a Signal of Altered Alternatives: Response to Change

The market mechanism rations scarce goods and services based on the costs of production (supply) and the benefits of consumption (demand). Buyers and sellers jointly determine the price at which a good is exchanged and the quantity that is exchanged, but in a competitive market no buyer or seller can individually influence the market outcome. The set of prices of goods and services existing at a point in time constitutes an opportunity set for buyers and sellers that influences their consumption and production decisions.

Consumers attempt to maximize their benefits from a given expenditure on consumer goods. The existing set of prices defines their opportunities. While the benefits of consumption are determined by consumers themselves, they must take the cost of consumption as given. Consumers do not control market prices. When market prices change, consumers' opportunities change. Consumers react by altering the quantities of goods they buy.

Producers seek to maximize profits from the production and sale of goods. The set of existing market prices determines the revenue that producers can expect to receive from product sales. Producers can influence costs, through the choice of inputs and technologies, but in a competitive market individual producers have no control over the market price. Any producer choosing to charge a price either above or below the market price loses profits. If market prices change, the set of profitable opportunities changes. Firms respond to the new alternatives by producing more or less of a product, by discontinuing production of an old product, or by initiating production of a new product. Production changes reflect changed alternatives.

Thus, market price is an important element in consumption and production decisions. A change in price signals to market participants that conditions have changed. Market participants respond to these signals by altering their behavior as the market moves to a new equilibrium. Although the notion of market equilibrium is important, it should not be overemphasized. Understanding economics requires understanding the human behavior that causes a market to move from one equilibrium to another equilibrium. This *process of adjustment* is most important. The economy is characterized by change. The market mechanism works precisely because it responds to new developments through adjustments in market price.

Change in Demand

A *change in demand* is represented by a shift of the demand curve to the left or right. When one of the factors affecting demand, other than the good's own price, changes, the demand curve shifts, establishing a new market equilibrium. Suppose that people's tastes for coffee increase. What happens in the coffee market? Consumers are willing to buy more coffee than they purchased previously at any market price. The demand for coffee increases (shifts to the right). The process of moving to a new price-output equilibrium is illustrated in four steps in Figure 3.9. The initial equilibrium in the coffee market is depicted in Figure 3.9 (a). The equilibrium price is P_e^0 and the equilibrium quantity is Q_e^0. The change in tastes causes the demand curve for coffee to shift to the right from D_0 to D_1 in Figure 3.9 (b). The maximum quantity of coffee consumers are willing to demand is now greater at every price.

The change in demand sets in motion a number of changes, leading to a new equilibrium price and quantity in the coffee market. Figure 3.9 (c) depicts these changes. The increase in demand causes a shortage at the original equilibrium price, P_e^0. The quantity demanded, Q_d, exceeds the quantity supplied, Q_e^0. P_e^0 is now a *disequilibrium price*. The excess demand leads to a rapid depletion of grocers' inventories of coffee. Grocers increase their orders of coffee from producers, but producers are able to supply more coffee only at higher prices. Grocers pass the higher prices along to consumers. As the price of coffee is bid up, the quantity demanded falls (along the new demand curve, D_1) and the quantity supplied increases (along the original supply curve). A new equilibrium, E_1, is established in the coffee market, as depicted in Figure 3.9 (d). Both the new price, P_e^1, and the new quantity, Q_e^1, are higher than the original price and quantity exchanged.

Note that the distinction between a change in *demand* (or *supply*) and a change in *quantity demanded* (or *supplied*) is important in the analysis of a market change such as an increase in demand for coffee. Increased preferences for coffee cause a *change in demand*: The demand curve shifts to the right. The increase in demand raises the price of coffee, and as the price of coffee rises the *quantity of coffee supplied* to the market increases along the supply curve from the old price, P_e^0 to the new price, P_e^1. A change in demand (supply) is represented by a shift in the demand (supply) curve. A change in quantity supplied (demanded) is represented by a movement along the supply (demand) curve.

Any change in market demand caused by changes in income, tastes, expectations, the prices of substitutes or complements, or the number of buyers changes the market equilibrium. An increase in demand causes market price and quantity to rise, while a decrease in demand causes the market price and quantity to fall.

Ceteris paribus, an increase in demand causes both equilibrium price and equilibrium quantity to increase. A decrease in demand causes both equilibrium price and equilibrium quantity to decrease.

Section Recap

Change in Supply

A *change in supply* is represented by a shift in the supply curve to the left or right. When one of the factors affecting supply other than the good's own price changes, the supply curve shifts, establishing a new market equilibrium. Three examples illustrate the process leading to a new market equilibrium when supply changes.

Suppose that an early frost in Brazil destroys the coffee crop. The market supply of coffee decreases as a result. Figure 3.10 illustrates the effect of the frost on the coffee market. The coffee market equilibrium before the early frost is illustrated in Figure 3.10 (a). The frost reduces the quantity of coffee available at any market price; it is as if the bad

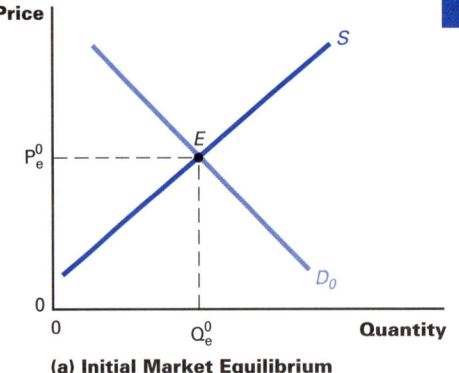

(a) Initial Market Equilibrium

Figure 3.9

Increase in Demand Alters the Market Equilibrium

(a) *Initial Market Equilibrium.* Before demand changes, the market is in equilibrium at a price of P_e^0 and a quantity of Q_e^0.

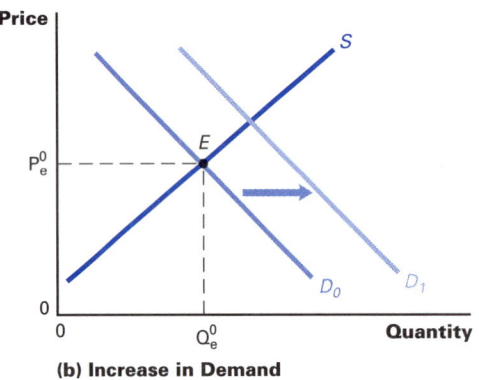

(b) Increase in Demand

(b) *Increase in Demand.* When one of the factors influencing demand changes, causing demand to increase, the demand curve shifts to the right to D_1. At any price, the quantity demanded on D_1 is greater than the quantity demanded on D_0.

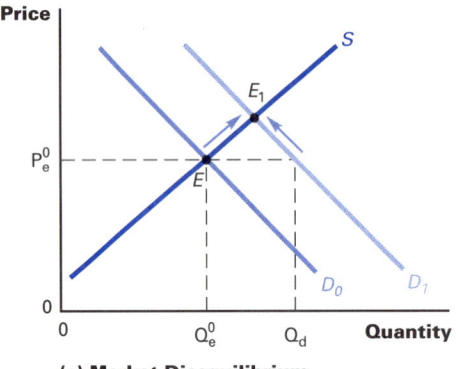

(c) Market Disequilibrium

(c) *Market Disequilibrium.* The increase in demand generates a disequilibrium at the initial price, P_e^0: Quantity demanded, Q_d, exceeds quantity supplied, Q_e^0. The shortage prompts consumers to bid up the price. Quantity supplied increases along S and quantity demanded decreases along D_1.

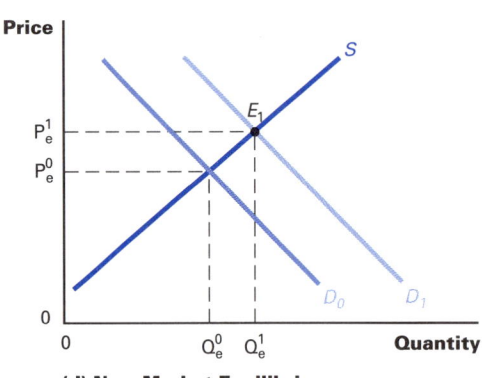

(d) New Market Equilibrium

(d) *New Market Equilibrium.* The price rises to P_e^1, the new equilibrium price. The equilibrium quality traded is Q_e^1. The increase in demand increases both the equilibrium price and quantity.

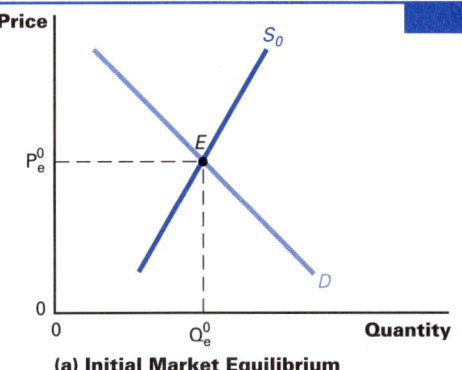

(a) Initial Market Equilibrium

Figure 3.10

**Decrease in Supply
Alters Market Equilibrium**

(a) *Initial Market Equilibrium.* Before supply changes, the market is in equilibrium at a price of P_e^0 and a quantity of Q_e^0.

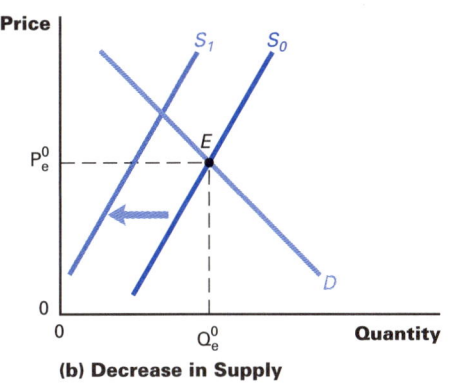

(b) Decrease in Supply

(b) *Decrease in Supply.* When one of the factors influencing supply changes, causing supply to decrease, the supply curve shifts to the left to S_1. At any price the quantity supplied along S_1 is less than the quantity supplied along S_0.

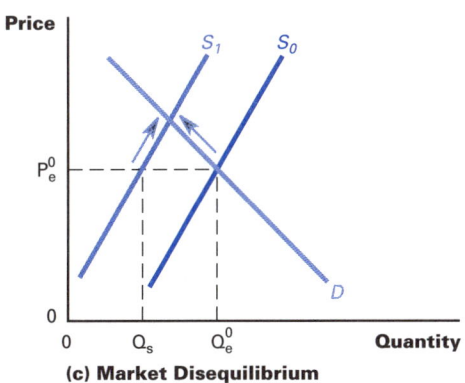

(c) Market Disequilibrium

(c) *Market Disequilibrium.* The decrease in supply causes a disequilibrium at the initial price, P_e^0: Quantity demanded, Q_e^0, exceeds quantity supplied, Q_s. The shortage prompts consumers to bid up the price. Quantity supplied increases along S_1 and quantity demanded decreases along D.

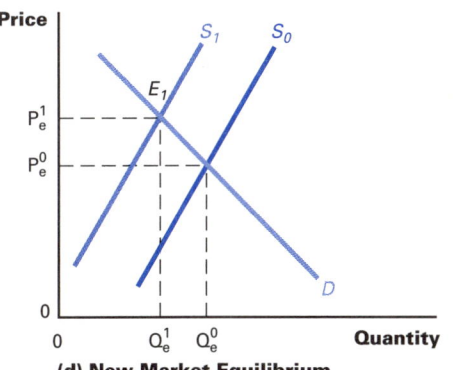

(d) New Market Equilibrium

(d) *New Market Equilibrium.* The price rises to its new equilibrium level, P_e^1. The equilibrium quantity traded falls to Q_e^1. The decrease in supply increases equilibrium price and decreases equilibrium quantity.

Why the DISAGREEMENT?

NAFTA: Some Farmers Are Not Swept Away

When the North American Free Trade Agreement (NAFTA) was being debated, it seemed that almost everyone had a stake in the outcome. Some industries expected to gain from the agreement as a result of the ability to expand into new markets. Others anticipated that they would be adversely affected through the loss of jobs or competition from less expensive foreign-made products. Consequently, it is not surprising that NAFTA generated a considerable amount of debate over its net

effects. Of particular interest is the debate that took place within the farming sector in Illinois. In 1993, the Illinois Farm Bureau voiced support for NAFTA. However, the Illinois Farmers Union opposed the agreement. Considering that both groups represent Illinois farmers, why the disagreement in their positions on this important issue?

At least part of the answer may be found by considering the case of corn. Corn comes in a number of varieties and has a number of uses. Field corn is used as feed for cattle and to produce ethanol, which can be used as an additive in gasoline. Farmers have been touting ethanol as one means of reducing our

dependence on foreign oil and reducing air pollution attributable to automobiles. Sweet corn is a popular vegetable, especially in the summer when people enjoy "corn on the cob." Broom corn is used for, among other things, producing brooms. In fact, broom corn was at the center of the debate.

As of 1993, brooms produced in Mexico and imported to the United States were subject to a 300 percent tariff. This provided protection to U.S. broom manufacturers, the largest of which was located in Arcola, Illinois. Although most of the broom corn used in the production of brooms is grown in Mexico and imported to the United States,

---

Figure 3.11

Effect of a Change in Tariffs on Broom Corn

(a) A reduction in tariffs on Mexican-grown broom corn causes a reduction in the demand for U.S.-grown broom corn. As a result, equilibrium price and quantity fall, adversely affecting U.S. broom corn growers.

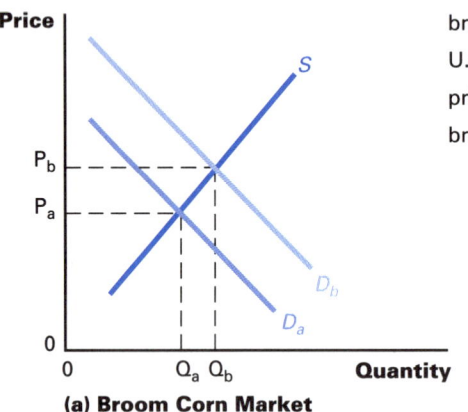

(a) Broom Corn Market

Continued

a number of farmers in the Arcola area still grow broom corn to meet part of the local demand. In their view, eliminating the tariff on Mexican brooms would seriously undercut both the U.S. broom manufacturers and U.S. broom corn growers.

Considering the relatively lower cost of Mexican-made brooms, the broom corn growers were right. This can help explain the position of the Illinois Farmers Union. But it also raises the question of why the Illinois Farm Bureau supported NAFTA. To answer this question, it is important to recognize that the Illinois Farm Bureau represents the interests of all of its members. These members grow a variety of crops ranging from different varieties of corn to soybeans to vegetable crops such as asparagus and tomatoes. In considering the effects of policies on its members, the Farm Bureau needs to consider the effects of changes in demand and supply at a number of different levels.

Consider Figures 3.11 (a) and 3.11 (b). Figure 3.11 (a) illustrates the market for broom corn grown in Illinois. The demand curve labelled D_b represents the demand for Illinois broom corn before the implementation of NAFTA. The demand curve labelled D_a represents demand for Illinois broom corn after the implementation of NAFTA. D_a reflects the effects of a decrease in the demand for Illinois broom corn resulting from the decrease in the effective price of foreign grown substitutes. As the figure clearly illustrates, the result of NAFTA is a reduction in the equilibrium price and quantity of broom corn produced in Illinois.

Figure 3.11 (b) depicts the demand and supply of all varieties of corn produced in Illinois. Once again, the demand curves labelled D_b and D_a represent the demand for Illinois corn before and after the implementation of NAFTA. However, unlike the case of broom corn, overall demand for corn increases as shown by the rightward shift of the demand curve. The increase in demand depicted in Figure 3.11 (b) reflects the expectation that NAFTA would open up new markets for other varieties of corn in Mexico, especially through the market for ethanol. The increase in demand results in an increase in the equilibrium price and quantity of corn produced in Illinois.

As Figures 3.11 (a) and 3.11 (b) illustrate, it is easy to see why such disagreement could occur. As we discussed in Chapter 2, specialization and trade can result in net benefits to society while imposing net costs on some individuals. This would appear to be the case for corn growers in Illinois.

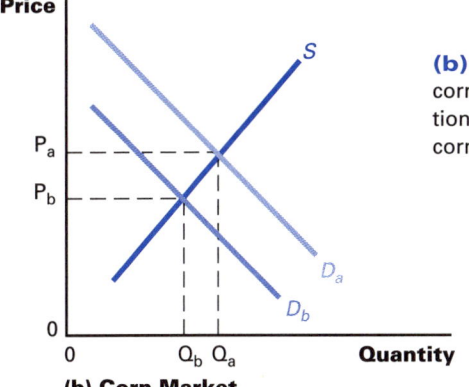

(b) Corn Market

Figure 3.11

Continued

(b) In the aggregate market for all varieties of corn, the overall effect of reduced trade restrictions is an increase in demand for U.S.-grown corn. Equilibrium price and quantity increase.

weather causes a large increase in the costs of production. Supply decreases and the coffee supply curve shifts to the left, to S_1 in Figure 3.10 (b). The change in supply causes a market disequilibrium at the original price, generating forces that push the market toward a new equilibrium.

The process of moving to a new equilibrium is illustrated in Figure 3.10 (c). At the original market price, P_e^0, excess demand now exists: The quantity demanded, Q_e^0, exceeds the quantity willingly supplied, Q_s. Consumers experience this shortage in the form of empty shelves in grocery stores. Producers ration their coffee supplies to retailers by raising the price they charge. Grocers pass the price increase along to consumers. By paying the higher price, the consumers who value coffee more highly bid the available coffee away from other consumers who value it less highly. As the price rises, the quantity of coffee demanded decreases along the demand curve. The price rise also causes an increase in quantity supplied along the new supply curve, S_1. These changes, caused by the rising price, gradually eliminate the shortage of coffee. A new equilibrium price is established when the quantity demanded again equals the quantity supplied, at a higher price. The equilibrium quantity exchanged in the market falls from Q_e^0 to Q_e^1 (Figure 3.10 (d)).

As this example clearly demonstrates, a decrease in supply increases market price and decreases market output. An increase in supply leads to a decrease in the equilibrium market price and an increase in output. To further illustrate the effects of a supply increase, consider the television market. Assume that technological improvements reduce the cost of producing television sets. What happens?

The pattern of changes is similar to the pattern in preceding examples. Technological change enables producers to produce TV sets at lower cost. The decrease in costs means that producers are willing to supply more TV sets than before, at any market price. Thus, the supply curve shifts to the right. The rightward shift of the supply curve creates an excess supply (surplus) at the original equilibrium price, generating pressure for price adjustment. Producers, competing to sell the now less costly TV sets, cut the market price in an effort to sell more sets. As the price falls, two effects are observed. First, the quantity willingly supplied decreases along the new supply curve. Second, the reduced price causes the quantity demanded to increase along the original demand curve. As the price falls, the surplus shrinks. At the new equilibrium price the quantity supplied just equals the quantity demanded. The increase in supply, caused by the technological advance, reduces the equilibrium price and increases quantity.

A change in input prices also causes a change in supply. Input prices influence supply through their effect on production costs. An increase in input prices increases costs, decreasing supply. Decreased input prices reduce costs and increase supply.

Supply also increases when restrictions on the sale of foreign-made goods in domestic markets are reduced or eliminated. Increased imports of foreign-made goods into a domestic market, such as the market for apples or wheat or VCRs, effectively increases the number of sellers. As the number of sellers increases, the supply curve shifts right. *Ceteris paribus*, this causes equilibrium quantity to increase while equilibrium price falls. Consumers in the domestic market are obviously better off, but domestic producers are worse off due to the fall in price. In January 1995, Japan allowed apples grown in the

United States to be sold in Japanese stores for the first time, a move that Japanese apple growers had vigorously opposed for years. Japanese consumers welcomed the imports. The price of U.S.-grown apples was 30 to 50 percent lower than the price of domestically grown apples.

Ceteris paribus, an increase in supply causes equilibrium price to decrease and equilibrium quantity to increase. A decrease in supply causes equilibrium price to increase and equilibrium quantity to decrease.

Section Recap

Change in Demand and Supply

The preceding examples demonstrated the way in which a market returns to equilibrium after it is disturbed by a change in demand *or* supply. Disequilibrium generates clear-cut responses by buyers and sellers, and their actions reestablish market equilibrium at a new price-quantity combination. When only demand or supply changes, the direction of change in price and quantity is clear.

What happens in a market when both supply and demand change? The answer is not so obvious. However, a little analysis allows us to identify the information needed to predict the price and quantity effects of a change in both demand and supply. Consider again the coffee market. What happens in this market when both supply and demand increase?

Suppose a fall in the price of labor decreases the cost of producing coffee. Supply increases; the supply curve shifts to the right. Figure 3.12 (a) illustrates the original and new equilibrium positions. An increase in supply, *ceteris paribus*, causes equilibrium price to fall to P_s and quantity exchanged to increase to Q_s. But what happens to price and quantity when demand also increases? If consumers' preferences for coffee increase, the demand curve shifts to the right, as in Figure 3.12 (b), increasing the market price to P_d and the equilibrium output to Q_d.

What are the combined effects on market price and quantity of an increase in both supply and demand? Quantity exchanged unambiguously increases – both a supply increase and a demand increase have a positive effect on the quantity exchanged. These changes reinforce one another, causing an even greater increase in equilibrium quantity. The price effect of a simultaneous increase in supply and demand is ambiguous, however. An increase in supply tends to depress market price, but an increase in demand pushes price up. The two forces counteract one another. Price might increase, decrease, or stay the same. In Figure 3.12 (c), the change in supply and the change in demand are superimposed on the same graph. If demand increases to D_1, the equilibrium price falls by a small amount, from P_e^0 to P_e^1. However, if demand increases by a larger amount, to D_2, the equilibrium price increases to P_e^2. If the demand and supply curves had shifted to the right by exactly the same amount (measured by horizontal distance), the price would not have changed. Note that we could produce the same set of possible outcomes by shifting the demand curve by a fixed amount and varying the amount by which supply increases.

The movement from P_e^0 to P_e^1 is representative of developments in many new product markets. After the product is introduced, both supply and demand increase. Costs of production fall as producers develop more efficient production techniques. Consumers increase their demand for the product as they become more familiar with it and identify the full range of benefits derived from the product. When pocket calculators were first introduced, basic units sold for well over $100. At that time, annual sales were only a fraction of today's sales. In the past fifteen years the costs of producing calculators have fallen further and faster than calculator demand has increased. Thus, we have experienced a steady decline in price while the quantity of calculators sold has increased.

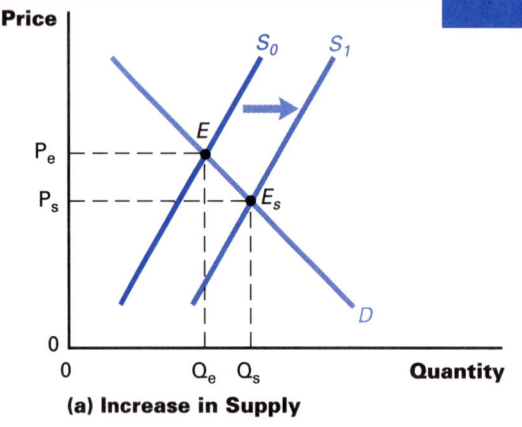

(a) Increase in Supply

Figure 3.12

Effect of an Increase in Both Supply and Demand

(a) *Increase in Supply.* The supply curve shifts from S_0 to S_1, reducing equilibrium price from P_e to P_s and increasing equilibrium price from Q_c to Q_s.

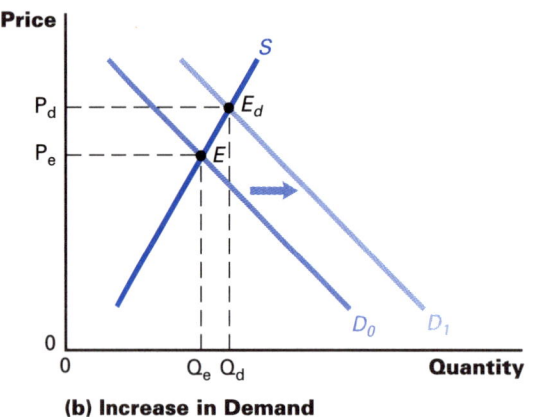

(b) Increase in Demand

(b) *Increase in Demand.* The demand curve shifts from D_0 to D_1, increasing equilibrium price from P_e to P_d and equilibrium quantity from Q_e to Q_d.

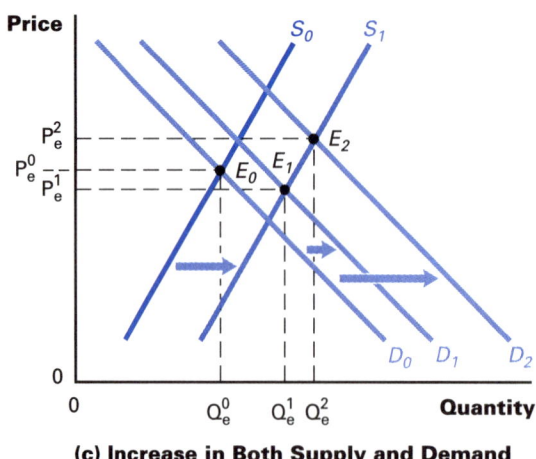

(c) Increase in Both Supply and Demand

(c) *Increase in Both Supply and Demand.* The supply curve shifts from S_0 to S_1 and the demand curve shifts from D_0 to either D_1 or D_2. Since both curves shift to the right, equilibrium quantity unambiguously increases. The direction of change in equilibrium price is less obvious, because the price effects of the two shifts offset each other. If the supply shift is larger than the demand shift, as when demand increases to D_1, price falls. If the supply shift is smaller than the demand shift, as when demand increases to D_2, price rises.

Other combinations of changes in demand and supply can produce more unusual results. Suppose the supply of oats was decreased by widespread crop failure. Consider what would happen if such a development was combined with a sudden increase in demand caused by reports that oat bran is a very healthful food (consumer preferences for oats increase).

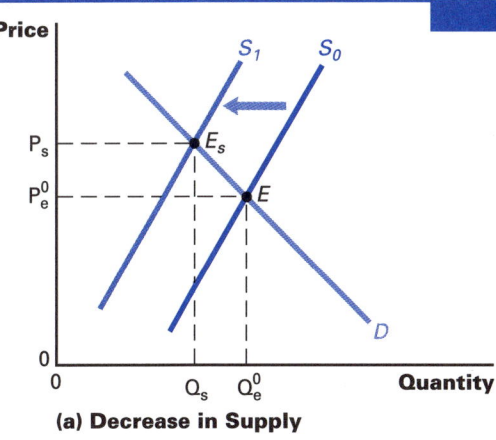

(a) Decrease in Supply

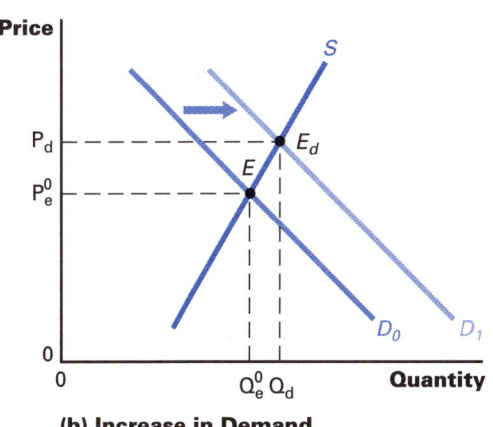

(b) Increase in Demand

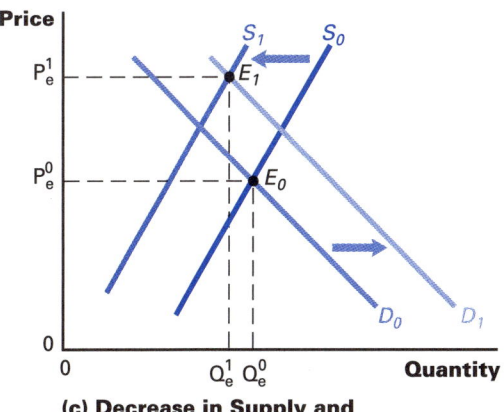

(c) Decrease in Supply and
Increase in Demand

Figure 3.13

Effect of a Decrease in Supply and an Increase in Demand

(a) *Decrease in Supply.* The supply curve shifts from S_0 to S_1, increasing equilibrium price from P_e^0 to P_s and decreasing equilibrium quantity from Q_e^0 to Q_s.

(b) *Increase in Demand.* The demand curve shifts from D_0 to D_1, increasing equilibrium price from P_e^0 to P_d and equilibrium quantity from Q_e^0 to Q_d.

(c) *Decrease in Supply and an Increase in Demand.* The supply curve shifts from S_0 to S_1 and the demand curve from D_0 to D_1. Each of the two changes pushes the price upward. Thus, equilibrium price unambiguously rises from P_e^0 to P_e^1. The direction of change in equilibrium quantity depends on the amount by which supply and demand change. If supply falls by a larger amount than demand increases, equilibrium quantity falls (as shown). If supply falls by a smaller amount than demand increases, equilibrium quantity rises (not shown).

ECONOMIC SENSE?

Ending the Free Lunch in Developing Countries

Many African countries have suffered the effects of famine in recent years. Images of starving children, their bellies bloated by the effects of malnutrition, appear in the media exhorting people to aid in the fight to end such suffering. Western countries have responded to this human tragedy with huge amounts of aid. During the 1980s, more than $1 billion was spent to ship millions of tons of food to those in need.[1] In 1991, West Africa received more than 54 million tons of beef from the European community.[2] While such aid certainly helps some segment of the population, it can also have adverse effects on the local economy. In fact, there is evidence which suggests that such aid has actually worsened the problem in some situations. Consequently, many observers have called for an end to shipments of free food in many situations. Does such a policy shift make economic sense?

Before we try to answer this question it is important to recognize what is not being proposed: an end to all food shipments. Certainly, in those cases in which starvation is imminent, food shipments are the appropriate response. However, when the problem is less severe, alternative strategies can produce better long-run results.

While food is a necessity, it nonetheless is subject to the same market pressures as any other good or service. Equilibrium price and quantity are determined by the interaction of supply and demand. Of particular relevance to this discussion is the effect of an increase in supply; while equilibrium quantity increases, equilibrium price falls. Therein lies the rub.

Most of the food donated to needy countries is either given out free or sold at extremely low prices. The effect is often to reduce

The effect of a combined decrease in supply and increase in demand is illustrated in Figure 3.13. The supply decrease causes equilibrium price to rise and quantity to fall, as in Figure 3.13 (a). Meanwhile, consumers are demanding greater quantities of oats at all prices, as shown in Figure 3.13 (b). Price and quantity exchanged would both increase in the absence of any decrease in supply.

The combination of decreased supply and increased demand produces the result illustrated in Figure 3.13 (c). Both the supply decrease and the demand increase put upward pressure on the price of oats, so the equilibrium price unambiguously rises. However, the reduced supply puts downward pressure on quantity, while the increased demand tends to increase quantity. The effect on the equilibrium quantity exchanged is ambiguous. If the supply shift is stronger, quantity exchanged falls; if the demand shift is stronger, quantity exchanged rises. As shown in Figure 3.13 (c), the supply shift is stronger: Equilibrium price rises and equilibrium quantity falls.

When both supply and demand in a market change simultaneously, the impact on price and quantity depends on the net effect of supply and demand changes. As a consequence, we must know the magnitude of the supply and demand changes to predict the direction of change in *both* price and quantity.

Section Recap

An increase in both demand and supply causes equilibrium quantity to increase, but has an indeterminate effect on equilibrium price. A decrease in both demand and supply causes equilibrium quantity to decrease, but has an indeterminate effect on equilibrium price. An increase in demand

the market price of food below the costs incurred by local producers. In effect, the food donations compete with local production and make farming unprofitable. Thus, local farmers do not have an incentive to continue to produce. The long-run implication is obvious; instead of reducing the problem of food shortages, food aid makes the problem worse since domestic production is undermined.

A number of alternatives have been suggested to avoid the problems described above. One alternative is to institute food-for-work programs. A number of such programs have been implemented in recent years, most notably in Ethiopia and Zimbabwe. In the latter case, people received food payments in return for work on the construction of wells, dams, and grain stores during the drought that occurred in 1992. The result was that few people died as a direct

result of starvation and farmers were ready for production in the following year.

Another alternative, advocated by Amartya Sen, an Indian economist, is to give the needy cash, rather than food. The idea is that by allowing individuals to purchase locally produced food, local markets, and in particular, producers, are strengthened. The question of which approach, work-for-food or cash-for-food, is better depends on the specific circumstances. It has been suggested that the former is likely to be better in situations in which markets are weak and there is a serious food shortage. The latter approach is likely to fare better when the opposite conditions prevail.

The preceding discussion illustrates once again what economists continually stress – incentives matter. While aid to starving countries is the morally correct

response, the form that such aid takes is critical. By providing aid that creates incentives for domestic production, both the short-run and long-run problems of food shortages can be addressed. Whether western countries would be willing to adopt or support such approaches as those suggested here is another matter. Food donations provide a way for governments to reduce excess food stocks resulting from domestic farm subsidy programs. Nonetheless, if we really want to help, simply sending people a free lunch is, in many cases, not the correct approach.

and a decrease in supply causes equilibrium price to increase but has an indeterminate effect on equilibrium quantity. A decrease in demand and an increase in supply causes equilibrium price to decrease, but has an indeterminate effect on equilibrium quantity.

Market Adjustments as Responses to Changed Alternatives

When the market is used to ration goods and services, market price plays a very important role. It provides information used by all buyers and sellers in making economic decisions. When any factor that affects supply or demand changes, market price changes. The change in price is a signal that conditions in the market have changed. Price changes influence the alternatives of consumers and producers, inducing them to alter their decisions. Seeking to maintain the benefits they derive from consumption, consumers respond to price changes by adjusting their purchases of goods and services. Seeking to maximize profits, producers respond to price changes by altering their production plans and output levels.

A new equilibrium market price reflects the effects of both the initial change in market conditions and consumer and producer responses. The key to understanding how the market allocates goods and resources is understanding how consumers and producers respond to price movements.

The attention given to market processes in this chapter should not obscure the fact that not all market solutions are socially desirable. Under certain conditions, market processes may not produce economically efficient outcomes. At other times, efficient market outcomes may not meet society's standards of equity or fairness, as when some people are unable to earn enough income to live at a socially acceptable level. In such instances, other decision-making mechanisms may augment or replace the market, even in an economy that relies on markets to coordinate most economic decisions. These issues are addressed in Chapter 5.

Summary

Scarcity of resources necessitates the rationing of goods to users. Every society must develop ways to reconcile competing claims on limited resources. Societies must decide what to produce, how to produce it, and to whom it will be distributed. These decisions can be made in centralized or decentralized ways. **Centralized decision making** occurs when government makes the important economic decisions. A **decentralized economy** is characterized by individual decision making. Such an economy typically relies on markets as the rationing device. Other rationing criteria exist. The choice of criteria affects only the nature of competition for scarce goods; competition itself results from scarcity.

A **market** is a process by which individuals freely negotiate the terms of exchange for goods and services. Market transactions are mutually beneficial exchanges with two sides: demand and supply.

On the demand side, consumers seek to maximize the benefits they derive from consuming goods and services. The quantity of a good purchased depends upon a number of factors, including price. The **law of demand** says that price and quantity demanded are inversely related. Other factors that affect demand include consumer income, tastes, expectations, the prices of other goods, and the number of consumers. When these factors change, the relationship between price and quantity demanded changes. This is called a *change in demand*.

On the supply side, firms produce goods and services to sell to consumers for a profit. The higher the market price, *ceteris paribus*, the greater the opportunity for profit. Thus, the **law of supply** states that a positive relationship exists between market price and quantities willingly supplied to the market. Other factors affecting the supply relationship include input prices, technology, other output prices, and the number of suppliers. Changes in these factors cause a *change in supply*.

The interaction of consumers and suppliers establishes a **market equilibrium** price at which quantity supplied equals quantity demanded. At any other price the market is in disequilibrium and pressures exist for the price to move toward the equilibrium price. These pressures arise from the behavior of consumers and producers adjusting their consumption and production to the market price.

A change in demand or supply shifts the demand or supply curve, creating a disequilibrium at the initial market price. The excess demand or supply causes consumers or producers to respond by bidding price up or down. As the price changes, quantities demanded and supplied change. Adjustments continue until quantity demanded again equals quantity supplied at a new equilibrium price.

The supply and demand, or market, model developed in this chapter is a specific application of the Fundamental Premise of Economics. The model has wide applicability, as subsequent chapters demonstrate.

Questions for Thought

Knowledge Questions

1. Explain the difference between centralized and decentralized decision making. Give an example of each kind of decision making in the U.S. economy.

2. How do universities typically ration the following goods and services?

   - Dormitory rooms

   - Athletic scholarships

   - Library books

   - Parking spaces

   - Textbooks

   - Football tickets

3. Explain the difference between scarcity and shortage.

4. What is the *law of demand*? Under what conditions is this law an accurate description of actual behavior?

Application Questions

5. "Health insurance that covers 100 percent of all medical expenditures encourages consumption of health services." Using a demand curve, justify this statement.

6. The demand and supply functions for sweatshirts (the basic grey kind) are as follows:

Demand		**Supply**	
Price	**Quantity Demanded (per period)**	**Price**	**Quantity Supplied (per period)**
$6	5,000	$6	8,002
5	6,000	5	7,335
4	7,000	4	6,668
3	8,000	3	6,001
2	9,000	2	5,334

   a. Graph the demand and supply functions for sweatshirts and find (approximately) the equilibrium price and quantity.

b. What effect will an increase in the price of gym shoes (a complement) have on the equilibrium price and quantity of sweatshirts, *ceteris paribus*? Explain the effect using your graph.

c. What effect will a wage increase for workers in the sweatshirt industry have on the equilibrium price and quantity of sweatshirts, *ceteris paribus*? Explain the effect using your graph.

7. "In the past five years the average price of our Chevrolets has risen about 6 percent a year and each year we have sold 10 percent more cars than the previous year." How can this car dealer sell more cars as the price of the cars increases?

8. Using a change in supply and/or demand, explain the following phenomena:

a. Afternoon movie prices are lower than evening prices.

b. Winter hotel rates in Florida are higher than summer rates.

c. Corn prices are higher in years of drought.

9. Is the ticket price for rock concerts typically set at the equilibrium level? Is it set above or below equilibrium? How is the disequilibrium eliminated?

Synthesis Questions

10. What factors influence the price of these goods: pork, toothpicks, condominiums, microcomputers. Which of these goods tend to experience both price increases and decreases? Which ones tend to decrease over time? Do any of the goods experience very little price fluctuation? Explain each response.

11. Explain what happens in the wheat market when a surplus exists. What happens to price and quantity? Why? Does the automobile market adjust to a surplus any differently? Explain.

12. The equations for the demand and supply functions in question 6 are as follows:

$$Q_d = 11,000 - 1,000P.$$
$$Q_s = 4,000 + 667P.$$

Solve for the equilibrium price and quantity. (Hint: At equilibrium, quantity supplied equals quantity demanded.)

Suppose the supply function changes to

$$Q_s = 1,000 + 667P.$$

Does supply increase or decrease? What is the new equilibrium price and quantity?

End Notes

[1] "Let Them Eat Cash?" *The Economist*, April 10, 1993, p. 47.

[2] "Overstuffing Africa," *The Economist*, May 8, 1993, p. 10.

Economic Efficiency:
A Measure of Market Performance

Overview

In this chapter we combine the concepts of mutually beneficial exchange and economic efficiency introduced in Chapter 2 with the supply and demand model presented in Chapter 3. We examine how, under well-defined conditions, a market equilibrium established by the interaction of supply and demand leads to economic efficiency. A graphical model of an efficient market equilibrium is developed, and the conditions that ensure the efficiency of market equilibrium are discussed. We demonstrate that market intervention, through price floors and ceilings, leads to inefficient market outcomes. We conclude the chapter with a discussion of situations in which a society might choose to be inefficient.

Learning Objectives

After reading and studying this chapter, you will be able to

1. Determine the social benefits of consumption from the demand curve and the social costs of production from the supply curve

CHAPTER 4

2. Identify the social net gain from producing and consuming a good

3. State the conditions necessary for a market equilibrium to be efficient, explain why it is efficient, and graphically illustrate your explanation

4. Define and illustrate consumers' surplus and producers' surplus

5. Explain why a price ceiling or floor causes market inefficiency

6. Discuss why society might decide to pursue an economically inefficient policy

Gains from Trade

Individuals and societies seek to obtain as much as they can from the limited resources they possess. Chapter 2 presented some examples of one way to increase the value of one's resources: mutually beneficial exchange. People trade with one another, giving up something of lesser value for something of greater value. Market transactions, explained in Chapter 3, are one form of mutually beneficial exchange. Consumers sacrifice income to buy goods or services whose consumption yields benefits to them. Producers sell to consumers when they can profit by the sale. Both parties to such voluntary exchanges are better off as a result of the exchange.

Economic efficiency is one benchmark against which the gains from market trades can be measured. Recall from Chapter 2 that *economic efficiency is the achievement of the maximum difference between benefits and costs*. When market decision making is employed to answer the three basic economic questions – what, how, and for whom to produce – society has the potential for achieving economic efficiency: generating the greatest net gain (benefits less costs) to society from its stock of resources. Thus, market decision making has the potential to make individual actions based on self-interest, consistent with the maximization of society's well-being.

Economic Efficiency of Market Equilibrium

Under well-defined conditions, which are discussed shortly, a market equilibrium is economically efficient. *In an efficient market, trading at the equilibrium price produces as large a net gain as possible for society, given consumer tastes and production costs*. The net gain produced by an efficient market can be illustrated with the supply and demand model.

Social Benefits from the Demand Curve

When we graph an individual's demand curve, we plot the maximum quantities of a good the person is willing to buy at various prices. When the price is very high, the quantity demanded is low; the consumer finds it beneficial to consume very few units of the good. As the price of the good falls, the consumer demands additional units of the good. At a lower price, the consumer gains by buying more of the good, because the marginal benefit of an additional unit of the good exceeds the (lower) price. The consumer purchases additional units of the good until the marginal benefit from consuming the good equals its price. Thus, the good's price measures the marginal benefit of the last unit of the good purchased. For example, if a person is willing to buy four pounds of oranges per week at a price of 60¢ a pound, the marginal benefit of the last pound of oranges purchased is 60¢. If the marginal benefit were less than 60¢, the final pound of oranges would not be purchased. Thus, the individual's demand curve provides us with a measure of the benefits the individual enjoys from the consumption of a good.

The market demand curve can also be used to measure the total benefits to *society* of consuming a particular good. To illustrate this, consider the demand for top-quality ground beef. The ground beef demand curve in Figure 4.1 (a) reveals that at a price of $3 per pound, U.S. consumers are willing to buy up to 40 million pounds of ground beef per month. If the price were $2.75 per pound, they would like another 40 million

Figure 4.1

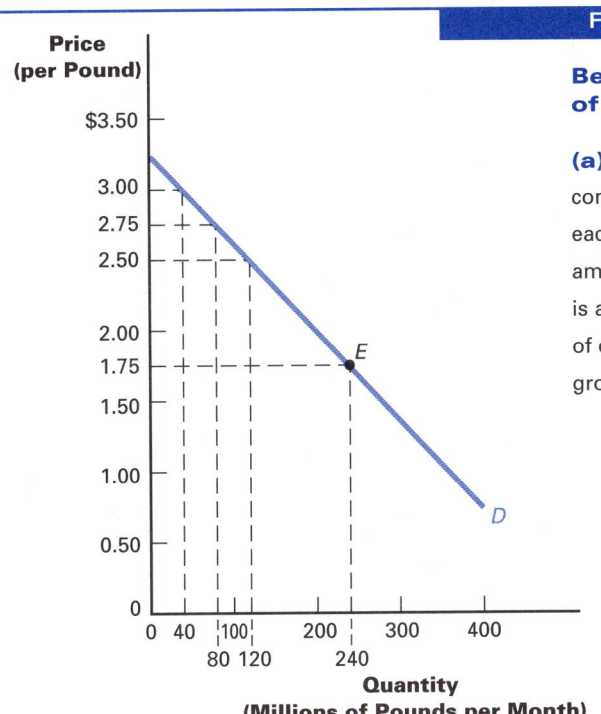

(a)

Benefits of Consumption of Ground Beef

(a) The demand curve shows consumers' willingness to pay for each quantity of ground beef. The amount consumers are willing to pay is a measure of the marginal benefit of consuming a particular quantity of ground beef.

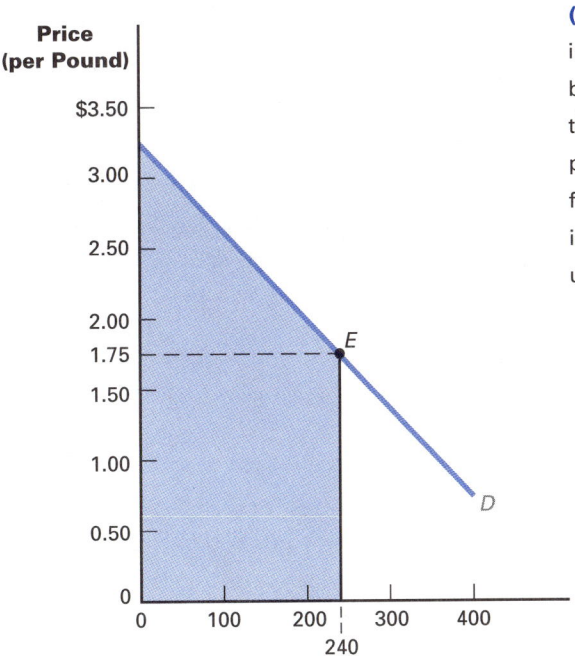

(b)

(b) The total benefits from consuming a particular quantity of ground beef can be calculated by adding up the willingness to pay for each pound. The total willingness to pay for 240 million pounds of ground beef is represented by the shaded area under the demand curve.

pounds; at a price of $2.50 per pound, yet another 40 million pounds; and at a price of $1.75 per pound an additional 120 million pounds (for a total of 240 million pounds of ground beef).

The demand curve shows us the benefit to consumers of each additional million pounds of ground beef. The vertical distance from the quantity axis to the demand curve measures the marginal benefit to consumers of a particular quantity of ground beef. By adding up the benefit of each additional million pounds, from the first million to the 240th million, we can derive the total benefit to consumers from consuming 240 million pounds of ground beef. Graphically, this amounts to adding up the area under the demand curve, up to 240 million pounds. Thus, the total social benefits derived from the consumption of 240 million pounds of ground beef equal the shaded area under the demand curve in Figure 4.1 (b).

Social Costs from the Supply Curve

The supply curve tells us the quantity willingly supplied at each market price. The supply curve reflects the marginal cost of production. Producers seeking to maximize profits will supply a unit of output only if the marginal benefit (the price received) equals or exceeds the marginal cost of production. The supply curve reveals the minimum price at which a producer will sell a unit of output. This price must be just equal to the marginal cost of production.

Consider the supply curve of top quality ground beef in Figure 4.2 (a). Producers are willing to supply 60 million pounds at a price of $1 per pound. At a price of $1.50 per pound they will supply an additional 120 million pounds (for a total of 180 million pounds), and another 60 million pounds will be produced if the price rises to $1.75 per pound. At a price of $1.75, a total of 240 million pounds of ground beef is produced each month. The supply curve identifies the price that is necessary to get each pound of ground beef produced. This price represents the marginal cost of each pound. Adding up the prices at which each million pounds is produced, up to 240 million pounds, yields the total social cost of producing 240 million pounds of ground beef. The shaded area under the supply curve between zero and 240 million pounds in Figure 4.2 (b) represents total social cost.

Society's Net Gain:
Costs and Benefits . . . Again

Having examined separately the benefits and costs of producing and consuming ground beef, we now look at the net gain (benefits less costs) from the ground beef market. In Figure 4.3 the market demand and supply curves have been graphed together. The equilibrium price of top quality ground beef, the price at which quantity demanded equals quantity supplied, is $1.75 per pound. At that price the quantity exchanged in the market is 240 million pounds per month.

The equilibrium market outcome is efficient when the marginal benefit to consumers of the last unit purchased equals the marginal cost to producers of supplying that unit. Such is the case at point E in Figure 4.3. To the left of point E the marginal benefit of an additional pound of ground beef exceeds its marginal cost. To the right of point

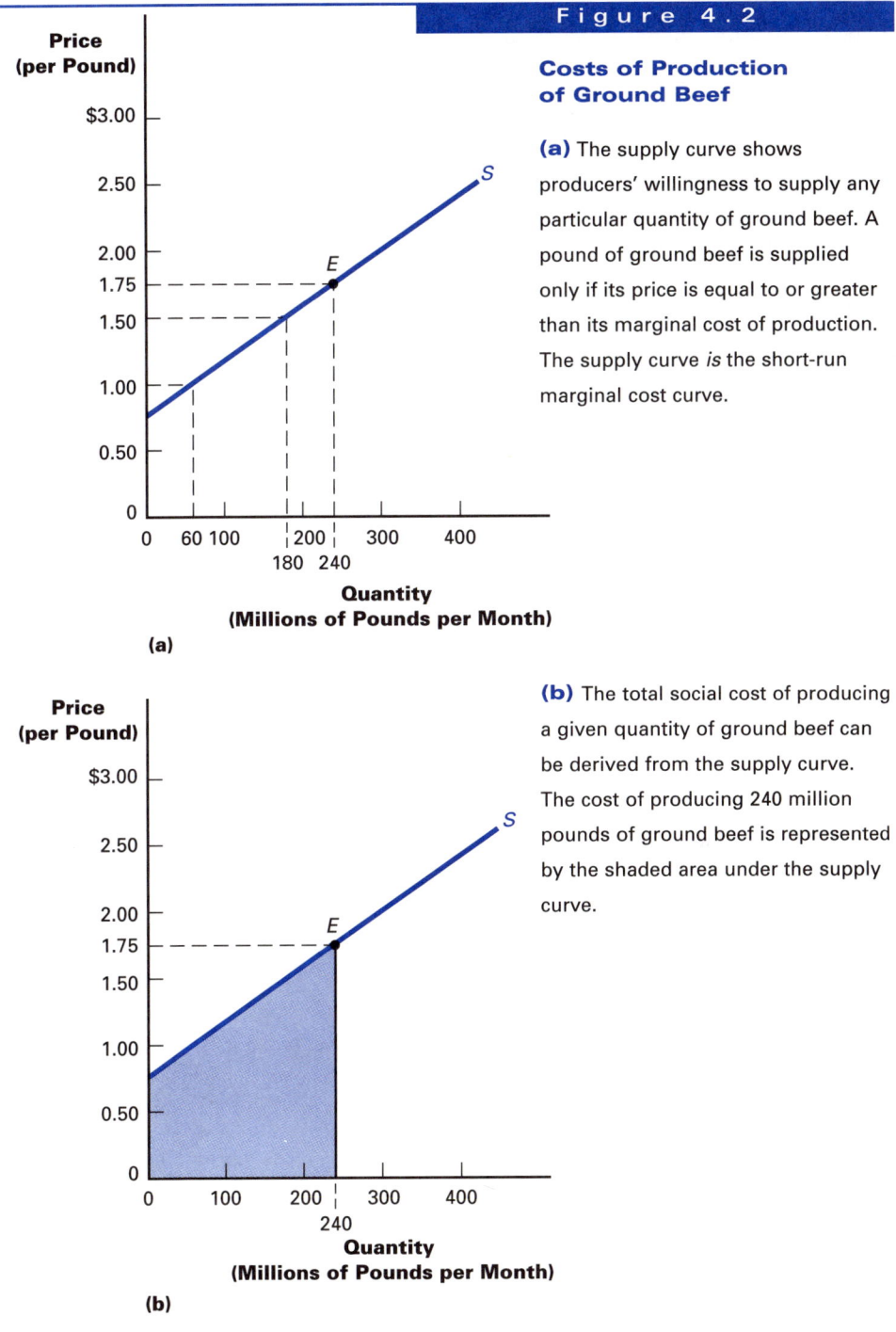

Figure 4.2

Costs of Production of Ground Beef

(a) The supply curve shows producers' willingness to supply any particular quantity of ground beef. A pound of ground beef is supplied only if its price is equal to or greater than its marginal cost of production. The supply curve *is* the short-run marginal cost curve.

(b) The total social cost of producing a given quantity of ground beef can be derived from the supply curve. The cost of producing 240 million pounds of ground beef is represented by the shaded area under the supply curve.

E the marginal cost of an additional pound exceeds its marginal benefit. Marginal benefit equals marginal cost at point E. Society's net benefit from the production and consumption of ground beef is maximized by producing and consuming 240 million pounds of ground beef per month.

Relationship Between Total and Marginal

Economists continually make comparisons at the margin, examining the change in one variable in response to a unit change in another variable. Since the efficiency of market equilibrium is most easily demonstrated when the relationships between marginal value and total value and marginal cost and total cost are understood, we will examine the relationship between total and marginal more closely.

Table 4.1 presents a hypothetical cost schedule for a small firm producing picnic tables. Column 2 indicates that the total cost of production rises as more picnic tables are constructed. Column 3 derives the marginal cost of producing each additional picnic table. The marginal cost of a particular table is simply the addition to total cost incurred in the production of that table. For example, the marginal cost of the third picnic table is the difference between the total cost of producing three tables and the total cost of producing two tables:

$$MC = \$180 - 110 = \$70.$$

Since marginal cost equals the change in total cost caused by producing an additional picnic table, the total cost of any particular number of tables equals the sum of the marginal costs of producing that number of tables. For example, the total cost of producing three tables is \$180. The sum of the marginal costs of producing the first three tables is \$50 + 60 + 70 = \$180. *The sum of marginal costs equals total cost.*

The same principle applies to marginal benefits and total benefits enjoyed by consumers. The total benefits from consuming a particular quantity of a good equals the sum of the benefits enjoyed from consuming additional units of the good up to that quantity, in other words the sum of marginal benefits. Table 4.2 illustrates this. Suppose consumers are willing to pay \$200 to buy one picnic table. The marginal benefit of the first table is \$200. Consumers are willing to pay \$160 to acquire a second table, \$120 for a third table, and \$80 for a fourth. The total benefits of purchasing and using four picnic tables equals the sum of the marginal benefits: \$560.

In mathematical terms, marginal cost equals the change in total cost divided by the change in the number of units produced:

$$MC = \Delta TC / \Delta Q.$$

Table 4.1

Costs of Producing Picnic Tables

Number of Tables	Total Cost	Marginal Cost
0	$ 0	
		$50
1	50	
		60
2	110	
		70
3	180	
		80
4	260	

To derive an accurate estimate of marginal cost, the change in quantity produced should be small (for example, one unit rather than 100 units). Marginal benefit equals the change in total benefit divided by the change in the number of units consumed:

$$MB = \Delta TB / \Delta Q.$$

Again, the change in quantity should be small.

Table 4.2

Benefits from Buying and Using Picnic Tables

Number of Tables	Total Benefit	Marginal Benefit
0	$ 0	
		$200
1	200	
		160
2	360	
		120
3	480	
		80
4	560	

Figure 4.3 illustrates this. In Figure 4.3 (a) the social benefits of consumption are represented by the shaded area (light and dark) under the demand curve, and the social costs are represented by the darker shaded area under the supply curve. For any given level of output up to 240 million pounds, the benefits of consumption exceed the costs of production. As output increases, the benefits of *additional* consumption decrease and the costs of *additional* production increase. The benefits of the 240 millionth pound just equal the costs of production. Beyond 240 million pounds, marginal costs exceed marginal benefits, since beyond that output level the supply curve lies above the demand curve.

The *net gain* from producing and consuming 240 million pounds of ground beef is the difference between total social benefits and total social costs. The net gain from the ground beef market appears in Figure 4.3 (a) as the lightly shaded area under the demand curve but above the supply curve, the triangular area labeled ABE in the figure. This area represents the gains to society from producing and consuming 240 million pounds of ground beef (sold at $1.75 a pound).

The net gains from exchange illustrated in Figure 4.3 (a) are enjoyed by two distinct groups, consumers and producers. Demand and supply analysis enables us to identify how the gains are distributed between the two groups.

Consumers' Surplus When society gains from an activity, both the size of the gain and how it is distributed to members of society are of interest. When the activity

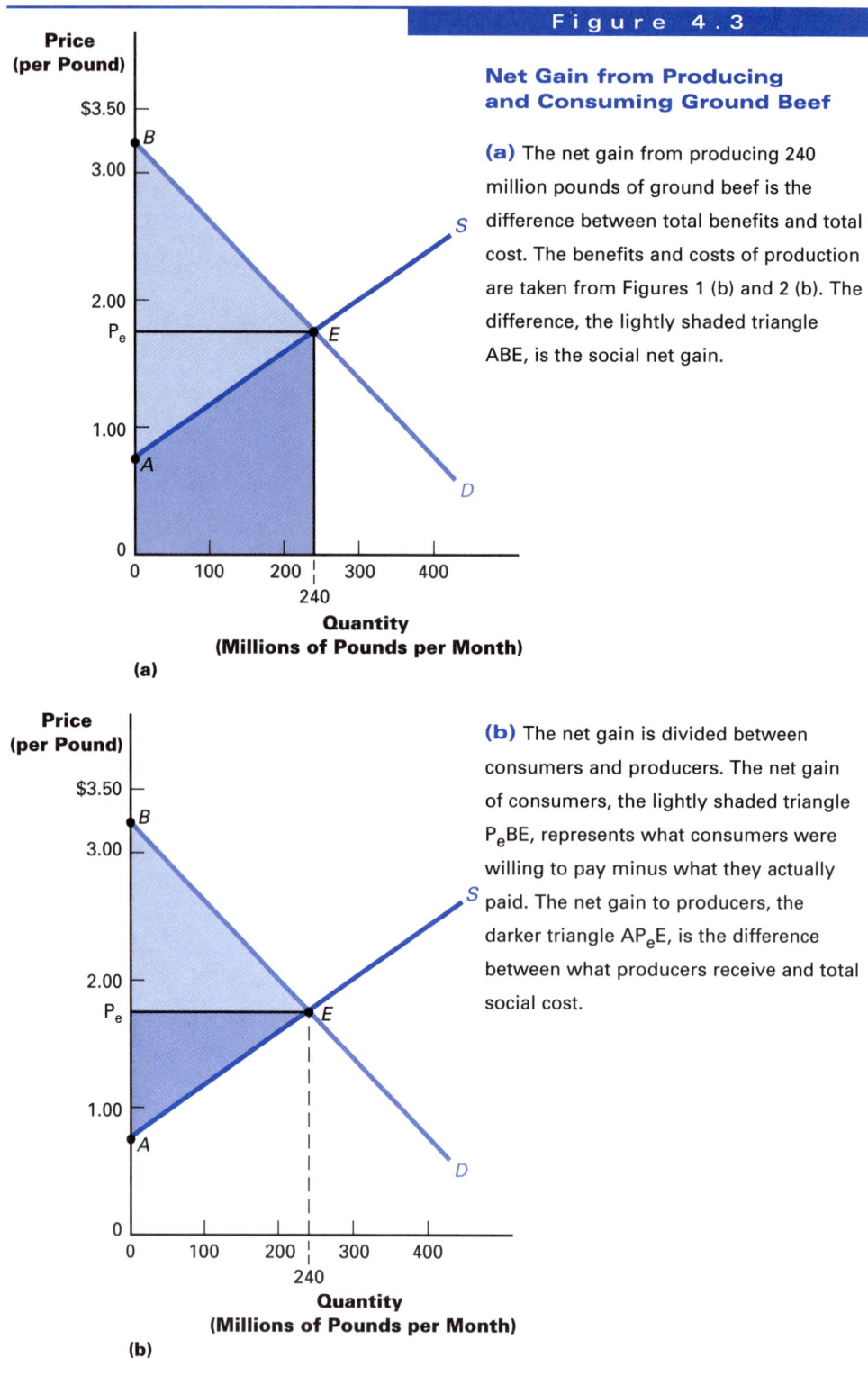

Figure 4.3

Net Gain from Producing and Consuming Ground Beef

(a) The net gain from producing 240 million pounds of ground beef is the difference between total benefits and total cost. The benefits and costs of production are taken from Figures 1 (b) and 2 (b). The difference, the lightly shaded triangle ABE, is the social net gain.

(b) The net gain is divided between consumers and producers. The net gain of consumers, the lightly shaded triangle P_eBE, represents what consumers were willing to pay minus what they actually paid. The net gain to producers, the darker triangle AP_eE, is the difference between what producers receive and total social cost.

in question is the production, exchange, and consumption of a good or service via the market mechanism, a straightforward way exists to identify the share of the gain that accrues to consumers and the share that goes to producers. Figure 4.3 (b) compares what consumers are willing to pay to what they actually pay for ground beef. The demand curve tells us what they are *willing to pay*. The market price of $1.75 is what they *actually pay* for each of the 240 million pounds of ground beef. The difference between what consumers are willing to pay and what they actually pay is **consumers' surplus**. In this example, consumers' surplus is the lightly shaded triangle P_eBE. This area pictures the consumers' share of society's net gain from producing and consuming top quality ground beef.

Total consumers' surplus is the summation of individual consumer's surplus. Suppose Vinita would be willing to pay up to $2 for a pound of ground beef. If the market price is only $1.75 per pound, she is required to pay less for a pound of ground beef than it is worth to her. She consumes ground beef worth $2 to her but pays only $1.75 for it. The difference, 25¢, is a measure of the consumer's surplus Vinita enjoys from the transaction.

Other consumers value ground beef differently than Vinita does. Dave would be willing to pay $2.25 for a pound of ground beef, so he enjoys consumer's surplus of 50¢, but Lisa would be willing to pay no more than $1.75 for a pound of ground beef, so she obtains no consumer's surplus from buying a pound. The ground beef is worth exactly what she must pay for it.

Total consumers' surplus is the sum of the consumer's surplus enjoyed by each individual consumer who buys ground beef at a price of $1.75 per pound. It is a measure of how much more consumers would have been willing to pay for 240 million pounds of ground beef than they actually paid.

Producers' Surplus The share of society's net gain accruing to producers is the difference between the price at which producers would have willingly produced and sold each pound of ground beef and the price at which they actually sold each pound. This difference is called **producers' surplus**. For any given quantity of ground beef the supply curve tells us the price at which producers would be willing to produce and sell the ground beef. The market price ($1.75) is the price at which each pound of ground beef actually sells. For every pound produced and sold – except the very last pound – producers would have been willing to sell at a price below the market price. The sum of the difference between market price and supply price for each pound of ground beef sold constitutes the producers' surplus associated with the ground beef market equilibrium. The darkly shaded triangle AP_eE in Figure 4.3 (b) illustrates producers' surplus.

Conditions for Efficient Market Outcomes Are Restrictive

The market is an attractive rationing mechanism because, under certain conditions, it produces efficient outcomes while allowing decentralized decision making, thus solving society's basic economic problems while preserving considerable individual freedom. In economic markets, the preferences of consumers and the costs of producers work through demand and supply to determine an equilibrium market price. This price rations the available quantity of goods on the basis of ability and willingness to pay.

Consumers' surplus:
The difference between the value of a good to consumers and the amount consumers paid to acquire the good.

Producers' surplus:
The difference between the revenue received by producers for a good and the opportunity cost of producing the good.

A market equilibrium is economically efficient only if the demand curve reflects true social benefits and the supply curve reflects true social costs. A number of situations exist in which the demand or supply curve might not represent true social benefits or costs. Although economists disagree among themselves about the exact conditions required for economic efficiency, three conditions are generally agreed upon: competition exists, all social benefits and social costs are incorporated into decision making, and the economy is relatively stable. These three conditions were implicitly assumed to hold in the discussion of market equilibrium and efficiency in Chapter 3 and in this chapter, though they sometimes fail to hold in real-world economies.[1]

Competition Exists The efficient operation of a market hinges on the presence of competition. By **competition**, an economist means a situation in which neither individual buyers nor individual sellers are able to influence the market price. In practice this means that the number of buyers and sellers is large enough to prevent one buyer or seller from affecting the market outcome. The presence of competition makes pursuit of private gain consistent with social well-being. Individuals cannot use their market power to transfer wealth from other market participants to themselves. For example, if one producer dominates a market, that producer can force the market price above the competitive equilibrium level by restricting the quantity of goods supplied to the market. In such a case, goods are not produced even though their marginal social benefits exceed their marginal social costs. The market outcome is inefficient.

All Social Costs and Benefits Are Incorporated in Decision Making Consumers make consumption decisions based on the benefits derived from consuming goods. Producers make supply decisions based on production costs. Economic efficiency presumes that all social benefits and costs are incorporated in the process that establishes market equilibrium. If some of the benefits of consumption go to people who do not pay for the goods or some of the costs of production are borne by someone other than producers, demand and supply do not reflect true social benefits and costs.

The emission of pollutants into the air or water by firms provides an example of a divergence between private costs and social costs. If no antipollution laws exist, firms will treat the air and public waterways as free pollution-disposal resources. Although the cost to firms of polluting is zero, members of society pay through poorer health, the attending higher medical bills, and a lower quality of life. Because firms do not consider the true social costs of their activities in this instance, they tend to overproduce goods and underproduce environmental quality. The market outcome is inefficient.

Stability of the Economy Economic stability has several dimensions. At the most basic level, there is the requirement of stable rules of the game governing activity in an economy. In particular, efficiently operating economies must have a stable system of **property rights** – legal rights to own and use property as the owners see fit within the limits prescribed by law. In the absence of firmly established property rights, people are unwilling to innovate and invest or even to work harder than necessary. (The low productivity of collective farms in the former Soviet Union is an example of this.

Competition:
A situation in which no individual buyer or seller is able to influence the market price.

Property rights:
Legal right to own and use property as the owner sees fit, within limits prescribed by law.

Since workers who produced a lot were paid no more than workers who produced little, workers had little incentive to work hard.) If property rights are not respected, people realize that any economic goods they manage to accumulate might be taken away from them. People will engage in risky, innovative activities – the kinds of activities that drive a dynamic economy – only if they believe they will get to enjoy the benefits of their activities.

A second kind of stability relates to the monetary system. Most market trades are carried out using money as a **medium of exchange** – an asset generally acceptable in exchange for other goods and services. The general acceptability of money facilitates trading, thus enabling extensive specialization in production to take place. Producers do not have to worry about being able to trade the products they produce for all the many products they want to consume. They simply sell their products for money and use the money to buy other goods and services.

An economy operates efficiently only if the monetary system is relatively stable. Uncertainty about the value of money in the present or in the near future can lead to serious inefficiencies as people fail to make beneficial exchanges because they fear the effects of monetary instability. Large changes in the **value of money** – what a unit of money will buy – can ruin some people while enriching others. Society as a whole suffers from such instability. Thus, governments have long regarded control of the value of money as a government right (though it is a right that has been abused repeatedly through the centuries).

Instability in the total flow of spending on goods and services in the economy can also reduce economic efficiency. If the flow of household spending in product markets declines sharply, the income received by producing firms falls. Lower incomes force firms to reduce their expenditures for productive inputs. Resources, including labor, are unemployed; the economy operates on the interior of its production possibilities frontier. Unemployed workers, lacking income, must reduce their purchases of goods and services. Thus, many potentially beneficial exchanges are forgone.

Medium of exchange:
An asset generally acceptable in exchange and used to make most purchases.

Value of money:
Quantity of goods and services a unit of money will buy.

The price-output equilibrium produced by a competitive market in which demand reflects all social benefits and supply reflects all social costs is efficient; it maximizes the net gains to society from producing and exchanging goods. When competition is absent, or when demand and supply in a market do not incorporate all social benefits and costs, the market outcome is inefficient.

Section Recap

Market Failure

When any one of the three conditions is not met, the market fails in the sense that the market outcome is economically inefficient. Market failure implies that society, through government, has the *opportunity* to improve its well-being by intervening in the market or by using some nonmarket rationing device to allocate resources. Government intervention certainly does not guarantee a social outcome superior to the market outcome, but the potential for improvement exists. Chapter 5 is concerned with when and how government should intervene to overcome market failures. Much of the rest of this book is devoted to two issues: (1) examining how markets work, so that the sources of market failure can be determined and possible solutions proposed, and (2) examining government economic policies to assess how well they have performed and how they might be improved. In the remainder of this chapter we assume that the conditions for market efficiency are met in order to examine how intervention in efficient markets leads to socially inefficient results.

Market Disequilibrium Generates Market Inefficiency

In a state of disequilibrium, the market price does not equate quantity demanded and quantity supplied. The resulting market outcome is inefficient. This section examines the social net gain from the ground beef market when the market price is below or above equilibrium. Comparing the net gain of each of these outcomes to that of the equilibrium case demonstrates the inefficiency associated with market disequilibrium, as well as the fact that *competitive markets maximize net social gains*. This demonstration sets the stage for a discussion of the efficiency effects of **price floors** – laws or regulations that hold the market price above its equilibrium level – and **price ceilings** – laws or regulations that hold the market price below its equilibrium level. The general discussion is then applied to agricultural policies designed to keep market prices above equilibrium and to rent controls designed to keep apartment rents below equilibrium levels.

Price floor:

A law or regulation holding the market price above its equilibrium level.

Price ceiling:

A law or regulation holding the market price below its equilibrium level.

Price Below Equilibrium

When market price is below its equilibrium level, a shortage develops – quantity demanded exceeds quantity supplied. Consider the situation illustrated in Figure 4.4 (a). When the price is $1.50, only 180 million pounds of ground beef are produced and sold, while 280 million pounds are demanded. Note that at 180 million pounds the marginal benefits of consuming more ground beef exceed the marginal costs of production. However, producers do not supply more ground beef because the marginal cost of supplying more than 180 million pounds exceeds the price of $1.50. When output for which benefits exceed costs is not produced, potential gains from trading are lost. The below-equilibrium price of $1.50 reduces the net social benefit from ground beef consumption by an amount equivalent to the shaded triangle, FCE.

Price Above Equilibrium

Market prices above equilibrium also cause market inefficiency. Producers supply quantities whose marginal cost exceeds their marginal benefit to consumers, thus reducing net social benefit. Suppose the price of ground beef is $2.25 a pound as in Figure 4.4 (b). At that price, 360 million pounds of ground beef are produced, while only 160 million are demanded. A surplus of ground beef is created by the above-equilibrium price. Note that beyond the equilibrium quantity of 240 million pounds the costs of production (measured by the area under the supply curve) exceed the benefits of consumption (measured by the area under the demand curve). Output whose production costs exceed consumption benefits is produced. Too many resources are allocated to beef production. If the surplus ground beef is distributed to consumers, the net gain at the equilibrium price, ABE, is reduced by the loss (the shaded triangle) EGF. If all or part of the surplus is destroyed, the loss is larger because consumers obtain no benefits from the surplus that is destroyed.

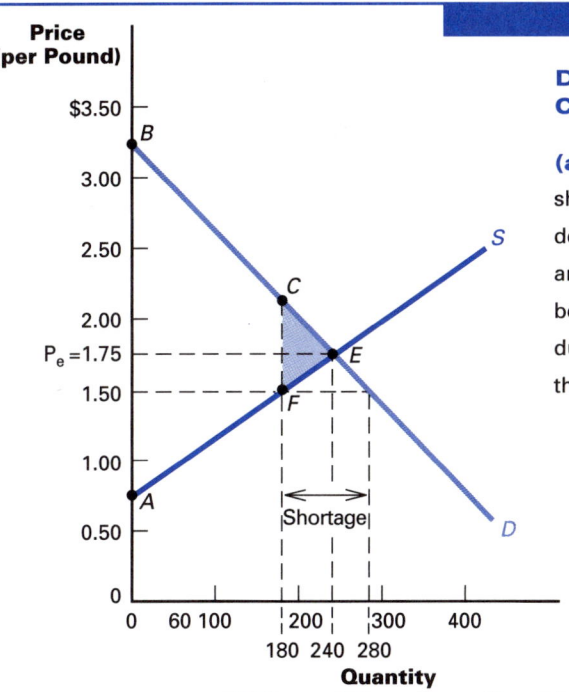

Figure 4.4

**Disequilibrium Prices
Cause Inefficiency**

(a) A below-equilibrium price causes a shortage: 280 million pounds are demanded but only 180 million pounds are supplied. Output for which the benefits exceed the costs is not produced. Social net gain is reduced by the shaded triangle FCE.

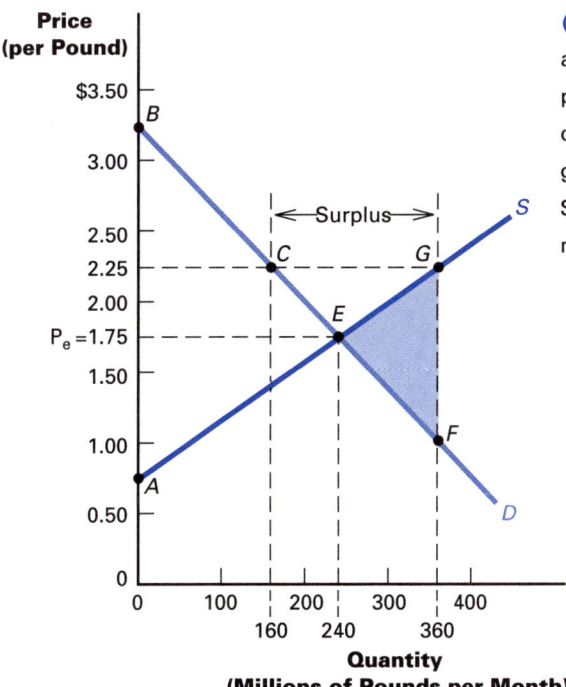

(b) An above-equilibrium price causes a surplus: 360 million pounds are supplied but only 160 million pounds are demanded. The last 120 million pounds generate greater costs than benefits. Social net gain is reduced by a minimum of the shaded triangle EGF.

These two cases illustrate the uniqueness of market equilibrium: *At the equilibrium price, only those units of output for which the marginal benefits equal or exceed the marginal costs are produced*. The net gain from production and consumption is maximized at this price. At any other price, producers either (a) fail to produce output for which the benefits exceed the costs (underallocate resources) or (b) produce output for which costs exceed benefits (overallocate resources).

The net gains to society are reduced when the market price is held either above or below its equilibrium level.

Section Recap

Price Controls Introduce Economic Inefficiencies

Price controls – floors or ceilings – prevent markets from moving to equilibrium. Efforts to intervene in markets to control prices are not uncommon. Governments often attempt to regulate prices through decrees or legislation, declaring that prices in some markets are too high or too low. Consumers sometimes successfully lobby their governments to hold the price of housing or fuel below the equilibrium level. On the other hand, businesses often lobby government to hold prices above equilibrium levels on products they produce or to prevent so-called unfair competition. Numerous examples of such market intervention in the U.S. economy have been documented.

Price Ceilings and Floors

A price ceiling prevents a price from rising above a certain level. In the mid–1970s, a price ceiling was placed on the retail price of gasoline. The price of some natural gas sold in interstate markets was limited by a price ceiling until 1989. A price floor prevents the market price from falling below a certain level. Since the 1930s the United States has had a minimum wage law establishing a price floor in the labor market. Employers cannot legally pay workers covered by the law less than the minimum wage.

When consumers and producers are free to trade, their actions establish a market equilibrium price that equates quantity demanded and quantity supplied. The market's rationing and allocating function is carried out by price adjustments in response to changes in factors that affect supply and demand. A price floor or ceiling prevents the market price from moving to the equilibrium level, thus disrupting this rationing and allocating function. Two examples illustrate this.

Rental Housing

Several U.S. cities, including New York, New York, and Berkeley, California, have rent control laws. These laws establish maximum rents that landlords can charge. Such laws were enacted because of the widespread belief that apartment rents were too high. Proponents of rent control (typically tenant groups) generally argue that shelter is a basic need and that society should not allow its price to be so high that families cannot afford decent housing. Opponents (landlords and economists) argue that rent controls fail to provide affordable housing to the poor, instead creating a host of problems not encountered when the price of housing is allowed to move freely.

The equilibrium price established in the rental housing market reflects the interaction of supply and demand. When a price ceiling is established below the equilibrium price, the market price cannot rise to the equilibrium level.[2] The effect of a price ceiling is illustrated in Figure 4.5. In the absence of intervention in this particular market, the equilibrium price for rental housing would be P_e = $600 per month, and the equilibrium quantity exchanged would be Q_e = 8000 units rented. However, a rent control law establishing P_c = $400 per month as the maximum rent prevents the market from reaching equilibrium. At the maximum legal price of $400 the quantity willingly demanded, 10,000 units, exceeds the quantity willingly supplied, 7000 units. The price ceiling generates excess demand for, or a shortage of, housing. In the absence of the price ceiling, consumers of housing would bid the price up, but the ceiling prevents the price from rising. Not all people who are willing to pay $600 per month for housing are able to obtain it.

When the price mechanism is not used to ration available housing, other rationing criteria arise. People who want rental housing must now look harder and spend more resources in the search. When an apartment is advertised for rent, many people respond. Apartment seekers try to be the first person to call the landlord. They might pay someone to help in finding an apartment or for information about upcoming vacancies. Or, prospective renters might offer bribes to landlords. Notice that, at Q_s = 7000 units in Figure 4.5, the price renters are willing to pay for rental housing ($700) exceeds the ceiling price. All or part of the difference could be offered as a bribe to a landlord and the renter would still benefit from the exchange.

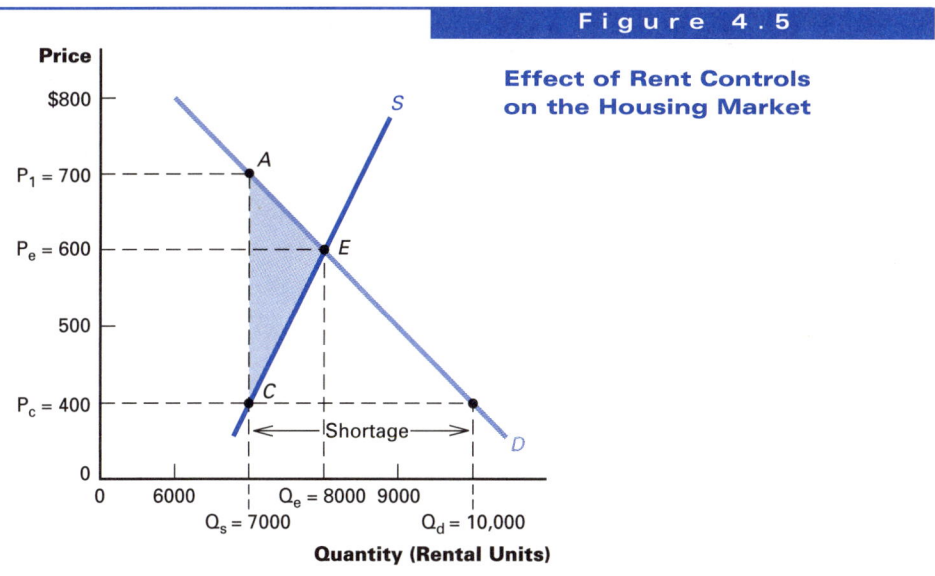

Figure 4.5

Effect of Rent Controls on the Housing Market

A rent control law establishes a price ceiling at P_c. Since P_c lies below the equilibrium price, P_e, a shortage of housing develops. At P_c, quantity demanded of Q_d=10,000 units exceeds quantity supplied of Q_s=7000 units. The rent control law prevents price from rising and eliminating the market disequilibrium and forces landlords to ration rental units by some other means. The net loss to society of the rent control law is represented by the shaded triangle CAE.

In these circumstances, landlords can choose to rent to whomever they please, using any criteria they like when choosing tenants. Some landlords might choose to practice racial discrimination. Some will charge fees for services usually included in the rent or for such necessities as keys. Realizing a shortage of housing exists, landlords have the incentive to allow the quality of housing to deteriorate. Lower-quality housing is less costly to maintain, thus enabling landlords to earn a profit even at the below-equilibrium rental price.

Although rent control laws lower the market price of housing, the total cost to renters may not fall. In addition, such laws create other problems: a shortage of housing, rationing of housing according to arbitrary criteria such as race or sex, bribery, and deterioration in the quality of housing. In cities that have maintained rent control laws for several decades, abandoned apartment buildings are common. When the condition of apartments becomes so bad that they can no longer be rented out, landlords board up the buildings and abandon them. The removal of apartments from the market worsens the housing shortage.

Price ceilings are also economically inefficient. The shaded triangle CAE in Figure 4.5 represents the net loss to society resulting from the price ceiling. Some socially beneficial trades are eliminated by the ceiling. Some consumers are willing to pay a price higher than both the ceiling price for rental housing and the marginal cost of providing the housing. Although both consumers and producers would benefit from trading, the price ceiling prohibits these mutually beneficial exchanges from taking place. As shown in Figure 4.5, the monthly loss in social welfare generated by rent control is $150,000 (the area of the triangle CAE $= 1/2 \times \$300 \times 1000$).

Agricultural Products

The prices of agricultural products, such as wheat, corn, cotton, and dairy, have fallen over time relative to the prices of most other goods. Technological advances in genetics, pesticides, fertilizers, and farm implements have reduced the marginal costs of production and increased the supply of agricultural products. Since large-scale operations are able to use modern techniques and materials more efficiently than smaller farms, many small farms have been caught in a cost-price squeeze: Their costs have not fallen as fast as the prices of their products. In an attempt to raise agricultural prices and incomes, the government, long ago, imposed price floors in various agricultural product markets.

The wheat market is a good example. The government maintains a support price, or price floor, for wheat. Figure 4.6 illustrates the effect of such a policy. In the absence of the price floor the wheat market would be in equilibrium at a market price of $P_e = \$3.20$ per bushel and quantity traded of $Q_e = 1800$ million bushels. The support price is designed to keep the wheat price above a certain level. This particular price floor is called a support price because, when necessary, the government takes action to support the price at $P_F = \$4$ per bushel. At the support price a surplus of wheat exists: The quantity supplied, $Q_s = 2000$ million bushels, exceeds the quantity demanded, $Q_d = 1500$ million bushels. In the absence of the price support policy, the price per bushel would fall from $P_F = \$4$ to $P_e = \$3.20$.[3]

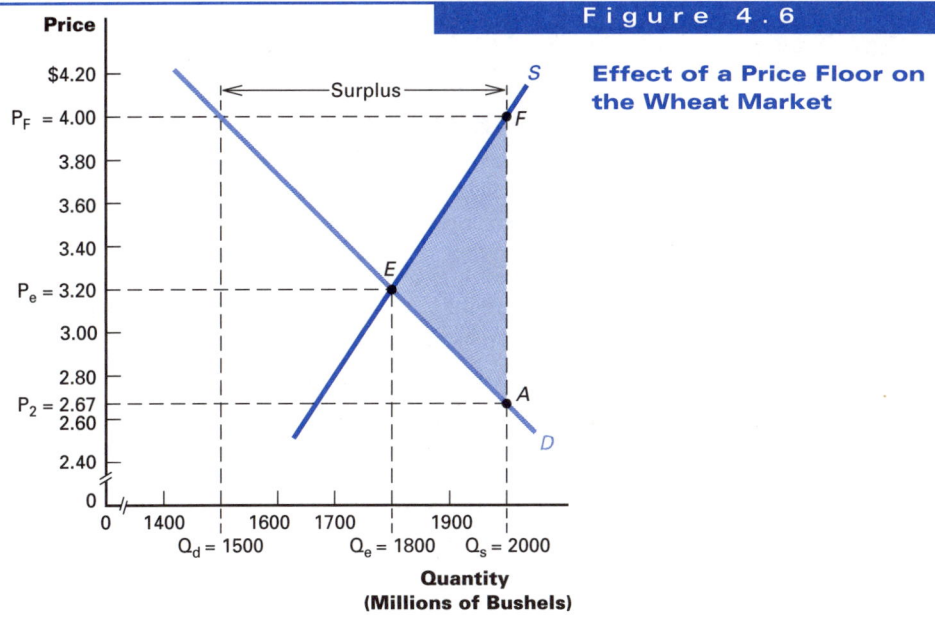

Figure 4.6

Effect of a Price Floor on the Wheat Market

An agricultural price support program establishes a price floor at P_F. Since P_F lies above the equilibrium price, P_e, it generates a surplus of wheat. At P_F, the quantity supplied of Q_s=2000 bushels exceeds the quantity demanded of Q_d=1500 bushels. The government stands ready to purchase the surplus wheat, since consumers will not buy it. If the government distributes the surplus wheat to those who value it most highly, the net social loss from the program is represented by the shaded triangle EFA. If the government destroys all or part of the surplus, the net social loss is even larger.

At the support price, farmers grow more wheat than consumers are willing to buy. The government maintains a price of $4 per bushel by being a consumer of last resort. At the support price, consumers are willing to buy only 1500 million bushels of wheat. To ensure that the market price stays at least as high as $4, the government must purchase the surplus wheat produced at the support price. Wheat farmers benefit from the guaranteed minimum price for wheat, but consumers pay a higher price for the wheat they purchase, as well as higher taxes to provide funds for the government purchase of surplus wheat. In addition, taxpayers must provide the funds to store and ultimately dispose of the grain. As in the case of rent control, the support program creates a number of problems that outweigh the benefits received by the favored group.

Price floors are also economically inefficient. Consumers improve their well-being by trading something of lesser value for something of greater value. Consumers exchange their income for wheat only when the wheat they obtain in return is more valuable to them than what they could have purchased with the income. The wheat price support causes wheat to be produced that would not be purchased voluntarily by consumers, that is, whose marginal cost exceeds its marginal value to consumers. If the surplus wheat is distributed to consumers, the net loss to society from the wheat price support program is represented in Figure 4.6 by the shaded triangle EFA, which in this example equals $133

Is It Better to Kill a Cow than to Kill a Program?

The Food Security Act of 1985 provided for the government purchase of whole dairy herds from dairy farmers. Cattle purchased under the program were to be exported or slaughtered. Officials expected the implementation of the act to result in the slaughter of 1.5 million dairy cattle by August 1987. The program was established to help reduce a huge surplus of dairy products that government price support programs helped to create. Price support programs had become very expensive. For example, in the 1980s the government annually spent over $2 billion on dairy price support purchases. Does it make economic sense for the government to purchase and slaughter millions of dairy cattle?

Whether the whole herd buy-out program makes sense depends upon one's point of view. People who believe that government should support the incomes of dairy farmers argued that the program makes sense in the context of the history of dairy policy. The program was simply the latest in a series of government interventions in the dairy market to increase prices and the incomes of dairy farmers. A system of price supports has held the market price above the equilibrium price since 1949, leading to, amomg other things, increased production and excess supplies.

The Food and Agriculture Act of 1977 increased price supports substantially, and dairy farmers responded by sharply increasing production. By 1983 the government was attempting to reduce output by taxing dairy men who received price support payments but did not reduce production. The attempt failed. Later that year the government began to pay farmers for every pound reduction of milk output below their previous output levels. The government also helped organize a massive promotion and advertising program to encourage increased milk consumption.

---

million ($1/2 \times \$1.33 \times 200$ million). If the surplus wheat is destroyed, the loss is much larger than EFA, since consumers are paying for the surplus production through higher prices and taxes but are enjoying no benefits from it. In fact, the Department of Agriculture estimated that the wheat price support system alone cost American taxpayers over $1.8 billion in 1988.[5] In addition, it is estimated that farm support programs cost U.S. consumers an average of $360 per person per year.[6]

The inefficiency that results from price floors has prompted increased efforts to eliminate or reduce the number of farm price support programs in the United States. Recent targets of the move toward increased efficiency include wool, mohair, and honey producers in the United States. In 1993, the Congress voted to eliminate honey subsidies immediately, resulting in a $23 million savings for U.S. taxpayers. The programs for wool and mohair, which cost $190 million annually, were allowed to operate for one more year, after which they were also scheduled to cease.

Agricultural price support programs are also quite prevalent in foreign countries. The members of the European Community (EC) all provide subsidies and price supports in their respective countries for a variety of agricultural products ranging from wine to cheese to wheat and corn. Such programs are estimated to cost EC consumers an average of $450 person per year. Japan has employed a number of measures designed to maintain the price of rice for a number of years to protect Japanese rice farmers. Rice costs Japanese consumers four to five times what it should. It has been estimated that,

Despite such policies, surpluses grew. By 1985 the government owned billions of pounds of surplus dairy products.[4] The government's only options are to destroy the surplus stocks or give them away to people who otherwise would not purchase dairy products. Huge quantities of surplus dairy products have been given away under various programs.

The whole herd buyout program is a logical policy in the context of this policy history. Since government price supports and government-supported research into milk production have been so important to the dairy industry for four decades, many government officials and politicians argued that ending supports would be excessively harmful to dairy farmers; the industry is dependent on the government's help. This put the government in an uncomfortable position: It is difficult, if not impossible, to reduce price supports or production without hurting the industry.

Viewed from the economic perspective developed in this book, the dairy support program does not make sense. The basic problem is that consumers are unwilling to pay a price that makes milk production at current levels profitable. Farmers produce output whose marginal costs exceed marginal benefits. As a consequence of the program, dairy prices are higher than they otherwise would be and taxpayers must pay higher taxes.

Programs such as the herd buyout program often do not achieve their primary objective – reduced surpluses – because of the actions of people who do not participate in the programs. For example, when some farmers sell out to the government, others who remain in business may profitably expand their own herds, offsetting the expected decrease in output. Furthermore, market intervention often creates problems in other markets. A successful buyout program would increase the number of cattle being slaughtered, depressing the market price of beef, making cattlemen worse off. Government concern about the possible effects on beef prices led lawmakers to place restrictions on the number of dairy cattle that could be slaughtered and to require the U.S. military to step up its purchases of beef, increasing the demand for beef and supporting beef prices.

Programs such as the whole herd buyout program would be unnecessary if dairy prices were not maintained at artificially high levels by government policies. None of these dairy programs makes sense on economic efficiency grounds. The buyout plan was designed to reduce government expenditures on the dairy programs, while continuing the price and income support programs that created the problem.

overall, farm support programs cost Japanese consumers as much as $600 per person per year. In Canada, milk is twice as expensive as it is in the United States. As we saw in Chapter 2, restrictions on free trade, such as policies that maintain agricultural prices above their competitive levels, end up costing consumers. In the case of agricultural support programs consumers are especially hard hit – through higher prices and increased taxes to support such programs.

Section Recap

Rent control laws hold the price of rental units below the equilibrium level. A shortage results, and the quality of rental housing deteriorates. Wheat price supports hold the price of wheat above the equilibrium level. A surplus results, and taxpayers and consumers lose more than producers gain.

Why Would Society Choose to Be Inefficient?

An economy is efficient when it uses all of its resources to produce at minimum cost those goods and services of most value to consumers. Since resources are scarce, it is costly to be inefficient; society goes without something it could have had. But societies have many, sometimes conflicting, goals, and efficient use of resources is only one of them.

Other Social Goals

In the United States the market mechanism is used to coordinate many individual decisions, in large part because it is consistent with two major goals: efficiency and individual liberty. However, intervention in a market or replacement of market decision making with some form of collective decision making is common when the market outcome is inconsistent with other social objectives. For example, ethical standards of fairness and justice lead us to refuse to trade some goods in markets: People are selected for human organ transplants on criteria other than ability to pay, and slavery – the sale and purchase of human beings – is forbidden.

A society can pursue any number of goals. The goals of economic efficiency and growth increase societies' overall standards of living. Societies place a high value on *national security. Individual liberty* and *equity* concerns are also important. Different cultures have different notions of fairness and justice, and these views shape the means by which decisions are made as well as the importance attached to various social goals.

Many decisions concerning social goals are made through collective means, including some through the political decision-making process. Criteria other than willingness to pay and economic efficiency are important in political decision making. The government purchases goods and services for national defense, but the production and sale of such goods is not subject to normal market forces. (This is one reason why we often read about problems between the government and its contractors.) National security is not left to the private market. (Chapter 5 discusses why these decisions are made collectively.) Government concerns about national security influence many other economic policy decisions. Some people even argue that the various agricultural programs are justified on national security grounds, an argument used to defend protection of other domestic industries from foreign competition.

Agricultural employment has shrunk so much that it now accounts for less than 3 percent of U.S. jobs. It could conceivably get even smaller if further productivity gains occur or U.S. consumers buy more agricultural products from other countries. Should we allow this vital industry to become so small? An adequate and secure food supply is important to society. If the United States were to become engaged in a major war and outside sources of food were suddenly cut off, we would be at a disadvantage if our domestic industry could not adequately respond to demand. Thus, some supporters of American agriculture argue that the inefficiency associated with agricultural programs is justified as part of the cost of our national security.

Noneconomic criteria often dominate political decision making. The United States was a rural society as recently as the early twentieth century. With their roots in agriculture, many Americans value the tradition of the family farm. In a market context, tradition may carry little weight, but in a political context, it might be important enough to persuade voters to support legislation to help maintain the well-being of those citizens still on the farm, even though it is economically inefficient.

Another element of the farm problem receives a great deal of attention in the political setting but much less in the market context. Economic losses are a signal to owners of resources that profitable opportunities in an industry are shrinking. Losses prompt resources to leave the industry, reducing supply and pushing up price. Resource mobility is important to the competitive functioning of markets. Our market model implicitly assumes that the movement of resources in and out of markets is costless. However,

W h y   W o u l d   S o c i e t y   C h o o s e   t o   B e   I n e f f i c i e n t ?

113

resource mobility is not costless. When a firm goes out of business, the firm's owners suffer losses and the firm's workers become unemployed. Such developments may impose hardships, at least temporarily, on individuals and families.

In a market context, adjustment costs are simply part of the price paid for the functioning of a healthy market and the efficiencies gained from the market. In a political decision-making context, however, such human costs may be accorded more importance. In the case of agriculture, mobility costs are high. People who have grown up on a farm, who are familiar only with a rural life, must change their way of life. They must look for employment elsewhere, and frequently they must move to a city. The costs of such a fundamental change in lifestyle can be very important in political decision making. Politicians may opt for policies that are inefficient economically because they want to reduce emotional and social costs.

Conflicting social goals make it difficult for government decisions to be satisfactory with respect to all social goals. In fact, most such decisions are compromises. Licensing health care practitioners may reduce competition and efficiency, but it improves the quality of health care for society. Requiring the use of seat belts restricts individual freedom, but it also saves lives. A random lottery military draft is an inefficient way to obtain human resources for the military, but it may be consistent with society's notion of selfless service to one's country. The government might respond to an international political development by eliminating trade with another country. By its action the government sacrifices some economic efficiency to achieve a political objective.

Income Redistribution

One of the three basic economic questions that all societies must answer is, For whom are society's goods and services produced? In a pure market economy, access to goods and services is determined by the resources one possesses. Markets ration goods to those willing to pay the most, and market outcomes are efficient, *given the existing distribution of income*. This point is an important one to remember. There is no efficient income distribution. Although a particular income distribution affects the outcomes of market transactions by affecting the structure of demand, it does not determine whether the market outcomes are efficient.

What people consider to be the best income distribution for society depends on their sense of fairness and equity; it is determined by normative considerations. Religious and ethical values have an important part to play in the economy as well, since they are important determinants of a society's goals and values. A wide array of programs designed to redistribute income currently exists.

Since a fair distribution of economic well-being is an important goal for most societies, they may choose to redistribute income in an attempt to achieve more equitable distributions. Although Americans value individual liberty, the U.S. government taxes workers to provide Social Security income to retirees. Therefore, some liberty is sacrificed to achieve the redistribution of income. We are willing to let a family's income be determined by the efforts of its members – and luck – only so long as the family is not too unfortunate. Employed workers are taxed to provide income to unemployed workers. Society provides a minimal income guarantee to low-income, single-parent families

Why the DISAGREEMENT?

Farm Programs: Welfare for the Wealthy?

The principles underlying current agricultural programs have not changed for fifty years, although these programs have been controversial since their inception. Disagreements flare up each time agricultural legislation is reconsidered and revised, a process recently occurring about every five years. Everyone involved in the legislative process understands that

U.S. agricultural policies are inefficient. However, a majority of legislators believes that the distributional benefits of the farm programs outweigh the costs of inefficient production. A vocal minority strenuously disagrees. Why the disagreement?

Without a doubt, the income redistribution aspects of farm policies underlie the longevity of the programs. Using farm programs as a way to redistribute income is legitimate, however, only if these programs are effective vehicles for

achieving the income redistribution goal. Let us assume that the specific objective of these policies is to provide income support to those farmers whose incomes are being eroded by the divergent trends in farm income and farm costs, especially those farmers who are financially distressed and are finding it difficult to generate enough income to finance their indebtedness. With these objectives in mind, two important questions arise: Who pays for the programs? Who benefits from the programs?

with young children. Such programs both satisfy notions of fairness and promote social stability.

Efficiency-Equity Tradeoffs

Although economic efficiency is independent of the initial distribution of resources in an economy, policies designed to redistribute income usually affect the efficiency of markets to some degree. By distorting the demands of consumers or the supplies of producers, redistributional policies drive the market price and output away from the equilibrium levels that would exist in the absence of intervention. Both consumers and producers lose. Some redistributional policies have only minor effects on the efficiency of markets, while others impose huge costs on society by reducing efficiency dramatically. Thus, if income redistribution is a social goal, it is important to design redistributional programs so that their negative effects on efficiency are minimized. Redistributional policies that reduce efficiency by an unnecessarily large amount make society poorer by eliminating the production of goods and services that could be used to satisfy wants.

Examples of redistributional policies that appear to have large negative effects on economic efficiency are not hard to find in the United States or abroad. For example, in Germany, unemployment insurance benefits are so generous that many unemployed workers remain unemployed for many months or even years. They refuse to accept jobs (to supply labor services) because the alternative of paid leisure is so attractive. This problem exists to a lesser degree in the United States as well. Another example of inefficiency created by a redistributional policy was the diversion of resources from productive uses into tax shelters that took place before income tax rates were lowered in the 1980s. Wealthy individuals, who faced marginal income tax rates (that is, tax rates on the last dollars of income earned) in excess of 50 percent, often preferred to invest in

The answer to the first question is well known. The burden of agricultural programs falls on consumers (who pay higher food prices) and taxpayers. The burden falls disproportionately on low-income consumers, because they spend a larger share of their income on food than do higher-income consumers.

Are the programs' beneficiaries financially troubled farmers? Unfortunately, the answer is, not in general. Consider the following evidence. Farms vary widely in size and in annual sales. Many farms are smaller than 100 acres and annually market less than $2,500 in products. Other farms consist of more than 5,000 acres and have annual sales in excess of $500,000. The financial well-being of the farm, its net income, and the value of government payments vary by farm size as well.

If we rank farms by size and the annual value of their sales and look at the amount of government support different farmers receive we see dramatic differences. In 1991, farms with 500 acres or more (about 357,000 farms) accounted for approximately 19 percent of all farms and 55 percent of all farm sales, resulting in average revenues of $252,400 per farm. The farms in this category also received nearly 77 percent of all government payments to farmers. Approximately 45,000 farms with 2,000 acres or more – 8 percent of all farms that received government payments – received 27 percent of total government payments, or an average of $31,633 per farm. By contrast, the 838,000 farms with less than 100 acres – approximately 44 percent of all farms – generated about 15 percent of total farm sales. Approximately 77,000 farms with less than 100 acres – 13.5 percent of all farms receiving government payments – received 2.2 percent of total government payments. The average payment to these farmers was $1,500 in 1991.[7]

The evidence suggests that agricultural programs do not work very well as income redistribution programs. They are financed primarily by the less well-to-do, and they distribute government payments primarily to relatively well-to-do farmers.

nonproductive ventures that exploited tax loopholes rather than investing in productive market activity. As a result, the U.S. government lost billions of dollars of tax revenue. In addition, the economy suffered because valuable resources were misallocated to nonproductive uses.

Since what constitutes a fair income distribution is more a matter of values than of analysis, economists have little if any comparative advantage in discussions of what the income distribution *should be*. However, once an income distribution goal has been set, economic analysis can contribute greatly to the achievement of that goal at a minimum cost to society.

Why Is Economic Efficiency So Important to Economists?

The topic of economic efficiency receives more attention than any other topic in Part I of this text and provides the motivation for much of the analysis in the remainder of the book. Why do economists devote so much attention to this particular social goal and relatively little to the other goals mentioned in this chapter? The reason for paying so much attention to economic efficiency is probably clear by now, but it bears repeating. Being economically efficient is the logical response to the basic economic problem of scarce resources relative to human wants. Economic inefficiency implies that society is failing to satisfy some wants that could be satisfied at no social cost.

The extent to which society is successful at achieving economic efficiency affects the achievement of other objectives. An efficient economy has more income to redistribute, should it choose to do so, than does an inefficient economy. Efficient environmental policies minimize the cost of protecting the air and water. An efficient economy promotes economic growth and the resulting increases in living standards. Other social goals may reduce the level of economic efficiency that could be achieved if efficiency were the *only* social goal, but that does not mean that the economy should not be as efficient as possible within the constraints imposed by other social goals.

Inefficient Markets and Government Intervention

This chapter has examined agricultural markets and policies as a vehicle for explaining and illustrating the notion of economic efficiency. Although agricultural policies generally have been poor policies from the perspective of economic efficiency, they have persisted for over fifty years in basically the same form.[8] The reason for the persistence of inefficient agricultural policies must be that they satisfy, to some degree, other social goals – equity, national defense, preserving tradition. Has the cost been worth it? Society – and its policymakers – must address this question, since it is clear that government intervention in otherwise competitive markets has been quite costly.

When markets do not meet the conditions necessary for efficient market outcomes, government intervention may be able to improve efficiency while simultaneously addressing other social goals. Chapter 5 considers in some detail the potential benefits from government intervention in imperfect markets.

Section Recap

Societies have many goals besides efficiency. Some of these goals may conflict with the goal of efficiency, leading governments to adopt inefficient policies. Still, given the other goals adopted by government, being as efficient as possible is important, since being inefficient needlessly reduces social welfare.

Summary

Economic efficiency is defined as the achievement of the maximum difference between benefits and costs. Under well-defined conditions the equilibrium achieved through market decision making is economically efficient.

Since a demand curve tells us how much consumers are willing to pay for each quantity of a good, we can calculate the total benefits from consuming a given quantity of a good by adding up the amount consumers are willing to pay for each additional unit. Similarly, the supply curve tells us the marginal cost of producing each unit of a good. The social cost of producing a given quantity of a good is calculated by adding up the marginal opportunity cost of producing each unit of output.

The net social gain from producing and consuming a good can be derived from market demand and supply by subtracting the cost of production from the benefits of consumption. The difference is the net gain to society. The net gain is greatest when the market price and quantity exchanged are the equilibrium price and quantity.

The net gain from an activity can be divided into **consumers' surplus** and **producers' surplus**. Consumers' surplus is the difference between what consumers would have been willing to pay to consume a given quantity of the good and what they actually had to pay. Producers' surplus is the difference between the price producers actually received for a good and the minimum price for which they would have produced and sold the good.

At least three conditions must be met for markets to operate efficiently. First, markets must be *competitive*. No single buyer or seller can use market power to affect the market price. Second, *private costs and benefits must equal social costs and benefits*. Third, the economy must be *stable* enough to permit people to engage in beneficial trades.

Disequilibrium market prices are inefficient relative to the equilibrium price. A market price below equilibrium leads to a shortage. Output for which the marginal benefits of consumption exceed the marginal costs of production is not produced. Resources are underallocated to this market, and mutually beneficial exchanges are not made.

A disequilibrium market price above equilibrium leads to a surplus; more output is produced than is consumed. Output for which the marginal production costs exceed marginal consumption benefits is produced. Resources are overallocated to this market.

Price floors and **ceilings** introduce inefficiency into market outcomes because they establish market prices above or below the equilibrium price. In the United States a system of price floors has long been used to support agricultural prices and to stabilize and enhance farm incomes.

The United States has maintained and expanded an array of programs that are clearly inefficient in an attempt to achieve other social goals. Economic efficiency is only one among many potentially conflicting goals. The desire to achieve an equitable income distribution often leads societies to alter the distribution of income generated by the market. In addition, once the government has intervened in a market, political decision making becomes an important influence. Political decision making is subject to different forces than market decision making.

Questions for Thought

Knowledge Questions

1. Explain why and how the benefits of consuming a given quantity of a good can be calculated from the demand curve.

2. When the market price is above the equilibrium price, as is the case with a price floor, resources are overallocated to the market. Explain what overallocation means.

3. Explain the concepts of consumers' and producers' surplus.

4. Why is economic efficiency important even in an economy that chooses to engage in massive income redistribution?

Application Questions

5. In Figure 4.3 point A is at a price of $0.75 and point B is at a price of $3.25. Calculate the net gain in dollars from producing and consuming 240 million

pounds of ground beef. (Hint: Remember the area of a triangle is equal to 1/2 × base × height.)

6. Describe the consumer's surplus that you gain when you purchase and consume one unit of a particular good.

7. Figure 4.4 (b) illustrates the impact of a $2.25 price floor on ground beef. What changes in demand or supply would make the price floor completely ineffective? Explain.

8. In Figure 4.4 (b), point F is at a price of $1 and point G is at a price of $2.25. What is the net loss to society of an above-equilibrium price *if the surplus production is distributed to those who value it most highly*? What can you say about the net loss to society if the surplus production is destroyed?

Synthesis Questions

9. Suppose that a rent control law is being considered for your college town. The law would keep apartment rents below present equilibrium levels.

   a. Who would favor the law? Who would oppose it? Why?

   b. How would your strategies for finding and renting an apartment be altered by the law?

   c. How would the behavior and policies of landlords be altered?

   d. Draw a graph, illustrating the inefficiency of this law.

   e. Can you think of an alternative policy that might address the problem of high rents, yet be less inefficient? Explain.

10. Suppose the social cost of production in a market exceeds the private cost of production (perhaps because firms ignore the social costs of pollution).

   a. Where does the social supply curve lie relative to the private market supply curve?

   b. Draw a graph showing the excess social costs of operating at the free market equilibrium level.

   c. Suppose the government imposes a tax on the good in question, increasing private production costs. Is such a tax inefficient *under these circumstances*? Explain your answer.

11. Explain why the efficiency of an economy is independent of the income distribution existing in the economy.

End Notes

[1] It should be noted that an efficient market outcome may be regarded as inequitable. If the initial distribution of wealth is very unequal – perhaps a few people are very wealthy and many are very poor – efficient markets will result in outcomes that are still unequal. Society may choose to intervene to adjust the initial distribution.

[2] A price ceiling is effective only if it is *below* the equilibrium price. If the price ceiling in Figure 4.5 were $P_1 = \$700$ per month instead of $400 per month, it would not affect the market outcome. Excess supply exists at a price of $700, and market forces would push the price down to its equilibrium level.

[3] A price floor is effective only when it is established above the equilibrium price. If the price support were set at P_2 in Figure 4.6, competition between consumers of wheat would push the price up to P_e.

[4] Bovard, J. *The Farm Fiasco*, San Fransisco, ACF Press, 1989.

[5] *Statistical Abstract of the United States*, 1990, Table No. 1126, p. 649.

[6] "Guilty on All Counts," *The Economist*, August 21, 1993, p. 51.

[7] The data reported here are from the *1992 Census of Agriculture*, Volume 1, Geographic Area Series, Part 51, United States Summary and State Data, AC92–A–51, U.S. Department of Commerce, Issued October 1994.

[8] It should be noted that, even in the face of massive government intervention, market forces dominate in the long run. The size of the agricultural sector has dwindled steadily throughout this century.

Decision Making in an Imperfect World

Overview

Our discussion of economic principles has covered a lot of territory. Chapter 1 examined the basic economic problem of scarcity, discussing the implications of this problem for decision making. Issues such as health care reform and improvements in environmental quality are vivid examples of the types of tradeoffs society must continually wrestle with. Chapter 2 considered specialization and exchange as the best means for meeting the wants of societies in the face of limited resources. Chapter 3 continued this discussion in more specific terms by discussing the market as the mechanism for specialization and exchange. By intentionally ignoring some real-world complications we developed a simple model of supply and demand that illustrates the gains associated with free trade. Chapter 4 used the market model to illustrate more formally the efficiency of market outcomes and the inefficiency that can accompany market intervention. We were careful to note that market outcomes are efficient only under well-defined conditions.

Chapter 4 also considered social goals that might conflict with efficiency.

In this chapter we look more closely at situations in which all the conditions necessary for economically efficient market outcomes are not met. When one or more of the conditions are not met, an opportunity exists for nonmarket decision making to improve on the market outcome. We discuss the kind of government decision making that might improve upon the market outcome; however, it is important to remember that government action does not ensure improvement. Some potentially serious problems are associated with government decision making just as with market decision making, and we identify and discuss several important potential problems with government action.

The topics discussed in this chapter serve as a guide and outline to the major economic issues developed and discussed throughout the remainder of the text.

Learning Objectives

After reading and studying this chapter, you will be able to

1. List and explain four conditions that can cause market outcomes to be inefficient

2. Define externality

CHAPTER 5

3. Explain the free rider problem

4. Provide three basic reasons why government action may not improve upon market outcomes

5. Apply basic economic principles to political behavior and explain the implications of this analysis for government decision making

The Market Mechanism Is a Decision-Making Device

A modern economy is an exceedingly complicated machine for getting things done. The number of different goods and services produced in an economy is difficult to imagine. Consider, for instance, the range of products available in a single grocery or hardware store, much less a shopping mall. How do people decide to produce all those products? What prompts individuals and companies to invent and develop the new products that are introduced each year? How do companies determine all the different jobs to be performed and then get people to do them? In the United States more than a hundred million people go to work each day at different jobs in hundreds of thousands of companies scattered all across the country. What ensures that enough clothes, computers, pencils, colas, office buildings, parks, books, and tomatoes are produced? What guarantees that there will be enough welders, programmers, salespersons, physicians, plumbers, secretaries, musicians, engineers, hair-stylists, and farmers to produce all these different goods?

The answer to all these questions seems a bit shocking. A market economy simply allows individuals to make their own decisions about what to consume and how to use time and other resources. All of these questions are answered through the process of individual decision making. In fact, decentralization works quite well most of the time.

Decentralized, but Interdependent, Decision Making

Decentralized decision making is possible because of the coordination provided by markets. In a market economy an individual's decisions are not made in isolation. Through the interaction of supply and demand, markets coordinate individual choices.

It is easy to forget the extreme interdependence of our decisions. When Harry decides to buy a new compact disc (CD), he goes to the music store and plunks down the $14 price of the CD. This is, of course, exactly the way most day-to-day purchases are made. It is useful to consider this simple decision more carefully, however. Harry's decision to purchase the $14 CD was influenced by the decisions of millions of other people: consumers, producers, and resource owners. The price was determined by both demand and supply. The demand for CDs depends on consumer tastes for CDs and all other products, as well as the incomes of consumers. The supply of CDs depends on the cost of resources necessary to manufacture CDs, and the cost of these resources depends on the outcomes of other markets. Technology influences the cost of producing the CDs and other products as well as the kinds of other products available. All of these forces influence the determination of a price for CDs. When any of these many factors changes, the price of CDs is affected, and Harry's consumption decision may be altered – which, in turn, affects the decisions of many other people.

Markets not only coordinate individual decisions, they actually promote specialization and interdependence. Economic decisions have to do with mutually beneficial exchanges. Harry trades $14 of money income for a CD because it is more valuable to him than anything else he could obtain with $14. The music store sells the CD for $14 because its owner is better off without the CD and with the money income. These mutually beneficial exchanges are made on the basis of comparative advantage.

Trade on the basis of comparative advantage increases economic well-being and encourages specialization. The gain from a trade is the difference between the value of what is given up and the value of what is acquired in trade. When people specialize in activities in which they have the lowest opportunity cost and trade for economic goods for which they have relatively high opportunity costs, the benefits of trade increase. Markets facilitate trade and specialization. One of the reasons that modern economies are so complex is the extensive specialization brought about by trading. The complexity of a modern economy masks these simple, but fundamental, patterns of specialization and interdependence.

How Markets Resolve Society's Three Economic Problems

In performing its rationing and allocating functions, the market mechanism resolves society's three basic economic problems.

What Is Produced? In a market system, consumers are free to consume those goods and services that they find most beneficial to them. Consumers buy goods for which the consumption benefits exceed the costs. Producers have an incentive to produce the goods that are most valuable to consumers, because producers benefit the most by satisfying consumer wants. In a market economy, consumers are sovereign. They vote with their dollars. Willingness to pay is reflected in higher prices, which attract more producers and lead to increased supplies.

How Are Goods Produced? Because prices moderate consumption and producers must compete for consumer dollars, producers have an incentive to keep costs down. If a producer is inefficient in production, a competitor will be able to produce the good at lower cost and attract customers away. There exists a strong incentive to be efficient in production, to use the best available technology, and to look for an even better technology for tomorrow.

For Whom Are Goods Produced? The goods and services produced in a market economy are rationed to those consumers willing and able to pay the highest price. Ability to pay is determined by income, which in turn reflects the quantity of resources owned and supplied to the market. Those who supply more resources and who supply those resources to the most highly valued uses have higher incomes. Since income determines one's command over other goods and services, the incentive to supply resources to their most productive employment opportunities is strong.

In a market economy, the distribution of income is unequal. High-income and low-income consumers bid for available goods and services. High-income individuals are able to buy more goods and services, but low-income consumers make offers sufficient to acquire goods in many markets. Not only ability to pay, but also willingness to pay, determine who gets available economic goods.

The Invisible Hand

The most important attribute of the market system is that it coordinates the decentralized, independent decisions of individuals in a systematic and beneficial way. We make decisions in our own self-interest, seeking to improve our economic well-being. When decisions are coordinated through the market mechanism, our rational, self-interested responses to changes in prices have unintended beneficial impacts on the economy. This is the rationing and allocating function that the market performs. If more people prefer to buy CDs rather than cassette tapes, they will bid CD prices up. The higher price will attract profit-seeking businesses, which will produce increased quantities of CDs. The increased supply moderates the increase in CD prices. Tape prices and quantities fall as consumers purchase more CDs and fewer tapes. No single planner directs that these changes be made. Individuals, acting in their own self-interest, bring about the changes.

The most important, and to many the most amazing, attribute of market decision making is that, under well-defined conditions and with a minimum of government involvement, the market achieves economic efficiency for society. When individuals are left alone and allowed to pursue their own private well-being, they unwittingly increase society's well-being. This beneficial social effect of the pursuit of individual self-interest was labeled the *invisible hand* by Adam Smith, the father of modern economics. In *An Inquiry into the Nature and Causes of the Wealth of Nations* (1776) he described it this way:

> As every individual…endeavors as much as he can…to [maximize his own economic well-being], every individual necessarily labors to render the annual revenue of the society as great as he can. He generally, indeed, neither intends to promote the public interest, nor knows how much he is promoting it….he intends only his own gain, and he is in this…led as if by an invisible hand to promote an end which was no part of his intention.[1]

This invisible hand is the most attractive attribute of the market mechanism: The individual pursuit of self-interest is consistent with society's achievement of economic efficiency. However, the invisible hand works to the benefit of society only if markets operate in a reasonably efficient manner. Market failure can lead to a sharp divergence between private and social benefits. The next two sections consider major causes of market failure and how society might act to overcome these failures through government policies.

Section Recap

Prices coordinate the interdependent decisions of millions of consumers and producers in a market economy. The market system allows individuals to make their own decisions, within the constraints imposed by resources and consumer preferences, thus maximizing individual liberty.

Problems for the Market

In this section we examine four circumstances in which the market mechanism fails to generate an economically efficient outcome: (1) lack of competition, (2) the presence of externalities, (3) the existence of public goods, and (4) the lack of economic stability. The causes of the problems are identified and possible corrective actions that could be taken by the government are discussed. The four cases account for many of the major economic problems that a society faces and for much of the debate and controversy surrounding economic policy.

Lack of Competition

The beneficial effects of the market mechanism are the result of competition among buyers and sellers. Competition limits the gains that accrue to people acting in their own self-interest. Consumers want to obtain the benefits of consumption at as low a price as possible, but the bids of other consumers for the same goods limit gains from consumption. Producers want to maximize profits, but the price they charge is limited by the competition of other firms seeking to sell to the same consumers. Competition makes earning profits more difficult.

In a world of scarce resources, benefits (consumption goods, profits) can be obtained only at a cost. Everyone would like to obtain benefits at as low a cost as possible. Thus, an incentive exists for both consumers and producers to attempt to minimize the competition they face. By reducing competition, consumers may be able to buy at a lower price or producers may be able to sell at a higher price.

Firms can benefit from a reduction in the competition they face by charging higher prices and thus earning larger profits. Firms can avoid competition in a number of ways, including by becoming large enough to prevent competitors from entering the market and by colluding with other sellers. When large firms employ mass production techniques to produce output, the investment in capital equipment can be enormous. The cost of constructing huge, expensive production facilities can discourage other firms from competing in the market. Firms also sometimes **collude** – agree to sell output at a specified price. If all firms agree, competition among them is effectively eliminated.[2]

Collude:
Agree to sell output only at an above-equilibrium price.

The effect of reduced competition is reduced output and higher prices. By restricting the quantity of goods supplied to the market, noncompetitive firms force the market price up. Consumers pay higher prices per unit for a smaller quantity of goods and lose the benefits of consuming some goods whose marginal social benefits exceed their marginal social costs.

In a modern economy a number of markets exist in which firms are large relative to the size of the market. The presence of relatively large firms usually means fewer firms in an industry. Examples of U.S. industries dominated by a few large firms are electrical equipment manufacturing, paper and paper products manufacturing, and the auto, chewing gum, and breakfast cereal foods industries. The smaller the number of competitors, the easier it is to organize and maintain a collusive agreement. Thus, the potential for market inefficiency due to lack of competition is high. In this setting, the potential exists for government action to improve upon the market outcome by penalizing collusion and taking other actions designed to reduce prices and increase output.

If government action is to reduce the inefficiency associated with a lack of competition, the specific market circumstances leading to reduced competition must be specified and government policies that address these circumstances must be developed. One of the major concerns of **microeconomics** – the study of consumer and firm behavior in individual markets – is how the structure of markets affects competition.

Microeconomics:
Study of consumer and firm behavior in individual markets.

Presence of Externalities

When making decisions, people pay attention to the benefits they enjoy and the costs they must bear. Our discussion of market decision making and supply and demand has implicitly assumed that the private costs and benefits motivating individuals equal the social (private and public) costs and benefits of their actions. We assumed that the price paid by a consumer reflects the social cost of producing the good, and that the private benefits from consumption and production equal the social benefits.

However, situations exist in which the costs or benefits of consumption and production activities are experienced by others without their consent. When a nonsmoker sits next to a smoker and breathes cigarette smoke, the nonsmoker's well-being is affected by the smoker's consumption behavior. The nonsmoker bears a cost because the smoker enjoys cigarettes. Commuters who drive during rush hours in large urban areas impose costs on other commuters by contributing to traffic congestion. Lost time and greater risk of accidents add to the normal costs of driving (such as fuel and wear and tear on the car).

Consider one more simple example. Suppose Sandi lives in a house in an old neighborhood in town, and one by one her neighbors begin to improve their homes by adding aluminum siding, renovating their plumbing and wiring, and landscaping their yards. Although Sandi makes none of these costly improvements, her house becomes more valuable, because it is now in a nicer neighborhood. The value of Sandi's house is increased by the actions of her neighbors. They incurred costs and benefits in the course of improving their homes. Sandi benefitted from their efforts at no cost to herself.

Externalities (spillover effects): Costs or benefits imposed on people not directly involved in a market exchange.

External cost: Cost of a market transaction imposed on someone other than the parties to the transaction.

External benefit: Gain from a market transaction going to someone other than the parties to the transaction.

These examples are instances of **externalities**, costs or benefits imposed on people who do not participate directly in a market exchange. Externalities are often called **spillover effects**, because the actions of producers or consumers spill over into the lives of other people. An **external cost** is a cost imposed by a market transaction on individuals who are not party to the transaction. Environmental pollution is an external cost associated with many different market transactions. When a manufacturer emits pollutants into the air or water, he avoids the cost of eliminating the pollutants, thus selling his product to consumers at a lower price than would otherwise be possible. However, others in society, including individuals who do not buy or benefit from the manufacturer's products, suffer the cost of the pollution. An **external benefit** is a benefit generated by a market transaction that accrues to individuals who are not party to the transaction. In the example above, Sandi gained economic benefits from the actions of her neighbors although she incurred no costs to obtain those benefits.

In market transactions in which social and private benefits and costs are equal, no externalities exist; all costs and benefits are included in the decision making of market participants. An externality causes social benefits or costs to exceed private benefits or costs. Since market participants pay attention only to the benefits and costs they experience, some benefits or costs are omitted from decision making. When externalities are generated by a market transaction, the market equilibrium outcome is not efficient.

The problems that externalities cause for the market mechanism are illustrated in Figure 5.1. Figure 5.1 (a) shows the effects of external costs on the market outcome. Assume that the suppliers in this market emit water pollutants in the process of producing their product. In making production decisions they are free to ignore the social costs of pollution. The production costs they incur are less than the social costs of producing the output. The difference between social and private costs is illustrated with two supply curves. Supply curve S_{Priv} reflects the private costs to producers and interacts with demand, D, to determine the market equilibrium price and output, P_P and Q_P. But S_{Soc} is the true supply curve, reflecting the cost to society of producing output. At every output level social costs exceed private costs. The vertical distance between the two supply curves measures the external costs of each unit of output. If there were no external costs,

Figure 5.1

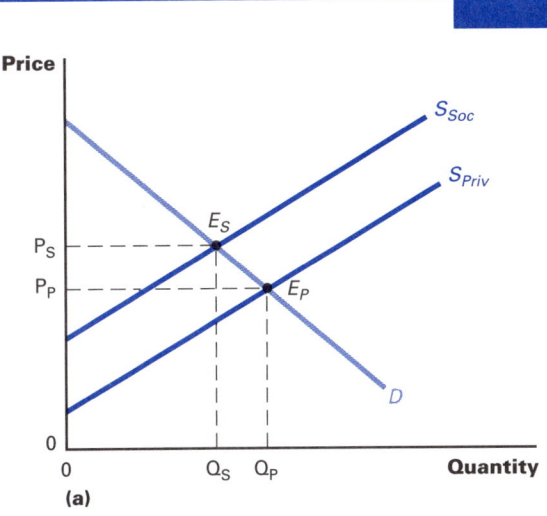

(a)

External Costs

(a) When private and social costs diverge, external costs exist. Producers fail to take into account all social costs. They behave as if the supply curve is S_{Priv} rather than the true social supply curve S_{Soc}. The result is an equilibrium at E_p rather than at E_s; market output is greater than the social optimum.

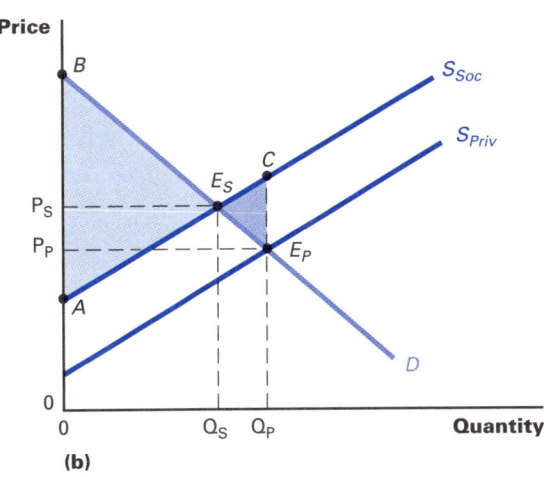

(b)

(b) For a market outcome to be efficient, a good should be produced until the marginal social benefits from consumption equal the marginal social costs of production. At Q_s, marginal social benefits equal marginal social costs. The net gain to society is ABE_s. However, failure to consider external costs causes resources to be overallocated to this market; production expands to Q_p units. Each additional unit between Q_s and Q_p generates social costs in excess of social benefits. The net gain to society from the production and consumption of the good is reduced by an amount equivalent to the area E_sCE_p.

that is, if producers were forced to pay all social costs when producing the product, the market equilibrium would be at E_S instead of E_P, at a higher price and lower output level.

Figure 5.1 (b) illustrates the inefficiency resulting from external costs. The social gain from producing the socially efficient amount of output, Q_S, would be ABE_S − the difference between social benefits and social costs. However, when the external costs are ignored by market participants, society produces output for which the social costs of production exceed the benefits, the increment to output $Q_P − Q_S$. Since some costs are ignored in the market, firms produce output that reduces the net gain by the amount E_SCE_P − the amount by which the total social costs of producing the output between Q_S and Q_P exceeds the social benefits from its consumption. Too much output is produced in markets with external costs. Stated differently, failure to take account of the external costs results in overallocation of resources to the production of the good.

External benefits cause economic inefficiency, but in a different manner than external costs. When social benefits exceed private benefits, resources are underallocated to the market and too little output is produced. Consider the benefits of vaccinating for contagious diseases. When a person is vaccinated against a disease such as measles, other people who associate with the vaccinated individual benefit from the vaccination. The probability that the individual's family, friends, and work associates will catch measles is reduced. Thus, the social benefit from a vaccination exceeds the private benefit.

Figure 5.2 (a) depicts this problem. Consumer demand is captured by D_{Priv}, which reflects the private benefits of vaccination against a contagious disease. Since external benefits exist, social benefits exceed private benefits. Demand curve D_{Soc} reflects social benefits − the benefits to vaccinated and unvaccinated people from vaccinations. The vertical difference between the two demand curves is a measure of the external benefits of vaccination received by unvaccinated people who are less likely to contract a contagious disease because other people have been vaccinated for it. Market equilibrium is determined by the interaction of consumers and producers, both of whom act only upon private benefits and costs. The result is an equilibrium at E_P. However, additional output beyond the Q_P level generates social benefits in excess of costs. Society benefits from the production of additional units of output (more vaccinations) up to output level Q_S. These units are not produced because the external benefits are ignored by market participants. Consequently, resources are underallocated to the market. The net gain to society is measured by $ABCE_P$ in Figure 5.2 (b). The gain could be increased by E_PCE_S if the external benefits were taken into account and output increased to Q_S, since social benefits exceed social costs for all the vaccinations between Q_P and Q_S.

When externalities exist, appropriate government actions can improve upon market outcomes. Government action that internalizes externalities by making decision makers take account of both private and external benefits and costs has the potential for moving the market outcome closer to the economically efficient level. Governments might intervene in the market through taxes or subsidies, enact some sort of regulatory policy, or assign ownership rights for previously public property to specific people or organizations.

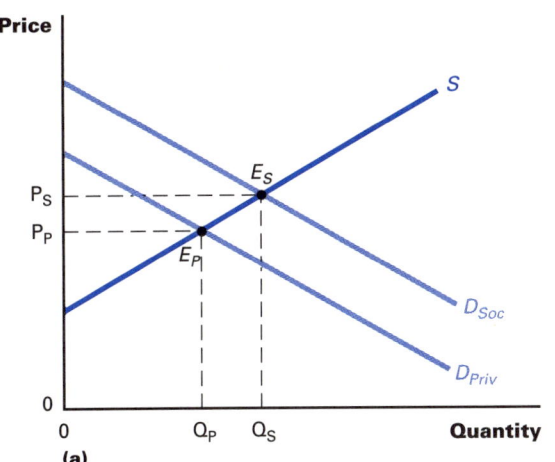

(a) External benefits arise when private and social benefits diverge. In this example, D_{Soc} represents social benefits and D_{Priv} represents only private benefits. The privately determined market equilibrium is at E_p rather than at E_s; market output is less than the social optimum.

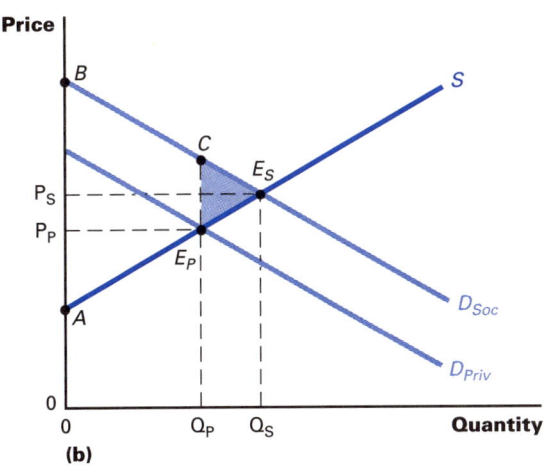

(b) The omission of external benefits from private decision making causes the level of output produced and consumed to fall short of the efficient level. With external benefits, society produces and consumes only Q_p units. However, the benefits of producing additional units of output exceed the costs until the output level Q_s is reached. Expanding production to Q_s would increase the net social gain from producing and consuming the good by an amount equivalent to the area E_pCE_s.

While such actions are potentially beneficial, in practice, making the appropriate corrections through government action is difficult.

Existence of Public Goods

Our study of the production and consumption of economic goods and services has thus far implicitly assumed that all goods and services are **private goods**, goods whose use by one person (in consumption or production) means that less is available for use by others. When a person buys a gallon of gasoline or a pizza, less gasoline and fewer pizzas are available for consumption by others. Markets do a good job of allocating resources when economic goods have this characteristic of privateness.

Private good:

A good whose use by one person reduces its availability for use by other people.

130

Public good:
A good whose use by one person does not reduce its availability for use by other people.

Some goods are not private goods, however. Some economic goods can be consumed by more than one person without reducing the quantities of the good available for use by other people who cannot be excluded from enjoying the benefits of the goods. Such goods are called **public goods**. The maintenance of city streets and highways is a public good. Once the pot-holes have been filled, everyone who drives on the roads benefits from the maintenance work, and one person's trip on the road does not reduce the supply of good roads available for others to use (ignoring congestion problems). National defense is another excellent example of a public good. When a nation establishes a given level of defense capability, it is consumed by all citizens. The consumption of defense by one person does not reduce the amount available for consumption by others. An idea or a technique is a public good. When someone discovers the biochemical process within the human body that causes cancer cells to develop and multiply, that understanding can be put to work to prevent cancer. The new understanding of the causes of cancer is a public good. The ideas are available for use by everyone, and the use of the ideas to save one person from cancer does not prevent the ideas from being used to save other people.

How does society decide the quantity of public goods to produce and who should pay for them? In the case of private goods, the market mechanism provides good answers to these questions. Private goods are produced when the benefits exceed the costs, and those consumers who value the goods the most – measured by willingness to pay – pay for the goods and consume them. However, the market mechanism is of little help in answering these same questions for public goods.

Free ride:
To consume without paying an appropriate price.

Unless consumers can be excluded from the consumption of public goods, they will not reveal their true willingness to pay for public goods. They have an incentive to **free ride** on other consumers. Consumers know that once national defense is provided, all will benefit regardless of how much any individual is willing to pay. National defense cannot be provided to only a select few who pay for it. If it is provided to one person, it is provided to everyone. Thus, individuals have an incentive to act as if the public good is of little or no value to them in the hope that they will enjoy the benefits of the good without having to bear the costs of providing it – the **free rider problem**.

Free rider problem:
Incentive for consumers of public goods to understate the true value of the good to them in order to reduce the amount they must pay to consume it.

Under such conditions, the market mechanism fails as an efficient rationing device. Consumers will not voluntarily pay an amount equal to the true benefits they receive from the public good. Instead, they act as if the value of the good is much less than it really is. Under such conditions, it might be impossible for any private producer to supply the public good profitably, and if some private producers could make a profit, the market equilibrium output would generally be less than the economically efficient output level. When public goods are provided by the market, resources are underallocated to the activity.

Public goods present a serious problem for markets. A more centralized decision-making process through some kind of government action is generally necessary to ensure that public goods are provided in quantities that approach efficient levels. The federal government provides national defense and collects taxes to pay the costs. Federal, state, and local governments tax their constituents to generate funds to construct and maintain roads. Note that sometimes governments can identify the primary beneficiaries of public goods and force them to pay the costs of providing the public goods. Many states have toll roads that are paid for only by the people who travel the roads. The federal government funds much of its highway construction by means of fuel taxes. Governments also provide direct research support and copyright and patent protection to those individuals who expend resources developing ideas of value to society, thus enabling researchers and inventors to benefit from the provision of public goods and increasing the supply of such goods.

In the area of public goods, the opportunities for socially beneficial government action are great. However, difficult problems still must be resolved for government action to produce efficient outcomes. A key problem is the determination of the economically efficient quantities of public goods to be produced. In addition, when public goods or services are produced in the public sector, or are produced by only one or two private producers who do not face competitive pressures, it is difficult to ensure that they are produced efficiently.

Lack of Economic Stability

A nation's government plays a vitally important role in the functioning of its economy. In market economies, an important function of the government is to establish the "rules of the game." A market economy functions through mutually beneficial exchange, which depends on the assignment of private property rights – private ownership of economic goods. Individuals must have a legal right to the goods or services they produce or purchase. Governments establish the systems by which ownership is defined and enforced.

The absence of secure property rights sharply reduces the incentive for individuals to invest and take risks in the hope of increasing their personal wealth. The entrepreneurship that drives dynamic market economies is likely to be absent. Instead, people are tempted to simply get by, since any excess goods and services beyond their immediate needs might be confiscated at any time. Long-range planning and the economic benefits that accompany it – saving, capital accumulation, and economic growth – depend on a system of stable property rights.

Governments also seek to promote a different kind of stability – macroeconomic stability – over shorter periods of time. As explained in Chapter 4, the uncertainty that accompanies monetary instability reduces economic efficiency. Market participants make more mistakes than they do in an environment of stable prices, and the amount of long-term contracting decreases. Some potentially beneficial exchanges are never made. Economic research has shown that a strong connection exists between the growth and variability of the money supply and the growth and variability of prices. Since national governments partially control the monetary system through regulation of banks and other financial institutions and through direct intervention in the system by government-controlled **central banks**, the responsibility for maintaining monetary stability falls on government.

Monetary policy – government control of the money supply as a means of influencing the overall level of economic activity – affects output and employment as well as prices. The process through which money affects the level of employment of society's

Central bank:
Governmental agency that controls a nation's money supply.

Monetary policy:
Government control of the money supply as a means of influencing the level of economic activity.

ECONOMIC SENSE?

Clearing the Air
on Smoking in Public

Recent years have witnessed a growing concern about the long-run health consequences of cigarette smoking. Most recently, studies have suggested that many people may experience serious health problems from the effects of second-hand smoke. This increased concern has resulted in more regulations governing smoking. The federal government regulates smoking on airlines, trains, and buses. Smoking is no longer permitted on commercial airline flights of less than six hours, which includes all domestic flights. Some cities have banned smoking in public places. In 1986, San Francisco adopted a relatively comprehensive ban, and in 1988, New York City enacted smoking restrictions. In 1993, Los Angles imposed a ban on smoking in all public eating establishments. Many firms have also adopted policies that substantially restrict the locations in which their employees are permitted to smoke, and the number of firms with such policies is growing. Do bans on smoking make economic sense?

By treating cigarette smoking as an economic good, we can use economic tools to analyze the problem. Cigarette smoking produces an external cost. Many nonsmokers dislike breathing cigarette smoke. In addition, growing evidence indicates that nonsmokers who breathe cigarette smoke suffer adverse long-term health consequences. Figure 5.3 illustrates the problem for society. Cigarette consumers and producers are able to ignore the external costs of smoking. As a result, the cigarette market equilibrium is E_1, with a lower price and higher output level than the socially optimal equilibrium that incorporates all social costs of smoking (E_2). This outcome is inefficient because resources are overallocated to smoking. The additional cigarette output $Q_1 - Q_2$ generates costs in excess of benefits.

Society would benefit if cigarette output were reduced to Q_2. The problem is how to achieve this market adjustment. Can market methods be used or is government action necessary? The government could simply ban all smoking. This strategy seems unlikely to succeed given the number of people who smoke. Because the benefits consumers enjoy from smoking exceed the social costs in some situations, society is better off in an efficiency sense if it allows smoking. A ban would cost society the net gain from Q_2 cigarettes. Such a ban could also be viewed as restricting individual freedom.

At the other extreme, market methods could be used to incorporate the omitted external costs into the decision making of cigarette consumers. If cigarette smokers were forced to compensate nonsmokers who breathe their smoke, the efficiency loss would be eliminated. The cost of smoking would rise, and less smoking would occur. However, this solution is exceedingly impractical because people consume a common property that is owned only by society at large – the air around us. (Cigarette smoke would not be a problem if each person had a private air supply.) It is difficult to imagine the chaos and the costs that would be generated by a system that requires each cigarette smoker to negotiate a payment to every nonsmoker exposed to second-hand smoke.

Macroeconomics:
Study of the behavior of the whole economy.

Fiscal policy:
Use of government powers to tax and spend to affect the level of economic activity.

resources is complex and is a major concern of **macroeconomics** – the study of the behavior of the economy as a whole.

Monetary policy is not the only tool of government stabilization policy. Governments also use **fiscal policy** – the power to tax and spend – as a tool to affect the level of macroeconomic activity. Through judicious use of its policy tools, government can to some degree smooth out *business cycles* – the periods of rapid expansion or contraction of economic activity that characterize market economies. Unfortunately, wide disagreement among economists exists as to what judicious use of policy tools is. This makes macroeconomics a somewhat unsettled, but very lively, area.

Section Recap

The outcomes produced by markets are not efficient if there is a lack of competition, if externalities cause private and social costs and benefits to diverge, if many goods are public goods,

The policies being adopted to deal with the smoking problem represent a compromise designed to achieve a feasible solution that moves society closer to the social equilibrium represented by Q_2. The adopted policies attempt to deal with the worst aspects of the externality, yet preserve some individual liberty for everyone. The bans have been adopted for situations in which smoke presents the worst problems for nonsmokers, such as in airline cabins. The bans usually provide arrangements whereby both smokers and nonsmokers have designated areas to which they can retreat to avoid offending others.

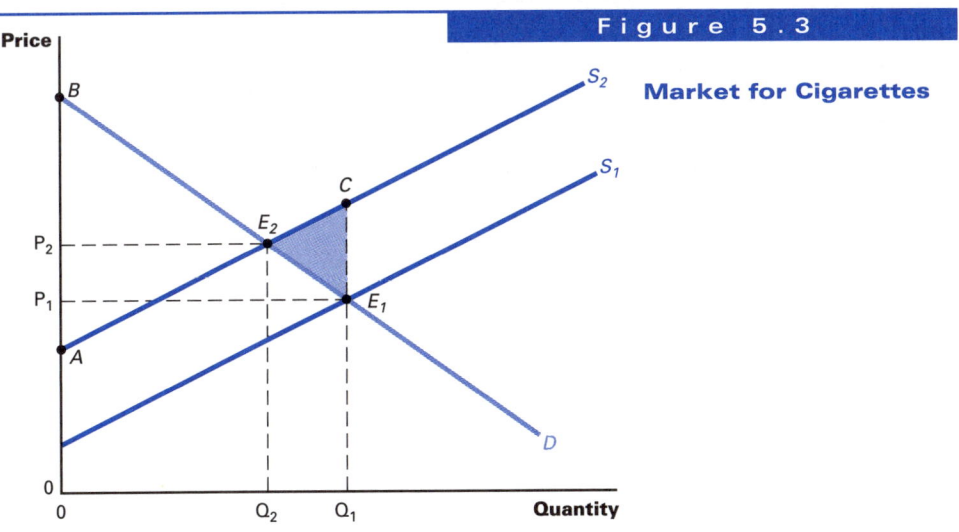

Figure 5.3

Market for Cigarettes

When nonsmokers breathe the smoke of cigarette smokers, they bear an external cost of smoking. If the full social costs of smoking were borne by smokers, the quantity of smoking would be reduced and society would be better off. Ignoring external costs, the cigarette supply curve is S_1. The social supply curve, which includes external costs, is S_2. At the privately determined market price of P_1 the quantity of smoking (Q_1) is inefficient, since the social costs of each additional pack of cigarettes smoked beyond Q_2 exceed the social benefits. The net social gain from smoking, ABE_2, is reduced by the amount E_2CE_1. Policies designed to reduce smoking or restrict where smoking can occur can move society closer to Q_2, thus generating a net social gain.

or if the economy is unstable because of a weak system of property rights or macroeconomic instability.

Opportunities for Collective Action

Centralized decision making addresses the same problems as market decision making. Society seeks to solve basic economic problems: what, how, and for whom to produce goods and services with the use of scarce resources. Government action may be a good alternative or supplement to market action when one or more of the four problems described above exists. When government action is taken in these instances, the primary objective is to do a better job of tackling the "what" and "how" questions facing society. Government does a better job when it improves upon the economic efficiency of the market outcome. Governments tackle the "for whom" question when they enact laws that alter the distribution of resources or income in society. Although economic efficiency is of concern when considering changes in the distribution of income, society's notions of equity or fairness often outweigh efficiency considerations, as we saw in Chapter 4.

Although government decision making offers an opportunity to improve on market outcomes when the market fails, government action does *not* ensure an improved outcome. A government solution could make the situation worse. For example, a governmental program to reduce pollution could be too costly: Pollution might be reduced, but at a cost in terms of forgone output that far exceeds the benefits of reduced pollution. Government efforts to manage the level of economic activity might turn out to be destabilizing, making inflation or unemployment worse than it was before the government intervention. Government regulation of firms might reduce competition among firms instead of increasing it.

Some government economic activities fail to improve on the market solution simply because policymakers do not have enough information to accomplish what they seek to do. Many examples of such governmental failures exist. Inefficiency has resulted when governments have attempted to replace the market with governmentally determined allocation of resources and have found that the information required to allocate resources was simply too great for central planners to comprehend. Other governments have engaged in active management of the macroeconomy in an attempt to maximize economic growth and stabilize employment. Often such activism has led to disappointing results – inflation, instability, and low growth rates. The complexity of the macroeconomy is so great that even policies designed by the brightest policymakers have had unintended consequences.

Government policies may prove to be less than optimal for another reason. Politicians and government officials sometimes have incentives to implement policies that fail to maximize net social benefits. The next section applies economic principles to the study of political behavior, an endeavor known as the **economics of public choice**.

Economics of public choice:

Application of economic principles to the study of political behavior.

The Economics of Public Choice

Economic analysis is based on the assumption that individuals choose among alternatives on the basis of expected net gain to themselves. The relative benefits and costs of an action determine whether it is chosen. The same general principle of economic decision making can be applied to political behavior. How do voters choose a candidate for whom to vote? They vote for the candidate who appears to support those programs and policies that will most benefit themselves. Politicians are elected if they appear to satisfy the preferences of a majority of the voters more than alternative candidates. Knowing this, candidates tend to support policies favored by a majority of their constituents. The point here is straightforward: In their roles as voters and politicians, individuals behave in a manner consistent with improving their well-being, just as they do in their roles as consumers and producers.

Economists have been applying basic economic principles to the study of political behavior for over three decades. The purpose of public choice analysis is to evaluate public decision making on the same terms as market decision making. We have already reviewed the conditions under which decentralized market decision making reconciles the pursuit of individual self-interest with the achievement of maximum social welfare. By analyzing public decision making in the same way, we seek to establish conditions under which such decision making leads to maximum social welfare as well.

The first question that public choice theory must address is very basic: Assuming that individuals pursue their self-interest, do forces exist that harmonize the interests of public decision makers with the social welfare? If the political marketplace is really competitive – potential candidates do not face extraordinary barriers when attempting to run for office, voters have good information on the positions of candidates and the actual voting records of incumbents, potential voters actually vote – elected officials will find it beneficial to represent the interests of their constituents. However, if such competition is absent, elected officials may benefit more by pursuing their private interests than by promoting the interests of society as a whole. In this case, public decision making may produce results that are both inefficient and inequitable. Unfortunately, a number of unique characteristics of the public choice process may bias the decisions of government officials against pursuing socially optimal policies. We consider potential problems first on the voter, or demand, side of the political marketplace, and then on the politician, or supply, side.

Voters as Consumers In a representative democracy, individual citizens elect representatives to make public decisions for them. They vote for the candidates they believe will best represent their interests. In turn, the political well-being of candidates depends in large part on their ability to satisfy the wishes of those they seek to represent. Political officeholders are agents of voters. When voters cast their ballots in support of a particular candidate, they expect the candidate to work to provide desired public goods and services. Voters are like consumers, using their political ballots to obtain desired public goods and services through their elected representatives.

Although consumers in markets and voters seeking to satisfy wants through the public sector are both motivated by individual self-interest, they face different constraints on their ability to acquire valuable goods and services. We mention three important differences.

Individual Voters Cannot Unbundle Goods and Services Because voters must support one person to represent them on a wide variety of public matters, they cannot vote for only those public goods and government policies they want. They must vote for one candidate who will support a number of different government policies, some of which inevitably run counter to their wishes. By voting for one candidate, voters opt for one bundle of goods instead of another. With one vote, individuals express their preferences on a wide range of government-provided goods and policies, such as national defense, support for higher education, welfare policy, and support for space exploration. Voters are able to register their preferences only weakly, compared to consumers who are buying private goods or services.

Furthermore, a politician must support the majority view or forgo reelection. There is an element of compulsion in public sector action that is absent in the market. Private consumers purchase and consume only the goods of most value to them; they do not purchase goods they dislike. However, voters who hold minority views are provided with public goods and government policies they may dislike.

Individual Voters Can Get a Free Lunch but Society Cannot   In the private sector all economic goods are costly. Consumers must sacrifice some of one good to obtain another. In less formal terms, *there's no such thing as a free lunch*. However, this fundamental rule does not apply to individual voters. A new government policy may benefit some voters at the expense of others. It is possible for governmental action to confer benefits on some voters at no cost to them. Rational individuals understand this possibility and support government actions that benefit them personally. People support tax laws that reduce their taxes – but someone must pay for government services. Senior citizens tend to support expanded Medicare benefits. Those of us in higher education tend to support increased funding for student loans and scholarships. Nearly everyone has some favorite public service that produces private benefits far in excess of individual costs.

Of course, society cannot get something for nothing. A governmental action that confers benefits on one group of voters must be paid for by someone else. Increased Medicare benefits make senior citizens better off at the expense of other members of society who must pay higher taxes or go without other government services. More generous loans and scholarships to college students help them finance their educations and increase the demand for the services of university faculty, but this increased support must be paid for by other taxpayers. An individual or group of individuals may be able to escape the resource constraint through some kind of government action, but society cannot escape it.

The Costs of Being Informed May Exceed the Perceived Benefits   If voters are to make choices that maximize their benefits, they must have good information about the candidates running for office. Poorly informed voters may vote for candidates who support positions quite different from those held by the voters. However, acquiring information about a politician's position on the full range of issues decided by the political process is costly. Time, effort, and perhaps money are required to collect the information needed to understand the issues confronting political decision makers. The expected benefits from collecting such information may be small for two reasons: (1) Individual voters gain or lose very little from many political decisions, and (2) a single voter is not likely to be able to change the outcome of the political decision-making process even if fully informed. When the costs of acquiring information exceed the expected benefits from having the information, voters may choose to remain ignorant of the issues being addressed by their elected representatives. Thus, the complaints frequently encountered in newspapers about uninformed voters often miss the point that it may be rational to be uninformed.

Since it is much less costly to choose a candidate by watching television news programs and advertisements and reading news coverage of speeches than it is to investigate detailed positions on a number of issues, many voters obtain their information about candidates secondhand. Political parties, or other kinds of labels, are shortcuts to identifying a candidate's position on issues.[3] Voters may also follow the advice given in particular newspapers or magazines because they find themselves in general agreement with the views of the editors.

Once elected representatives are in office, voters tend to ignore how they vote on most issues. Rarely do voters attempt to persuade their representatives to change their positions on political issues. For many people the perceived benefits of such investments are not large enough to outweigh the costs. Such an attitude may lead to the adoption of legislation that benefits a few at the expense of many.

The problem with the view that ignorance of the political process is rational is that the majority of voters may ultimately lose control of government to a minority who aggressively work to ensure passage of legislation favoring them. The proper functioning of an elected representative government depends on the existence of an informed electorate. To the extent that the electorate is uninformed about the issues confronting public decision makers, the public decision-making process tends to be dominated by special-interest groups that forcefully pursue legislation beneficial to their members, even if the legislation is harmful to society as a whole. The ultimate result of rational ignorance, then, may be the conversion of representative government into a political contest among interest groups seeking to use government for their own private ends, whatever the social consequences.

Political markets may fail to produce socially beneficial outcomes because voters must vote for a bundle of governmentally provided goods, rather than for individual goods; some voters may attempt to transfer wealth from other voters; and voters may be uninformed about the positions adopted by their representatives.

Politicians as Suppliers Political candidates and politicians, like other decision makers, are motivated by self-interest. They seek to supply, or produce, the public sector goods, services, and policies demanded by their constituents. The motivation for a private sector firm is profits. The motivation for a politician is reelection. Politicians respond to their constituents because they want to be reelected.[4]

At first glance such an incentive structure for politicians may seem reassuring in the sense that one can expect politicians to be responsive to the voters. Producer response to the dollar votes of consumers is part of the process that makes markets good rationing devices: Consumers get what they are willing to pay for. In a truly competitive political market, elected representatives would have powerful incentives to represent the wishes of their constituents on many, if not most, issues. Unfortunately, the problems on the demand (or voter) side of the political market, combined with some additional problems on the supply (or politician) side, imply that the desire of politicians to be reelected, and their responsiveness to voters, is not necessarily consistent with achievement of overall social welfare. Two important biases can affect the decision making of politicians.

The Power of Special Interests The equal distribution of votes in a democracy (one person, one vote) does not ensure that political power is equally distributed. A **special-interest group** is a well-defined, usually relatively small, group of individuals whose economic well-being is jointly determined and significantly influenced by particular economic events, policies, or laws. Examples of special-interest groups include firms in various industries (such as oil, auto, steel, computer, or agriculture) or groups of industries (such as the National Association of Manufacturers or the Chamber of Commerce); occupational groups (American Medical Association, trade unions, American Bar Association, or other professional organizations); or special-interest organizations (such as the National Rifle Association and Common Cause).

Special-interest group:
Cohesive group of individuals with a common interest in some economic or social issue.

138

Finding the Right Prescription for Health Care Reform

Health care reform was one of the hot issues in the 1992 Presidential campaign. Most people – Republican and Democrat, rich and poor – appeared to agree that the health care system in the United States needed changing. The rising cost of health insurance, skyrocketing costs for many health-related services, and the mountains of paperwork that occupy an increasing amount of everyone's time were all cited as symptoms of a health care system in trouble. Presidential candidate Bill Clinton made health care reform one of the cornerstones of his campaign. In September, 1993, after several months of work by the President's Task Force on Health Care Reform, President Clinton took his proposal for health care reform to the public. While the proposal's basic guiding principles – to provide care to more people more efficiently – were generally agreed upon, differences of opinion gradually began to surface. Indeed, many observers predicted that health care reform would be extremely difficult to achieve. They were right: The Congress did not pass any form of health care reform legislation in 1994. Since so many people agreed with the call for health care reform, as well as the general principles laid out in the Administration's plan, why is there such disagreement over what to do?

To begin, it is worth considering the nature of health care in an economic context. As the example of the external benefits of vaccinations we considered earlier in this chapter illustrates, some forms of health care involve externalities. In addition, because some of the

Under certain circumstances special-interest groups can wield disproportionate influence in political decisions. Since these groups stand to gain substantial private benefits from favorable political decisions, they are willing to provide substantial support to politicians who, in turn, support their causes. If the benefits of a particular piece of legislation accrue to a special-interest group, while the costs of the legislation are spread over a large number of individual taxpayers, a strong incentive exists for politicians to accept the special-interest group's assistance and support its preferred position. When the costs are spread over a large number of voters, the cost to each individual is small. Thus, voters have little incentive to be informed on the issue or to expend resources to oppose the special-interest group's actions.[5]

An example illustrates the interest group problem. In 1980, U.S. auto makers appealed for protection from Japanese imports. A year later, President Reagan announced a voluntary export restraint agreement with Japan that limited the number of cars Japanese auto makers could export to the United States each year. The result was substantially increased benefits (profits) for domestic manufacturers and higher prices for automobiles sold in the United States.[6] United States auto makers and autoworkers benefitted from the quota (restriction on imports). The costs of the quota were spread over a large number of consumers who had only one thing in common: They purchased automobiles. Although the cost increase for each purchaser was not small, the benefits enjoyed by the owners and employees of U.S. automobile companies were huge by comparison.

Shortsightedness of Political Decision Making Another important bias in political decision making arises in the timing of the receipt of benefits and payment of the costs of political actions. Since the politician's objective is to be elected (and then be reelected)

benefits from the consumption of health care are enjoyed by many individuals simultaneously (at no cost to them), it has characteristics of a public good. As we have already seen, in the case of externalities and public goods, the private market will fail to produce the economically efficient level of output. In such cases, intervention by the government is warranted. The fact that people generally agree that some form of health care reform is needed is consistent with that conclusion. However, this says nothing about the extent or nature of government involvement that is warranted. And herein lies the rub.

The reason for the disagreement lies in the fact that there are so many special interest groups that stand to gain, or lose, as a result of health care reform. For example, many members of Congress expressed serious concern over how to pay for the new health plan. They argued that the Administration's proposal to mandate the provision of health insurance by all employers would impose an especially harsh burden on small businesses. The American Medical Association argued that the plan would lead to the rationing of health care and restrict the ability of doctors to do their job in the way they considered best. Researchers in the field of medicine expressed fears that cost-cutting efforts would seriously restrict their ability to search out new cures for medical ailments because of the high costs that this type of research often entails.

Disagreements also arose over the types of medical care that would be covered by the basic plan. Services such as mental health treatment, abortion, and treatment for drug and alcohol dependency were (and to some extent continue to be) at the center of such disagreements. Many people expressed concerns about being required to share the costs of services that they are opposed to on moral or other grounds.

At the time that this text was being written, the debate over health care reform was not resolved. Thus, it is not clear how such issues were, or are yet to be, resolved. In any event, it is clear that special interests will have a significant effect on the final outcome, regardless of what economic analysis might suggest to the contrary.

and since most terms in office last only a few years, political decision making tends to be shortsighted. Political action is biased toward those laws and policies that generate benefits now and postpone costs until later. If voters are shortsighted, valuing today's benefits more highly than tomorrow's costs, politicians can benefit by promoting policies that produce immediate benefits, even if the long-term costs exceed the long-term benefits. Unfortunately, the best economic policy may be the one that imposes costs today and yields benefits tomorrow.

Examples of shortsighted political behavior are not hard to find. The savings and loan crisis provides a recent example. In the early 1980s hundreds of the nation's savings and loan associations (S&Ls) were *insolvent* – the value of their liabilities (what they owed) exceeded the value of their assets (what they owned). Rather than taking immediate action to close the insolvent institutions, the agency regulating S&Ls, the Federal Home Loan Bank Board (FHLBB), lowered its regulatory standards. Neither Congress nor the Reagan administration objected to the reduction in standards. They wanted to avoid the cost of closing insolvent S&Ls and seemed to hope that the problem would cure itself; if left alone, insolvent S&Ls might once again become profitable. The lower standards permitted the FHLBB to allow many insolvent S&Ls to continue to operate. Losses mounted throughout the 1980s, and the eventual cost to the government (and taxpayers) of the S&L bailout turned out to be many times what the cost would have been in the early 1980s.

Political Self-Interest versus Society's Economic Well-Being Our brief discussion of the economics of public choice provides an illustration of human behavior in the context of scarce resources. We have examined political behavior as a response to the incentives that individuals face as voters and as politicians. This approach to governmental decision making is a powerful tool for anticipating the actual expected benefits of government decision making. Public choice analysis also leads us to conclude that a number of rather powerful forces can cause government action to fail. These forces influence individual behavior in such a manner that governmental decision making can fail to improve upon more decentralized decision-making approaches. Understanding these forces enables us, as citizens of a democracy, to calculate the true social benefits of turning decisions over to the political process.

<table>
<tr><td>Section Recap</td><td>Politicians may fail to represent the interests of their constituents because of special-interest group influences or shortsightedness.</td></tr>
</table>

Summary

The market mechanism is an amazingly effective device for rationing and allocating resources. Markets permit complex modern societies to function relatively well with very little centralized direction by coordinating individual decisions. Under well-defined conditions, market economies achieve economic efficiency.

Four factors can prevent these conditions from being met: (1) lack of competition in markets, (2) the existence of externalities, (3) the existence of public goods, and (4) economic instability. Any of these factors can cause market outcomes to be inefficient. Lack of competition raises prices and reduces output. **External costs** cause resources to be overallocated to markets, prices to be too low, and output to be too high; **external benefits** cause an underallocation of resources to the market, with both price and output falling below efficient levels.

Public goods permit individuals to attempt to **free ride** on others, by understating the value of the goods to them. The result is an underallocation of resources and low price and output relative to the efficient outcome. Economic instability can cause a number of problems that lead to reduced economic efficiency.

When these factors exist, government decision making may be able to improve upon the market outcome. The government might intervene in the market or simply shift the decision making from the private to the public sector. However, it is important to stress that government action does not necessarily improve upon a market outcome. Government action can fail, too.

The situations that cause problems for markets can also cause problems for government decision making. Government action can fail because society simply does not have enough information or understanding to resolve the problem. In this case government action has no clear advantage over the market approach.

Rational political behavior can prevent government action from improving upon the market mechanism. The incentives that voters and politicians face can cause government action to be biased against efficiency. The **economics of public choice** demonstrates that voters are often rationally ignorant, that special-interest groups can wield political power in their favor and at the expense of others, and that political decisions are biased toward immediate, short-run action, which may not be the most efficient solution to a problem.

Questions for Thought

Knowledge Questions

1. Distinguish between a private and a public good.

2. Distinguish between microeconomics and macroeconomics. Why is an understanding of microeconomics important to the study of macroeconomics?

3. Define externality.

4. What are the goals of a politician?

5. Is it possible to be rationally ignorant? What impact does such behavior have on society?

Application Questions

6. In a market economy consumers and producers act in their own self-interest. How does competition ensure that their actions promote social welfare?

7. List five situations leading to externalities. Are they external benefits or costs? Has society attempted to solve any of these five problems? How?

8. Explain why an economic incentive to litter exists. Is litter more of a problem (a) in movie theaters, (b) along highways, or (c) in your neighborhood? Why?

9. Are the following goods private or public?

   • City park

   • National defense

   • Garbage collection

   • Fire protection

   • Postal service

10. Do you know the name of your Congressional representative? Does he or she favor

    a. Subsidies to agricultural producers?

    b. Student loans for higher education?

    c. Restrictions on Japanese imports?

    How might these policies benefit or harm a college student?

Synthesis Questions

11. In recent years the People's Republic of China (PRC) has adopted the use of the market in many situations in order to improve the performance of its economy. This

change is a drastic one for a communist government that has for many years refused to adopt decentralized decision making, calling it inconsistent with its political and social values. What does this recent change tell us about the PRC's economic goals in the 1990s?

12. The distribution of income is not a factor determining the achievement of economic efficiency in an economy. Can you explain why? Can you explain how income redistribution policies might introduce some economic inefficiency?

End Notes

1 Adam Smith, *An Inquiry into the Nature and Causes of the Wealth of Nations.* Oxford University Press, Oxford, 1976, p. 456.

2 Though a proponent of free markets, Adam Smith was well aware of the harmful effects of collusion. Once again quoting from *The Wealth of Nations,* p. 145: "People of the same trade seldom meet together, even for merriment and diversion, but the conversation ends in a conspiracy against the public, or in some contrivance to raise prices."

3 Labels such as "environmentalist" or "pro-life" can convey substantial information about the positions candidates will adopt as legislators, since voting in opposition to such labels is easy to detect. Voters who feel betrayed can then punish their legislator by voting for his or her opponent in the next primary or general election. Thus, adopting specific labels constrains the voting patterns of legislators.

4 Some public choice studies have assumed that politicians are income maximizers who seek to use their political powers to increase their incomes as much as possible. Maximizing reelection chances and maximizing income produce different behavior in some instances. We will examine only the reelection assumption in this text.

5 Donald Wittman has argued that special-interest groups do not wield as much power as most people think, because even small costs imposed on many voters can cost an incumbent dearly in the next election. If even a small percentage of voters change their votes because of the costs imposed on them by the incumbent, the incumbent could lose. See "Why Democracies Produce Efficient Results," *Journal of Political Economy* 97 (December 1989), pp. 1395-1424. Of course, Wittman's argument assumes that incumbents do not have other advantages that give them market power, which itself is an arguable proposition.

6 Charles Collyns and Steven Dunaway, economists at the International Monetary Fund, estimated that the voluntary export restraint added over $1600 to the average price of a new automobile in 1984. "The Cost of Trade Restraints: The Case of Japanese Automobile Exports to the United States," IMF *Staff Papers* 34 (March 1987), pp. 150–75.

Part II:Basic Economic Model

The Elasticity of Demand

Overview

In May 1995 the Clinton Administration announced that it was considering the imposition of 100 percent tariffs on 13 Japanese-made luxury cars in retaliation for what the administration considered unfair trade practices by Japan. In the United States, import dealerships quickly came out in opposition to the tariffs, claiming that they would virtually wipe out sales of the affected cars in the United States. As a result, affected dealerships would incur substantial losses and would have to lay off many of their employees. To what extent does economic theory support the dealerships' claims?

In Chapter 3 we established the relationship between the price of a good and the quantity demanded – the law of demand. The fact that the demand curve is downward sloping means that consumers will buy more of a good when its price decreases and less when its price increases. But how much more (or less)? Just how responsive are consumers to price changes? Our objective in this chapter is to develop a quantitative measure of the sensitivity of quantity demanded to a change in market price. This measure of responsiveness is called the *price elasticity of demand*. We will see that, depending on the price elasticity of demand, changes in price can cause the total amount of money spent on a good to increase, decrease, or stay the same. We will also consider the factors that influence the price elasticity of demand.

This chapter also examines the responsiveness of quantity demanded to other factors that influence consumer demand, such as income and the price of related goods. The concept of the elasticity of supply is also briefly considered.

Learning Objectives

After reading and studying this chapter, you will be able to

1. Define the general concepts of elasticity and price elasticity of demand

2. Identify the major factors that influence price elasticity of demand

CHAPTER 6

3. Calculate the price elasticity of demand and distinguish between elastic and inelastic demand

4. Explain how total revenue (expenditures), price changes, and the price elasticity of demand are related

5. Explain how the price elasticity of demand determines who will bear the burden of a tax on a good

6. Identify and describe other measures of elasticity of demand

Changes in Price and Quantity Demanded

In Chapter 3 we examined an important first question about consumer behavior: What is the general relationship between price and the quantity demanded of a good? According to the law of demand, quantity demanded and price are inversely related. We observe the implications of the law of demand in everyday life. Sales events by merchants such as clothing outlets and electronics stores are used to reduce inventories of goods such as seasonal clothing and the current year's models of TVs, VCRs, and so on.[1] Policymakers also recognize the importance of the law of demand. Taxes are often used to raise the effective price of many goods such as gasoline. Among other things, the price increase that results from the tax is intended to raise revenue for the government and induce people to reduce the quantity purchased.

We now turn to an extremely important second question about the relationship between price and quantity demanded: How much of a change in quantity demanded do we expect to see when the price of a good changes by a given amount? If a store manager marks down the price of her goods by 20 percent, how much will quantity demanded increase? In addition, what will happen to the total amount of revenue that is earned from the sale of the goods whose price has now been reduced?

Figure 6.1 shows three different demand curves, D_1, D_2, and D_3, which each represent the demand for a different good. At price P_0, the quantity demanded is the same for each demand curve. In addition, a price decrease to P_1 causes quantity demanded to increase in each of the three cases because the demand curves are all negatively sloped.

Figure 6.1

Responsiveness of Quantity Demanded to a Change in Price

This figure shows that for the three demand curves, D_1, D_2, and D_3, the quantity demanded at price P_0 is the same. A price decrease to P_1 causes quantity demanded to decrease, but the extent of the increase in quantity demanded differs for each demand curve. The responsiveness of quantity demanded to a change in price is measured by the price elasticity of demand.

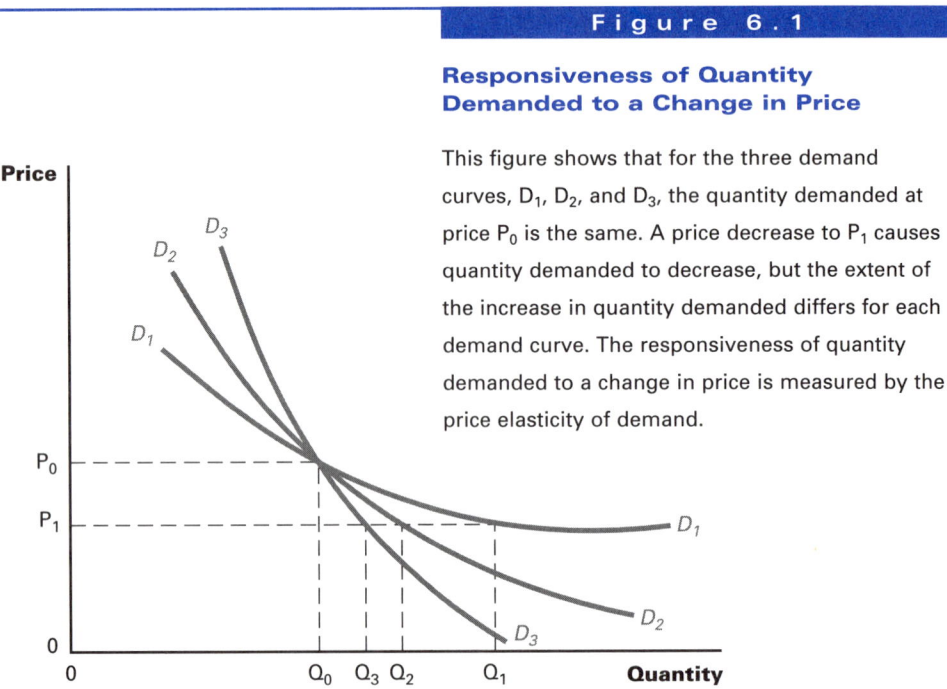

However, although quantity demanded increases in all three cases, the *amount* of the increase differs for each demand curve. How can the differences in consumer responses associated with each demand curve be measured, and why are the responses different?

Consumer Responsiveness to Price Changes

The knowledge that quantity demanded decreases when price increases, and increases when price decreases, is useful for understanding and predicting consumer behavior. However, knowledge of the specific extent of such responses to price changes is even more useful. Consumer responsiveness to price changes is measured by the **price elasticity of demand**, which describes the relationship between a change in quantity demanded of a good or service and a change in price.

Your own responses to price changes vary depending on the good in question and the size of the price change. For example, if the price of pizzas tripled, you might reduce significantly the number of pizzas you purchase in a given time period. The same would probably be true if the price of Big Macs tripled. On the other hand, a tripling of the price of notebook paper might have virtually no impact on the quantity that you consume. An individual's responses to changes in the prices of different goods vary. The responses of different individuals to a change in the price of a particular good vary as well. As a consequence, we need a method for measuring the change in quantity demanded *relative* to the size of the price change. A relative measure is needed because changes in different measures are being compared. In the case of movements along a demand curve, we are comparing a change in dollar price to a change in physical units of a good.

Economists measure the relative changes in quantity demanded and price by comparing the *percentage* change in quantity demanded to the *percentage* change in price. The resulting ratio is called the **coefficient of elasticity** (e_d), or:

$$e_d = -\frac{\text{\% change in quantity demanded}}{\text{\% change in price}}$$

An important qualification must be stated regarding the preceding formula. According to our formula, e_d is negative. Technically, the price elasticity of demand is the ratio of a positive and a negative number. Thus, the ratio has a negative sign. This negative value arises because demand curves are negatively sloped. However, because the ratio is always negative, the negative sign is usually dropped from use. We will observe this practice in the remainder of the chapter.

Why is the coefficient of elasticity calculated using percentages rather than absolute changes? To answer this question, suppose we are interested in the responses of consumers in a medium-sized city to price changes for three different goods. The three goods, the price changes, and the resulting changes in quantity demanded are given in Table 6.1. In columns (A) and (B) both price changes and quantity changes are in absolute terms. For example, when the price of coffee increases by 75¢, daily coffee consumption decreases by 1,000 cups. A small absolute change in price causes a large absolute decrease in coffee consumption. However, the opposite occurs for compact disc (CD) players. Can we

Price elasticity of demand:
The relationship between a change in quantity demanded of a good or service and a change in price.

Coefficient of elasticity:
The ratio of the percentage change in quantity demanded to the percentage change in price.

Table 6.1

Consumer Responses to Price Changes

Good Consumed	(A) Price Increase	(B) Decrease in Daily Consumption	(C) % Δ in Price	(D) % Δ in Quantity Demanded	(E) The Ratio (D)/(C)
Coffee	25¢/cup	1,000 cups	100%	25%	0.25
Fresh Bagels	50¢/pkg.	200 pkg.	33%	90%	2.73
Compact Disc Players	$75/unit	40 units	25%	25%	1.00

make a concrete judgment about the sensitivity of consumers to price changes for these two goods based on absolute changes in price and quantity? No, we cannot.

Information on absolute changes in price and quantity is inadequate for making judgments about consumer responses to price changes. Assessing consumers' sensitivity to price changes requires information on the size of the price change *relative* to the price of the product and on the size of the change in quantity demanded *relative* to the total quantity demanded. This information is also provided in Table 6.1. Note that columns (C) and (D) provide a different type of information from that found in columns (A) and (B). In particular, columns (C) and (D) tell us the percentage increase in price and the resulting percentage decrease in quantity demanded for each of the three goods. In column (E) the price elasticity of demand has been calculated using the definition above.

The percentages reported in columns (C) and (D) of Table 6.1 provide useful information with respect to the sensitivity of quantity demanded to changes in price. The increase in the price of coffee represents a doubling of price. However, this relatively large increase in price causes only a 25 percent reduction in the quantity of coffee consumed each day. This price-quantity change yields an elasticity coefficient of 0.25. (The elasticity coefficient is a pure number; there are no units attached to it.) On the other hand, the increase in the price of a package of fresh bagels is just 33 percent, but it induces a reduction in quantity demanded of 90 percent. The price elasticity of demand for fresh bagels is 2.73.

The elasticity coefficient is useful for comparing consumers' responses to the price changes of different goods. A price change of 10 percent affects the quantity of fresh bagels demanded by much more than the quantity of coffee demanded. Based on the information in Table 6.1, a 10 percent increase in price would cause coffee consumers to decrease the quantity demanded of coffee by 2.5 percent. However, the same 10 percent increase in the price of fresh bagels would cause the quantity demanded of bagels to decrease by 27.3 percent. Coffee consumers clearly are less sensitive to price changes than are bagel consumers.

Using the elasticity coefficients in column (E) of Table 6.1, the three goods in our example can be ranked according to the responsiveness of consumers to price changes.

Consumers are least sensitive to changes in the price of coffee and most sensitive to changes in the price of fresh bagels. Their sensitivity to changes in the price of CD players lies somewhere between that of the other two goods. What differences in coffee, fresh bagels, and CD players or in consumers' tastes for these goods can explain this particular ranking? This question and its answer are discussed at length later. However, we must first resolve a potential problem in the calculation of elasticity coefficients.

For a movement along a demand curve, price elasticity of demand measures the percentage change in quantity demanded *relative* to the percentage change in price. The resulting ratio is a pure number that measures the sensitivity of quantity demanded to price changes.

Section Recap

Calculating the Coefficient of Price Elasticity

Calculating elasticity can be thought of as a two-step process. The first step involves calculating the percentage changes in price and quantity demanded from information on the old and new prices and quantities. In the second step, the ratio of the percentage change in quantity demanded to the percentage change in price is calculated.

One potential source of confusion in the calculation of elasticity must be identified and resolved. The problem is how to calculate the percentage changes in price and quantity. The elasticity calculations in Table 6.2 illustrate this problem. The formula for the coefficient of elasticity can be rewritten as:

$$e_d = \frac{\dfrac{\text{change in quantity}}{\text{quantity}}}{\dfrac{\text{change in price}}{\text{price}}}$$

However, when we actually calculate an elasticity coefficient with this formula, we face a complication: Should the changes in price and quantity be divided by the initial price and quantity or by the new price and quantity? Columns (C) and (D) in Table 6.2 indicate that this decision can have an important impact on the elasticity calculation. Column (C) contains the calculated elasticity for the price and quantity changes in the illustration above using the initial price and quantity. Column (D) contains the same calculation using the new price and quantity. As indicated by the comparison of columns (C) and (D), depending on the specific price and quantity amounts and the size of the changes relative to these amounts, one can get dramatically different elasticity estimates.

Because the objective of the elasticity calculation is to obtain a specific measure of the sensitivity of consumers – measured by quantity responses – to price changes, it is important that we adopt one method for elasticity calculations and use it consistently. *For discrete price changes the most appropriate method of calculating the elasticity coefficient uses the average of the two prices and the two quantities.* This method has been used to calculate the elasticities in Column (E) of Table 6.2. Notice that use of the average price and quantity yields elasticity estimates that lie between the estimates derived using either the old or the new price-quantity combination. The average price and quantity demanded yield a single

| Table 6.2 | | | | | |

The Price Elasticity Calculation

	(A) Price	(B) Quantity	Elasticity (C) Initial Price and Quantity	(D) New Price and Quantity	(E) Average Price and Quantity
Coffee			0.25	0.67	0.43
Old	25¢	4000			
New	50¢	3000			
Change	25¢	1000			
Fresh Bagels			2.70	36.36	5.74
Old	$1.50	222			
New	$2.00	22			
Change	$0.50	200			
CD Players			1.00	1.67	1.29
Old	$300	160			
New	$375	120			
Change	$ 75	40			

estimate of the price sensitivity of consumers over the range of prices between the old and new price. The following formula employs the average price and quantity demanded to calculate price elasticity:

$$e_d = \frac{\dfrac{\text{old Q} - \text{new Q}}{\text{old Q} + \text{new Q}}}{2}\Bigg/\dfrac{\dfrac{\text{old P} - \text{new P}}{\text{old P} + \text{new P}}}{2}$$

This formula can be reduced to

$$e_d = \frac{\Delta Q}{\Delta P} \times \frac{\text{old P} + \text{new P}}{\text{old Q} + \text{new Q}}$$

By using this formula we will eliminate any question about the appropriate procedure. We can then concentrate on the implications of the estimate rather than its validity.

Section Recap

In order to be consistent in our measurement of price elasticity of demand over different ranges on a demand curve, the percentage changes in price and quantity demanded are based on the *average* of the old and new values for price and quantity demanded.

Elastic versus Inelastic Demand

According to the elasticity estimates in Table 6.2, coffee drinkers are relatively insensitive to price changes. People who buy fresh bagels, on the other hand, are relatively sensitive to a change in price. Mathematically, the absolute value of the coefficient of elasticity ranges from zero to infinity.

At one extreme, the quantity demanded of a good may be totally insensitive to a change in price – consumers purchase the same quantity of the good no matter how high or low its price is. In this case the percentage change in quantity demanded is 0, regardless of the value of the percentage change in price. Therefore, the coefficient of elasticity is equal to 0.[2] In such a case demand is said to be **perfectly inelastic**. A perfectly inelastic demand curve is pictured in Figure 6.2 (a). An individual addicted to a drug or alcohol might have a demand curve for the addictive good that is perfectly inelastic, at least over a wide range of prices. The same is true of individuals who require specific medications, such as insulin, to maintain their health.

At the other extreme is **perfectly elastic demand**. When demand is perfectly elastic the value of the coefficient of elasticity is infinity. A perfectly elastic demand curve is shown in Figure 6.2 (b). Consumers will purchase all the available quantity at one price but purchase none at a higher price and infinite amounts at any lower price. A good example of such a demand curve is the demand curve for an individual farmer's corn or wheat. The farmer faces a perfectly elastic demand curve because he can sell any amount he grows at the market price, but no one will offer more than the market price.

A third unique elasticity coefficient divides all other elasticity coefficients into one of two categories: inelastic and elastic. When the percentage change in quantity demanded is equal to the percentage change in price the coefficient of elasticity is equal to 1. In this case demand is **unitary elastic**.[3] A unitary elastic demand curve is depicted in Figure 6.2 (c). The elasticity definition implies that an entire demand curve can have unitary elasticity only if for any price change the percentage change in quantity demanded is equal to the percentage change in price.

When the elasticity coefficient is between 0 and 1, demand is **inelastic**. Consumers are relatively insensitive to price changes. Examples of goods and services for which demand is inelastic include electricity, clothing, and medical care. When the elasticity coefficient is greater than 1, demand is **elastic**. Consumers are relatively sensitive to price changes. Examples of goods and services for which demand is elastic include china and glassware, and restaurant meals.

The Difference between Price Elasticity and Slope An understanding of the technical side of the price elasticity of demand is enhanced by an important consideration. The price elasticity of demand along a segment of a demand curve is not the same thing as the slope of that segment of the demand curve.[4] A slope calculation incorporates only information about the extent of change in one variable as the other variable changes. An elasticity coefficient incorporates both the value of the two

Perfectly inelastic demand:
The percentage change in quantity demanded is 0, regardless of the value of the percentage change in price; the coefficient of elasticity equals 0.

Perfectly elastic demand:
The percentage change in quantity demanded is infinite for a price decrease, regardless of the value of the percentage change in price; the coefficient of elasticity equals infinity.

Unitary elastic demand:
The percentage change in quantity demanded is exactly equal to the percentage change in price; the coefficient of elasticity equals 1.

Inelastic demand:
Quantity demanded is relatively unresponsive to a change in price; the coefficient of elasticity is greater than 0 but less than 1.

Elastic demand:
Quantity demanded is relatively responsive to a change in price; the coefficient of elasticity is greater than 1.

The Elasticity of Demand

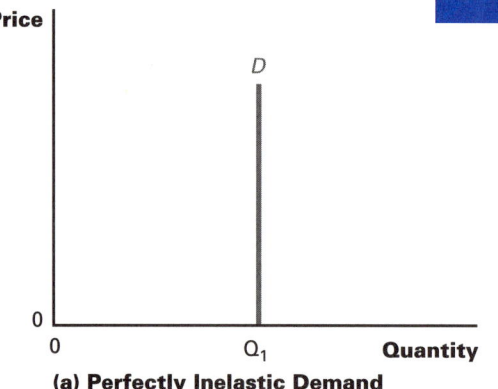

(a) Perfectly Inelastic Demand

Figure 6.2

Price Elasticity of Demand

(a) *Perfectly Inelastic Demand.* The demand curve is vertical. The coefficient of elasticity is 0. **(b)** *Perfectly Elastic Demand.* The demand curve is horizontal. The coefficient of elasticity is ∞. **(c)** *Unit Elastic Demand.* The coefficient of elasticity is 1 at every point of the demand curve.

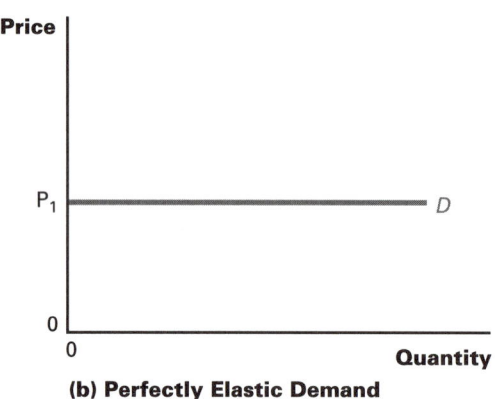

(b) Perfectly Elastic Demand

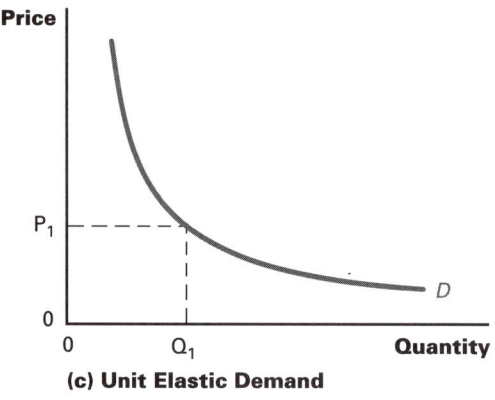

(c) Unit Elastic Demand

variables, price and quantity, at a particular point, and information about the extent of change in quantity demanded as price changes.

For a demand curve that is a straight line, the slope is constant; the slope does not change as we move along the demand curve. However, for the same demand curve, price elasticity varies depending on the particular range of the demand curve in question. Consider, for example, the linear demand curve for office visits per year to a medical clinic depicted in Figure 6.3. Because it is linear, the demand curve has a constant slope. In this example, the slope is equal to –0.01. However, the price elasticity of demand varies along the demand curve. Two price changes are identified in Figure 6.3. One change shows an increase in price from $18 to $19 per office visit, and the other change shows an increase in the price of an office visit from $5 to $6.

Because the demand curve is linear, the change in quantity demanded must be the same for equivalent price changes: A $1 increase in the price of an office visit reduces the number of visits by 100 (per year). However, the price elasticity of demand for the two price changes is quite different. The $18 to $19 price range has an elasticity coefficient of 0.44 associated with it, but the $5 to $6 price range has an elasticity coefficient of 0.11. The demand curve has a constant slope, but its elasticity is greater at the higher price (between A and B) than at the lower price (between E and F).

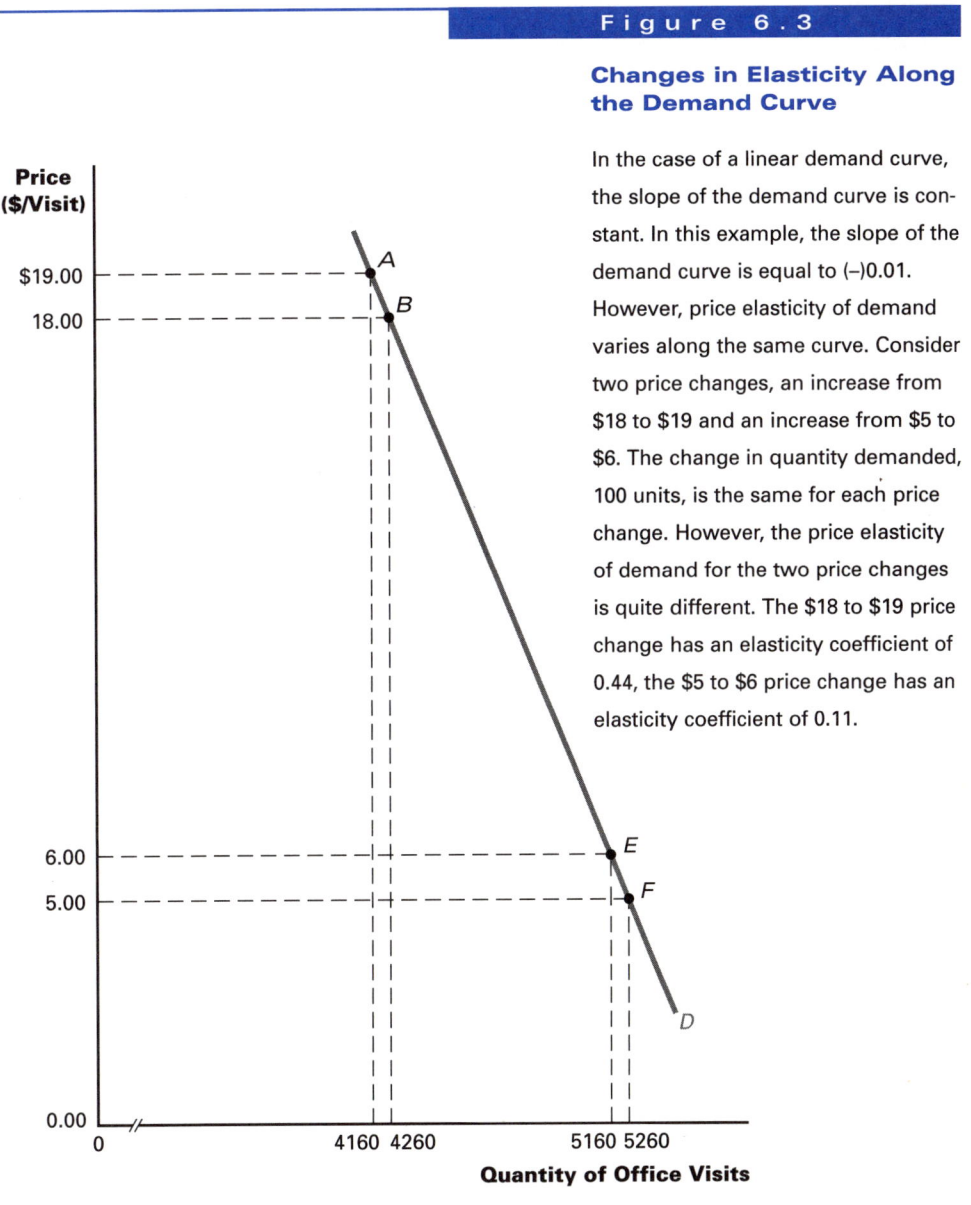

Figure 6.3

Changes in Elasticity Along the Demand Curve

In the case of a linear demand curve, the slope of the demand curve is constant. In this example, the slope of the demand curve is equal to (−)0.01. However, price elasticity of demand varies along the same curve. Consider two price changes, an increase from $18 to $19 and an increase from $5 to $6. The change in quantity demanded, 100 units, is the same for each price change. However, the price elasticity of demand for the two price changes is quite different. The $18 to $19 price change has an elasticity coefficient of 0.44, the $5 to $6 price change has an elasticity coefficient of 0.11.

The Economist's TOOL KIT

Point Elasticity

Arc elasticity:
The price elasticity of demand between any two points on a demand curve.

In our discussion of the price elasticity of demand we have focused on the calculation of **arc elasticity** – the elasticity between two points on a demand curve. However, it is also possible to calculate the price elasticity of demand at a single point on the demand curve. This value is referred to as the **point elasticity of demand**. The formula for calculating the point elasticity of demand is derived from the same premise as the arc elasticity of demand. Recall that elasticity is measured as:

$$\frac{\% \,\Delta Q}{\% \,\Delta P}.$$

Point elasticity of demand:
Price elasticity at a single point on a demand curve.

This can be rewritten as

$$\frac{\Delta Q/Q}{\Delta P/P} = \frac{P}{Q} \times \frac{\Delta Q}{\Delta P}.$$

Section Recap

Price elasticity of demand is not the same as the slope of the demand curve. In general, elasticity varies along the demand curve. When the percentage change in quantity demanded is greater than the percentage change in price, demand is elastic. When the percentage change in quantity demanded is less than the percentage change in price, demand is inelastic.

Consumer Response to Price Reexamined: Price Elasticity and Total Revenue

According to the law of demand, when the price of a good changes, the quantity demanded changes in the opposite direction. Consequently, a price change can cause total expenditures (total spending) on a good to increase or decrease. Stated differently, *in almost all cases a price change will cause the amount of **total revenue** received from the sale of a good to change*. Total revenue from a good is the product of its market price, P, and the quantity, Q, of the good demanded, or P × Q, which is, in turn, equal to total expenditures. The price elasticity of demand allows us to determine the specific relationship between price changes and changes in total revenue.

Total revenue:
The product of a good's market price and the quantity of the good purchased.

A price increase with no change in quantity demanded will cause an increase in total expenditures and hence total revenues. However, as we have already seen, according to the law of demand a price increase leads to a reduction in the quantity demanded. Thus, a price increase tends to increase total revenue, but at the same time, total revenue tends to decrease because quantity demanded decreases. The net effect of a price change on total revenue is determined by the size of the change in price relative to the size of the change in quantity demanded.

For a linear (straight line) demand curve of the form

$$Q = a - bP ,$$

b represents the slope of the demand curve, that is, $b = \Delta Q/\Delta P$. For a given combination of P and Q on the demand curve, denoted $P^\star$ and $Q^\star$, point elasticity is calculated as

$$\frac{P^*}{Q^*} \times b.$$

This last formula further emphasizes the difference between the price elasticity of demand and slope. The calculation of the point elasticity requires *both* the slope of the demand curve and the values of price and quantity for the point in question on the demand curve. Examination of this last formula also highlights the relationship between point elasticity and arc elasticity. In particular, arc elasticity incorporates the average of the old and new values of price and quantity when calculating elasticity over a range on a demand curve. P^* and Q^* are simply the mathematical limits of the averages of the old and new prices and quantities as the differences between the old and new values approach zero.

Point elasticity is useful when we are interested in the effects on quantity demanded of very small changes in price. However, in situations in which price changes are substantial, arc elasticity provides more useful information.

Referring to the definition of the price elasticity of demand, when demand is inelastic, that is, when $e_d < 1$, the percentage change in quantity demanded is smaller than the percentage change in price. This means that the change in price has the greater effect on total revenue. Consequently, *when demand is price inelastic, total revenue moves in the same direction as price and in the opposite direction of quantity demanded*. This result is illustrated in Figure 6.3. Between points A and B, and E and F, demand is price inelastic. As such, when price decreases from $19 (point A) to $18 (point B), total revenue declines from $79,040 ($19 × 4160) to $76,680 ($18 × 4260). In a similar fashion, when price decreases from $6 (point E) to $5 (point F), total revenue decreases from $30,960 to $26,300.

On the other hand, when demand is elastic, that is, when $e_d > 1$, the percentage change in quantity demanded is larger than the percentage change in price. This means that the change in quantity demanded has a greater effect on total revenue than the change in price. Consequently, *when demand is price elastic total revenue moves in the opposite direction of price and in the same direction as quantity demanded*.

With unitary elasticity the percentage change in quantity demanded exactly offsets the percentage change in price. Thus, *when demand is unit elastic a price change has no effect on total revenue*. The relationships between price elasticity, price changes, and total revenue changes are summarized in Table 6.3.

The relationship between elasticity, price changes, and changes in total revenue highlights an important fact: Higher prices do not always mean an increase in total revenue. The impact of a price change on total revenue depends on the price elasticity of demand for the product. This relationship implies that an understanding of consumer sensitivity to price is important to firms attempting to maximize profits.

Table 6.3

The Relationship Between Elasticity, Changes in Price, and Changes in Total Revenue

Demand Is:	Elasticity Coefficient	Relationship Between Change in Price and Change in Total Revenue
Inelastic	0 to 1	Price increases, total revenue increases Price decreases, total revenue decreases
Unit Elastic	1	Price increases} no change in Price decreases} total revenue
Elastic	> 1	Price increases, total revenue decreases Price decreases, total revenue increases

Table 6.4 contains information on price, quantity demanded, and total revenue for a linear (straight line) demand curve. As the table indicates, when price decreases from $18 to $10, quantity demanded and total revenue both increase. Hence, over this range, demand is elastic. However, as price decreases from $10 to $2, quantity demanded increases but total revenue decreases. Over this range, demand is inelastic.

As an illustration of the implications of the relationship between the price elasticity of demand and total revenues, consider the case of legalized gambling. In many

Table 6.4

Price Changes, Total Revenue, and Elasticity: An Illustration

Price	Quantity Demanded	Total Revenue	Elasticity
$18	1	$18	
			5.67
16	2	32	
			3
14	3	42	
			1.86
12	4	48	
			1.22
10	5	50	
			0.82
8	6	48	
			0.54
6	7	42	
			0.33
4	8	32	
			0.18
2	9	18	

states, including Illinois, New York, and California, gambling is an important source of tax revenues. In addition, lawmakers are strongly tempted to place a high tax rate on gambling, both because of the potential revenues it could generate and because such so-called sin taxes are politically attractive. However, the price elasticity of demand for gambling has been estimated to be approximately 1.59, indicating that demand is relatively elastic.[5] This estimate suggests that states might actually increase their total tax revenue by decreasing tax rates (which affect the price of gambling) and thereby increasing the total amount of revenue to which the tax rate is applied.

Section Recap

Price elasticity of demand, price changes, and changes in total revenue are related. When demand is elastic, a price increase will result in a decrease in total revenues. When demand is inelastic, a price increase will cause total revenues to increase. If demand is unit elastic, a change in price will leave total revenues unchanged.

Price Discrimination Have you ever tried to figure out the strategy behind the rather complicated pricing of airline tickets? For travel between two points such as Chicago and San Francisco there is a variety of fares, and the lowest fare might be less than half the highest fare – even though the cost of carrying an additional passenger is the same regardless of the fare charged. The fare for which you are eligible depends on factors such as how long you plan to stay, how early you make your reservation, and which day of the week you travel. The pricing of airline tickets is an example of **price discrimination**, the practice of charging different customers different prices for the same good or service when price differences are not justified on the basis of cost differences. Firms attempt to price discriminate because willingness to pay for a service and price elasticity vary across consumers and because raising the price to some customers and lowering it for others can increase total revenue.

Price discrimination: The practice of charging different prices to different consumers of the same good or service.

Some people, such as many businesspeople who must travel on short notice, have an inelastic demand for air travel. Other people, such as those who are taking trips for pleasure or who can plan a trip well in advance, have an elastic demand. An airline can take advantage of these differences if it can identify each of the different groups. If the firm raises air fares for those whose demand is inelastic, it increases total revenue. Moreover, the firm can lower fares for those with elastic demand and raise total revenues further!

The variety of air fares available for flights to the same location is an example of price discrimination. There are many other examples of firms charging different prices to consumers whose elasticities of demand differ. For example, a variety of businesses charge lower prices to children and senior citizens. Restaurants, movie theaters, and other public transportation companies also practice this kind of price discrimination.

Price discrimination is based on the fact that certain groups are more sensitive to prices; therefore, reduced prices have a much bigger impact on the quantity consumed by those groups. In the case of children, requiring them to pay the regular price for a meal or a ticket would simply make it too expensive for many families to dine out or go to the movies. Consequently, firms that do not price discriminate lose sales not only to children, but also to their parents, who might otherwise purchase the good or service. In the case

Operating in the Inelastic Portion of the Demand Curve

We have established a distinct relationship among a price change, the price elasticity of demand, and the resulting change in total revenue earned by a firm. Table 6.4 illustrates this relationship. Beginning at a quantity demanded of zero, as we decrease price, quantity demanded and total revenue increase; we are operating in the elastic portion of the demand curve. However, beyond a certain point, further decreases in price cause total revenue to decrease. In this range, the demand curve is inelastic. If we assume that the objective of a firm is to maximize its profits (the difference between the total rev-

enues it receives and the total cost of producing the output it sells), it would seem logical that firms should always operate in the elastic portion of the demand curve. So long as demand is price elastic, a decrease in price will result in an increase in both sales and the total revenue earned by the firm. However, if the firm continues to lower price and expand output into the inelastic range of the demand curve, total revenue will decrease.

However, inspection of Table 6.5 suggests that, in many situations, this is not the case. Many firms, agricultural firms for example, appear to operate in the inelastic portion of the demand curve for their products. As such, when price decreases, although quantity demanded increases, total revenue

decreases. This suggests that increased sales will result in a decrease in profits for the firm. In light of these observations it is worth asking: Does such behavior – operating in the inelastic portion of the market demand curve – make economic sense?

The answer to this question is, it depends. In the case of many markets, such as those for most agricultural products, the answer is yes because the market demand curve for the good is *not* the demand curve faced by the individual firm. Instead, the supply side of the market is characterized by a large number of firms that are each small relative to the market. (You will recall from Chapter 3 that the market supply curve is the horizontal

of senior citizens, many people are on low, fixed incomes that, in turn, restrict quantity demanded. A reduction in price for certain groups – price discrimination – increases the total quantity demanded without requiring the firm to reduce price on the previous units sold.

Price Elasticity and the Incidence of a Tax

Another important implication of the price elasticity of demand concerns the effect that imposing a tax on a good will have on the equilibrium price and quantity demanded. Federal, state, and local governments tax various goods and services to raise needed revenues. So-called "sin taxes" on such items as liquor, beer, wine, and cigarettes are a good example. In most cases, the tax, which is calculated either as a percentage of the purchase price or a flat amount (as in the case of excise taxes on tires and gasoline), is imposed on the seller of the good. The seller then tries to pass the tax along to the buyer in the form of a higher price. However, the question of how much of the tax is ultimately paid by the consumer rather than by the seller – the *incidence of the tax* – depends on the price elasticity of demand. The following example illustrates this concept.

Most states and the federal government impose taxes on gasoline to raise revenues needed to finance road construction and repairs. Assume that the government is consid-

sum of the individual firms' supply curves.) The output produced by each firm satisfies only a small amount of the total market demand. Each firm faces a demand curve for its product that is much more elastic than the market demand curve.

In Chapter 11 we will develop the theory of a perfectly competitive market. It is sufficient at this point to note that a perfectly competitive market is characterized by a large number of firms that are each small relative to the market in which they operate. As a result, firms in this type of market take the market-determined price as given; they sell as much or as little output as they want at the market price. This means that the demand curve faced by the individual firm is perfectly elastic. The firm's only decision is what level of output to produce and sell. Agricultural markets are considered to be among the best approximations to a perfectly competitive market.

So long as it is profitable to do so, each firm will increase its output. However, the decisions of the individual firms have no effect on market price and therefore do not influence the behavior of other firms in the market. In addition, because price does not change with a change in the firm's output level, total revenue moves in the same direction as quantity. When the firm increases its output, total revenue increases; when the firm decreases its output, total revenue falls. Thus, as a group, it is not irrational for firms to operate in the inelastic portion of the market demand curve.

As a side note, this discussion suggests an interesting solution to the problems confronting farmers that we hear about so frequently in the news, in particular, the seeming lack of profits. To be specific, by reducing market supply, as a group, farmers would move up the market demand curve for their product, causing an increase in price and a

decrease in quantity demanded. However, total revenues would increase at the same time farmers' costs are going down (assuming costs decrease with a reduction in output). Profits would increase! There are problems with this strategy. First, an explicit agreement by farmers to decrease supply, known as collusion, would be illegal. Second, even if collusion were not illegal, it would require that all producers behave in a like manner, reducing supply. Given the large number of farmers, this is unlikely to happen. Instead it is likely that more than a few individuals would cheat on the agreement in an effort to increase profits even more.

In conclusion, operating in the inelastic portion of the demand curve may make economic sense, depending on the structure of the market in question. In addition, there are sound reasons why this behavior is unlikely to change.

ering increasing the tax on gasoline by 5¢ per gallon. In Figure 6.4, the supply curve labeled S_B is the supply curve for gasoline before the proposed tax increase. The initial average price of gas is $1.15 a gallon (for unleaded regular). The imposition of the tax would shift the supply curve up vertically by the amount of the tax (5¢) to S_A, since sellers would try to pass on the entire tax to consumers. If consumers paid the entire tax increase the price of gas would increase to $1.20 per gallon. However, because demand is not perfectly inelastic, the new equilibrium price is less than $1.20; it is $1.19. The increase in market price of 4¢ is the portion of the tax paid by consumers. Suppliers pay the remainder of the tax, 1¢. In this example, consumers would pay 4¢ of a 5¢ tax, or 80 percent of the tax. Suppliers would pay the other 20 percent.

As the preceding example illustrates, the extent to which a tax can be passed on to consumers depends upon the consumers' quantity response to price changes. When demand is inelastic, as it is for gasoline, consumers absorb most of a tax increase. However, suppliers pay at least part of the tax unless demand is perfectly inelastic. (If the demand curve in Figure 6.4 were vertical the price would have increased by exactly 5¢, the full amount of the tax increase.) On the other hand, consumers do not bear as much of the burden of a tax on goods for which demand is very elastic. Suppliers cannot shift the burden to consumers because an elastic demand means that consumers have alternatives; they will substitute other goods for the good being taxed.

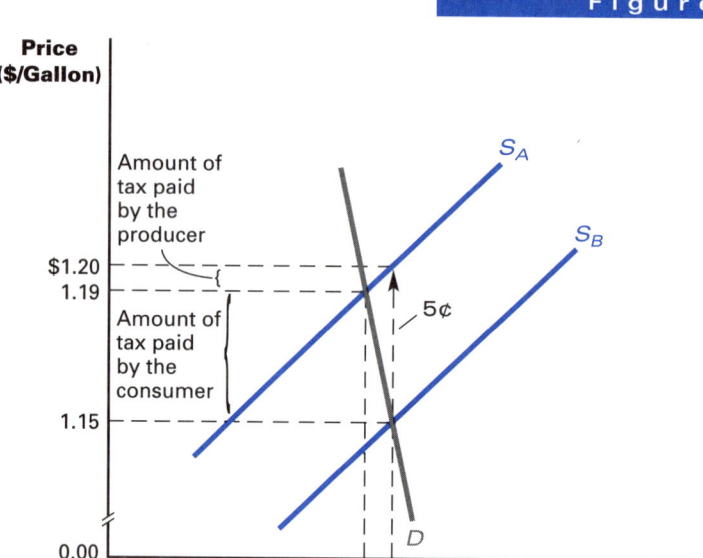

Figure 6.4

Elasticity of Demand and the Incidence of a Tax

The supply curve labeled S_B is the supply curve for gasoline before the tax increase of 5¢ per gallon. The imposition of the tax shifts the supply curve up vertically by the amount of the tax (5¢) to S_A. The pretax price of gasoline was $1.15 per gallon. If consumers paid all the tax increase, the price of gas would increase to $1.20 per gallon. However, because demand is not perfectly inelastic, the new equilibrium price is less than $1.20; it is $1.19. The increase in market price of 4¢ is the part of the tax consumers pay. Suppliers pay the remainder of the tax, 1¢.

Section Recap

The incidence of a tax – the amount of a tax on a good that is borne by producers versus consumers – is determined by the price elasticity of demand. When demand is price elastic, the majority of the tax is borne by producers. When demand is inelastic, the majority of the tax is borne by consumers.

Determinants of Price Elasticity of Demand

We now return to an important question that was raised but not answered when we first introduced the concept of elasticity. What factors influence the price elasticity of demand for a good or service? Price elasticity of demand varies widely – across different goods and across consumers of the same good. Economists have estimated price elasticities of demand for many goods. Estimated elasticities for selected products and services are presented in Table 6.5. As the data in Table 6.5 indicate, elasticity estimates vary widely. Can this extensive variation in elasticity be explained? What attributes of the products, or the consumers, account for these differences?

| Table 6.5 |

Selected Estimates of the Price Elasticity of Demand

Good or Service	Short-run Price Elasticity	Long-run Price Elasticity
Clothing and shoes	0.20	N.A.
Housing	0.30	1.88
Medical care	0.31	N.A.
Tobacco products	0.46	1.89
Radio and TV repair	0.47	3.84
Movies	0.87	3.67
China and glassware	1.54	2.55
Automobiles and parts	1.87	2.24
Restaurant meals	2.27	N.A.
Household electricity use[1]	0.30	0.72
Household natural gas use[1]	1.38	2.12
Gasoline[2]	0.43	N.A.
Fresh fruit[3]	3.02	N.A.
Milk[3]	0.54	N.A.
Chicken[3]	0.80	N.A.
Bread[3]	0.29	N.A.

Sources: Unless otherwise indicated, estimates are taken from Houthaker, H.S., and L.D. Taylor, *Consumer Demand in the United States*, Cambridge, MA: Harvard University Press, 1970.

[1] Lakshmanan, G.R. and W. Anderson, 1980, "Residential Energy Demand in the United States," *Regional Science and Urban Economics*, 10: 371–86.

[2] Archibald, R. and R. Gillingham, 1980, "An Analysis of the Short-Run Consumer Demand for Gasoline Using Household Survey Data," *The Review of Economics and Statistics*, 62: 622–28.

[3] Heien, D.M., 1982, "The Structure of Food Demand: Interrelatedness and Duality," *American Journal of Agricultural Economics*, 64(2): 213–21.

N.A. = Not Available

Available Substitutes

The most important influence on price elasticity of demand is the availability of substitutes for a good. When substitutes for a good or service exist, a consumer has consumption alternatives. Depending on how close these substitutes are, even a small price increase can prompt consumers to switch to one of the alternatives. The estimated elasticity for fresh bagels (in Table 6.2) suggests that, as a group, consumers are quite sensitive to changes in the price of fresh bagels. This sensitivity arises because of the many close substitutes for fresh bagels: frozen bagels, other fresh rolls, and other prepackaged or frozen rolls.

There are many other goods for which the price elasticity of demand is relatively high. There are a number of close substitutes in the fast food market – McDonald's, Burger King, Taco Bell, and Kentucky Fried Chicken, just to name a few. Consumers are sensitive to a change in the price of a given product in this market due to the wide variety of available substitutes. In a similar manner, the price elasticity of demand for new Toyota passenger cars is relatively high because of the close substitutes available – used Toyotas and other new and used passenger cars (as well as other means of transportation such as trucks or buses).

The inelastic demand category includes such goods as cigarettes and coffee. Consumers are relatively insensitive to price changes for these goods because they *perceive* few, if any, close substitutes. In some objective sense, a wide variety of liquid refreshments are substitutes for coffee: tea, water, milk, soft drinks. However, for coffee drinkers who drink coffee because of its caffeine content and flavor, there are few good substitutes. For these consumers, an increase in the price of coffee has only a small effect on consumption. Cigarette smoking is addictive; thus, smokers are insensitive to cigarette price changes. To smokers, no good alternatives exist. Returning to our air travel example, trips taken on short notice are motivated by the need to get somewhere quickly. There are no close substitutes for air travel for such trips. Consequently, the demand for this kind of air travel is quite inelastic. What matters in determining price elasticity of demand is the consumer's perception of the available substitutes.

The availability of substitutes also depends on the definition of the product or service category. Generally, price elasticity of demand is greater for the more narrowly defined categories of goods or services. We can talk about automobiles, or new automobiles, or new GM automobiles, or new Pontiac Firebird automobiles. The price elasticity of demand for these groups increases as the category becomes more narrowly defined because the range of available substitutes increases. The demand for salt is very inelastic; it has few substitutes. The demand for Morton salt is less inelastic because other brands of salt are available. Even less inelastic (more elastic) is the demand for Morton salt at a particular grocery store. Alternatives include Morton salt sold at other stores.

Cost of the Good Relative to Total Income

Another influence on price elasticity of demand is the size of the expenditure on a good relative to the consumer's total income. The price of white bread is relatively low and, furthermore, its price is an insignificant fraction of most individual or family incomes. If the price of a loaf of white bread doubled, it would have almost no impact on quantities consumed. (Even at the doubled price a household would now spend perhaps $7 or less every week on white bread.) On the other hand, as Table 6.5 indicates, an increase in the price of restaurant meals, which command a relatively larger percentage of a household's income, would lead to a significant percentage reduction in the quantity demanded. The same is true of such big-ticket items as automobiles, TV sets, and home computers. As such, there is a positive relationship between the cost of a good relative to total income and the price elasticity of demand.

Time and the Availability of Substitutes

Time can affect price elasticity of demand in two ways. Often the adjustments that consumers wish to make in response to price changes take time. The full adjustment to a price change can take a relatively long time. Consequently, the longer the period of time available for adjustment, the more elastic is demand for the good or service.

For example, the full response to an increase in the price of fresh vegetables takes little time. There is little difference between the short-run and long-run price elasticities for vegetables. The adjustment to an increase in the price of heating fuel takes much longer, as all homeowners discovered in the 1970s and early 1980s. A relatively rapid increase in the price of fuel oil and then natural gas eventually caused marked consumer adjustments. However, in the short run, consumers had few alternatives. They turned down their thermostats, substituting a colder house and more clothing for fuel consumption. In addition, many consumers purchased portable space heaters. They also improved the seals around windows and doors.

Over a longer period of time consumers had additional alternatives: installation of storm doors and windows, added insulation, and even more efficient heating systems. Wood-burning stoves also became popular due to the relatively low cost of firewood. With even more time consumers were able to consider buying new houses with energy-saving features including solar heat, or even earth homes that are partially underground. The initial reduction in the quantity of fuel used was relatively small, but the adjustment continued over time. The long-run price elasticity of the demand for energy is greater than the short-run elasticity.

Some consumption activities have a time dimension. If we want to fly to New York City this week for an important meeting, we will be relatively insensitive to air fare changes. Our demand will be relatively inelastic because there are few good alternatives to air travel if we really want to travel 2,000 miles and still work four days this week. On the other hand, if we plan to fly to the West Coast for a vacation next year, we will be more sensitive to air fare changes because we have more alternatives to choose from over the course of a year, including a change in the specific date of the vacation or the possibility of taking the train or driving our own car.

Table 6.5 includes estimates of both the short-run and the long-run price elasticity of demand for a variety of goods and services. As the data indicate, long-run price elasticity is larger than its short-run counterpart for each of the goods and services listed. This reflects the increased flexibility consumers have to adjust to a change in price as the length of the adjustment period increases.

Luxuries versus Necessities

Consumers are also more or less sensitive to a change in the price of a good depending on whether they consider the good to be a luxury or a necessity. The price elasticity of demand tends to be relatively low for necessities such as basic food items. By definition, a necessity is something that the consumer must have. In contrast, luxury items are goods

Why the DISAGREEMENT?

An Addiction to Prohibition?

Society has long viewed the use of illegal drugs, including heroin and cocaine, as detrimental to social welfare. Many people believe criminal activities such as robbery, theft, and murder are a direct result of drug abuse. In addition, drug abuse results in a decrease in worker productivity and, hence, lost output. To address the problems attributed to drug abuse, many societies have passed laws that prohibit the use of many substances. In response to such prohi-

bitions, law enforcement agencies have concentrated on attempting to eliminate, or at least reduce, the available supply of illegal drugs. In addition, people convicted of selling or using illegal drugs face the prospect of stiff penalties. However, an increasing number of individuals have questioned the effectiveness of this approach and have instead argued for the legalization of many drugs.[6] Why is there such fundamental disagreement over policy in this area?

The arguments for each of the respective policies can be couched

in economic terms. Supporters of prohibitions argue that this approach has an immediate effect on the amount of drug use. Intercepting shipments of drugs before they reach the street reduces the available supply. In addition, severe penalties for convicted drug dealers raise the expected costs of doing business and thereby reduce the incentive to enter the market as a supplier. At the same time, penalties for drug users (consumers) reduce the expected benefits of consumption, decreasing the demand for drugs.

---

that the consumer can more easily do without. The price elasticity of luxury items tends to be higher than that of necessities. Examination of Table 6.5 supports this distinction. The price elasticity of demand for items such as bread, milk, and chicken is relatively low (<1) while the price elasticity of demand for china and glassware, and restaurant meals is considerably higher.

We are now in a position to consider, at least qualitatively, the possible effects of the threatened 100 percent tariff on Japanese luxury cars that was discussed at the beginning of this chapter. Recall that U.S. dealerships declared that such a tariff would drive sales of the affected models to 0. This assertion implies that, over the relevant price range, the price elasticity of demand for these cars is very high. A quick review of the determinants of elasticity tends to support this argument. Consider first the question of available substitutes. While it is true that luxury cars differ in a variety of characteristics, it is also true that in addition to the affected models there are a number of other luxury cars to choose from, including Mercedes, BMW, Jaguar, Lincoln, and Cadillac.

A second consideration is the price of a luxury car as a percentage of total income. The cars in question were priced roughly in the $26,000 to $50,000 range. A 100 percent tariff would effectively double the price of such cars (assuming quantity demanded was unchanged after the price increase). Clearly, this type of purchase constitutes a significant portion of most peoples' incomes (in 1994, the average household income in the United

The overall result of the anticipated decrease in the supply of and demand for drugs is a reduction in the use of illegal drugs and an increase in social welfare. Supporters of prohibitions also argue that legislation/decriminalization of drugs would lead to an increase in drug consumption.

Proponents of the legalization, or decriminalization, of drugs argue that, in fact, increased penalties for selling and buying drugs do not affect the market significantly. They maintain that the demand for illegal drugs is relatively inelastic because drugs are addictive. As such, supply reductions that drive up the price simply result in an increase in criminal activity such as robbery and theft as users scramble to obtain the means to support their drug habits. Furthermore, higher drug prices create an incentive for new suppliers to enter the market in pursuit of larger profits.

Proponents of legalization assume that the legalization of otherwise illegal drugs would increase the drug supply and reduce the profitability of the industry for the criminal element. The high profits associated with drug dealing would disappear with the introduction of additional suppliers and the resulting decrease in prices. Proponents also argue that, subsequent to legalization, the government could tax the sale of these drugs. The relatively inelastic demand would ensure a steady flow of tax revenues, which could then be used to fund efforts to monitor the industry and pay the costs of programs designed to help drug addicts. Finally, proponents of the case for legalization argue that it would free up law enforcement resources currently committed to trying to reduce the supply of drugs. These resources could be used in other areas of law enforcement.

Clearly, economic analysis provides only part of the analysis relevant to formulating sound social policy in this area. Moreover, the arguments that have been noted here only consider the effects of policy in the market for illegal drugs. The implications of effects such as spillovers into other markets resulting from a possible increase in the level of drug abuse have not been addressed. However, this discussion does demonstrate that there are no simple solutions to this difficult social problem.

States was approximately $39,000). Finally, as the term used to describe such cars implies, we are dealing with a luxury item as opposed to a necessity.

All of the factors considered above point to a relatively high price elasticity of demand coefficient for the affected automobiles. While we cannot say what the precise value of the elasticity coefficient is, we can say that there is strong qualitative evidence supporting the affected dealers' claims that such a tariff would be extremely bad for their business.

Availability of substitutes, the cost of a good relative to total income, the time period in question, and the type of good (luxury versus necessity) all affect the price elasticity of demand for a good or service. In general, an increase in any one of the first three factors will cause the price elasticity of demand to increase. In addition, the price elasticity of demand tends to be higher for luxury goods than necessities, *ceteris paribus*.

Section Recap

Other Measures of Elasticity

The concept of elasticity is general. It is the percentage change in one variable that is caused by a percentage change in another variable. If a change in X causes a change in Y, we would define the elasticity of Y with respect to X as the ratio of the percentage change in Y to the percentage change in X. Economists use this elasticity concept to measure not only the price elasticity of demand but also a variety of other relationships. Three of these other elasticity measures are defined below.

Income Elasticity of Demand

Income elasticity of demand:

A measure of the responsiveness of quantity demanded to a change in income.

The **income elasticity of demand** measures how responsive consumer demand for a good or service is to a change in income. The income elasticity of demand (e_I) is calculated as the percentage change in quantity demanded (holding price constant) that is induced by a percentage change in income, that is:

$$e_I = \frac{\% \text{ change in quantity demanded}}{\% \text{ change in income}}$$

Table 6.6

Selected Estimates of the Income Elasticity of Demand

Good or Service	Short-run Income Elasticity	Long-run Income Elasticity
Non-Durables		
Spectator sports	0.46	1.07
Clothing	0.95	1.17
Shoes	0.9	1.50
Gasoline and Oil	0.55	1.36
Foreign travel by U.S. citizens	0.24	3.09
Dental services	0.28	1.00
Potatoes[1]	−0.81	N.A.
Pork[1]	0.33	N.A.
Beef[1]	1.27	N.A.
Fresh fruit[1]	1.99	N.A.
Household electricity use[2]	0.30	0.72
Household natural gas use[2]	N.A.	2.00
Durables		
Furniture	2.60	0.53
Household Appliances	2.72	1.40
Automobiles	5.50	1.07

Sources: Unless otherwise indicated, estimates are taken from Houthaker, H.S., and L.D. Taylor, *Consumer Demand in the United States,* Cambridge, MA: Harvard University Press, 1970.

[1] Heien, D.M., 1982, "The Structure of Food Demand: Interrelatedness and Duality," *American Journal of Agricultural Economics,* 64(2): 213–21.

[2] Lakshmanan, G.R. and W. Anderson, 1980, "Residential Energy Demand in the United States," *Regional Science and Urban Economics,* 10: 371–86.

N.A. = Not Available

Income elasticity can be positive or negative because an increase in income can cause quantities consumed to increase (normal goods) or decrease (inferior goods). Estimates of the short-run and long-run income elasticity of demand for a variety of goods and services are presented in Table 6.6.

As we saw in Chapter 3, increases in income cause people to consume more of most goods. For example, we would expect to observe an increase in the amount of dining out as a result of an increase in income. In a similar fashion, many families might purchase a second or third car as a result of an increase in income. The income elasticity of demand enables us to predict the amount by which demand will increase for a given increase in income. For normal goods such as those in the examples above, the income elasticity of demand is positive – a percentage increase in income leads to a percentage increase in demand.

In contrast to the previous examples, we demand consumer durables, like TV sets, stereo systems, refrigerators, washing machines, or cars, for the services they provide over a period of time. Because these purchases can be moved up or delayed in time, their income elasticity is greater in the short run than in the long run. It is again a question of alternatives. For these products consumers have more flexibility in the short run.

Income elasticity of demand is negative for inferior goods – goods for which demand decreases as income increases. A percentage increase in income leads to a percentage decrease in demand. Macaroni and cheese is considered by many to be an inferior good. Consequently, when income increases, the demand for macaroni and cheese decreases. As indicated in Table 6.6, the income elasticity of demand for potatoes is negative. This suggests that, on average, consumers consider potatoes to be an inferior good.

Cross-Price Elasticity of Demand

Changes in the price of one good can also affect the demand for other goods. The extent of such an impact is measured by the **cross-price elasticity of demand**: the ratio of the percentage change in quantity demanded of one good (holding its price constant) to the percentage change in the price of another good. The cross-price elasticity of demand between two goods, X and Y, is calculated as:

$$e_{x,y} = \frac{\%\ \text{change in quantity demanded of good X}}{\%\ \text{change in the price of good Y}}$$

Estimates of the cross-price elasticity of demand for specific goods are summarized in Table 6.7. As the data in Table 6.7 indicate, substitute goods such as butter and margarine and beef and pork have positive cross-price elasticities. The positive sign on the elasticity estimates reflects the positive relationship between the quantity demanded of a good and the price of its substitutes. Complementary goods have negative cross-price elasticities. The negative sign reflects the fact that when the price of a good increases (or decreases), the quantity demanded of its complements moves in the opposite direction.

Cross-price elasticity of demand:

A measure of the responsiveness of the quantity demanded of one good to a percentage change in the price of another good.

Table 6.7

Selected Estimates of the Cross-Price Elasticity of Demand

Goods	Price Elasticity
Margarine with respect to price of butter	1.53
Fresh fruit with respect to price of processed fruit	1.96
Butter with respect to price of bread	0.09
Fresh fruit with respect to price of fresh vegetables	−0.02
Pork with respect to price of beef	0.36
Chicken with respect to price of pork	0.30
Electricity with respect to price of natural gas[1]	0.80

Sources: Unless otherwise indicated, estimates are taken from Heien, D.M., 1982, "The Structure of Food Demand: Interrelatedness and Duality," *American Journal of Agricultural Economics*, 64(2): 213-21.

[1] Lakshmanan, G.R. and W. Anderson, 1980, "Residential Energy Demand in the United States," *Regional Science and Urban Economics*, 10: 371-86.

Producers of close substitutes are especially interested in cross-price elasticities. For example, changes in the price of one breakfast cereal can affect the sales of other breakfast cereals. The producers of corn flakes would like to know, and they attempt to estimate, the cross-price elasticity of demand for corn flakes with respect to the price of Wheaties. They are interested in how much the quantity demanded of corn flakes will increase (or decrease) when the price of Wheaties increases (or decreases).

Producers are also interested in the cross-price elasticities of complements. When OPEC imposed the oil embargo in 1974 and began to dramatically increase the price of oil, gasoline prices quickly followed. As a result, consumers began to alter their demand for automobiles, increasing purchases of smaller, more fuel-efficient cars. Auto manufacturers can use estimates of the cross-price elasticity between gasoline and fuel-efficient cars to predict increases in demand (as well as decreases in demand for less fuel-efficient autos) that would result.

Price Elasticity of Supply

In this chapter the focus has been on the demand curve and thus price elasticity of demand. However, elasticity of supply is also an important measure of price response. The **price elasticity of supply** is the ratio of the percentage change in quantity supplied to the percentage change in market price. Determinants of supply elasticities are discussed in later chapters.

Summary

The **price elasticity of demand** is the ratio of the percentage change in quantity demanded to the percentage change in price. This measure captures the sensitivity of con-

Price elasticity of supply:

A measure of the responsiveness of the quantity supplied to a percentage change in market price.

sumers to price changes. When consumers are relatively insensitive to price changes, demand is said to be **inelastic** – the elasticity coefficient is between 0 and 1. When consumers are relatively sensitive to price changes, demand is said to be **elastic** – the elasticity coefficient ranges from 1 to infinity.

Because the coefficient of elasticity is the ratio of the percentage change in quantity demanded to the percentage change in price, it tells us the relationship between price changes and resulting changes in total revenue from a good. When the price of a good for which demand is inelastic increases, total revenue from the sale of the good increases. For goods whose demand is elastic, a price increase causes total revenue to decrease.

The price elasticity of demand also provides information on the incidence of a tax – the amount of a tax on a good that is borne by producers versus consumers. When demand is price elastic, the majority of the tax is borne by producers. When demand is inelastic, the majority of the tax is borne by consumers.

The degree to which consumers respond to a change in price, and therefore the price elasticity of demand, is heavily influenced by the availability of substitutes. Other factors that influence the price elasticity of demand include the percentage of total income accounted for by the good in question, the time period under consideration, and the type of good (luxury versus necessity).

A number of other measures of elasticity can be calculated that provide additional insights into the responsiveness of demand. The **income elasticity of demand** measures the responsiveness of demand to changes in the level of income. The **cross-price elasticity of demand** measures the responsiveness of demand for one good to changes in the prices of complements and substitutes.

Questions for Thought

Knowledge Questions

1. Define the price elasticity of demand. What does the price elasticity of demand measure?

2. Can you think of a good or service for which demand is generally elastic (or inelastic), but for which your own demand is inelastic (or elastic)? How do you explain the difference?

3. Summarize the relationship between elasticity, price changes, and changes in total revenue.

4. Explain the relationship between the price elasticity of demand and the incidence of a tax imposed on a good. Under what circumstances will consumers, as opposed to producers, pay the larger share of the tax? Why?

Application Questions

5. Salt was taxed for hundreds of years. In fact, at times French monarchs generated as much as 10 percent of their royal income from a salt tax. What attributes made salt a good commodity to tax?

6. The price of a good whose elasticity is 1.5 has just decreased by 10 percent. Will the quantity consumed increase or decrease? By what percent? What will happen to the total expenditures on the good? Why?

7. Calculate the price elasticity of demand for wheat in the two situations below:

    The Wheat Market

    Farmer Brown's Wheat

    Old price: $3.40/bu

    Old quantity: 2.5 billion bu

    New price: $3.20/bu

    New quantity: 2.525 billion bu

    Old price: $3.40/bu

    Old quantity: 28,000 bu

    New price: $3.20/bu

    New quantity: 35,000 bu

    Can you account for the difference in elasticities?

8. In the ten years between 1971 and 1981, the price of gasoline increased by more than 350 percent, from an average of about 36¢ to about $1.31 per gallon. Assuming that the short-run and long-run price elasticity of demand for gasoline are approximately equal, what happened to total household spending on gasoline during this period? Explain.

Synthesis Questions

9. Assuming the income elasticity of demand for margarine is negative, describe the effect associated with an increase in the income of margarine consumers on the demand for butter.

10. If a university wishes to increase its tuition revenue, should it increase or decrease tuition rates? Why?

11. What effect does price discrimination have on the total amount of a particular good sold relative to the amount sold if only a single price were offered?

12. Assume that the demand curve for a particular good can be written as:

    $Q = 15 - 2P.$

    Assuming that P = 5, calculate the point elasticity of demand. In addition, calculate the price elasticity of demand over the range P = 5 to P = 7. How do your estimates of the point and arc elasticity differ? Why?

End Notes

1 Sales events are also used to bring customers into the store in the hopes that they will see other items they might consider purchasing.

2 Recall that, by definition, a ratio in which the numerator takes the value of zero is equal to zero.

3 A demand curve that is unitary elastic is represented by an equilateral hyperbola of the form:

$$x = a/y^M$$

where x is quantity, y is price, and $M = 1$.

4 A demand function is a functional relationship between two variables (price and quantity); therefore, we can calculate the slope of the curve representing the function.

5 D.B. Suits, 1979, "The Elasticity of Demand for Gambling," *Quarterly Journal of Economics*, Vol. 93, No. 1: 155-62.

6 See, for example, "Bring Drugs Within the Law," *The Economist*, May 15, 1993, pp. 13-14.

The Theory of Consumer Behavior

Overview

In the United States alone there are more than 250 million consumers. Each consumer makes many consumption decisions every day and literally thousands of decisions in a year. Although some of these decisions are made with considerable care, many are made on the spur of the moment. Some of the more important decisions include where to live, what kind of residence to occupy, what to wear, what to eat, how to get from place to place, and how to spend leisure time. Thousands of choices exist; the variety of alternatives is truly astounding.

The logic of individual choice and the concepts of scarcity, choice, and opportunity cost represent the foundation on which economic theory is built. Beginning with this chapter, we examine these concepts from the viewpoints of the individual consumer, producer, and resource owner. In particular, we consider the specific choice problems of consumers (on the demand side of the market) and producers (on the supply side of the market), and we show how they use the basic economic principles developed in Part 1 in their decision-making processes.

This chapter, which introduces the consumer choice problem, has two objectives. The first is to demonstrate how the Fundamental Premise of Economics can be applied to the consumption decisions of individuals. The second is to provide a rationale for the law of demand, which states that the market price and quantity demanded of a product are inversely related. We will see that the consumer's desire to maximize his or her well-being is, in fact, the reason for negatively sloped demand curves.

Learning Objectives

After reading and studying this chapter, you will be able to:

1. Explain the basic consumer choice problem

2. Explain the concept of a *utility function*

CHAPTER 7

3. Explain the concept of the marginal rate of substitution

4. Explain the condition that is met when a consumer is maximizing his or her benefits from consumption

5. Explain how a change in price results in a downward-sloping demand curve by referring to the substitution and income effects

6. Describe various types of transactions costs and their influence on the consumer's decision-making behavior in actual practice

The Consumer Choice Problem

In Part 1, we introduced the basic economic problem of scarcity and the fundamental proposition that individuals seek to maximize their economic well-being. We demonstrated, through a variety of examples, that trade and exchange are motivated by the desire of individuals – consumers and producers – to improve their well-being. To achieve that end, individuals choose those alternatives for which the net benefit – the difference between benefits and costs – is greatest.

The logic that underlies the notion that individuals seek to maximize net benefits is compelling. However, many of us nonetheless are curious about why people make a particular consumption choice. Our curiosity often derives from the fact that someone we know has faced the same decision as we have, but has chosen a different alternative. For instance, you may own a sport utility vehicle while your friends own compact economy cars or mini vans or, in some cases, have no car at all. Why didn't these people buy the same type of car you did?

Other very good reasons exist for wanting to understand consumption behavior. Business firms earn their incomes by providing goods and services to consumers. Firms must know what appeals to consumers if they are to increase their sales and incomes. Whether you want to own a bicycle shop, manage a biotechnology company, or work in a health maintenance organization (HMO) will depend to some extent on information you have about consumer demand for bicycles, biotechnology, and health care.

Economists have a special interest in consumer behavior. To the extent possible, a society's resources are used to satisfy the wants of individual members of society. Consumer behavior affects the extent to which wants are satisfied through its influence on the kinds of goods produced in the economy, the manner in which wants are satisfied, and the stock of resources available in the future. Consumption spending accounts for about two thirds of all spending in the U.S. economy (the other third is accounted for by business, government, and foreigners). Consequently, changes in consumer spending can also contribute to changes in the price level and the level of unemployment in the economy. All of these issues are important to economists.

The consumer's problem can be stated very simply. We assume that consumers have unlimited wants and face an incredible array of choices when making consumption decisions. However, all consumers have limited resources. This constraint is usually reflected in a limited amount of income per time period. As a result of the income constraint, all consumers must make choices. They cannot have everything they would like.

Given a set of market-determined prices, a consumer can buy any one of a number of different combinations of goods he or she might consider purchasing with a limited income. Each combination will yield some amount of benefits to the consumer. However, once a particular combination is purchased, no other combination can be purchased in the same time period. Thus, the consumer's problem is deciding how to allocate limited income in such a way that maximizes benefits from consumption. This brings us to the question, What condition characterizes the combination of goods that maximizes the benefits a consumer derives from his limited income?

Consumer Utility

The condition that is satisfied when a consumer is maximizing his benefits from consumption is derived from the theory of utility maximization. This theory has evolved considerably over time. When it was originally developed, the concept of utility was used to refer to the amount of satisfaction, or pleasure, an individual derives from consumption activities. Moreover, it was assumed that utility was measurable, that is, the amount of utility derived from consuming a combination of goods could be quantified. In addition, it was assumed that the utility one person derives from consuming a combination of goods could be compared to the utility another person would derive from the same combination. However, over time this earlier concept of utility has been discarded.

Economists now recognize that utility is not something that can be measured like the number of apples in a box or shares of stock in a company, or the weight of cattle or square footage of apartment floor space. In modern economic theory, the concept of a **utility function** has come to refer to the preference ranking that an individual attaches to various combinations of goods and services she might buy. Thus, if we say that an individual derives greater utility from one combination of goods than she does from some other combination, we are simply saying that the individual prefers the first combination to the second. Consequently, the first combination yields greater benefits to the consumer. However, we are not saying anything about the actual *amount* of benefits or the difference in benefits the consumer derives from each combination. In addition, we can't compare one person's utility from a particular combination of goods to the utility another person derives from the same combination. Interpersonal comparisons of utility are not possible.

Utility function: The preference ranking a consumer applies to various combinations of goods he can purchase with his limited income.

We can summarize the relationship between the theory of utility maximization and the benefits a consumer derives from consumption activities as follows. Because the consumer has limited income, she must make choices. To be specific, she must select, from all the available combinations of goods she can buy, that combination that maximizes her benefits from consumption. The theory of utility maximization establishes the condition that is met when a consumer is purchasing the most preferred combination of goods (given her limited income). The combination that is most preferred is the one that yields the maximum benefits to the consumer. Once we have identified the utility-maximizing condition, we will use it to predict how a consumer responds to a change in the price of a good, *ceteris paribus*.

The consumer's problem is deciding how to allocate her limited income among consumption choices. The combination of goods that maximizes the consumer's benefits is that combination most preferred by the consumer. The theory of utility maximization establishes the condition that is met when the consumer is purchasing the most preferred combination of goods.

Section Recap

Basic Assumptions

The theory of consumer behavior is based on a few simple yet powerful assumptions. These assumptions are used to construct a model that enables us to predict how a consumer will react to a change in the price of a good, *ceteris paribus*. As we will see shortly, these assumptions yield downward-sloping demand curves for goods, as were described in Chapter 3. The assumptions we consider here concern the consumer's objectives, the nature of the consumer's preferences for different combinations of goods and services, and the consumer's subjective valuation of one good in terms of another. To illustrate these assumptions we will consider the case of a consumer, let's call her Nadine, who has to decide how to allocate her income between two goods, compact discs (CDs) and bungee jumps.

Consumers are rational First and foremost, we assume that consumers are rational decision makers; consumers attempt to maximize their benefits from consumption. Given a limited amount of income, a set of goods and services with market-determined prices from which to choose, and individual tastes and preferences, consumers attempt to make themselves as well off as possible. Thus, Nadine's problem is to select that combination of CDs and bungee jumps that maximizes her benefits from consumption. If we were to assume that consumers are not rational it would allow for some rather strange behavior. It is also worth noting that studies of consumer behavior consistently support the assumption of rationality. This is true even in the case of people – chronic psychotics – who are considered to be irrational in the psychological meaning of the word.[1]

Consumers have well-behaved preferences. We also assume that for any two combinations of goods, A and B, the consumer might consider, one of the following three possibilities is true:

1. A is preferred to B.

2. B is preferred to A.

3. A and B are equally preferred (the consumer is indifferent between A and B).

This assumption is equivalent to saying that, at a point in time, the consumer knows her tastes and preferences and is able to rank any two combinations of goods on the basis of those preferences. We also assume that the consumer's preferences are consistent in the following sense. In the case of three different combinations of goods, A, B, and C, if the consumer prefers A to B and prefers B to C, then it is automatically true that the consumer prefers A to C.

Table 7.1 describes various combinations of CDs and bungee jumps that Nadine might consider. We assume that Nadine can compare these combinations to one another and say, with certainty, that she prefers one to the others or that she is indifferent between two or more of the combinations in the table. Moreover, if Nadine asserts that she prefers combination D to combination B and that she prefers combination B to combination A, then it is also true that she prefers combination D to combination A.

Table 7.1

Combinations of CDs and Bungee Jumps

Combination	Bungee Jumps	Compact Discs
A	1	18
B	2	13
C	2	12
D	3	12
E	3	6

Consumers prefer more to less To illustrate this assumption, assume that Nadine is currently consuming combination C in Table 7.1. As a result, she is enjoying the level of benefits associated with combination C. What the "consumers prefer more to less" assumption says is that, holding the amount of the other good consumed constant, an increase in the amount of either bungee jumps or CDs consumed will leave Nadine better off. Thus, if Nadine were to go from consuming 2 bungee jumps and 12 CDs (combination C) to consuming either 3 bungee jumps and 12 CDs (combination D) or 2 bungee jumps and 13 CDs (combination B), her benefits from consumption would increase. In terms of her utility function, combinations B and D are both preferred to combination C. The fact that going from C to either B or D causes benefits to increase also means that the additional, or marginal, benefit that Nadine derives from consuming an additional unit of either good is positive. Increasing the amount of one good Nadine consumes, *ceteris paribus*, results in an increase in Nadine's benefits from consumption.

Consumers are willing to make tradeoffs The "consumers prefer more to less" assumption concerns the situation in which consumption of at least one good increases, while consumption of all other goods is held constant. We also assume that a consumer would be willing to give up some amount of one of the goods she is currently consuming to increase her consumption of some other good while leaving her benefits from consumption unchanged. In other words, the consumer would be willing to substitute some amount of one good for some amount of another good, utility held constant. In this case, what we are interested in is the *amount* of one good that must be given up to obtain one more unit of some other good, while leaving total utility and total benefits from consumption unchanged.

The maximum amount of CDs Nadine is willing to give up to consume an additional bungee jump while holding utility constant is called Nadine's **marginal rate of substitution** (MRS) of bungee jumps for CDs.[2] Thus, when we write $MRS_{BJ, CD}$ we are referring to the MRS of bungee jumps for CDs. In other words, substituting bungee jumps for CDs, the MRS is maximum number of CDs Nadine is willing to give up for an additional bungee jump while leaving total utility unchanged. Mathematically the MRS of bungee jumps for CDs is written as

Marginal rate of substitution:

The maximum amount of one good the consumer is willing to give up to consume an additional unit of another good while leaving total utility unchanged.

$$MRS_{BJ,\ CD} = \frac{\Delta CD}{\Delta BJ}$$

Referring again to Table 7.1, assume that Nadine is indifferent between combinations B and E. This means that combinations B and E yield the same utility; they are equally preferred by Nadine. From this we can infer that in going from combination B to combination E the MRS of bungee jumps for CDs is seven; Nadine is willing to give up a maximum of seven CDs to consume one additional bungee jump while holding utility constant.

Diminishing marginal rate of substitution The final assumption we make regarding consumers' preferences concerns the effect that consumption of additional units of one good has on the individual's MRS. Quite simply, we assume that, holding utility constant, as additional units of a good are consumed, the value of each additional unit, measured by amount of other goods the individual is willing to forgo, declines. Returning to Nadine's situation, as she consumes additional bungee jumps, the value of each additional bungee jump, measured by the number of CDs she is willing to forgo, decreases. Thus, the MRS of bungee jumps for CDs is declining. The MRS between two goods is not constant; it depends on the quantities of goods that are currently being consumed.

Section Recap

The theory of consumer behavior assumes that consumers are rational (they attempt to maximize their benefits from consumption given their income constraint), their preferences are well-behaved, they prefer more to less, and they are willing to make tradeoffs in consumption that leave total benefits unchanged. The marginal rate of substitution of X for Y – measured by the amount of Y a consumer is willing to give up to consume an additional unit of X – is assumed to decrease as additional units of X are consumed.

The Utility-Maximizing Condition

We have already noted that the consumer's consumption choices are constrained by her limited income. We can examine the implications of the budget constraint by considering Nadine's problem in greater detail. Assume that the prices of compact discs (CDs) and bungee jumps are $10 and $60. Assume also that Nadine has a total of $240 to spend each month on these two goods. Figure 7.1 illustrates various combinations of CDs and bungee jumps Nadine can purchase given her monthly income and the market-determined prices of the two goods. If Nadine spends all of her money on CDs, she can purchase a total of 24 ($240/$10) CDs each month (combination A). Conversely, if she spends all of her money on bungee jumps, she can purchase a total of four ($240/$60) bungee jumps per month (combination D). Other combinations of CDs and bungee jumps are also possible; for example, two bungee jumps and 12 CDs (combination B), or three bungee jumps and six CDs (combination C). The line in Figure 7.1, labeled BC_1, that connects the maximum combinations of the two goods Nadine can buy illustrates her **budget constraint**. She can purchase any combination of bungee jumps and CDs that lies on or to the left of this line.

Budget constraint:
The amount of money income the consumer has available to allocate among the goods and services he wishes to consume.

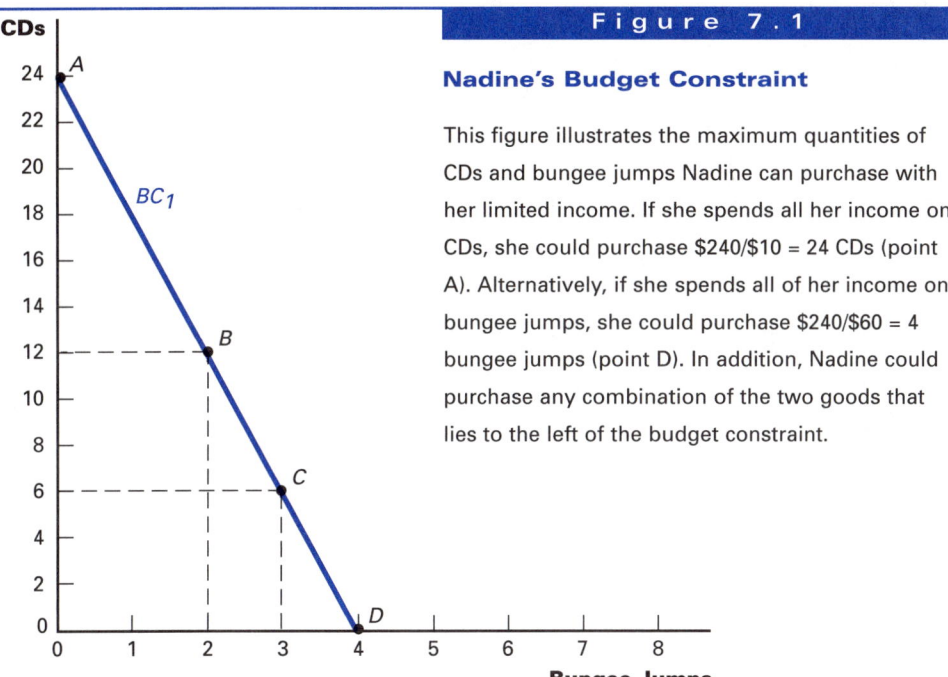

Figure 7.1

Nadine's Budget Constraint

This figure illustrates the maximum quantities of CDs and bungee jumps Nadine can purchase with her limited income. If she spends all her income on CDs, she could purchase $240/$10 = 24 CDs (point A). Alternatively, if she spends all of her income on bungee jumps, she could purchase $240/$60 = 4 bungee jumps (point D). In addition, Nadine could purchase any combination of the two goods that lies to the left of the budget constraint.

Nadine's problem is deciding how many CDs and how many bungee jumps to buy with her limited income. In making her consumption decision, Nadine compares the rate at which she is willing to trade off CDs for bungee jumps – her MRS of bungee jumps for CDs – to the market-determined exchange rate between the two goods, measured by the ratio of their respective prices. According to the theory of utility maximization, when Nadine is consuming the combination of bungee jumps and CDs that maximizes her benefits (subject to her budget constraint), the MRS between bungee jumps and CDs is equal to the ratio of the market prices of the two goods. *In the more general case in which a consumer is purchasing a number of different goods, utility, and therefore the benefits from consumption, are maximized when the consumer purchases the combination of goods such that, for any two goods, the MRS between the two goods is equal to the ratio of their market prices.* We will call this the **utility-maximizing condition**.

Mathematically, Nadine's benefits from consumption are maximized when she allocates her limited income between bungee jumps and CDs such that

$$\frac{\Delta CD}{\Delta BJ} = \frac{P_{BJ}}{P_{CD}}$$

In words, this condition states that, to maximize her benefits from consumption, Nadine should purchase the combination of bungee jumps and CDs such that, for the last bungee jump purchased, the rate at which she personally is willing to substitute an additional bungee jump for CDs (that is, the number of CDs she is willing to give up to purchase another bungee jump) is equal to the market-determined rate of exchange between the two goods.

Utility-maximizing condition:

Utility, and therefore the benefits from consumption, are maximized when the consumer purchases the combination of goods such that, for any two goods, the MRS between the two goods is equal to the ratio of their market prices.

Because the per unit price of bungee jumps is $60 and the per unit price of CDs is $10, the right-hand side of the equation that describes the utility-maximizing condition is six. This number tells us that, based on their respective market prices, one bungee jump is six times as expensive as one CD. Thus, six CDs must be forgone to consume an additional bungee jump. If Nadine's MRS between bungee jumps and CDs – the rate at which she is willing to give up CDs to consume additional bungee jumps – is also equal to six, Nadine can do no better than the current combination of the two goods.

To see why the utility-maximizing condition holds when Nadine maximizes her benefits from consumption, consider what it means when this condition is not satisfied. First, assume that Nadine were to consume a combination of CDs and bungee jumps for which the MRS of bungee jumps for CDs equals twelve. This means that, given her current consumption choice, Nadine is willing to forgo twelve CDs to consume an additional bungee jump. Because the ratio of the price of bungee jumps to the price of CDs is six, it is clear that

$$\frac{\Delta CD}{\Delta BJ} = 12 > \frac{P_{BJ}}{P_{CD}} = 6.$$

The number of CDs Nadine is willing to give up to gain an additional bungee jump while holding utility constant is greater than the number of CDs she would actually have to give up. Based on the market prices of the two goods, Nadine only has to give up six CDs to consume the additional bungee jump. Thus, she could consume the additional bungee jump and still have six CDs left over that she would have been willing to sacrifice. Nadine will see her benefits from consumption increase by increasing her consumption of bungee jumps at the expense of CDs. In addition, because the MRS of bungee jumps for CDs is assumed to decrease as additional bungee jumps are consumed (holding utility constant) the left-hand side of the previous equation will begin to fall, moving toward equality with the right-hand side. Nadine should continue to substitute bungee jumps for CDs until the two sides of the equation are equal.

Next, consider the situation in which Nadine has decided to consume a combination of bungee jumps and CDs such that

$$\frac{\Delta CD}{\Delta BJ} < \frac{P_{BJ}}{P_{CD}} = 6.$$

In this case, the MRS between bungee jumps and CDs is less than six. The value Nadine attaches to the additional bungee jump, measured by the number of CDs she is willing to give up, is less than the number of CDs she must give up given the per unit prices of the two goods. Thus, Nadine is better off by reducing her consumption of bungee jumps and increasing her consumption of CDs. Making this adjustment will cause the MRS of bungee jumps for CDs to increase and move toward equality with the ratio of market prices.

Section Recap

According to the theory of utility maximization, when the consumer is purchasing the combination of goods that maximizes her benefits, the MRS between any two goods is equal to the ratio of the market prices of the two goods. If this condition is not met, utility, and therefore the benefits from consumption, would be increased by altering the combination of goods consumed.

Derivation of the Demand Curve

Having identified the condition that is satisfied when the consumer is purchasing the benefit-maximizing combination of goods, we can now ask the question, How will the consumer respond to a change in the price of a good she is currently consuming? To answer this question, let's assume that Nadine has decided that, given her budget constraint, her most preferred, or benefit-maximizing, combination of CDs and bungee jumps is three jumps and six CDs. This corresponds to point C in Figure 7.1. Now assume that the price of bungee jumps is reduced from $60 per jump to $30 per jump. How will Nadine respond?

The decrease in the price of bungee jumps will cause Nadine's budget constraint to rotate out from BC_1 to BC_2 as illustrated in Figure 7.2. With the decrease in the price of bungee jumps, if she were to allocate all of her income ($240) to bungee jumps, Nadine could now consume twice as many jumps as she could before the price decrease. Because the price of CDs has not changed, the maximum number of CDs she can consume is still 24. Because the new budget constraint, BC_2, lies to the right of the original constraint, BC_1, it is clear that with the exception of combination A, Nadine is now able to consume more of both goods with the same limited amount of income. Thus, her benefits from consumption will increase. But the question remains, What is Nadine's new bene-

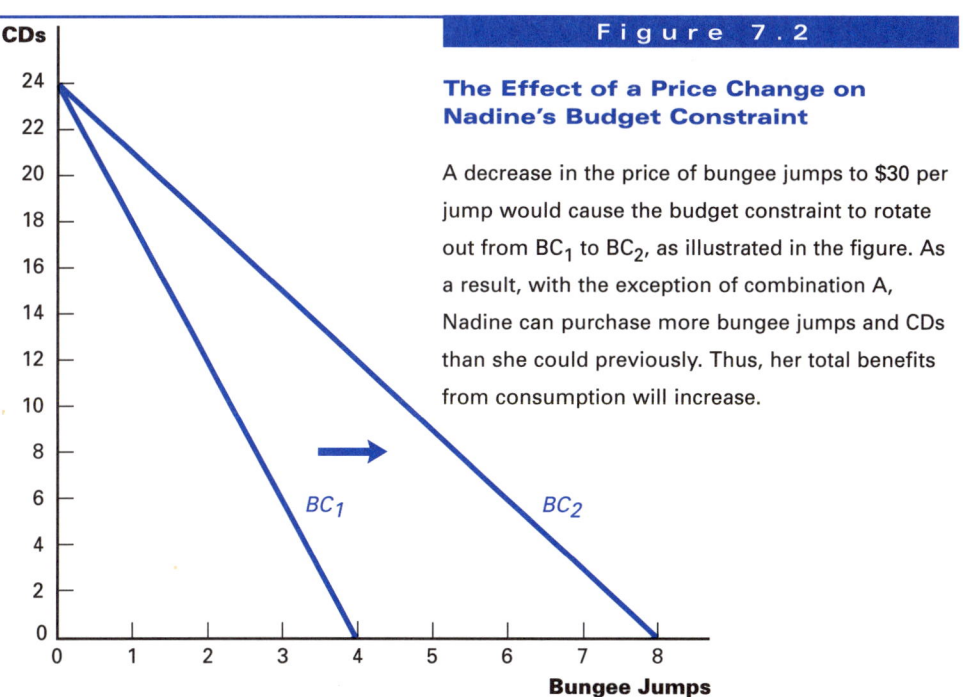

Figure 7.2

The Effect of a Price Change on Nadine's Budget Constraint

A decrease in the price of bungee jumps to $30 per jump would cause the budget constraint to rotate out from BC_1 to BC_2, as illustrated in the figure. As a result, with the exception of combination A, Nadine can purchase more bungee jumps and CDs than she could previously. Thus, her total benefits from consumption will increase.

fit-maximizing combination of bungee jumps and CDs? In general, the answer is that Nadine will respond by consuming more bungee jumps, and possibly more CDs as well.

Because we assumed that Nadine was maximizing her benefits from consumption by consuming combination C on the original budget line, we were therefore implicitly assuming that

$$\frac{\Delta CD}{\Delta BJ} = 6 = \frac{P_{BJ}}{P_{CD}} = 6.$$

However, the decrease in the price of bungee jumps has caused the ratio P_{BJ}/P_{CD} to fall as well, in this case, from six ($60/$10) to three ($30/$10). Thus, with the price decrease, Nadine is no longer in equilibrium because

$$\frac{\Delta CD}{\Delta BJ} = 6 > \frac{P_{BJ}}{P_{CD}} = 3.$$

To reestablish equilibrium, and increase her benefits from consumption, Nadine must increase her purchase of bungee jumps. This will cause the MRS between bungee jumps and CDs to decrease from six to some smaller number. In turn, the two ratios – Nadine's MRS of bungee jumps for CDs and the ratio of the prices of the two goods – will move back toward equality. *Thus, the decrease in price of bungee jumps will cause the quantity demanded of bungee jumps to increase; the demand curve for bungee jumps is downward sloping.* The effect of the decrease in price on quantity demanded can be decomposed into two distinct effects, which we describe next.

Income and Substitution Effects

The following discussion explains in more detail the reasoning that causes economists to argue that demand curves are negatively sloped. A price change has two effects on a consumer's economic well-being and behavior. First, when the price of one good changes, *ceteris paribus*, the good becomes less expensive (if its price decreases) or more expensive (if its price increases) relative to other goods. At the same time, a change in the price of a good, *ceteris paribus*, causes the *purchasing power* of a fixed amount of money income to increase (in the case of a price decrease) or decrease (in the case of a price increase).

Substitution effect:

Consumers purchase more (less) of a good whose price has fallen (risen) relative to the prices of its substitutes, utility held constant.

The **substitution effect** refers to the consumer's response to a change in the *relative* prices of two goods, while holding total utility constant. The term *relative prices* refers to the price of one good measured as the amount of other goods that an equivalent amount of money would buy. In the example we have been considering, the initial price of a bungee jump was $60 and the initial price of a CD was $10; thus, the relative price of a bungee jump was six CDs. The decrease in the price of bungee jumps from $60 to $30 has caused the relative price of jumps to fall from six CDs to three CDs.

In order to isolate the substitution effect, that is, the effect of the change in relative prices, we need to hold all other factors constant. As we have already noted, a change in the price of one good, *ceteris paribus*, alters both the good's relative price and the consumer's purchasing power. The substitution effect considers the effect of the price change on consumption holding the consumer's utility level constant. In this way, the effect of the price change on the consumer's purchasing power is ignored. According to the substitution effect, when the price of one good (for example, bungee jumps) decreases relative to the prices of other goods (for example, CDs), a consumer will substitute more of the good whose price has fallen for other, relatively more expensive goods. In Nadine's situation, we noted that as a result of the decrease in the price of bungee jumps,

$$\frac{\Delta CD}{\Delta BJ} = 6 > \frac{P_{BJ}}{P_{CD}} = 3.$$

Holding utility constant, to once again satisfy the utility-maximizing condition, Nadine must increase her purchase of bungee jumps and purchase fewer CDs in the process. This will cause the MRS between bungee jumps and CDs to decrease from six to some smaller number. In turn, the two ratios – Nadine's MRS of bungee jumps for CDs and the ratio of the prices of the two goods – will move back toward equality. Thus, Nadine will substitute additional units of the now cheaper bungee jumps for the relatively more expensive CDs while leaving total utility unchanged. *According to the substitution effect, the decrease in price causes an increase in quantity demanded.*

The substitution effect is illustrated graphically in Figure 7.3. Point A represents Nadine's consumption of bungee jumps before the price change – three jumps at a price of $60 per jump. According to the substitution effect, after the price of bungee jumps falls to $30 Nadine will increase her consumption of bungee jumps to something like Q_2. The change in the quantity demanded of bungee jumps resulting from the substitution effect is the amount $Q_2 - 3$.

The **income effect** refers to the effect of a price change on the consumer's purchasing power, or real income. When the price of a good is reduced, the consumer can continue to buy the same quantities of goods she purchased before the price change. However, because the price of at least one good is now lower, the consumer has some income left over that can be used to buy additional units of the good whose price has fallen (as well as of other goods). Thus, Nadine will use the increase in purchasing power to purchase additional bungee jumps, as well as possibly more CDs. *Thus, according to the income effect, a decrease in price leads to an increase in quantity demanded:* the essence of a downward-sloping demand curve.

Income effect:
The change in real purchasing power that results from a change in the price of a consumption good, *ceteris paribus.*

The income effect is also illustrated in Figure 7.3. Quantity demanded increases by some additional amount, the difference between Q_3 and Q_2 as a result of the income effect. Thus, the decrease in the price of bungee jumps has led to an increase in quantity demanded. Together, the substitution and income effects cause quantity demanded to increase by the amount $Q_3 - 3$. Connecting points A and B, which corresponds to the price-quantity combination of $30 and Q_3, yields the familiar downward-sloping demand curve introduced in Chapter 3.

In summary, according to the substitution and income effects, a decrease in the price of a good causes an increase in quantity demanded for two reasons. First, since the good is less expensive relative to other goods, the consumer substitutes the good for others. Second,

Figure 7.3

The Substitution and Income Effects

The substitution effect is illustrated in this figure. Point A represents Nadine's consumption of bungee jumps before the price change – three jumps at a price of $60 per jump. According to the substitution effect, after the price of bungee jumps falls to $30 Nadine will increase her consumption of bungee jumps to something like Q_2. Quantity demanded increases by some additional amount, the difference between Q_3 and Q_2, as a result of the income effect. Together, the substitution and income effects cause quantity demanded to increase by the amount $Q_3 - 3$. Connecting points A and B yields the familiar downward-sloping demand curve introduced in Chapter 3.

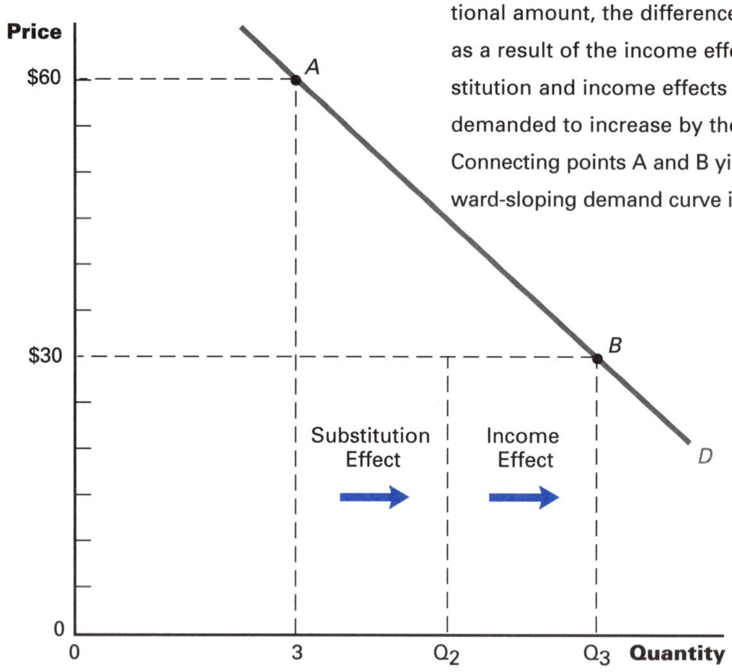

the decrease in price causes real income, or purchasing power, to increase. This prompts the consumer to purchase additional quantities of goods. The two effects reinforce each other. If price had increased, the two effects would have worked together in the opposite direction, leading the consumer to buy less of the now more expensive good.

We have used the consumer's utility-maximizing condition to derive the law of demand. In essence, we have applied the Fundamental Premise of Economics to the individual consumption decision. We have concentrated on a relatively simple case to highlight the fact that the theory of consumer behavior is just a specific case of the general welfare-maximizing behavior of rational individuals.

Section Recap

The law of demand is a result of the substitution and income effects of a price change. In particular, if the price of a good falls, *ceteris paribus*, consumers will substitute more of the good for other, relatively more expensive goods. In addition, the decrease in price increases consumers' purchasing power, enabling them to increase their consumption of the good whose price has fallen, as well as other goods.

Consumer Decision Making in Practice

It is not atypical for someone to come away from his first reading of the theory of consumer behavior rolling his eyes skyward and muttering about "this ridiculous marginal rate of substitution versus price ratio business!" The theory of consumer behavior gives some people the impression that economists believe consumers are just microcomputers with arms and legs, but without souls, who spend three quarters of their time making careful calculations to ensure that benefits are maximized and the other quarter of their time consuming the goods and services so carefully chosen. This impression is mistaken. Consumption is the objective of all economic activity. The benefits of consumption are the comfort, the joy, the excitement, the pure pleasure of satisfying one's wants. To maximize his benefits from consumption, a rational consumer satisfies the utility-maximizing condition established in this chapter: Consume goods and services in quantities such that the marginal rate of substitution is equal to the ratio of market prices for each pair of goods consumed.

This is not meant to suggest that whenever someone makes a decision concerning the consumption of a particular good that he explicitly considers the marginal rate of substitution between the good and every other good he is currently consuming. Instead, what we are arguing is that whenever someone consumes what he considers to be the best combination of goods and services, he has implicitly set the MRS equal to the price ratio for all pairs of goods.

Transactions Costs in the Theory of Demand

The primary concern of economists is with the relationship between the opportunity cost of consumption and its benefits. We have generally assumed that the opportunity cost of consumption is captured in the market price of the good. In many instances, however, the market price of a good accounts for less than the full opportunity cost of consumption. The difference between the full opportunity cost and the market price is called the **transactions cost** of consumption. Although transactions costs take a variety of forms, they all have the same impact on consumer behavior – the cost of consumption is greater than the market price.

Transactions costs: Any of the opportunity costs of consumption that are not incorporated in the market price of a good or service.

Transactions costs include all costs (except price) that are incurred in the process of purchasing and consuming a good or service. Waiting costs, taxes of different kinds (especially so-called nuisance taxes), contractual costs (which can be substantial when buying consumer durable goods), and the expected costs of risks assumed in consumption (for example, penalties if caught consuming illegal goods or services) are all examples of transactions costs. All these costs drive a wedge between the market price of a good and the true opportunity cost of consumption.

Time spent in making a transaction is a transaction cost. We typically do not think too much about this cost, but sometimes it is an important part of the opportunity cost of consumption. If a service station in town advertises its gasoline for 70¢ a gallon, it will attract considerable attention because this price is below the market price. Many people will attempt to take advantage of the offer. Consequently, although you can buy the gasoline for 70¢ a gallon, you may have to wait in line for a long time. Waiting is a transaction cost that will influence your gasoline consumption decision.[4]

186

Sorry, But the Price is too Low

In Chapter 3 we developed the concept of the law of demand; the quantity demanded of a good and its price are inversely related. We reinforced the concept in this chapter by identifying the utility-maximizing condition and using it to derive a downward-sloping demand curve. Starting from a position of consumer equilibrium, we showed that if the price of a good decreases, *ceteris paribus*, the quantity demanded of the good will increase. However, a recent article in *The Economist*[3] quotes the mar-

keting manager of a luxury goods firm as saying, "Our customers do not want to pay less. If we halved the price of all our products, we would double our sales for six months and then we would sell nothing." What are we to make of this statement in light of the law of demand and theory of choice? Does it make economic sense?

A turn-of-the-century American economist named Thorstein Veblen considered just this issue. A central theme in Veblen's book, *The Theory of the Leisure Class*, is that as individuals become wealthier, they desire to display (or flaunt) their wealth to others. Such displays are

accomplished through the purchase of expensive, and often exclusive, items ranging from designer clothing and lavish houses to expensive jewelry. Veblen referred to this sort of consumer behavior as "conspicuous consumption." According to Veblen, the consumption of expensive goods demonstrates that such individuals are members of the upper class and distinguishes them from members of the lower class. Stated in more formal terms, according to the theory of conspicuous consumption, as wealth increases, so does the demand for more expensive goods. Importantly, this increase in demand does not

---

Information costs:
The costs incurred in gathering information to be used in making a consumption decision.

Mobility costs:
The expense, time, and effort spent traveling to a particular location to complete a transaction for a consumption good.

Decision-making costs:
The time, effort, and risk involved in making a consumption decision.

The theory of consumer behavior we have developed in this chapter assumes that individuals are rational and informed and that transactions costs are zero. That is, for simplicity we have assumed away the frictions of the real world. Although these frictions do not alter the consumer's decision-making rule (that is why we initially assumed them away), they do change the manner and sometimes the outcomes of the decisions we make. Let's consider three types of transactions costs: (1) **information costs**, (2) **mobility costs**, and (3) **decision-making costs**.

Information Costs The assumption that consumers are fully informed decision makers implies that their consumption decisions are made with knowledge of all available consumption alternatives and prices. In actual practice, consumers may not be fully informed – for good reason. The acquisition of information is costly. For relatively inexpensive purchases, acquiring information on all alternatives may not be worth the additional cost. If you want to buy a personal stereo, such as a Sony Walkman, you might visit two stores and see five to ten similar products. Additional visits to other stores might enable you to see a few more stereos. However, the chances are low of saving a great deal of money as a result of the continued search for additional information. This possible gain must be weighed against the costs of additional store visits.

On the other hand, consumers who are making major purchases, such as automobiles, houses, a college education, or consumer durables will spend considerable amounts of time and money collecting information. The potential gains from this process are sub-

depend on whether the more expensive item is any more useful than less expensive substitutes that serve the same function.

Conspicuous consumption was certainly evident in the 1980s. Brand names such as Louis Vuitton, Christian Dior, Cartier, Rolex, Mercedes, and BMW seemed to spring up everywhere. In fact, this was the result of at least two forces: consumers' desire to purchase such items and more aggressive marketing strategies on the part of producers. However, this still does not answer the original question, Why do people prefer to pay more, rather than less, for such items?

The answer can be found by considering the effect of price on the marginal benefits of such goods. In the usual situation, the benefit the consumer receives from consuming an additional unit of a good is assumed to be independent of the good's price. The marginal benefits an individual derives from the consumption of a good are determined by the characteristics of the good. The marginal rate of substitution, the price of the good relative to the prices of the other goods and services the individual wants to purchase, and the consumer's budget constraint then interact to determine the quantity of the good that will be purchased. As price decreases, more is purchased, and vice versa.

In the case of luxury goods, however, one of the important characteristics is the good's price. Remember that part of the reason for purchasing such goods is to advertise your wealth to others and to distinguish yourself as a member of the upper-income class. Thus, a higher price increases the benefits obtained from the consumption of the good. A lower price reduces total benefits; the marginal benefit from consumption of additional units of a good is diminished as price falls. If the MRS for the good falls more quickly than its relative price, it will create an incentive for consumption of the good to decrease.

Viewed in this light, conspicuous consumption makes economic sense. Recall that one of the determinants of demand is tastes and preferences. We noted in Chapter 3 that economists do not have a great deal to say concerning this subject. However, it is clear that as the preference for a good increases, so will demand. *Ceteris paribus*, the result is an increase in willingness to pay. It would appear that the manager of the luxury goods store understands basic economic principles very well.

stantial in this kind of purchase. Notice that these costs are transactions costs for the purchase. One reason we are a little uncomfortable with the theory of consumer behavior is that we know consumers are not fully informed. However, consumers use the same benefit-cost calculation that they use to make their consumption choices when deciding how much information to acquire.

Mobility Costs A second cost associated with consumption decisions, but ignored so far, is mobility costs. It takes time to go from one place to another. Movement is costly. We expend resources directly on some transportation source such as a car or bus. In addition, time is a scarce good and therefore costly. Travel time requires a sacrifice. Thus, mobility costs can affect the outcome of consumption decisions. If we want to purchase a beverage for a small dinner party, we will purchase it from the least-cost supplier. However, time can be an important factor in the decision. If we decide to make the purchase only a half-hour before the party, the proximity of the supplier will be an important factor in the purchase decision. We may buy the beverage at a higher price than we know is available elsewhere because we can get it from a nearby location and therefore make the purchase in a shorter period of time.

In deciding how far to travel for the beverage, we had good, complete information and we opted for a higher-priced purchase. However, notice the decision-making process. We wanted a beverage for a party in thirty minutes. That is not the same kind of consumption purchase as a beverage for a party next week. Having the beverage fifteen minutes sooner is more valuable to us than the increase in the purchase price. We recognized

Why the DISAGREEMENT?

The Poverty Programs Controversy

Programs to reduce poverty are probably the government's most controversial domestic programs. The debate over the appropriate extent of support provided and the structure of the programs is, it seems, never ending. Ever since Michael Harrington's book, *Hunger in America* (1963), startled the country with a vivid depiction of poverty in the United States, and President Lyndon Johnson launched the War on Poverty in the 1960s, the country has been embroiled in a public debate of the relative benefits and costs of antipoverty programs. Although there have been repeated calls for welfare reform, the general

structure of these programs has changed little since they were first established more than thirty years ago, and total funding has increased substantially. In 1995, the Congress proposed radical changes in the federal government's welfare programs. Although most people agreed that such programs need to be changed, there was nonetheless disagreement about the specific types of changes that should be made. Why have these programs generated so much disagreement?

Statistics suggest that it is not a general unwillingness to support worthwhile causes, including caring for the poor and destitute, that accounts for the emotional intensity of the debate. In 1985, Americans contributed an estimated $70 bil-

lion to private charitable and philanthropic organizations. However, it is important to note that a contribution to a private charitable organization, such as the Salvation Army or United Way, differs from support provided for a government poverty program in at least one important aspect — the contribution to the charity is voluntary, and support provided for government programs through the payment of taxes is not.

The proponents of relying primarily on voluntary contributions to fund antipoverty efforts believe that the net benefits associated with this approach outweigh the net benefits associated with government-sponsored programs. From an economic perspective, an individual chooses to donate to a charity just

---

that the full cost of the beverage included both the price of the beverage and the travel time to make the purchase. Remember that good decision making requires the identification of the true costs and benefits of each alternative.

Decision-Making Costs The third type of cost involves the decisions themselves. One of the reasons that the utility-maximizing condition bothers many people when they are first exposed to it is that it suggests that we spend an inordinate amount of time making decisions. In fact, you may have wondered at one point or another how a consumer could really focus on this condition and still have time to consume anything. This insight is an important one. The very process of decision making itself is costly; it takes time and effort and requires the expenditure of resources. Thus, we would expect these costs to affect consumption decisions to some extent. Do I really want this item enough to justify the required expenditure? This question is one we have all asked ourselves at one time or another.

Our uncertainty about the extent to which we will benefit from a consumption good makes the decision itself costly. This risk is much like the risk a businessman faces in deciding to start a business. He believes that he will be able to make a profit, but he is not guaranteed a profit. The risk that we assume in either of these decisions is the source of a

as he chooses to purchase a consumer good. He compares the benefits to the cost. In this case, the cost is the amount of the donation. The benefit from a donation is the satisfaction derived from the gift. Consumers have favorite charities or causes that are especially important to them. Alternatively, they might make a donation in their own names, obtaining both satisfaction from the use to which the donation is put and recognition for their support. A donation is made when the benefit from a dollar spent on a gift is higher than the benefit per dollar spent on the available consumption alternatives. Overall, there is a net gain – both the donor and the recipient gain from the charitable contribution.

Unlike charitable donations, tax payments to support poverty programs are not voluntary. In addition, the taxpayer has very little control over the cause to which the taxes go. Thus, to some taxpayers these payments represent sacrifices –

costs incurred – with little or no benefit in return. In effect, society requires them to make an exchange by which their own welfare is reduced rather than enhanced. Moreover, the beneficiaries of these tax payments are viewed as receiving resources – income or services – with little or no sacrifice. The resource constraints under which we all live make the idea of a free lunch attractive to everyone. Consequently, it should not be surprising that when one individual is required to sacrifice for someone else's benefit, dissatisfaction frequently surfaces.

On the other hand, proponents of government-sponsored anti-poverty programs feel that the government is better equipped to address the problems of the needy than are private individuals and organizations. In this case, it could be argued that the government is in a much better position to identify the individuals most in need of assistance. As such, there is less

risk that truly needy individuals will be overlooked when aid is distributed. In addition, it could be argued that funneling funds through a single distribution point makes it possible to compare the benefits of providing assistance to alternative groups. This improves the likelihood that funds will be distributed where they are most highly valued. The result is that benefits from such programs are maximized by having the government allocate funds to those individuals it identifies as having the greatest need.

Clearly, the arguments on both sides merit consideration. In addition, it is clear that no simple solution to the debate over the appropriate form of income redistribution will be forthcoming soon. However, application of the basic elements of consumer theory helps explain why different individuals take the position they have on this issue.

decision-making cost. Consumers do make mistakes. They overestimate consumption benefits, or they make purchases based on erroneous or incomplete information. However, in the long run their reaction to these mistakes is consistent with the theory of consumer behavior: When consumers become aware of the problem they correct the mistakes.

Decision-making costs do have an impact on consumer decisions. Although we have assumed that consumers maximize their benefits from consumption, we have provided no further information about the specific nature of this goal. For instance, are consumers maximizing lifetime benefits when they make consumption decisions today or when they made them last year? This question is a difficult one to answer. In reality, the precise framework within which consumers attempt to maximize benefits varies across consumers. Among consumers with similar incomes, some might live for today while others might essentially live for tomorrow. These orientations suggest different consumption patterns. The differences arise because of different values placed on goods available today versus goods available tomorrow.

None of these real-world complications voids the theory of consumer behavior. They simply change the manner in which the utility-maximizing condition is applied in actual practice.

Section Recap

Transactions costs, such as information costs, mobility costs, and decision-making costs all affect consumer decision making by increasing the full opportunity cost incurred in consuming a particular good. However, they do not alter the utility-maximizing condition.

Indifference Curves Analysis

This section presents a more technical approach to the concepts of utility maximization and the law of demand.[5] It is intended to provide additional insights into the derivations of the utility-maximizing condition and the downward-sloping demand curve.

The Utility Function and Indifference Curves

The theory of consumer behavior assumes that consumers have a well-behaved set of preferences. In particular, we assume that more is preferred to less and that, holding total utility constant, the value of additional units of a good declines as more of it is consumed. The implication of these assumptions is that in the process of choosing between two goods and holding total utility constant, the amount of one good that a consumer is willing to give up to get one more unit of the other good becomes smaller and smaller. Alternatively, the consumer must receive larger and larger amounts of one good in exchange for each additional unit of the other good given up to still maintain the same level of total utility.

This concept is illustrated in Table 7.2, which identifies specific combinations of two goods, jeans (J) and shirts (S), that yield the same level of utility for a representative consumer. As the table indicates, holding utility constant, as the individual consumes additional units of one good, the amount of the other good the consumer is willing to give up decreases. For example, to increase his consumption of shirts from one to two units, the consumer would be willing to give up four pairs of jeans. To increase his consumption of shirts from two units to five units, he would only be willing to give up three pairs of jeans, an average of one pair of jeans for each additional shirt.

The information in Table 7.2 is also plotted in Figure 7.4. The resulting curve is called an **indifference curve**. It locates all the combinations of jeans and shirts that yield the same level of total utility. A consumer receives the same amount of total utility from any combination of goods on a given indifference curve. As such, the consumer is indifferent between the combination of jeans and shirts associated with point A and the combination associated with point B.

Indifference curve:

All combinations of two goods, X and Y, that yield the same level of total utility.

Indifference Curves and the Marginal Rate of Substitution

We have already noted that the rate at which a consumer is willing to exchange one good for another and still remain at the same level of total utility is known as the marginal rate of substitution, or MRS. The MRS between two goods also equals the ratio of the **marginal utility** (MU) of one good to the marginal utility of the other, where marginal utility is defined as the change in total utility attributable to a one-unit change in the consumption of a good.

Marginal utility:

The change in total utility from consuming one more unit of a good or service.

Table 7.2

Alternative Combinations of Two Goods That Yield the Same Level of Utility for a Representative Consumer

Utility	Quantity of Jeans Consumed	Quantity of Shirts Consumed
15	9	1
15	5	2
15	2	5
15	1	9

   The relationship of the rate at which a consumer is willing to trade one good for another and the ratio of their marginal utilities is derived as follows. First, the MRS between two goods is measured holding total utility constant. In addition, we assume that, *ceteris paribus*, consuming an additional unit of a good causes total utility to increase; marginal utility is positive. Thus, it follows that reducing the consumption of a good, *ceteris paribus*, causes total utility to decrease. In order for total utility to remain unchanged, the gain in total utility attributable to the increased consumption of one good must be exactly offset by the reduction in total utility attributable to the decreased consumption of another good. In each case, the change in total utility is equal to the change in the number of units consumed multiplied by the marginal utility of each of those units. Thus, in the case in which a consumer is giving up shirts to consume additional pairs of jeans, the restriction that total utility remain unchanged requires that:

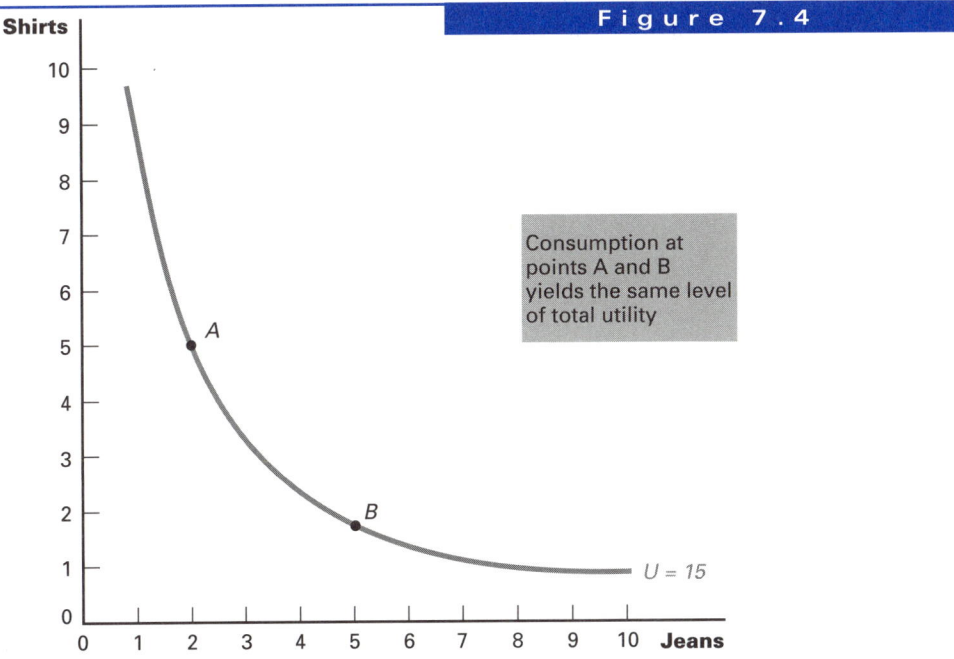

Figure 7.4

Consumption at points A and B yields the same level of total utility

$U = 15$

Alternative Combinations of Two Goods, Utility Held Constant

This figure depicts the various combinations of two goods, jeans and shirts, that yield a constant level of utility. As such, the consumer is indifferent between (receives the same amount of utility from) the combination of jeans and shirts associated with point A and the combination associated with point B.

$$\Delta J \times MU_J + \Delta S \times MU_S = 0.$$

Because ΔS is negative, the previous equation can be rewritten as

$$\Delta J \times MU_J = \Delta S \times MU_S.$$

Finally, rearranging terms yields

$$MU_J/MU_S = \Delta S/\Delta J.$$

Indifference curve map:

A set of indifference curves, each of which is associated with a different level of total utility; moving up to the right (away from the origin) moves the consumer to higher levels of utility

The right-hand side of the last equation is the consumer's MRS of jeans for shirts. It tells us how many shirts he is willing to give up to purchase an additional pair of jeans. The left-hand side of the equation is the ratio of the marginal utility of jeans to the marginal utility of shirts; in other words, the MRS of jeans for shirts.

Figure 7.5 depicts an **indifference curve map**. Each indifference curve, for example, the curve labeled U_1, locates all the combinations of jeans and shirts among which the consumer is indifferent. Note that the indifference curves are convex to the origin, that is, they are bowed in toward the origin. The slope of an indifference curve at any point is simply the MRS of jeans for shirts, MU_J/MU_S.

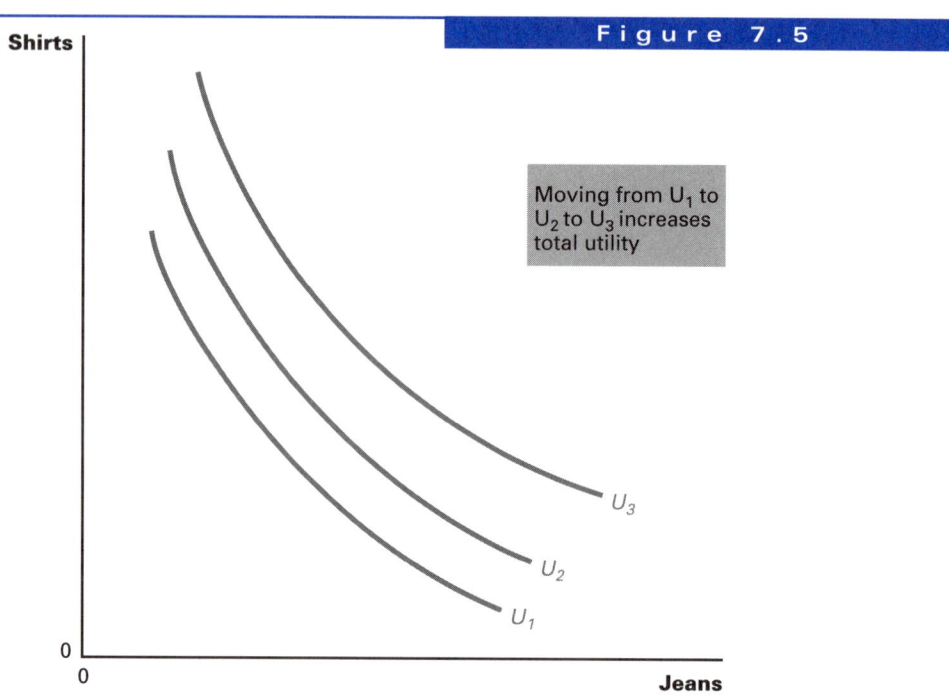

Figure 7.5

Moving from U_1 to U_2 to U_3 increases total utility

An Indifference Curve Map

This figure depicts an indifference curve map. Each indifference curve, for example, the curve labeled U_1, locates all the combinations of jeans and shirts that yield the same amount of total utility. The slope of an indifference curve at any point is the negative of the MRS of jeans for shirts, MU_J/MU_S. The fact that the indifference curves are convex to the origin reflects the fact that as we move down an indifference curve the MRS decreases. Moving up to the right (away from the origin) moves the consumer to higher levels of utility.

Moving up to the right (away from the origin) moves the consumer to higher levels of utility. U_3 is associated with a higher level of utility than U_2, and U_2 is associated with a higher level of utility than U_1. To maximize utility, a consumer will seek to consume a combination of goods that lies on the highest indifference curve possible.

The Budget Constraint

The consumer is constrained, however, by the amount of income available for consumption. In the simple case being considered here, in which only two goods are being consumed, the budget constraint can be written mathematically as:

$$M \geq P_J J + P_S S$$

where M represents money income, and P_J and P_S are the prices of jeans and shirts. The budget constraint simply states that total expenditures on the combination of goods purchased must be less than or equal to available income.

A budget constraint has been graphed in Figure 7.6. The slope of the budget constraint is $-P_J/P_S$. The slope is found by solving the budget constraint for S, that is:

$$M = P_J J + P_S S$$
$$P_S S = M - P_J J$$
$$S = M/P_S - (P_J/P_S)J$$

Figure 7.6

The Consumer's Budget Constraint

Assuming that the consumer is purchasing only jeans and shirts with a fixed amount of income, M, the budget constraint can be graphed as shown in this figure. The slope of the budget constraint is $-P_J/P_S$. If the consumer spends all of his income on shirts, he can purchase M/P_S units of shirts. Alternatively, if the consumer spends all of his income on jeans, he can purchase M/P_J units of jeans. In addition, the consumer can purchase any combination of the two goods that lies on, or to the left of, the budget constraint.

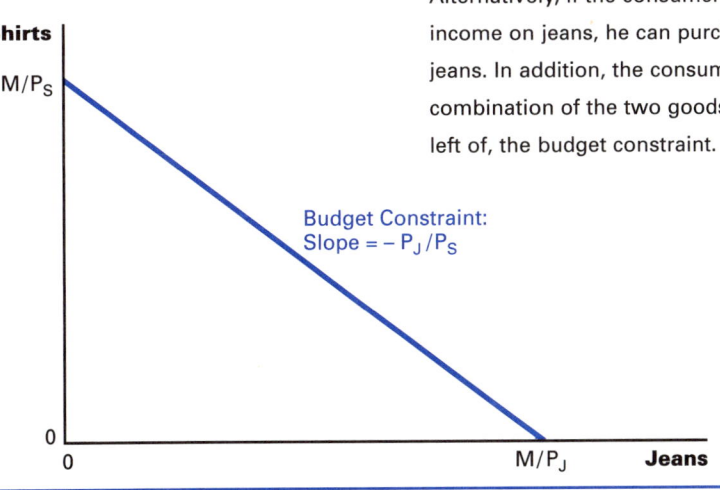

Budget Constraint:
Slope = $-P_J/P_S$

If the consumer spends all of his income on shirts, he can purchase M/P$_S$ shirts. In a similar fashion, if the consumer spends all of his income on jeans, he can purchase M/P$_J$ pairs of jeans. In addition, the consumer can purchase any combination of shirts and jeans that lies on, or to the left of, the budget constraint.

Utility Maximization

To maximize utility, the consumer purchases that combination of goods that lies on the highest indifference curve he can attain given his budget constraint. The information in Figures 7.5 and 7.6 has been combined in Figure 7.7, which illustrates the utility-maximizing level of consumption for our consumer. Note that, as it is drawn, the consumer's budget constraint is just tangent to indifference curve U$_2$, at point C. The consumer maximizes his utility by consuming the combination of jeans and shirts associated with point C, J$_C$ and S$_C$. At point C, the MRS of jeans for shirts is equal to the slope of the budget constraint, P$_J$/P$_S$ or:

$$\frac{MU_J}{MU_S} = \frac{P_J}{P_S}$$

Figure 7.7

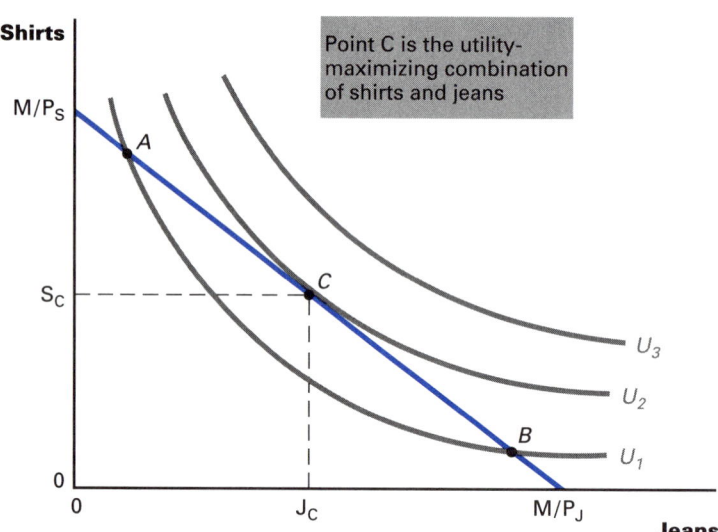

Point C is the utility-maximizing combination of shirts and jeans

Utility Maximization in the Case of Two Goods

The information in Figures 7.5 and 7.6 has been combined here to illustrate the utility-maximizing level of consumption. Utility is maximized by consuming the combination of goods associated with point C, J$_C$ and S$_C$. At point C, the consumer's budget constraint is just tangent to the indifference curve U$_2$, and the MRS of jeans for shirts is equal to the slope of the budget constraint. Points A and B are also attainable by the consumer since each point lies on the consumer's budget constraint. However, if the consumer moves to any point other than C, such as A or B, he will automatically place himself on a lower indifference curve.

Recalling that the ratio of the marginal utilities is another expression for the MRS of jeans for shirts, this is equivalent to the utility maximizing condition derived earlier in the chapter.

To see why point C maximizes utility, consider points A and B. Both of these combinations of jeans and shirts are attainable by the consumer because each point lies on the consumer's budget constraint. However, each of these points lies on indifference curve U_1, which is associated with a lower level of total utility than U_2. In fact, if the consumer moves to any other point (on or inside his budget constraint) except point C, he will automatically place himself on a lower indifference curve.

Deriving the Demand Curve

The indifference curve map and the budget constraint can also be used to derive the demand curve for a good. As an illustration, assume that the price of jeans increases from P_J to P_J'. This has the effect of causing the budget constraint to rotate in toward the origin, as illustrated in Figure 7.8 (a). Note that the budget constraint still intersects the vertical axis at M/P_S because the price of shirts and the level of income have not changed. Hence, the consumer can still purchase the same number of shirts as before. However, because the price of jeans has increased, the consumer is able to purchase fewer pairs of jeans. As shown in Figure 7.8 (a), if the consumer were to spend all of his income on jeans, he could only purchase M/P_J' units.

Because the budget constraint has now rotated, it is tangent to a lower indifference curve, in this case U_1. Point D is now the utility-maximizing combination of jeans and shirts. The increase in the price of jeans has forced the consumer to a lower level of utility. In addition, the consumer is now consuming fewer pairs of jeans (as well as fewer shirts).

The demand curve for jeans is derived in Figure 7.8 (b). At the initial price, P_J, the consumer purchased J_C units of jeans. Once the price of jeans increased to P_J', the consumer reduced his purchases of jeans to J_D units. As we would expect, the demand curve for jeans is downward sloping, as shown in the figure.

The Substitution and Income Effects Additional insights into the theory of demand can be seen by focusing on Figure 7.8 (a), which has been recreated in Figure 7.9. The increase in the price of jeans from P_J to P_J' caused purchases of jeans to fall from J_C to J_D. This reduction in jeans purchased can be broken down into two components: the substitution effect and the income effect.

Recall that the substitution effect states that when the price of a good increases, the consumer will consume less of the good and increase consumption of other, relatively less expensive goods. The substitution effect is seen graphically when a line is constructed, parallel to the new budget constraint and just tangent to the original indifference curve. The dashed line that is tangent to U_2 at point E has been so constructed. The quantity of jeans associated with point E, J_E, is the quantity of jeans that would be consumed after the price increase, but holding utility constant. Consumption of jeans has fallen by the amount $J_C - J_E$. (Note that consumption of shirts has increased.)

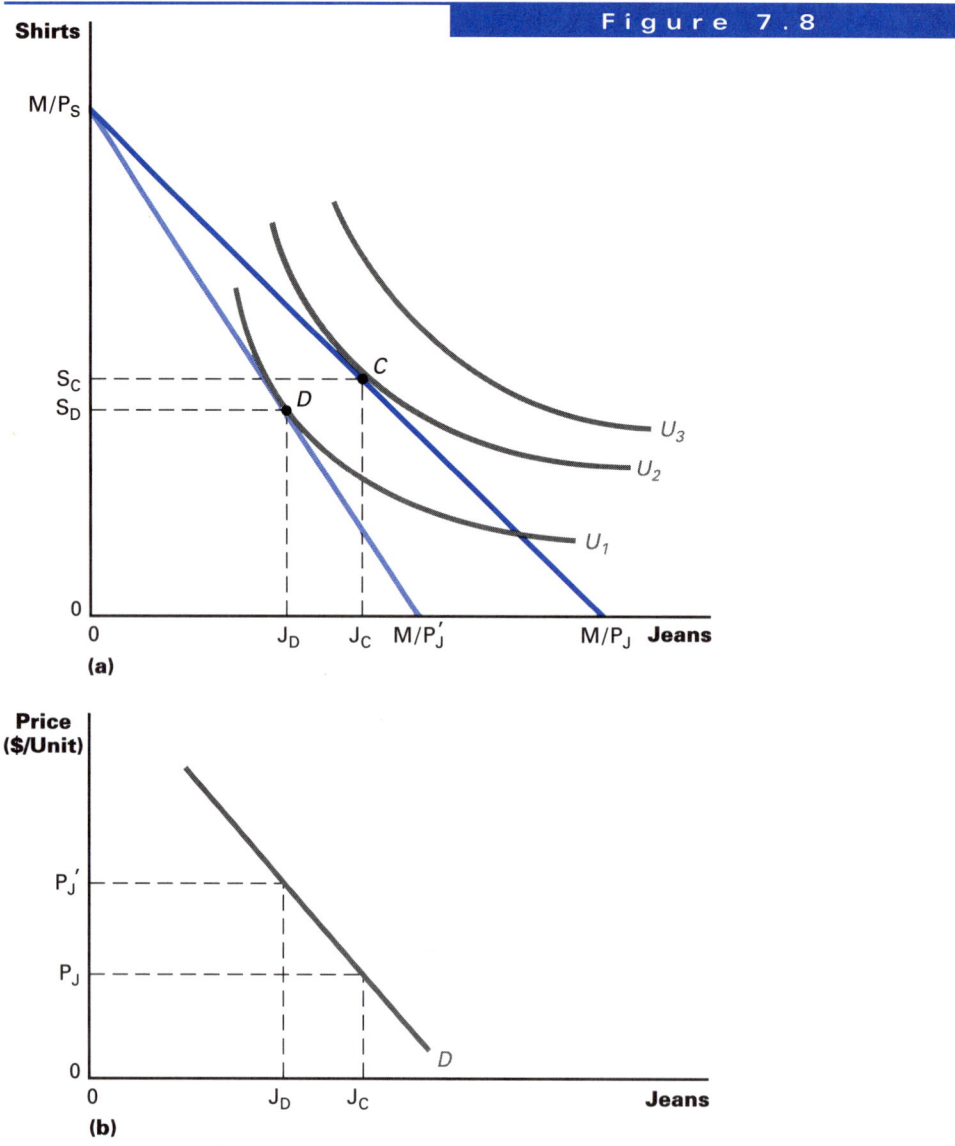

Figure 7.8

(a)

(b)

Deriving the Demand Curve for Jeans

If the price of jeans increases from P_J to P_J', the budget constraint will rotate, as illustrated in Figure 7.8 (a). Because the price of shirts and the level of income have not changed, the consumer can still purchase the same amount of shirts as before. However, because the price of jeans has increased, the consumer now is able to purchase only M/P_J' units. Point D is the new utility-maximizing combination of jeans and shirts. The demand curve for jeans is derived in Figure 7.8 (b). At the initial price, P_J, the consumer purchased J_C units of jeans. Once the price of jeans increased to P_J', the consumer reduced his purchases of jeans to J_D units. The demand curve for jeans is downward sloping.

Figure 7.9

The Substitution and Income Effects with Indifference Curves

The substitution effect is illustrated by constructing a line parallel to the new budget constraint and tangent to the original indifference curve, as shown by the dashed line tangent to U_2 at point E. J_E is the quantity of jeans that would be consumed after the price increase holding utility constant. The income effect is shown by the movement from J_E to J_D. This is the amount by which consumption of jeans declines as a result of the reduction in purchasing power associated with the increase in the price of jeans. The substitution and income effects combine to cause the consumption of jeans to decrease from J_C to J_D.

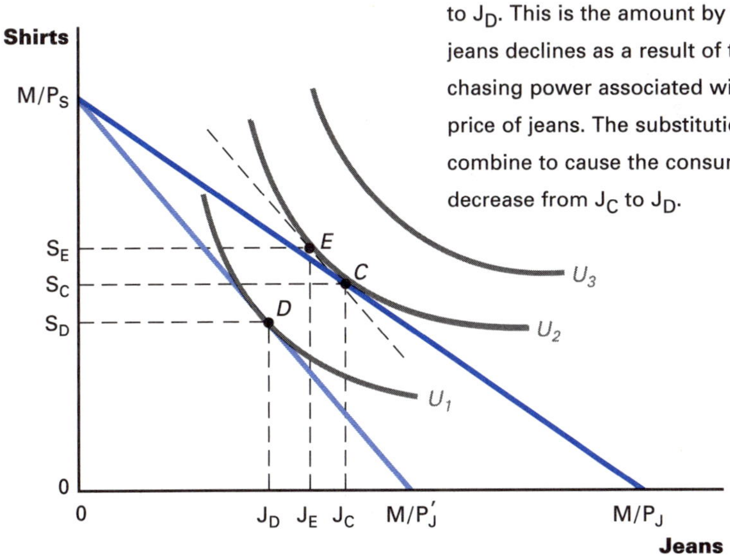

The income effect is shown by the movement from J_E to J_D. This is the amount by which consumption of jeans declines as a result of the reduction in purchasing power associated with the increase in the price of jeans. Once again, the substitution and income effects combine to cause the consumption of jeans to fall from J_C to J_D.

Summary

In this chapter the fundamental proposition of economics has been applied to a specific set of decisions: the choices of individual consumers. The consumer seeks to maximize her benefits from the consumption of economic goods and services. However, since the consumer has limited resources or income, she must make choices. In particular, given various combinations of goods she might purchase, she must select the combination that maximizes her benefits from consumption subject to her budget constraint.

The theory of consumer behavior is based on a set of simple but powerful assumptions. We assume that consumers are rational (they attempt to maximize their benefits from consumption given their income constraint), their preferences are well-behaved, and they prefer more to less. In addition, consumers are willing to make tradeoffs in consumption that leave total utility, and total benefits, unchanged. The amount of one good, Y, a consumer is willing to give up to consume an additional unit of another good, X, is called the **marginal rate of substitution (MRS)** of X for Y. The MRS of X for Y is assumed to decrease as additional units of X are consumed.

According to the theory of utility maximization, utility, and therefore the benefits from consumption, are maximized when the consumer purchases the combination of goods such that, for any two goods, the MRS between the two goods is equal to the ratio of their market prices. In other words, the rate at which the consumer is willing to trade one good for another is equal to the market-determined rate of exchange between the two goods. This is referred to as the **utility-maximizing condition**.

The result of utility-maximizing behavior is that the quantity of a good that is willingly consumed is inversely related to market price: Demand curves are negatively sloped. The **substitution effect** and the **income effect** help explain why demand curves are downward sloping. According to the substitution effect, consumers will purchase additional quantities of a good when its price declines because the good is now less expensive relative to other goods. The income effect suggests that as the price of a good falls, a person's purchasing power increases, enabling her to purchase more of the good.

In many cases, the market price of a good understates the true opportunity cost of consumption. **Transactions costs**, including **information costs, mobility costs**, and **decision-making costs**, can all increase the effective price of purchasing and consuming a good or service.

Questions for Thought

Knowledge Questions

1. Explain the concept of consumer utility. Can utility be measured in the same way that the amount of output produced by a manufacturer is measurable? Why?

2. What is the utility-maximizing condition? Explain the meaning of this condition in your words.

3. In your words, how do the substitution effect and the income effect explain the downward-sloping demand curve?

4. What is the difference between the cost of watching a baseball game on TV and going to one at the ball park? What is the difference in benefits gained from each?

Application Questions

5. Referring to the example involving Nadine, assume that the price of CDs doubles (to $20) while the price of bungee jumps remains at $60. How will this affect Nadine's budget constraint? Illustrate the effect graphically. What will happen to Nadine's consumption of CDs? Explain your reasoning by referring to the substitution and income effects.

6. Explain, in terms of the utility-maximizing condition, the effect of an increase in the transactions costs associated with a particular good on the demand for that good.

7. The development of the fast food industry is often attributed (in part) to the increased number of women, especially married women, working outside the home. Explain this argument. What is the full opportunity cost of a meal prepared at home?

8. Assume that an individual is currently using all of his income to consume two goods – X and Y. If the prices of X and Y are $3 and $8, respectively, and the MRS of X for Y is four, is this individual maximizing his benefits from consumption? If not, what should he do to increase benefits?

Synthesis Questions

9. A local record store sells CDs with quantity discounts. The first two CDs are sold at their list price, but the third CD is sold at a 10 percent discount and the fourth CD at a 20 percent discount. Use the substitution effect and income effect to explain this pricing policy.

10. The theory of consumer behavior asserts that individuals derive benefits from consuming goods and services. Their limited incomes prevent them from satisfying all wants. Yet consumers typically do not spend all of their income. They save part of it. How can savings be consistent with benefit-maximizing behavior?

11. Use the utility-maximizing condition to explain how an increase in the price of one good causes the demand for its substitute to increase.

12. Subsequent to the Iraqi invasion of Kuwait in August 1990 the price of a gallon of gas rose by more than 30 percent in most parts of the United States. Use the substitution and income effects to analyze the effects of this price change in the markets for gas and fuel-efficient cars.

Appendix to Chapter 7

Overview

The discussion presented here constitutes an alternative approach to explaining the theory of utility maximization. This approach is one that is traditionally found in introductory textbooks. It relies on the assumption that utility can be quantified and, as such, provides a more concrete discussion of the theory of utility maximization presented in the main part of the chapter.

Total versus Marginal Utility

In establishing a decision-making rule for consumers a distinction is made between the *total utility* derived from consuming a good and the *marginal utility* derived from consuming one more unit of the good. As the term suggests, for a single good or service, *total utility refers to the utility received from all units of the good or service consumed.* However, for decision-making purposes, it is important to pay attention to the marginal utility of consuming one more unit of the good. *Marginal utility is the additional utility the consumer receives from consuming one more unit of the good or service.*

To illustrate the notions of total and marginal utility and the relationship between the two measures, consider Nadine's consumption of compact discs (CDs). The number of CDs that Nadine might consume (per month) is listed in column (A) of Table 7.3. Column (B) contains the total utility that Nadine derives from consuming a given quantity of CDs.

Table 7.3

Nadine's Utility from Compact Disc Consumption

(A) Number of CDs (per month)	(B) Total Utility (in units of utility)	(C) Marginal Utility (in units of utility)
0	0	–
1	250	250
2	290	40
3	320	30
4	345	25
5	365	20
6	380	15
7	390	10

Column (C) indicates the marginal utility derived from consuming each additional CD. Notice that utility is measured in units. Only Nadine knows the significance of a unit of utility. All we know for sure is that more units (more CDs) are associated with greater total utility. The total utility column indicates that no utility is obtained when no CDs are consumed and that the total utility from CD consumption increases as the number of CDs purchased each week increases. When Nadine buys six CDs per month, she gets 380 units of utility.

The marginal utility column (C) tells us the addition to total utility associated with the consumption of each additional CD. Notice that the marginal utility of any specific level of CD consumption is equal to the difference in total utility between that level and the previous one. For example, the marginal utility of the fourth CD is 25 units, which is the difference between a total utility of 345 units (for four CDs) and 320 units (for three CDs). In general, marginal utility is the addition to total utility derived from consuming one more unit of a good.

Having developed an understanding of the concept of marginal utility, we can now examine the rule consumers follow to maximize the total amount of utility gained from consumption of a combination of goods and services. However, to do this, we need to be able to directly compare the consumer's gains from consumption with the opportunity cost of consumption. For most transactions in a market economy, the opportunity costs of consumption are measured in terms of market prices.

Marginal Utility versus Price

Thus far, we have concentrated on the total and marginal utility of a single good. However, consumers purchase many different goods. Also, consumers face a budget constraint that limits the amount of money the consumer can spend per time period. How do consumers decide how much they will buy to maximize their utility from the consumption of many different goods?

To achieve maximum utility from limited income, consumers compare the ratio of marginal utility (MU) to price (P) across all goods – that is, they compare the ratio MU/P for each good or service they buy. The ratio MU/P measures the additional utility per additional dollar spent on the good in question. In the simple case in which an individual is consuming only two goods, A and B, the factors that must be considered are the individual's total income (or money available to spend), the prices of the two goods, and the marginal utility function for each good. An individual can consume more of each good so long as the total amount spent on the two goods is no greater than the individual's total income.

To see how an individual maximizes utility, consider the following example. Nadine has $240 that she can spend each month, and the only two goods that she purchases are bungee jumps and CDs. Nadine's problem is deciding how to allocate her income between bungee jumps, priced at $60 per unit, and CDs, priced at $10 per unit, in such a way that her total utility from consuming bungee jumps and CDs is maximized. Table 7.4 contains information on the total utility (TU), marginal utility (MU), and marginal utility per dollar spent (MU/P) for each unit of bungee jumps and CDs purchased.

Which combination of goods should Nadine purchase? To answer this question, note that MU/P is 10 for the first CD, and MU/P is 1.5 for the first jump. Hence, Nadine will buy the first CD at a cost of $10 because, per dollar spent, she gains more utility from the CD. In deciding on how to spend the remaining $230 ($240 − $10) the next choice is between the first jump, for which MU/P is 1.5, and the second CD, for which MU/P is 4. Nadine gains more marginal utility per dollar spent on the second CD than the first jump, and therefore she will buy a second CD. The same is true when comparing the third, fourth, and fifth CDs to the first jump. In comparing the first jump to the sixth CD,

Table 7.4

Nadine's Utility from the Consumption of Bungee Jumps and Compact Discs

	Bungee Jumps				CDs		
Number of units	TU_{BJ}	MU_{BJ}	MU_{BJ}/P_{BJ}	Number of units	TU_{CD}	MU_{CD}	MU_{CD}/P_{CD}
0	0	–	–	0	0	–	–
1	90	90	1.5	1	250	250	10
2	180	90	1.5	2	290	40	4
3	270	90	1.5	3	320	30	3
4	360	90	1.5	4	345	25	2.5
5	450	90	1.5	5	365	20	2
6	540	90	1.5	6	380	15	1.5
7	630	90	1.5	7	390	10	1
8	720	90	1.5	8	390	0	0

Per-unit price of jumps = $60

Per-unit price of CDs = $10

however, the jump now yields an equivalent amount of marginal utility per dollar spent (1.5 = 1.5). Because Nadine has $190 left ($240 − $10 − $10 − $10 − $10 − $10) she can buy the first jump and the sixth CD. She will then have $120 left ($240 − $10 − $10 − $10 − $10 − $10 − $60 − $10).

In deciding which additional goods to buy, Nadine will continue to compare MU/P for the next unit of each good. Nadine's utility-maximizing combination of bungee jumps and CDs is three jumps and six CDs. With this combination, MU/P for the third jump is equal to 1.5, which is, in turn, equal to MU/P for the sixth CD. Nadine has exhausted her income since (3 × $60) + (6 × $10) = $240. In addition, the total utility associated with this combination is 650. There is no other combination that Nadine can afford that will yield greater total utility from the consumption of bungee jumps and CDs.

As the preceding example suggests, in the case of two goods an individual maximizes utility by purchasing the combination of goods A and B such that:

$$\frac{MU_A}{P_A} = \frac{MU_B}{P_B}$$

and all income is spent. In words, the marginal utility of the last dollar spent on good A is equal to the marginal utility of the last dollar spent on good B. Rearranging terms yields

$$\frac{MU_A}{MU_B} = \frac{P_A}{P_B}.$$

This is the utility-maximizing condition derived in the section on indifference curves analysis and is equivalent to the expression for the utility-maximizing condition derived earlier in the chapter.

Using the approach described here, consumers rank all purchases based on the marginal benefit–marginal cost ratio, MU/P. (Remember that the benefits are subjectively determined by the consumer.) They then make their purchases based on this ranking, always spending on the good whose next unit has the highest marginal benefit–marginal cost ratio. The ratio gives the consumer a measure of the benefits per dollar of expenditure. Consumers seek the greatest possible gain from each dollar spent. They therefore buy goods and services in a manner that keeps these ratios equal at the margin across all goods and services.

Deriving the Demand Curve

The utility-maximizing condition is used to determine how much of each good a person will consume given a set of prices and a fixed amount of income. The question that arises now is, What if prices change? We can now use this rule to derive the demand curve for a particular good.

Referring again to Nadine's decision problem, assume that the per-unit price of bungee jumping falls from $60 to $30. The effect of this decrease in price is illustrated in

Table 7.5

The Effect of a Change in Price on Nadine's Utility from the Consumption of Bungee Jumps and Compact Discs

Number of units	TU_{BJ}	MU_{BJ}	MU_{BJ}/P_{BJ}	Number of units	TU_{CD}	MU_{CD}	MU_{CD}/P_{CD}
0	0	–	–	0	0	–	–
1	90	90	3	1	250	250	25
2	180	90	3	2	290	40	4
3	270	90	3	3	320	30	3
4	360	90	3	4	345	25	2.5
5	450	90	3	5	365	20	2
6	540	90	3	6	380	15	1.5
7	630	90	3	7	390	10	1
8	720	90	3	8	390	0	0

Per-unit price of jumps = $30

Per-unit price of CDs = $10

Table 7.5. Table 7.5 is the same as Table 7.4, with the exception that the fourth column, labeled MU_{BJ}/P_{BJ} has now changed, reflecting the change in the price of jumps. After the price change, the ratio MU_{BJ}/P_{BJ} is now larger for each jump, as indicated in Table 7.5. Using the utility-maximizing condition, Nadine will now purchase seven jumps and three CDs. With this combination, the marginal utility per last dollar spent on jumps is equal to the marginal utility per last dollar spent on CDs, and Nadine's income is exhausted ($7 \times \$30 + 3 \times \$10 = \$240$). Note that, as a result of the decrease in the price of jumps, the number of jumps Nadine purchased has increased.[6]

Nadine's adjustment to the change in the price of jumps is illustrated graphically in Figure 7.10. When the price of jumps was $60 per unit, Nadine purchased three jumps. This price-quantity combination is associated with point A in Figure 7.10. After the price decrease, from $60 to $30, the quantity demanded of jumps increased from three to seven. Nadine moved from point A to point B. Connecting points A and B yields a downward-sloping curve that is, in effect, Nadine's demand curve for bungee jumping. It has been constructed by holding income and the prices of other goods constant and allowing only the quantity demanded to change as prices vary. Using the utility-maximizing condition, we have shown that the demand curve is downward sloping.

Figure 7.10

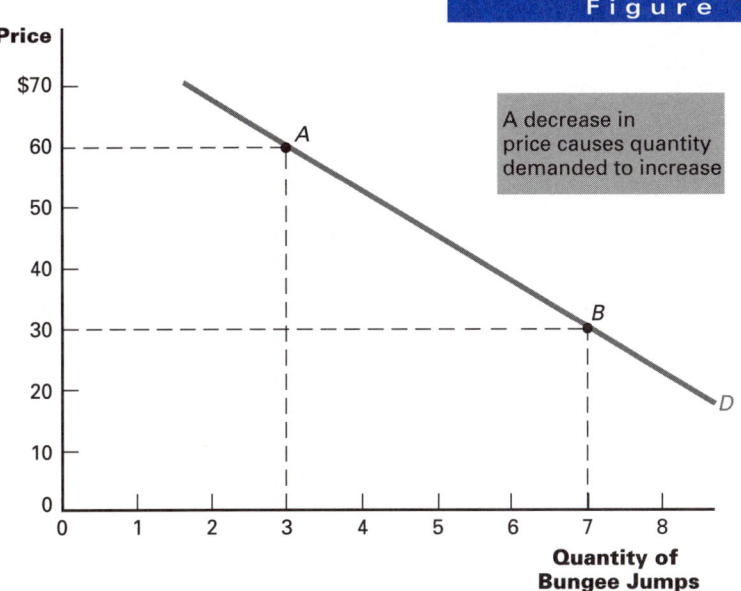

A decrease in price causes quantity demanded to increase

Utility Maximization and the Law of Demand

If a consumer is initially maximizing her utility and then the price of a good decreases, the ratio MU/P is no longer equal across all goods. To once again maximize her utility, the consumer will purchase additional units of the good whose price has decreased. All else constant, a decrease in price has caused an increase in quantity demanded; the demand curve is downward sloping.

End Notes

[1] Battalio, *et al.*, 1973, "A Test of Consumer Demand Theory Using Observations of Individual Purchases," *Western Economic Journal*, Vol. 11: 411–28.

[2] In a similar manner, we could talk about the MRS of CDs for bungee jumps.

[3] "The Luxury Goods Trade: Upmarket Philosophy," *The Economist*, December 26, 1992-January 8, 1993, pp. 95–8.

[4] Because a demand curve incorporates transactions costs, any change in transactions costs will change the cost of consumption and therefore the demand for the product. An increase in transactions costs reduces the gain from consumption and shifts the demand curve to the left. A decrease in such costs shifts the demand curve to the right.

[5] This section is included for those interested in a more technical treatment of the theory of utility maximization. It can be omitted without any loss of continuity.

[6] It is also worth noting that the demand for CDs has decreased, even though the price of CDs has not changed. This is explained by the fact that CDs and bungee jumps are both sources of entertainment for Nadine. Hence they are substitutes. Because the price of a substitute (bungee jumps) has fallen, the demand for CDs has decreased – the demand curve for CDs has shifted left – as was described in Chapter 3.

Entrepreneurial Behavior

Overview

Many people share a common dream–they want to become their own boss. What they really want is to start and operate their own business. This fact is attested to by the large number of new businesses started each year (and most of which fail shortly thereafter). Success stories such as those of Henry Ford, Sam Walton, and Steve Jobs and Steve Wozniak (who started Apple Computers) have inspired countless other individuals to take on the challenge of organizing and operating a business. In some cases, the business consists of a single or a few individuals. In other cases, the business might grow into a large corporation, as Apple Computer did in the 1980s.

Like consumers, firms differ in many dimensions. They vary in size, ranging from conglomerates with worldwide operations and thousands of employees to small one-person operations in local communities. They employ different production technologies and use different kinds of resources. They may produce basic commodities such as sand, lumber, corn, or oil, or they may produce exotic and unique products: Rolls-Royces, Cray computers, nuclear power plants, artificial hearts. However, just as we assume that all consumers have a common objective–utility maximization–we assume there is an element common to all firms: They are all in business to make a profit.

In the previous chapter we saw that consumers choose the goods and services they consume by weighing the benefits of consumption against the costs, measured by market prices. In this chapter, we begin an equally close look at economic behavior on the supply side of the market: the decision making of firms. To analyze the behavior of the broad range of firms that exist, we need a means of categorizing firms. Consequently, in this chapter we explore alternative methods of categorizing firms. Depending on how firms are categorized, we can say more or less about how they behave when they attempt to maximize the amount of profit they earn. We conclude the chapter by examining the profitability of U.S. businesses in the recent past.

Learning Objectives

After reading and studying this chapter, you will be able to:

1. Describe three approaches that can be used to categorize the range of firms that operate in the U.S. economy

2. Explain the advantages and disadvantages of the three legal forms of business organization

CHAPTER 8

3. Identify the major characteristics that distinguish the different types of market structures that exist in the economy

4. Describe the behavior of profits earned by U.S. businesses over the past two decades

ECONOMIC SENSE?

Inventing Products for Consumers Who Don't Exist

All around the world, a strange phenomenon is taking place. Seemingly intelligent people are dreaming about products that do not exist, which they intend to produce with unknown techniques and sell in nonexistent markets to consumers who have expressed no demand for them. Say all you want about "hard-headed businessmen," these folks sound crazy. Yet they are drawing many economies into the modern world and are pushing the developed economies into previously undreamed-of areas. Does it make economic sense?

Economists are good at explaining how firms should organize the production of existing products sold in well-developed markets. When it comes to explaining how new goods are invented and sold in newly created markets, we're not so adept. Yet, the overwhelming importance of creativity and inventiveness becomes more and more obvious. An economic revolution has taken place in the last two or three decades, and it is showing no signs of letting up. The creators of the revolution are the entrepreneurs who dream about what isn't and cause it to become.

Standard microeconomic theory pays relatively little attention to the creation of information, production processes, and markets. It pays a lot of attention to how consumers maximize benefits by choosing among known alternatives and how firms maximize profits by efficiently utilizing resources to produce goods for which markets already exist. However, goods, production techniques, and markets must be created by someone. Entrepreneurs are the motivating force in dynamic economies. They envision products that will meet needs, figure out how to produce them, then creatively market the products, generating the demand for them as they go.

Consider the goods you routinely use or hear about that would have been unimaginable in 1960:

The Entrepreneurial Challenge

As the first step in our analysis of the behavior of firms we need to address the question, Why do firms exist? In brief, firms facilitate the efficient allocation and organization of productive resources. We have already seen how specialization can enable individuals to consume more output than they could otherwise. Firms take advantage of the benefits of specialization by bringing together the inputs needed to produce a particular product. Within the firm, inputs such as capital and labor have specialized functions, and each input contributes to the production of the firm's output. The problem for the firm is deciding the types and quantities of inputs it should purchase to achieve its objectives.

Generally speaking, the decision making of firms is quite like that of consumers. In both cases, the decision maker chooses among available alternatives to maximize well-being: Consumers maximize utility, firms maximize profit. This decision process requires that the decision maker–consumer or producer–evaluate the costs and benefits of each alternative. However, many supply decisions have an element of *riskiness* associated with them that is absent from most consumption decisions.

A business firm attempts to make a profit by purchasing resources, combining them in a way that yields a consumer good or service, and then selling the good or service at a price that is at least as great as the cost of production. The real problem for the firm is that there is never any guarantee that consumers will pay a high-enough price and buy enough

multifunction calculators that cost almost nothing; air bags that prevent you from putting your face through the windshield in an auto accident; genetic testing that can pinpoint the likelihood of genetically transmitted diseases; laser surgery that can correct near-sightedness; microwave ovens that cook a hot dog in 38 seconds; electronic transmitters that unlock car doors from a distance; personal computers that hold entire encyclopedias on CD-ROM files. The list could go on indefinitely. Someone envisioned each of these incredible goods or services, persuaded investors to fund research on them, and marketed them to a public that was previously unaware of its unmet needs.

Such creativity appears in "low-tech" markets as well. The managers of a newly privatized watch factory in Russia turned an outmoded Soviet production facility into a profitable business by thinking creatively about marketing. They produce watches based on 24-hour periods for sale in Siberia, where the long, dark winter makes it difficult to tell day from night. They produce a nautical watch with a display that makes it easy for sailors to tell when their eight-hour shifts end. Their technology may be old, but their market vision is keen, and the factory prospers.[1]

Peasants migrate from the countryside to Lima, Peru and establish "informal" markets of many kinds. Unable to navigate the byzantine regulations choking the officially recognized market economy, these peasants use their numbers to slowly take over parts of the city, turning them into centers of market activity. Where once economic stagnation and government corruption were the rule, a vibrant market economy has emerged. Creative entrepreneurs have met unsatisfied demands and have profited by doing so.[2]

Entrepreneurship involves not only creativity; it also entails a willingness to take risks. No one is ever certain, before the fact, whether the new technology will really work. No one knows whether consumers will buy an entirely new product or respond to a new marketing approach. For every successful product or market innovation, many innovations fail. That's what makes investing in the stock market so uncertain. Until a product is actually produced and marketed, we can only guess what its reception will be. Thus, we can only guess what the value of the companies listed on the stock exchange will be in future years.

Does it make sense to go out on a limb by promoting new technologies, new products, and new marketing techniques? Absolutely. Creativity pays — but not every time.

---

units of the good for the firm to earn a profit. The firm must make an educated guess about the expected demand for the product.

In addition, firms must incur costs before they earn revenues. Production takes time. Resources must be purchased and production facilities established before there is output to sell to consumers. The producer must be able to finance production during the time between the purchase of inputs and the sale of outputs. The firm incurs debts before it has a chance to sell its product and generate revenue. A firm's success is uncertain. Getting into business to sell a product is risky. One can win big or lose big!

It is this aspect of supply that makes entrepreneurship important. An **entrepreneur** is a person who organizes, manages, and assumes the risks of a business enterprise. In a market economy characterized by competition and resource mobility, this riskiness persists over time. Even an established and very profitable firm can become unprofitable and fail if its owners or managers do not continue to study consumer wants, seek product improvements or new products, look for new production technologies, and respond to changes in market conditions. All of these decisions involve some uncertainty and risk. Business success requires the continued willingness to assume risks.

Clearly, understanding how a firm's decision-making process works requires an understanding of many interrelated issues such as how output is produced, how costs are determined, and how much revenue the firm can expect to earn from a particular level of

Entrepreneur:
A person who organizes, manages, and assumes the risks of a business enterprise.

output. However, before we can begin to address these specific questions, we need to group firms together into broad categories to simplify our analysis.

Section Recap

Like consumers, firms attempt to maximize their well-being, which is measured by profits. However, unlike most consumption decisions, production decisions involve an element of risk. Entrepreneurs assume the risks of a business enterprise.

Ways to Categorize Firms

Because we have such a rich diversity of firms in an economy, we can categorize them in a number of ways. In this section, we identify three different ways we can group firms.

Industries

Industry:
A grouping of firms that produce a similar product

Firms can be grouped according to the products they produce. These groupings are called **industries**. When we speak of the auto industry, the construction industry, the pharmaceutical industry, or the wholesale trade industry, we are referring to those firms that produce similar products: automobiles and trucks, residential and commercial buildings, drugs, or the distribution of goods from manufacturers to retailers. These industry groupings can be quite general, such as the manufacturing industry, or very specific, such as the lumber and wood products industry. Table 8.1 displays a list of general industry categories taken from an industry classification scheme adopted by the federal government. The major industry categories comprise more detailed industry categories, listed under each of the major categories.

Firms within each of the industry categories are similar in many respects. They sell products in the same or related markets and thus face similar market conditions–changes in demand, new technological developments, competition from other sectors, or cost pressures. Within an industry, firms use generally similar production processes. The relative size of these industries reflects patterns of consumer tastes, the nature of society's resource endowment, the level of economic development, and other characteristics of the economy. For example, measured by levels of employment, the agricultural sector in the United States has been shrinking since the turn of the century, the manufacturing sector has stabilized at a level achieved in the 1960s, and the service and government sectors have grown considerably.

Legal Structure

Business firms also can be categorized according to one of three basic legal structures: sole proprietorship, partnership, and corporation. A firm's legal structure affects how much control its owners have over the business, the firm's access to financial resources, and the liability (legal responsibility) of the owners for the financial obligations of the firm. The characteristics of each legal form of business are discussed in turn.

Sole proprietorship:
A business that is owned by a single person

Sole Proprietorship The simplest form of business organization is one that is owned and operated by a single individual; thus it is called a **sole proprietorship**. The owners of these businesses are self-employed. They have complete control over all business

Table 8.1

The Standard Industrial Classification of Businesses

Agriculture, Forestry, and Fishing
  Agricultural production - crops
  Agricultural production - livestock
  Agricultural services
  Forestry
  Fishing, hunting and trapping

Mining
  Metal mining
  Coal mining
  Oil and gas extraction
  Nonmetallic minerals, excluding fuels

Construction
  General building contractors
  Heavy construction, excluding buildings
  Special trade contractors

Manufacturing
  Food and kindred products
  Tobacco products
  Textile mill products
  Apparel and other textile products
  Lumber and wood products
  Furniture and fixtures
  Paper and allied products
  Printing and publishing
  Chemicals and allied products
  Petroleum and coal products
  Rubber and miscellaneous plastics products
  Leather and leather products
  Stone, clay, and glass products
  Primary metal industries
  Fabricated metal products
  Industrial machinery and equipment
  Electronic and other electric equipment
  Transportation equipment
  Instruments and related products
  Miscellaneous manufacturing industries

Transportation and Public Utilities
  Railroad transportation
  Local and interurban passenger transit
  U.S. Postal Service
  Water transportation
  Transportation by air
  Pipelines, excluding natural gas
  Transportation services
  Communications
  Electric, gas, and sanitary services

Wholesale Trade
  Wholesale trade - durable goods
  Wholesale trade - nondurable goods

Retail Trade
  Building materials and garden supplies
  General merchandise stores
  Food stores
  Automotive dealers and service stations
  Apparel and accessory stores
  Furniture and home furnishings stores
  Eating and drinking places
  Miscellaneous retail

Finance, Insurance, and Real Estate
  Depository institutions
  Nondepository institutions
  Security and commodity brokers
  Insurance carriers
  Insurance agents, brokers, and service
  Real estate
  Holding and other investment offices

Services
  Hotels and other lodging places
  Personal services
  Business services
  Auto repair, services, and parking
  Miscellaneous repair services

(Continued on next page)

Table 8.1 Continued

The Standard Industrial Classification of Businesses (Continued)

Services (Continued)	Public Administration
Motion pictures	Executive, legislative, and general
Amusement and recreation services	Justice, public order, and safety
Health services	Finance, taxation, and monetary
Legal services	Administration of human resources
Educational services	Environmental quality and housing
Social services	Administration of economic programs
Museum, botanical, zoological gardens	National security and international affairs
Membership organizations	
Engineering and management services	
Private households	
Services, not elsewhere classified	

Source: United States, Office of Management and Budget, *Standard Industrial Classification Manual,* 1987.

decisions and are personally responsible for all obligations assumed by the business. In a very real sense, the owner is the business. The business itself is not recognized as a legal entity separate from the owner. The owner is legally responsible for contracts entered into between the firm and other individuals or businesses. When legal action is taken against the firm, it is the owner who is sued.

Sole proprietorships are numerous, but they tend to be small. Business situations in which we frequently encounter sole proprietorships include small retail operations such as ice cream stores and cleaning establishments, general contractors and builders, and real estate agents. As shown in Table 8.2, in 1990, there were more than 14.7 million nonfarm sole proprietorships in existence. About 80 percent of them had annual sales of less than $50,000, and only 1.5 percent had sales in excess of $500,000 annually.

Sole proprietorships tend to be small for very good reasons. The sole proprietor, while enjoying the important advantage of being in complete control of the business, faces two severe limitations in this business form. First, the law makes no distinction between the owner and the business; the owner is personally liable for the financial obligations of the firm. This liability is unlimited; the owner's personal assets can be taken to satisfy the firm's creditors.

Financial capital:

The money firms acquire from lending institutions and individuals to finance production activities, including current production, expansion, product development, and so forth.

Second, proprietorships have limited access to the financial resources necessary for growth. It is costly for a firm to expand production or to develop new or improved products. These costs are incurred before the firm is able to sell the additional or new products. Thus, the firm must have access to financial resources, referred to as **financial capital**, to finance these activities. A sole proprietor's ability to raise financial capital to support growth of the business is limited. If the business is to remain a sole proprietorship, funds for research, development, and growth must be generated by the firm or borrowed. Borrowing opportunities are constrained by the characteristics of the business form; loans

Table 8.2

Number and Annual Sales of Firms by Legal Form of Business Organization, 1990

Legal Structure	Size of Firm by Annual Sales			
	Under $50,000	$50,000–$499,999	Over $500,000	Total
Number of Firms (1,000s)				
Nonfarm Sole Proprietors				
Number of firms	11,856	2,726	200	14,782
% of total	80.2	18.4	1.4	100
Partnerships				
Number of firms	1,186	273	94	1,553
% of total	76.4	17.6	6.1	100
Corporations				
Number of firms	1,131	1,521	1,065	3,717
% of total	30.4	40.9	28.7	100
Annual Receipts ($billions)				
Nonfarm Sole Proprietors				
Receipts	$127	$387	$216	$731
% of total	17.4	52.9	29.5	100
Partnerships				
Receipts	$9	$67	$465	$541
% of total	1.7	12.4	85.9	100
Corporations				
Receipts	$14	$317	$10,583	$10,914
% of total	0.1	2.9	97.0	100

Source: U.S. Department of Commerce, Bureau of the Census, *Statistical Abstract of the United States*, 1994, Table 832.

are secured by the personal assets of the owner. In summary, sole proprietorships tend to be very small businesses that are owned and managed by one person. Owners of these firms have limited access to financial capital and bear all the risks – including legal liability – of doing business.

Partnership A **partnership** differs from a sole proprietorship in only one way: There are two or more joint owners of the business. Some of the more common examples of partnerships include many law and accounting firms, construction companies, consulting firms, and medical clinics. In a partnership, decision-making power is shared by the owners; each partner has the power to act for the partnership. Each partner is personally liable for the obligations of the firm, and the owners face unlimited liability for the firm's actions.

Because the assets of more than one person are available to secure loans, the partnership arrangement improves the firm's ability to raise financial capital for expansion of the business. However, the firm's decision making may be somewhat more complicated in a partnership

Partnership:
A business that is owned by two or more people. Each partner is personally liable for all of the firm's obligations.

than it is in a sole proprietorship because ownership is shared. Dissolution of a partnership can be difficult and costly. Partners must find other individuals who are willing to purchase the firm. If new owners cannot be found, the firm's assets must be sold off.

One variation on the partnership as a form of business is the *limited partnership*. Under this kind of partnership there are two kinds of partners: general and limited partners. General partners are just like the partners of a simple partnership: They have full control of the business and bear unlimited personal liability for the firm's actions. However, a limited partner has no management control or responsibility and bears only limited liability for the firm's actions. A limited partnership is a means for acquiring additional financial resources for the firm. The ownership rights of limited partners are determined by the financial investment they make in the partnership. Their risk is limited to the investment they have made in the firm. If the firm fails, the most they lose is the amount of their investment.

In 1990, there were about 1.55 million partnerships, 76 percent of which had annual sales of less than $50,000. About 6 percent of all partnerships had sales in excess of $500,000. Partnerships tend to be larger than proprietorships, in part because of better access to resources for growth and expansion. Nevertheless, most partnerships are relatively small firms, though somewhat larger than sole proprietorships.

Corporation:
A legal business entity that is owned by a group of individuals. The corporation can sue and be sued, but the liability of each owner is limited to the amount of money he or she has invested in the firm.

Corporation The **corporation** is itself a legal entity and therefore is quite different from a sole proprietorship or partnership. A corporation has the legal powers and rights of an individual. A corporation can enter into legally enforceable contracts with individuals or other corporations. A corporation can sue and be sued for its actions. However, its owners cannot be sued. Thus, the owners of a corporation face *limited liability* – they are liable only to the extent of their investment in the firm.

Corporations must be licensed by a state and are governed by a charter that describes the structure of the corporation and its principal activities. As a general rule, the owners of the corporation select a board of directors and a chairperson who are responsible for overseeing the operations of the corporation. The board usually employs managers to make the firm's decisions and manage the firm's day-to-day business activities. Consequently, the owners of the corporation have only indirect control of the firm..

The corporation is the dominant form of business organization in the United States. In 1990, there were about 3.7 million corporations, approximately 30 percent of which had annual sales of less than $50,000. Another 29 percent had sales in excess of $500,000. However, a glance at Table 8.2 reveals a clearer picture of the importance of corporations in the economy. If we arbitrarily consider all firms with sales in excess of $500,000 a year as large, then large firms account for only a small fraction (6.8 percent) of the total number of firms, but they account for 92.4 percent of annual sales. Furthermore, corporations alone account for 90 percent of total annual sales. Large corporations account for only 5.3 percent of all firms, but they account for 87 percent of annual sales. (These figures would be basically the same if we defined large as sales in excess of $1 million a year.) Large firms are a fact of life in the U.S. economy and other developed economies, and most large firms are corporations.

Financial Capital for the Corporation. An important advantage of the corporate form of business organization, as compared to sole proprietorships and partnerships, is the corporation's ability to obtain financial capital. A corporation can acquire the funds to support its growth and expansion from three sources: (1) the sale of ownership shares in the business, (2) its own profits, and (3) borrowing from financial institutions or individuals. The extent to which a corporation relies on each source depends on the relative cost of each funding source.

When a firm sells ownership shares of the company, it is said to sell **stock** in the company. The owners of the firm are then **stockholders**. Funds acquired through the sale of stock represent *equity capital* because the stockholders have an ownership stake in the company. Different kinds of stock exist, and each kind carries different ownership rights. The basic form of equity ownership is *common stock*. Common stockholders share in the control of the business and its profits and losses. However, they share in the control of the company only very indirectly, mainly by voting for or against the management team hired by the company and for or against very broad decisions or policies.

Shares of stock:
Certificates of ownership in a company. Stockholders are the owners of the firm.

Firms decide how much of the profits are returned to stockholders. These returned profits are called **dividends** and are paid per share of stock outstanding. Firms typically pay out only part of their profits as dividends. Those profits retained by the firm, called **retained earnings**, are reinvested in the firm and support activities such as research, product development, and expansion. This part of the firm's profits can be indirectly beneficial to stockholders. If reinvested profits increase the value of the firm, the price of the firm's shares of stock will rise. Shareholders may then sell their holdings at a higher price than they paid for them. Often, rapidly growing firms will pay no dividends, reinvesting all profits in the business. Shareholders gain only from the increasing value of the company as reflected in its stock price.

Dividends:
The amount of profit per share of stock outstanding that is paid to the firm's stockholders.

Retained earnings:
Profit that the firm reinvests in the business to support activities such as research, product development, and expansion.

Common stockholders share in the firm's losses, too. They receive their share of profits (their dividends) only after all the firm's creditors have been paid. If the firm fails, they lose their investment in the company; that, however, is the sole extent of their liability.

Firms also borrow financial capital. They typically borrow for short-term needs by obtaining loans from financial institutions, such as banks, thrift institutions, or insurance companies. Such loans are an important source of financial capital for proprietorships and partnerships. However, they are a relatively expensive source of funding. To reduce the cost of borrowing, corporations issue **bonds** to obtain most of their borrowed funds. A bond is a promissory note: The purchaser loans a fixed amount, called the principal, to the firm in return for its promise to pay the bondholder a fixed amount of interest each year and to repay the face amount of the note – the amount borrowed – at a specific time in the future. The length of time for which the bond is issued is called its **maturity**. The bond *matures* after this period of time has elapsed. At the date of maturity the company pays back the principal amount of the bond. Most of this borrowing is long term, and bonds are often issued for ten to thirty years. A bond is a contract between the issuing corporation and the bondholder. If the interest is not paid on time, the bondholder can legally force the firm to make the payment, even if the firm must liquidate its assets to do so.

Bond:
A note that promises to pay its holder a specified amount of interest plus the face amount of the bond at a specified point in the future.

Maturity:
The length of time for which a bond is issued.

When someone buys a share of common stock in a corporation, he or she purchases an ownership share for an indefinite period of time. When someone buys a thirty-year corporate bond, the company has thirty years before it must repay the principal. What if both of these individuals wanted to liquidate their respective investments after two years? The corporation would not buy the stock back, nor would it redeem the bond before the maturity date (except under exceptional circumstances). Each investor would have to find another individual willing to buy the stock or bond at an acceptable price.

When a corporation issues new shares of stock or new bonds, their prices are established in the *primary market* — the market for new stocks and bonds — and are determined by the willingness of investors to buy the new stock or bonds. Stocks and bonds are generally referred to as **securities**. **Securities markets** are *secondary markets* in which existing shares of stock or bonds are bought or sold. It is in these markets that the price of an existing share of stock or a bond is determined by the market forces of supply and demand. The existence of these markets allows corporations to issue new shares of stock and new bonds at higher prices because potential investors know they can sell their investments at any time.

In summary, corporations constitute the dominant legal form of business structure in the United States. Corporations have the advantage of being able to raise large amounts of financial capital through the sale of stocks and bonds. Owners of corporations enjoy limited liability; however, they have only indirect control over the decisions made by the firm.

Market Structure

A third approach to categorizing firms in the economy is based on the type of market in which a firm operates. **Market structure** (or *industry structure*) refers to the characteristics of output markets that influence the behavior of firms. These characteristics include the number of firms in the market, the size of the firms, and the variety of products produced by the firms. This chapter and the several that follow examine the economic behavior of firms, focusing on how their decision making and actions are influenced by these various characteristics.

These characteristics affect firm behavior because they determine the *degree of competition* in a market. If we think of the degree of competition as measured on a continuum, at one end we would have very competitive industries. A competitive industry is typically characterized by many small firms that produce a very similar product (where small is defined as share of the market output accounted for by each firm). Agriculture and retail trade are two broadly defined industries characterized by strong competition.

At the other extreme are industries comprised of only one firm. These industries are called *monopolies*. It is difficult to imagine a pure monopoly industry. Most industries have at least a few competing firms, and firms that produce similar, but not identical, products can be considered competitors for these so-called monopolies. One example of a monopoly industry is cable TV. At present, there is only one supplier of the service — cable TV — in a given geographic region. Other examples of monopoly involve *regulated monopolies*. A regulated monopoly is a single firm that is given the legal right to be the only producer

Security:
The physical evidence of ownership of debt, such as a stock certificate or promissory note.

Securities markets:
Secondary markets in which existing shares of stock or bonds are bought and sold.

Market structure:
The caracteristics of output markets including the number of firms in the market, the size of the firms, and the variety of products produced by firms, that influence the behavior of firms.

in an industry (usually in a limited geographic region). These firms are typically public utilities, such as electric power or natural gas companies.

Between the two extremes of competition and monopoly are all kinds of industries with varying degrees of competition. The extent of competition influences the pricing, output, and resource-utilization decisions of firms. Chapters 11 through 13 discuss the impact of market structure on the behavior of firms in much more detail. We introduce the notion of market structure now because it is an important way to categorize firms. As the concepts presented in the next few chapters are developed, market structure will take on even more importance as a factor in understanding the behavior of firms and the public regulation of the actions of firms.

Firms can be categorized according to the industry in which they operate, their legal structure – proprietorship, partnership, or corporation – or on the basis of the type of market structure in which they operate. Of these, market structure focuses on the characteristics of output markets that influence the pricing and output behavior of firms, and hence is the basis for analyzing the economic decisions firms make.

The Firm's Objective: Profit

We have just detailed several ways to classify differences in firms: different products, different legal forms of organization, and varying degrees of competition. Although firms differ in various ways, they *all* have one thing in common: They are in business to make a **profit**. Profit is the incentive for production. *In our analysis of the behavior of firms, we assume that the firm's objective is to maximize profits.*

Profit:
The difference between total revenue and total cost.

Although profit plays a central role in the behavior of firms, it can be a confusing concept. As we will see in Chapter 10, the economist's definition of profit differs from the approach used by accountants. At this point, it is sufficient to note that while profit is generally defined as the difference between total revenues and total costs, the definition of costs varies depending on one's perspective.

Profitability of American Business

Since the accounting definition of profit is the only widely available, systematic measure of profits, we will use this profit measure to describe the size and variation of profit levels in the U.S. economy. In addition, we will restrict our discussion to profits earned by corporations. This focus is not only convenient in terms of the profit data available, but it is also a relatively accurate depiction of the size of all profits since, as we have already noted, corporations account for about 90 percent of all business sales in the United States.

National income:
The total annual income paid to all owners of resources. It is the sum of all wages, rent, interest, and profit.

Aggregate Profits   The most useful way to describe profits is in relative terms. In 1994, corporate profits were $556 billion.[3] It is difficult to assess this profit level unless we have a benchmark against which to compare it. **National income** is the total annual income paid to all owners of resources. Comparing corporate profits to national income tells us that in 1994, pre-tax profits were 10.1 percent of national income. By comparison, the largest component of national income is compensation of employees (wages, salaries, and fringe benefits). In 1994, employee compensation was 73.2 percent of national income.[4] Table 8.3 shows pre-tax profits as a share of national income for the years 1961 to 1994. On average, pre-tax profits have amounted to about 9.6 percent of national income during this period.

Two other kinds of profit measures are given in Table 8.3 as well. After-tax profits are calculated as a share of stockholder equity (the aggregate value of ownership shares), and as a share of annual sales. By comparing after-tax profits to stockholder equity we get a crude measure of the annual return on a dollar invested in the company. The profits-to-sales ratio is a measure of the after-tax profit earned per dollar of revenue earned by the firm. After-tax corporate profits averaged about 10.6 percent of stockholder equity and about 4 percent of sales during this period.

Variations in Profit Levels While the aggregate value of profits remains a fairly stable share of national income over time, profit levels vary by industry, and industry profits fluctuate widely from year to year. Annual profits are reported for several manufacturing industries for selected years in Table 8.4. The variation in profits across industries and years is evident. For the entire manufacturing sector, profits increased by about 15 percent

Table 8.3

Corporate Profits in the United States: 1961–94

Year	Profits as % of of National Income[1]	Profits as % of Stockholder Equity[2]	Profits as % of Annual Sales[2]
1961-65	13.0	10.7	4.9
1966-70	11.7	11.6	4.9
1971-75	9.8	11.9	4.6
1976-80	9.9	14.7	5.3
1981-85	7.8	11.2	4.1
1986-90	8.6	12.5	4.7
1990	8.5	10.7	4.0
1991	8.5	6.3	2.4
1992	8.4	2.2	0.8
1993	9.5	8.1	2.8
1994	10.1[3]	16.4[3]	5.6[3]

[1] Pre-tax, with inventory valuation adjustment and capital consumption allowance.

[2] After taxes, manufacturing firms only.

[3] Average through first three quarters of 1994.

Source: Economic Report of the President, 1995, Tables B-24 and B-94.

Table 8.4

Corporate Profits: Selected Years and Manufacturing Industries (Billions of Dollars)

Manufacturing Industry	1980	1981	1990	1991	1994[1]
All Manufacturing	75.8	87.4	109.1	90.1	143.3
Durable Goods					
Total	17.9	18.1	39.2	30.3	70.3
Primary Metal Industries	2.6	3.0	3.3	1.1	0.6
Fabricated Metal Products	4.3	4.4	6.1	5.3	9.0
Industrial Machinery and Equipment	7.5	8.2	9.6	4.3	7.9
Electronic and other Electrical Equipment	5.0	4.9	7.9	9.2	21.4
Motor Vehicles and Equipment	−4.3	0.2	−2.2	−5.6	8.8
Other	2.8	−2.7	14.6	16.0	22.6
Non-durable Goods					
Total	57.8	69.3	69.9	59.8	73.0
Food and Kindred Products	6.0	9.0	14.0	17.7	20.3
Chemicals & Allied Products	5.5	7.6	16.2	15.5	18.4
Petroleum and Coal Products	33.6	38.6	17.3	5.0	6.6
Other	12.9	14.2	22.5	21.6	27.8

[1] Data for 1994 are seasonally adjusted estimate of annual profits based on third quarter data.

Source: Economic Report of the President, 1995, Table B-92.

between 1980 and 1981; at the same time miscellaneous durable goods industries as a group went from positive profits to a loss. Large differences also are evident in the change in profits across industries. The automobile industry went from a net loss to positive profits, while fabricated metal products profits rose by only 2.3 percent. Between 1980 and 1981, profits generally increased. Profits generally decreased between 1990 and 1991 and then once again increased between 1991 and 1994. Again, there was wide variation in the change across industry categories. Profit levels are volatile because profit is a relatively small residual; it is the difference between revenues and costs, and on average is only about 4 percent of revenues. *Thus, small changes in revenues or costs can cause large relative changes in profits.*

Section Recap

Economists assume that the firm's primary objective is to maximize profits. As a percentage of national income, corporate profits vary from year to year, but have averaged about 9.6 percent over the past 30 years. Profits also vary considerably across industries, and within industries over time.

Why the DISAGREEMENT?

Taxing
Corporate Profits

Over the past two decades, the federal government's annual deficits have been large. Consequently, its total debt (the net accumulation of deficits over time) has grown dramatically. The ballooning debt has met with increasing criticism and demands that the government's books be balanced. There are two ways to accomplish this task: cut government spending or increase taxes. The latter option has raised a number of issues, not the least of which is who should be taxed. Interestingly, during the budget negotiations in 1995, many members of the Congress, as well as President Clinton, were calling for a tax *decrease* for many Americans at the same time that they were proposing ways to decrease, and eventually eliminate, the federal deficit.

An especially contentious issue is the way the U.S. tax code treats corporate earnings. Many individual taxpayers believe that the corporate profits tax is too low and that there are too many tax "loopholes" for corporations. Stories about corporations that avoid paying any taxes in a particular year invariably produce a surge of public resentment and demands that Congress alter the tax code to ensure that corporations pay their "fair share" of taxes. However, some observers, including many economists, have suggested that rather than increasing the corporate tax rate, the tax on corporate profits should be reduced or eliminated. Why the disagreement?

It is easy to understand the position of the average tax-paying citizen. The taxable portion of personal income is taxed at rates ranging from 15 percent to 39.6 percent, depending on the individual's total income. In 1994, personal income taxes accounted for 43 percent of the federal government's income. In contrast, corporation taxes accounted for only 11 percent of the government's total revenues. However, the average household income was approximately $39,000, while many corporations earned profits in the hundreds of millions of dollars. From the individual's perspective it would appear

Summary

This chapter provides an introduction to the behavior of decision makers on the supply side of the market and a broad description of the business sector in the United States. The three legal forms of business are **sole proprietorships, partnerships**, and **corporations**. The first two forms are simple organizational arrangements that make it easy for anyone to start a business. For legal purposes the owners and the business are one and the same entity. Owners of these businesses have strong management control but face unlimited liability as well as serious limits in financing business growth.

The corporation is by far the dominant form of business, accounting for almost 90 percent of all business sales. Corporations are separate legal entities, limiting the owners' liability. The corporation has a range of options for raising capital, including the sale of common stock, the issuance of bonds, and borrowing from financial institutions.

Market structure refers to characteristics of output markets that influence the behavior of firms through their impact on the degree of competition the firm faces. Industries with many small firms tend to be very competitive, while industries with only a few firms tend to be less competitive. When the industry is composed of only one firm, called a **monopoly**, the firm faces little competition.

that corporations are in a much better position to pay taxes than are most individual households.

One of the main arguments for reducing or eliminating the amount of taxes paid by corporations is based on the issue of double taxation. Under the current tax system, the net income of a corporation is taxed at the applicable corporate profits tax rate. However, the net income is then distributed to the corporation s shareholders as dividends or kept by the corporation in the form of retained earnings. Retained earnings are used for such things as plant expansions, acquisition of other businesses, and so forth. According to current tax laws, however, profits that are distributed to shareholders in the form of dividends are considered personal income. They are taxed a second time, this time at the marginal tax rate to which the individual is subject. In effect, these corporate profits are taxed twice.

Stockholders consider this to be unfair. In effect, they are paying taxes twice on the same income – once in their role as owners of the firm and a second time in their role as individuals who are paid dividends on their investment.

In addition to the question of fairness, double taxation of corporate profits also affects the incentives for people to invest in corporations and corporations' incentives to pursue profitable opportunities. If individuals believe that the net return on their investment in a corporation is reduced by the corporate profits tax, they may seek alternative investments that are not as closely tied to production and economic growth. To the extent that double taxation reduces the demand for stocks, stock prices and therefore the amount of money firms can raise by issuing additional shares will be lower as well. This may, in turn, create an increased

incentive for corporations to borrow needed funds from banks and other lending institutions rather than raise needed cash through the sale of additional stock. The increased demand for loans puts additional upward pressure on interest rates, making borrowing costlier for everyone. At the same time, corporations may spend an inordinate amount of time and resources on ways to reduce the appearance of profitability to minimize their tax burden.

There is little doubt that the corporate profits tax will remain a part of the tax structure for the foreseeable future. Congressional efforts to reduce or eliminate this tax would be tantamount to political suicide. However, there are some serious questions about the appropriateness of this type of tax and whether a better, more economically efficient approach could be developed.

Corporate profits vary considerably from year to year. On average, pre-tax corporate profits have amounted to about 9.6 percent of national income over the 1961-1994 time period. During that same time period, after-tax profits have amounted to about 10.6 percent of stockholder equity and 4 percent of annual sales.

Questions for Thought

Knowledge Questions

1. Explain the difference between a partnership and a corporation.

2. Explain the difference (to the firm) between common stock and corporate bonds.

3. Why is the stock market a secondary market?

4. What characteristics are considered in differentiating firms on the basis of market structure?

Application Questions

5. Suppose one firm controls all bauxite (an ore from which aluminum is made) in the world. Is this firm a monopolist? Explain.

6. Assume that the XYZ firm currently has 1,000,000 shares of common stock outstanding, and it has decided to issue an additional 50,000 shares of common stock. In the short run, what effect would this have on the average price of a share of XYZ's stock?

7. According to the data in Table 8.2, in 1990, less than 2 percent of nonfarm sole proprietorships had annual sales in excess of $500,000, while 29 percent of all corporations had sales in excess of $500,000. What characteristics of these two legal structures help to explain this difference.

Synthesis Questions

8. Assume that a firm is currently deciding whether to sell bonds or issue new shares of common stock to raise funds for a planned expansion of its production facilities. Which approach would you recommend to the firm? Why?

9. Assume that you have been offered the opportunity to invest in a new business and that you have a choice between forming a partnership and becoming a limited partner. Which option would you choose and why?

10. According to Table 8.2, in 1990 there were 14,782 nonfarm sole proprietorships versus 1,553 partnerships in the United States. Use the concept of transactions costs developed in Chapters 2 and 7 to explain why individuals might be more inclined to operate a sole proprietorship than form a partnership.

End Notes

[1] Anita Raghavan, "Profits? No, Please! A Russian Concern Finds Success a Bear," *The Wall Street Journal*, November 10, 1993, pp. A1, A9.

[2] The creation of the informal economy in Peru is detailed in Hernando de Soto, *The Other Path: The Invisible Revolution in the Third World*, New York: Harper & Row, 1989.

[3] *Economic Report of the President*, 1995, Table B-24.

[4] *Economic Report of the President*, 1995, Table B-25.

Production Costs

Overview

In early 1995 the managing director of Olivetti, an Italian information technology firm, announced that his company was undertaking a number of significant steps in response to declining profits. Among these was a 40 percent reduction in its workforce, including a large number of jobs described as "middle-management" positions. A number of other firms have also taken the corporate "downsizing" route in the 1990s, including General Motors, IBM, Boeing, and McDonnell-Douglas, to name a few. In the case of U.S. companies, it is especially noteworthy that this emphasis on downsizing came at a time when the economy was growing robustly and many firms were seeing profits increase. This suggested to some people that firms should be hiring additional employees, rather than laying people off. However, the behavior of these and other firms emphasizes the fact that minimizing costs is just as important as increasing revenues when it comes to the firm's primary objective – profit maximization.

Profit is measured as the difference between total revenue and total costs. The measurement of total revenue is fairly straightforward; it is the product of the number of units of output sold and the average price per unit of output. Measuring total costs, however, is a somewhat more complicated matter. When economists talk about total costs, they are referring to the *full opportunity costs* of production. As we will see momentarily, the full opportunity costs of production often include more than simply the expenses incurred in the purchase of productive inputs such as labor, capital and raw materials. The firm needs to take care to ensure that all of the costs incurred are considered when calculating the amount of profit earned. Identification of all of the firm's costs is also necessary to ensure that the costs of producing each level of output are as low as possible.

We begin the chapter by considering the firm's short-run costs, including the different types of costs that can be incurred, and a variety of measures of short-run costs. We also consider the distinction between the short run and the long run as it relates to the firm's planning decisions. Issues related to the firm's long-run decision-making process are also introduced in this chapter. Since firms can vary all inputs in the long run, the long-run objective of a firm is to employ all resources in the combination and amount that minimize costs.

Learning Objectives

After reading and studying this chapter, you will be able to:

1. Distinguish between explicit and implicit costs

2. Distinguish between a short-run and a long-run decision

CHAPTER 9

3. Explain what a production function is and distinguish between fixed and variable costs

4. Explain the relationship between diminishing marginal returns and short-run marginal cost

5. Distinguish between marginal and average product functions, and marginal and average cost functions

6. Describe the firm's long-run cost-minimization rule and use it to explain the firm's responses to input price changes

7. Describe how economies of scale affect the size of the firms in an industry

Total costs of production:
The full opportunity costs of all resources used in the production of the firm's output, including both explicit and implicit costs.

Explicit costs:
The out-of-pocket expenses incurred by a firm; they involve the expenditure of money to buy resources, raise financial capital, and so on.

Implicit costs:
The opportunity costs of using resources that are already owned by the firm.

Normal profit:
An implicit cost incurred by the firm; the amount of payment that is just sufficient to keep the entrepreneurs/owners in business.

Explicit versus Implicit Costs

The **total costs of production** are the full opportunity costs of all resources used in production of the firm's output. However, accounting for the full opportunity costs of production is complicated. When inputs are purchased in a market, their purchase prices are their opportunity costs. These costs are **explicit**. Hourly wages or monthly salaries are paid for labor. Machinery is purchased or rented. Raw materials are bought in markets. The cost of funds obtained from bond sales is determined by the interest rate paid to obtain the borrowed funds. Explicit costs involve the expenditure of funds by the firm to acquire the resource in question.

However, some resources used in production are not purchased in a market. In many instances, the firm owns resources that it may or may not use in the production process. Using these resources is costly so long as they have alternative uses. These costs are **implicit**; the firm does not pay an individual or another firm for the use of these resources. Implicit costs are measured by the value of the opportunity forgone when the resources are used in production.

There are many examples of implicit costs. For instance, when a firm uses retained earnings (profits that are not distributed to the firm's owners) to finance an expansion of its production facilities, it does not pay interest charges as it would have to if it had sold bonds or borrowed money to raise the needed funds. Nevertheless, it incurs a cost. Retained earnings could be invested in financial markets. The rate of interest that the retained earnings would earn in the market is the implicit cost of using these funds for expansion. It is a real cost incurred by the firm, and it should be included in the firm's assessment of the costs and benefits of expansion.

One of the most important resources in the production of goods and services is *entrepreneurial ability*, that difficult-to-define willingness to assume the risks associated with organizing and managing a firm. The owners of the firm contribute their entrepreneurial ability to the production process. In addition, the owners of the firm often invest their own financial assets in the business. The provision of these resources – risk taking and financial assets – is costly, and their owners will use them elsewhere unless they are compensated. The combined payments for risk taking and the financial assets of owners that is just sufficient to keep the entrepreneurs/owners in business is called **normal profit**. Normal profit is another implicit cost of production. If the firm's owners cannot earn a normal profit, this implies that their personal resources have more valuable alternative uses. The firm's owners would therefore be better off to shut down and divert these resources to their higher-valued uses.

Section Recap

The total costs of production include both explicit costs – any out-of-pocket expenditures on productive inputs – and implicit costs – the opportunity costs of resources already owned by the firm. Normal profit, the payments for risk taking and the financial assets of the firm's owners, is another implicit cost of production.

Short Run versus Long Run

The firm makes myriad decisions in its effort to maximize profits. It must choose a product to produce and sell. It must decide on a particular production technology to use to produce the good or service. After the firm is in business, it must be ready to make decisions of all kinds in response to changes in the market. In all of these decisions, the firm has a range of alternatives to choose from. One of the most important determinants of the alternatives available to a firm in its decision making is the time dimension of the decision.

For convenience we will distinguish between long-run and short-run decisions and will use this important distinction throughout the rest of the book. A **long-run decision** for a firm is a planning decision. In the long run, a firm is free to vary all its inputs. The decisions to enter a new business or build a new plant are long-run decisions. The choice of a least-cost combination of *all* inputs, or the technology that embodies this combination, is a long-run decision. Long-run decisions are based on expectations about future prices and costs. The decision maker is free to consider a wide range of alternatives and faces few constraints.

A **short-run decision**, on the other hand, is a constrained decision. A firm's short-run decisions center on how to use existing plant and equipment efficiently. In the short run, at least one of the firm's input levels is fixed. For example, in the short run the firm's production technology and its stock of capital equipment are fixed. The firm's short-run profit-maximizing decision is to choose an output level (and levels of inputs that can be varied in the short run) that maximizes profit.

The short run is not a chronological period of time but rather is defined by the firm's production technology. For example, it may take an electrical utility five or more years to vary all of its inputs. It takes a long time to build a new power-generating plant. (It has taken from ten to twenty years to build some nuclear power plants.) On the other hand, an entrepreneur in retail trade may be able to vary all of his inputs within a six-month period. A retail store can be built from scratch and stocked for business in a matter of months. This implies that the short run is approximately five years in the electrical utility industry but only six months in retail trade. The nature of the firm's business determines the length of the short run.

This distinction between short run and long run is a general one. It can be used to characterize all kinds of decisions, not just those made by firms. Before a semester begins, you decide whether to work or go to school or which courses to take. If you decide to go to school and enroll in five classes, you may consider dropping one of the courses during the semester. The decision to take five courses in this semester was a long-run, planning decision; the decision to drop a course is a short-run decision that is influenced by the fact that you are enrolled in four other courses. The decision to buy a car is a long-run decision based on the expected benefits and costs of the car. The decision about how much to use the car – once you have purchased it – is a short-run decision. The constraint is the particular car that you own.

Long-run decision: A planning decision. In the long run, all inputs are variable, including the amount of capital stock employed by the firm.

Short-run decision: A constrained decision. In the short run, the amount of at least one of the inputs employed by the firm is fixed.

Sunk Costs

Sunk cost:

A cost that has been incurred in the past that can no longer be recovered. Sunk costs are irrelevant for current decisions.

Decisions should be based on the full opportunity costs of different alternatives. Sometimes, however, it is difficult to distinguish between the full opportunity costs of an action and costs that have already been incurred – **sunk costs**. Historical costs are sunk costs because they have been paid in the past and a decision today will not alter them. Thus, *sunk costs are irrelevant to today's decision making and should be ignored*. When a firm is deciding whether to produce another unit of its output, it should consider only the extra costs of the unit such as those for materials and labor. The cost of an existing machine used to produce the unit should be ignored. The firm owns the machine, and its cost is not altered by producing one more unit (ignoring depreciation).

What about other decisions? Should the tuition cost of a course be considered when trying to decide whether you should drop the course? No, unless you will get a tuition refund. The tuition cost was incurred in the past when you made the long-run decision and, after any refund period has expired, dropping the course will not change that cost. What matters for this decision is the future costs incurred and benefits received by continuing in the course. Tuition has become a sunk cost.

What costs do you consider when trying to decide whether to drive your car or fly from San Diego to Chicago? Only the cost of driving your car versus the cost of the air fare is relevant. The cost of driving your car includes only those costs actually incurred for this trip. The cost of the car purchase is sunk and therefore irrelevant. However, a drive of this length does reduce the value of the car because of wear and tear on the car. This change in value, called *economic depreciation*, is a true opportunity cost of the trip and should be considered in this decision. In addition, do not forget to include the opportunity cost of your time. It takes longer to drive than it does to fly.

In the next section we see very explicitly how profit-maximizing firms ignore sunk costs in their short-run decisions. Remember that only the true costs of an action or decision should be included in the decision-making process. Sunk costs should be ignored. Good economic decision making is forward thinking.

Section Recap

Long-run decisions are planning decisions, since all inputs are variable in the long run. In the short run, at least one input is fixed. Hence, short-run decisions are constrained to focus on how to use existing fixed inputs efficiently. In either case, sunk costs are nonrecoverable and should therefore be ignored in the decision-making process.

The Short-Run Production Process

To be able to calculate the short-run costs of producing various levels of output a firm needs certain information. First, it needs to know the types and quantities of inputs it will use in the production process. In addition, it needs to know the per-unit price of each input. Combining this information with any implicit costs yields the total cost of each level of output the firm produces. The prices of inputs purchased by the firm are determined in the market for each input. The quantities of each input required to produce a particular level of output are determined by the firm's production function.

In order to maximize profit, the firm attempts to select the production function that, given the prices of the inputs used by the firm and any implicit costs, will minimize the total costs of production incurred by the firm. However, once the firm has selected a production function, it is fixed in the short run. The decision to change the firm's production function is a long-run decision and will be addressed in a later section.

Production Function

To understand the short-run relationship between output and costs, we must first understand the physical process of production. The technical relationship between the quantity of inputs required to produce a good and the quantity of output produced is called a **production function**. The production function determines the maximum output that can be produced from a given quantity of inputs (and a given level of technology). Thus, *the production function embodies productive efficiency – the process of getting the maximum output from a given quantity of inputs.*

Production function:

Determines the maximum output that can be produced from a given quantity of inputs (and a given level of technology).

As an illustration, assume that a production process requires only capital (K) and labor (L) to produce output (Q). The general production function is then expressed as:

$$Q = f(K,L)$$

That is, output is a function of capital and labor. To know how much capital and labor are required to produce a given amount of output, we would have to know the specific mathematical form of the production function. In many cases, the production function for an actual firm may be so complex that it is very difficult to characterize mathematically. However, the general principles of production and cost that are explained in this chapter with a simple two-input production function apply even to firms with very complex production processes.

In the short run, the firm employs at least one input that is fixed in amount; it cannot vary the quantity of this input. Capital is usually fixed in the short run. Mathematically, we can express this condition as:

$$K = \overline{K}$$

where the bar indicates that capital is constant or fixed in amount. Thus, the short-run production function becomes:

$$Q = f(\overline{K},L)$$

or simply:

$$Q = f(L)$$

In the short run, the firm's level of output is determined by the quantity of labor employed with a fixed stock of capital equipment. (Dropping K in the second equation simply reflects the fact that for this production function, a change in L is the only source of a change in Q.)

Production Costs

A simple example of a short–run production function for snow removal in a parking lot is given in Table 9.1. In this example, output is measured as cubic yards of snow removed per minute. The short-run production function is illustrated in the first two columns of the table. The first column shows the amount of labor employed. The second column shows how much output is produced for each amount of labor (assuming a fixed stock of capital, in this case, three snowplows). Notice the output pattern. As more and more labor is added to the production process, output increases, but ultimately it increases by smaller and smaller amounts.

Marginal physical product:

The change in total output resulting from the employment of an additional unit of a variable input.

The change in output associated with an additional unit of the variable input (labor in this example) is called its **marginal physical product** (MP) and can be written, in the case of labor (L), as:

$$MPL = \Delta Q / \Delta L.$$

The marginal product of the variable input is important in the firm's decision-making process. It tells the firm how much additional output will be produced by adding one more unit of the input to the production process. The third column of Table 9.1 shows the marginal product associated with each unit of labor. Note that the marginal product of labor rises from 20 units to 28 units as we employ the first 3 units of labor. However, beginning with the fourth unit of labor, marginal product begins to decline, falling to 5 units of output for the seventh unit of labor.

Law of diminishing returns:

At some point, the marginal physical product of an input begins to decline.

This pattern of diminishing marginal productivity for the variable input occurs in every short-run production function. It is the **law of diminishing returns** in production. *Diminishing returns occur in the short run because more and more of one input is being added to a production process with at least one fixed input. The amount of additional output that can be produced*

	Table 9.1		

Short-Run Production Function for Snow Removal

Measures of Daily Productivity

Units of Labor Per Day	Total Output	Marginal Product	Average Product
0	–	–	–
1	20	20	20.0
2	45	25	22.5
3	73	28	24.3
*4	99	26	24.8
5	121	22	24.2
6	136	15	22.7
7	141	5	20.1

Capital units = 3

* Diminishing marginal returns are incurred with the fourth unit of labor.

in this case is physically limited by the amount of the fixed input. In Table 9.1, the law of diminishing marginal returns occurs between the third and fourth units of labor employed.

To better understand this concept, note that the firm in our example has three machines – snowplows – that produce the firm's output – snow removal. At least one worker must operate the plows. Additional workers will increase output. One or two additional workers can increase output significantly. Each worker is able to spend more time operating machines and less time running between them. As we add more than three workers, however, fewer ways exist for them to increase output. They can operate the plows while other workers rest, or they can take care of all the other tasks while three workers only operate the plows. However, as more and more workers are added, less and less additional output is produced. At some point, an additional worker might actually reduce output by simply getting in the way and reducing the productivity of other workers.

As another example, suppose we are growing mushrooms in a cave that has one acre of growing space. In the short run, we are stuck with that one acre. We can add more workers, more fertilizer, or more of any other input in the mushroom-growing production process and increase output. However, as we add more and more of these variable inputs, additions to output begin to decline. What we can get out of one acre of land (in a cave or not) is limited. Diminishing marginal productivity occurs in the short run because at least one input cannot be varied.

A concept closely related to marginal product is average product. The **average product of a variable input (AP)** is defined as output per unit of the variable input. In the case where labor is the variable input,

$$APL = Q/L.$$

Average productivity for each unit of labor is presented in the fourth column of Table 9.1.

Average product of a variable input:
The amount of output per unit of the variable input employed.

All three measures of output, or productivity, are graphed as functions of the labor input in Figures 9.1 (a) and (b). In Figure 9.1 (a) we have drawn the production function. Output increases as more units of labor are added, but the rate of increase in output decreases with additional units of labor. The marginal product of labor and the average product of labor are illustrated in Figure 9.1 (b). Initially, both marginal product and average product increase as units of labor are increased. However, the marginal product of labor begins to decline when diminishing marginal productivity sets in. This occurs at point B in Figure 9.1 (b). The average product of labor continues to rise until marginal product and average product are equal. Once marginal product falls below average product, beyond point C in Figure 9.1 (b), average product begins to decline as well. This relationship is also shown numerically in Table 9.1.

A production function determines the maximum amount of output that can be produced with a given set of inputs. In the short run, at least one input to the production function is fixed. Consequently, marginal product exhibits diminishing returns. Marginal product begins to decrease at the point where diminishing returns sets in.

Section Recap

232

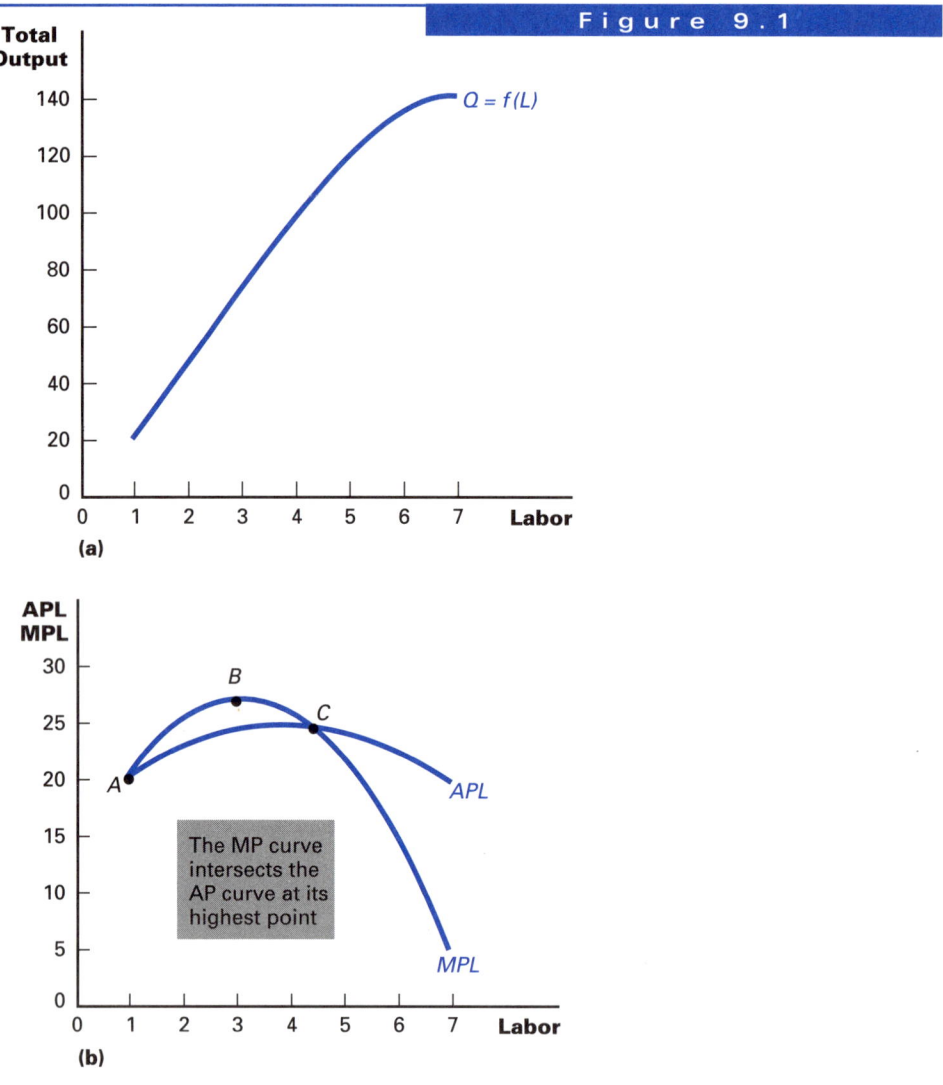

Figure 9.1

The Short-Run Production Function, Average Product (AP), and Marginal Product (MP)

The production function illustrated in 9.1 (a) is drawn assuming a fixed amount of capital and only one variable input, labor. As the amount of labor increases, output increases as well, but ultimately it increases by smaller and smaller amounts. The average product (AP) and marginal product (MP) functions are graphed in 9.1 (b). When MP is greater than AP, AP is rising and the MP curve intersects the AP curve at its maximum (point C).

The Firm's Cost Functions

Total cost:

The sum of the costs of each input (fixed and variable) used in production.

The production function is one important determinant of production costs. It determines the kind and quantity of inputs required for a given level of output. The other determinant of costs is input prices. The firm pays the market price for each input that it purchases to use in production. Therefore, for any given level of output, the **total cost** of production (TC) is just the sum of the costs (price times the quantity) of each input used in the production process (plus any implicit costs).

In the short run, at least one input is fixed and other inputs are variable. **Fixed cost** does not vary with output. Total fixed cost (TFC) is the sum of all costs that do not vary with output. In our example, the fixed cost is the cost of capital. Other examples of fixed costs include overhead expenses, the building in which the firm is located, and the entrepreneur's opportunity costs. In the short run, fixed costs are sunk costs. They are incurred regardless of the level of output. Thus, in making short-run output decisions, fixed costs are ignored.

Fixed cost:
Any cost that does not vary with output. In the short run, fixed costs are sunk.

Variable cost varies directly with the quantity of output produced. Total variable cost (TVC) is the sum of all costs that vary directly with the quantity of output produced. Examples of variable costs include some labor costs, the costs of raw materials, and the cost of energy used in the production process. Because all costs are either fixed or variable, it is the case that:

Variable cost:
Any cost that varies directly with the quantity of output produced.

TC = TFC + TVC.

The cost functions for the production function example in Table 9.1 – the snowplow operation – are calculated in Table 9.2 and graphed in Figure 9.2. The cost figures in Table 9.2 are calculated on the assumption that the price of a unit of labor is $30, the price of capital per unit per day is $25, and the amount of capital is fixed at three units (the snowplows). Because more output is produced only with more inputs, total cost increases as output increases.

In the short run, the change in total cost resulting from a change in the level of output is equal to the change in total variable cost. Total fixed cost, by definition, is constant with respect to output changes. In our example, the cost associated with the three snowplows does not change, regardless of the amount of snow that is removed. However, as we

Table 9.2

Short-Run Cost Functions for Snow Removal

Total Output	Total Fixed Cost	Total Variable Cost	Total Cost
0	75	0	75
20	75	30	105
45	75	60	135
73	75	90	165
99	75	120	195
121	75	150	225
136	75	180	255
141	75	210	285

Capital units = 3 (snowplows)

Capital price per day per unit = $25

Labor price per day = $30

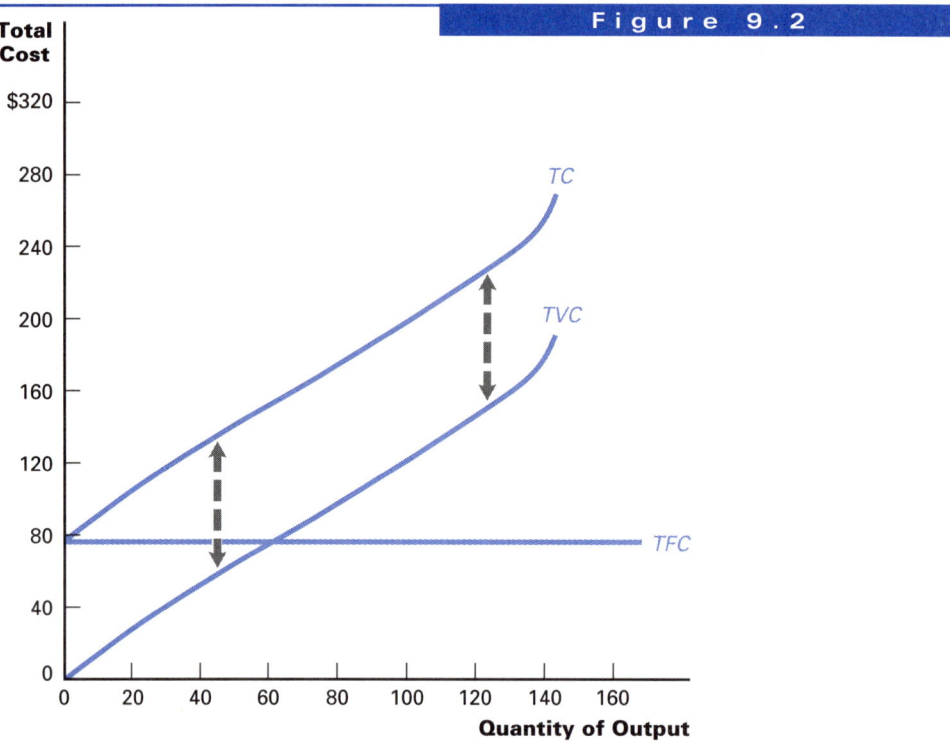

Figure 9.2

Total Cost Functions

This figure illustrates the total cost functions in Table 9.2. The price of labor is $30/unit, the price of capital is $25/unit, and capital is fixed at three units. Because fixed costs do not vary with the level of output, total fixed cost (TFC) appears as a horizontal line at $75. Total costs (TC) and total variable costs (TVC) increase with the level of output. The vertical difference between TC and TVC is TFC.

add more or less labor, total cost and total variable cost increase or decrease accordingly. Total cost and total variable cost differ by the amount of total fixed costs.

The shape of the total cost function is determined by the production function. Notice that total cost begins to rise rapidly beyond an output level of 135 units. This rapid increase is caused by the diminishing marginal productivity of the labor input. We are paying the same price for each additional worker, but each additional worker is adding less and less output to production. Thus, the cost of each additional unit of output begins to rise rapidly. We see this influence more clearly in other measures of cost.

Two other kinds of cost measures are important for the firm's decision making – average cost and marginal cost. We can define three different average cost functions, one for each of the total cost functions noted above.

Section Recap

Total costs are the sum of total fixed costs and total variable costs. Fixed costs are associated with the fixed inputs to the production process. Variable costs are associated with the variable inputs to the production process.

1. **Average total cost** (ATC) is total cost per unit of output:

   ATC = TC/Q

   This cost measure is also popularly referred to as *unit cost* of production, the average total cost of a unit of output.

2. **Average variable cost** (AVC) is total variable cost per unit of output:

   AVC = TVC/Q

3. **Average fixed cost** (AFC) is total fixed cost per unit of output:

   AFC = TFC/Q

Fixed costs are constant in the short run. Therefore, as output increases, average fixed cost steadily declines. Furthermore, since

TC = TVC + TFC

it is also true that

ATC = AVC + AFC.

Thus, we need only work with two of these functions and we can always derive the third one. We will use average total cost and average variable cost explicitly in our analysis of the firm's supply decisions. However, remember that we can always calculate average fixed cost since average fixed cost equals average total cost minus average variable cost.

The other cost function that is very important in the firm's decision-making process is **marginal cost** (MC) – the addition to total cost associated with the production of an additional unit of output:

MC = ΔTC/ΔQ.

The marginal cost of a unit of output is the additional cost the firm incurs by producing that one unit of output.

The average and marginal cost functions calculated for the total cost functions in Table 9.2 are presented in Table 9.3 and are graphed in Figure 9.3. In Figure 9.3, each cost function tells us the value of that particular cost measure at each level of output. For example, to find marginal cost, average variable cost, average fixed cost, and average total cost for 45 units of output, draw a vertical line at 45 units on the output scale (horizontal axis). The point at which the vertical line intersects each cost function is the cost at that output level. Cost is read off the vertical axis. Compare the values for the four cost functions at 45 units of output on the graph in Figure 9.3 with the values in Table 9.3.

The average total cost, average variable cost, and marginal cost curves are U-shaped; they initially decrease as output increases and then begin to increase with further increases in output. This general pattern is a result of the law of diminishing marginal returns in the production function. Consider first the marginal cost curve. It is a mirror image of the marginal product curve. As illustrated in Table 9.3, when marginal product rises, marginal cost falls; when marginal product falls, marginal cost rises. (Note in Table 9.3 that when three units of labor are employed, marginal product is at its maximum and marginal cost is at its minimum.) Additional workers are hired at a constant price per worker, but these

Average total cost:
Total cost per unit of output.

Average variable cost:
Total variable cost per unit of output.

Average fixed cost:
Total fixed cost per unit of output.

Marginal cost:
The addition to total cost associated with the production of an additional unit of output.

Table 9.3

Short-Run Production and Cost Functions

Units of Labor Per Day	Measures of Daily Productivity			Total Costs ($)			Average Costs ($/unit)			
	Total Output	Marginal Product	Average Product	Total Fixed Cost	Total Variable Cost	Total Cost	Fixed	Variable	Total	Marginal Costs
0	–	–	–	75	0	75	–	–	–	–
1	20	20	20.0	75	30	105	3.75	1.50	5.25	1.50
2	45	25	22.5	75	60	135	1.67	1.33	3.00	1.20
3	73	28	24.3	75	90	165	1.03	1.23	2.26	1.07
*4	99	26	24.8	75	120	195	0.76	1.21	1.97	1.15
5	121	22	24.2	75	150	225	0.62	1.24	1.86	1.36
6	136	15	22.7	75	180	255	0.55	1.32	1.88	2.00
7	141	5	20.1	75	210	285	0.53	1.49	2.02	6.00

Figure 9.3

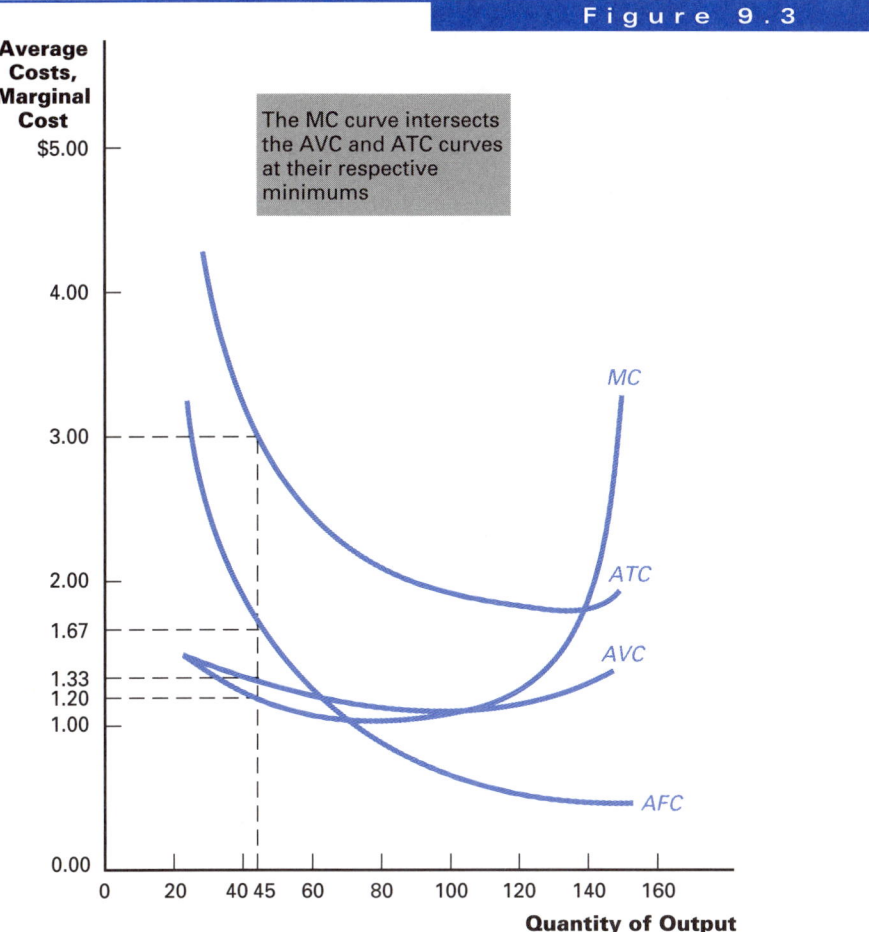

The MC curve intersects the AVC and ATC curves at their respective minimums

The Firm's Short-Run Cost Functions: AFC, AVC, ATC, and MC

This figure illustrates the firm's average and marginal cost curves. Costs are read off the graph by drawing a vertical line at the level of output of interest. For forty-five units of output, AFC = $1.76, AVC = $1.33, ATC = $3.00, and MC = $1.20. AFC is equal to the vertical difference between ATC and

additional workers initially add more and then later add less to total output. Because marginal product ultimately decreases in the short run, marginal cost ultimately increases. *Short-run rising marginal cost is caused by diminishing marginal productivity.*

What about the shape of the average variable cost curve? It is a mirror image of the average product curve. The initial increase in marginal product causes average product to rise; in other words, the initial decrease in marginal cost causes average variable cost to fall. However, at some input level, between three and four units in our example, marginal product begins to fall, thus marginal cost begins to rise. The increasing cost of production at the margin eventually pulls average variable cost up. This occurs at the level of output where marginal cost begins to exceed average variable cost. The U-shape of the average total cost function is also the result of the behavior of marginal cost.

Average-Marginal Relationships: A Hint

It is worthwhile to stop and consider the relationship between an average and a marginal function in more general terms. In this chapter we have examined average and marginal productivity as well as average and marginal cost. At other places in the book we use other average and marginal concepts. The relationship between average and marginal productivity, average and marginal cost, or average and marginal anything is a mathematical one. A more familiar example illustrates the relationship.

Suppose your grade in your economics course is to be determined by your average score on nine different exams. Table 9.4 contains your score on each exam, your total points, and your course average. On the first exam you score 100 points. Having taken only one exam, your average score is 100 points. On the second exam, you score 85 points (this is the marginal number of points), and this reduces your average grade to 92.5 points [(100 + 85)/2]. The third exam reduces your average further: You score 70 points and your average falls to 85 points [(70 + 85 + 100)/3]. When you realize that this trend will give you a low semester grade, you work harder and your exam scores begin to climb. On the next two exams you score 75 and then 80 points, respectively. Although your average continues to fall, it falls more slowly. On the sixth exam your score of 85 points actually causes your average point total to rise for the first time. Your later exam scores are higher, pulling your semester average up even farther.

Notice two very important points:

Average total cost and average variable cost differ by the amount of average fixed cost. (Or stated in mathematical terms again: ATC − AVC = AFC.) Thus, at any output level, the vertical distance between the average total cost and average variable cost functions is equal to average fixed cost. As output increases, the amount of fixed cost per unit of output declines. Thus, average fixed cost is downward sloping over the entire range of output.

Relationship Between Marginal Cost and Average Cost Marginal cost – the cost of an additional unit of output – may differ from average cost. If it is higher than the average, it will cause the average to rise; if it is lower than the average, it will cause the average to fall. As a consequence of this relationship between the margin and the average, the marginal cost curve cuts the average total cost curve at the minimum point of the latter. So long as marginal cost is less than average total cost, average total cost will fall. But the moment marginal cost exceeds average total cost, average total cost will rise. The same is true of the relationship between marginal cost and average variable cost.

The average-marginal relationship holds for any variable, be it exam scores, costs, revenues, productivity, or whatever. What happens at the margin is the crucial issue in

Table 9.4

Relationship Between Marginal and Average Exam Scores

Exam Number	Marginal Exam Grade	Total Exam Points	Average Exam Score
1	100	100	100.0
2	85	185	92.5
3	70	255	85.0
4	75	330	82.5
5	80	410	82.0
6	85	495	82.5
7	90	585	83.6
8	95	680	85.0
9	100	780	86.7

1. Your average score reflects your total exam performance. It is a record of your performance on all previous exams. It tells us nothing about how you will do on the next exam. The same relationship holds for average and marginal costs. Average cost tells us the cost of producing a given quantity of output. It does not tell us the cost of the next unit of output.

2. Your marginal test scores affect your average score. Your score on the next exam, the marginal exam, or your score on the last exam tell us about your current performance. The marginal scores affect the average. If your score on the next exam is above your average, it will cause the average to rise. If it is equal to the average, the average will not change. If it is lower than the average, it will cause the average to decline.

decision making. It tells us the consequence of a specific action. The average, on the other hand, describes what has happened in total. It reflects not only the change at the margin, but also the accumulated value of all the previous units of the variable in question.

Section Recap

Increasing short-run marginal cost is a result of diminishing marginal productivity. In turn, MC determines the shape of the average total cost and average variable cost functions. So long as marginal cost is less than ATC (AVC), ATC (AVC) will decline. When MC exceeds ATC (AVC), ATC (AVC) will begin to rise.

Short-Run Cost Functions

The short-run cost functions capture the relationship between output and costs – variously defined – in the short run. Given a set of cost functions for a firm, we can determine the change in costs – total, average, or marginal – associated with a particular change in output. Some general patterns in costs are illustrated by the representative set of short-run cost functions in Figure 9.4. These cost functions have the same general shape as those in our

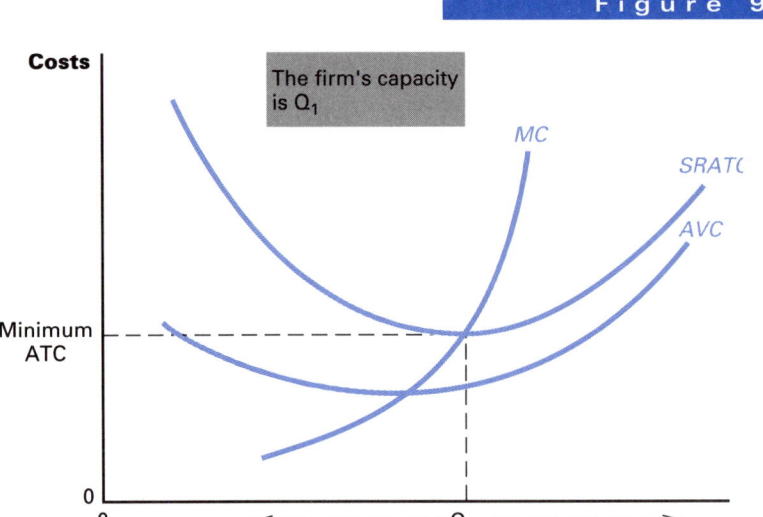

Representative Short-Run Cost Functions

The cost functions illustrated here are representative of the short-run costs incurred by many firms. The short-run ATC and AVC curves are U-shaped. In addition, the MC curve intersects the ATC and AVC curves at their respective minimums. So long as MC is less than ATC and AVC, respectively, ATC and AVC are each declining. However, when MC exceeds AVC, AVC begins to increase. The same is true for ATC.

example. In addition, the marginal cost curve intersects both the average variable cost curve and the average total cost curve at their respective minimum points. This relationship holds for all short-run production processes. Mathematically, marginal cost will always intersect the average cost functions at their minimum points.

Short-run capacity:
The level of output at which the average total cost of production is minimized.

Short-Run Capacity of the Firm The short-run capacity of a firm is defined as the level of output at which average total cost is at a minimum. It is an optimal level of output in the sense that average total cost is minimized. In Figure 9.4 the short-run average total cost function (which has been labeled SRATC to avoid any confusion between the short run and the long run) reaches a minimum at Q_1. Hence, Q_1 is the short-run capacity of the firm. Note that if output is less than or greater than Q_1, average total cost is higher.

When a firm produces at an output level below its capacity, it is *under-utilizing* its existing plant and equipment. For example, referring to Figure 9.4, when output is less than Q_1, the firm is producing below capacity. In this case, average total cost is high because of the firm's high average fixed cost. Recall that fixed costs are usually associated with the firm's capital. By expanding output to Q_1, the firm makes more efficient use of its capital stock, and average fixed costs and average total costs decline.

On the other hand, when a firm produces a level of output that exceeds its capacity, it is *over-utilizing* its plant and equipment. Referring once again to Figure 9.4, if output exceeds Q_1 the firm's average total cost rises because of high marginal costs. At output levels above Q_1 diminishing marginal productivity has pushed marginal costs above average total cost. In the snowplow example, capacity is exceeded when the sixth worker is hired (see Table 9.3).

The U-shaped pattern of short-run average costs is one reason why the choice of a production technology is important to the firm. The firm wants to keep costs as low as possible. In addition, it wants to use a short-run production technology that will allow it to produce at the capacity output level. To do this, the firm must correctly anticipate the volume of its sales. If it anticipates sales of 1 million units a month but only has sales of 250,000, it is stuck with excess capacity and high average total costs in the short run. On the other hand, firms can suffer from underestimating sales. If sales are 1.5 million units a month, the firm's capacity is being overutilized and average total costs are high for another reason. The high output level is associated with low marginal productivity of the variable inputs, raising marginal cost and average total cost.

Determinants of Short-Run Costs At the beginning of the chapter we said that short-run costs are determined by the production function and input prices. This causal relationship can now be illustrated using the cost functions we have developed. Figure 9.5 illustrates two sets of cost functions, $SRATC_1$ and MC_1, and $SRATC_2$ and MC_2. Costs increase when the prices of variable inputs increase or the production function changes so that more variable inputs are required to produce the same amount of output. If either of these changes occurs, the cost functions shift up, for example from $SRATC_1$ to $SRATC_2$. Costs decrease when the prices of variable inputs are reduced or the production function changes so that fewer variable inputs are required to produce the same amount of output. If either of these changes occurs, the cost functions shift down, for example from $SRATC_2$ to $SRATC_1$. (Note that because these changes affect variable costs, the average variable cost curve shifts as well.)

Another determinant of costs is taxes. One of the costs of doing business is paying the taxes that have been levied on business firms by governments. Thus, taxes are part of the costs of production. A tax increase raises costs; a tax decrease lowers costs. Assume, for example, that a firm's costs are characterized by MC_1 and $SRATC_1$ in Figure 9.5. If a tax is placed on each unit of the good produced, it causes both the marginal cost and average total cost curves to shift up vertically (by the amount of the tax) to MC_2 and $SRATC_2$.

This section has described and explained the short-run relationship between output and costs. In the next section we continue our discussion of production costs by taking a look at the firm's long-run decision-making process.

242

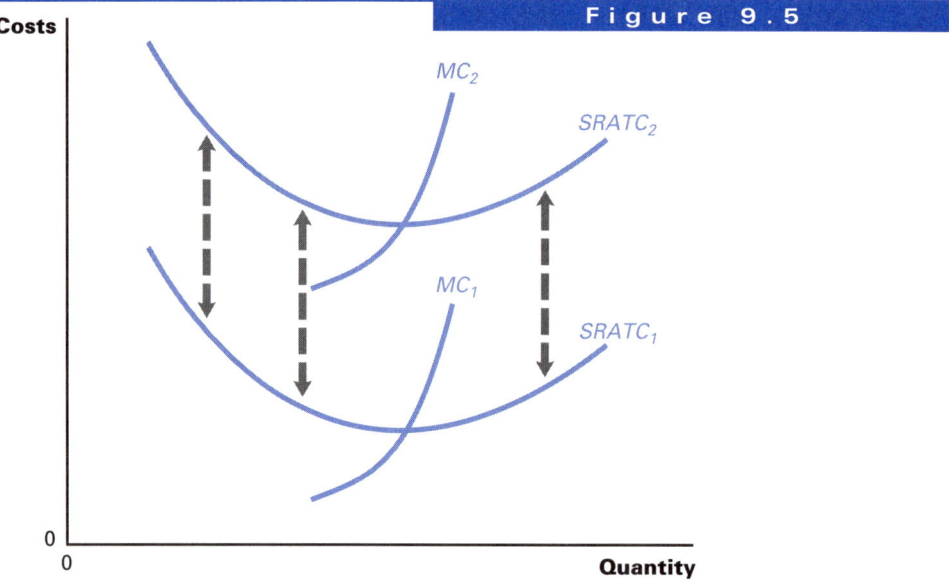

Figure 9.5

Changes in Short-Run Costs

This figure illustrates two sets of cost functions, $SRATC_1$ and MC_1, and $SRATC_2$ and MC_2. Costs increase when input prices increase or the production function changes so that more inputs are required to produce the same amount of output. If either of these changes occur, the cost functions shift up, for example from $SRATC_1$ to $SRATC_2$. If costs decrease, the cost functions shift down, for example from $SRATC_2$ to $SRATC_1$.

Section Recap

When a firm operates at capacity in the short run it is utilizing its fixed inputs efficiently. Changes in the prices of variable inputs or the production function can cause the firm's short-run cost functions to shift up or down.

Long-Run Production Costs

The firm's long-run decisions are planning decisions. Decisions to start a new business firm, to alter the firm's capacity, or to go out of business are all long-run decisions. In making long-run decisions, the firm faces fewer constraints than it does in the short run because it is free to vary all of its inputs. *In the long run, all inputs are variable.* On the other hand, the firm faces more uncertainty when making long-run decisions because these decisions are based, by necessity, on *anticipated* production costs and product demand.

A firm enters a particular market or industry to earn profits. It attempts to maximize long-run profits by choosing a short-run production technology that minimizes costs. This decision is a challenging one because the firm has to predict future product demand, technological developments, and changes in input prices. Our discussion of capacity utilization has already illustrated the importance of correctly anticipating demand. Once a production process has been chosen, the firm is stuck with it in the short run. If the firm has erred in anticipating product demand, it will experience higher production costs (and reduced profitability) due to either overutilization or underutilization of the firm's capacity. For this reason we want to pay careful attention to the firm's long-run choice of a production technology.

Long-Run Cost Minimization

Let's consider a simplified version of the complex long-run decision of a firm seeking to maximize profits. Suppose that the firm knows the annual output it will produce and the input prices it must pay for the resources it employs. To maximize profits, the firm must choose from among the available production technologies the one that minimizes its costs of production. The choice of a production technology, or a short-run production function, is the same as the choice of a cost-minimizing combination of inputs.

In a way, the firm's choice of input combinations is very similar to the consumer's choice of a utility-maximizing combination of consumer goods. Consumers want to get as much benefit as they can for each dollar they spend on goods and services. In a like manner, the firm wants to get as much output as possible for each dollar that it expends on resources. What matters in the firm's decision is the productivity of the inputs and their costs. The firm compares the benefits of employing a particular input to its cost and then compares the gain from one input to the gain from another. We know from the previous sections that the benefit of an input to the firm is the input's contribution to output – its marginal product.

We can state the firm's decision rule for long-run cost minimization formally. Suppose again that there are only two inputs, capital and labor. For a given expenditure on capital and labor, the firm minimizes its production costs by employing capital and labor in quantities such that the marginal product of capital per dollar expended on it is just equal to the marginal product of labor per dollar expended on it:

$$\frac{MP_K}{P_K} = \frac{MP_L}{P_L}$$

Unless this equation is satisfied, the firm can simply alter the ratio of capital and labor employed and increase output without increasing costs. For example, if the ratio of marginal product to price for capital exceeds that for labor, the firm can reallocate its expenditures from labor to capital (reducing its employment of labor and increasing its employment of capital with no change in total expenditures) and increase output because the firm gets more output from a dollar spent on capital than it does from a dollar spent on labor. When such a reallocation occurs, the two ratios converge because of diminishing marginal productivity. As the firm hires more capital, the marginal product of additional units of capital declines; as the firm reduces its employment of labor, the marginal product of the marginal unit of labor rises.

As an aid to better understanding this concept, consider the following numerical example. Assume that a firm can purchase labor for $9 per unit and capital for $7 per unit. In addition, the firm is faced with the long-run production function in Table 9.5. Note

Why the DISAGREEMENT?

Excess Capacity in the Electric Utility Industry

Over the past two decades a number of electric utility companies began construction of nuclear power plants to meet the anticipated demand from their customers. However, utility companies' efforts to pass on the construction costs of these plants to consumers have met with considerable resistance. Aside from the issue of the degree of safety associated with this type of electric power generation, many electricity customers

and consumer advocacy groups have questioned whether these plants are really needed. They have argued that, in many cases, the production capacity of the utility far exceeds demand. Utilities, on the other hand, have argued that this excess capacity is justified. Why the disagreement?

Part of the answer to this question lies in the fact that utilities have a responsibility known as the *obligation to serve*. According to the obligation to serve, utilities must maintain sufficient generating capacity to provide service to all customers who demand it and are will-

ing and able to pay for it. Utilities argue that, to be able to meet their obligation to serve, they must maintain excess generating capacity — capacity that exceeds the normal level of demand. The excess capacity serves as a backup in the event of a failure of one of the firm's regular generating units or when a generating unit requires regular maintenance. In addition, the excess capacity can be used to provide additional power when extreme weather conditions, such as a prolonged heat wave, cause a surge in demand for electrical power.

that the firm can produce 150 units of output by hiring 3 units of labor and 2 units of capital, or 2 units of labor and 3 units of capital. If the firm decides on the first combination (3L and 2K) the total cost of production is $41 [(3 × $9) + (2 × $7)]. However, it is also the case that

$$\frac{MP_K}{P_K} = \frac{32}{7} > \frac{22}{9} = \frac{MP_L}{P_L} ,$$

which indicates that this is not the cost-minimizing combination of resources for producing 150 units of output. In fact, if the firm hires one less unit of labor and one more unit of capital (2L and 3K) it will still produce 150 units of output, but the total cost is now only $39 [(2 × $9) + (3 × $7)]. In addition,

$$\frac{MP_K}{P_K} = \frac{21}{7} = \frac{27}{9} = \frac{MP_L}{P_L} .$$

The long-run cost minimization rule also suggests the firm's long-run response to changes in relative input prices. In the short run, an increase in the price of one or more inputs, *ceteris paribus*, leads to higher costs because the firm cannot substitute among all inputs in the short run. At least one input is fixed. However, in the long run, all inputs are variable. Consequently, if, for example, the price of labor rises relative to the price of capital, firms have an incentive to substitute capital for labor. Assuming that the firm is initially employing an efficient combination of labor and capital, if the price of labor does rise, the ratios of productivity per dollar are no longer equal:

Utilities have also defended the recent expansion in generating capacity on the grounds that, because of the obligation to serve, the utility must predict what demand will be in five to ten years so that it can begin construction now on plants that will be necessary to meet future demand. The growth in demand that was predicted for the 1980s and 1990s was based on the growth of demand in the 1960s and 1970s. It only became apparent in the late 1980s that demand was not growing as rapidly as had been predicted earlier.

Critics respond that many utilities are maintaining a level of excess capacity that far exceeds the level necessary to ensure adequate service and enable utilities to meet their obligation to serve.

Critics argue that the overexpansion by utilities has caused fixed costs to be much greater than they would be if the utilities had planned more carefully and developed a level of capacity more consistent with the level of demand for electricity. As we will discuss in Chapter 13, the price of electric service is regulated by government and is based on the utility's costs of production. As such, an increase in average costs often leads to higher prices for electricity. Critics maintain that because of the utilities' overexpansion, customers are being forced to pay a per-unit price that exceeds the price that would prevail if the utilities had behaved in a more efficient manner.

Many critics have also argued that utilities purposely overbuilt in

an effort to earn additional profits. Stated briefly, utilities are allowed to charge a price that enables them to pay all of their fixed and variable costs that are determined to have been prudently incurred. The price is also set such that the utility has the potential to earn a profit, specified as a maximum percentage of total fixed costs. As fixed costs increase, it is argued, so do total profits.

It is easy to see why there is such disagreement over this issue. Utilities must meet their legally imposed obligations. At the same time, customers want electric service provided at the lowest cost possible. Both sides of the argument have merit. It is also obvious that the disagreement will not be resolved easily or quickly.

Table 9.5

A Long-Run Production Function Using Capital and Labor

Labor	Total Product of Labor	Marginal Product of Labor	Capital	Total Product of Capital	Marginal Product of Capital
0	0	0	0	0	0
1	30	30	1	40	40
2	57	27	2	72	32
3	78	21	3	93	21
4	92	14	4	106	13
5	98	6	5	109	3

$$\frac{MP_K}{P_K} > \frac{MP_L}{P_L}$$

The firm's cost–minimizing response is clear: Hire more of the now relatively cheaper input (capital) and reduce employment of the now relatively more expensive input (labor). The firm substitutes capital for labor until the marginal product–price ratios are once again equal.

Firms, like consumers, are sensitive to the prices of the goods and services they buy. When factor prices change, firms adjust their input purchases to get as much productivity as they can for each dollar spent. When the price of labor rises relative to the prices of other inputs, firms try to economize on labor by substituting other inputs for labor. For example, in some assembly work, auto manufacturers substitute robots for humans. The Coast Guard is automating its remaining manned lighthouses to reduce the cost of providing navigational assistance to ships. When the price of gold rises, dentists seek to employ alternative metal alloys in crowns and bridges. When the price of energy rose rapidly in the 1970s, firms substituted more capital or labor for energy in their production processes by employing more fuel-efficient equipment and adopting more labor-intensive technologies.

Substitution in production is generally a long-run process. None of the substitution examples just mentioned can be carried out in the short run. It takes time to make these kinds of changes, and the amount of time required varies widely, depending on the nature of the production process. It takes years to substitute nuclear fuel for coal in the production of electricity, but only weeks or months to substitute bigger, more automated tractors for farm labor. In the short run, the firm's response to input price changes is limited to changes in output. However, in the long run, the firm has more options. It can vary its usage of all inputs by adopting a new production function with a different mix of inputs.

Section Recap

In the long run, all inputs are variable. Hence, the firm's objective is to hire the combination of inputs for which marginal product divided by price is equal for the last unit of each input employed.

Long-Run Average Cost

In the long run, there is a least-cost combination of inputs for producing each level of output. If we express these least-cost input combinations in terms of average or unit cost, we can examine the relationship between long-run average cost and the level of expected or planned output. The function that relates long-run average cost (LRAC) to the planned output level is called the **long-run average cost curve**. A long-run average cost curve is illustrated in Figure 9.6.

Long-run average cost curve:

The cost of producing different levels of output when all inputs are allowed to vary; it shows the effect on average total cost when the capacity of the firm is varied.

The long-run average cost curve shows the cost of producing different levels of output when all inputs are allowed to vary. The long-run average cost curve can be considered a *cost frontier* because it separates the set of attainable levels of cost from those that are unattainable, given input prices and the present state of technology. Those points below the long-run average cost curve are unattainable cost levels. Those points above the curve are attainable.

The long-run average cost curve is often called a *planning curve* or *envelope curve*. This terminology reflects the fact that the long-run average cost function is not a cost function for a particular production technology. Instead, the long-run average cost function is derived from a set of short-run average total cost functions. As we move from left to right in Figure 9.6, the amount of capital associated with each short-run average total cost curve is increasing. Consider, for example, a retail firm's decision of how much floor space to

Figure 9.6

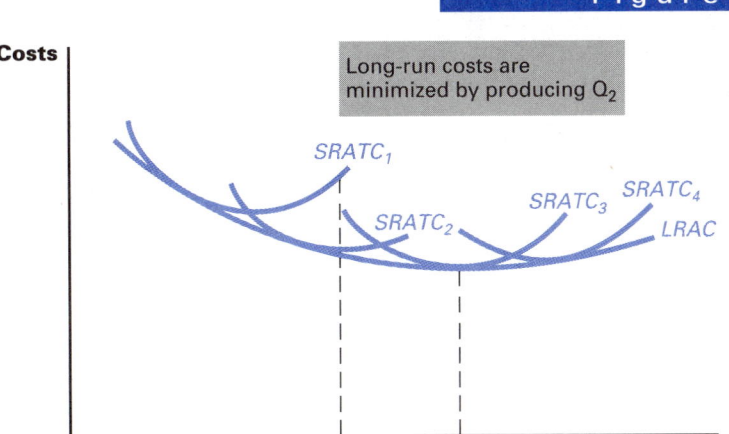

The Long-Run Average Cost Curve

The long-run average cost curve (LRAC) shows the average cost of production when all inputs are allowed to vary. Each short-run average cost curve is drawn for a given level of the fixed input. As we move to the right, the amount of the fixed input is increasing. At output levels below Q_2, as capacity expands, LRAC declines due to economies of scale. As capacity expands beyond Q_2, however, LRAC begins to increase, due to diseconomies of scale.

occupy. Once the firm selects a certain amount of square footage, its capacity is fixed in the short run. A decision to expand the amount of floor space it employs is a long-run decision. Expanding to a larger size moves the firm to a new short-run average total cost curve that is to the right of the previous one. In a similar manner, a decision by a manufacturing firm to add an additional assembly line is a long-run decision that would move it to a new short-run average total cost curve.

Firms adopt a particular short-run function when they choose a short-run production technology to employ. The firm's long-run decision problem is to choose that combination of inputs and capacity that minimizes production costs. In Figure 9.6, a firm can produce Q_1 units of output with three different short-run cost functions, but only one cost function, $SRATC_2$, minimizes the cost of producing Q_1 units of output.

Economies of Scale

What is the relationship between the planned output level and average total costs? The long-run average cost curve in Figure 9.6 has been drawn such that average total costs decrease as planned output increases up to a point (Q_2). Beyond Q_2 average total costs begin to increase with larger planned output levels. Since we are assuming that input prices are constant, the reduction in costs (the negatively sloped portion of the long-run average cost curve) must come about because output is increasing faster than the increase in costs

Production Costs

Taking Stock of Managers' Performance

In recent years, a growing amount of attention has focused on the amount of pay received by the managers of many of the largest businesses in the United States. In many instances, the compensation received by managers in the United States is more that 100 times as large as the amount received by their counterparts in Europe and Japan. The multimillion dollar earnings of the presidents and CEOs of such firms as Chrysler, Ford, H.J. Heinz, Kodak, and others have left many stockholders angry and embittered, especially in light of the fact that in many cases managers continue to earn huge amounts, even when the company is losing money. In effect, the high cost of manager compensation adds to firms' losses.

A large portion of the financial renumeration received by many managers comes in the form of stock options, which give the recipient the option to buy a certain number of shares at a predetermined price — which is usually set below the market price. The idea is that by providing compensation in the form of shares in the company, the recipient — the manager — has an incentive to ensure that the company performs as well as possible. However, once the shares are purchased, they can then be sold at the market price, resulting in an immediate profit for the person holding the option. A question that many observers have raised is, Does this type of compensation make economic sense? More and more, analysts are concluding that the answer to this question is a resounding No!

It has been estimated that more than half of all stock options are turned into cash within the first

---

Economies of scale:
An increase in the capacity of the firm results in a decrease in the average total cost of production.

as the scale (size) of operations increases. A firm is said to experience long-run **economies of scale** when average total costs fall as the scale of production increases.

Economies of scale arise because of specialization and substitution among inputs. With a larger scale of operations, firms can employ many inputs in more specialized, and usually more productive, ways. Capital equipment with very specialized functions can be employed when the expected volume of output is large. In addition, firms can take advantage of a greater division of labor, allowing workers to specialize in specific tasks. The division of labor itself can result in increased productivity. Moreover, the resulting increase in experience achieved by workers who specialize in certain tasks also increases productivity. The assembly line has become synonymous with mass production technologies. In assembly line production, the manufacturing process has been broken down into literally hundreds or thousands of separate, small steps performed by different workers.

The increased employment of capital relative to labor and other inputs is an important source of improved productivity as well. The cost of developing and adopting technologically advanced capital equipment is high. However, its cost per unit of output can be very low if the scale of production is large enough. A firm that expects to produce and sell a hundred hamburgers a week will employ less capital equipment and less specialized capital equipment than a firm expecting to produce ten thousand hamburgers weekly. The larger firm can reduce its average total costs by spending more on automated, specialized

year they are granted.[2] This type of behavior suggests that individuals who receive such options are concerned more with short-run than long-run gains. Theoretically, one could hold on to shares that have been purchased with an option with the expectation that improved performance by the firm will result in an increase in the stock's price. Thus, over the long run, the return on the stock would increase. On the other hand, sale of the stock shortly after the option is converted increases the certainty of the size of the resulting payoff. In addition, the amount of compensation received as a result of such options is less dependent on the performance of the company.

Analysts point out that the problem is not so much with the fact that stock options are offered as part of a manager's compensa-tion. Rather, the problem is that the stocks purchased with the options can be resold at any time thereafter. The upshot is that with the current system, one of the incentives managers might other-wise have to ensure the company's success – large profits translate into higher stock prices – is lost. This approach stands in contrast to compensation systems in Europe and Japan, which tie increased compensation, in the form of perks such as large expense accounts and housing allowances, to the company's performance. Under this approach, the level of compensa-tion is dependent on how well the company does. Thus, the incentive for managers to perform is pre-served.

Some firms in the United States have begun to address the prob-lems with the current approach by imposing new rules on how stock options can be used. For example, the head of Kodak instituted a requirement that the top 40 man-agers in that firm must invest one to four times their base salary in shares of Kodak stock between 1993 and 1998. In 1990, Chrysler instituted a requirement that each of its top managers must hold the equivalent of one year's salary in the form of shares in the company.

Requirements such as those imposed at Kodak and Chrysler strengthen the link between the compensation received by man-agers and the firm's performance. As such, managers have an incen-tive to pay closer attention to the firm's performance – both short-run and long-run – in an effort to maxi-mize profits – and their own well-being.

capital and less on labor. (Check out the difference in equipment in a McDonald's fran-chise and a local mom-and-pop hamburger stand – if you can find a mom-and-pop place!)

The shape of the long-run average cost curve in Figure 9.6 also suggests that a firm can become too big. At output levels beyond Q_2, economies of scale have been exhausted, and average total costs begin to rise as planned output increases. A firm that produces at a capacity level beyond Q_2 is experiencing **diseconomies of scale**. The explanation for diseconomies of scale is simply that the firm grows so large that it becomes increasingly difficult to manage. The difficulties encountered in managing such a large firm introduce inefficiencies into its operations. As an example, Ford produces its F-series pick-up truck at three separate plants. The average total cost of producing all of the output at a single plant would be greater than the minimum average total cost of production at each of the three individual plants.

In some industries, average total costs are invariant with respect to the planned volume of output. This case is known as **constant economies of scale**. For a firm faced with con-stant economies of scale, the long-run average cost curve appears as a horizontal line.

The precise relationship between the scale of operations and average total cost will vary by industry and change over time as technology changes. The potential for significant economies of scale is greater in the production of electricity than in the manufacture of fine furniture. Technological change can increase or decrease economies of scale. New

Diseconomies of scale:
An increase in the capacity of the firm results in an increase in the average total cost of production.

Constant economies of scale:
An increase in the capacity of the firm has no effect on the average total cost of production.

developments in papermaking technology may lead to smaller paper mills with average total costs as low as those of the large mills currently in use. It is interesting to note, however, that the new Japanese automobile assembly plants, which utilize the latest technology, have capacities that range from 220,000 to 270,000 units – the same as Henry Ford's 1920 Model-T plants.

Section Recap

The long-run average total cost curve reflects the effects of increasing the scale (capacity) of the firm. Economies of scale are associated with decreasing long-run average total costs. Diseconomies of scale are associated with increasing long-run average total costs.

Technology and Production Costs

The cost of production is the full opportunity cost of all resources used in producing a good or service. Cost is determined by two factors: input prices (including implicit costs) and technology. The prices of inputs used in production are determined by the market forces of supply and demand. Technology determines the kind and quantity of resources necessary to produce a good or service. A variety of technologies that employ different kinds and combinations of inputs may be available for producing a given good. Some require more labor relative to capital and other inputs – **labor-intensive production**. Others use more capital relative to labor and other inputs – **capital-intensive production**. The technologies also may differ according to the desired output per period of time. The long-run problem for the firm is to choose the production technology that minimizes the costs of production, given the kinds of inputs required for production, relative input prices, expected product price, and expected levels of production per period of time.

Technology plays a key role in determining the overall level of economic well-being in society. It is the constraint that determines the minimum level of cost that can be achieved in the accomplishment of a specific objective, for example, the production of one hundred automobiles. Technological change reduces costs by permitting society to achieve the same level and quality of output with less costly or fewer inputs. Technological change creates new production processes that allow us to produce new goods and services of more value than existing goods and services. Over time, technological change lowers the minimum level of costs that can be achieved in the economy.

Isoquants, Input Prices, and Least-Cost Production

This section presents a more technical approach to the relationships between the firm's production function, input prices, and the least-cost method of producing a given level of output.[1] It is intended to provide additional insights into the derivation of these relationships.

Labor-intensive production:

Use more labor relative to capital and other inputs.

Capital-intensive production:

Use more capital relative to labor and other inputs.

The Production Function and Isoquants

The firm's production function tells us how much output can be produced from a given level of inputs and a particular technology. Assume that we are looking at a production process that uses only two inputs – capital (K) and labor (L). Various combinations of the two inputs can be employed to produce a specific level of total output, that is, the inputs can be substituted for each other. However, according to the law of diminishing marginal productivity, additional units of each input yield increasingly smaller additions to total output, all else constant. The implication of this assumption is that, as the amount of one input employed is decreased by a particular increment, the additional amount of the other input that must be employed to continue producing the same level of output must increase.

This concept is illustrated in Table 9.6, which identifies specific combinations of the two inputs, K and L, that yield the same level of total output for the firm. As the table indicates, to maintain a constant level of total output, as the amount of one input employed is decreased by one unit, the *additional* amount of the other input the firm employs must increase. For example, if the firm reduces the amount of capital employed from five units to four units, it must increase the employment of labor by ten units. When employment of capital decreases from four units to three units, employment of labor must increase by fifteen units, and so forth.

The information in Table 9.6 is also plotted in Figure 9.7. The resulting curve is called an **isoquant**, or *equal output* curve. It locates all the combinations of K and L that yield the same level of total output; that is, the firm produces the same quantity of total output from any combination of inputs on a given isoquant.

Isoquants and the Marginal Rate of Technical Substitution

The rate at which a firm can substitute one input for the other and still produce the same level of total output is known as the **marginal rate of technical substitution**, or MRTS. The MRTS between L and K is equal to the negative of the ratio of their

Isoquant:
All the combinations of a set of inputs that yield the same level of total output.

Marginal rate of technical substitution:
MRTS between two inputs, for example, labor (L) and capital (K), is equal to the negative of the ratio of their marginal products, or MP_L/MP_K.

Table 9.6

Alternative Combinations of Two Inputs That Yield the Same Level of Total Output for a Representative Firm

Total Output	Amount of Capital Employed	Amount of Labor Employed
300	5	10
300	4	20
300	3	35
300	2	55
300	1	90

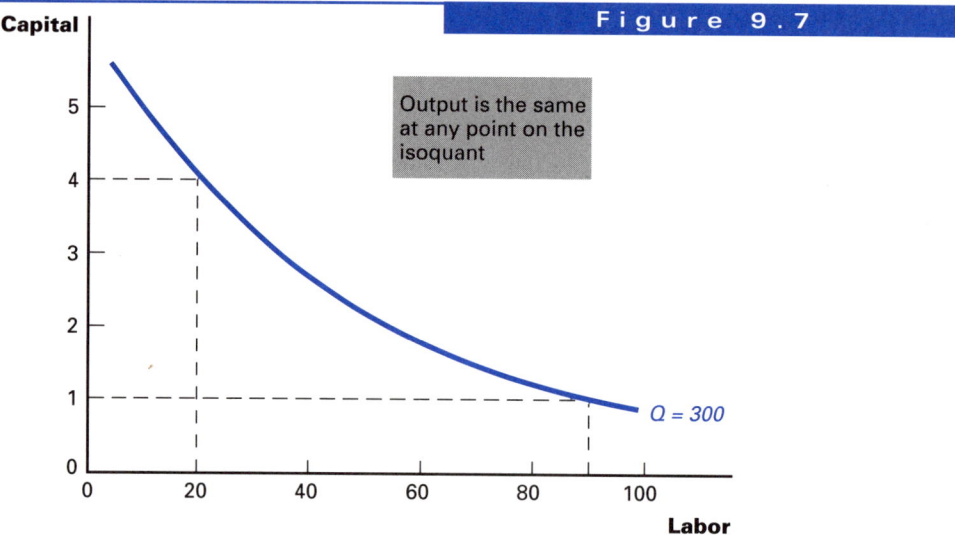

Alternative Combinations of Two Inputs, Total Output Held Constant

This figure depicts the various combinations of two inputs, labor (L) and capital (K), that yield a constant level of total output. The resulting curve is called an isoquant, or "equal output curve." It locates all of the combinations of K and L that yield the same level of total output.

marginal products, MP_L/MP_K. In most cases, the MRTS is assumed to change as we alter the combination of the two inputs employed (holding total output constant).

Isoquant map:

All the output levels that can be produced with a set of inputs; moving up to the right (away from the origin) moves the firm to higher levels of total output.

Figure 9.8 depicts an **isoquant map**. Each isoquant – for example, the isoquant labeled Q_1 – locates all of the combinations of the two inputs K and L that can be used to produce the same level of total output, Q_1. Note that the isoquants are convex to the origin; that is, they are bowed in toward the origin. This feature is due to the assumption of diminishing marginal productivity of each input. The slope of an isoquant at any point is simply the MRTS between L and K, MP_L/MP_K. Moving up to the right (away from the origin) moves the firm to higher levels of total output. As such, Q_3 is associated with a higher level of total output than Q_2, and Q_2 is associated with a higher level of total output than Q_1.

The Isocost Line

The firm's objective is to produce a given level of output at least cost. The firm is constrained, however, by the prices of the inputs used in the production process. In the simple case in which only two inputs are being used, the firm's total cost (TC) function is written as:

Isocost line:

All the combinations of two inputs that result in the same total cost.

$$TC = P_L L + P_K K$$

where TC represents total cost, and P_L and P_K are the prices of labor and capital. The total cost function is used to derive a set of **isocost lines**, or *equal cost lines*. Each isocost line locates all the combinations of the two inputs that result in the same total cost.

Figure 9.8

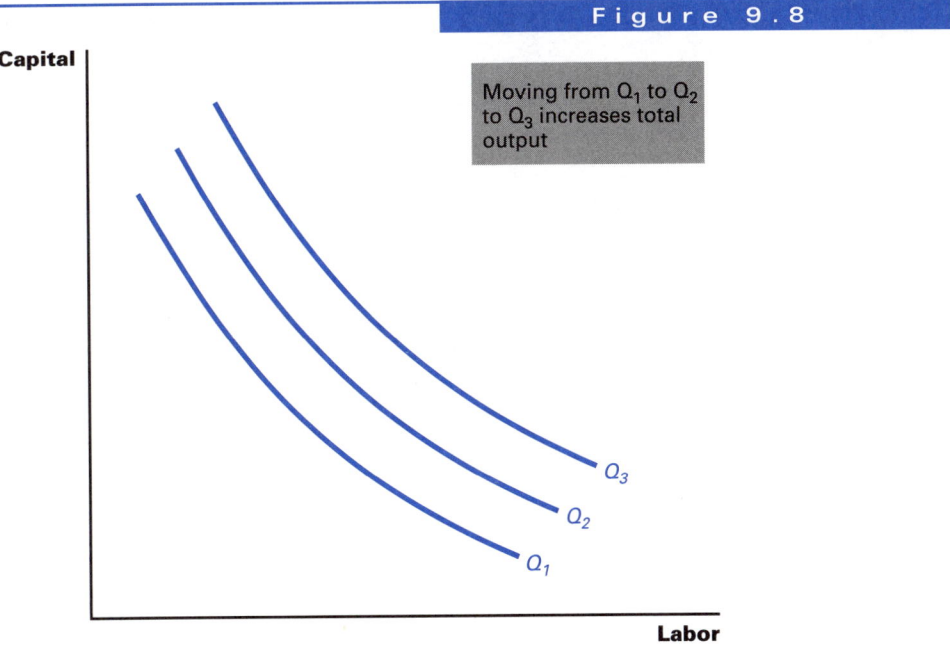

Capital

Moving from Q_1 to Q_2 to Q_3 increases total output

Q_3

Q_2

Q_1

Labor

An Isoquant Map

This figure depicts an isoquant map. The isoquants are convex to the origin due to the assumption of diminishing marginal productivity of each imput. The slope of each isoquant at any point is the MRTS between labor and capital, $-MP_L/MP_K$. Moving up to the right (away from the origin) moves the firm to higher levels of total output.

A series of isocost lines has been graphed in Figure 9.9. Note that the isocost lines are parallel. The slope of each isocost line is $-P_L/P_K$. The slope is found by solving the total cost function for K and holding total cost constant, that is:

$$TC = P_L L + P_K K$$
$$P_K K = TC - P_L L$$
$$K = TC/P_K - (P_L/P_K)L$$

As we move up to the right (out from the origin), total costs increase — each isocost line is associated with a higher level of total costs.

Least-Cost Production

To produce a given level of output efficiently, the firm will employ that combination of resources that minimizes the total costs of production. The information in Figures 9.7 and 9.9 has been combined in Figure 9.10, which illustrates the cost-minimizing combination of resources for producing output level Q_1. The firm will minimize the costs of producing Q_1 units of output by employing the combination of inputs associated with point C, L_C and K_C. Note that, as it is drawn, the isocost line labeled TC_2 is just tangent to the isoquant labeled Q_1, at point C. Therefore, the two curves have the same slope at that point. Stated differently, the MRTS between L and K is equal to the slope of the isocost line, P_L/P_K, or

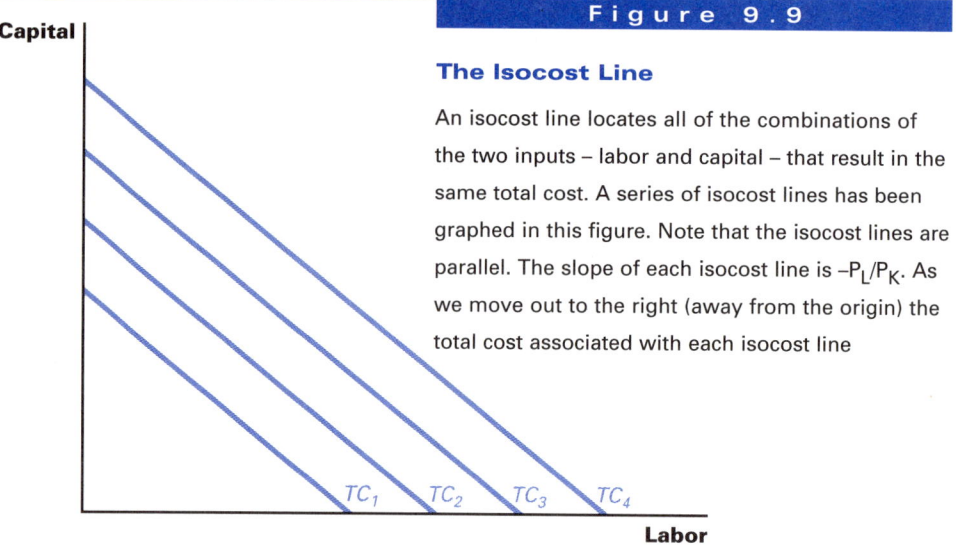

Figure 9.9

The Isocost Line

An isocost line locates all of the combinations of the two inputs – labor and capital – that result in the same total cost. A series of isocost lines has been graphed in this figure. Note that the isocost lines are parallel. The slope of each isocost line is $-P_L/P_K$. As we move out to the right (away from the origin) the total cost associated with each isocost line

$$\frac{MP_L}{MP_K} = \frac{P_L}{P_K},$$

which can be rewritten as

$$\frac{MP_L}{P_L} = \frac{MP_K}{P_K}$$

This is the rule for least-cost production we derived earlier in the chapter.

To see why point C minimizes costs, consider points A and B. Both of these combinations of L and K could be employed to produce Q_2. However, each of these points lies on a higher isocost line than isocost line TC_2. Each of these isocost lines corresponds to a greater level of total costs. In fact, if the firm employs any combination of resources to produce Q_2 other than the combination associated with point C, it will automatically increase its total costs of production.

The Effect of a Change in Relative Input Prices

Assume that the price of labor increases from P_L to P_L^*. This would have the effect of causing the isocost line to rotate and become steeper, as illustrated in Figure 9.11. Isocost line TC^* reflects the increase in slope resulting from the increase in the price of labor to P_L^*:

$$\frac{P_L^*}{P_K} > \frac{P_L}{P_k}.$$

Also:

$$\frac{P_L^*}{P_K} > \frac{MP_L}{MP_k}$$

at point C on isoquant Q_1. As Figure 9.11 indicates, to once again produce Q_1 at least cost, the firm must increase the amount of capital employed and decrease labor, that is, substitute capital for labor. Failure to do so would put the firm on a higher isocost line, which is shown by the dashed line passing through point C.

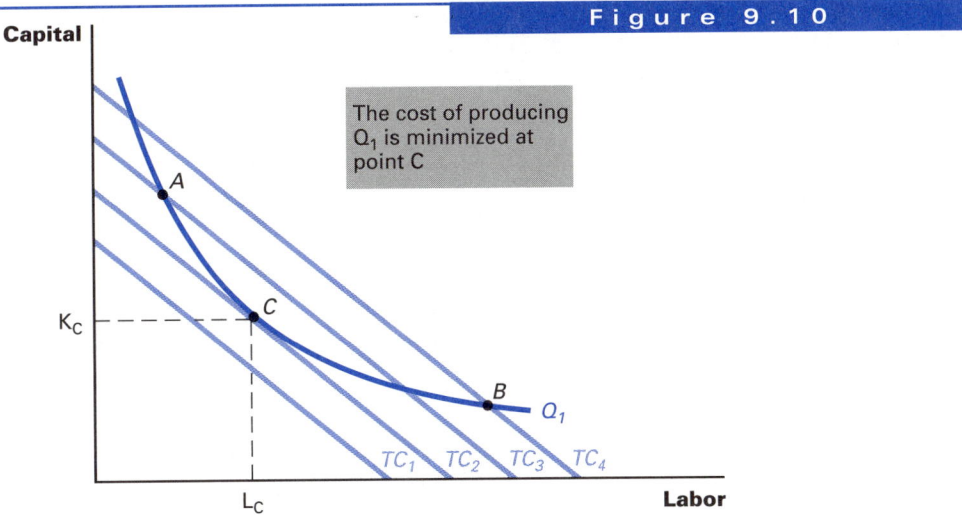

Figure 9.10

The cost of producing Q_1 is minimized at point C

The Least-Cost Input Combination

The information in Figures 9.7 and 9.9 has been combined in this figure, which illustrates the cost-minimizing combination of resources for producing output level Q_1. The firm will minimize the costs of producing Q_1 units of output by employing the combination of inputs associated with point C, L_c, and K_c. At this point the MRTS between labor and capital is equal to the slope of the isocost line, $-P_L/P_K$. The combinations of labor and capital associated with points A and B could also be employed to produce Q_2. However, each of these points lies on a higher isocost line than isocost line TC_2 and therefore corresponds to a greater level of total costs.

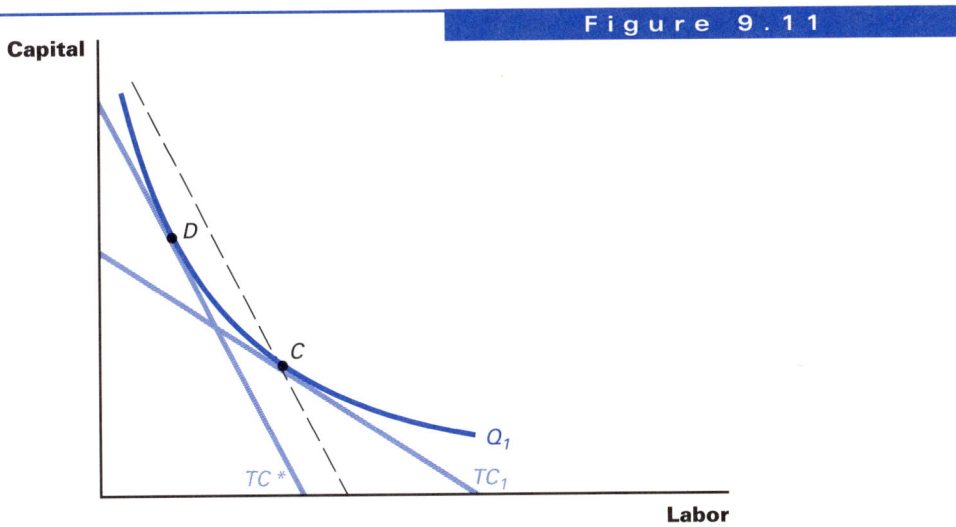

Figure 9.11

The Effect of a Change in Relative Input Prices

Assume that the price of labor increased from P_L to P_L^*. This would have the effect of causing the isocost line to rotate and become steeper. Isocost line TC* reflects the increase in slope resulting from the increase in the price of labor to P_L^*. To once again produce Q_1 at least cost, the firm must substitute capital for labor. Failure to do so would put the firm on the higher isocost line that is shown by the dashed line passing through point C.

Once the firm substitutes capital for labor, and moves to point D, the condition for least-cost production is once again met:

$$\frac{MP_L}{MP_K} = \frac{P_L{}^*}{P_K}$$

and

$$\frac{MP_L}{P_L{}^*} = \frac{MP_K}{P_K}.$$

Summary

A firm exists to earn a profit. It attempts to accomplish this objective by purchasing raw materials, labor, and other inputs, combining these inputs in a manner determined by existing technology to produce an output, and then selling this output to consumers at a price that is at least as high as the cost of producing the good. The firm's costs are determined by the prices of the inputs it must purchase, the particular technology employed in production, and any implicit opportunity costs. The technology determines the kind and quantity of inputs required to produce the good.

The **total costs of production** include both explicit and implicit costs. **Explicit costs** include any out-of-pocket expenditures on productive inputs. **Implicit costs** consist of the opportunity costs of resources already owned by the firm. The combined payments for risk taking and the financial assets of owners that are just sufficient to keep the entrepreneurs/owners in business are called **normal profit**. Normal profit is another implicit cost of production.

A **short-run** decision concerns how to use existing plant and equipment efficiently. In the short run, at least one input employed by the firm is fixed and cannot be varied. On the other hand, a **long-run** decision is a planning decision. The firm can vary all of its inputs. The choice of a least-cost combination of inputs for an expected level of output is a long-run decision.

A **sunk cost** is not a true opportunity cost of an action. It is a cost that has already been incurred and cannot be altered by a future decision. Sunk costs are ignored in economic decision making.

The firm's short-run costs are determined by the prices of any inputs it must purchase, the firm's **production function**, and any implicit opportunity costs. The production function is the technical relationship between the quantity of inputs employed and the level of output. In the short run, both input prices and the production function are assumed to be fixed.

Marginal physical product measures the change in output associated with a change in the quantity of a variable input employed in production. The marginal product of a variable input is subject to the **law of diminishing returns** – marginal productivity ultimately decreases as more and more units of the input are added to production.

The relationship between production costs and output is measured in various ways. **Average total cost**, or **unit cost**, is the cost per unit of output. We also distinguish between **average variable cost** and **average total cost**. **Marginal cost** is the change in total cost associated with a one-unit change in the level of output. The firm's short-run marginal costs ultimately increase because of diminishing marginal productivity. Average and marginal cost functions are generally U-shaped over the relevant range of output.

In the long run, all inputs are variable. The firm is choosing a set of inputs that minimizes its cost of producing an anticipated volume of output. Once the firm makes this choice it is back in a short-run position. The firm seeks to employ inputs in a combination such that the marginal physical productivity per dollar spent on each input is equal across all inputs. If the firm fails to achieve this position, it can increase output with no change in costs by simply reallocating its spending on inputs.

The **long-run average cost** curve is the locus of all points representing the least-cost input combination (measured by average total cost) for each output level. If the long-run average cost curve is downward sloping, there are **economies of scale** in the industry: The larger the expected volume of output for a firm, the lower are its average total costs. **Diseconomies of scale** imply rising average total costs as firm size increases.

Questions for Thought

Knowledge Questions

1. Explain what is meant by the *full opportunity costs of production*.

2. Why is normal profit considered a cost of production?

3. Define the following terms: marginal product, average product, total cost, variable cost, fixed cost, average total cost, average variable cost, average fixed cost, marginal cost.

4. Distinguish between economies of scale, diseconomies of scale, and constant economies of scale.

Application Questions

5. When demand for a firm's product increases, the firm can take a number of steps to increase quantities supplied to the market. Some are listed below. Rank them by how quickly the firm can implement them. Explain your ranking. Which actions are short run and which are long run?

    a. Begin a second production shift by hiring more workers.

    b. Build a second production line in the existing plant.

    c. Buy more materials and increase the rate of production per day.

    d. Deplete product inventories.

    e. Build a second manufacturing plant.

6. A firm's short-run production function is:

Units of Labor/Day	Units of Output/Day
5	120
6	140
7	155
8	165
9	168

The price of labor is $20 per day. Ten units of capital are used each day, regardless of output level. The price of capital is $50 per unit.

a. Calculate the marginal product of each unit of labor input.

b. Calculate total, average, and marginal costs.

c. Graph the average and marginal cost functions.

7. Assume that a firm is faced with the following short-run cost functions:

Output	Average Variable Cost	Average Total Cost
0	0	0
1	25	55
2	21.2	36.3
3	19.2	29.2
4	18.8	26.3
5	19.4	25.4
6	21.2	26.2

a. What is the amount of the firm's fixed costs? What is the average fixed cost of each level of output?

b. Calculate the marginal cost of each unit of output.

c. At what point do diminishing marginal returns set in? How do you know?

8. Use the firm's long-run cost-minimizing decision rule to explain the differences in the relative use of capital and labor in agriculture in the United States and the People's Republic of China.

Synthesis Questions

9. Suppose that you have signed a twelve-month lease on an apartment for $200 a month, anticipating that you will be in school this coming summer as well as this academic year. However, you have obtained a summer job elsewhere. What is the minimum amount of rent for which you would be willing to sublet your apartment rather than let it sit empty for the summer? Explain your reasoning.

10. A sales manager is responsible for two sales representatives. One rep has had average monthly sales of $10,000 for the past six months. His sales in the last three months have been $10,000, $8,000, and $5,000, respectively. The other rep has averaged $5,000 monthly in the last six months, with monthly sales of $4,500, $5,500, and $6,500 in the last three months. With which sales rep should the sales manager spend more time? Why?

11. Explain overutilization of capital. What would prompt a firm to produce in this situation? Explain.

12. Marginal cost can be calculated as Wage/MP in the example in Table 9.2 and in Question 6 above. Explain why ΔTC/MPL = Wage/MP in these examples.

13. Referring to Table 9.3, assume that a tax of $2 per unit is imposed on the firm's output. Recalculate the marginal cost, total cost, and average cost functions. Does the level of output at which average total cost and average variable cost are at a minimum change? Why or why not?

End Notes

[1] This section is included for those interested in a more technical treatment of the theory of cost minimization. It can be omitted without any loss of continuity.

[2] "Managers as Shareholders," *The Economist*, January 23, 1993, pp. 19-20.

Revenues and Profit Maximization

Overview

From 1984 to 1987, manufacturers of motor vehicles and related equipment saw their profits decline by almost 60 percent. Profits rebounded somewhat in 1988, but in 1990 and 1991 the industry incurred a net loss. Profits rebounded again in 1993 and 1994. Other industries experienced quite different patterns with respect to changes in profits. For example, the primary metals industry saw profits increase by almost 580 percent between 1986 and 1989. These examples raise a number of questions, among them, How do firms select the profit-maximizing (or loss-minimizing) output level, and how can firms continue to operate when they incur a loss? The purpose of this chapter is to shed some light on these and related questions. The short-run profit-maximizing behavior of the firm is the focus of the chapter. The relationships that are established in this chapter form the basis of the analyses in Chapters 11–13.

The short-run problem for a firm is to determine the output level that maximizes profits. To calculate the amount of profit associated with any output level it is necessary to identify the relationships between inputs and outputs on the cost side, and outputs and prices on the revenue side. In Chapter 9 we defined production costs as the full opportunity costs of production, highlighting normal profit as one component of costs. In addition, we considered the time dimension of the decisions of firms, making an important distinction between short-run and long-run decisions.

On the cost side, we defined both average and marginal cost. On the revenue side we will define and use both average and marginal revenue. We then determine the firm's short-run profit-maximizing rule. One of the important conclusions of this chapter is that, regardless of the type of market in which they operate, all firms follow the same rule to maximize profits.

Learning Objectives

After reading and studying this chapter, you will be able to:

1. Define economic profit and explain its relationship to normal profit

2. Explain the difference between economic profit and accounting profit

CHAPTER 10

3. Explain the differences between a price-taking firm and a price-searching firm

4. Explain how firms identify the short-run profit-maximizing (or loss-minimizing) level of output

5. Determine the amount of profit (loss) associated with the profit-maximizing (loss-minimizing) level of output for a firm

6. Explain the firm's shutdown point and breakeven point

Economic Profit

In general terms, profit is measured as the difference between total revenue and total cost. Total cost and total revenue are determined by how much output is supplied to the market and purchased by consumers. Supply decisions, in turn, depend on the actual or anticipated benefits and costs of producing goods and services. The total costs of production are the full opportunity costs of all resources used in production of the firm's output. As we saw in Chapter 9, the full opportunity costs of production are equal to the sum of explicit and implicit costs. The revenue generated by the sale of a firm's output constitutes the benefits of production and is determined by the demand curve for the firm's output.

Economic profit:

The difference between total revenue and the total costs of production (including normal profit).

Having established the determinants of the firm's costs and revenues we are in a position to define **economic profit**. Economic profit is the difference between total revenue and the total costs of production:

Economic Profit = Total Revenue – Total Costs of Production [including normal profit]

It is important to keep the distinction between economic profit and normal profit in mind. Normal profit is an implicit cost of production. It is the amount of money the entrepreneur could earn by employing the resources he or she owns in the next best alternative. Economic profit is the revenue earned by the firm in excess of its total (explicit plus implicit) costs of production.

When total revenues equal total costs, economic profit is zero. In this case the firm is earning a normal profit, which is acceptable to the firm. All costs are covered, including payments to the entrepreneurs/owners for their contributions, and each input receives as payment the value of its opportunity cost – the highest payment the inputs would receive in the market (in the next best alternative). If economic profit is positive, resources in the firm are receiving higher payments than can be received elsewhere. If economic profit is less than zero, the firm is experiencing losses. Resources employed by the firm are earning payments that are less than they would receive elsewhere.

Table 10.1 illustrates the cost and revenue conditions faced by Jim and Stella, who are considering whether to enter the frozen yogurt business. According to information in Table 10.1, Jim and Stella can expect to incur $108,600 in explicit costs each year. In addition, Jim and Stella are currently working as mid-level managers for a small manufacturing concern and are each earning $40,000 per year. Thus, Jim and Stella's projected total economic costs are $188,600 per year. The questions for Jim and Stella are, What are their projected revenues per year and how much economic profit can they expect to earn?

Based on the information in Table 10.1, so long as Jim and Stella can expect to earn more than $188,600 they should go into business for themselves. Revenues in excess of $188,600 would mean that Jim and Stella would earn positive economic profit. If total revenues are exactly equal to $188,600, based on their net income, they would be indifferent between staying at their current jobs and going into business for themselves. In this case, Jim and Stella would be earning a normal profit; economic profit would be zero. Earning any amount of revenues less than $188,600 would leave Jim and Stella with an economic loss.

Table 10.1

Projected Costs of Jim and Stella's Fabulous Frozen Yogurt

Explicit Costs

Building (rent)	$55,000
Equipment (lease)	$11,000
Ingredients	$9,000
Utilities	
(electricity, gas, phone)	$3,600
Labor	$30,000

Implicit Costs

Jim and Stella's current incomes	$80,000

Total Economic Costs	$188,600

Economic Profit Is Not Accounting Profit

By now you have noticed that the economic definition of profit is different from the meaning of profit as it is used in everyday conversation. In everyday use, the term *profit* refers typically to the revenue left over after paying the bills. This definition is common terminology for profit as it is defined in an accounting sense. **Accounting profit** *is the difference between total revenue and explicit, or accounting, costs. The implicit costs of production, including normal profit, are omitted from an accountant's definition of profit.*

Referring again to Table 10.1 we can see that, using the accounting definition of profit, Jim and Stella would show a profit so long as total revenues exceed $108,600. However, if total revenues are less than $188,600, Jim and Stella would not be doing as well, in terms of net income, as they would by avoiding the frozen yogurt business and staying at their current jobs. This illustrates the importance of distinguishing between economic profit and accounting profit. When deciding whether to start a business or stay in business, focusing on economic profit provides a better picture of the true net benefits of the alternative choices the decision maker faces. Thus, the different meanings given to the notion of profit arise for good reasons.

Economists are concerned with the true social cost of producing economic goods. *Normal profit is the minimum payment just sufficient to attract the firm's owner(s) into business and, consequently, preclude their employment elsewhere. Economic profit is the difference between total revenues and total opportunity costs, including normal profit.* The absence of normal profit will cause the owners of firms to exit the industry in search of more profitable employment opportunities for their entrepreneurial contributions.

Accountants are concerned with other problems. It is the accountant's responsibility to maintain systematic records of the financial transactions of businesses. To carry out this task, many accounting conventions, or rules, have been established to ensure that financial records are maintained similarly in all businesses. These conventions are required because some transactions, such as depreciation expenditures, are difficult to measure and because regulations and tax laws require certain kinds of information.

Accounting profit: The difference between total revenue and explicit, or accounting, costs.

Why the DISAGREEMENT?

Do Firms Maximize Economic Profits?

A central theme in this chapter is that firms maximize profits. Our model of decision making by firms is based on this assumption. Without it, our predictions of firm behavior could be quite different than they are. Although this assumption is a common one among economists, some people, including some economists, believe that firms do not seek to maximize profits. They contend that firms have other objectives or that it is simply too difficult or costly for a firm to seriously attempt to maximize profits. Why the disagreement over firms' objectives?

Some analysts argue that corporations choose to maximize sales instead of profits. Corporations are run by management teams that must answer to the owners, but owner control of management is weak and indirect. Thus, management objectives rather than owner objectives are more important in understanding the behavior of firms, and managers tend to be more interested in sales volume than in profit levels. Sales are important to managers because the size of the firm has such a big impact on the economic well-being of management. All of the benefits of being a manager – salary, fringes, power, prestige – are more directly related to the size of the firm than to profits. If the level of profits is acceptable to the owners, then the managers will seek to maximize the firm's sales.

Another argument against the assumption of profit maximization derives from the importance of corporations as a form of business. According to this argument, corporations do not maximize profits or, for that matter, anything else (such as sales). They are "satisficers" rather than "maximizers." Because corporations are large organiza-

---

The appropriate and systematic accounting of a firm's financial affairs is important to the owners and managers of the firm (they use this information to make decisions), to other businesses who buy from or sell to the firm, to the stockholders of the firm, and to various taxing authorities. Of foremost importance to all these groups is the financial viability of the firm. In an accounting sense, profit is a residual, the part of total revenue that remains after explicit costs have been paid. This accounting profit includes both normal and economic profit. Owners of firms, as well as these other groups, are not concerned about the distinction made by economists; they simply prefer more profit to less.

Thus, the two definitions of profit arise because of two different interests. Economists are concerned with one set of problems and the business community with another. It is important to keep this distinction in mind as we analyze the behavior of firms. We note one more time: *Normal profit is a cost of production while economic profit is the difference between total revenue and total costs.*[1]

Section Recap

Firms attempt to maximize economic profit, which is the difference between total revenues and total costs (explicit and implicit), including a normal profit. Economic profit differs from accounting profit to the extent that accounting profit does not account for implicit costs, including a normal profit.

tions managed by a great number of people, the decisions of firms are generally compromises between management groups with different responsibilities, objectives, and perspectives. Management by compromise makes it difficult for the firm to maximize anything. Decision making is slow, reactions to new situations take time, and outcomes reflect efforts to satisfy different groups within the firm as much as efforts to improve the firm's profits. This environment generates behavior that is designed to achieve satisfactory levels of profits or sales.

How do economists respond to these arguments that firms do not maximize profits? Generally, they defend profit maximization as the firm's primary objective. Several arguments support their defense. The first point is an important one: Firms come into existence to make a profit, and they cease to exist if they are unsuccessful at it. An entrepreneur decides to risk scarce resources in anticipation of a gain. If the gain does not materialize, the entrepreneur is worse off. The failure to actively seek profit, even if one experiences losses along the way, is counter to the Fundamental Premise established in Chapter 1: In a world of scarcity, individuals act to make themselves better off.

A second argument concerns the possible effects of a firm's failure to maximize profits. In short, such firms are at risk of being taken over by another firm or group of individuals. Although takeovers can be initiated for a variety of reasons, one distinct possibility is the failure of the current management to maximize profits. This failure can lead to an undervaluation of the firm's assets. Outside individuals view such situations as a way to realize a quick gain. Hence, the threat of a takeover is another motivation for profit maximization.

A point raised in connection with consumer behavior is also relevant here. In reality, firms are more complex than we have assumed them to be. For instance, managers must make decisions that will have effects far into the future, even though they do not know what the future holds. Thus, their decision making is based on expectations that may or may not be realized. In addition, although we use as a model a firm that produces and sells one product, firms are constantly developing improved or new products, and many firms sell more than one product. Decisions about how to allocate resources among these competing ends are quite complex and are based on imperfect information. Thus, while firms seek to maximize profits, it may be difficult to discern their pursuit of profit even if maximizing profits is their objective.

The Firm's Output and Revenue

The primary purpose of this chapter is to establish the relationship among costs, revenues, and profits for a firm. In Chapter 9 we solved one piece of the puzzle: the relationship between inputs, outputs, and the costs of production. We now turn to the next question: What is the relationship between output and revenue for the firm? Once this question is answered, we can address the issue of profit maximization.

The input-output-cost relationships established in Chapter 9 apply to all firms, regardless of size or other characteristics. However, a firm's output-revenue relationship is determined by the demand curve for its product. There are two broad categories of firms based on product demand curves, and these categories reflect the market structure in which the firm operates. Firms are either *price takers* or *price searchers*. The demand curve faced by a price-taking firm is perfectly elastic (horizontal). The demand curve faced by a price-searching firm is negatively sloped.

Price-Taking Firms

A firm is a **price taker** when its output decision has no effect on market price. The firm takes the market price as given. The type of market structure in which price-taking firms operate is called a perfectly competitive market. The perfectly competitive market structure is analyzed in detail in Chapter 11. Our focus here is on the revenue functions of the

Price-taking firm:
Takes the market price as given; the output decisions of the individual firm have no effect on market price.

price-taking firm and their implications for the firm's determination of the profit-maximizing level of output.

A price-taking firm's demand curve is illustrated in Figure 10.1 (b). Note that the market demand curve, shown in Figure 10.1 (a), is downward sloping, but the firm's demand curve is perfectly elastic at the market equilibrium price, P_e, which is established by the interaction of market supply and demand. The firm can produce at any output level, for example Q_1 or Q_3, and receive the same per-unit price for its product, P_e.

The revenue functions for a price-taking firm are defined as follows:

1. As we noted in Chapter 6, **total revenue** (TR) is simply the product of market price and the quantity of output produced:

   $$TR = P \times Q$$

2. **Average revenue** (AR) is total revenue per unit of output:

   $$AR = TR/Q = (P \times Q)/Q = P$$

3. **Marginal revenue** (MR) is the change in total revenue associated with a one-unit change in output:

   $$MR = \Delta TR/\Delta Q = (P \times \Delta Q)/\Delta Q = P$$

Total revenue:
The product of market price and the quantity of output produced and sold.

Average revenue:
The amount of revenue per unit of output sold.

Marginal revenue:
The change in total revenue associated with a one-unit change in output.

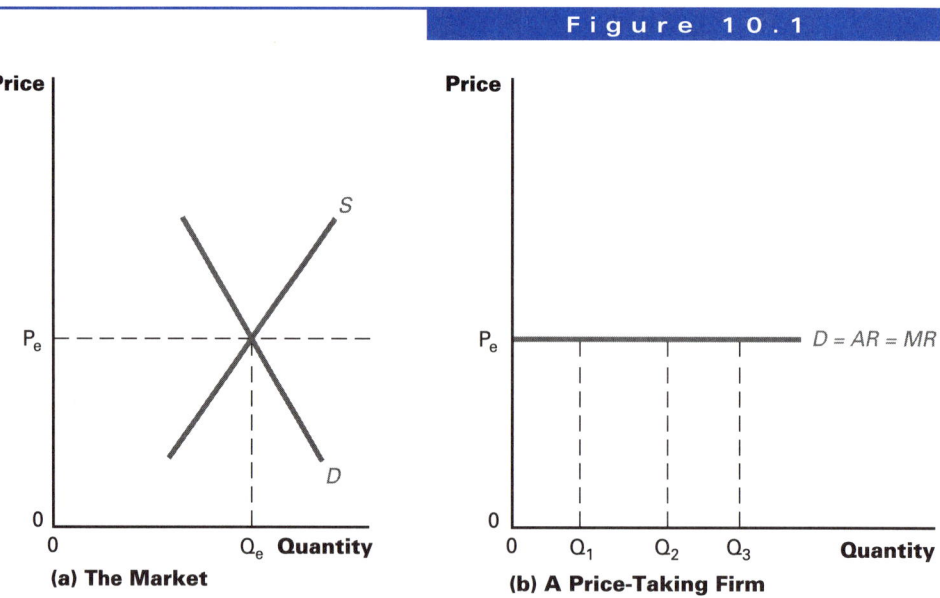

Figure 10.1

(a) The Market

(b) A Price-Taking Firm

The Price-Taking Firm's Revenue Functions
(a) *The Market* (b) *A Price-Taking Firm*

A price-taking firm's demand curve is illustrated in this figure. Note that the market demand curve is downward sloping but that the firm's demand curve is perfectly elastic at the market equilibrium price, P_e. The firm can produce at any output level, for example Q_1 or Q_3, and will receive the same per unit price for its product, P_e. Consequently, P = MR = AR for the price-taking firm.

266

Because price takers can sell more of a product without affecting its price, the addition to total revenue from an increase in output of one unit is just the market price. Consequently, average and marginal revenue are the same. Moreover, because the firm's output decisions do not affect market price, average revenue and marginal revenue are constant. Referring to Figure 10.1, the average revenue function and the marginal revenue function are shown by a horizontal line that intersects the vertical axis at P_e. As this example suggests, the price-taking firm's demand curve is also its average revenue curve and its marginal revenue curve.

Table 10.2 illustrates the revenue functions for a representative price-taking firm. The equilibrium market price of the output produced and sold by the individual firm is assumed to be $6 per unit. We can see in Table 10.2 that as output increases, so does total revenue. However, because the per-unit price the firm receives for its output does not change with the level of output, marginal revenue and average revenue are constant and equal to market price.

Price-Searching Firms

A firm that has some degree of price-setting power is a **price searcher**. These firms face negatively sloped demand curves and *search* for the profit-maximizing price-output combination. Price-searching firms operate in market structures characterized by some degree of imperfect competition. Price-searching firms operate in one of three different market structures – monopolistic competition, monopoly, or oligopoly. These market structures are described in detail in Chapters 12 and 13.

Because price-searching firms face negatively sloped demand curves, their revenue functions differ in some respects from those of the price taker. Like the price taker's, the price searcher's demand function is also its average revenue function because:

$$AR = TR/Q = (P \times Q)/Q = P.$$

Price-searching firm:

Has some degree of market power; the output decisions of a price searcher affect market price.

Table 10.2

Revenue Functions for a Price-Taking Firm

Total Output	Per unit Price	Total Revenue	Average Revenue	Marginal Revenue
1	$6	$ 6	$6	$6
2	6	12	6	6
3	6	18	6	6
4	6	24	6	6
5	6	30	6	6
10	6	60	6	6
50	6	300	6	6
100	6	600	6	6
200	6	1200	6	6

However, in contrast to the price-taking firm, the price searcher s marginal revenue function is different from its demand function (and average revenue function). Consequently, for all levels of output greater than one unit, price and marginal revenue differ. Recall that:

$$\Delta MR = \Delta TR / \Delta Q .$$

Price changes as output changes for the price searcher. As we move down the demand curve and output increases, price decreases. Because price equals average revenue, average revenue also decreases. Marginal revenue decreases as well, but faster than average revenue – marginal revenue is less than price. When the price-searching firm sells one more unit of output, it gains revenue equal to the new lower market price for the extra unit sold. However, the previous units of output are now sold at the lower price as well, so the firm loses revenue on all the units that were previously sold at the higher price.

Table 10.3 illustrates the problem for the price-searching firm. Because it faces a negatively sloped demand curve, additional output can be sold only by lowering price. When price falls from $7 to $6.50, output increases by one unit. The additional output generates $6.50 in additional revenue. However, all units of output are sold at the $6.50 price. Before the output increase, three units were sold at $7 each. The price reduction caused revenue on these units to fall by $1.50 ($.50 × 3 units). Thus, the change in total revenue associated with an increase in output of one unit is $6.50 − $1.50 = $5.00 and:

$$MR = \Delta TR / \Delta Q = \$5 / 1 = \$5$$

When price is $6.50, AR is $6.50 and MR is $5.

Both the average revenue and marginal revenue functions for the price-searching firm are graphed in Figure 10.2. The average revenue curve is simply the demand curve for the firm's output. As shown in the graph, the marginal revenue curve lies below the average revenue curve. In fact, when the demand curve is linear (a straight line), the marginal revenue curve is exactly twice as steep as the demand curve. When demand is negatively sloped, marginal revenue falls as output increases. For price searchers, $P = AR > MR$.

Table 10.3

Revenue Functions for a Price-Searching Firm

Output	Price	Total Revenue	Average Revenue	Marginal Revenue
1	$8	$ 8	$8	$8
2	7.5	15	7.5	7
3	7	21	7	6
4	6.5	26	6.5	5
5	6	30	6	4
6	5.5	33	5.5	3
7	5	35	5	2
8	4.5	36	4.5	1
9	4	36	4	0

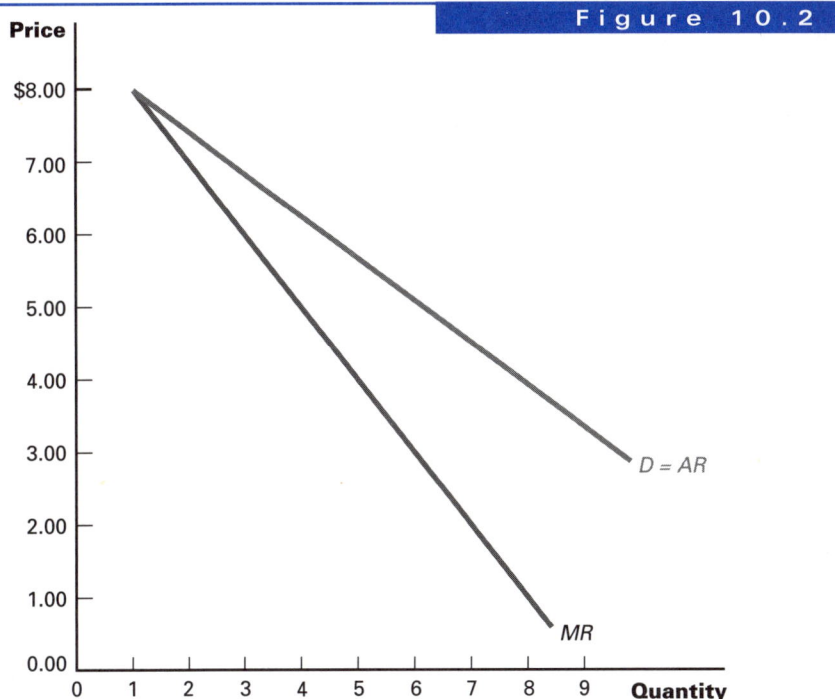

Figure 10.2

The Price-Searching Firm's Revenue Functions

This figure illustrates the problem for the price searcher. Because the firm faces a negatively sloped demand curve, additional output can be sold only by lowering price. As this figure shows, the MR curve lies below the AR curve. When demand is negatively sloped, MR falls as output increases, causing AR to decrease as well. For price searchers, P = AR > MR.

The cost functions that were defined in Chapter 9 apply to all firms, regardless of market structure. The marginal revenue functions defined above are different for price–taking and price–searching firms because the demand curves faced by these two kinds of firms are different. The remainder of this chapter focuses on the rule firms in any market structure use to maximize profits.

Section Recap

Price-taking firms take the market price as given. For the firm, price is invariant to the level of output; therefore, price and marginal revenue are equal. Price-searching firms face a downward-sloping demand curve; as they increase output, per-unit price declines. Consequently, at each output level, marginal revenue is less than price.

Short-Run Profit Maximization

We now have the tools needed to establish the firm's rule for maximizing profits (or minimizing losses) in the short run. It is important to note that this rule is the same regardless of whether the firm is a price taker (perfect competitor) or a price searcher. We consider the case for the price taker first.

Profit Maximization for the Price-Taking Firm

The short-run situation of a price-taking firm is as follows:

- At least one of the firm's inputs is fixed; thus, the firm faces rising marginal cost.

- The firm takes input prices as given.

- The firm takes market price as given; thus, marginal revenue is constant.

The short-run situation for a price-taking firm is illustrated graphically by putting the cost and revenue functions together, as in Figure 10.3. Now we are able to see the importance of the output–cost and output–revenue relationships. In the short run, the firm can control only one variable that affects costs or revenue: output. Therefore, *the short-run profit-maximizing decision for the price-taking firm is an output decision.*

A price-taking firm maximizes short-run profits by producing the level of output at which marginal revenue equals marginal cost. To see that this is the case, consider the output levels identified in Figure 10.3. At Q_1, marginal revenue, which equals market price, P_1, exceeds marginal cost. That is, $P_1 > MC_1$ at Q_1. Producing another unit of output adds to total profit (the difference between total revenue and total cost) because marginal revenue exceeds marginal cost. In more general terms, the additional benefits of another unit

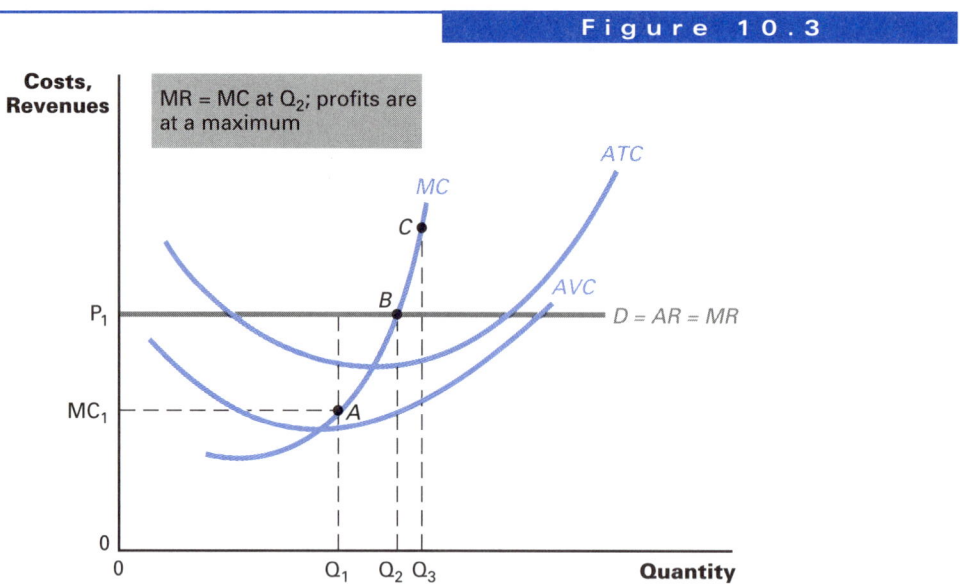

Figure 10.3

Determination of the Profit-Maximizing Level of Output: The Case of the Price-Taking Firm

The output level that maximizes the price-taking firm's short-run profits is found where marginal revenue and marginal cost are equal. At Q_1, marginal revenue exceeds marginal cost. MC at Q_1 is MC_1. So long as MR > MC, the firm increases profits by increasing production. At output level Q_2, MR equals MC (point B). For units of output beyond Q_2, for example, output level Q_3, MC exceeds MR: Producing more than Q_2 units reduces profits.

of output – measured as marginal revenue – are greater than the additional costs – measured as marginal cost. So long as marginal revenue is greater than marginal cost, the firm increases profits by producing one more unit. However, as output increases, marginal cost rises. At output level Q_2, marginal revenue, or market price, is just equal to marginal cost (point B). For units of output beyond Q_2, such as Q_3, marginal cost exceeds marginal revenue: The cost incurred to produce an additional unit of output exceeds the benefit – the marginal revenue that is earned. Producing more than Q_2 units reduces profits. Thus, *the firm maximizes short-run profits by producing the output level at which MR = MC.*

Profit Maximization for the Price-Searching Firm

In the case of the price-searching firm, the demand curve faced by the firm is downward sloping. The short-run cost and revenue functions for a price-searching firm are illustrated in Figure 10.4. According to the rule for profit-maximization – produce the level of output at which MR = MC – the firm should produce Q_2 units of output and charge a price of P_2 if it wishes to maximize profits. To see that this is the profit-maximizing level of output, consider the output levels Q_1 and Q_3. At output level Q_1, marginal revenue is greater than marginal cost and the firm can add to its profit by increasing the level of output. This is true for all levels of output less than Q_2. On the other hand, if the firm decides to produce at Q_3, it will be adding more to its costs than to its revenues because the addition to total cost, mar-

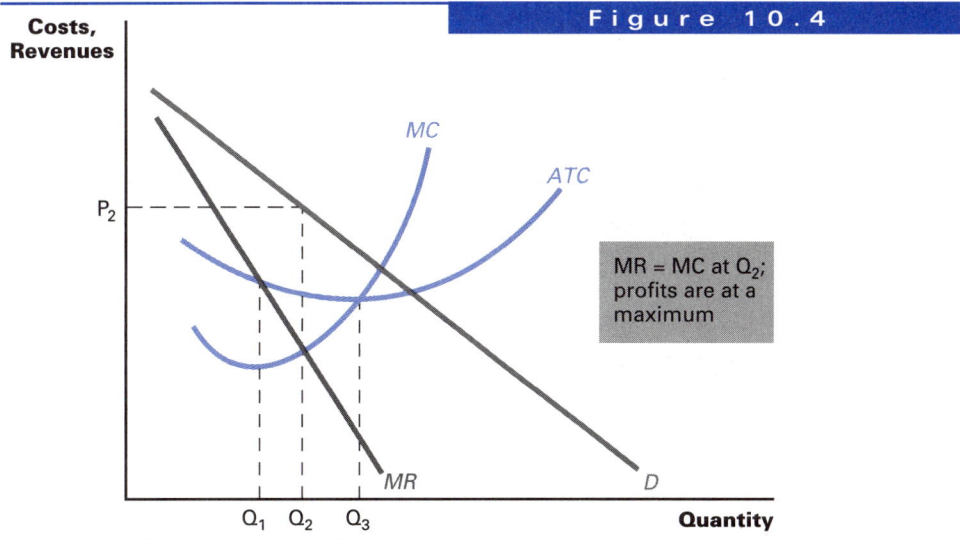

Figure 10.4

MR = MC at Q_2; profits are at a maximum

Determination of the Profit-Maximizing Level of Output: The Case of the Price-Searching Firm

The output level that maximizes the price-searching firm's short-run profits is found where marginal revenue and marginal cost are equal. At Q_1, marginal revenue exceeds marginal cost. If another unit of output is produced, it adds to total profit (the difference between total revenue and total cost) because MR > MC. So long as MR > MC, the firm increases profits by producing one more unit. At output level Q_2, MR is just equal to MC. For units of output beyond Q_2, for example, output level Q_3, MC exceeds MR: Producing more than Q_2 units reduces profits.

ginal cost, is greater than the addition to total revenue, marginal revenue. This is true for any level of output greater than Q_1. Hence we have shown that *price-searching firms also maximize profits by producing the level of output at which MR = MC*, just as in the case of the price taker.

In the case of both the price-taking firm and the price-searching firm, profits are maximized by producing the level of output at which MR = MC.

Determination of Profit...or Loss

As we saw in the previous section, the demand curve for the individual price-taking firm's product is perfectly elastic. The firm can produce as much output as it wants and sell it at the market price. The firm has no incentive to lower price in order to increase sales. On the other hand, if the firm tries to raise its price above the market price, consumers will simply switch to one of the firm's competitors. Therefore, *for the price-taking firm, the problem of profit maximization is strictly an **output** decision*.

In the previous section we established the rule for determining the profit-maximizing output level – produce the level of output at which marginal revenue equals marginal cost. Now we want to measure the amount of economic profit or loss associated with a chosen output level.

Referring to Figure 10.5 (a), which illustrates demand and supply for a good produced in a competitive market, the equilibrium market price is P_1 and equilibrium market output is Q_M. The representative firm depicted in Figure 10.5 (b) takes P_1 as given. In the previous section we showed that market price equals average revenue. We also showed that, because the perfectly competitive firm is a price taker, the per-unit price of output is constant; marginal revenue is also equal to market price. Finally, because consumers are willing to pay the same price, P_1, for each unit of output the firm produces, the marginal revenue curve is also the firm's demand curve:

$$P = AR = MR = D$$

For the firm depicted in Figure 10.5, profits are maximized at Q_1, the output level at which marginal revenue equals marginal cost. (Note that Q_1 is a small fraction of Q_M.) Having determined the profit-maximizing output level, total economic profit, or loss, can be calculated in the following manner.

1. Calculate total revenue. Total revenue is equal to price times quantity. Thus, at the profit-maximizing level of output, total revenue is:

$$TR = P_1 \times Q_1$$

    The calculation of total revenue for the firm is illustrated in Figure 10.5 (b). It is equal to the rectangle $0P_1BQ_1$.

2. Calculate total cost. The second step is to calculate total cost at output level Q_1. Because

$$ATC = TC/Q$$

it is also true that

$$TC = ATC \times Q$$

Figure 10.5

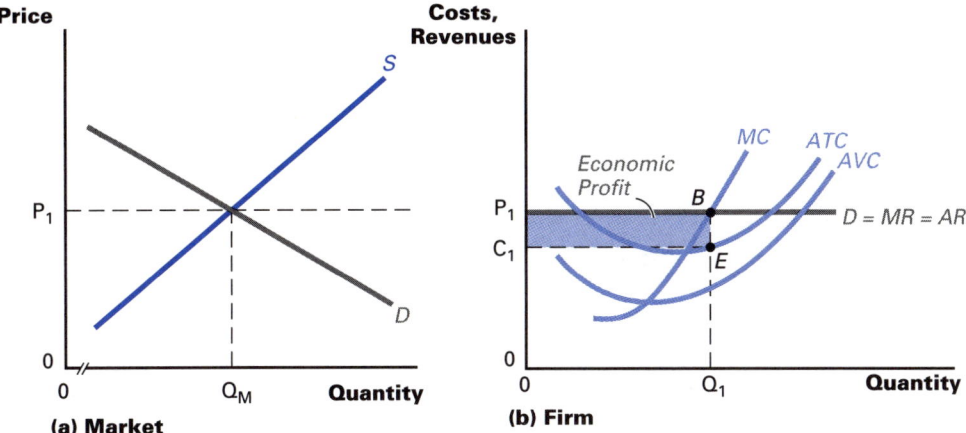

**Measuring Economic Profit for a Price-Taking Firm:
Positive Economic Profit (a)** *Market* **(b)** *Firm*

In this example, the market price is P_1, and the profit-maximizing level of output is Q_1. Total revenue is equal to the rectangle $0P_1BQ_1$. Total cost is equal to the rectangle, $0C_1EQ_1$. The economic profit earned by producing Q_1 units of output is equal to the rectangle C_1P_1BE.

In Figure 10.5 (b), we see that at Q_1, average total cost is C_1, which is found by locating the point at which the vertical line from Q_1 intersects the ATC curve. The total cost of producing Q_1 is therefore

$$TC = C_1 \times Q_1 \, ,$$

which is equal to the rectangle, $0C_1EQ_1$, in Figure 10.5 (b).

3. Calculate economic profit. Economic profit is the difference between total revenue and total cost. The economic profit earned by producing Q_1 units of output is equal to the rectangle C_1P_1BE, in Figure 10.5 (b). Given market price P_1 this firm earns positive economic profit by producing at Q_1, the output level at which marginal revenue equals marginal cost. At any other output level, total profit is lower.

The profit-maximizing output level and amount of profit are determined for any price level in the manner described in the above example. Suppose, for example, that price decreases from P_1 to P_2, as illustrated in Figure 10.6. Given this new market price, the profit-maximizing output level falls to Q_2 because marginal revenue equals marginal cost at this lower output level. Total revenue is now $Q_2 \times P_2$, or the rectangle $0P_2FQ_2$. Since average total cost at Q_2 is also P_2, total cost is $Q_2 \times P_2$, or the rectangle $0P_2FQ_2$. Thus, total revenue is equal to total cost, and economic profit equals zero. (Remember that normal profit is considered a cost of production; it is part of total costs.)

The same approach is used to measure the amount of profit (or loss) earned by a price-searching firm. Figure 10.7 illustrates the situation faced by a price searcher. Once again, the firm maximizes its profits by producing the level of output at which MR = MC, in

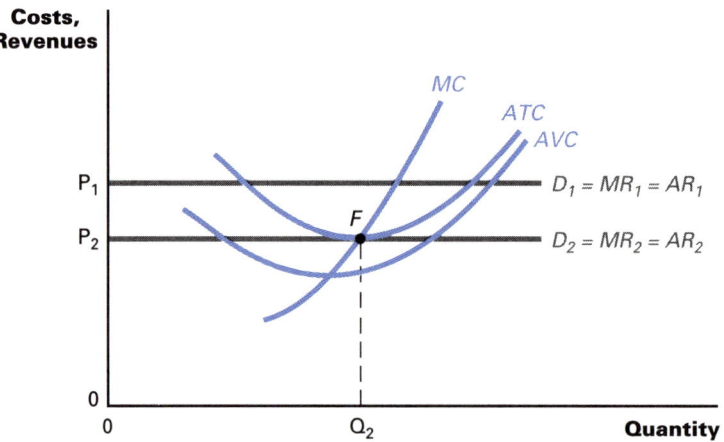

Figure 10.6

Measuring Economic Profit for a Price-Taking Firm: Zero Economic Profit Zero

Assuming that price falls from P_1 to P_2, at the new market price, the firm will maximize profits by producing output level Q_2. Total revenue is now equal to the rectangle $0P_2FQ_2$. Since ATC at Q_2 is also P_2, total cost is also equal to the rectangle $0P_2FQ_2$. Thus, total revenue equals total cost, and economic profit is zero.

this case, Q^*. According to the demand curve, the maximum price the firm can charge for each of the Q^* units of output is P^*. The average total cost of producing Q^* units of output is C^*. Thus, in this case, the price–searching firm is earning economic profit equal to the rectangle C^*P^*BE.

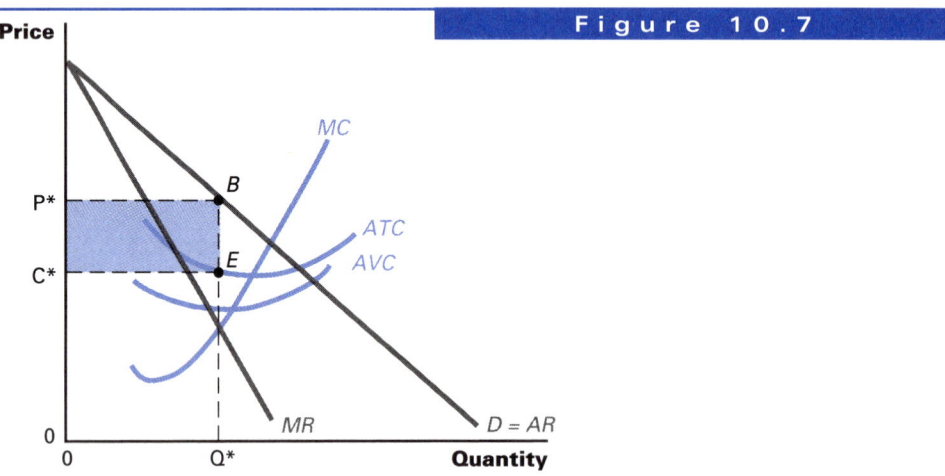

Figure 10.7

Measuring Economic Profit for a Price-Searching Firm

This figure illustrates the situation faced by a price searcher. The firm maximizes its profits by producing Q^* and charging price P^*. The average total cost of producing Q^* is C^*. Thus, in this case, the price-searching firm is earning economic profit equal to the rectangle C^*P^*BE.

Economic profit is equal to total revenue minus total cost. So long as average revenue exceeds average total cost at the profit-maximizing level of output, economic profit is positive.

To Produce or Not to Produce

In Figure 10.6, the firm is earning zero economic profit. When price equals average total cost at the profit-maximizing level of output, as it does in this example, total revenue equals total cost. If the market price is less than average total cost at the profit-maximizing level of output the firm will suffer a loss. To see that this is the case, recall that price equals average revenue. If average revenue is less than average total cost, on average, the firm pays out more than it takes in on each unit of output produced. Figure 10.6 illustrates the situation for a price-taking firm, but this relationship holds regardless of whether the firm is a price taker or a price searcher.

If market price equals average total cost at the profit-maximizing level of output, that is, the output level at which marginal revenue equals marginal cost, total revenue equals total cost and economic profit is zero. This price-output combination is called the **breakeven point**. So long as price (and therefore average revenue) exceeds average total cost at the profit-maximizing level of output the firm earns positive economic profit. If price, and therefore average revenue, is less than average total cost at the profit-maximizing level of output the firm suffers losses. At the breakeven point economic profit equals zero.

In the short run, the firm is an active business. Its objective is to maximize profits or minimize losses. Its profits (or losses) are determined only by its production decision – how much output it produces. What should the firm do when price is less than average total cost and the firm is incurring losses? Should it produce and, if so, how much should it produce to minimize losses?

When market price is less than average total cost but greater than average variable cost, the firm minimizes losses by continuing to produce the output level at which marginal revenue equals marginal cost. Such a situation is depicted in Figure 10.8 for the case of a price-taking firm. At the market price P_3, marginal revenue equals marginal cost when Q_3 units are produced. However, at that output level, price is less than average total cost. Total revenue is equal to the rectangle $0P_3IQ_3$ ($P_3 \times Q_3$). Total cost is equal to the rectangle $0C_3HQ_3$ ($H \times Q_3$). Because total cost is greater than total revenue, the firm suffers an economic loss equal to the rectangle P_3C_3HI.

Why does the firm continue to produce at all when it is incurring losses? Recall that total cost is the sum of total fixed costs and total variable costs. If the firm does not produce at all, its losses are equal to its total fixed cost. However, so long as price is greater than average variable cost, the firm can generate revenues in excess of total variable cost. By producing at Q_3, the firm can pay all of its variable costs and have some revenue left to pay part of its fixed costs, thus reducing the losses it suffers in the short run. Consequently, *when price is less than average total costs but greater than average variable cost at the output level at which marginal revenue equals marginal cost, the firm minimizes its losses by continuing to produce.* This conclusion applies to both price-taking and price-searching firms.

Breakeven point: Assuming the firm is following the rule for profit maximization, the price-output combination at which price equals average total cost and economic profit is therefore zero.

276

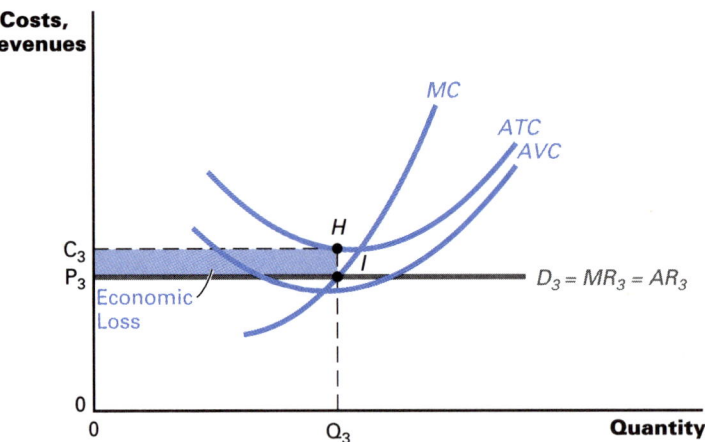

Figure 10.8

**Short-Run Economic Loss for a Price-Taking Firm:
Price Greater than AVC**

When market price is less than ATC but greater than AVC, to minimize losses the firm produces the output level at which MR = MC. At the market price P_3, MR equals MC at Q_3, and at that output level P_3 < ATC. Total revenue is equal to the rectangle $0P_3IQ_3$. However, total cost is equal to the rectangle $0C_3HQ_3$. Because total cost is greater than total revenue, the firm suffers a loss equal to the rectangle P_3C_3HI.

However, when market price is less than average variable cost at the level of output at which MR = MC, the firm minimizes losses by shutting down. If the market price equals average variable cost at the level of output at which MR = MC, the firm's total revenue equals its total variable costs and the firm incurs a loss equal to its total fixed costs. This price-output combination is called the **shutdown point**. When price is less than average variable cost at the loss-minimizing output level, the firm is not generating enough revenue to pay all of its variable costs, let alone any fixed costs. In this situation, the minimum loss incurred is the firm's fixed costs. Any production at all increases the loss to more than just fixed costs. Figure 10.9 illustrates the shutdown point for a price-taking firm. At a price equal to P_4:

$$\text{TR} = P_4 \times Q_4 = \text{TVC}$$

If the firm produces Q_4, its loss is exactly equal to its total fixed costs, or the rectangle P_4C_4YZ. At any price below P_4, the loss from production would increase – the firm would incur losses equal to its fixed costs *plus* part of its variable costs. Thus, *when price is less than average variable cost at the level of output at which MR = MC, the loss-minimizing output level is zero output – no production.* Once again, this conclusion applies to both price-taking and price-searching firms.

Figures 10.10 (a) and (b) illustrate the breakeven and shutdown points for a price-searching firm. In Figure 10.10 (a), the profit-maximizing price and output are P_1 and Q_1. In this case, price, which equals average revenue, is equal to the average total cost of pro-

Shutdown point:
Assuming the firm is following the rule for profit maximization, the price-output combination at which price equals average variable cost. If price falls below this level, the firm minimizes losses by shutting down.

Figure 10.9

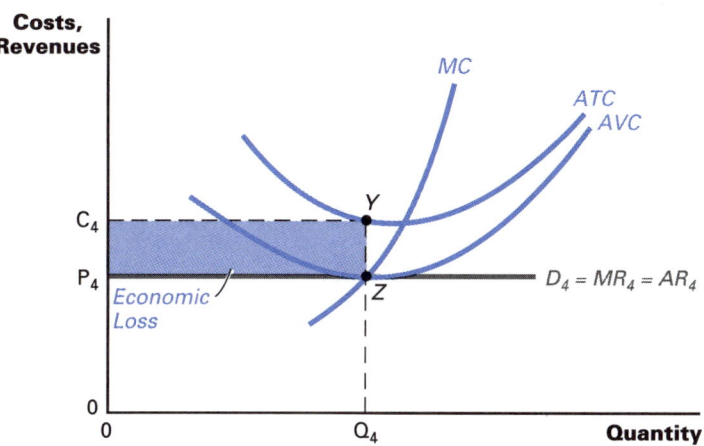

The Shutdown Point

When price is less than AVC at the profit-maximizing level of output, the firm shuts down. It cannot generate enough revenue to pay all of its variable costs, let alone any fixed costs. At a price equal to AVC, in this case P_4, $TR = P_4 \times Q_4 = TVC$. The firm's loss is equal to its TFC, the rectangle P_4C_4YZ. At any price below P_4, which is referred to as the shutdown point, if the firm continues to operate, the losses from production will increase. At prices below P_4 the loss-minimizing output level is zero output – no production.

ducing each of the Q_1 units of output. Thus, the firm in Figure 10.10 (a) is just breaking even. In Figure 10.10 (b), the profit-maximizing price and output are P_2 and Q_2. In this case, price is equal to average variable cost. The firm's total revenue is equal to the rectangle $0P_2IQ_2$, which also equals total variable cost. However, total cost is equal to the rectangle $0C_2HQ_2$. The difference between the firm's total revenue and its total cost, the rectangle P_2C_2HI, is equal to the firm's total fixed costs. Hence, the firm is indifferent between continuing to operate and shutting down; in either case, its losses equal its total fixed costs.

So long as $P > AVC$ at the profit-maximizing level of output, the firm minimizes losses by continuing to produce. If $P < AVC$ at the profit-maximizing level of output, the firm minimizes losses by shutting down.

Section Recap

Sunk Costs Again

In the short run, fixed costs are sunk costs and are ignored in the firm's decision-making process. We have just seen this in our analysis of short-run profit-maximizing behavior. However, our approach to the firm's short-run profit-maximizing decision may seem a bit strange to those who work in business or have studied business. You may be thinking, the firm has to pay its fixed costs first, then worry about its variable costs. How can it ignore its fixed costs? Of course, the firm does pay its fixed costs, and in a broad, long-run sense, it cannot ignore them.

Figure 10.10

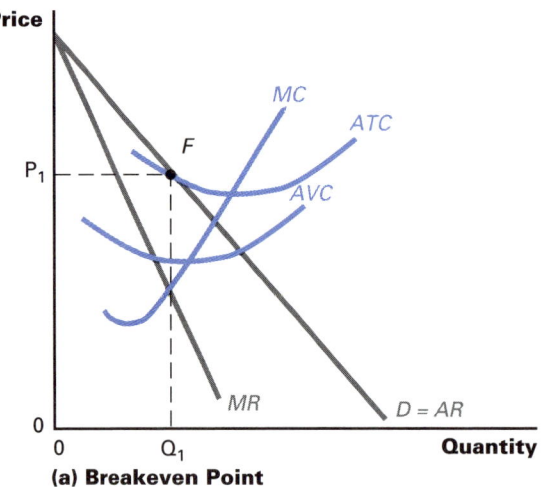

(a) Breakeven Point

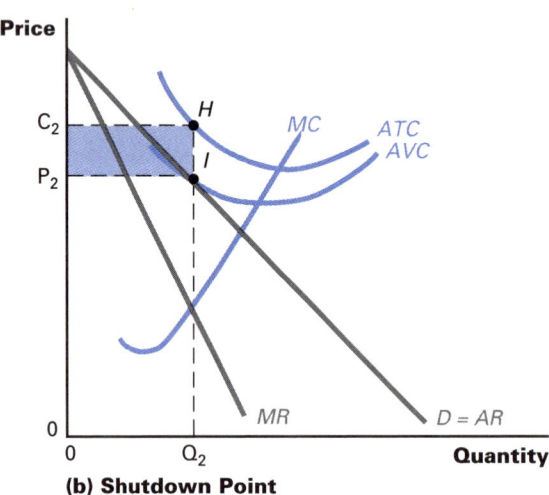

(b) Shutdown Point

**The Breakeven and Shutdown Points for a
Price-Searching Firm (a)** *Breakeven Point* **(b)** *Shutdown Point*

In Figure 10.10 (a), the profit-maximizing price and output are P_1 and Q_1. Price, which equals average revenue, is equal to the average total cost of producing Q_1, and economic profit is zero; the firm is breaking even. In Figure 10.10 (b), the profit-maximizing price and output are P_2 and Q_2. Price is equal to average variable cost. The firm's total revenue, the rectangle $0P_2IQ_2$, equals its total variable cost. Total cost is equal to the rectangle $0C_2HQ_2$. The difference between total revenue and total cost, the rectangle P_2C_2HI, is equal to the firm's total fixed costs. Hence, this firm is indifferent between continuing to operate and shutting down; in either case, its losses will equal its total fixed costs.

The analysis of the firm's behavior has focused, thus far, on the short run. A firm incurs the obligations of its fixed costs when it decides to go into business. The decision to go into business is a long-run decision based on *anticipated* prices, revenues, and costs.

However, once the firm is in business, it is operating in the short run. The price-taking firm has no control over market prices or its cost structure (determined by the production function) in the short run. Its short-run problem is how to maximize its welfare given that it is in business and has certain fixed-cost obligations.

Once in this short-run situation, how does the firm maximize its welfare? It produces additional output if the additional revenue exceeds the additional cost incurred. The cost of additional output is the cost of the variable inputs. If the revenue from production is at least as great as the variable costs incurred, the firm is better off producing output. Any additional revenue in excess of variable costs can be used to pay off part of the firm's fixed costs. However, if the revenue generated by producing output is less than the additional costs of production (the variable costs), the firm is better off shutting down. If the firm continued to produce, it would pay not only all of its fixed costs out of its pocket, but some variable costs as well. The profit-maximizing (loss-minimizing) firm pays attention to the actual costs and benefits of a decision. In the short run, when deciding what level of output to produce, fixed costs are sunk costs; they are ignored.

This does not imply, however, that losses are totally ignored. When a firm incurs short-run losses, it has important long-run decisions to make. It will continue to incur losses only if it believes that demand for its product will rise in the future, thus pushing up the market price. The firm also must be able to finance its short-run losses. To some extent, these decisions are related. A firm can borrow to cover its short-run losses only if lenders believe the firm will become profitable in the future.

Supply Decisions in a Dynamic Economy

In this chapter, we have derived a relatively simple decision rule for short-run profit maximization: Produce that level of output at which marginal revenue equals marginal cost. The decision rule was explained using an abstract picture of the firm's cost and revenue functions. Actually implementing this rule in a complex and dynamic economy is quite a challenge. Consumer demand, and therefore product prices, are changing all the time. Input markets are also dynamic; changes in supply and demand in these markets cause input prices to change. Technological developments alter production processes as well, making existing technologies less productively efficient than new ones.

To maintain their competitiveness and productive efficiency, firms must attempt to anticipate new developments and respond quickly to changes in market prices and cost conditions. While the firms' short-run options are limited, they must make adjustments quickly to maximize profits. Further complicating matters, these decisions are being made at the same time that firms are considering and making long-run decisions.

Summary

Firms are in business to make a profit. Although firms differ in many respects, we assume that they all seek to maximize profits. **Normal profit** is a part of the opportunity cost of production. It is the payment that is just sufficient to motivate the entrepreneur to assume the risks of supply.

Does It Make ECONOMIC SENSE?

Losses? What Losses?

In recent years a number of companies that have traditionally been considered the leaders in their industries have fallen on hard times. General Motors incurred losses for several years and had to reorganize and cut costs to return to profitability. IBM, the leader in computing equipment, found itself in a similar position. The airline industry has been plagued by recurring losses for an extended period of time. In 1982, Gannett Company, a company that owns many local newspapers in the United States, launched a national daily newspaper called *USA Today*. It suffered losses each year of operation, accumulating operating losses in excess of $250 million by mid-1989. Moreover, these loss figures underestimate the true losses incurred by excluding the costs of literally hundreds of person-years of work from reporters, editors, and other personnel that *USA Today* "borrowed" from other Gannett papers. These figures also omit the capital expenditures on plant and equipment for the paper. Considering the fact that firms are in business primarily to make a profit it is worth asking, Does it make economic sense for a business to continue operating in the face of huge losses?

For many firms, the answer is yes! The decision to start up and maintain a business is a long-run decision. In the case of *USA Today*, Gannett decided to start the paper based on its expectations concerning the potential for success — the potential for profits — over time. Gannett believed that a newspaper like *USA Today* could become a profitable business, but it would take time. Costs were expected to exceed revenues for a number of years because circulation of the paper was expected to grow slowly,

Economic profit is the difference between total revenue and the total opportunity cost of production, which includes normal profit. When a firm is earning zero economic profit, all factors of production are receiving payments equal to their highest-valued employment opportunity. When economic profit is greater than zero, resources are earning more than their next highest-valued earnings opportunity. Economic profit is not equivalent to accounting profit. Accounting profit omits normal profit and other implicit costs of production.

The output-revenue relationship for a firm depends on the shape of the firm's demand curve. A firm is a **price taker** if its demand curve is perfectly elastic or a **price searcher** if its demand curve is negatively sloped. Since price is invariant with respect to output for a price taker, revenue per unit of output (**average revenue**) and the change in revenue associated with a change in output (**marginal revenue**) are constant and equal to market price.

For a price searcher, price falls as output expands. Thus, average and marginal revenue fall as well, and marginal revenue is less than average revenue.

In the short run, firms seek to maximize profits by producing at the output level at which the difference between total cost and revenue is the greatest. That output level is the one at which marginal revenue equals marginal cost.

A firm earns economic profits when market price (average revenue) exceeds average total cost at the profit-maximizing level of output. Economic profit is zero when market

causing subscription and advertising revenue to grow slowly. On the other hand, initial costs would be high. Actual revenue and cost experienced by the paper over its first seven years of operation were close to initial projections. For the managers of *USA Today* the short-run problem was to minimize the losses while continuing to make the expenditures that contribute to growth in the paper's popularity.

In the case of established firms such as General Motors, IBM, and various airlines, losses are viewed from a long-run perspective. These firms have historically produced healthy profits. However, the environment within which each of these firms operates is constantly changing. Technological advances in the computer industry have resulted in a considerable increase in the number of competitors and the level of competition in the computer industry. In a similar fashion, rising fuel costs, changing consumer preferences, and an increase in competition from foreign producers have altered significantly the picture in the auto industry. Deregulation and a corresponding increase in competition among carriers led to numerous significant changes in the airline industry. Thus, IBM, General Motors, and the airlines must continually make adjustments to maintain their competitive edge and profitability. Many of the changes that must be made can only be accomplished over time. In the interim, losses are a very real possibility.

An ever-present decision in a business experiencing steady losses is, "Should we halt production and shut down the business or continue production in the face of losses?" This decision has to be made (or reassessed) based on changing expectations about future revenues and costs, not the losses previously suffered. Past losses are sunk costs; decisions today will not alter those losses. The relevant questions are about the future. Are revenues growing as anticipated? Are costs in line with projections? Do we still believe the business can be profitable given more time and effort?

The managers of firms such as General Motors, IBM, the airlines, and Gannett continue to believe in the long-run profitability of their respective firms. Whether their beliefs will turn out to be correct in the long run remains to be seen.

---

price equals the average total cost at this output level. If price falls below average total cost at the profit-maximizing level of output, the firm will minimize losses by continuing to produce so long as market price exceeds average variable cost. If price is less than average variable cost, losses are minimized by shutting down and producing nothing.

Questions for Thought

Knowledge Questions

1. Define the following terms: total revenue, average revenue, marginal revenue, and compare and contrast the total revenue, average revenue, and marginal revenue functions for a price-taking firm and a price-searching firm.

2. Explain the rule firms follow to determine the profit-maximizing (loss-minimizing) level of output.

3. Define the firm's breakeven and shutdown points. Do these concepts differ depending on whether we are talking about a price-taking versus a price-searching firm?

4. Explain why fixed costs are sunk costs in the short run.

Application Questions

5. When a price-taking firm earns zero economic profit, its short-run average total cost is at a minimum. Explain why and illustrate graphically.

6. Referring to Table 9.3 in Chapter 9, and assuming the firm is a price taker, determine the firm's profit-maximizing level of output and calculate the amount of profit (or loss) when the price is $1, $2, and $6.

7. Graphically illustrate the situation in which a price-searching firm would minimize its losses by shutting down as opposed to continuing to operate in the short run.

8. Assume that you have been offered a job that pays $40,000 per year. In addition, you have the opportunity to start your own business. The revenues are expected to be $100,000 per year and explicit costs will be $62,000. Which employment option would you choose and why?

Synthesis Questions

9. Assume a price-searching firm is currently producing the profit-maximizing level of output and is earning positive economic profits. Illustrate this situation graphically. Now assume there is a decrease in the incomes of consumers in the market for the firm's output. What will happen to the firm's profit-maximizing output level and price and the amount of profit earned by the firm? Illustrate these effects graphically.

10. It has been observed that price-searching firms operate only in the price-elastic portion of the demand curve for their output. Using the graphical model of the profit-maximizing level of output for a price-searching firm, show why this is true.

11. In the example involving Jim and Stella, we stated that so long as expected revenues are equal to $188,600, Jim and Stella are indifferent between going into the yogurt business and staying at their current jobs. Can you think of a reason why they might nonetheless prefer to go into the yogurt business? Can you provide an economic rationale for this decision?

12. Assume that a price-taking firm is producing the profit-maximizing level of output and is earning positive economic profit. Illustrate this situation graphically. Now assume that there is an increase in the number of firms in the market in which this particular firm is operating. What will happen to the firm's profits? Why? Illustrate these effects graphically.

End Notes

[1] In the remainder of the text, when we use the term *profit*, we are referring to economic profit, unless otherwise specified.

The Perfect Competition Model

Overview

The political changes in Eastern Europe and the former Soviet Union have resulted in a radical transformation of the affected economies. In particular, these changes have spawned a distinct, if not always steady, movement in the direction of increased reliance on "market forces," as opposed to command-and-control regimes, to determine the allocation of scarce resources. While this shift has not been greeted enthusiastically by everyone, its backers continue to argue on its behalf, citing the efficiency of markets. At the same time, many voices in the United States have called for increased reliance on "market forces" rather than government intervention in determining the answers to such questions as what to produce and how to produce. In both of these cases, the faith expressed in market forces is based on the model of a competitive economy, one in which output decisions are determined by the market forces of supply and demand.

In this chapter we develop the model of a perfectly competitive market. Although the model simplifies reality in a number of ways, it allows us to identify key factors that influence the behavior of profit-maximizing firms and determine the efficiency of market outcomes. In so doing, the perfect competition model serves as a benchmark by which we can evaluate market structures that more closely approximate those actually observed in our economy. These other market structures are considered in Chapters 12 and 13.

We begin the chapter with an examination of the basic characteristics of a perfectly competitive market. We then consider the short-run and long-run profit-maximizing behavior of the perfectly competitive firm. Several examples of competitive markets in action are used to highlight the role of competitive markets as rationing and allocating mechanisms. These examples demonstrate the power of the consumer in a market economy and reveal the means by which perfectly competitive markets generate long-run economic efficiency.

Learning Objectives

After reading and studying this chapter, you will be able to:

1. Describe the perfectly competitive market structure

2. Identify the perfectly competitive firm's short-run supply curve

CHAPTER 11

3. Explain how long-run market equilibrium in a perfectly competitive market is reestablished once it has been disturbed

4. Construct the long-run supply curve for constant-cost and increasing-cost industries

5. Explain how the model of a perfectly competitive market illustrates the concept of economic efficiency

Characteristics of a Perfectly Competitive Market

In Chapter 8 we introduced a variety of criteria for categorizing firms in the economy, including the type of output produced, the legal framework, and market structure. The third approach – market structure – is the one most often used by economists to study the behavior of firms. As this chapter and the next two illustrate, the type of market structure in which a firm operates has important implications for such things as the types of decisions the firm makes, the potential for the firm to earn economic profits over the long run, and the extent to which the firm behaves in an economically efficient manner. Important determinants of the answers to these questions include the size of individual firms relative to the market, the characteristics of the output produced by the firms that compete with each other, and the degree of resource mobility in the market.

Perfect competition:

A large number of relatively small price-taking firms that produce a homogeneous product and for whom entry and exit are relatively costless.

The model of **perfect competition** serves as a benchmark for analyzing how efficiently different market structures allocate society's scarce resources. As we will see below, a perfectly competitive market achieves an efficient allocation of resources. Consequently, we can use the results of this model to assess the degree of inefficiency associated with the outcomes in imperfectly competitive markets. The following conditions are assumed to characterize a perfectly competitive market.

1. Firms in the market are all small relative to the size of the market. A perfectly competitive market consists of a relatively large number of small firms; the output of each firm makes up only a very small proportion of total market output. Therefore, changes in a single firm's output level, even large changes, have little or no measurable effect on total market supply and therefore no influence on market price. Good examples of perfectly competitive markets include agricultural markets and some resource or raw materials markets. In the U.S. wheat market, for example, there is a very large number of wheat producers, and each producer is responsible for a relatively small amount of total market output.

2. Firms in the market produce a homogeneous product. The firms in a perfectly competitive market produce and sell homogeneous (identical) products – each unit of market output is a perfect substitute for another unit. Consequently, buyers are indifferent between suppliers. Buyers of wheat are indifferent as to which wheat farmer produced the wheat they purchase. Farmer Jones's wheat is identical to Farmer Brown's wheat.[1]

3. The market is characterized by freedom of entry and exit. In a perfectly competitive market, there are no barriers to entry or exit. Resources are assumed to be mobile (they can be shifted into and out of the market costlessly) and, as a consequence, firms can enter or leave a perfectly competitive market costlessly. If existing firms in the market are earning economic profits, new firms will be attracted and will enter the market. If existing firms are incurring economic losses, this will eventually drive at least some firms out of the market. In our wheat example, if wheat farmers incur losses, some farmers will switch to other crops. On the other hand, if

wheat farmers earn economic profits, other farmers will switch to wheat in an effort to capture part of the profits.

As a result of these characteristics, firms in a perfectly competitive market are price takers. The individual firm's output decision does not influence market price. Rather, market price is determined by the interaction of market demand and supply. The individual firm takes the market price as given in deciding how much output to produce. Wheat producers are price takers. The output decisions of individual wheat producers have no impact on the market price of wheat.

Perfectly competitive markets are characterized by a large number of small firms that produce a homogeneous product and by resource mobility. Perfectly competitive firms are price takers.

Section Recap

Short-Run Equilibrium for the Perfectly Competitive Firm

In Chapter 10 we established the rule the firm follows to maximize profits or minimize losses: Produce the level of output at which marginal revenue equals marginal cost, or MR = MC. In addition, we saw that a price-taking firm faces a perfectly elastic demand curve for its product. Recall that in the case of the price-taking firm the demand curve for its product intersects the vertical axis at the market price. In addition, the firm's demand curve is also its marginal revenue curve and its average revenue curve; marginal revenue and average revenue are both constant.

Figures 11.1 (a) – (d) depict a series of short-run situations that a perfectly competitive firm might encounter. In Figure 11.1 (a) the market price is P_1. Following the profit-maximizing rule, the firm produces Q_1 units of output, the level of output at which MR = MC. Because the firm's average revenue, equal to P_1, is greater than average total cost (C_1) at the profit-maximizing level of output, the firm is earning economic profit equal to the rectangle C_1P_1AB. In Figure 11.1 (b), market price is P_2 and the profit-maximizing level of output is Q_2. In this situation, total revenue, represented by the rectangle $0P_2EQ_2$, is equal to total cost (represented by the same area). Thus, the firm is earning zero economic profit, that is, a normal profit. In Figure 11.1 (b) the firm is operating at its breakeven point.

Figure 11.1 (c) and Figure 11.1 (d) illustrate situations in which the firm is incurring short-run economic losses. In Figure 11.1 (c), given the market price of P_3 the firm's loss-minimizing level of output is Q_3. Producing this level of output the firm incurs economic losses equal to the rectangle P_3C_3FG. However, because price, and therefore average revenue, is greater than the average variable cost of producing Q_3, the firm is earning enough revenue to pay all of its variable costs and part of its fixed costs. Thus, the firm should continue to operate in the short run to minimize its losses. Figure 11.1 (d) depicts the firm's shutdown point. At the market price P_4, the firm produces output level Q_4. In this situation, total revenue is equal to total variable cost, the rectangle $0P_4HQ_4$. As a result, the firm is incurring losses equal to its total fixed costs. Thus, the firm is indifferent between

Figure 11.1

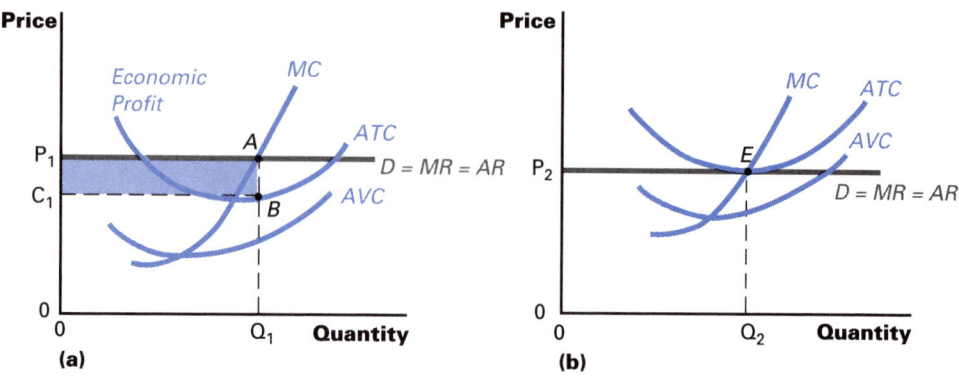

(a)

(b)

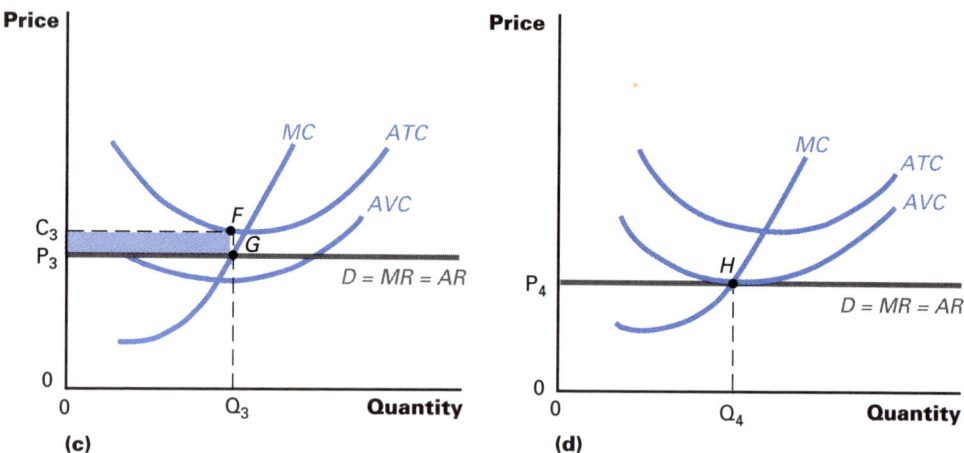

(c)

(d)

Short-run Equilibria for a Perfectly Competitive Firm (a) *Positive Profits* (b) *Breakeven* (c) *Economic Losses* (d) *Shutdown*

In Figure 11.1 (a) the market price is P_1. At the profit-maximizing output level, Q_1, the firm will earn economic profits equal to the rectangle C_1P_1AB. In Figure 11.1 (b), market price is P_2, and the profit-maximizing level of output is Q_2. Total revenue equals total cost. Thus, the firm is earning zero economic profit. In Figure 11.1 (c) the market price is P_3, and the loss-minimizing level of output is Q_3. Producing this level of output the firm incurs economic losses equal to the rectangle P_3C_3FG. Figure 11.1 (d) depicts the firm's shutdown point. At the market price P_4, the firm produces output level Q_4. In this situation, the firm is indifferent between continuing to operate and shutting down. However, if price falls below P_4, the firm should shut down, limiting its losses to its total fixed costs.

continuing to operate and shutting down. However, if price falls below P_4, the firm would be better off by shutting down and limiting its losses to its total fixed costs. If the firm were to continue to operate, total revenues would not be sufficient to cover all of the firm's variable costs, let alone any of its fixed costs.

Short-Run Supply Curve for the Price-Taking Firm

As summarized in the previous section, the decision rule for maximizing profits (and minimizing losses) says that the price-taking firm produces the output level at which marginal revenue (which equals price) equals marginal cost so long as the market price exceeds average variable cost. If the firm's marginal cost function and the market price are known, we can determine the firm's output level.

As the series of examples in Figure 11.1 clearly demonstrates, the firm's marginal cost curve, above its intersection with the average variable cost curve, tells us the quantity of output supplied by the firm at every market price. Therefore, *the firm's marginal cost curve above the minimum of the average variable cost curve is the firm's short-run supply curve.* The short-run supply curve for a typical price-taking firm is illustrated in Figure 11.2. Given the firm's short-run cost functions and its decision rule to produce the output level at which marginal revenue equals marginal cost, changes in price from P_1 to P_4 trace the short-run, positively sloped supply curve of the firm.

Figure 11.2

Short-Run Supply Curve for a Price-Taking Firm

The firm's MC curve, above its intersection with the AVC curve, determines the quantity of output supplied by the firm at each market price. Therefore, the firm's MC curve above the AVC curve is the firm's short-run supply curve.

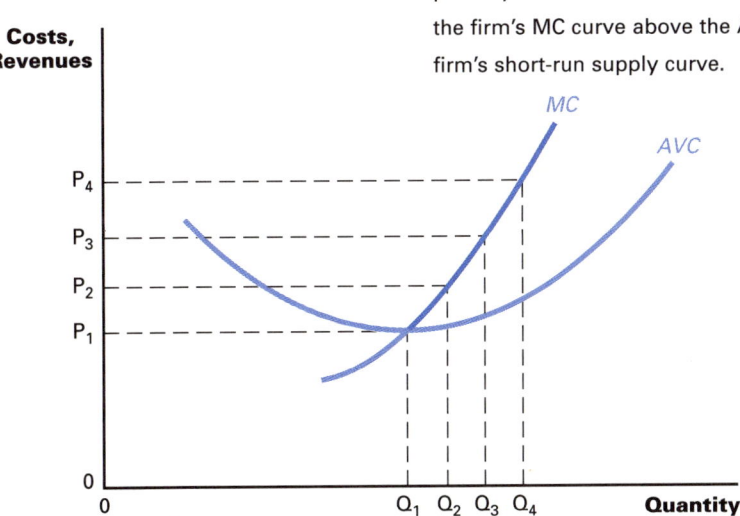

When supply curves were first introduced in Chapter 3 we said that they reflect the opportunity cost of production. Now we can see that point more clearly. The firm's supply curve is its marginal cost curve, which tells us the additional cost to the firm of producing each additional unit of output. The market short-run supply curve is the horizontal sum of these individual supply curves. That is, we sum up the quantity of output each firm is willing to produce at each price. The resulting price-quantity combinations constitute the market supply curve.

Section Recap

The firm's short-run supply curve is its marginal cost curve above minimum AVC. The market short-run supply curve is the horizontal sum of the individual firms' supply curves.

Perfect Competition and Rational Behavior

Our next step is to take a close look at market decision making in action. We will see how the utility-maximizing behavior of individual consumers and the profit-maximizing behavior of individual producers generate the outcomes observed in markets. These market outcomes are also considered in terms of their broad, economy-wide implications. It was argued in Chapter 4 that competition is an important prerequisite for economic efficiency. The focus now shifts to the characteristics of a perfectly competitive economy that constitute conditions for achieving economic efficiency.

Implicit in the definition of perfect competition is the assumption of costless information and mobility. In other words, we assume that economic decision makers are aware of all the alternatives available to them. They know the prices of all goods and inputs, and they are aware of differences in profit levels across markets. In addition, we assume that decision makers and resources can move from market to market in a costless fashion. If information and mobility are costless, individuals will acquire all information and therefore have perfect information. In addition, they will move when and where necessary at no cost to take advantage of opportunities – they are perfectly mobile.

We know that these assumptions are unrealistic. Information is costly to acquire, and getting around is also costly. However, these assumptions are simplifications that permit us to concentrate on the issues important in understanding how markets operate. Relaxing these assumptions does not alter the basic principles derived from this abstract economic model. In fact, after acquiring an understanding of this perfect market model, we can then use the model to deduce market developments that arise because of costly information and mobility.

As a preface to the following examples of competitive markets in action, it is useful to recall the Fundamental Premise of Economics and an important assumption about information and mobility. The Fundamental Premise is a basic assumption about human behavior. It says that individuals behave rationally – in making decisions people choose the alternative that maximizes their net gain from each decision. Consumers seek the best price for what they buy. Entrepreneurs seek the most profitable business ventures.

Individuals look for the highest-paying jobs. Investors search for the highest-yielding investment alternatives. This rational behavior is the force that drives markets to equilibrium.

The Dynamics of the Market Mechanism: Long-Run Equilibrium

Chapter 3 introduced supply and demand analysis and illustrated how markets work. We examined the process by which market equilibrium is disturbed by a change in some factor affecting supply or demand and then is reestablished by further changes in the market. Now we return to this equilibrium process with a better understanding of both consumer and producer behavior in competitive markets. We will again illustrate the disturbance of market equilibrium and the return to a new equilibrium. However, this time the process is examined in more detail by relying on the profit-maximizing behavior of price-taking firms and the assumptions just reviewed in the previous section.

Demand Changes in Perfectly Competitive Markets

Consider a specific market: the market for wood pencils. Assume that all pencils produced in this industry are exactly alike. The industry produces a homogeneous product. For the purposes of our example, assume that pencils are all No. 2 yellow wooden pencils. If the industry is perfectly competitive, firms are price takers. The many individual firms in the industry each face a perfectly elastic demand curve, and firms can enter and exit the market freely.

What happens in the pencil market when an increase in the demand for pencils disturbs the pencil market equilibrium? How is a new equilibrium reestablished, and how does the new equilibrium compare to the original one? To answer these questions, consider Figure 11.3.

Initial Equilibrium Figure 11.3 (a) depicts the market for pencils, and Figure 11.3 (b) depicts the cost and marginal revenue curves for a representative firm. The market supply curve, S_1, is the horizontal sum of the individual firms' marginal cost curves. The market demand curve, D_1, is the horizontal sum of all the individual consumers' pencil demand curves. The market and the firms in the market are initially in equilibrium at a price of P_1. Market output is Q_{M1}.

The equilibrium price, determined by the interaction of supply and demand, is taken as given by each firm. Each firm sets its output level, Q_{F1} in Figure 11.3 (b), such that its marginal cost is equal to marginal revenue (the market price). Since at Q_{F1}, market price also equals the firm's short-run and long-run minimum average total (unit) cost, the firm's total revenue equals total cost and economic profit is zero. The market and each firm in the market are in long-run equilibrium – there is no pressure for market price to rise or fall. In addition, there is no incentive for firms to leave or enter the market. Existing firms are earning a normal profit. The fact that each firm is operating at the minimum of the

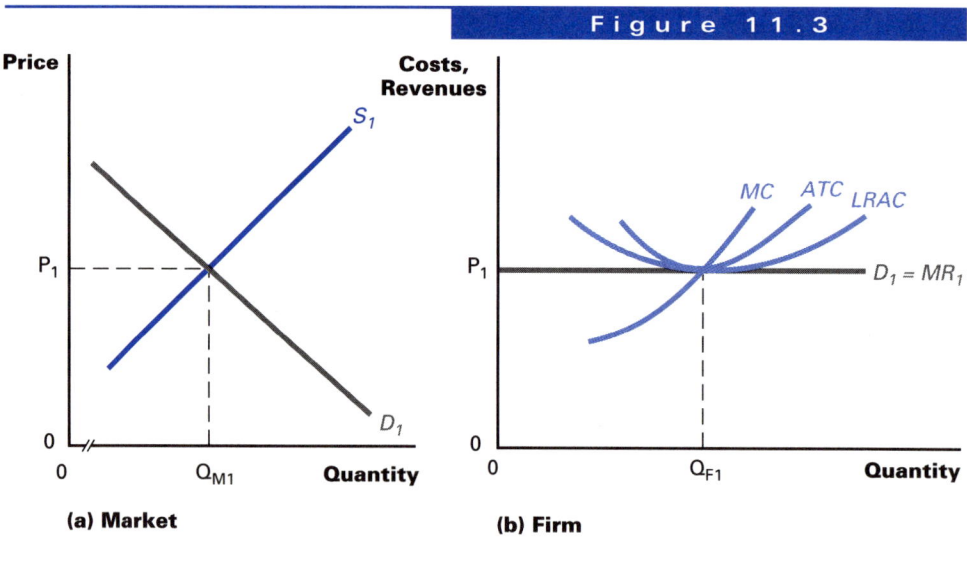

(a) Market   (b) Firm

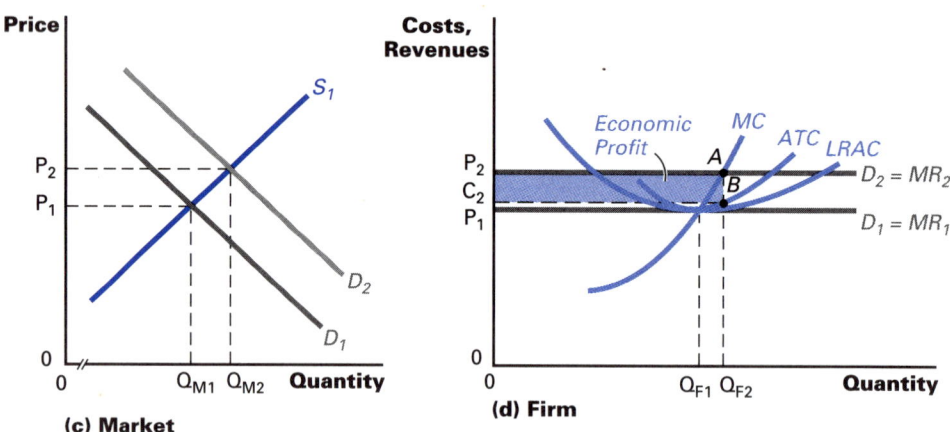

(c) Market   (d) Firm

Short-run Adjustment to a Change in Demand
(a) *Market* (b) *Firm* (c) *Market* (d) *Firm*

Figures 11.3 (a) and (b) depict the market for pencils and the situation for an individual firm, respectively. Initially, equilibrium price is P_1, market output is Q_{M1}, the firm's output level is Q_{F1}, and economic profit is zero. As shown in 11.3 (c), an increase in demand shifts market demand from D_1 to D_2, and market price increases from P_1 to P_2. Each firm increases output from Q_{F1} to Q_{F2}, as illustrated in Figure 11.3 (d), and the quantity supplied to the market increases from Q_{M1} to Q_{M2}. In the market, a new short-run equilibrium is reached at P_2 and Q_{M2}. Each firm is now earning economic profit equal to the rectangle C_2P_2AB.

long–run average cost curve indicates that firms are using the optimal plant size. New firms cannot enter and operate at lower cost than the firms currently operating in the market.

Increase in Demand Now assume that consumer demand for pencils increases. An increase in demand occurs when any factor affecting consumer demand changes in the appropriate direction. For example, the demand increase could be caused by an increased preference for pencils, an increase in the price of substitutes for pencils, or an increase in the incomes of pencil consumers. The increase in demand shifts market demand from D_1 to D_2, as shown in Figure 11.3 (c).

Short-Run Response to Increased Market Price The increase in market demand causes market price to increase from P_1 to P_2. Following the short-run profit-maximization rule, each firm responds to the higher market price by increasing output from Q_{F1} to Q_{F2}. [This increase in output is illustrated in Figure 11.3 (d).] As each firm increases its output, the quantity of pencils supplied to the market increases from Q_{M1} to Q_{M2}. In the market, a new short-run equilibrium is reached at P_2 and Q_{M2}. Note that the new higher market price is greater than the firm's average total cost at Q_{F2} units of output, as illustrated in Figure 11.3 (d). Consequently, each firm is now earning economic profit equal to the shaded rectangle C_2P_2AB. The increased willingness to pay for pencils has created short-run economic profits for existing firms.

Long-Run Market Adjustment The short-run increase in market price and the increased production and profits of existing firms are really only the beginning of the market adjustment to a new long-run equilibrium. As we have already noted, firms in this industry are now earning positive economic profits. However, these so-called excess profits over and above normal profits attract attention. Entrepreneurs notice the increased profits in the industry and are attracted to them. Additional resources are brought into the industry as new firms enter. The increase in the number of firms increases market supply and market output increases.

This long-run increase in supply is illustrated as a shift in market supply from S_1 to S_2 in Figure 11.4 (a). The increase in market supply causes output to increase, but this, in turn, causes market price to fall from P_2 back toward P_1. The decrease in market price erodes economic profits and reduces the incentive for additional firms to enter the market. In addition, existing firms reduce production to continue to maximize profits in the face of the now-declining price. As shown in Figure 11.4 (b), each firm's output eventually returns to Q_{F1} and price returns to P_1, a price at which the firms in the market earn zero economic profits.

New Long-Run Market Equilibrium Established The market has now returned to long-run equilibrium after the initial equilibrium was disturbed by the increase in pencil demand. Once all adjustments have occurred, the new long-run market equilibrium is at the old price P_1, but at a higher level of output, Q_{M3}. Firms are earning only normal profit, and there is no pressure in the market for price to change.

Let's summarize what has happened in the pencil market. Consumers decided that pencils were more valuable than they were previously – they were willing to pay more for pencils. Consumers signaled this change in the value of pencils through their spending: They began to buy more pencils at the old equilibrium price, bidding up the price. As the

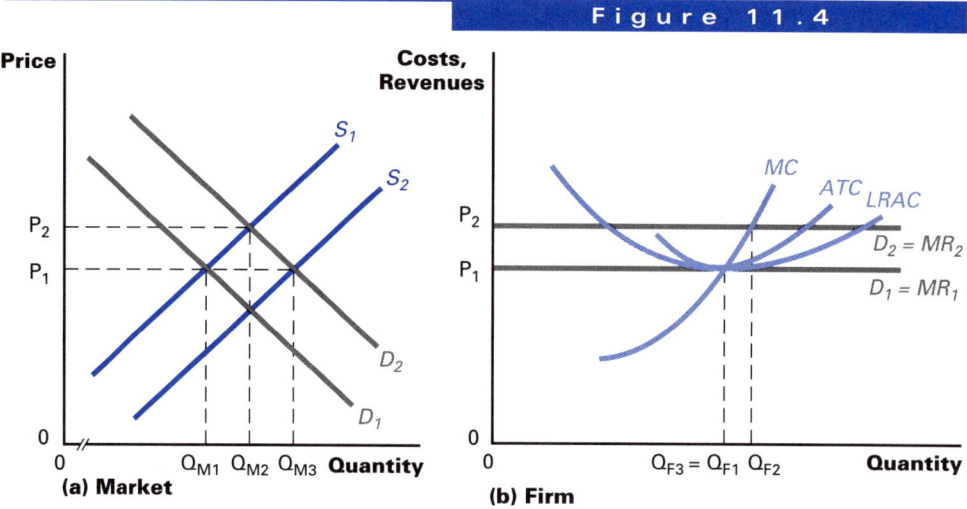

Figure 11.4

The Long-run Market Adjustment (a) *Market* **(b)** *Firm*

Over the long run, as new firms enter and existing firms increase production, market supply increases, shifting market supply from S_1 to S_2 in Figure 11.4 (a). Output increases, but market price also decreases, reducing the incentive for entry into the market. Existing firms reduce production to maximize profits in the face of the now-declining price. As shown in Figure 11.4 (b), firm output eventually returns to Q_{F1}, price returns to P_1, and firms once again earn zero economic profit. The long-run market equilibrium price and quantity are P_1 and Q_{M3}.

market price rose, firms began to earn economic profits. The higher–than–normal profits attracted resources into the market from elsewhere in the economy. The resources were able to move because we assumed resource mobility. The increased number of firms, competing with one another, bid the market price down until all economic profits had been eliminated. At the new market equilibrium the economy produces more pencils than before, at the initial market price. At the new long-run equilibrium, pencils are produced at minimum unit cost and sold to consumers at a price that just equals the unit cost.

Decrease in Demand A decrease in market demand brings about opposite adjustments. If consumer demand for pencils decreases, firms that had been earning zero economic profits begin to incur losses because price, and hence marginal revenue, has declined. In the short run, firms respond by reducing output to once again equate marginal revenue with marginal cost. However, firms are now incurring economic losses. Consequently, further changes will occur over the long run.

The economic losses eventually drive some firms out of the industry. They move to other industries with better profit prospects. As firms depart the industry, market supply decreases, driving up market price. The rise in market price reduces and ultimately eliminates losses, prompting increased output from the remaining firms. A new long-run market equilibrium is established at the original market price, but at a reduced output level. There are fewer firms in the industry, and they are earning no economic profit.

Again, the market mechanism has performed its rationing and allocating function. If consumers value pencils less, they indicate this change by purchasing fewer pencils. The fall in market price generates losses for pencil firms. These losses signal entrepreneurs that too many resources are being employed in producing pencils and so drive resources out of the pencil market and into some other, more profitable, industry. Finally, the pencil price remains the same in the long run, just equal to the cost of production.

Assuming a perfectly competitive market is initially in long-run equilibrium, an increase (or decrease) in demand will result in economic profits (or losses) for existing firms. However, entry or exit by firms will eventually eliminate any short-run profits or losses.

Section Recap

Long-Run Supply

Constant-Cost Industries In our pencil market example, after all adjustments to the increase in the demand for pencils had taken place, the equilibrium market price returned to its original level of P_1. This type of industry is called a **constant-cost industry**. In this type of industry, input prices, and therefore short-run and long-run costs, remain constant when the level of output and the demand for resources (inputs) change. As a consequence, the optimal plant size is left unchanged.

Figure 11.4 has been recreated in Figure 11.5. For the market depicted in Figure 11.5, the long-run supply curve is shown by the curve labeled S_{LR} in Figure 11.5 (a). The long-run supply curve is found by connecting the market equilibrium price-quantity combinations that exist before the change in demand and after the change in demand and all supply adjustments have occurred. *The long-run supply curve for a constant-cost industry is horizontal (perfectly elastic).*

Constant-cost industry:
Input prices are invariant to the level of output, causing the long-run supply curve for the market to be horizontal.

Increasing-Cost Industries An industry in which an increase in the supply of a good puts upward pressure on input prices is called an **increasing-cost industry**. In this case, an increase in the demand for inputs causes input prices to rise – there is a movement up the supply curve(s) of the input(s). An increasing-cost industry is illustrated in Figure 11.6. Assume that demand has increased, as in our previous example, causing market price to rise from P_1 to P_2. As firms respond by increasing output and additional firms enter the market, market supply increases. However, because it is an increasing-cost industry, production costs are also increasing. The increase in costs is the result of increased demand for inputs whose supply is less than perfectly elastic. Consequently, the short-run and long-run cost curves in Figure 11.6 (b) begin to shift up as supply increases. In this case the new equilibrium price is P_3, and the equilibrium market quantity is Q_{M3}. Firms once again earn zero economic profit.

Note that *in the case of an increasing cost industry, the long-run supply curve, S_{LR}, is upward sloping.* This reflects the fact that as output increases, production costs are also increasing.

Increasing-cost industry:
Input prices are an increasing function of the level of output, causing the long-run supply curve for the market to be upward sloping.

Figure 11.5

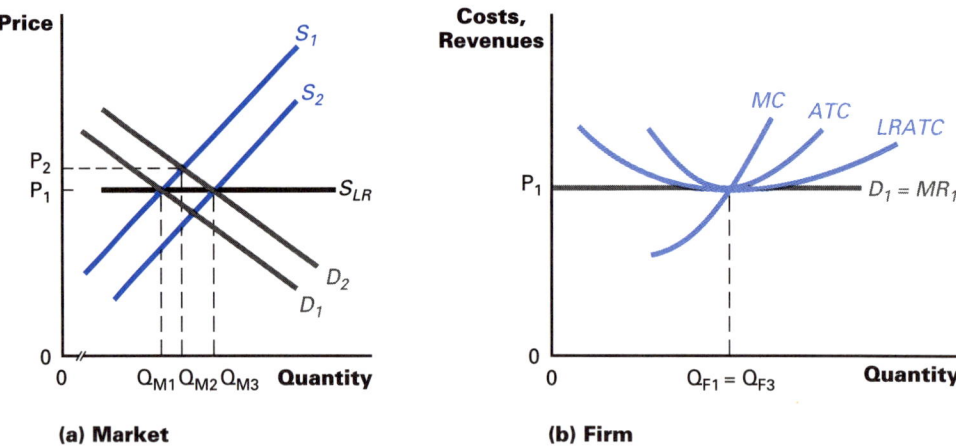

Price | **Costs, Revenues**

(a) **Market** (b) **Firm**

Long-Run Supply in a Constant-Cost Industry
(a) *Market* (b) *Firm*

Figure 11.4 has been recreated in this figure. After all adjustments to the increase in the demand for pencils have taken place, the equilibrium market price is at its original level of P_1. In this type of industry, which is called a **constant-cost industry**, costs remain constant when the level of output and hence the demand for resources (inputs) change. The long-run supply curve for a constant-cost industry is horizontal (perfectly elastic), as shown by the heavy black line labeled S_{LR} in Figure 11.5 (a).

Hence, over the long run, as supply increases, so does the price that a firm must receive to earn a normal profit.

In a constant-cost industry, long-run supply is perfectly elastic; a change in demand does not affect the long-run equilibrium market price. In an increasing-cost industry, the long-run supply curve is upward sloping; an increase in demand leads to an increase in the long-run equilibrium market price.

Consumer Sovereignty

In the examples above, changes in consumer demand caused long–run changes in the market that were consistent with consumer preferences. More or fewer pencils were produced depending on whether consumers valued pencils more or less. Market sensitivity to consumer preferences is a general attribute of competitive markets: Markets respond when

Figure 11.6

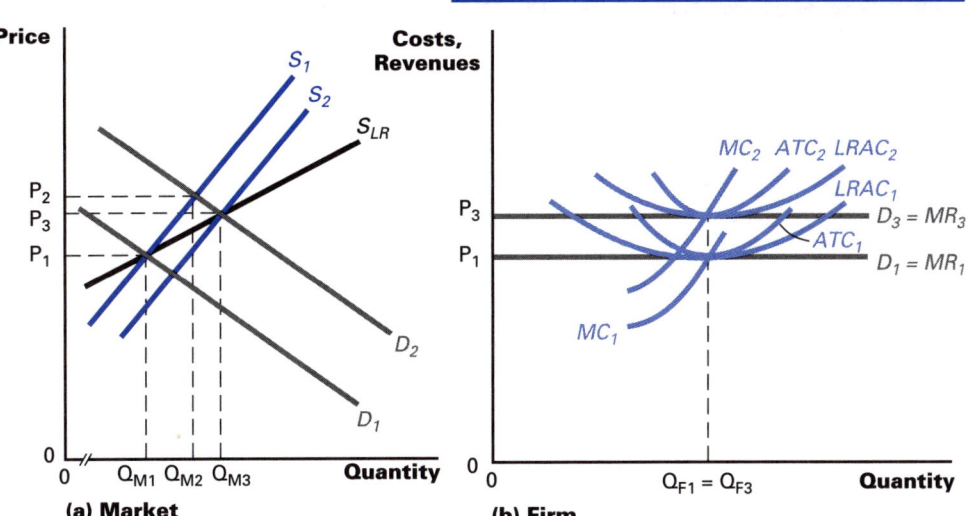

Long-Run Supply in an Increasing-Cost Industry (a) *Market* **(b)** *Firm*

This figure illustrates the situation for an **increasing-cost industry**. In this case, an increase in the demand for inputs causes input prices, and therefore costs, to increase. Assuming that demand has increased, market price will rise from P_1 to P_2 [Figure 11.6 (a)], causing market supply to increase. However, production costs are also increasing. Consequently, the cost curves in Figure 11.6 (b) shift up as supply increases. The new long-run market equilibrium price is P_3, equilibrium quantity is Q_{M3}, and firms once again earn zero economic profit. In the case of an increasing-cost industry, the long-run supply curve, S_{LR}, is upward sloping.

consumers express their preferences through their spending on goods and services. This power of consumers in competitive markets is called **consumer sovereignty**.

In a competitive market economy it is the consumer who decides what is produced. Consumers influence the price of economic goods through their willingness to pay for such goods. Consumers compete for goods by bidding up market prices. Higher prices mean increased opportunities for profit on the supply side of the market. Profit-maximizing producers seek out these opportunities by producing more of the goods valued highly by consumers. Changes in consumer preferences lead to changes in market prices. Producers respond to higher prices by reallocating resources to the production of the now more valuable goods and away from production of less valuable goods.

Consumer sovereignty:

The ability of consumers' preferences to influence the level of output in competitive markets.

Production Costs and Efficiency

One of the conditions necessary for efficient market outcomes is that markets be competitive. If we assume all other conditions – for example, perfect information and perfect

Does It Make # ECONOMIC SENSE?

Bailing Out the Farm Credit System: Who Bought the Farm?

From 1985 to 1987, the Farm Credit System – which was created to facilitate the provision of credit to farmers for the purchase of land, equipment, and seed – lost approximately $5 billion in loan defaults. The defaults occurred primarily because low crop prices prevented farmers from repaying loans for farm land. The problem was compounded by a decrease in land prices that made it impossible for farmers to pay off the debt by selling their land. In turn, the growing losses of the Farm Credit System made it more difficult for the system to raise additional funds through bond sales, thus threaten-ing the supply of credit to an already weakened farm sector.

As the financial health of the Farm Credit System deteriorated, calls for some kind of bailout plan arose. Support for a bailout was based on a number of arguments. A bailout of the Farm Credit System was consistent with many other government farm programs that are designed to provide assistance to those in need during difficult eco-nomic times. In addition, society historically has seemed generally willing to provide special treatment to the farm population. Finally, con-cerns about the impact of additional agricultural problems on the overall economy seem to have influenced Congress. After considerable debate, Congress passed controver-sial legislation in December 1987 that provided for a $4 billion injec-tion of new funds into the Farm Credit System and reorganized the system of credit banks that serve farmers. In light of the existing losses and the fact that the bailout plan was projected to cost taxpay-ers in excess of $1 billion[2] it is worth asking, Did additional sup-port for the Farm Credit System make economic sense?

First, consider the financial cri-sis at the farm level. Farmers are price takers. No individual farmer can affect the price of his product, and the prices of agricultural prod-ucts can vary considerably from year to year. For a growing season (even for several seasons) – the short run in agriculture – land is the fixed input for the farmer. The farmer decides on an expected

mobility – are met, the long-run equilibrium output level of perfectly competitive firms is economically efficient.

Economic Efficiency in the Long Run

In the short run, every firm maximizes profits by producing the level of output at which marginal revenue equals marginal cost. Because the perfectly competitive firm's demand curve is perfectly elastic, price equals marginal revenue, and the profit-maximization deci-sion rule becomes:

$$P = MR = MC$$

We have also shown that the firm produces the level of output at which marginal revenue equals marginal cost in the long run as well. It is also the case in the long run that market price equals the minimum short-run and long-run average total cost of production, or:

$$P = MR = MC = \text{minimum ATC} = \text{minimum LRAC}$$

This unique level of output is ensured in the long run by the resource mobility that we assumed as an attribute of perfectly competitive markets. In the absence of freedom of entry into and exit from a market, firms could earn economic profits in the long run. The market equilibrium price would then exceed the minimum average cost of production.

short-run output to produce to maximize short-run profits. (The output is "expected" because the farmer has only imperfect control over the relationship between inputs and output.) Prices fluctuate from year to year, but so long as the farmer s revenues are at least equal to his total costs over a period of several years, short-run losses are not a serious problem. Economic profit from the good years can be used to catch up on mortgage payments for the land.

However, if annual losses occur over several consecutive years, the farmer runs into financial difficulties and may have to sell his land and equipment to pay his debts and then leave farming for some other kind of work. If the value of the farmer's land and equipment is insufficient to pay off the debts, the farmer may be forced into bankruptcy. The steep decline in land values and the decrease in farm prices in the early and mid-1980s forced many farmers into precisely this situation.

Opponents criticized the bailout plan for several different reasons. Further aid to agriculture represented further government support to one particular sector of the economy and set a precedent for increased government intervention in private markets. Opponents also argued that a bailout would provide additional support for farmers to remain in an industry already suffering from excess supply and was, therefore, inefficient. As farmers leave the industry, supply decreases, causing an increase in market price. Assuming resource mobility, exit would continue until price rose high enough that the remaining farmers could earn a normal profit. The bailout effectively reduced the incentive for resource owners to exit from agriculture, even though losses in the farm sector suggest that those resources are more valuable in other markets. Finally, the bailout was opposed as simply being too expensive. The federal government's continued deficits created serious macroeco-

nomic problems. The bailout plan made it that much more difficult to resolve the government's spending problems.

The economic arguments would appear to provide the most support for the position maintained by the opponents of the bailout. However, as the preceding discussion suggests, the motivation for this particular policy derived as much from considerations about what the government *ought* to be doing with regard to agricultural policy (a normative question) as it did from consideration of the plan's relative economic costs and benefits (a positive question). Economic analysis provides only one piece of information that policymakers use in their decision-making process. In the case of the Farm Credit System, it is reasonable to conclude that other concerns played a dominant role.

Because, in long-run equilibrium, price equals minimum short-run and long-run average total cost, firms are using the existing plant size as efficiently as possible. In addition, they are using the most efficient capacity, or scale of plant. The assumptions that characterize a perfectly competitive market ensure that firms will employ the efficient level of capacity in the long run. To see why, assume that firms are not operating at minimum long-run average cost. In this case, a new firm could enter the market with a more efficient plant size, that is, the plant size associated with minimum long-run average cost. The firm could then charge a price for its product that is lower than the price charged by existing firms but greater than its average total cost; thus, the firm would earn economic profit. Buyers would switch to the lower-priced product, and existing firms would incur economic losses. In the long run, the remaining firms would be forced to switch to the plant size associated with the minimum long-run average cost to avoid additional economic losses.

In addition to producing at minimum average cost in both the short run and the long run, perfectly competitive firms produce the level of output at which price equals marginal cost. This condition is referred to as **allocative efficiency**. When price equals marginal cost, the value to consumers, measured by price, of the last unit of the good purchased is just equal to the value of the additional resources, measured by

Allocative efficiency:

Results when P = MC for the last unit of output produced; the value of the variable inputs used to produce the last unit of output equals its value to consumers.

marginal cost, used to produce it. If price is less than marginal cost, too many resources are going into production of the good in question. The value of the resources used to produce the units of output for which price is less than marginal cost exceeds the value of those units of output. The opposite is true in the case in which price is greater than marginal cost.

The market outcome is economically efficient because firms have no price-setting power. In addition, freedom of market entry and exit ensure that competition will drive the price down to the minimum average total cost of production in the long run.

In the long run, perfectly competitive firms employ the efficient capacity; in other words, they operate at minimum LRAC. In addition, they are allocatively efficient because P = MC for the last unit of output produced.

Cost Changes in Perfectly Competitive Markets

We have considered how a competitive market adjusts to changes in demand. The question we now address is, What happens when the costs of production change?[3] Does the perfectly competitive market handle such changes as well as it does demand-side changes? The answer is yes. In fact, the supply-side changes are handled in a very similar fashion.

Increased Input Prices   Suppose that the price of labor employed by pencil manufacturers rises. In the short run, this increased input price increases production costs. However, in the short run, firms are stuck with their existing production technology. They cannot substitute relatively less expensive inputs for the more expensive labor. Figure 11.7 illustrates the problem for pencil producers. The initial effect of the input price increase is depicted in Figures 11.7 (a) and (b). The long-run market equilibrium quantity, Q_{M1}, is disturbed by the increase in production costs. The short-run cost curves shift up from ATC_1 to ATC_2, and from MC_1 to MC_2, as shown in Figure 11.7 (b). As a result, the firm's short-run supply function decreases – each firm now supplies less output at each market price. The decrease in supply for each firm translates into a decrease in market supply, represented by the shift in market supply from S_1 to S_2 in Figure 11.7 (a).

Because these price-taking firms have no control over market price they reduce output to Q_{F2}, following their profit-maximizing decision rule. However, so long as market price remains at P_1, firms incur economic losses. The losses incurred by each firm are equal to the rectangle P_1C_2FG. These losses cause a further adjustment to occur: Some firms also begin to leave the market. This causes the supply curve to shift further to the left, to S_3 in Figure 11.7 (a). Because the number of firms and output of the remaining firms have both declined, market output falls to Q_{M2} at the initial price of P_1.

With the decrease in market supply, there is a shortage of pencils at P_1 – quantity demanded exceeds quantity supplied by the amount $Q_{M1} - Q_{M2}$. Competing for the quantity of pencils available, consumers bid the market price up. Referring to Figure 11.7 (c), as the market price rises from P_1 to P_2 along S_3, the short-run losses incurred by the remaining firms in the industry are reduced. In their efforts to maximize profits, firms

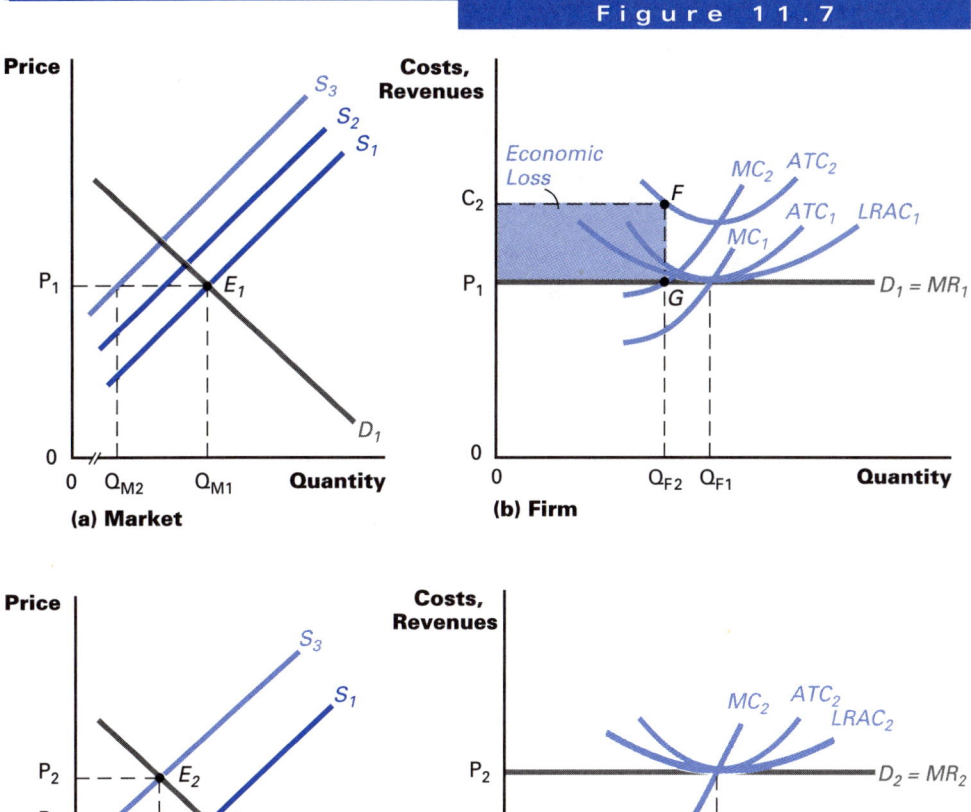

Figure 11.7

The Effect of an Increase in Input Prices
(a) *Market* (b) *Firm* (c) *Market* (d) *Firm*

This figure illustrates the effect of an increase in input prices. The increase in costs causes market supply to shift from S_1 to S_2 in Figure 11.7 (a). Firms reduce output to Q_{F2}, incurring economic losses equal to the rectangle P_1C_2FG, which causes some firms to exit, shifting market supply to S_3. Market output falls to Q_{M2}. At the initial price of P_1 there is a shortage; thus, conumers bid the market price up. Figure 11.7 (c) illustrates the new long-run market equilibrium, E_2. Market price, P_2, is higher, and output, Q_{M3}, is reduced. As shown in Figure 11.7 (d), each firm is once again earning a normal profit because $P = MC = $ minimum average total cost.

increase output as price rises.

Figure 11.7 (c) illustrates the new long–run equilibrium, E_2. Compared to the initial long–run equilibrium, E_1, market price (P_2) is higher and output (Q_{M3}) is reduced. The increased cost of producing pencils has been passed on to consumers through the higher market price. As shown in Figure 11.7 (d), the remaining firms are once again earning a normal profit since price equals marginal cost equals minimum average total cost.

Note that the increase in the market price of pencils is not the result of a direct action by firms. They are price takers and have no direct control over price. Rather, the decisions that they made as they sought to minimize their losses caused market supply to be reduced, and competition among consumers bid the market price up. Fewer pencils are produced at the new equilibrium because consumer demand is negatively sloped. Pencils are now more costly for society to produce. The market mechanism has translated these increased costs into higher pencil prices. The reduced quantity of pencils produced is rationed to those who value pencils the most.

The new equilibrium established at E_2 ignores another long-run process set in motion by the increased price of labor. In the short run, firms have no alternative but to absorb the higher costs and adjust output downward. However, over time, firms look for ways to offset the increased production costs. If firms were employing a cost-minimizing combination of inputs before the labor price increase, the price increase has caused them to be in long-run disequilibrium. Productivity per dollar spent on labor is now reduced. Firms therefore search for new input combinations to reduce costs. As they adjust their input mix by installing new production processes, to the extent that production costs are reduced, their short-run costs would shift down again. The extent to which less costly input combinations can be found depends on the nature of the production process and the time available to make the adjustment. Generally, the potential for substitution is greater the longer the period of time in question.

Technological Change Production costs can also be altered by changes in technology. Generally, we think of technological change as an advance: New technologies lower costs or make possible the production of new products. In perfectly competitive markets, the cost savings from technological change are passed on to consumers in the form of lower prices. Figure 11.8 illustrates the process by which this occurs.

Referring to Figure 11.8 (a), at an initial long-run equilibrium position with a market price of P_1 and market output of Q_{M1}, firms are earning zero economic profit. As shown in Figure 11.8 (b), price equals marginal cost equals minimum average total cost, and each firm is producing Q_{F1} units of output. Now assume there is an improvement in technology that increases the productivity of labor used to produce pencils. When the new technology is adopted by the firm, its short-run costs fall. As shown in Figure 11.8 (b), the firm's cost curves shift down from ATC_1 to ATC_2 and MC_1 to MC_2, shifting its supply curve to the right.

With the new marginal cost function, MC_2, the firm sets output at Q_{F2}, where P_1 equals the new marginal cost. At output level Q_{F2} each firm is earning economic profits, shown by the rectangle C_2P_1HI. However, these profits will not persist. The existence of economic profits causes new firms to enter the market.

Market price initially remains at P_1. However, as each price-taking firm increases its output and the number of firms in the market increases, market supply shifts to the right

Figure 11.8

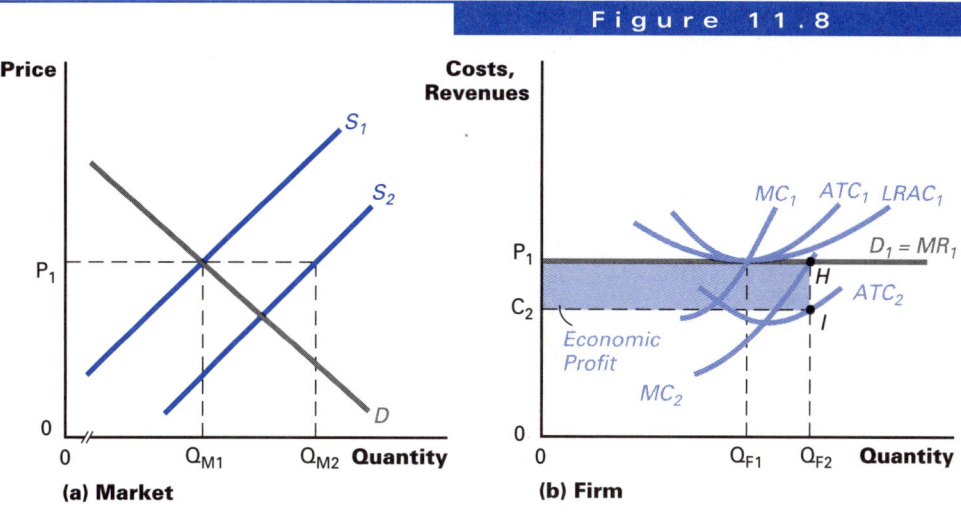

(a) Market   (b) Firm

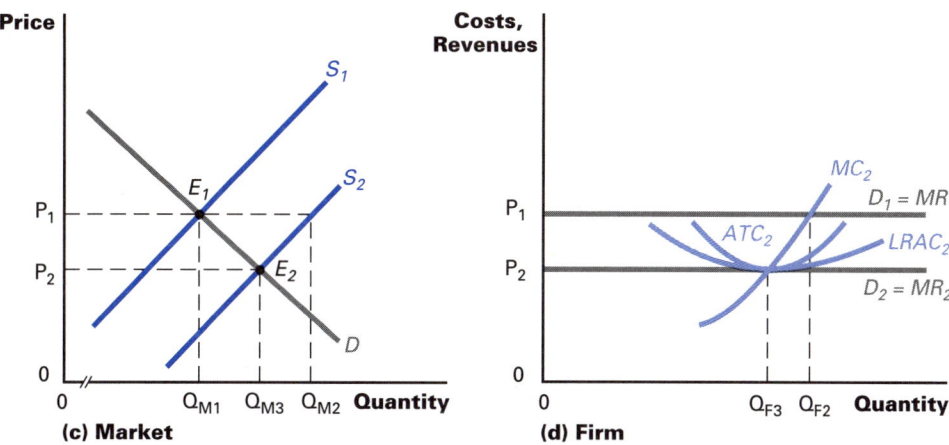

(c) Market   (d) Firm

The Effects of an Improvement in Technology
(a) *Market* (b) *Firm* (c) *Market* (d) *Firm*

Adoption of a new technology causes the firm's cost functions to shift down to ATC_2 and MC_2. Firms increase output to Q_{F2} and earn economic profit, shown by the rectangle C_2P_1HI. Entry by new firms and increased output by existing firms causes market supply to shift right from S_1 to S_2, creating excess supply [Figure 11.8 (a)]. As market price falls to P_2, each firm's output is decreased to Q_{F3}, and economic profits are reduced to zero [Figure 11.8 (d)]. Long-run equilibrium is reestablished at E_2 with an equilibrium price and quantity of P_2 and Q_{M3}, respectively [Figure 11.8 (c)].

from S_1 to S_2 in Figure 11.8 (a). At the new market output level of Q_{M2} the quantity supplied exceeds quantity demanded by the amount $Q_{M2} - Q_{M1}$, putting downward pressure on market price. Producers compete with one another to sell the excess supply. Market

Why the # DISAGREEMENT?

Quotas on
American Jobs?

Over the past two decades, U.S. demand for foreign-made autos has steadily increased. Japan's share of the U.S. auto market in 1990, including imports and models built in the United States, increased to approximately 28 percent. In response to this trend, U.S. auto makers have consistently maintained that foreign competition adversely affects the domestic economy by taking away jobs from American workers. To offset these job losses, these auto makers and the United Auto Workers union (UAW) frequently demand that trade restrictions, such as quotas, be imposed on autos imported from Japan. Partly in response to these demands, Japanese imports were capped in 1981.

In 1991, Ford, Chrysler, and the UAW once again demanded that Japan be forced to reduce the number of Japanese autos sold in the United States to preserve domestic jobs and protect the domestic auto industry.[4] However, most economists disagreed with this strategy. They argued that it would be costly not only to Japanese auto makers, but to U.S. consumers and labor as well. Why the disagreement?

Proponents of trade restrictions argue that restrictions are necessary to protect domestic industries and jobs because imports reduce the demand for domestically produced autos. This decrease in demand results in unemployment, which leads to further reductions in demand for goods and services and pushes the economy toward recession. Proponents of trade restrictions also contend that the competition from imports is unfair because foreign producers enjoy much lower costs of production (usually as a result of lower labor costs) than do domestic competitors. Finally, many proponents argue that trade restrictions are necessary to ensure the self-sufficiency of the economy and to minimize the degree to which the United States becomes dependent on foreign-produced goods.

Opponents of trade restrictions contend that free trade is necessary to maximize social welfare. In par-

---

price is bid down. As market price falls, each firm's output is decreased and its profits are reduced.

A new long-run equilibrium is established at E_2 in Figure 11.8 (c). Market equilibrium price is reestablished at P_2, and the new equilibrium quantity is Q_{M3}. As shown in Figure 11.8 (d), market price has fallen to the level of the new lower minimum average total cost for each firm. As a result of entry by new firms, economic profits disappear. Firms once again earn only a normal profit. Competition has eroded the profits that arose from the technological innovation, and the cost savings have been passed on to consumers. They now get pencils at a lower price and, as a result of the lower price, the equilibrium quantity of pencils consumed in the economy has increased.

Section Recap

A change in production costs or technology will cause a change in the long-run market equilibrium price and level of output in a perfectly competitive market.

General Equilibrium in the Economy

This chapter has focused on the dynamics of the market mechanism, closely examining how the rational decision making of consumers and price-taking producers in competitive markets keeps markets moving toward equilibrium. Market equilibrium can be disturbed by many different factors – shifts in demand, changes in relative factor prices, and

ticular, they point out that free trade provides a greater degree of competition and moves producers closer to the efficient level of production. The entry of Japanese and other foreign automobile manufacturers into the U.S. market has more than quadrupled the number of competitors. As the number of foreign firms in the market increases, more of the pressures of competition are brought to bear on domestic producers. Firms in the market seek out the least-cost method of production in an effort to earn short-run economic profits, resulting in a more efficient use of resources. Competition also drives the equilibrium market price toward the lowest possible level. Overall, free trade allows consumers to choose from a wider array of goods, and this results in a higher level of consumer well-being.

To the extent that foreign competition is reduced, so is the pressure to minimize costs and, therefore, prices. In fact, the restric-tions imposed on Japanese imports in 1981 resulted in a dramatic increase in the average price of a new car. Over the period from 1981 to 1989, the amount of time it took a family earning the median house-hold income to earn enough money to buy a new car rose from 18.7 weeks to 24.7 weeks.

In the most recent debate, opponents of restrictions on the number of imported Japanese autos further argued that the adverse effects of restrictions would not be limited to domestic consumers. Citing the increased number of Japanese autos pro-duced in the United States, critics point out that restrictions would also result in the loss of many domestic jobs. Japan's share of the domestic car market, including imports and models built in the United States, rose from approxi-mately 20 percent in 1985 to roughly 28 percent in 1990. However, over this same time period, the share of all autos sold in the United States that were built in Japan fell from roughly 20 percent to about 18 percent. Reducing the number of Japanese autos sold in the United States would result in fewer sales of both foreign-made and American-made Japanese autos. This would, in turn, translate into fewer jobs for American auto-workers.

There is no doubt that free trade can lead to a more efficient use of the world's resources or that the economies that engage in free trade experience an increase in the level of available consumption opportunities. However, it is also clear that free trade can have adverse effects on specific domes-tic industries. The debate over free trade involves the issue of eco-nomic efficiency as well as issues of fairness and the benefits to the individual versus the benefits to the economy as a whole. Viewed in this light, it is easy to see why this dis-agreement exists.

changes in technology, to name a few – but the market mechanism acts to reestablish a new equilibrium when such disturbances occur. We have illustrated these market dynamics by taking a close look at individual markets. However, we do not want to lose sight of the big picture.

All markets in an economy are tied together. A change in one market causes changes in other markets. The changes in these markets cause further changes. In a sense, every-thing depends on everything else. This interrelatedness is illustrated in the *circular flow model* in Figure 11.9. A change in the pencil market will affect all other markets. If demand for pencils increases, more pencils will be produced at a higher pencil price. Because con-sumers have limited incomes, the increased spending on pencils must be balanced by decreased spending (decreased demand) for other goods. To produce more pencils, more labor is employed in the pencil industry. This additional labor must come from other industries.

An increase in the demand for labor pushes the price of labor up, and therefore the costs of producing other goods rise as well. These costs are translated into price increases by the resulting decrease in product supply. These price changes cause consumers to adjust their spending on consumer goods. In addition, the higher price of labor causes firms to try to substitute alternative inputs for labor. Thus, the demand for other inputs will

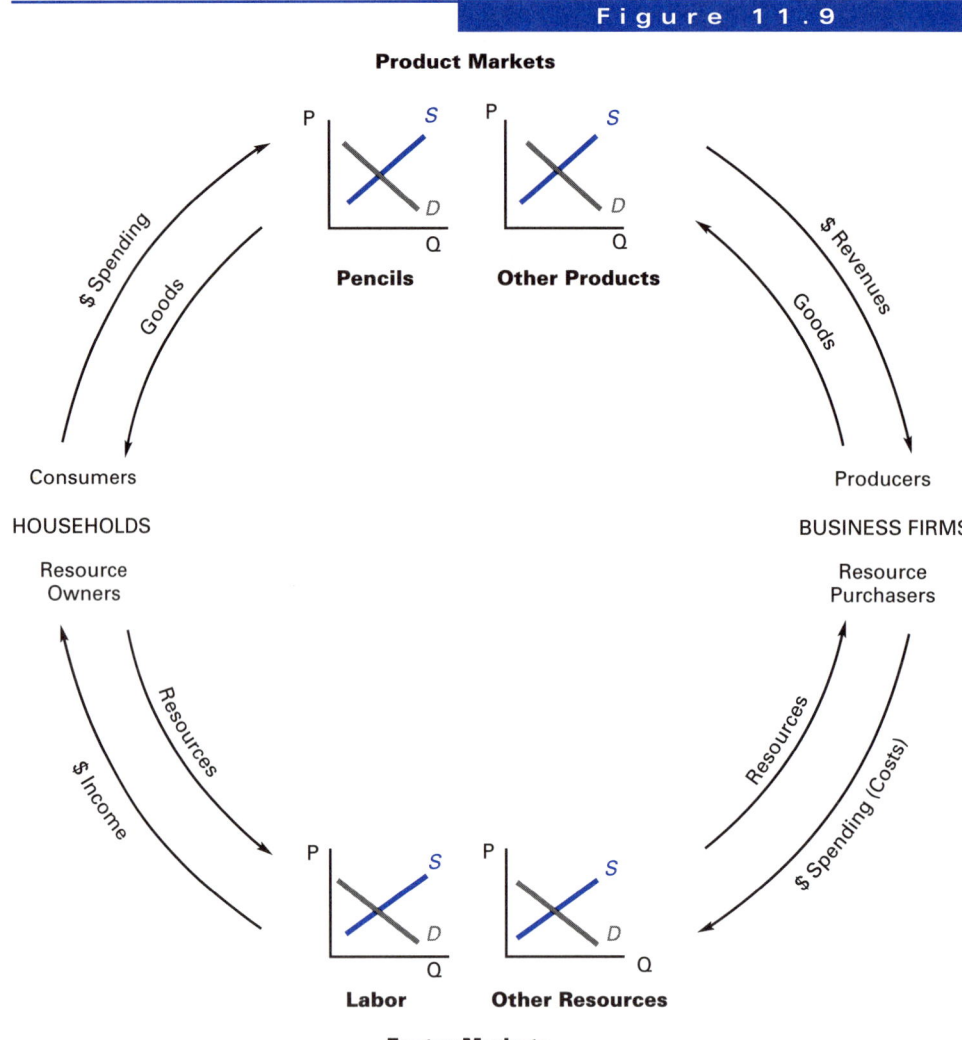

Figure 11.9

Product Markets

Pencils **Other Products**

$ Spending

Goods

Consumers

HOUSEHOLDS

Resource
Owners

$ Income

Resources

$ Revenues

Goods

Producers

BUSINESS FIRMS

Resource
Purchasers

Resources

$ Spending (Costs)

Labor **Other Resources**

Factor Markets

Circular Flow Model of the Economy

This model illustrates the interrelatedness of the product and resource markets in the economy. A change in demand or supply in a particular market sets in motion a series of reactions that work their way through the other markets in the economy until general equilibrium is once again established.

Partial equilibrium analysis:

Focuses on the conditions necessary for equilibrium in a particular market, independent of other markets in the economy.

General equilibrium analysis:

Is concerned with the relationships across markets and the conditions necessary for equilibrium in all markets simultaneously.

increase, causing price changes in other input markets. These price changes will alter costs again, affecting product market supply.

These simple examples highlight the interrelatedness of all markets. When we focus on the equilibrium outcome in one particular market, we are concerned about a **partial equilibrium**. When we focus on the relationships across markets and the equilibrium conditions in all markets, we are concerned about **general equilibrium**. In this chapter, partial equilibrium analysis has been used to illustrate the characteristics of a perfectly competitive market economy that is in general equilibrium. *If all markets are perfectly com-*

petitive and are in long-run equilibrium, consumers are buying goods and services in the quantities that maximize their utility. The prices prevailing in the economy are equal to the minimum unit cost of production. Producers are earning only normal profits, and consumers are getting the goods that are most valuable to them at exactly the social opportunity cost of producing them. The economy has achieved economic efficiency.

Of equal importance, if a change occurs in any one market to disturb this economy-wide equilibrium, it sets in motion market forces that will reestablish a new equilibrium with different market prices and outputs, but with the same economic efficiency characteristics.

For simplicity, we will continue to rely on partial equilibrium analysis to explain the decisions of economic agents and to examine the implications of those decisions for society. It is assumed that each market constitutes a small part of the total economy and that the effects of a change in one market on all other markets are small. However, keep in mind the interrelatedness of markets. The scarcity of resources causes economic decisions to have effects throughout the economy in addition to the immediate effects that are easily observed.

Costs and Benefits Again: The Invisible Hand of the Market

The power and efficiency of the market mechanism are captured in the dynamics of the market. It is the way that a market economy and, in particular, a perfectly competitive market economy, handles change that best illustrates the amazing power of the market. The merits of a perfectly competitive market economy are summarized in the two points discussed below.

Perfectly Competitive Markets Allocate Resources Efficiently

Goods and services are allocated to their highest-valued use. Consumers who value goods the most are willing to pay the highest price for them. Inputs are allocated to their highest-valued uses. The value of an input is determined by its use in production. Owners of inputs want to maximize the value of their resources − the firms bidding the most for inputs will be those firms responding most closely to consumer preferences.

Only goods for which consumer benefits exceed the opportunity cost of production are produced, and those goods are produced at minimum opportunity cost. On one hand, market competition is a cruel taskmaster. Competition keeps long-run market prices at the level of production costs. Only normal profits are earned in the long run. On the other hand, the market rewards increased productivity and lower costs. Producers have an incentive to minimize costs today and look for ways to reduce costs in the future in an effort to earn short-run economic profits. The cost savings from technological change are passed along to the consumer in the long run.

Economic Efficiency Is Achieved Through an Invisible Hand

The market mechanism is a decentralized decision-making institution. No one individual or group of individuals directs the economy's decision making. Instead, individuals are left alone to pursue their own individual self-interest. Consumers seek to maximize utility, producers seek to maximize profit, and resource owners seek to maximize income. However, competition limits the harm that the self-interested action of one person can impose on others. In fact, competition between decision makers has the curious effect of preventing individual gain at the expense of others and promoting a cooperation between and specialization among individuals that ensures maximum social welfare. This effect is the *invisible hand* of which Adam Smith spoke. Each individual pursues his or her own self-interest and in doing so contributes to the achievement of maximum social welfare. Consumers seek the benefits of consumption at the lowest cost possible, but competition from other consumers limits their gains. Producers seek maximum profits, but competition among producers ensures that they earn only normal profits in the long run.

The Perfectly Competitive Market Model in the Science of Economics

It should be clear from the discussion in this chapter, as well as the treatment of markets and efficiency in Chapters 3 – 5, that the perfectly competitive market model is a very special and important one in economics. At this point in your study of economics, the careful attention that is paid to the case of perfect competition may be somewhat puzzling. For this reason we end this chapter by devoting a few pages to the role of the perfectly competitive model in economic analysis.

The Economic Problem and Economic Efficiency

The basic economic problem for any society is one of scarce resources with which to satisfy unlimited individual wants. The central purpose of an economic system is to allocate resources and distribute economic goods in a manner that satisfies the greatest amount of wants. A perfectly competitive market economy is indeed such an economic system. Society obtains the maximum value from its stock of resources. One of modern society's major goals – satisfaction of the maximum amount of wants possible – is thereby achieved.

The perfectly competitive market model is a theoretical benchmark against which we evaluate other markets. We know that few actual markets approach perfect competition. However, by constructing a perfectly competitive market model we identify those characteristics of consumers, firms, resource owners, and market structures that are necessary for achieving an important social goal, economic efficiency. This theoretical framework can be used to examine actual market conditions, understand why actual market outcomes are not efficient, and develop policies to promote more competition and increase economic efficiency.

The perfectly competitive model is an attractive economic system to many societies, not only because of its efficiency properties, but also because it is consistent with another valued social goal – individual freedom. Recall that the value of any good is derived from the satisfaction it provides to individuals. Individuals express the value they attach to specific goods through their dollar votes. We measure this value by individual willingness to pay for a good. The value of a good to society is the sum of these individual valuations.

These individual votes are coordinated by the market mechanism. Resources are free to move to their best opportunities, and "best" is defined by resource owners. Individuals are free to pursue their own self-interest. The market mechanism coordinates these decisions, limits the power of any one decision maker, and provides incentives that make individual self-interest consistent with achievement of society's maximum economic well-being.

Perfect Competition Is a Reference Point

The perfectly competitive market model is built on a handful of key assumptions reviewed earlier in this chapter. When these assumptions do not hold, market outcomes are altered – they diverge from the optimal outcomes of perfectly competitive markets. We investigate the characteristics and operations of actual markets by considering the impact that changing or relaxing these key assumptions has on long-run market equilibrium. We compare the characteristics of observed markets and their outcomes to the perfectly competitive model. For instance, the last section of this chapter discusses some of the implications of more realistic assumptions about the availability of information and mobility. In Chapter 12 it is assumed that firms are price searchers instead of price takers. In Chapter 13 we look at how restrictions on resource mobility affect market outcomes. The array of government policies designed to promote competition or replace the market mechanism in certain markets is considered in Chapters 12-14.

A Close Approximation to Perfect Competition

The model of perfect competition is an extremely simple and abstract view of a market economy. However, the simplifying assumptions that are made serve a very important purpose. We have established the conditions necessary for an economic system to fully achieve its primary goal. It is a powerful model that serves as a useful benchmark for us in many of the following chapters.

Unfortunately, such an abstract model can be misleading. Because of its simplicity it may appear to be of little use in understanding the economy. Our concentration on basic decision rules and simple examples may make the model seem even more unrealistic. Consider the example illustrating the firm's decision rule for short-run profit maximization as a case in point. It was assumed that there were only two inputs, capital and labor, employed in a well-defined production process. The important entrepreneurship input, which includes the skill employed in following a decision rule, was ignored. The firm's competition consisted of a large number of virtually identical firms producing identical products with identical production functions. The adjustments to changes in market price were explained as if they were almost automatic. This determinism and lack of ambiguity in the model can make it seem so far from reality that the important insights from the exercise are missed, or at least discounted. We hope you fight off this almost instinctive reaction. The discussion that follows is intended to help you.

Imperfect Information and Mobility

Consider a market economy that only approximates perfect competition. Assume that both information and mobility are not perfect, but that all firms are price takers. Because decision makers have limited information, they make many decisions based on *anticipated* future market conditions. In addition, costly mobility slows market responses and changes the structure of some markets. What implications do these changes have for the performance of the economy?

In effect, information and mobility become economic goods – they are costly to produce. The amount of information acquired by a decision maker will depend on the expected benefits from having the information and the cost of acquiring it. If the purchase of information is thought of as any other good, the optimal amount of information is that amount at which the marginal cost is just equal to the marginal benefit. Consider the firm's behavior in this context. It might, for example, not know exactly how much output is produced by a given combination of inputs. It certainly cannot foretell the future. It does not know what future market prices for its product or its inputs will be. Furthermore, different firms may have different amounts of information and make different decisions based on available information.

By assuming that information is costly and that expectations are important, we have made firm decision making much more challenging. Entrepreneurial skill becomes important, and firms can make mistakes. For example, firms must choose a particular production technology and determine firm size based on the *expected* volume of output. With costly information, the kinds of technologies and the size of firms will vary within the industry. Thus, different firms will be stuck with different unit costs in the short run. Competition will drive the market price down to the level of minimum unit costs – those firms with relatively high unit costs will be driven from the market. Only those firms with the lowest production costs will stay in the market over the long run.

When new technological advances occur, some firms are slower than others to adopt them. It is often unclear initially what the cost saving from such investments will be. However, competition in the market will penalize late action to adopt cost-saving technology. Those firms that act quickly will push costs lower, expand output, earn more short-run economic profit, and weaken the market position of higher-cost firms. Downward pressure on market price is a strong incentive to use the least-cost technology.

Now consider responses to market price changes. Price increases generate short-run economic profits, attracting the attention of entrepreneurs and resource owners. As firms expand and new firms come into the market, price is pushed down, eliminating economic profit. In a world of costly information and mobility, this adjustment process is slower and less smooth. When the market price rises, it is not known if this is a permanent or temporary change. If an existing firm believes the price increase is temporary and does not expand when other firms do, it forgoes economic profit that accrues to other firms. It is also possible for the market to overreact to an increase in price. In the long run, new firms enter the market in response to the price increase. The increased supply depresses market price so that the new equilibrium is at a higher market output level and a price below the short-run higher price.

It is also possible for too many new firms to come into the market. If an entrepreneur believes the price increase is permanent, starts up a new firm, and then discovers it was only a temporary increase, he or she will face losses. Moreover, supply can increase so much that market price will be depressed below the original price, causing firms to experience losses. Refer to Figure 11.7 again. If too many firms enter the market in response to the price P_2 (at which existing firms are earning economic profits), supply will shift to the right, beyond S_2, and market price will fall below the long-run equilibrium price of P_1. The losses cause further adjustments – this time a reduction in market supply pushing the price back up to the long-run equilibrium level.

This pattern of oscillation around a new equilibrium position is attributable to incorrect expectations about the price change and to the time and expense of changes in capacity. Some entrepreneurs may interpret the increase in market price as a signal of further price increases, leading them to build too much capacity for the actual volume of sales. In addition, it takes time to make a long-run decision to start a business or add capacity. By the time some firms can make a decision and complete construction of production facilities, the increase in output from other new firms may have caused prices to stabilize or begin to fall.

Costly mobility also implies that the movement of resources and the transportation of goods are costly. Resources are attracted to the most profitable alternatives. However, now the price differences between alternatives must be large enough to more than offset the costs of mobility. Resource owners are less sensitive to relative differences in prices. Firms must employ inputs to ship output to consumers. These transportation or mobility costs cause firms' production costs to vary. Therefore, regional or local markets with different equilibrium prices can exist in the long run. For example, farmers are price takers. However, the market price they receive for their output depends, in part, on the costs of transporting it to the market. These price differences persist in the long run.

When we allow for imperfect information and mobility, our model of the economy begins to take on a closer resemblance to the economy that we observe. It is in a constant state of flux. Changes are occurring continuously all over the economy, and markets are adjusting constantly. The adjustments to change are not smooth. New firms are being organized every day as other firms are going out of business. Some markets are expanding while others are shrinking. New technologies and products are being introduced daily.

Some firms seem poorly managed and fail in a short period of time, but other firms are well managed and seem always to be in the right place at the right time. The frictions of real life slow the dynamic process of adjustment to equilibrium. Long-run equilibrium may never be reached, but the economy is always moving toward it. The market mechanism establishes an incentive structure that rewards behavior consistent with the achievement of economic efficiency.

If the economy were filled with only price-taking firms, the overall economy would function much like the perfectly competitive market model. The market mechanism rewards firms for producing the goods that are the most valuable to consumers. The pursuit of economic profit drives producers to be responsive to consumers' preferences. Competition among firms erodes short-run profits, and firms produce output at minimum unit cost. In the long run, economic profit is zero. Consumers not only obtain goods they most value, they obtain them at a price equal to the social opportunity cost of production.

This chapter has laid the groundwork for a closer look at the complexities of a market economy and has established a reference point for evaluating economic performance. Perfect competition is a benchmark by which we evaluate other market structures. The next few chapters take a closer look at the economic implications of price-searching firms and the lack of resource mobility.

Section Recap

The model of perfect competition serves as a benchmark to assess the efficiency of alternative market structures.

Summary

The firms that operate in a perfectly competitive market are price takers. Perfectly competitive markets are characterized by a large number of firms that are small relative to the market. As a result, no individual firm is able to exert any influence on market price. Firms in a perfectly competitive market produce a homogeneous product, and there is a high degree of resource mobility – ease of entry and exit. As a result, over the long run, short-run profits (or losses) are eliminated. The price-taking firm's short-run marginal cost curve (above its intersection with the average variable cost curve) is the firm's short-run supply curve because it reveals the level of output the firm will produce at every market price.

If a perfectly competitive market is initially in long-run equilibrium, firms are earning zero economic profits. A product price increase will cause existing firms to increase output, and positive profits will be generated that will attract additional resources into the market in the long run. When supply increases, market price is bid down, economic profits are competed away, and the market returns to a new long-run equilibrium at which price equals marginal cost equals minimum average total cost for all firms.

A change in costs causes a similar market adjustment. A decrease in costs causes unit cost to fall below the market price, generating economic profits. Firms expand output, following the marginal revenue equals marginal cost rule. The increased production at the initial market price leads to excess supply in the market. The market price gets bid down, profits are eroded, and a new long-run market equilibrium is established at a lower price and increased output level. Economic profit is again zero.

When perfectly competitive markets reach their long-run equilibrium, economic efficiency is achieved: Only those goods and services for which consumer willingness to pay exceeds the social opportunity cost of production are produced and consumed. In such an economy consumers are sovereign.

In addition, goods and services are produced at the minimum opportunity cost of production. Competition among producers and the mobility of resources between markets ensure that market price is always bid down to minimize unit cost in long-run equilibrium.

When all markets in a perfectly competitive economy are in long-run equilibrium, **general equilibrium** is achieved. In most of our analyses and examples we concentrate on only one or two markets, and thus a **partial equilibrium**. However, it is important to remember that market outcomes are interrelated. Developments in one market cause changes in many other markets. It is this complex interrelatedness across markets that makes the market mechanism such a powerful decentralized decision-making tool.

The perfectly competitive market is a simple, abstract market model. Careful attention is devoted to it because it serves as a starting point, or benchmark, for our analyses of other kinds of markets that more closely resemble the kind of markets we actually observe. By carefully studying this perfect market model we are better able to understand the way our economy actually operates and to design policies that can help us alter those market outcomes with which society is dissatisfied.

Questions for Thought

Knowledge Questions

1. Summarize the basic characteristics of a perfectly competitive market.

2. Distinguish between partial and general equilibrium.

3. What assumptions in the perfect competition model ensure that economic profit is zero in the long run? Explain.

4. What assumptions in the perfect competition model ensure that price equals the minimum average cost in the long run? Explain.

Application Questions

5. Assume the government decides to impose a per-unit tax on a good that is produced in a perfectly competitive market.

    a. Graphically illustrate the short-run effect of the tax in the market for the good and on the cost conditions faced by a representative firm in the market.

b. Explain the adjustment process to long-run equilibrium in the market. What has happened to long-run equilibrium price and output as a result of the tax? What has happened to the number of firms in the market? Why?

6. Suppose that the market for raw cotton is perfectly competitive and that the development of synthetic fibers reduces the demand for cotton.

a. What happens to the market price of cotton? What is the short-run response of cotton producers to the change in the price of cotton? Explain the sequence of events.

b. What is the long-run response in the market? Assuming that the cotton market is a constant-cost industry, how do the new long-run equilibrium price and quantity compare to the initial equilibrium price and quantity?

Illustrate, graphically, your answers to a and b.

7. Assume that the market for a good produced by firms in an increasing-cost industry is currently in long-run equilibrium. Now assume that there is a decrease in the market demand for the good. Analyze the short-run effects of the decrease in demand on equilibrium market price and output. What has happened to the profits of each of the firms in the industry? Over the long run, what will happen to the number of firms in the industry and to each firm's average costs? Why?

8. Scarce resources cause all market outcomes to be interrelated. Explain how a change in price affects another market in the four cases below:

a. An increase in college tuition on the pizza market.

b. An increase in the price of wheat on the pizza market.

c. A decrease in the price of computers on the shirt market.

d. An increase in the price of copper on the computer market.

Synthesis Questions

9. Referring to Question 6 above, suppose that the government establishes a program to support the price of cotton by being the consumer of last resort to ensure that the price does not fall below the initial equilibrium. That is, the government simply buys any cotton consumers are not willing to purchase at the initial equilibrium price. What will happen in the cotton market when demand decreases? Explain how the new long-run equilibrium would differ from the one in Question 6. What are the implications for economic efficiency?

10. Is consumer sovereignty a normative or positive concept? Explain why you answered as you did.

11. Explain why producers would like to restrict or eliminate competition from other firms.

12. Assume that the production technology changes for a good that is currently pro-
    duced in a perfectly competitive market. In particular, the new technology is such
    that the marginal costs of production for a single firm decline over the entire range
    of the demand curve for the good in question. How would this affect the number
    of firms that operate in this market? Explain.

End Notes

[1] Actually there are several different kinds of wheat. But it is easy to grade wheat to
determine what kind it is, and different prices are established for each kind. A market
exists for each kind, and the markets are large enough that wheat farmers, regardless of
the kind of wheat they grow, are price-taking firms.

[2] "Senate Approves $4 Billion in Aid to Farming Banks," *The New York Times*, December
5, 1987, pp. D5.

[3] This discussion should not be confused with the analysis of an increasing-cost industry.
In the latter, costs increase as a result of a change in the demand for inputs, which was
caused by a change in demand for the product.

[4] J.B. White and J. Mitchell, "Detroit Rolls Out Old Ploy: Quotas," *The Wall Street Journal*,
January 14, 1991, p. B1.

Small Firm Behavior: The Imperfect Competition Model

Overview

In Chapter 11 we developed the model of a perfectly competitive market. As we pointed out at the end of the chapter, this model is an abstraction. Very few, if any, actual markets meet all the characteristics of a perfectly competitive market. Many markets, such as the markets for groceries, gasoline, fast food, and clothing, are characterized by a large number of firms that are small relative to the market they serve. However, firms within each of these markets usually charge a range of prices, rather than a single "market" price, for the goods or services they produce. In addition, the products offered are not homogeneous (as is the case in perfect competition). Instead, firms offer a wide variety of similar, but not identical, products and services. For instance, convenience stores such as 7-Eleven or Circle K offer many of the same products as major supermarkets, but they provide the additional benefit of being close by, thus reducing travel time for many customers. In a similar manner, gas stations offer varied services and products, fast food restaurants offer different products (Big Mac versus Whopper), and clothing stores offer different brands and styles. In all of these examples, consumers have a range of prices and products to choose from.

This chapter relaxes some of the assumptions of the perfect competition model and examines the resulting effects on economic efficiency. In effect, we are introducing some of the complexities of actual markets into our analysis. The model that results is one that more closely approximates many of the markets we observe. The implications of this model for efficiency are evaluated using perfect competition as the benchmark.

In this chapter we develop the model of *monopolistic competition*. Monopolistically competitive markets are characterized by many small firms, each of which possesses at least some degree of market power. Firms behave as price searchers. An important result of our analysis is that although competition ensures that monopolistically competitive firms earn zero long-run economic profits, nonetheless each firm produces output inefficiently. However, the fact that monopolistically competitive firms produce a differentiated product also means that consumers enjoy a greater variety of choices with respect to specific goods and services than they would in a perfectly competitive market.

Learning Objectives

After reading and studying this chapter you will be able to:

1. Describe the basic characteristics of a monopolistically competitive market

2. Describe the two major forms of product differentiation

CHAPTER 12

3. Explain how price and output are determined in a monopolistically competitive market in the short run

4. Explain how monopolistically competitive markets move from short-run to long-run equilibrium

5. Discuss the differences, in terms of efficiency, between perfectly competitive markets and monopolistically competitive markets

6. Describe how government regulation can benefit firms in monopolistically competitive markets

Real People, Space, and Time

In the simple model of consumer choice behavior, and in the model of perfect competition, information and mobility are assumed to be costless. Decision makers – both consumers and producers – possess perfect information regarding the choices they must make. Also, as supply and demand conditions change in individual markets, resources are assumed to move between markets until equilibrium is once again reached. However, in most situations information and mobility are not costless. In addition, consumers have heterogeneous (varied) tastes, exhibiting preferences for a wide variety of goods and services with varying characteristics. These facts explain why we observe the types of markets described in the chapter overview.

Costly Information and Mobility

Costly information and mobility have important and predictable implications for the structure of a market. Because resources are not perfectly mobile, different producers of the same good may end up paying different prices for what is essentially the same resource. Consequently, it is possible for different prices to exist for the same good across different locations. In addition, because information is costly, consumers (and resource owners) may not be aware of the fact that different prices exist for the same good. In either event, the result is that there is no single equilibrium price for the good in question.

A look around us confirms the argument that, for many goods and services, there exists a set of prices, rather than one single price, even within the same city. A check at different supermarkets, convenience stores, and the corner mom-and-pop store will yield a range of prices for the same product. Why is this the case? One possibility is that consumers are not aware of all the prices being asked for a given item. This is a result, at least in part, of the fact that it takes time to observe all the prices for the good in question.

Finding the lowest price for a given product is costly; it takes time and effort. To the extent that time is spent gathering information on competing prices, that time cannot be spent doing anything else. Consequently, an efficient use of time requires the consideration of the opportunity cost of time spent in a specific endeavor.

In addition to the time spent looking for the lowest price for a given good or service, traveling to the location of the firm offering the lowest price also takes time. In many cases, a consumer may be aware that the lowest price for a particular good is charged at a firm across town, while the same good can be had for a slightly higher price from a firm that is much closer. In this case, the savings in travel costs associated with going to the nearby firm may outweigh the extra cost paid for the good. Consequently, it is the case that even if a product is homogeneous in respects other than location, firms may have some control over price. Interstate travelers know that gas stations located next to an interstate exchange on the outskirts of a city generally charge a higher price for a gallon of gas than firms located in the middle of town. While interstate travelers could drive to gas stations in the middle of town that may offer lower prices, the inconvenience and time spent may not be worth the savings in reduced prices.

Heterogeneous Consumer Tastes

Variations in consumers' tastes also affect product price and the range of products offered by firms by expanding the market for substitute goods and services. Firms respond to variations in consumers' tastes through **product differentiation** on the basis of one or more characteristics of the product. Product differentiation enables a firm to fill a niche in a particular market. To the extent that consumers attach different values to specific characteristics of a product or service, firms can charge different prices depending on the characteristics their product offers.

Product differentiation: Variations in one or more characteristics of a good that are designed to distinguish the good from its competitors.

A relatively large number of gas stations operate in most cities. Moreover, a number of different brands of gasoline are often available in the same city, and even on adjoining street corners, suggesting a high degree of competition among firms. However, gas stations differ in a number of ways. Some gas stations promote the ability of their gas to clean your carburetor. Others advertise the quality of the service they provide. Still other stations offer a number of products in addition to gas. Many of these items are periodically put on "sale" in an effort to attract customers who will also buy gas while they're picking up the sale item. The upshot of this product differentiation is that we frequently observe a range of prices for gasoline.

Fast food restaurants also offer differentiated products. In this case, product differentiation occurs on several levels. Some firms offer quicker service than others. Other firms specialize in different products – hamburgers versus chicken versus fish. Firms also differentiate their products on the basis of the quantity and type of inputs used – "one-third pound of all-U.S. beef." Once again, a primary result of this differentiation is that prices differ across firms.

In both of the above examples, product prices differ on the basis of consumers' tastes and preferences and consumers' valuations of the different characteristics each firm offers. However, it is also important to note that product differentiation can allow firms to satisfy a greater range of tastes and preferences than a homogeneous product could. In this sense, firms are simply responding to market forces.

We have talked about some specific kinds of complexities observed in consumer and firm behavior. The question we turn to next is, What impact do these phenomena have on the behavior of firms?

For many goods, consumers are faced with a range of prices rather than a single price. Price differences can be the result of costly information and mobility and product differentiation designed to satisfy heterogeneous consumer tastes.

Section Recap

Monopolistic Competition

The world we have described above is clearly different from the world implied by perfect competition. A perfectly competitive market is characterized by a large number of small

Monopolistic competition:
A market characterized by a large number of relatively small price-searching firms, resource mobility, and product differentiation.

firms that produce a homogeneous product. As a result, each firm is a price taker and, in the long run, economic profit is equal to zero. However, as we have just seen, in many instances markets are characterized by a large number of small firms that produce a heterogeneous product. In fact, as the examples cited above suggest, this type of market pervades our economy. This market structure is referred to as **monopolistic competition**.

Monopolistically competitive markets are similar to perfectly competitive markets in some respects – there is usually a large number of firms, each firm is small relative to the market, and resources are assumed to be mobile, that is, there is ease of entry and exit. However, these two markets differ in one important aspect – perfectly competitive firms produce a homogeneous product, while firms in a monopolistically competitive market produce differentiated products. As a result, monopolistically competitive firms are able to exercise some degree of control over price, regardless of the source of the product differentiation.

A *monopoly market*, which is discussed in detail in Chapter 13, consists of a single seller of a good or service. *The fact that sellers can differentiate their product on whatever basis is the monopoly element of monopolistic competition.* Because the monopolistically competitive firm somehow distinguishes its product from that of its competitors, it acts as a price searcher. However, because there are many close, if not perfect, substitutes for its product, the demand curve faced by the monopolistic competitor is affected by the decisions of other firms.

Because there are many small firms in a monopolistically competitive market, individual firms constantly face the threat of competition. The high degree of resource mobility in these markets increases this threat. The individual firm must therefore constantly strive to distinguish itself from its competitors in an effort to earn economic profits.

Short-Run Profit Maximization

Before analyzing the short-run behavior of a monopolistically competitive firm, we need to summarize the major characteristics of a monopolistically competitive market. They are:

1. A large number of small firms. Monopolistically competitive markets consist of a large number of firms. The output of each firm is relatively small compared to the market as a whole.

2. Ease of entry and exit. As in the case of perfect competition, ease of entry and exit is assumed in monopolistic competition – there is a high degree of resource mobility.

3. Product differentiation. The output of the firms in a monopolistically competitive market is differentiated. Products can be differentiated on the basis of one or more characteristics, including product quality, advertising claims, consumer perceptions, location, and availability. Product differentiation is the source of the monopoly element in these markets.

Monopolistically competitive markets are characterized by a large number of firms that each produce a small share of total market output, and a high degree of resource mobility. Because firms
sell a differentiated product, each firm acts as a price searcher.

Like firms in a perfectly competitive market, monopolistically competitive firms seek
to maximize profits. However, *unlike perfectly competitive firms, which are price takers, monopolistically competitive firms act as price searchers. As a result of product differentiation, monopolistically
competitive firms face a downward-sloping demand curve.*

Perfectly competitive firms are price takers because price is the only factor that distinguishes one firm's output from that of the other firms – output is homogeneous. For
firms to compete effectively, they cannot raise their price above the market-determined
price (quantity demanded would fall to zero). Product differentiation enables the monopolistically competitive firm to alter the price it charges without losing all its customers. The
decision to buy a particular product is based not only on price, but on the specific attributes of that product as well. However, the monopolistically competitive firm's price-setting
power is not unlimited. Ease of entry and exit in the market and the large number of competitors limit the individual firm's ability to set price.

Figure 12.1 illustrates the short-run position faced by a monopolistically competitive
firm. Note that the demand curve is downward sloping – the result of product differentiation. Because each firm is a price searcher, it seeks out the price–quantity combination
that maximizes economic profits.

Figure 12.1

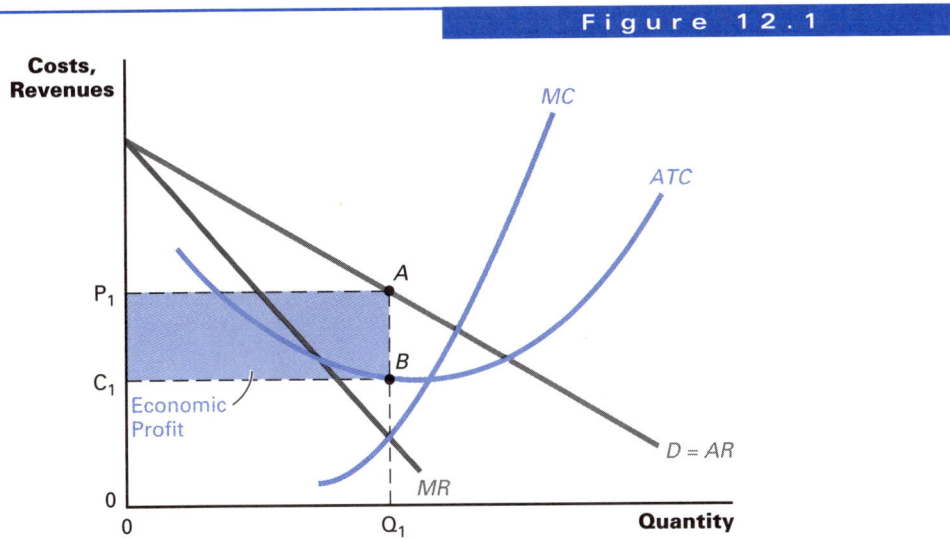

Short-Run Economic Profits for a Monopolistically Competitive Firm

This figure illustrates the position faced by a monopolistically competitive firm. Using the MR =
MC rule, the profit-maximizing level of output is Q_1. According to the demand curve, D, the firm
can charge a price of P_1 for each of the Q_1 units of output. Total revenue is therefore equal to the
rectangle $0P_1AQ_1$. Total cost is equal to the rectangle $0C_1BQ_1$. Thus, in the short run, this firm is
earning economic profit equal to the area C_1P_1AB.

The cost curves in Figure 12.1 are of the standard form developed in Chapter 9. The average total cost curve is U-shaped, and marginal cost cuts the average total cost curve at its minimum point. (For expositional ease, the average variable cost curve is not shown.) In addition, the demand curve and the average revenue curve are the same. However, unlike the case of perfect competition, the marginal revenue (MR) curve is *not* the same as the firm's demand curve. As we saw in Chapter 10, when the demand curve is downward sloping, the marginal revenue curve lies below the demand curve.

The rule for profit maximization is that firms maximize profits (or minimize losses) by producing the level of output at which marginal revenue equals marginal cost. For the firm depicted in Figure 12.1, the profit-maximizing level of output is Q_1. The demand curve, D, indicates that the firm can charge a price of P_1 for each of the Q_1 units of output. The average total cost of producing Q_1 units is found by locating the point at which the vertical line drawn at Q_1 intersects the average total cost curve and then reading the corresponding dollar amount off the vertical axis. Thus, in this case the average total cost of producing Q_1 units is C_1.

Recall that profit (or loss) is the difference between total revenue and total cost. For the firm in Figure 12.1, total revenue is equal to the rectangle $0P_1AQ_1$. Total cost is equal to the rectangle $0C_1BQ_1$. Thus, in the short run, this firm is earning economic profit equal to the rectangle C_1P_1AB.

In Figure 12.1, the firm is earning positive economic profit. However, it is also possible for firms in monopolistically competitive markets to earn economic profit equal to zero or incur an economic loss in the short run. These situations are illustrated in Figure 12.2. The firm depicted in Figure 12.2 (a) is earning zero economic profit. Note that at the profit-maximizing level of output, Q', price, P', and average total cost, C', are equal. Therefore, total revenue is equal to total cost, and economic profit is zero.

In Figure 12.2 (b), marginal revenue equals marginal cost at output level Q^*. At this level of output, the price charged, P^*, is less than average total cost, C^*. Total revenue is equal to the rectangle $0P^*FQ^*$. Total cost is equal to the rectangle $0C^*EQ^*$. Thus, the firm is incurring an economic loss equal to the rectangle P^*C^*EF. However, assuming that P^* is greater than average variable cost, by producing Q^* the firm is minimizing the loss it incurs in the short run. (Recall that so long as the firm is earning a price that is greater than its average variable costs of production, it should continue to produce in the short run.)

Section Recap

Monopolistically competitive firms maximize profits by producing the level of output at which MR = MC. They may earn economic profit or normal profit, or incur economic losses in the short run.

Long-Run Equilibrium Position

In the long run, monopolistically competitive firms earn zero economic profits. The question we consider now is, How does the adjustment process (from the short run to the long run) work, and how is this long-run equilibrium outcome characterized?

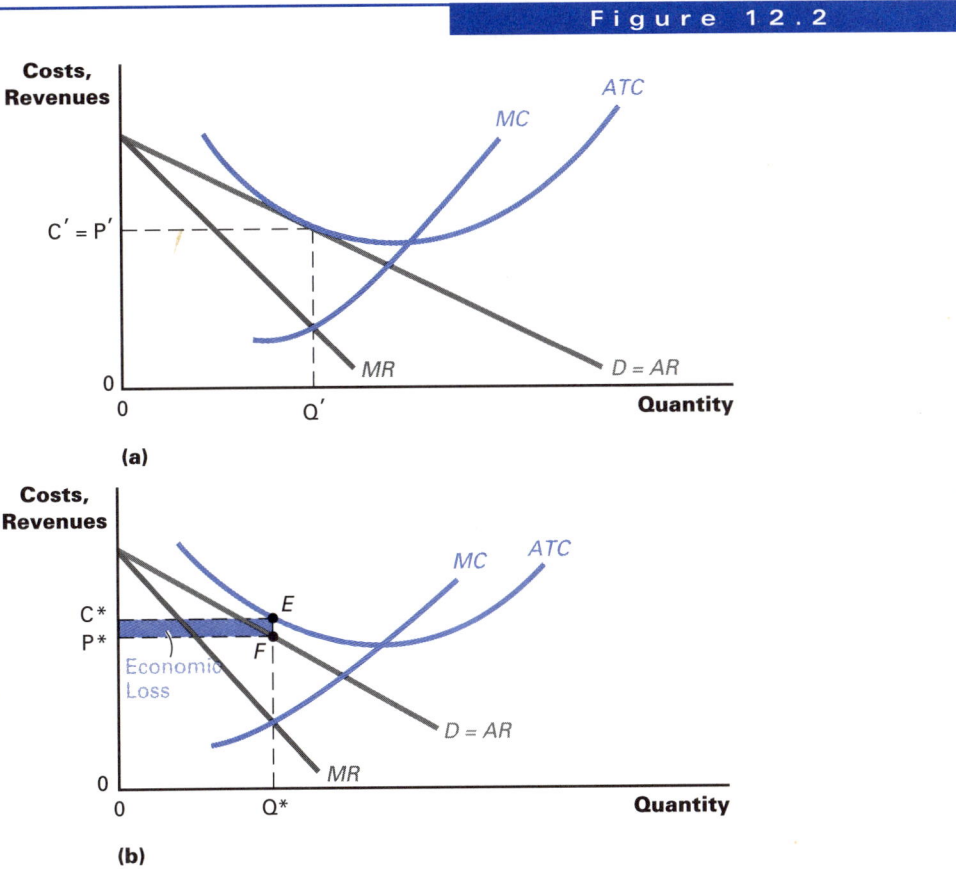

(a)

(b)

Normal Profits and Economic Losses

For the firm depicted in Figure 12.2 (a), at the profit maximizing level of output, Q', price, P', and average total cost, C', are equal. Therefore, TR = P' x Q' = TC and economic profit is zero. In Figure 12.2 (b), MR = MC at the output level Q*. Total revenue is equal to the rectangle 0P*FQ*, and total cost is equal to the rectangle 0C*EQ*. Thus, the firm is incurring an economic loss equal to the rectangle P*C*EF. However, assuming P* > AVC of producing Q*, the firm is minimizing the loss it incurs in the short run.

Market Forces Eliminate Economic Profits

Consider once again the case depicted in Figure 12.1, which has been recreated in Figure 12.3. In the short run, the firm is earning an economic profit. These profits act as a signal to other firms to enter the market in an effort to compete for these profits. (Recall that entry and exit are assumed to be relatively costless in a monopolistically competitive market.) We can analyze the effect of the increase in the number of firms competing in the market as follows.

As new firms enter the market, the number of available substitutes for the good in question increases. In turn, the share of customers buying the output of any specific firm falls as some buyers switch to the newly offered products. Consequently, the demand for each firm's output decreases. Assuming the available pool of customers is constant, the

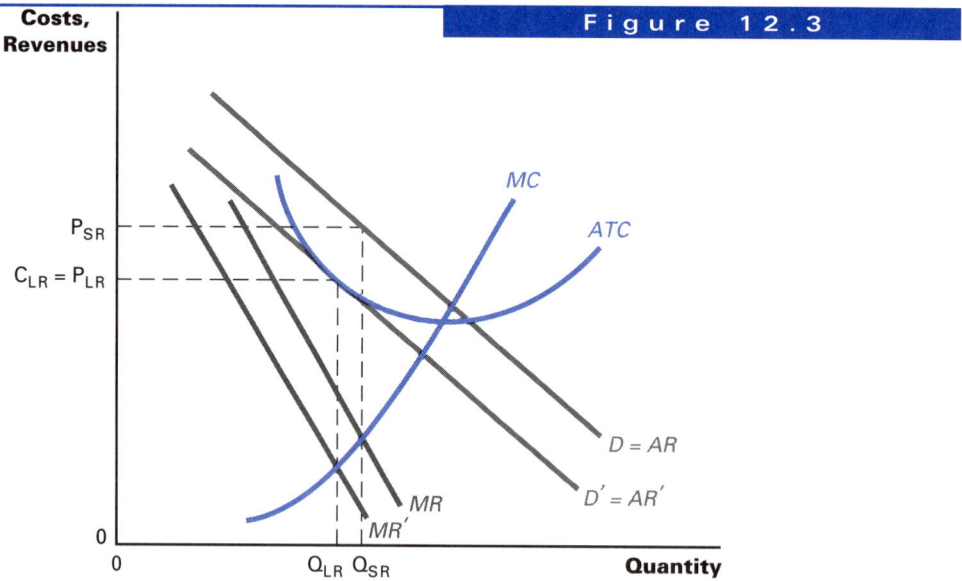

The Adjustment to Long-Run Equilibrium

In this figure, the firm is initially earning positive economic profit. This creates an incentive for other firms to enter the market. As the number of substitutes increases, the demand curve faced by the individual firm shifts left and becomes more elastic, as shown by the demand curve D'. In long-run equilibrium, the demand curve is tangent to the ATC curve at the level of output at which MR = MC. At output level Q_{LR}, TR = TC. Thus, the firm is earning zero economic profit. However, the firm is operating inefficiently; it could increase output and lower the average total cost of production.

demand curve faced by each individual firm shifts to the left. In addition, as the number of substitutes for a given good increases, the demand for any specific good becomes more elastic. These two effects are shown graphically by the demand curve labeled D' in Figure 12.3. Note that relative to the original demand curve D, D' has shifted left. Firms continue to enter the market until demand for the individual firm's output falls to where price is equal to average total cost.

In long-run equilibrium, the demand curve faced by the firm is just tangent to the average total cost curve at the level of output at which marginal revenue equals marginal cost. In Figure 12.3, equilibrium occurs at the output level Q_{LR}. At this level of output, price, P_{LR}, equals average revenue which equals average total cost, C_{LR}, and therefore, total revenue equals total cost. Thus, the firm is earning zero economic profit.

However, because the demand curve is downward sloping, the point at which it is tangent to (touches) the average total cost curve is to the left of the minimum average total cost of production – the firm is not operating at capacity. The firm is therefore operating at an inefficient level of output. The firm could increase output and lower its average total cost of production. However, doing so would force the firm to incur an economic loss. It is also the case that price is greater than marginal cost for the last unit produced.

In our example of the gas stations located at different points in the city, it is reasonable to assume that, to the extent that a particular firm is earning economic profit, this would attract other firms into the market. In particular, assuming that economic profits are being earned by existing sellers, we would expect to see an increase in the number of such firms operating close to the interstate exchanges. The level of output sold by each firm would fall and entry would continue until all existing economic profits had been competed away. In addition, it is likely that sellers would attempt to differentiate their products on the basis of particular characteristics such as service and possibly the sale of additional goods, such as refreshments.

As another example, consider the recent boom in the quick-service oil-change business. A large number of firms specializing in this type of service entered the market in a remarkably short period of time. This quick entry reflects the high degree of resource mobility in this particular market and the effect of existing profits on the incentive for new firms to enter. Firms in the market compete on the basis of price, location, and a variety of services in addition to simply changing the oil in a person's car.

In the fast food industry, firms are constantly offering new and different products to attract customers and earn economic profit. Competitors respond by offering similar products to retain their existing customers. These firms also compete on the basis of service. For example, it is now almost impossible to find a fast food restaurant that does not have a drive-up window.

In all of the above examples there is a common thread – firms will compete on any basis that makes a difference to consumers. The result of this intense competition is to constantly drive economic profits in the market to zero.

In summary, the two most important features of long-run equilibrium in monopolistically competitive markets are the following:

1. In the long run, firms earn zero economic profit. As the preceding analysis indicates, in the long run, firms in monopolistically competitive markets earn zero economic profit. Recall that for perfectly competitive markets, long-run economic profit equals zero as well.

2. Long-run inefficiencies exist. In the long run, firms produce at an average total cost that is greater than the minimum average total cost possible. Consequently, fixed inputs are used inefficiently. In addition, long-run price is greater than marginal cost. Hence, resources are allocated inefficiently.

Due to competition for economic profits and a high degree of resource mobility, in long-run equilibrium, monopolistically competitive firms earn zero economic profit.

Section Recap

Efficiency Implications

From the perspective of economic efficiency, monopolistic competition compares unfavorably with perfect competition. When a perfectly competitive market is in equilibrium, price is equal to marginal cost and each firm in the market is operating at the minimum of its average total cost curve. Thus, the allocatively efficient level of output is produced and the firm is using its plant size as efficiently as possible.

As Figure 12.3 illustrates, however, the long-run price charged by the monopolistic competitor is greater than the marginal cost of production. Hence, *the monopolistically competitive firm is allocatively inefficient.* In other words, the value of the output produced, measured by price, is greater than the value of the additional resources used to produce the last unit of output, measured by marginal cost. Society would prefer more of the good in question.

We also noted that in equilibrium, production does not occur at the minimum point on the average total cost curve. As such, the monopolistically competitive firm is using its available plant size – its capacity – inefficiently. A smaller number of firms could produce the same total amount of output at a lower average total cost and still earn a normal profit by setting price equal to the minimum average total cost.

From the strict viewpoint of economic efficiency, monopolistic competition compares unfavorably with perfect competition. However, it is worth noting that, in many cases, the loss of efficiency may not be particularly great. Note that the more elastic is the demand curve faced by the monopolistic competitor, the closer will be equilibrium price and output for the monopolistically competitive firm and the perfectly competitive firm. In addition, the monopolistically competitive firm will move closer to the minimum of average total cost as the demand curve becomes more elastic.

This comparison is illustrated in Figure 12.4. If the market is perfectly competitive, equilibrium output and price will be Q_{PC} and P_{PC}. If, on the other hand, the firm is

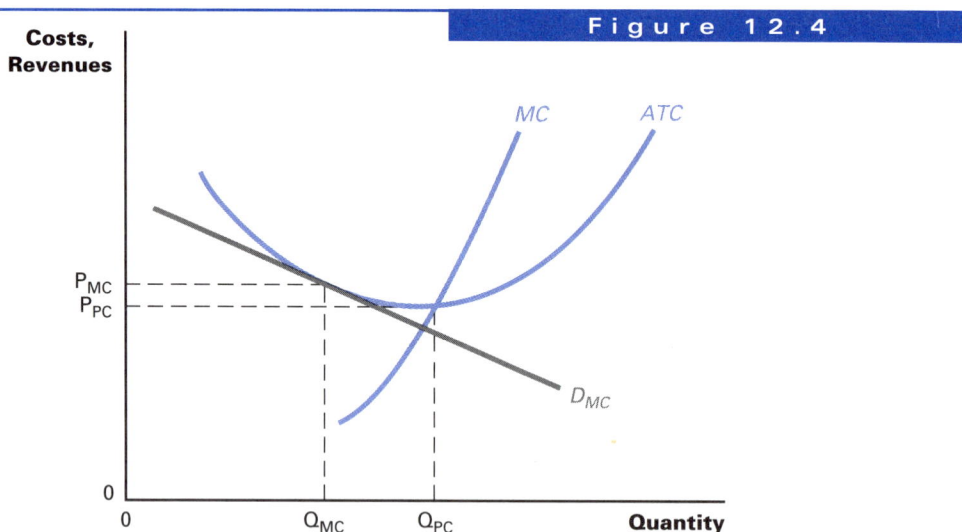

Figure 12.4

Equilibrium and Efficiency:
Perfect Competition versus Monopolistic Competition

In a perfectly competitive market, equilibrium output and price will be Q_{PC} and P_{PC}. If, on the other hand, the firm is operating in a monopolistically competitive market, and faces the demand curve labeled D_{MC}, equilibrium output and price will be Q_{MC} and P_{MC}. However, the difference between the two sets of equilibria disappears as the demand curve faced by the monopolistically competitive firm becomes more elastic.

operating in a monopolistically competitive market and faces the demand curve labeled D_{MC}, equilibrium output and price will be Q_{MC} and P_{MC}. Equilibrium price is higher for the firm in monopolistic competition, and equilibrium output is lower. However, the differences between the two sets of equilibria disappear as the demand curve faced by the monopolistically competitive firm becomes more elastic.

In addition, monopolistic competition provides a benefit to consumers that is absent in the case of perfect competition – increased choice. As a result of product differentiation, consumers have a set of alternatives from which they can make their selections of what to consume. Thus, it is possible for a greater range of consumer tastes and preferences to be satisfied. As a consequence, the total amount of consumer satisfaction associated with the consumption of a particular good or service may be greater than it would be if the good were produced in a perfectly competitive market. The large number of monopolistically competitive markets in our economy testifies to the fact that consumers prefer a wide variety of choices.

In the long run, monopolistically competitive firms do not make efficient use of their capacity. In addition, they produce an inefficient level of output. However, they offer consumers the benefit of increased choice relative to perfectly competitive markets.

Section Recap

Competitive Pressure

One of the most important similarities between firms in a perfectly competitive market and those operating in a monopolistically competitive market is the extent of competition. In both cases, firms are subjected to the constant pressure of competition. Each firm seeks to maximize profits. Yet firms have only limited control over the forces influencing profitability, and the amount of control depends on the market structure in which the firm operates.

Because firms in a perfectly competitive market are price takers, their only control over profits lies on the cost side. Such firms can earn short-run economic profits by reducing average (unit) costs. However, the creation of these short-run economic profits simply increases the incentive for competition by other firms. In the long run, economic profits equal zero.

On the other hand, firms in a monopolistically competitive market are price searchers. Each firm faces a negatively sloped demand curve. Therefore, these firms have a degree of control over price as well as their costs, and they can compete on the basis of price. Monopolistically competitive firms also rely heavily on **nonprice competition**, such as product differentiation and advertising, to gain more customers at any given price, and they work to keep reducing unit costs. Nonetheless, long-run market adjustments drive economic profit to zero.

The Incentive to Escape Competition

The constant competitive pressure of profits creates an incentive for firms to try to escape competition. After all, it is competition that eventually eliminates any economic profits. Of

Nonprice competition: Activities such as product differentiation and advertising, which are designed to increase the demand for a firm's output.

Shaking Up the Fast Food Industry

The fast food industry offers consumers a wide range of choices. A drive through most cities and towns in the United States confirms that consumers face a formidable array of different brand names and product types from which to choose. In addition, it is interesting to note the seeming regularity with which new firms enter the market in a particular area and existing firms offer new products. It is also interesting to note the number of firms that go out of business in this industry and the rate at which products are dropped as new ones are added. This phenomenon is referred to as a *shakeout*.

Shakeouts occur as a result of the intense competition for economic profits. If a new product line proves to be profitable for a firm, duplication by other firms is the usual result. Duplication leads to an increase in supply and the elimination of profits. Firms respond to the erosion of profits by developing new products. Given the rate at which shakeouts occur, the fast food industry would appear to be characterized by excess supply, suggesting that firms earn little if any economic profits. In light of these observations, it is worth asking, does the type of behavior witnessed in the fast food industry make economic sense?

Recall from our discussion of monopolistically competitive markets that firms are constantly striving for new ways to earn short-run economic profits. One of the primary means of achieving this objective is through product differentiation. In the market for fast food, there is

course, the desire to avoid competition is not confined to profit-maximizing firms. Consider a student about to take an exam. Knowledge of the questions and answers on the exam, before the fact, would ensure the student of a high grade. In a sense, a high grade is not unlike economic profit for the firm. Note that this knowledge in effect relieves the student of the need to compete for the high grade. In a similar manner, resource owners would like to be able to sell their resources in markets free of competition. In this way, resource owners would be able to maximize the potential gains that could be realized from the sale of their resources.

Firms can escape the pressures of competition in two ways. The first is to differentiate the product in such a way that there are no, or very few, substitutes for the product in question. As the number of available substitutes for a product or service declines, the pressure of competition is reduced. The second approach involves the imposition of restrictions on the mobility of resources, in particular, restrictions on market entry. As resource mobility is reduced, once again, competitive pressures will decline.

Firms in monopolistically competitive markets have relied on both of these approaches to reduce competitive pressures. In many cases, firms have relied on a combination of these approaches.

Product Differentiation

We introduced the notion of product differentiation in the course of identifying the principal characteristics of a monopolistically competitive market. Product differentiation gives firms some control over product price. While product differentiation can be either real or

substantial variety in the tastes of consumers. Children tend to prefer fun foods and are often drawn to products that capitalize on a currently popular theme such as a cartoon program or movie. Many adults, on the other hand, prefer foods that emphasize a healthy diet and good nutrition.

Tastes differ within groups as well. One adult may prefer salads while another prefers fish to beef. In addition, different individuals may have a preference for different types of sandwiches: bacon and cheese hamburger versus a ham and cheese sandwich versus a chicken sandwich. Different children, on the other hand, may have a preference for one fast food chain over another due to a particular commercial. (Note that adults are also subject to the persuasive elements of advertising.)

Firms are aware of the considerable divergence among tastes and preferences. They also know that, although a product may be selling well today, it is always possible that entry by a competitor will reduce the demand for their product. Firms in the fast food industry have responded to this threat by offering a wide variety of substitutes rather than a single product. In addition, firms are constantly developing new products designed to attract new customers and, they hope, increase profits. Ultimately the purpose of product innovation is to maximize the demand for fast food. Although the introduction of a new product might reduce the demand for one of their existing lines, firms expect that the increase in the number of new customers realized from the new product will more than offset any loss that occurs. However, this behavior also results in intense competition, which leads to frequent shakeouts in the industry.

The conclusion is that, from the firm's perspective, the type of behavior examined here makes economic sense. Although firms and products continue to come and go, the primary motivation is short-run profits. So long as firms are able to differentiate their products, and in so doing retain existing customers and attract new ones, economic profits can be earned.

---

imagined, it has the effect of distinguishing competitors from each other and creating what are essentially different markets for a particular good or service.

Real product differentiation occurs when similar products differ as a result of actual characteristics such as quality of inputs or location of the firm and the consequent availability of the product. For example, certain brands of bread claim that only the "choicest" ingredients are used. Other brands claim that all the ingredients are purely natural. In a similar fashion, different brands of blue jeans differ in price, at least in part due to the varying quality of the denim used to make them.

Real product differentiation: Similar products differ as a result of actual characteristics such as quality of inputs or location of the firm.

In our example of the gas stations located next to the interstate exchanges and in the middle of town, the same product is differentiated on the basis of convenience. Interstate drivers could travel a short distance and pay a higher price or travel a longer distance and pay a lower price. The seller simply takes advantage of the opportunity cost of travel time in setting price at each location.

In other cases, firms claim that their product is unique. For example, many fast food restaurants claim to use a specific method or secret ingredients in preparing the food items they serve. Kentucky Fried Chicken claims that its secret recipe of eleven different herbs and spices results in a fast food unlike any other. The objective of such devices is to eliminate competition from other producers. In any case, real product differentiation distinguishes a particular good from its competitors.

Imagined product differentiation is the result of efforts such as advertising or packaging that create the impression that two or more products are different when, in fact, they are composed of exactly the same inputs. Imagined product differentiation can also be the

Imagined product differentiation: The result of efforts such as advertising or packaging that create the impression that two or more products are different when, in fact, they are composed of the same inputs.

result of the individual's personal assessment of the good or service in question. Regardless of the type of differentiation employed, however, the result is that a consumer is willing to pay different prices for what is, at least to some degree, the same product.

In contrast to perfectly competitive markets, in which advertising is virtually nonexistent, monopolistically competitive markets are characterized by extensive advertising. Many monopolistic competitors – clothing manufacturers, fast food chains, and soft drink beverages, to name a few – rely heavily on advertising to distinguish their product from that of their competitors. The purpose of advertising is to highlight the differences among competing goods and services. Such advertising can be designed to inform consumers about real differences among competing products, or simply to persuade them. A considerable amount of advertising is also used to develop and maintain brand loyalty by creating an image of the type of people who consume a particular product. Consider, for example, the commercials used to advertise different brands of jeans such as Levi's and Lee, and soft drinks such as Pepsi, Coke, and 7-UP.

Proponents of advertising argue that it yields benefits to consumers because it provides valuable information they can use in their decision-making process. However, critics of advertising argue that the primary purpose of advertising is simply to persuade rather than to inform. They also argue that advertising does little to alter the share of the market controlled by each firm in the market. Thus, advertising simply raises the costs of production and hence the price charged for each unit of output. Proponents of advertising respond to this criticism by arguing that advertising has the effect of increasing the level of output sold and, in so doing, moves firms down along their long-run average total cost curve, reducing the average total costs of production. Whether advertising is, in fact, beneficial is a matter of considerable debate, as the foregoing suggests. In any event, it is a tool that is heavily relied on to differentiate products from one another.

Product differentiation is intended to reduce the price elasticity of demand. As demand becomes more price inelastic, the quantity demanded becomes less sensitive to price changes. This enhances the firm's ability to earn economic profits. More importantly, as demand becomes more price inelastic, it is easier to maintain economic profits over a period of time. Price inelasticity implies a lack of available substitutes.

Although product differentiation can benefit the firm in the short run, its long-run effectiveness is limited because of the continuous pressure exerted by competition. Although a firm may differentiate its product in the short run, competitors are constantly looking for ways to eliminate the source of the differentiation. In the case of real product differentiation, competitors are constantly seeking ways to copy or duplicate the product in question or produce a better product. In the case of advertising, firms are constantly competing with each other to persuade customers that their product is superior. The result is that the effects of a particular type of product differentiation rarely last long. Therefore, firms must be constantly looking for new ways to differentiate their product. It also provides the basis for reliance on a second means by which competition is reduced – government regulation.

Product differentiation – whether real or imagined – is designed to increase short-run economic profits. Advertising may serve to highlight real product differences or may simply be designed to persuade customers that there are product differences that do not, in fact, exist.

Government Regulation

When people think of government regulation of a market or industry, they usually think in terms of efforts designed to promote competition or otherwise protect consumers. A large body of government legislation and regulation is designed to provide quality assurances for consumers. However, from an economic perspective, the effect of much of this regulation is to actually limit the amount of competition in particular markets.

There are many examples of restrictions on market entry. The requirement that a firm possess a license to sell alcohol is a classic example. In most areas, a bar, liquor store, restaurant, or other similar establishment cannot sell alcoholic beverages without a license. From society's perspective, the purpose of this restriction is to ensure that some measure of control is exercised over alcohol consumption. The growing emphasis on alcohol awareness and the threat posed to society by those who drink and drive reflects the benefits society associates with such restrictions. From an economic perspective, however, this restricts the available supply and pushes price above what it would be in the absence of such a restriction.

Establishments such as beauty parlors and barber shops, various medical practitioners, and taxi cab services must obtain a license to operate in many parts of the country. In fact, almost 500 occupations require a license in various locations in the United States. Such occupations range from doctors to septic-tank cleaners and beekeepers. In many situations, the number of available licenses is limited. (See the box on taxi cab decontrol.) In addition, individuals who want to work in these jobs must pass a test or otherwise be certified first.

In each of the examples just noted, government has regulated otherwise competitive markets in an effort to ensure product quality and promote the interests of consumers. However, such regulation also promotes the interests of the firms left operating in the affected market. This is especially true in the case in which regulation takes the form of restrictions on entry into the market. As a result of restricted entry, firms can charge a higher price than they would be able to in an unregulated setting.

Although regulation of monopolistically competitive markets is designed to protect the consumer and, in many cases, maintain product quality, it is often the case that producers realize long-term benefits as well. As Figures 12.1 and 12.3 illustrated, although it is possible for a monopolistically competitive firm to earn economic profits in the short run, over time those economic profits will be competed away. However, if entry is limited, as is the case in many regulated monopolistically competitive markets, economic profits can persist over the long run. In addition, the price paid remains higher than it would be in the presence of increased competition. Thus, producers gain at the expense of consumers, who are left paying a higher price.

332

Taxi Decontrol: Who's Being Taken for a Ride?

With the introduction of the Model-T Ford in the 1920s, the taxi business experienced a tremendous surge in supply. In effect, the cost of entry into the market was reduced substantially. However, the surge in supply resulted in cutthroat competition. In addition, the level of safety decreased as an increasing number of inept drivers entered the market. Customers were also increasingly faced with having to pay unreasonably high prices to dishonest drivers in situations in which the customer was unaware of the true market price.

Many cities throughout the United States responded to this situation by regulating the local taxi industry. In many situations, strict limits were imposed on the number of taxis that could operate in a city and the fares that could be charged. Interestingly, although many of the limits on the number of permitted taxis were set in the 1930s, in many cities the same restrictions are still in place. For example, the number of cabs that can legally operate in New York City has been set at 11,787 since 1937. In addition, it was not until 1990 that Boston raised the limit, established in 1934, on the number of permitted taxis. Regulation of the taxi industry is not unique to the United States. In Japan, the Transport Ministry sets the fares that can be charged by all taxi firms.[1]

The failure to update restrictions on the number of permitted taxis, combined with population growth, has created a considerable amount of excess demand for taxi service in many cities, especially during periods of peak demand. In response to this problem, many cities have begun to consider either decontrolling their taxi market or, at least, easing restrictions on entry and rates for service to improve the level of service available to customers. However, such moves toward deregulation have met considerable resistance from the taxi industry, which argues that deregulation is not in the consumer's interest. Proposals to deregulate the taxi industry in Japan have met with similar resistance. Why the disagreement?

The principal argument by proponents of deregulation is rather straightforward. If restrictions were eased, competition would increase along with the number of taxis in the market. This increase in competition would move rates toward the economically efficient level and ensure that the quality of service is maintained at an acceptable level.

Section Recap

Government regulation that restricts entry into a market in an effort to protect consumers' interests also has the effect of increasing the potential for existing firms to earn economic profits.

Summary

This chapter has examined a second form of market structure – **monopolistic competition**. Although monopolistic competition is similar to perfect competition in many respects – large number of relatively small firms, ease of entry and exit, and long-run economic profits equal to zero – there are some important differences. In particular, monopolistically competitive firms sell a product that is **differentiated**.

In the short run, monopolistically competitive firms can earn economic profits, break even, or incur a loss. However, over the long run, the presence of profits or losses and the associated entry into or exit from the market will force all firms to a situation in which economic profit is equal to zero.

Compared to the perfectly competitive market, the long-run equilibrium in a monopolistically competitive market is inefficient. In particular, at the equilibrium level

In effect, competition would ensure that inefficient providers of taxi service are forced out of the business while providing a level of supply consistent with the demand for taxi service.

Proponents of deregulation also point out that restrictions on entry into the taxi industry create incentives for illegal behavior, such as black markets in taxi service. These markets are not subject to the safety regulations that have been designed to protect the welfare of consumers and the general public. Deregulation would eliminate the incentive for black markets and facilitate the maintenance of minimum safety standards.

Opponents of deregulation point to the experiences of cities that have attempted to eliminate restrictions on the taxi industry. Beginning in the 1980s, a number of cities, including Seattle and San Diego, began to lift restrictions on rates and entry into the taxi market. However, in both cases, subsequent to decontrol, ceilings were imposed on rates to prevent price gouging. In addition, San Diego reimposed restrictions on entry into the market.

Opponents of deregulation point out that many of the problems that arose subsequent to deregulation reflect the nature of the industry. For example, price gouging is rather easy when it comes to out-of-town customers who are unfamiliar with local rates and the distance that must be traveled to get from one point to another. This lack of information makes it nearly impossible to determine whether a reasonable rate is being charged for taxi service. Opponents also point out that open entry makes it very difficult to monitor the large number of independent taxis attracted into the market. To the extent that individual cab drivers exhibit behavior that reflects poorly on the city, this can damage the city's image and have adverse effects on its tourist industry.

Finally, in many cities the legal right to operate a taxi has, in and of itself, become a very valuable commodity. For example, in New York City a permit to operate a taxi was worth more than $130,000 in 1989. That figure rose to $210,000 in 1994. In Boston, a permit sold for $95,000 during the same time period. In San Diego, permit values rose to $15,000 subsequent to the reimposition of restrictions on entry. Obviously, the elimination of restrictions on entry would eliminate the value of these permits, resulting in a substantial economic loss for their owners who, not surprisingly, oppose deregulation.

The experiences of cities such as Seattle and San Diego would suggest that, at the least, the effects of deregulation in the taxi market are mixed. In addition, it appears that at least some form of regulation will be imposed on most taxi markets for the foreseeable future. This reflects the unique character of the taxi industry and the competing goals, protection of customers and the pursuit of economic profits, that guide the behavior of regulators and firms, respectively.

---

of output, price exceeds marginal cost and the firm is allocatively inefficient. In addition, firms are operating at a point to the left of the minimum of their average total cost curve.

Because competition increases the elasticity of demand for a product and reduces economic profits, monopolistically competitive firms attempt to reduce competition wherever possible. Two basic approaches are relied on – product differentiation and government regulation.

Product differentiation can be either **real** or **imagined**. Real product differentiation is the result of some difference in the quality of inputs used, the production process employed, or some similar attribute. Imagined product differentiation is generally the result of advertising. The result of product differentiation is that monopolistically competitive firms behave as price searchers as opposed to firms in perfect competition, which are price takers.

Product differentiation has the effect of reducing the number of available substitutes for a particular good or service. As such, demand is less elastic and the firm is able to exercise greater control over the price charged and, consequently, profits.

Government regulation is usually employed in monopolistically competitive markets to limit the amount of competition. While the stated purpose of such regulation is to protect the consumer by maintaining product quality, regulated firms can also benefit. In particular, restrictions on entry into markets limit the available supply and can result in the realization of economic profits by existing firms over the long run.

Questions for Thought

Knowledge Questions

1. List and briefly describe the major characteristics of a monopolistically competitive market.

2. Briefly describe what is meant by the term product differentiation. What is the difference between real and imagined product differentiation?

3. What is the objective of regulation of monopolistically competitive markets?

4. Describe the basic similarities and differences between perfectly competitive and monopolistically competitive markets.

Application Questions

5. Assume that firms in a monopolistically competitive market are currently experiencing economic losses.

   a. Construct a graph that illustrates this situation.

   b. Verbally and graphically describe the adjustment in the market to long-run equilibrium.

6. Good X is produced in a monopolistically competitive market. In addition, each of the firms in the industry uses essentially the same technology. Competitors distinguish their individual products primarily on the basis of imagined product differentiation. Assume that one of the firms in the market discovers a new production process that substantially reduces the unit costs of production. Verbally and graphically analyze the effects of this discovery on long-run equilibrium in the market.

7. Graphically analyze the effect of government regulation that restricts entry of new firms into the market on the long-run equilibrium in a monopolistically competitive market.

8. Analyze, graphically and verbally, the short-run and long-run effects of an increase in demand for a good produced by a monopolistically competitive firm.

Synthesis Questions

9. Perfect competition results in the economically efficient level of output and price while monopolistic competition offers consumers a greater degree of choice among competing goods. Which market structure do you think better serves the interests of the consumer? Of society? Why?

10. Advertising is a central feature of monopolistic competition. However, viewpoints differ considerably with respect to the value of advertising. Use the Fundamental Premise of Economics to analyze the value of advertising. Does consideration of the Fundamental Premise tend to support the use of advertising?

11. Discuss the implications of perfect competition versus monopolistic competition as they relate to the concept of consumer well-being. Which market structure do you think better serves the objective of utility maximization?

12. Regulation of seemingly competitive markets is supposedly intended to protect consumers. However, it is clear that in many instances one of the results of regulation is an increased price for the good in question. Can you think of an economic argument that would justify this increased price?

End Notes

[1] This discussion is based on "Cab Decontrol Is Hailed and Booed," *Insight*, Dec. 5, 1988, and "Where To? Japan's Taxi Plan Shows Deregulation May Be Slow," *Far Eastern Economic Review*, November 11, 1993, p. 66.

Large Firm Behavior: The Imperfect Competition Model

Overview

In early June 1995 IBM announced its intention to acquire Lotus Development Corporation, a major developer of computer software programs. Later that same month, Lotus agreed to accept IBM's offer. Analysts saw the merger as an effort by IBM to increase its share of the personal computer market and consolidate its market power. In particular, they viewed the move by IBM as an attempt to move ahead of another software giant, Microsoft, in the business of computer networking. Microsoft was also busy trying to increase its size during the same period. In addition to proposed acquisitions of software lines developed by competitors, Microsoft was making a bid to enter the market for on-line services as part of its Windows 95 operating system. Beyond being competitors in the same industry, IBM and Lotus have something else in common; they are both major players in the computer industry that are bent on increasing their size and market power. This raises a number of questions, not the least of which is, What effect does a firm's size relative to the market have on the efficiency of resulting market outcomes?

In the last chapter, we examined the pricing and output behavior of firms that operate in monopolistically competitive markets. We assessed the implications of this type of market structure for economic efficiency by comparing it to the perfect competition model. In this chapter we consider markets dominated by one or a few firms. Now we will be examining markets with potentially much less competition than is found in either perfect competition or monopolistic competition.

Both perfect competition and monopolistic competition are market structures characterized by a large number of competing firms that are able to earn no long-run economic profit. Competition and resource mobility combine to erode any short-run economic profit. In contrast to these markets, many industries in the United States consist of only one or a few firms, each of which controls a large share of the total output in a market. Examples include electric and natural gas utilities in a geographic region and the automobile, flat glass, steel, petroleum, breakfast cereal, chewing gum, and cigarette industries. Firms in industries such as these may possess considerable market power because there is little resource mobility. Both the reasons for and the consequences of this lack of mobility are discussed in this chapter.

Learning Objectives

After reading and studying this chapter, you will be able to:

1. Describe the various types of barriers to entry into a market

2. Explain the implications of resource immobility for long-run economic profits

CHAPTER 13

3. Describe the short-run and long-run equilibrium conditions for a monopolist and the implications for efficiency

4. Describe the situation of a natural monopoly

5. Describe the major characteristics of an oligopoly

6. Explain the role of collusion in the price-setting behavior of oligopolistic firms, and discuss the major obstacles to successful collusion

7. Explain how government regulation and mergers enable a firm to avoid the pressures of competition

Resource Immobility and Competitive Pressure

As we have already seen, in perfectly competitive markets competition for economic profits reallocates resources to their most highly valued uses and leads to the efficient use of those resources. A key factor in competitive markets is resource mobility. Competition and resource mobility combine to ensure that the number of firms competing in a market will adjust such that the price of the good is equal to the marginal opportunity cost of production. In contrast to the perfectly competitive situation, many markets in the U.S. economy are characterized by a small number of large firms. The popular view is that the firms in these markets possess considerable market power and that competition and resource mobility are both absent. If resources are immobile, the forces of competition are weakened, short-run economic profits can persist into the long run, and inefficiency can result. In this chapter we examine the origins of this type of market structure and the efficiency of outcomes in such markets.

Barriers to Entry

Barrier to entry:
Anything that restricts the free flow of resources among profitable employment alternatives.

The immobility of resources is the result of **barriers to entry**. An entry barrier is anything that restricts the free flow of resources among profitable employment alternatives. The control of specific resources, the control of a particular production process or specific products, economies of scale, and legal restrictions are all barriers to entry.

Control of Resources A firm or small number of firms may gain control of a resource or group of resources. For example, ALCOA for a long time controlled most of the world's known supplies of bauxite, a raw material essential to the production of aluminum. In a similar fashion, the De Beers diamond syndicate controls approximately 85 percent of the world's diamond supply. To the extent that one or a few firms control a resource that is necessary for the production of a particular good and there are no good substitutes for this resource, these firms may be able to earn long-run economic profit: Other, new firms will be unable to enter the market and compete. Consequently, there will be no competition from new firms to bid product price down to unit cost.

Control of Production Processes and Products One or a few firms may have exclusive rights to a production process for a particular good. In this case, entry is restricted to the extent that alternative (substitute) production processes are not available. So long as potential competitors are unable to develop processes that can be used to produce a comparable product, the existing firm, or firms, will be able to exercise considerable market power.

Patent:
Issued by the government, it entitles its owner to exclusive rights to a production process for a period of seventeen years.

To protect its rights to a particular production process, a firm (or an individual) can apply for a **patent**. A patent entitles its owner to exclusive rights to the process for a period of seventeen years. Other firms are legally prohibited from using the production process during that time. A patent serves two purposes. On the one hand, it acts as an inducement to firms to develop new, and possibly more efficient, production processes in their pursuit of economic profits. The patent guarantees the firm that it will be able to enjoy the benefits of research and development and not have to share those benefits with its competitors for a period of time. On the other hand, patents limit the degree of competition that arises in a particular market. For many years Xerox held a patent on plain-paper copying and IBM held patents on tabulating machines. These patents insulated their owners from competitive pressure for a period of time.

In addition to holding a patent on a production process, it is possible to hold a patent on a particular good. In 1995, the U.S. Patent and Trademark Office issued new guidelines that would make it easier to obtain a patent for software programs contained on CD-ROMs, disks and other memory devices. Many firms in the computer industry reacted positively to the Patent Office's move. However, some firms disagreed, arguing that such patents would stifle innovation. Indeed, to the extent that there is a significant demand for a good, the owner of the patent is able to exercise considerable control over pricing and output in the market. Patents can therefore act as a significant barrier to the production of particular goods.

Patents prevent the production of exact duplicates of a good. They do not, however, restrict the production of substitutes. Guitar manufacturers in the United States have long held patents on specific models of guitars such as the Gibson Les Paul, the Fender Stratocaster, and the line of Martin acoustic guitars. However, in recent years a number of Japanese firms have successfully entered the guitar market with a series of models that are very similar to their U.S. counterparts. This example highlights the fact that in some situations patents may be imperfect or weak barriers to entry. (It also illustrates, once again, the power of the desire for profits.)

Economies of Scale In Chapter 9 we discussed the concept of economies of scale. Economies of scale occur when the long-run costs of production decrease as the scale of operation of a single firm increases. When economies of scale are substantial, it is possible for one or a few firms to control the market. Potential competitors who attempt to enter the market with a smaller scale of operation will incur higher average production costs than a larger, existing firm. Thus, the new firm cannot charge as low a price as the existing firm and remain profitable.

The existence of economies of scale implies that the costs of entry into the market may be substantial. A large scale of operation is usually associated with a high level of fixed costs, which are, in turn, the result of large capital requirements. The auto and steel industries exemplify this situation. In this case, entry is limited by the sheer magnitude of the financial requirements of entry into the market.

Legal Barriers In some instances, the government may eliminate the potential for entry into a market through the granting of a *franchise* or a *license* to operate in a particular market. Electric, natural gas, water, and local telephone companies, for example, are usually granted a franchise in a particular service territory. These firms are the sole producer of the good or service in question in that territory. However, as we shall see shortly, the pricing and output decisions of these firms are usually regulated in an effort to generate the economically efficient level of output.

340

Cornering the Market on Genetically Engineered Cotton

Genetic engineering has received a growing amount of attention in recent years as scientists continue to make progress in this important field. Much of the attention has focused on the debate over the extent to which genetic engineering should be used to increase productivity in agriculture. However, a recent decision by the U.S. Patent Office has also created quite a stir.

In 1992, the Patent Office awarded two broad patents to W.R. Grace and Co., a specialty chemical concern, for a genetically engineered strain of cotton plant. However, the patents covered more than the specific strain in question. In fact, the patents awarded to Grace and Co. were for *all* strains of genetically engineered cotton. As word of the decision spread, it was met with varying degrees of disbelief. The Patent Office (and W.R. Grace) believed the patent was justified, but almost no one else agreed. The

Patent Office's decision was subsequently challenged by a number of organizations, including the U.S. Agriculture Department. In December 1994 the Patent Office reversed its ruling.[1] However, Grace expressed its intention to fight the ruling, expressing confidence that the patents ultimately will be reconfirmed. In light of the continuing controversy it is worth asking, Why the disagreement?

As we have already noted, the primary justification for patents is to create an incentive for individu-

Until recently, cable television represented an exception to the rule. In most locations in the United States, a single provider of cable television is granted a license to serve a particular area. Between 1984 and 1993, the pricing and output decisions of these firms were not regulated. However, in response to a growing number of complaints, Congress passed legislation in 1992 that reestablished limited regulation of the rates charged for cable television. The effects of this reregulation are discussed in Chapter 14.

As the preceding discussion suggests, barriers to entry are seldom perfect or permanent. In all market structures both existing firms and potential new entrants respond to the incentive for additional profits. To this end, firms are constantly looking for new production techniques and alternative resources that will result in lower production costs and enable the firm to earn economic profits. In addition, legislative and regulatory restrictions are constantly changing. When AT&T was broken up in 1984, the market for telecommunications equipment broadened considerably.

Section Recap

Barriers to entry can limit the degree of competition in a market. Sources of barriers to entry include exclusive control of resources, patents, economies of scale, and legal barriers such as franchise agreements.

Long-Run Economic Profits

Markets dominated by a small number of firms differ from the market structures we have analyzed in earlier chapters in a very important way. In the long run, it is possible for firms in markets with one or a few firms to earn positive economic profits. This potential is the direct result of the entry barriers that restrict resource mobility in such markets.

als and firms to expend time, effort, and money on research and development. So long as the developers of a new product or production process can receive a patent, they are assured of receiving at least some amount of the benefits from their efforts as well. That patents do not last forever reflects the importance of competition in a market economy. Once the patent expires, other firms can develop the same good or use the same production process. In this way, the forces of competition are brought to bear, encouraging the economically efficient market outcome. In the case of genetic engineering, supporters of patents for specific processes cite the significant research and development costs such efforts entail, and the consequent need for

some guarantee that the successful firm's efforts will be adequately rewarded.

The patents that were initially awarded to W.R. Grace, however, would have forced any entity that developed *any* other strain of genetically engineered cotton to pay royalties to W.R. Grace for the next seventeen years. In effect, W.R. Grace would be able to profit from the research efforts of others. Thus, other firms would have less of an incentive to expend resources on research directed at the development of new strains of genetically engineered cotton, since any firm marketing a new strain of genetically engineered cotton would have to compensate W.R. Grace. This would reduce the net revenues the firm would realize for its efforts,

limiting the amount of research-related costs a firm could afford to incur while still earning a profit.

If the cotton patents are reconfirmed, the development of genetically engineered strains of other crops might also be affected. W.R. Grace has begun to work on acquiring patents in the United States and Europe for strains of genetically engineered soybeans. If these patents are approved, they would have the same adverse effects on the incentives of other firms in the soybean market.

The ability to patent a new good or production process clearly creates incentives for research and development. However, it is equally clear that for the type of patent considered here, the outcome would likely be less than efficient.

Recall from our previous discussions that short-run economic profits attract additional resources into a market. As firms compete for short-run profits, additional resources are allocated to the production of a good, supply increases, price falls, and economic profits disappear. In addition, firms have an incentive to reduce their average total costs of production to the lowest point possible. However, if resources are immobile, the reallocation process is disrupted.

Figure 13.1 illustrates the situation faced by a firm that controls a significant share of a market in which resources are immobile. The firm is a price searcher and faces a downward-sloping demand curve. Profits are maximized by producing the level of output at which marginal revenue equals marginal cost – in this case, Q_1 – and charging the price P_1. The firm is earning economic profits equal to the rectangle C_1P_1AB. However, due to resource immobility, competitive forces do not erode profits. Consequently, these short-run economic profits can persist into the long run. Figure 13.1 depicts both the short-run and the long-run positions for the firm. Note that if resources were mobile, additional firms would enter the market and entry would continue until economic profits were driven to zero.[2]

Because price is greater than marginal cost, the firm depicted in Figure 13.1 is producing a level of output that is allocatively inefficient, that is, it is too low. This outcome is the result of the small number of firms and the corresponding lack of competition and, therefore, the benefits of competition. However, as we have already noted, many industries characterized by a few firms that are large relative to the market are also characterized by economies of scale. Economies of scale imply that, in order to minimize the average (unit) costs of production, the industry should consist of only one or a few relatively large firms. Consequently, we are often confronted with a tradeoff. In particular, one of the conditions

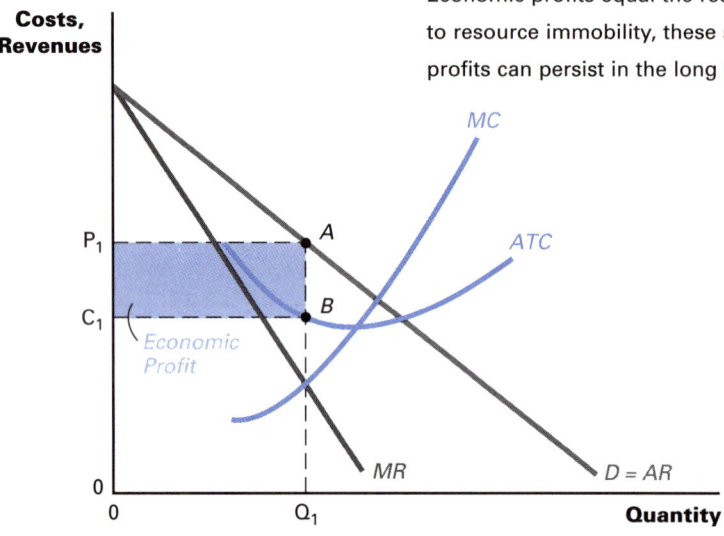

Figure 13.1

Short-Run and Long-Run Equilibrium for a Price-Searching Firm

This figure illustrates the situation faced by a firm that controls a significant share of a market in which resources are immobile. Profits are maximized by producing Q_1 and charging the price P_1. Economic profits equal the rectangle C_1P_1AB. Due to resource immobility, these short-run economic profits can persist in the long run.

that encourages an efficient level of output – a large number of competing firms – may result in unit costs that are higher than they would be otherwise. This tradeoff complicates the question of what to do when this type of market structure arises.

Section Recap

Barriers to entry can enable firms to earn economic profit in the long run. When economies of scale are a factor, there is a tradeoff between the efficient level of output and efficient production.

Monopoly

Thus far, our analysis of markets dominated by one or a few firms has focused on the sources of market power. We now turn to the specific question of how prices and output levels are determined by firms in this type of market structure and the implications for economic efficiency. We begin with the case of **monopoly**, a market comprised of a single firm.

Monopoly:

A single firm that produces all the output in a particular market.

A firm is a monopolist if it is the only producer of a good for which no close substitutes exist. Familiar examples of monopolies include electric and natural gas utilities, local telephone companies, Amtrak rail service, and public transportation in a particular city. Note that in all of these examples there is a single provider of the particular good or service. If we think in more general terms – energy, communications, or transportation services – substitutes, although imperfect, do exist. Natural gas can be substituted for electric service in many uses, taxicabs and personal cars can be substituted for bus service, and telegrams can be substituted for phone calls. Nonetheless, there is only one producer of the specific good or service in each location.

From a theoretical perspective, the monopoly model is the direct opposite of perfect competition. Recall that the perfect competition model enabled us to identify the conditions that characterize efficiency in production. In contrast, the monopoly model enables us to identify the effects on efficiency of the complete absence of competition.

The major characteristics of the monopoly market structure are summarized as follows:

1. A single firm. Monopoly implies the existence of a single firm in the market. Although imperfect substitutes for the good or service may exist, the monopolist is the only producer of the good. The monopoly may be defined geographically. There are a large number of electric utilities in the United States; however, there is only one provider of electricity in a specific geographic region. In a similar fashion, there is only one provider of natural gas or local telephone service in a particular geographic region.

2. Barriers to entry. Monopoly is the result of one or more barriers to entry. Consequently, the monopolist is able to operate in a relatively competition-free environment. This fact has important implications for the distinction between short-run equilibrium and long-run equilibrium for the monopolist.

Because the monopolist is the only firm in the market, it faces the market demand curve for the good. As a result, the monopolist is a price searcher. Like firms in any other market structure, the monopolist maximizes profits by producing the level of output at which marginal revenue equals marginal cost.

A monopoly market is characterized by a single firm and significant barriers to entry. A monopolist is a price searcher.

Section Recap

Short-Run and Long-Run Profit Maximization

Following the rule for profit maximization, firms in all market structures produce the level of output at which marginal revenue equals marginal cost. To this extent, the monopolist behaves in the same manner as monopolistically competitive and perfectly competitive firms. In addition, because it is a price searcher, given the profit-maximizing level of output, the monopolist seeks to identify the maximum price it can charge for its output.

Short-Run Profit Maximization Figure 13.2 illustrates the situation faced by a monopolist. Note that the monopolist depicted in Figure 13.2 faces the same type of short-run cost curves faced by firms in the other market structures that we have analyzed. However, unlike the firms in the other market structures, the monopolist's demand curve is the market demand curve. Since the market demand curve is downward sloping, the monopolist's marginal revenue curve lies below the demand curve. Once again, the demand curve is also the average revenue curve.

To maximize profits, the monopolist produces the level of output at which marginal revenue equals marginal cost, Q_1. The monopolist's ability to set price is constrained only by the demand curve for the good or service. According to the demand curve in Figure 13.2, the highest price consumers will pay for Q_1 units of output, and therefore the highest price the monopolist can charge, is P_1.

Profits, once again, are calculated as the difference between total revenue and total cost. The average total cost of producing Q_1 units of output is C_1. Consequently, by producing Q_1 units of output and selling them at a per-unit price of P_1, the monopolist is earning economic profits equal to the rectangle C_1P_1AB.

In the situation depicted in Figure 13.2, the firm is earning an economic profit. However, the fact that a firm is a monopolist does not ensure the realization of economic profits. Remember that the monopolist's price-setting power is limited by the demand curve for the good. Consider, for example, Figure 13.3 (a). In this case the profit-maximizing level of output is Q' and the corresponding price is P'. At the profit-maximizing level of output the firm is earning zero economic profit. The combination $P' - Q'$ is this monopolist's breakeven point.

Figure 13.3 (b) illustrates a case of economic loss for a monopolist. At the profit-maximizing level of output, average revenue, P^*, is less than average total cost, C^*. Hence, this monopolist is incurring an economic loss equal to the rectangle P^*C^*EF. However, so long as P^* is greater than the average variable cost of producing Q^*, the monopolist should continue to operate in the short run.

Long-Run Profit Maximization For firms that operate in perfectly competitive and monopolistically competitive markets, long-run economic profits equal

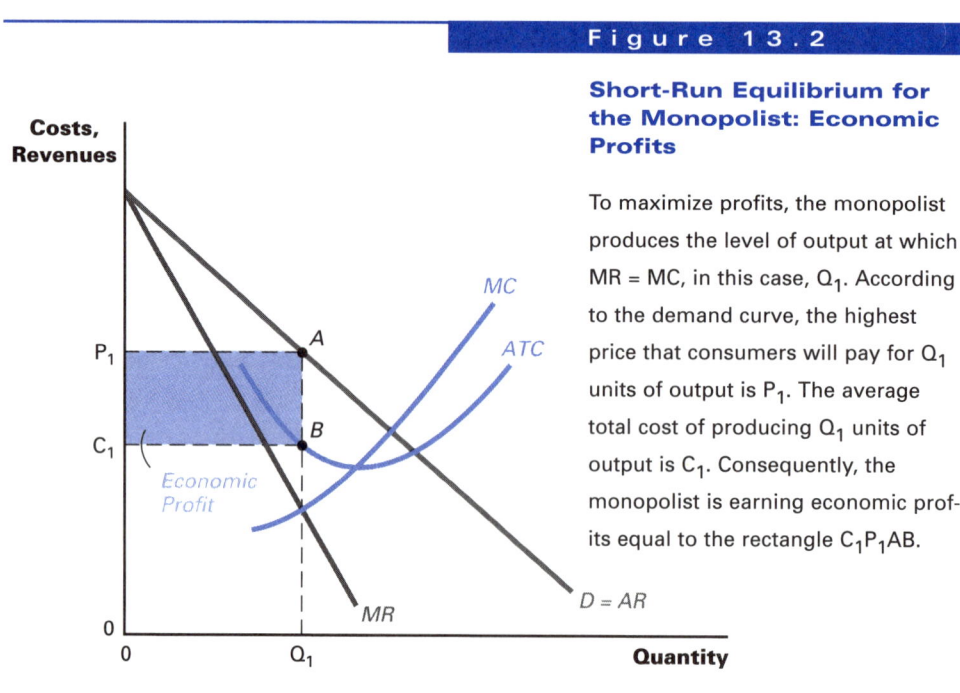

Figure 13.2

Short-Run Equilibrium for the Monopolist: Economic Profits

To maximize profits, the monopolist produces the level of output at which MR = MC, in this case, Q_1. According to the demand curve, the highest price that consumers will pay for Q_1 units of output is P_1. The average total cost of producing Q_1 units of output is C_1. Consequently, the monopolist is earning economic profits equal to the rectangle C_1P_1AB.

Figure 13.3

Alternative Short-Run Equilibrium Situations for the Monopolist (a) *Breakeven* (b) *Economic Loss*

The fact that a firm is a monopolist does not ensure the realization of economic profits. In Figure 13.3 (a), the profit-maximizing level of output is Q' and the corresponding price is P'. In this situation, the monopolist is earning zero economic profit. In Figure 13.3 (b), at the profit-maximizing level of output average revenue, P^*, is less than average total cost C^*. Hence, this monopolist is incurring an economic loss equal to the rectangle P^*C^*EF.

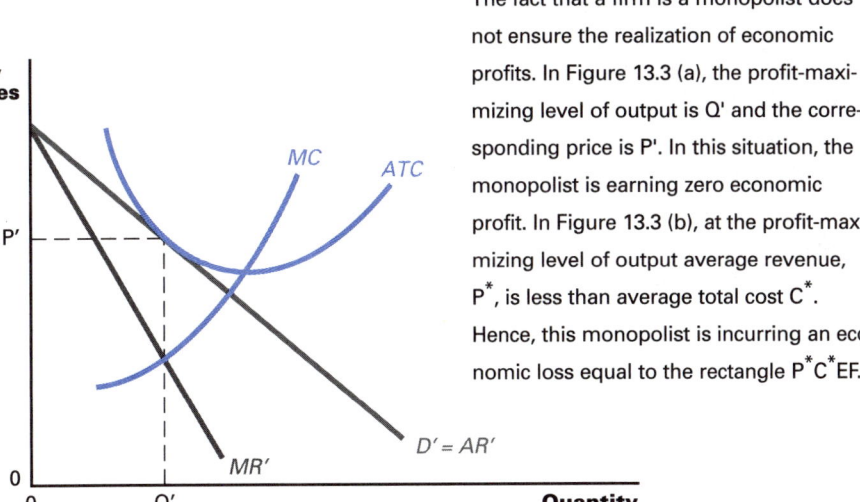

(a)

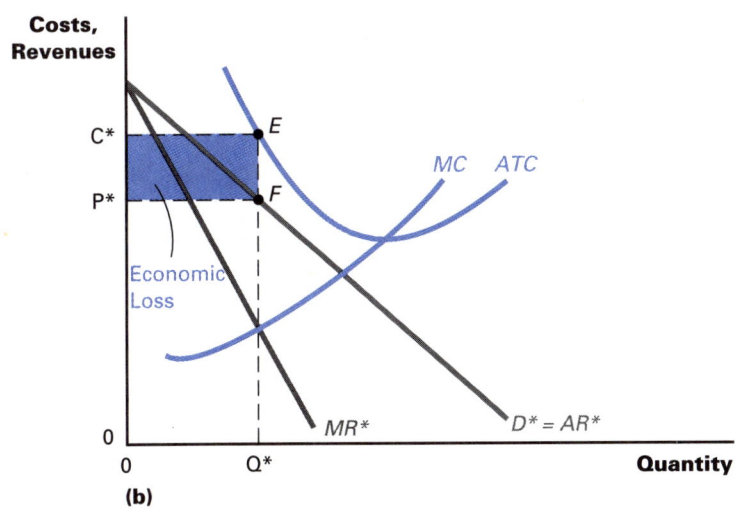

(b)

zero. This is the direct result of resource mobility. *The fact that resource immobility eliminates competition enables a monopolist who is earning economic profits in the short run to continue to do so in the long run, so long as demand and cost conditions remain unchanged. In addition, the monopolist has the potential to increase profits through technological innovation that reduces the costs of production.*

Long-run profits are not guaranteed, however. As we saw in Figure 13.3 (b), demand and cost conditions may actually result in a loss for the monopolist. Short-run economic profits persist in the long run only so long as there are no adverse changes in demand or cost conditions. In addition, for short-run economic profits to persist in the long run, the barriers to entry that gave rise to the monopoly must remain intact. If the firm's monopoly position is the result of a patent that expires, new firms may enter the industry. In a similar fashion, if new sources of scarce inputs are developed by potential competitors, the monopolist's position will be eroded. Technological change can also alter economies of scale. In the last decade we have witnessed a considerable increase in the number of competitors in the market for long-distance telephone service. The potential for competition in the cable TV industry is also increasing. Telephone companies are poised to enter this lucrative market. At the same time, cable TV companies are contemplating competing with telephone companies for the provision of local telephone service. These topics are considered in greater detail in Chapter 14.

Section Recap

A monopolist has the potential to earn economic profit in both the short run and the long run. However, the fact that a firm is a monopolist does not guarantee economic profit (or even a normal profit).

Efficiency Implications

In the case of perfect competition, firms acting in their own self-interest end up promoting society's welfare. In particular, perfectly competitive firms produce the allocatively efficient level of output, since price equals marginal cost for the last unit of output produced. Also, because each firm operates at the minimum of its long-run (and short-run) average total cost curve, perfectly competitive firms use their capacity efficiently. However, a profit-maximizing monopolist will, in most cases, violate both of these conditions. Consequently, an unrestricted monopoly market generates equilibrium market outcomes that are economically inefficient.

Figure 13.4 illustrates the demand and cost conditions for a particular good. Assuming that all the output is produced by a single firm, the profit-maximizing price and level of output are P_M and Q_M. If, instead, the industry were characterized by a high degree of competition, the marginal cost curve would represent the sum of the marginal cost curves of all the firms in the industry.[3] Price would be set equal to marginal cost, the level of output would be Q_C, and the corresponding price would be P_C.

As we can see from Figure 13.4, left on its own the monopolist will produce a level of output that is too low (since $Q_M < Q_C$) and charge a price that is too high ($P_M > P_C$). *Monopoly is allocatively inefficient because, at the profit-maximizing level of output, price is always greater than marginal cost. Hence, too few resources are allocated to the good in question. It is also the case in most instances that the monopolist does not operate at the minimum of its average total cost curve and therefore does not make efficient use of its capacity.*

One final note with respect to Figure 13.4 concerns the triangle ACF. This area represents consumer and producer surplus that would be realized if the market were perfectly competitive, but is lost if the market is served by an unrestricted monopolist. If the market were perfectly competitive, consumer surplus would be equal to the area P_CEC.

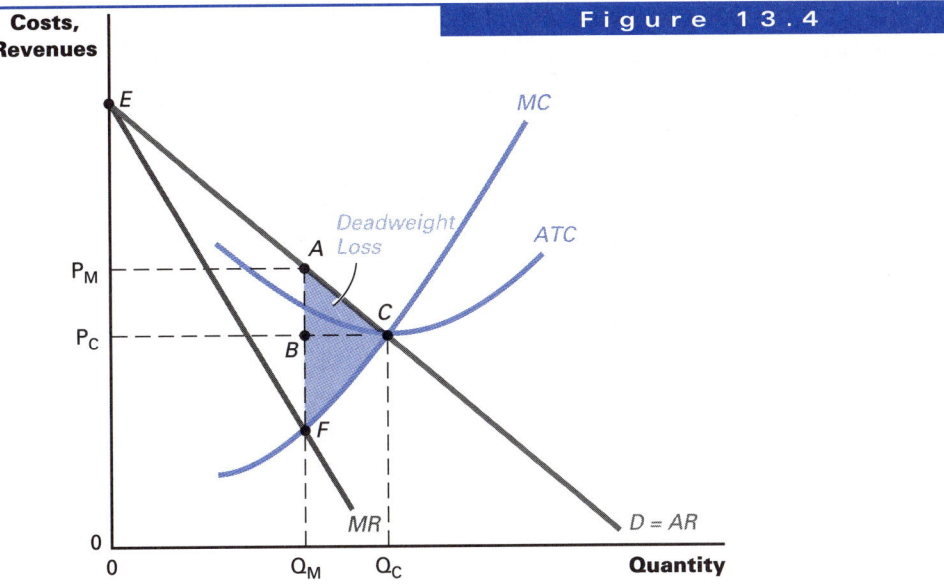

Figure 13.4

Equilibrium Price and Output: Monopoly versus Perfect Competition

Assuming that the industry is controlled by a monopolist, the profit-maximizing price and level of output would be P_M and Q_M. If we instead assume that the industry is perfectly competitive, price would be set equal to marginal cost, at P_C, and the level of output would be Q_C. (Note that in this case, this would be long-run equilibrium for the competitive industry because price is at the minimum of the ATC curve.)

However, because the monopolist is able to restrict output and raise price, consumer surplus is reduced to the area P_MEA. The amount of consumer surplus represented by the area $P_C P_M$AB is transferred to the monopolist in the form of producer surplus. The area ABC is lost consumer surplus. In a similar fashion, the triangle BCF represents lost producer surplus. The combined loss of producer and consumer surplus, shown by the triangle ACF, is referred to as a **deadweight loss**. It is a benefit that is lost to everyone – it is not captured by consumers or the firm. Deadweight loss is another cost of unrestricted monopoly.

Deadweight loss:
The combined producer and consumer surplus that would be realized in a perfectly competitive market but are lost in a monopoly situation.

Unrestricted monopoly results in an inefficient level of output and use of resources. As a result, society incurs a deadweight loss.

Section Recap

Natural Monopoly

A **natural monopoly** is a special case of the monopoly market structure. A natural monopolist has a long-run average cost curve that is downward sloping over the relevant range of output. The most common examples of natural monopolies are regional electric and gas utilities and local telephone service. The key point with respect to a natural monopoly is that one firm can produce all of the output demanded in the market at a lower per-unit cost than can two or more firms.

Natural monopoly:
The long-run average costs of production are decreasing over the relevant range of output.

Figure 13.5 illustrates the cost and demand conditions for a natural monopoly. The long-run average cost curve, labeled LRAC, and the long-run marginal cost curve, labeled LRMC, represent the long-run costs incurred by the monopolist. (Recall that long-run cost curves reflect the effect on average costs of allowing the plant size to vary.) For the firm illustrated in Figure 13.5, the long-run marginal cost curve lies below the long-run average cost curve. Recall that so long as marginal cost is less than average cost for a given level of output, average cost will decline. The demand curve represents total market demand for the good in question.

In Figure 13.5, the demand curve intersects the long-run average cost curve to the left of the average cost curve's minimum. Consequently, one firm can produce all the output demanded in the market at a lower average per-unit cost than could two or more firms. More importantly, the marginal costs of production – both short-run and long-run – and therefore the amount of resources used to produce a given level of output are minimized by having a single producer. If two or more firms were to operate in the industry, the marginal cost of production would necessarily be higher than the marginal cost of production incurred by a single producer because each firm would produce a level of output that is less than Q_E.

From the viewpoint of efficiency, *if a market is a natural monopoly, production by a single firm is preferred to a competitive market because average (unit) costs are minimized.* However, as we have already seen, in the absence of intervention in the market, the profit-maximizing

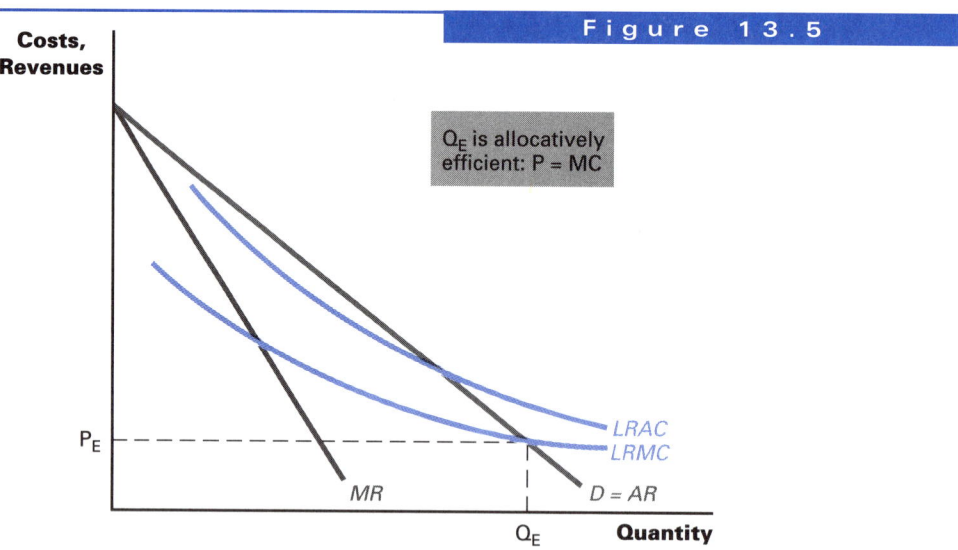

Figure 13.5

Q_E is allocatively efficient: P = MC

Demand and Cost Conditions for a Natural Monopoly

In a natural monopoly, the costs of production decline over the relevant range of output. The socially efficient level of output occurs where P = MC, in this case at Q_E. The socially efficient price would be P_E. Two or more firms operating in this industry would divide up the total amount of output, and each would produce at a higher marginal cost than P_E.

monopolist will produce a level of output that is less than the economically efficient amount. As illustrated in Figure 13.6, the price and level of output that correspond to point M on the demand curve represent the profit-maximizing price-output combination for an unregulated natural monopolist. However, the economically efficient level of output, which occurs where price equals marginal cost, is located at point E on the demand curve.

The efficiency problem is further complicated by the fact that if the monopolist is forced to produce the efficient level of output, the monopolist will incur a loss. In Figure 13.6, the efficient price and level of output are P_E and Q_E. However, the average total cost of producing Q_E units of output is C_E. Clearly, P_E is less than C_E. If the firm is forced to produce at point E, it would incur an economic loss represented by the rectangle $P_E C_E AE$ in Figure 13.6. A rational monopolist forced to produce this output level would simply cease production altogether.

Economic policymakers, therefore, face a dilemma. If the monopoly is prohibited and the industry is instead populated by many smaller competitive firms, the result is that output is produced inefficiently – output is produced at a higher average and marginal cost than if produced by a monopolist. Consequently, resources are wasted. Alternatively, if the monopolist is allowed to operate without restrictions, it will produce an inefficient level of output because price is greater than marginal cost. Policymakers have responded to this dilemma by seeking to take advantage of the lower production costs while denying the monopolist its market power. Natural monopolies are allowed to operate, but in a regulated environment.

Figure 13.6

Natural Monopoly and Output

The profit-maximizing natural monopoly will produce the level of output at which MR = MC, in this case, at point M on the demand curve. The corresponding level of output is Q_M. If, instead, the monopolist was forced to produce the efficient level of output, production would occur at point E on the demand curve, and the price and level of output would be P_E and Q_E. However, the average cost of producing Q_E is C_E. Consequently, the monopolist would incur an economic loss equal to the shaded area.

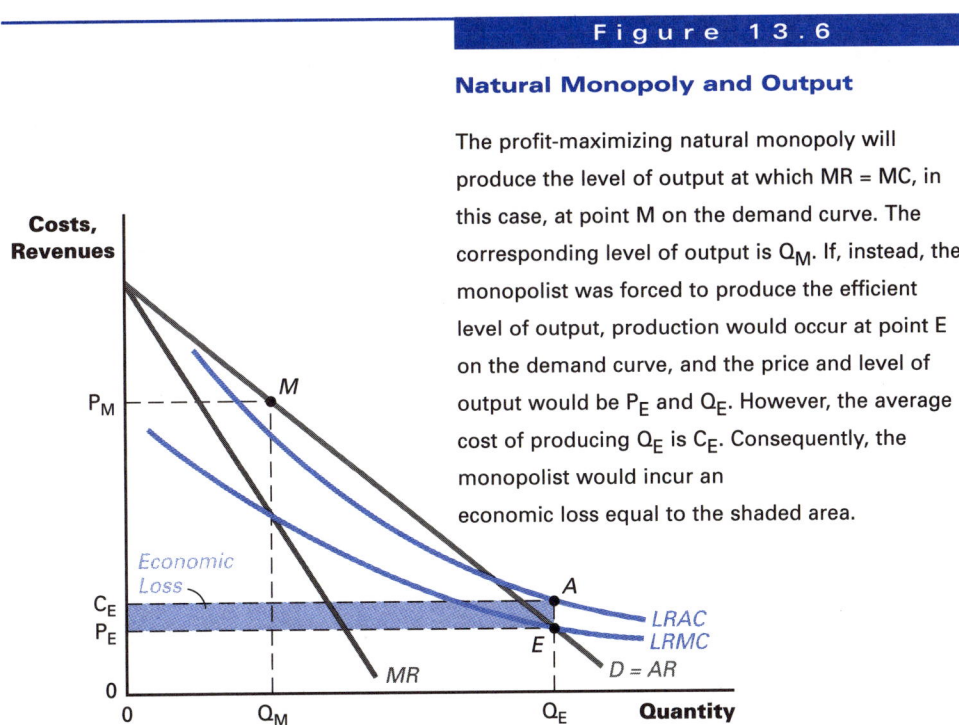

Section Recap

In a natural monopoly, production costs are minimized by allowing a single firm to produce all the output in the market. However, the unrestricted natural monopoly does not have an incentive to produce the allocatively efficient level of output.

Rate–of–return regulation:

Prices are set at a level that will cover the costs of production and provide the firm's investors with a competitive rate of return on their investment.

Revenue requirement:

The amount of money a regulated firm such as a utility must earn to be able to cover its production costs and earn a normal profit.

Regulation of Natural Monopoly The behavior of a regulated monopoly such as an electric or natural gas utility is usually governed by some form of regulatory commission. The major objectives of the commission are to ensure that costs are reasonably and prudently incurred and that the rates firms are allowed to charge are justified by the costs of production. In determining the price(s) that the regulated firm will be allowed to charge its customers, regulatory commissions have traditionally relied on what is referred to as **rate–of–return regulation**. In this form of business regulation, prices are set at a level that covers the costs of production and provides the firm's investors with a competitive rate of return on their investment.

The critical determinant of the actual rates that are charged under rate–of–return regulation is the **revenue requirement**. The revenue requirement is determined by the *rate of return*, the *rate base*, and *operating expenses*. The rate of return refers to the amount of profit the firm is allowed to earn, expressed as a percentage of the rate base. The rate base refers to the total costs of capital (less depreciation) to which the rate of return is applied. Operating expenses consist of the variable costs of production.

Mathematically, we can write the revenue requirement as:

$$RR = ror(RB) + OE$$

where RR is the revenue requirement, *ror* is the rate of return, RB is the rate base, and OE represents variable operating expenses. As an example, assume that the competitive rate of return for a particular electric utility is determined to be 10 percent, the rate base is equal to $10 million, and operating expenses equal $2 million. Then, the firm would be allowed to collect $3 million [= (.1)10 million + 2 million] in total revenue over a given time period (usually one year). To generate this total amount of revenue, specific rate schemes must be developed and approved by the regulatory commission.

The objective of rate–of–return regulation is to encourage the efficient allocation of resources. However, one obvious problem associated with the rate–of–return approach to rate setting is that there is a clear disincentive for regulated firms to control costs. As the rate base increases, the amount of profits a firm is allowed to earn will increase as well. While firms must be able to justify additional costs that they want to add into the rate base, it is often difficult for the staff of a regulatory commission to determine whether such costs are, in fact, justified.

Another problem with rate–of–return regulation is that although it results in an improvement over the unregulated monopoly, the resulting level of output nonetheless is inefficient. In Figure 13.7, the curve labeled D represents the demand for electric power in a particular geographic region. The long-run marginal and average costs of production incurred by the electric utility are measured by the curves labeled LRMC and LRAC. As shown here, the long-run average cost curve has been constructed to reflect both the

Figure 13.7

Rate-of-Return Regulation and the Level of Output

The LRAC curve is constructed to reflect the costs of production and a fair rate of return for the producer. If a single price is charged to all customers, equilibrium will occur at point F on the demand curve. The firm will earn a normal profit because AC = AR. The application of block pricing could result in production at point E, the efficient level of production. With block pricing, different prices are charged for different levels of output. Excess profits earned on units of output to the left of Q_1 are used to offset the losses incurred on units of output between points Q_1 and Q_E.

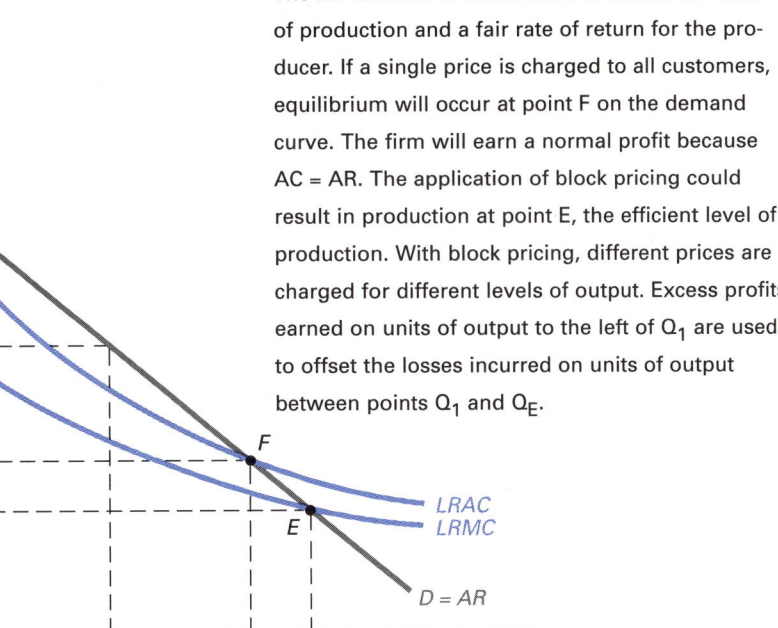

average costs of production and the rate of return, r^*, that has been established by the governing regulatory body.[4] That is, we have simply incorporated the rate of return into long-run average cost.

The economically efficient level of electricity production occurs at point E on the demand curve. However, a firm producing at point E would incur an economic loss. Assuming that a single price is charged for each unit of output, the largest amount of output that the firm could produce and still earn a normal profit is Q_F. This level of output falls short of the efficient amount.

One way to deal with this problem is through the application of **block pricing**. With block pricing, different units of output are sold at different prices. In effect, the sale of some units results in a rate of return in excess of r^* while the sale of other units generates a rate of return below r^*. These latter units correspond to the levels of output between Q_F and Q_E in Figure 13.7. The end result is that the pluses and minuses cancel out, the firm earns an average rate of return equal to r^*, and the efficient level of output is produced.

A simple form of block pricing is illustrated in Figure 13.7. To ensure the efficient level of output, a price of P_E must be charged for the level of output Q_E. Assume that, in fact, this price is charged for the units between Q_1 and Q_E. Clearly, because price is less than average total cost, the firm incurs a loss on these units of output. However, to offset

Block pricing:

A pricing technique in which a regulated firm is allowed to sell blocks of output at different prices to simultaneously earn a normal profit and produce the efficient level of output.

ECONOMIC SENSE

Rethinking Regulation of Natural Monopolies

As discussed in this chapter, certain industries, such as electric and natural gas utilities and local telephone service, traditionally have been viewed as natural monopolies. This characterization is the result of high fixed costs of production and corresponding economies of scale. Policymakers have responded to these market characteristics by granting franchises to individual firms to operate in a specified service territory. The prices these firms can charge their customers have, in turn, been set using rate-of-return regulation. However, recently there has been a movement toward abandoning rate-of-return regulation in favor of alternative regulatory methods and, in the extreme, reliance on the

forces of competition to determine market prices. In light of the characteristics of these markets and the long history of the prevailing approach to price setting, it is worth asking, Does this make economic sense?

To answer this question, we need to consider two factors: (1) the incentives associated with rate-of-return regulation versus alternative regulatory approaches, and (2) the changing nature of many industries that heretofore have been viewed as natural monopolies. With respect to incentives, recall from our discussion of rate-of-return regulation that prices are set by determining the amount of revenue the firm must receive to cover all of its reasonably and prudently incurred costs, plus a reasonable rate of return. Critics of this approach have

argued that, in fact, there is little incentive for firms to hold down costs or engage in research that would reduce the costs of production. Any savings would simply be passed along to customers, rather than enjoyed by the firm in the form of increased profits.

An alternative to rate-of-return regulation that has received increased attention uses price caps that are adjusted on a periodic basis. In fact, a version of price caps, referred to as RPI-X, has been in use in Great Britain for the last few years.[6] In principle, the method is straightforward. Based on the regulated firm's current costs of production, the regulatory authority sets the maximum price the firm can charge during a specific year. Then, for the next few years the price ceiling rises by an amount

the loss, the firm could charge a price of P_1 for the units of output between 0 and Q_1. The sale of the first Q_1 units generates economic profits (since price is greater than average total cost), which can be used to offset the losses incurred on the $Q_E - Q_1$ units sold at the lower price.

Even in the case of block pricing, however, potential problems exist. To be specific, income redistribution occurs because different consumers end up paying different prices for the same product. Those individuals paying higher prices subsidize the purchases of consumers who enjoy the lower price. In our example, customers who consume the first Q_1 units pay an average per-unit price greater than average total cost while customers consuming the units between Q_1 and Q_E pay the lower price of P_E.

Price discrimination – the practice of charging different prices to different customers of the same good or service – is also utilized to affect the level of total output. In the case of electricity and natural gas, for instance, rates are often based on customer classifications – industrial, commercial, and residential – with customers in each class paying rates either above or below the actual average cost of service. The fact that residential demand for electricity is more inelastic than commercial or industrial demand is used in the rate-setting process. This reflects the recognition that if rates are set too high for

Price discrimination:
The practice of charging different prices to different buyers of the same good or service.

equal to the rate of inflation minus some predetermined percentage. For its part, the firm can reduce costs as much as possible and realize the savings in the form of increased profits. After the time period covered by the initial price cap has passed, the price cap is reset, reflecting the reductions in costs that have occurred. In this way, the firm's customers also get to enjoy the benefits of reduced costs in the form of lower prices, but with a lag. Using this method, the firm has the incentive to reduce costs that is absent under rate-of-return regulation.

The second factor is the changing nature of many industries that have traditionally been viewed as natural monopolies. Consider first the electric utility industry. Electricity production can be divided into three activities: generation, high-voltage transmission, and low-voltage distribution (to individual customers). The latter two activities are still considered to be natural monopolies due to the large fixed costs associated with the system of wires used to trans-

mit and distribute electricity and the duplication of costs that would occur if two firms were to compete in the same area. However, generation technologies have been progressing rapidly, to the point where it is now possible for many smaller generators to produce electricity at costs that are comparable to those incurred by much larger generating units. States such as California and Illinois have begun to address the growing potential for increased competition at the generation stage by considering significant changes in the way that generators' prices are regulated. In California there is considerable interest in relying much more on competitive forces to set prices not only for industrial and commercial customers, who have various options available to them in terms of supplies of electricity, but for residential customers as well.

The potential for competition in the provision of local telephone service also has grown rapidly. In their book *Toward Competition in Local Telephony*, William Baumol and Gregory Sidak identify a number of potential competitors for local tele-

phone carriers, including the long-distance carriers, local carriers that operate in adjacent areas, cable television firms, cellular and other wireless telephone services, and local fiber-optic networks. Although the authors do not propose that regulation of local telephone carriers be completely abandoned in favor of reliance solely on competitive forces, they make a strong case that competitive pressures will go a long way toward containing costs and the price of local telephone service.

In summary, it appears that increased reliance on alternatives to rate-of-return regulation, including alternative regulatory methods and competition, would make economic sense. Regulation has always been considered a second-best solution compared to the outcome produced by a competitive market. Thus, any change that moves us in the direction of a competitively determined solution should be preferred, at least on economic efficiency grounds.

customers whose demand is more elastic, the customers will simply switch to relatively lower-priced substitutes. This would, in turn, mean even higher rates for the remaining customers who must bear the fixed and variable costs of production.[5]

The pricing and output decisions of natural monopolies are often regulated. Rate-of-return regulation, combined with techniques such as block pricing and price discrimination, is intended to simultaneously provide producers a fair rate of return and consumers an allocatively efficient level of output at a fair price.

Section Recap

Oligopoly

Like the model of perfect competition, the monopoly model provides us with useful insights. An important conclusion of the monopoly model is that, left unchecked, economic inefficiency – which results from an absolute lack of competition – may be substantial. We now modify the monopoly model to consider the situation in which a market is dominated by a few firms. This type of market structure is called **oligopoly**. The big corporations that we hear about daily and that together account for most of the output (in dollar terms) of the economy are oligopolists.

Oligopoly:
A small number of firms dominate the market; the economic well-being and behavior of the firms are mutually interdependent.

We want to examine the profit-maximizing behavior of oligopolists and the market outcomes associated with this behavior, just as we have analyzed the behavior of firms in other market structures. However, our treatment of oligopoly differs from our handling of the other three market structures in one important way. In the cases of perfect competition, monopolistic competition, and monopoly we were able to describe the equilibrium market outcomes in unambiguous terms. We will not be able to do that in the case of oligopolists because of the unique nature of oligopolistic markets. *In an oligopoly there are only a few rival firms whose economic well-being and behavior is **mutually interdependent**. One firm's actions influence the actions of other firms.* Consequently, market outcomes can be quite ambiguous. We will describe and explain the source of this interdependence among firms, the alternative outcomes we expect to observe, and the features of the market environment that account for these different outcomes.

Mutual interdependence:
One firm's actions influence the actions of other firms in a market.

General Characteristics

Examples of oligopolies include the steel, auto, breakfast cereal, and chemical manufacturing industries. A small number of firms that serve a local market, such as three grocery stores in a large city, would be considered an oligopoly as well. Oligopolists may produce a homogeneous or a differentiated product. For example, firms in the steel or chemical industries may produce essentially the same product. Firms in the auto or breakfast food industries, on the other hand, produce differentiated products. The following is a summary of the major characteristics of oligopolistic markets:

1. Small number of dominant firms. Oligopolists are often large firms, each producing a significant portion of total market output. In some cases, a market may actually consist of hundreds of firms. However, to the extent that the market is dominated by one or a few firms, it is considered to be an oligopoly.

2. Mutual interdependence. Because the market is dominated by a few firms, the price and output decisions of one firm affect the profitability of the remaining firms in the market. Mutual interdependence is an incentive to develop alternatives to price competition in the pursuit of economic profit.

3. Barriers to entry. Like monopoly markets, oligopoly markets are usually characterized by considerable resource immobility, especially economies of scale. Barriers to entry limit the threat of competition and facilitate the ability of firms to earn long-run economic profit.

4. Homogeneous or differentiated product. As the examples cited above indicate, the output of an oligopolistic market may be either homogeneous or differentiated.

Like monopolies, oligopolistic firms are price searchers. Firms that produce a differentiated product each face their own downward-sloping demand curve. For firms that produce a homogeneous product, mutual interdependence causes the individual firm's demand curve to be downward sloping.

Oligopolies are characterized by a small number of firms that produce a large share of market output, mutual interdependence among firms, and barriers to entry. Oligopolists are price searchers.

Market Concentration The size of oligopolistic firms and the small number of firms in an industry have often led individuals to associate "bigness" and "fewness" with less competition and greater profits. The degree of concentration in an industry or market refers to the share of the total market output produced by one or more firms. A **concentration ratio** is a measure of industry concentration. For example, a four-firm concentration ratio is the percentage of sales in an industry accounted for by the four largest firms. Concentration ratios can also be constructed with respect to the amount of physical output, the amount of labor employed, and so forth. Four-firm and eight-firm (directly analogous to the four-firm measure) concentration ratios for selected industries are presented in Table 13.1.

A high four-firm concentration ratio indicates that most of the sales or output (or whatever) in the industry are accounted for by the four largest firms. It also suggests the presence of barriers to entry into the market. However, it does not necessarily imply that there are only a few firms in the industry. Hence, it is possible to have an industry that is

Concentration ratio:

A measure of market concentration, that is, the extent to which one or more firms control the level of production in an industry.

Table 13.1

Four-Firm and Eight-Firm Concentration Ratios for Selected Industries: 1987

SIC Code	Industry	Four-Firm Concentration Ratio	Eight-Firm Concentration Ratio	Herfindahl-Hirschman Index[a]
2043	Cereal Breakfast Foods	87%	99%	2207
2066	Chocolate and Cocoa Products	69%	82%	1835
2067	Chewing Gum	96%	100%	D[b]
2082	Malt Beverages	87%	98%	D
2251	Women's Hosiery, Except Socks	61%	72%	1501
2296	Tire Cord and Fabric	91%	99%	D
2771	Greeting Cards	85%	89%	2830
3211	Flat Glass	82%	D	1968
3333	Primary Aluminum	74%	95%	1934
3711	Motor Vehicles and Car Bodies	90%	95%	D
3721	Aircraft	72%	92%	1686
3996	Hard Surface Floor Coverings	82%	99+%	2550

[a] for 50 largest firms

[b] D = Data withheld to avoid disclosing data for individual companies.

Source: U.S. Department of Commerce, 1987, Census of Manufactures, Subject Series MC87-S-6, *Concentration Ratios in Manufacturing*; Washington, DC, 1992, pp. 6-6, 6-7.

essentially oligopolistic, but in which the number of firms is large. For example, there were 717 firms operating in the photographic equipment and supplies industry in 1987. However, the four largest firms produced 77 percent of the output of the industry.

Historically, four-firm (and eight-firm) concentration ratios were relied on to assess the degree of competition in an industry. More recently, the Herfindahl-Hirschman Index (HHI) has been used by the U.S. Justice Department to assess the degree of concentration in a particular industry.[7] It has been argued that the HHI provides a more accurate measure of the overall degree of concentration because the HHI takes account of all the firms in the industry, rather than just the top four or top eight. The HHI is calculated as the sum of the squares of the market shares (percentages) of each of the firms in the industry. The formula for the HHI is:

$$HHI = S_1^2 + S_2^2 + S_3^2 + ... + S_n^2$$

where S_1 through S_n are the market shares of each of the n firms.

Table 13.2 illustrates the effect that use of the HHI has on measures of concentration relative to the four-firm concentration ratio. According to guidelines developed by the Justice Department, a market with an index of less than 1000 is unconcentrated, a market with an index between 1000 and 1800 is moderately concentrated, and a market with an index in excess of 1800 is highly concentrated. Table 13.1 also reports the HHI for the industries listed.

Section Recap

Measures of market concentration, such as concentration ratios and the Herfindahl-Hirschman Index, are used to determine the extent to which an industry is dominated by one or a few firms.

Short-Run Profit Maximization: Competition Among Rivals

Unlike the other market structures we have analyzed – perfect competition, monopolistic competition, and monopoly – the profit-maximizing decision of an oligopolist is difficult to analyze graphically. This is a direct result of the mutual interdependence of the firms in

Table 13.2

A Comparison of the Four-Firm Concentration Ratio and the Herfindahl-Hirschman Index

Industry Structure	Four-Firm Concentration Ratio	Herfindahl-Hirschman Index
Single firm	100	10,000
4 equal-sized firms	100	2,500
6 equal-sized firms	67	1,667
8 equal-sized firms	50	1,250
10 equal-sized firms	40	1,000

the industry. In response to a decision by one firm to increase (or decrease) the price of its product, the other firms may alter their prices as well.

Because of this mutual interdependence, competition among firms may lead to reduced profits for everyone in the long run. To see that this is the case, consider the following example. Assume that an industry is made up of only two firms, A and B, each of which is initially operating at a profit-maximizing level of output (and is earning economic profits). Now assume that Firm A lowers its price in an effort to increase its sales and profits. Initially, when Firm A lowers its price it attracts customers away from Firm B. So long as marginal revenue is greater than marginal cost for the additional units sold, Firm A's profits increase in the short run at the expense of Firm B. However, the price cut by Firm A and the resulting increase in its profits creates an incentive for Firm B to cut its price as well in an attempt to regain lost profits. If Firm B responds to Firm A's price reduction by lowering its price, each firm will produce roughly the same share of market output that it did initially. However, the price the firms receive for each unit of output will be lower. Assuming that average costs have remained the same, each firm's economic profits have declined.

Figures 13.8 (a) and 13.8 (b) illustrate the situation described above. Initially each firm is producing Q_1 units of output and charging a price of P_1. Because price (which equals average revenue) is greater than average total cost, each firm is earning an economic profit. If Firm A lowers its price to P_2, it will attract buyers away from Firm B and sell more output. Firm A is now operating at point 2 in Figure 13.8 (a). The decrease in price by Firm A has the effect of shifting Firm B's demand curve to the left, to D_2 in Figure 13.8 (b). (Firm B's demand curve shifts left because the price of a substitute – the output of Firm A – has decreased.) Firm B is now selling less output at the original price of P_1. However, Firm B will respond by lowering its price to P_2 to regain its lost customers. As Firm B lowers its price, Firm A's demand curve shifts left to D_2 in Figure 13.8 (a). Firm A's output falls back to Q_1. Once all adjustments have taken place, each firm's output level is unchanged, but price and profits have declined.

This action-reaction scenario suggests that competition among oligopolists may lead to reduced profits for each firm. Since competition makes each firm worse off, it is a no-win situation. This motivates firms to look for other strategies to increase economic profits. Not surprisingly, cooperation among firms is an attractive alternative.

It is in the interest of oligopolists to agree to work together to jointly set price and output in the market. If they do, the industry, in effect, becomes a shared monopoly. Consider again the situation of Firms A and B. If the firms agree to divide up the market among themselves, each firm can produce the level of output that maximizes profits. Because they have agreed not to compete with each other on the basis of price, each firm can continue to earn economic profits over the long run, provided demand and cost conditions do not change. Entry barriers prevent competition from others, and economic profits persist in the long run.

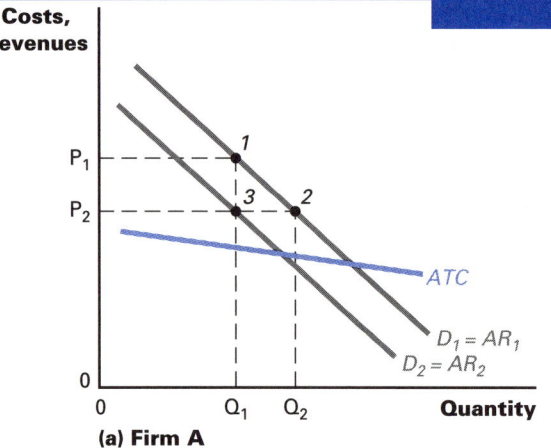

(a) Firm A

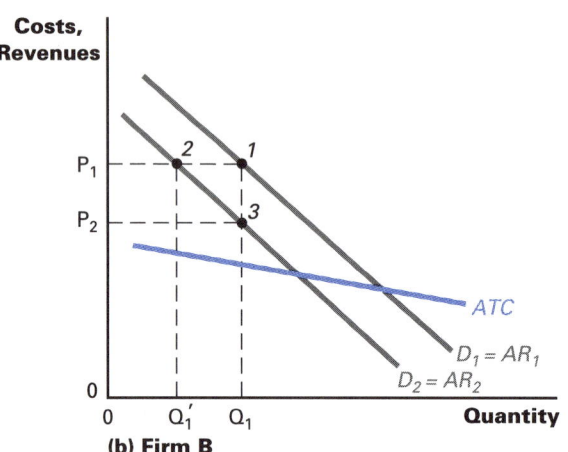

(b) Firm B

Figure 13.8

The Interdependence of Pricing Decisions by Firms in Oligopoly

Figures 13.8 (a) and (b) illustrate the situation for two firms – A and B – that each produce Q_1 units of output and charge a price of P_1. Because P = AR > ATC, each firm is earning an economic profit. Assuming Firm A lowers its price to P_2, it will attract buyers away from Firm B and will move to point 2 in Figure 13.8 (a). The decrease in price by Firm A has the effect of shifting Firm B's demand curve to the left, to D_2 in Figure 13.8 (b). Firm B will respond by lowering its price to P_2 to regain its lost customers. As Firm B lowers price, this causes Firm A's demand curve to shift left to D_2 in Figure 13.8 (a) and Firm A's output falls back to Q_1. Once all adjustments have taken place, each firm's output level is unchanged, but price and profits have declined.

Section Recap

As a result of mutual interdependence, oligopolistic firms that attempt to compete on the basis of price will end up losing profits. This creates an incentive for firms to cooperate with one another.

Alternatives to Competition

Collusion Among Rivals

We have assumed that the objective of all firms in all markets is to maximize profits. Yet we have learned that competition limits the opportunity to earn economic profit. Thus, there is an incentive for a firm to escape competition in any market setting. **Collusion** refers to the act of firms working together (cooperating) to establish the price and level of output in a particular market. By colluding with each other, firms hope to escape, or at least lessen, the pressures of competition. However, the opportunity to collude successfully depends on the structure of the market in which the firms operate.

Perfectly competitive markets are characterized by a large number of small firms. The firms in the market have absolutely no market power and take price as given. The fact that

Collusion:

The act of firms working together (cooperating) to establish the price and level of output in a particular market.

each firm produces a homogeneous product eliminates the possibility of escaping competition through product differentiation. In addition, because of the large number of firms, it would be extremely difficult, if not impossible, to coordinate efforts to restrict market output as a means of forcing up the market price. The only alternative available to competitive firms is to reduce costs, which results in short-run economic profits.

Monopolistic competition affords the individual firm greater opportunities for escaping the pressures of competition. Product differentiation and, in some cases, the effects of regulation lessen the competitive pressures faced by the firm. However, the facts that firms are small relative to the market, that there is usually a large number of firms, and that entry is relatively easy – resources are mobile – all serve to maintain a fair degree of competitive pressure. Just as in the case of perfect competition, the likelihood of successful collusion is extremely small.

We have already seen that the potential costs of competition among oligopolists – loss of both market share and economic profit – can be high. Hence, there is a strong tendency for firms in this situation to seek out alternatives to competition. Cooperation and, in particular, collusion are such alternatives. The fact that oligopoly is characterized by a small number of firms enhances the attractiveness of this alternative.

Explicit collusion among firms is illegal in the United States. Specific laws have been passed (which are discussed in Chapter 14) that prohibit firms from working together to set price and the level of output in a particular market. Collusion nonetheless occurs and can take a variety of forms. These include the formation of cartels, price leadership, and secret agreements among firms.

Cartels A **cartel** consists of a group of firms that have explicitly and openly agreed to work together to set the price that will be charged in a particular market. A cartel also sets production quotas for each participant. The quotas are designed to ensure that price is not driven below the agreed-upon level. The most widely recognized example of a cartel is the Organization of Petroleum Exporting Countries (OPEC). OPEC is legally able to operate because it is an international organization and is not prohibited by any international law. The International Tin Cartel is another example of a cartel that operated successfully for many years.

Cartel:
A group of firms that have explicitly and openly agreed to work together to set the price that will be charged in a particular market.

Price Leadership **Price leadership** refers to a situation in which one firm in an industry establishes the market price and the remaining firms in the industry follow suit. Successful price leadership requires implicit agreement among firms as to who the price leader will be. A number of instances of price leadership have occurred in the United States. U.S. Steel historically took the lead in setting price in the steel industry.[8] R. J. Reynolds assumed a similar role in the tobacco industry. Price leadership is usually the result of dominance in the industry by one firm. However, instances can also arise in which the least-cost producer in the industry emerges as the price leader.

Price leadership:
A situation in which one firm in an industry establishes the market price and the remaining firms in the industry follow suit.

The price leader benefits from its role in two ways. First, it is able to set a price that enables it to earn economic profit without concern about potential price reductions by rival firms. In addition, the price leader can exercise its price-setting power in such a way

Game Theory and the Prisoner's Dilemma

The mutual interdependence of the firms in an oligopoly is similar to the problem faced by two individuals involved in a game. In chess, for example, one player's choice of which piece to move depends, in large part, on how she thinks her opponent will respond. In other games, such as cards, players must select strategies that they believe will yield the greatest payoff given their opponents' potential actions.

The study of game theory is devoted to the analysis of strategic behavior under uncertainty. In part, game theory allows one to identify the solution to a problem that achieves a particular goal. For example, one strategy is to behave so as to minimize the maximum loss that could be incurred in a particular situation. Alternatively, the player may wish to maximize the minimum gain possible.

One particular game, which closely resembles the situation faced by many oligopolistic firms, is known as the *prisoner's dilemma*. In its generic form, two individuals must select one of two behaviors. However, the payoff associated with each behavior depends on what the other player does. As an illustration, consider the situation faced by two firms that constitute a market. Depending on how each firm prices its output, each firm will earn varying levels of profit. The possible payoffs are shown in Table 13.3, which is referred to as a *payoff matrix*.

Table 13.3 indicates that if both firms charge a price of $10, each will earn $200 of profit (payoff 1). In addition, if both firms raise their price to $12, each firm's profits will increase to $250 (payoff 3). However, the individual firm's profits will be greatest if it holds its price constant and the other firm raises its price (payoffs 2a and 2b). Each firm must decide whether to charge $10 or $12 per unit. (This is the dilemma.) If Firm A decides to charge $12 and Firm B follows suit, both firms win. However, if Firm B charges $10, Firm A loses. So long as one firm believes that the other may lower its price, each firm maximizes its minimum payoff (profit) by charging a price of $10. In this situation, this is the equilibrium strategy.

Note that the situation in Table 13.3 is very similar to that faced by Firms A and B in Figure 13.8. In particular, if each firm originally sells its output at a per-unit price of $12 and either firm lowers its price, the eventual outcome will be a loss of profits for both firms — assuming the other firm follows suit. (If the second firm does not follow suit, its profits will fall even further.) If, instead, each firm is initially charging a per-unit price of $10, an increase in price by either firm will cause its profits to fall. The other firm will increase its profits by continuing to charge the original price of $10. Clearly, the actions of the firms are mutually interdependent.

Table 13.3

Payoff Matrix for Two Competing Firms

			Firm B Price $10	Firm B Price $12
	P	$10	$200, $200 (A) (B) (payoff 1)	$300, $150 (A) (B) (payoff 2a)
Firm A	rice	$12	$150, $300 (A) (B) (payoff 2b)	$250, $250 (A) (B) (payoff 3)

that the other firms in the industry are able to make a small profit as well. The continued presence of the smaller firms shields the dominant firm from charges of monopolization of the market or possession of excessive market power.

Price leadership, although not necessarily intentional, is observed on a regular basis in the automobile industry. Each year, one or another of the three major U.S. producers announces its price changes for the upcoming model year. The remaining firms follow with announcements, usually a week or so later. Generally, the price adjustments are strikingly similar. In this case, the firms in the industry take turns being the price leader. This same general phenomenon is also observed with respect to rebate programs. When one of the three manufacturers announces a set of rebates for selected models, the other manufacturers are often quick to follow with similar programs.

Secret Agreements Situations have arisen in which firms have worked together, secretly (and illegally) to control the price in a particular industry. In one of the more famous cases, a group of firms, including Westinghouse and General Electric, worked together to fix prices in the heavy-duty electric equipment industry. Once the plan was uncovered, the Justice Department brought suit against the offending companies. The trial that followed resulted in fines for twenty-nine companies and jail terms for many of the individuals involved.

Regardless of the specific form of collusion, the result is that firms in the industry are able to act jointly as a monopolist. By cooperating with each other, they are able to maximize the joint profits in the industry. However, because a number of firms are working together, they must agree on a number of issues including what the price should be and the level of output each firm should produce. Depending on the nature of the output produced, such agreements can be quite complicated.

At one extreme, firms producing a homogeneous product have a rather simple problem. Once the profit-maximizing price is determined, it is simply a matter of determining what share of the market each firm will control. At the other extreme, if the firms produce a differentiated product, there will almost certainly be a set of prices rather than a single price. Dividing up market shares will consequently be more difficult to agree upon.

Collusion enables firms to escape the pressures of competition and can increase economic profits. There are a number of forms of collusion including cartels, price leadership, and secret agreements.

Section Recap

Successful Collusion

For a collusive agreement to be successful, it is important that all of the firms involved implement the terms of the agreement. However, there is a strong incentive for individual firms to cheat. Consequently, the behavior of individual parties to the agreement must continually be monitored.

Cheating is a considerable obstacle to successful collusion. This results from the conflict between the individual firm's welfare and the welfare of the group as a whole. Each firm in the agreement recognizes that there are benefits from collusion and benefits from cheating on the agreement once it has been reached. Whether a given firm actually cheats on the agreement will depend on the benefits and costs of doing so.

On the one hand, a collusive agreement benefits each firm by protecting it from the adverse effects of competition from its rivals. Adherence to the agreement by all of the firms involved ensures that the joint profits of the parties to the agreement are maximized. So long as all firms continue to cooperate, and demand and cost conditions are not adversely affected, economic profits will persist over the long run.

On the other hand, cheating offers a single firm the possibility of additional benefits. If the other participating firms all adhere to the terms of the agreement, the remaining firm can cheat on the agreement by lowering price and increasing output and its share of profits. To the extent that the firm does not cheat, these potential benefits are forgone.

Cheating can take a number of forms. For example, a firm might offer secret discounts to buyers and increase its sales as a result. So long as price remains above the average total cost of production for all the additional units sold, the firm will increase its profits. The cheating firm can also increase sales by offering a higher level of quality than its competitors at the going price. The provision of extra benefits such as buyer credit and extended warranties can also increase the firm's sales at the expense of its rivals.

Cheating is obviously a major obstacle to successful collusion among firms in an industry. However, the success of a cooperative agreement among firms depends on a number of other factors as well. These factors include: (1) the degree of product differentiation, (2) the extent of cost differences among firms, (3) the number of firms involved, and (4) the availability of substitute products produced by firms outside the industry. Market conditions such as the stability of demand – is demand increasing, decreasing, or staying the same? – also affect the ability to successfully collude.

Product differentiation complicates efforts to agree upon prices and the market share to be controlled by each firm. In addition, differences in product quality among firms make it easier for individual firms to hide discounts (to cheat on the agreement). As cost differences among firms become larger, identifying a price or set of prices that benefits all the firms becomes more difficult. Once again, cost differences create an incentive to cheat. As the number of firms in the market increases, it is more difficult to police the agreement and ensure adherence to the agreement by each of the firms involved. It is this fact that renders collusion unworkable in the case of perfect competition or monopolistic competition. The availability of substitutes from other firms outside the industry has a similar effect.

The stability of market demand and its effect on the ability of firms to collude successfully is best illustrated by reference to the near-collapse of OPEC in the mid-1980s. The oil market experienced a large increase in supply and a simultaneous decrease in the rate of growth of demand. The resulting excess supply put substantial downward pressure on oil prices, and many of the members of OPEC began to undercut the cartel's agreed-upon minimum price to bolster their sagging profits. As a consequence, the pump price of gasoline fell in some places to well below a dollar per gallon. Finally, in late 1988, the cartel reached a new agreement to once again reduce output and raise prices in an effort to regain their control of world prices. However, in 1989, evidence suggested that members were already cheating on the new agreement.

The degree to which collusion is successful depends on a number of factors, including the degree to which firms cheat, the degree of product differentiation, the extent of cost differences among firms, the number of firms involved, and the availability of substitute products produced by firms outside the industry.

Government Regulation and Cartel-Like Behavior

Government regulation has, on occasion, served to strengthen the cartel-like behavior of firms in an oligopoly. This is especially true when regulation results in the establishment of barriers to entry in the industry. Examples of industries in which this has occurred include the Interstate Commerce Commission's regulation of the trucking and railroad industries and the Civil Aeronautics Board's regulation of the airline industry. In each of these cases, one of the major results of regulation of the industry was the creation of cartel-like conditions that led to significant profits for firms in each industry.

Regulation in each of these industries focused, in part, on the number of firms that could enter and compete in the industry. In each case, it was argued that an excess of competition would result in reduced quality of service to the firms' customers. Therefore, entry into the market was restricted. However, the restrictions on entry also allowed firms to work more closely to establish prices and available levels of service. In addition, regulation had the effect of preventing any firm from cheating, since prices were legally enforced. It is interesting to note that these same industries have been the target of deregulation in recent years. The effects of deregulation are discussed in Chapter 14.

Mergers

Mergers between firms can also provide a means of reducing the degree of competition faced by individual firms and enhancing their market power. There are several types of mergers. A **horizontal merger** is a merger into a single firm of two or more firms producing the same or similar products. The merger of USAir Group, Inc. and Piedmont Airlines, which was initiated in 1987 and completed in 1989, and the merger of Chrysler and American Motors are examples of horizontal mergers. A **vertical merger** is a merger into a single firm of two or more firms at different levels in the chain of production. A merger between a grain distributor and a breakfast food company would be a vertical merger. The merger between IBM and Lotus Development Corporation referred to at the beginning of this chapter is another example of a vertical merger. When two or more firms whose outputs are unrelated merge, it is referred to as a **conglomerate merger**. A merger between an oil company and a retail chain, such as the merger between Mobil Oil and Montgomery Ward, would be a conglomerate merger. In 1993, Viacom, a communications conglomerate, and QVC, the home shopping cable TV network, made competing bids to purchase Paramount. The eventual merger of Paramount with Viacom amounted to a conglomerate merger.

Horizontal merger: A merger into a single firm of two or more firms producing the same or similar products.

Vertical merger: A merger into a single firm of two or more firms at different levels in the chain of production.

Conglomerate merger: A merger between two or more firms whose outputs are unrelated.

The effect of a merger, in particular, a horizontal or vertical merger, on competition and economic efficiency depends on the specific market situation. In the case of a horizontal merger, if the merger results in a significantly higher degree of market concentration, it could open the door to collusive behavior on the part of the dominant firms. This is so if for no other reason than that the *potential* for successful collusion is now greater. On the other hand, a horizontal merger can result in the realization of greater economies of scale. To the extent that prices decline as a result of the decrease in costs, consumers could benefit from the merger.

Vertical mergers also have the potential to create substantial competitive advantages for a firm. For example, if a firm takes control of a supplier of a vital input, the firm may experience lower costs in the short run, enabling it to reduce prices. This would benefit consumers, who would be able to purchase the product at a lower price. However, it may also drive other firms out of the market. Recall our earlier discussion about the different barriers to entry. In the long run, it is likely that the firm could establish what amounts to a monopoly position by controlling all or most of the available supply of an input to the production process. Consumers would then bear the costs of the inefficiencies associated with monopoly.

As the foregoing discussion suggests, the ambiguity of the outcome of a particular merger makes the evaluation, and therefore the regulation, of mergers difficult. This difficulty has led to considerable disagreement over the benefits and costs of mergers within the U.S. economy as well as economies worldwide, and the appropriate policy to adopt with respect to proposed mergers of various types. Over time, the attitude toward mergers has shifted, and mergers are now treated much more leniently than they once were. The current policy toward mergers is discussed in detail in Chapter 14.

Section Recap

Like collusion, government regulation and mergers can enable firms to escape or reduce the pressures of competition. However, there may be benefits to both consumers and firms, as when product quality is improved or production costs, and therefore prices, are reduced.

Oligopoly: Economic Profits and Efficiency

Economic Profits

Recall once again that *oligopoly is, in part, a result of barriers to entry. It is possible for firms to earn economic profits in both the short run and the long run. However, economic profits are not guaranteed.* Indeed, many of the oligopolistic industries in the United States have experienced losses over the last decade. Whether a firm actually earns economic profits in the short run depends on the demand and cost conditions faced by the firm. In this respect, firms in an oligopoly are faced with essentially the same situation as a monopolist. These similarities can extend into the long run as well.

Both the steel and auto industries were hard hit by the effects of recession and competition from foreign producers in recent years. The steel industry experienced losses as a result of competition from foreign producers, most notably Japan and West Germany, who enjoyed the benefits of more modern production methods that result in lower average costs. In the late 1970s and early 1980s the auto industry felt the effects of recession and the shift in consumers' tastes toward smaller, more fuel-efficient cars. The auto industry was also adversely affected by slumping car sales in the early 1990s. GM, for example, lost $17 billion between 1990 and 1993, before seeing its profits rebound in 1994.

Economic Efficiency

The fact that oligopolistic firms are able to exercise considerable economic power suggests that such firms may take advantage of that power and earn economic profits at the expense of efficiency. However, as we have already noted, it is often the case that oligopolies arise as a result of the existence of significant economies of scale. This implies that oligopoly is economically desirable to the extent that the average costs of production are minimized through the existence of a small, as opposed to a large, number of firms in the industry. However, it may or may not be the case that society actually benefits.

The fact that a particular good is produced at the lowest possible average cost does not ensure that the price paid for the good accurately reflects that cost. Indeed, as we have already seen, there is a strong incentive for firms in an oligopoly setting to collude and behave, in effect, like a monopolist. In this case, the price of the good will exceed the marginal cost of production, resulting in allocative inefficiency.

In addition to the potential benefits associated with economies of scale, some economists have argued that as a result of the larger pool of resources that they are able to draw on, firms in oligopolistic (and monopolistic) markets have a greater ability to invest in research and development (R&D). R&D can lead to increased economies of scale, improved product quality, and new products, all of which can result in improved social welfare.

As the preceding discussion suggests, the ability of oligopolistic firms to earn economic profits is not guaranteed. In addition, the efficiency effects of oligopoly are unclear. In fact, many economists maintain that in certain situations, the fact that an industry is dominated by a few firms may not have any adverse effects on efficiency.

The Theory of Contestable Markets One theory that has received increasing attention over the last few years maintains that oligopoly may be quite efficient due to the competitive pressures that exist despite the small number of firms in the industry. The **theory of contestable markets** maintains that so long as entry and exit are costless, firms will produce at minimum cost and earn no economic profits.

Briefly, costless entry and exit imply that there are potential competitors that could enter the market and operate at the same level of costs as existing firms. Moreover, the potential competitors could leave the market without the loss of capital. Thus, in contestable markets there are no sunk costs. It is also assumed that consumers in contestable markets are not influenced by such factors as brand loyalty and instead will purchase the lowest-priced product available.

In a contestable market, existing firms are faced with the threat of hit-and-run entry by firms outside the industry. Outside firms are able to enter the market, undercut the price of existing firms, and draw customers away from existing firms before the existing

Theory of contestable markets:
So long as entry and exit are costless, firms will produce at minimum cost and earn no economic profits, regardless of the other characteristics of the market.

firms are able to respond. As soon as economic profits disappear, the new entrants leave. Because of the threat of hit-and-run entry, existing firms are forced to set their prices at the competitive level on a permanent basis. If they do not, they run the risk of attracting entrants and incurring short-run economic losses.

The following two examples illustrate this situation. The first example involves airline service between two cities.[9] Airline equipment, which consists primarily of airplanes, is highly mobile. In effect, entry and exit into specific markets is costless. Thus, airlines can move into and out of markets at minimal cost. The resulting threat of hit-and-run entry puts downward pressure on prices for air travel.[10] Hotels and motels, on the other hand, involve considerable sunk costs (it is not simply a matter of picking up a hotel and moving it to a new location). Thus, the threat of entry, at least in the short run, is much less. The hotel industry is not contestable.

Under the assumption that entry and exit are costless, the number of firms operating in the market, that is, the degree of market concentration, is largely irrelevant. The mere threat of viable competition creates an incentive sufficient to induce existing firms to produce and price efficiently. Although the theory of contestable markets is not applicable in all cases, it nonetheless suggests that in many instances oligopoly and monopoly may better serve society's interest in efficiency than would perfect competition or monopolistic competition.

Because of the potential for inefficiency, the U.S. government has actively sought to exert a degree of control over oligopolistic markets. As we discussed above, direct regulation has been relied on in some instances to control the behavior of firms in a particular industry. At a more general level, a body of law called *antitrust legislation* has been developed that imposes specific restrictions on the behavior of firms. This legislation, the purpose of which is to prevent the formation of monopolies and excessive market concentration, is one of the major topics of the next chapter.

Section Recap

Oligopolistic firms may or may not earn economic profits in the short run and long run. In addition, the efficiency effects of oligopoly are unclear. The theory of contestable markets suggests that, in fact, the behavior of oligopolistic firms may be similar to that of perfect competitors.

Summary

This chapter has examined the behavior of markets that are characterized by a small number of firms that control the majority of output in the industry. In the extreme case, a single firm controls the market. This type of market structure is called **monopoly**. The situation in which the market is dominated by a few large firms is called **oligopoly**.

Monopoly and oligopoly are the result of **barriers to entry**, which result in resource immobility and impede the level of competition that exists in affected markets.

It is possible for a monopolist to earn economic profits in both the short run and the long run. However, economic profits are not guaranteed. Although a monopolist acts as a price searcher, its ability to set price is limited by the market demand curve – the monopolist cannot set a price for a level of output that is higher than consumers are willing to pay. Consequently, depending on demand and cost conditions, it is also possible for a monopolist to incur an economic loss.

A **natural monopoly** is the result of economies of scale. In this case, efficiency is best served by having a single firm produce for the market. One firm can satisfy market demand at a lower average cost than could two or more firms. However, the considerable market power enjoyed by natural monopolists has led to regulation to limit that power and protect the interests of consumers. Regulation of natural monopolies usually relies on **rate-of-return regulation**. This approach involves establishing a price for the good or service in question that simultaneously is fair to the consumer and allows the producer to earn a fair return on investment.

Oligopoly is similar to monopoly to the extent that it is possible for firms to earn economic profits in both the short run and the long run. It is also true that oligopoly generally results in an inefficient level of output.

Firms in an oligopolistic setting have a strong incentive to avoid competing with each other. As a consequence, firms seek alternatives to competition. These alternatives often consist of some form of **collusion**, including the formation of **cartels, price leadership**, and the use of **secret agreements** among firms to fix price and limit output.

Government regulation and mergers can both result in cartel-like behavior by firms and allow firms to reduce or avoid competition. Although the purpose of government regulation is to protect the interests of consumers, regulation that limits entry into certain markets may reduce the level of competition and the incentive for firms to price at marginal cost.

Although oligopoly is often associated with an inefficient level of output, economies of scale can result in lower costs than would exist under competitive conditions. Consequently, it may be desirable to have the government intervene in the market by means of direct regulation or through the enforcement of antitrust legislation.

Questions for Thought

Knowledge Questions

1. List and describe the major characteristics of monopoly and oligopoly. How do these two market structures differ from the other market structures we have considered?

2. How is it possible for monopolists and oligopolistic firms to earn long-run economic profits?

3. What is the principle behind rate-of-return regulation, and how does it work? What are the advantages and disadvantages of rate-of-return regulation?

4. What are the principal forms of collusion? How does each one work to control price and the level of output in an oligopoly?

Application Questions

5. Assume that you are the economic advisor to a regulatory commission that is in the process of determining the rates to be paid by three separate classes of customers of a natural gas utility. Assume that the rate base is $5 million; operating expenses are $30,000; the rate of return has been set at 10 percent; and marginal cost equals average revenue equals 5¢ at 10 million units of output. Determine the amount of revenues the utility should be allowed to collect. Will this utility be able to produce the efficient level of output and cover costs by charging the same price to customers in all three classes? Why?

6. Many economists and policymakers argue that when a market is characterized as a natural monopoly, regulation is the appropriate policy response. Do you agree or disagree with this view? Does your response differ depending on the particular situation? Why or why not?

7. In recent years, OPEC has had difficulty ensuring that the individual members abide by the agreed-upon price and output quotas of the cartel. What factors do you think are most responsible?

8. Construct a graph that depicts a monopolist earning economic profits. Now assume that as a result of a shortage of an essential resource, costs increase and force the monopolist to incur a loss. Graphically illustrate the increase in costs and explain what will happen over the long run.

Synthesis Questions

9. "Because of the huge data requirements and the uncertainty as to what the competitively determined equilibrium would be, an unregulated monopoly is preferred to a regulated monopoly." Do you agree or disagree with this statement? Why?

10. The majority of utilities in the United States are privately owned and operated, but subject to rate-of-return regulation. However, some utilities are publicly owned and operated. These publicly owned utilities usually are not controlled by a regulatory commission. In your opinion, which approach is more beneficial to society and why?

11. Construct a demand curve for a single oligopolistic firm that illustrates the mutual interdependence among firms in an oligopolistic market. (Hint: Your demand curve should not be a straight line.)

12. Economies of scale often force a tradeoff between producing efficiently and producing the efficient level of output. Compare and contrast the benefits of producing efficiently and producing the efficient level of output. Which do you think is more important from the perspective of society's welfare?

End Notes

[1] "Agency Deals Blow to Patents Held by W.R. Grace," *The Wall Street Journal*, Dec. 9, 1994, p. B5.

[2] See the discussion of long-run equilibrium for the monopolistically competitive firm in Chapter 12.

[3] This assumes that cost conditions are the same in both situations.

[4] It should be noted that a normal rate of return is included in all the ATC curves throughout the text. However, in the case of rate-of-return regulation, the normal rate of return and the rate of return selected by the regulatory body may differ.

[5] Individual customer classes are often subdivided into different rate classes according to usage levels as well.

[6] "Incredible," *The Economist*, March 11, 1995, p. 74.

[7] Market concentration is one of the pieces of information used in determining whether a firm is in violation of the antitrust laws. See Chapter 14 for further discussion.

[8] Interestingly, however, the price of steel did not necessarily change every time U.S. Steel changed its price. In some cases, when the new price was announced, the other firms did not follow. The announced price was then rolled back to the original price.

[9] This example is taken from Baumol, Panzar, and Willig, *Contestable Markets and the Theory of Industry Structure*, New York: Harcourt Brace Jovanovich, 1982.

[10] Whether the airline industry can actually be considered a contestable market is the subject of some debate, as is discussed in Chapter 14.

The Regulation of Business Behavior: Policy in Transition

Overview

In 1992, Congress passed legislation that mandated the regulation of many of the rates charged by cable television companies. The question of whether such legislation was needed had been debated ever since rates were deregulated in 1984. However, an increasing number of complaints by disgruntled customers finally resulted in Congressional action. Although it is still too early to determine the overall effect of the new regulations, there are indications that regulators may have "missed the mark" in terms of the intended outcome of reregulation. Cable companies responded to the new regulations with new types of pricing structures and changes in the rates for certain unregulated services. This example illustrates the difficulties encountered when government undertakes efforts to remedy a *market failure*, that is, the failure of the market to produce the efficient level of output.

In this chapter we consider three approaches government can use to attempt to improve market efficiency in the event of market failure: direct regulation, antitrust legislation, and direct government ownership and operation of specific businesses. We consider the objectives of each approach, its economic ramifications, and the impact it has had on efficiency in the markets where it has been used.

In this chapter we also examine the trend toward deregulation of previously regulated markets and analyze the impacts of deregulation. In the course of our analysis, we identify effects of regulation that may, in fact, argue for deregulation of specific markets.

Before proceeding, it is worth noting that economists are divided on the question of when competitive pressures are weak or nonexistent and, therefore, when and where intervention in the market is desirable. For example, there is considerable disagreement over issues such as whether the bigness of a firm, in and of itself, implies a lack of competition and is therefore bad from an economic efficiency perspective. Two questions you should ask yourself as you read this chapter are, Does the policy being discussed appear to be warranted on efficiency or equity grounds, and what have the actual results of the policy been?

Learning Objectives

After reading and studying this chapter, you will be able to:

1. Identify market conditions that can lead to market failure and government intervention

2. Describe the alternatives available to policymakers when a lack of competition results in inefficient market outcomes

CHAPTER 14

3. Explain how government ownership addresses the problem of market failure

4. Describe the evolution of antitrust legislation and its impact on monopolies and oligopolies

5. Discuss the potential problems associated with direct regulation and the rationale for deregulation of previously regulated markets

6. Summarize the potential benefits of deregulation

Lack of Competition and Inefficient Outcomes

Our analysis of the economic behavior of firms operating in different market structures has demonstrated that in a market economy, competition is important for the promotion of economically efficient prices and output levels. A lack of competition can result in long-run economic inefficiency. In Chapters 12 and 13 we saw that in imperfectly competitive markets, the equilibrium output level is generally too low (allocatively inefficient) and the equilibrium price is too high. Long-run economic inefficiency is referred to as **market failure**.[1]

Market failure:

The forces of supply and demand do not yield the economically efficient level of output.

Traditionally, the degree of competition in a particular market has been viewed as being closely related to the number of firms in the market. The monopoly market structure constitutes the polar opposite of perfect competition. The monopolist is the only producer in the industry; it is constrained only by the market demand curve when setting price. As we saw in Chapter 13, an unconstrained monopolist produces an inefficient level of output relative to the perfectly competitive market.

Oligopolistic markets are often characterized by a lack of competition as well. Consequently, the general results associated with monopoly – a level of output that is below the economically efficient level and a price that is too high – have traditionally been associated with oligopoly. However, more recently, economic theories such as the theory of contestable markets have challenged the validity of this long-held view.

The potential market inefficiencies associated with monopoly and oligopoly have been of much greater concern to policymakers than the inefficiencies associated with monopolistic competition. In part, this is due to the importance of monopoly and oligopoly markets relative to the value of all goods and services produced in the economy. Also, as we noted in Chapter 12, much of the policy directed at monopolistically competitive markets has focused on limiting competition in these markets rather than increasing it. The bulk of this chapter therefore focuses on the approaches that policymakers have taken to address the potential lack of competition associated with monopoly and oligopoly.

Can Market Failure Be Corrected?

Can market failure be corrected? The answer is a qualified yes. According to economic theory, appropriately designed policies can result in a more efficient level of output than would occur in the absence of such policies. In effect, policies can be designed that force producers to provide the economically efficient level of output. However, efforts to remedy market failures can also take us further away from the economically efficient outcome. Indeed, economists and policymakers increasingly have questioned the actual gains associated with intervention in many markets.

When market failure occurs, an opportunity exists for government to take action to improve on the market outcome. A quick glance at the historical record shows that government has not been shy about assuming this role. The substantial body of antitrust legislation, the large number of administrative agencies created to regulate specific industries and activities, and the vast body of regulations these agencies have developed are all evidence of government attempts to alter market outcomes. While the specific reasons for regulation vary, *economic efficiency has traditionally been a major objective of government intervention in markets.*

A lack of competition in a market can lead to market failure, that is, an inefficient level of output. Government has employed a variety of measures to remedy market failure.

Collective Decision-Making Options

The government can use three alternatives to influence economic activity: (1) direct government ownership, (2) the establishment and enforcement of legislation to promote a competitive environment, and (3) direct regulation of firm behavior. In all three cases, the actions involved affect, either directly or indirectly, the exercise of **property rights** by private individuals. Consequently, before we examine these various policy options, it is important that we have a clear understanding of what we mean by the term property rights.

Property rights:
The legally sanctioned control that an individual exercises over a collection of goods, resources, and services.

Definition of Property Rights

The concept of property rights refers to the legally sanctioned control that an individual exercises over a collection of goods, resources, and services. For example, in a capitalist economy such as that of the United States, individuals possess the property right to their labor skills. Similarly, when a person purchases a productive resource such as land, he or she is able to exercise a property right (within legal limits) over that land. The same is true for capital and technological innovations.

Society determines, through its system of laws, how property rights are to be established and exercised. Property rights are continually exercised and exchanged in day-to-day transactions. In the context of production, producers obtain the property rights to labor through the payment of wages and salaries. The goods produced are then sold at the market price. In the cases of monopoly and oligopoly, and to a lesser extent monopolistic competition, that price may exceed the costs of production. In such cases, the corresponding level of output falls short of the efficient level. Society may, therefore, determine that it is in the interest of economic efficiency and social welfare to limit, or otherwise control, the property rights exercised by producers.

Government Ownership of Business

One means of remedying market failure is to substitute government ownership and operation of industry for that of the private sector. This approach is more widespread in other economies than in the United States. In many socialist economies, for example, most productive resources are owned by the government. However, the federal, state, and local governments in the United States have on occasion opted to own and operate specific

Does It Make ECONOMIC SENSE?

Regulating the Internet

Over the past few years the Internet, which was created more than two decades ago, has experienced a huge surge in popularity. "Surfing the net" has become a favorite pastime for many individuals, from students to professors to homebodies to CEOs. The volume and diversity of information that can be accessed through the Internet and the World Wide Web have gained it the nickname the "information superhighway." However, at the same time that the Internet's popularity has been growing, so has concern over the types of information that can be accessed. Parents and others have become increasingly concerned over the amount of sexually explicit material that is available. In addition, law enforcement officials see on-line information on terrorism training and other illegal activities as a potential inspiration for criminal behavior.

Concerns such as these have prompted lawmakers and others to propose various laws and regulations to govern what goes on the Internet.[2] For example, in March 1995, Georgia passed legislation banning on-line terrorism training and indecent material aimed at minors. At roughly the same time, U.S. Senator James Exon proposed legislation that would make it a crime to create or solicit indecent material on-line. However, the Internet is not so easy to control. In fact, there is no single location from which the Internet emanates. Instead, it is a patchwork of networks. In addition, it is extremely large: It reaches 180 countries and serves literally millions of people. Given the characteristics of the Internet and the customer base it serves, does regulation of the Internet make economic sense?

On one hand, it is clear that many people consider some of the material on the Internet immoral or otherwise offensive. In addition, it is reasonable to expect that some of this information will impose costs on society, such as when individuals are duped into participating

businesses in lieu of private ownership combined with some form of legislated or regulatory control.

Public enterprise:
A government-owned business.

Government-owned businesses, known as **public enterprises**, are usually found in situations perceived to be natural monopolies. State and local governments own and operate utilities such as water and sewage treatment, and to a lesser extent, electric and natural gas utilities. The United States Postal Service and the Tennessee Valley Authority are examples of federally owned businesses.

Policy Objectives A number of objectives are associated with government ownership of business. The most important of these are to ensure that: (1) the good or service is provided at a competitive price, (2) the product meets minimum quality standards, and (3) the good or service is available to all who need or desire it.

In some instances, production of a particular good or service may require substantial capital outlays that private industry is not willing to undertake. If the government feels that the good or service is socially beneficial, the government may choose to undertake production of the good. Public transportation and municipally owned water companies are good examples. In other cases, although private business may be willing to undertake production of the good, policymakers may feel that greater control could be exercised, and greater efficiencies achieved, through public ownership. This may occur when it is believed

in illegal pyramid schemes, someone learns how to commit a crime and then follows through on the act, or teenagers are encouraged to run away from home by people conversing through a bulletin board. However, it is also true that many of these same activities are currently accomplished through other communications media. This raises the question of why the Internet is being singled out. There is also a question as to whether existing laws address the problems in question so that new legislation would simply duplicate existing laws.

The more important issue concerns the problem of transactions costs. First, experts predict that developing legislation and regulations that can withstand challenges on the basis of constitutional law will be extremely difficult. Freedom of speech issues will be especially difficult. Second, the sheer number of people who use the Internet and the number of exchanges that take place on a daily basis are a problem. Policing the activities on the Internet will require a considerable amount of manpower. More than 8,000 companies have their own "home page" on the World Wide Web, not to mention the thousands of individuals who have created home pages as well. The director of the Federal Communications Commission has described the effort that would be required to enforce Senator Exon's proposal as a "Herculean task."

Alternatives to direct regulation exist. In many cases, people can block out offensive material found on the Internet. Software programs are being developed that parents could use to limit their children's access to the Internet. More simply, parents can actively participate in screening what their children access on the Net. In the case of adults, people can simply avoid those areas of the Net they find offensive. As for illegal activities such as pyramid schemes, laws already on the books can be used to prosecute violators.

The Internet poses major difficulties insofar as regulation is concerned. The large number of parties potentially affected, the rather amorphous character of the Internet itself, and the potential for violators of the law to appear and disappear almost instantly all stand in stark contrast to the more familiar regulatory scenarios. The costs that are likely to be incurred in any serious effort to actually police the Internet and enforce whatever regulations are passed are likely to be astronomical. At a time when government is attempting to downsize, it would seem to make much more sense to rely on people to make their own decisions regarding what to access. In those situations in which truly illegal activities are taking place, it would appear that existing laws would suffice.

that the costs incurred in monitoring and enforcing restrictions on privately owned firms would be excessive.

Lack of Competitive Pressure One of the most obvious drawbacks associated with government ownership of business is the lack of competitive pressure. We have already noted that in most instances government ownership involves a monopoly. In addition, there are usually legislated restrictions on entry by private firms into the industry. Consequently, the only pressure to produce efficiently comes from within the organization and, to a lesser extent, from voters.

One example in which competitive pressures have come to bear on a government-owned business is in the overnight shipment of mail. A number of privately owned firms including Federal Express, Emery, UPS, and DHL have entered this market in recent years. The result has been increased competition for a share of the overnight-delivery market and mail service in general. Although the United States Postal Service has experienced a decline in business as a result of the creation of this specialized market, consumers have clearly benefited. Individuals can now select from a number of different providers of overnight delivery service and a range of options with respect to guaranteed delivery terms (e.g., next morning, next afternoon, second business day) and corresponding prices.

Although economists have shown that under certain circumstances publicly owned firms can generate the same results that would occur in a competitive environment,[3] concerns about the prospects for efficiency resulting from government ownership of business are noteworthy. In particular, the objectives of the firms' managers and problems such as the information needs associated with a government-owned monopoly raise questions about the actual degree of efficiency that can be realized.

Political Issues It is not clear whether government ownership actually results in an economically efficient outcome. In particular, questions arise concerning the motivations of politicians. Public ownership of business is ultimately the result of an act by the governing political body. Public ownership may be pursued for the benefits it will generate for specific segments of society rather than society as a whole. In addition, concerns have been expressed about how staffing decisions for government-owned firms are made. This concern is reflected in Ambrose Bierce's definition of a lighthouse as a "tall building on the seashore in which the government maintains a lamp and the friend of a politician."[4] Finally, the possibility exists that the staff of the government-owned firm may use the firm as a vehicle to further objectives other than economic efficiency.

Section Recap

Government has three alternatives when it wants to influence economic activity: direct ownership, legislation, and regulation. The overall effect of direct ownership on the efficiency of a market is not clear.

Establishment and Enforcement of Rules for a Competitive Environment

A second approach to ensuring economic efficiency in the event of market failure involves the imposition of laws concerning the accumulation and exercise of specific types of property rights. A large body of law, known as **antitrust legislation**, has been developed over time. The purpose of this legislation has been to establish rules that firms must follow in their decisions on production, how large the firm will be, and other relevant factors. Of particular importance are the restrictions on the size a particular firm can assume relative to the industry in which it operates. Laws have been developed that limit the ability of firms to acquire competitors and accumulate additional property rights to productive resources.

Antitrust legislation:
A body of law that establishes rules firms must follow in their decisions on production, how large the firm will be, and other relevant factors that influence the efficiency of market outcomes.

Historical Development of Antitrust Legislation One of the major characteristics of an oligopolistic industry is the high degree of interdependence among firms. We saw in Chapter 13 that interdependence creates an incentive for firms to avoid competing with each other. In the extreme, firms may form cartels or other similar collusive arrangements to avoid competition. Firms involved in these interactions conspire to restrict output and raise price in an effort to maximize profits. In essence, the firms behave collectively as a monopoly supplier of the good or service in question.

One of the earliest forms of such behavior in the United States entailed the formation of **trusts**. A trust consists of a group of firms that agree to work together to restrict the level of total output in their efforts to maximize profits. In effect, the firms in a trust act as a monopolist.

Trust:
A group of firms that agree to work together to restrict total output in order to maximize profits.

The *Sherman Antitrust Act*, passed in 1890, was designed to counteract the effects of trusts by prohibiting their formation and operation. In particular, the Sherman Act states that "every contract, combination in the form of a trust or otherwise, or conspiracy, in restraint of trade or commerce among the several States, or with foreign nations" is illegal. It also states that any person or group of individuals who attempts to monopolize trade between the states or with foreign nations is guilty of a felony.

Several other important pieces of antitrust legislation followed the Sherman Antitrust Act. The *Clayton Act*, passed in 1914, was intended to strengthen the Sherman Act by prohibiting specific monopolistic practices. Outlawed practices include (1) price discrimination[5] that is not justified by cost differences, (2) the use of exclusive, or *tying contracts* (which require the buyer to purchase other goods or services from the seller of the good in question and not from competitors), (3) the acquisition of stock in competing companies if that acquisition would lessen competition, and (4) the establishment of interlocking directorates (in which the same individual sits on the board of directors of two or more competing firms) if the result would be a lessening of competition.

The *Federal Trade Commission Act*, which was also enacted in 1914, established the Federal Trade Commission (FTC). The FTC is responsible for investigating charges of anticompetitive practices and prosecuting individuals or firms charged with unfair practices.

The *Robinson-Patman Act* of 1936, the *Wheeler-Lea Act* of 1938, and the *Celler-Kefauver Act* of 1950 all amended the Clayton Act in various ways. The Robinson-Patman Act broadened the Clayton Act's restrictions on price discrimination. The Wheeler-Lea Act focused on unfair or deceptive practices and, in particular, false or deceptive advertising. The Celler-Kefauver Act dealt primarily with mergers. Specifically, Celler-Kefauver disallowed vertical and conglomerate mergers that resulted in a substantial lessening of competition. Recall that a vertical merger involves the combining of firms that operate at different stages in the production process. For example, the purchase of a steel company by an auto manufacturer would constitute a vertical merger. A conglomerate merger occurs when firms producing unrelated products combine to form a single company. Horizontal mergers, which involve firms producing the same product, had already been addressed in the Clayton Act.

Impact of Antitrust Legislation   The actual impact of antitrust legislation has varied over time. In large part, this is due to the varied interpretations that courts have applied to these statutes. In particular, over time there has been disagreement as to whether bigness per se is a violation of the antitrust statutes or whether the behavior of the firm should be of paramount concern. These shifts in interpretation are best illustrated by reference to a series of landmark court cases.

Bigness versus Behavior   The first set of cases involved the American Tobacco Company (1911), Standard Oil (1911), and U.S. Steel (1920). In the course of hearing these cases, courts developed the doctrine of the **rule of reason**, which stated that only business practices that were considered unfair (such as pricing below cost to drive competitors out of business) or illegal could be considered unreasonable. Businesses guilty

Rule of reason:
Only business practices that are considered unfair or illegal should be considered unreasonable.

of such practices would be in violation of the Sherman Act. In the cases involving the American Tobacco Company and Standard Oil, the Supreme Court maintained that the behavior of each company was clearly unreasonable because they had engaged in unreasonable restraints on trade. Therefore, they were in violation of the Sherman Act. However, in a case brought against U.S. Steel, the court held that although U.S. Steel controlled approximately 60 percent of the market, it did not behave in an unreasonable manner. Therefore, U.S. Steel was not found to be in violation of the Sherman Act.

The rule of reason focused on the behavior of firms rather than solely on their size. However, in 1945, the Supreme Court reversed itself in a case involving ALCOA. Specifically, the Court ruled that the mere size of a firm could and, in the case of ALCOA with 90 percent of the aluminum market, did constitute a violation of the Sherman Act.

The Court's ruling in the ALCOA case constituted a major departure from previously held views on the distinction between mere size and the behavior of the firm. The ALCOA decision raised questions about the legality of any firm holding a significant share of the total market. Since the ALCOA case, however, views have moderated, and behavior has once again become the more crucial issue. Two important cases, involving IBM and AT&T, illustrate this change.

The Justice Department first filed suit against IBM in 1969, alleging that IBM "attempted to monopolize and has monopolized . . . the general-purpose computer and peripheral equipment industry." The suit charged that in addition to using anticompetitive techniques, such as pricing schemes designed to discourage the entry and reduce the competitiveness of producers of peripheral equipment for computers (for example, software), IBM controlled over 70 percent of the market for mainframe computers.

During this time, IBM was also involved in a number of civil suits brought by individual firms. In many of these cases, IBM either won the case outright or reached a settlement agreed upon by all the involved parties. Then, in 1982, the Justice Department dropped its case against IBM, concluding that IBM no longer monopolized the computer industry. This decision reflected a changing attitude toward the existence and behavior of large firms and the ability of the government to fashion a result more efficient than that which could be determined by the market.

Another recent major antitrust case involved AT&T's monopolization of the telecommunications industry. A series of suits initiated by the federal government culminated in a suit brought in 1974. In that suit, the Justice Department argued that AT&T should be broken up, charging that the company was using its monopoly over local markets to retain control of the long-distance market by preventing potential competitors from hooking up to local transmission lines.

In what many observers considered a surprising move, AT&T agreed, in 1982, to dissolve its existing structure. Specifically, AT&T agreed to divest itself of parts of Western Electric (its equipment manufacturer) and its local telephone companies. In return, AT&T was allowed to retain its long-distance service operations and most of Western Electric and was granted permission to enter the data communications (information services) market.

While the AT&T breakup can be considered at least a partial victory for competition, it is important to note that the case against AT&T centered primarily on the firm's behavior, rather than on its size. The IBM case focused primarily on IBM's size relative to the industry and was ultimately found to be without merit. In a case brought against the Du Pont Company in 1947 (and decided in 1956), it was argued that Du Pont held a virtual monopoly in the cellophane market. However, by interpreting the cellophane market to include all substitutes for cellophane, such as wax paper and aluminum foil, the court concluded that Du Pont was innocent of any wrongdoing. Each of these cases points to a clear trend away from the emphasis on the size of a firm relative to the market in which it operates. In the AT&T and IBM cases, the decision ultimately centered on the firm's behavior. In the Du Pont case, the pivotal issue centered on defining the relevant market.

Merger Efforts by the government to control the market power of firms have also focused on mergers. Recall that the Clayton Act and Celler-Kefauver Act addressed the practice of horizontal, and vertical and conglomerate mergers, respectively. Horizontal and vertical mergers were discouraged by the government as recently as the early 1970s. Two cases exemplify the government's earlier position. In 1962, the government blocked a merger between Brown Shoe and Kinney Shoe, although they ranked only third and eighth in the industry. In 1966, the Supreme Court found a merger between Von's Grocery and Shopping Bag, the third- and sixth-largest supermarket chains in Los Angeles, to be illegal, citing concern over a "trend toward concentration," although the firms had a combined share of only 7.5 percent of the market.

For a time, the FTC and the Justice Department also vigorously pursued efforts to block conglomerate mergers when it was felt that domination of a market would result. In these cases, suit was brought on the grounds that the proposed merger had the *potential* to threaten competition in the affected markets. Almost half of the cases brought by the government in the 1960s and early 1970s were successful. However, after 1973, the burden of proof was placed on the government to show that the proposed merger would *actually* reduce or eliminate competition. This change in the burden of proof substantially reduced the ability of the government to block conglomerate mergers.

Since 1973, government actions designed to block potential mergers have dropped significantly. Conglomerate mergers have drawn considerably less attention. Since the early 1980s, many vertical and horizontal mergers have been given approval as well. For example, between 1982 and 1986, the Federal Trade Commission and the Justice Department brought actions against only fifty-six of the more than 7,700 mergers that were reported.[6]

In 1994, the value of mergers and acquisitions involving U.S. companies was approximately $344 billion. In the first six months of 1995, this value exceeded $164 billion, and over $334 billion in merger activity took place worldwide during this same time period. Some of the more significant deals during 1995 included the acquisition of Lotus Development Corp. by IBM (for $3.5 billion), Seagram Company's purchase of 80 percent of MCA Inc. (for $5.7 billion), and a merger of two of the largest financial payment processors in the United States, First Data Corp. and First Financial Management Corp ($6 billion).[7] In late July 1995, Kimberly-Clark acquired Scott Paper at a reported cost of $6.8 billion to make it the second largest personal care company in the United States.

Since 1982, the Justice Department has relied on new sets of guidelines, including the use of the Herfindahl-Hirschman Index (HHI),[8] to gauge the effects on market concentration of potential vertical and horizontal mergers. The five-part process established by the 1982 Guidelines for evaluating horizontal mergers includes (1) identification of the relevant market involved, (2) calculation of the HHI before and after the merger, (3) evaluation of the likelihood of entry into the market by new firms, (4) evaluation of other factors that might affect the likelihood of successful collusion, and (5) evaluation of any efficiency effects resulting from the proposed merger.

Many analysts view the new merger guidelines as a more economically defensible approach to merger policy. By assessing such questions as ease of entry into the market, the potential benefits with respect to cost savings, and the likelihood of successful collusion, attention is focused on the efficiency implications of the proposed merger. Although disagreement still exists over matters such as the level of the HHI that constitutes excessive market concentration, the general conclusion is that the new guidelines have resulted in a more efficient approach to policy on mergers.

The switch to the new guidelines has resulted in a tendency toward a more lenient view of mergers than was the case previously. This approach reflects, in part, the effects of the theory of contestable markets discussed in Chapter 13. Recall that a market is contestable if it is possible for firms to enter and leave the market at minimal cost. This threat of hit-and-run entry forces existing firms in the industry to set prices at the competitive level. Mergers between firms in a contestable market should not have an effect on the ability of firms to sustain long-run economic profits or the efficiency of the new equilibrium.

The new approach to mergers is also indicative of a clear shift in views on how the size of the firm affects the potential for competition and the economic efficiency of the resulting market equilibrium. This new attitude is exemplified by the merger between Chrysler and American Motors, which was announced in March 1987 and finalized in the fall of that year. Other examples of significant mergers that have occurred in recent years include the merger of USAir Group, Inc., and Piedmont Airlines, the acquisition of Ozark Airlines by TWA, the merger of Northwest and Republic Airlines, the takeover of Kraft by Phillip Morris, the merger of R.J. Reynolds and Nabisco, and the mergers of IBM and Lotus Development Corp. and Kimberly-Clark and Scott Paper referred to earlier.

The preceding examples should not be taken to suggest that all proposed mergers are approved. In the late 1980s, the Justice Department blocked the proposed acquisitions of Dr. Pepper by Coca-Cola and 7-Up by PepsiCo. In 1993, the Justice Department forced Goldman, Sachs and Co. to sell a 20 percent stake in National Gypsum Co. In addition to its 20 percent share of National Gypsum, Goldman owned 43 percent of USG Corp., the largest gypsum maker in the United States. (Gypsum is used to make wallboard, which is used in housing construction.) USG and Gypsum make more than one-half of all the wallboard sold in the United States. During the same year, the Justice Department also filed suit against General Motors in an effort to block the sale of one of its automatic transmission divisions to a competitor. The suit argued that the sale could result in higher prices, a reduction in technological innovation, and poorer service. In 1995, Microsoft Corp. dropped its plans to acquire Intuit, Inc. after the Justice Department sued to block Microsoft's purchase of the maker of personal finance software.

Antitrust legislation addresses issues including trusts, competitive practices, size and behavior of firms, and mergers between firms. Over time, there has been considerable variation in the interpretation and enforcement of specific antitrust laws.

Section Recap

Regulation of Firm Behavior

A third approach to addressing market failure is the use of direct regulation. This approach, most often associated with natural monopolies, was analyzed at some length in Chapter 13. In the case of natural monopolies, the objectives of direct regulation are to ensure that the efficient level of the good or service is produced and that it is offered for sale at a so-called fair price, which allows firms to earn a normal profit. The issue of property rights arises in the sense that although the objective of regulators is to achieve an efficient level of output, they are restricted from forcing businesses to use their property (capital and resources) in such a way that the businesses would incur an economic loss.

As we saw in Chapter 12, direct regulation has also been employed to *limit* the amount of competition in a market, for example, by limiting the number of taxi cabs that are allowed to operate in a market. In effect, restrictions are imposed that limit who may exercise property rights in a particular market. Although someone may possess the property rights to resources (a driver's license and a car) that would enable him to produce and compete in a market (the taxi cab market), entry may be barred.

The ostensible objective of regulation of competitive markets is to maintain product quality and otherwise protect the interests of consumers. The concern is that excessive competition might result in inferior goods or services as firms cut costs in their efforts to compete and earn profits. Interestingly, while we might be tempted to conclude that firms would resist any type of regulatory restrictions, many economists and policymakers have argued that some industries want to be regulated as a way of establishing a legally sanctioned cartel with the attendant benefits (such as a reduction in competitive pressures).

The question of when, or whether, to regulate is a subject of considerable debate among economists. The evidence on the effects of regulation, while not conclusive, does raise questions about the extent to which regulation actually results in greater economic efficiency. The issues involved include the following:

1. The possibility of regulatory capture: Regulatory capture refers to the fact that many of the individuals who staff regulatory agencies are former employees of the firms being regulated. In addition, many agency employees who return to the private sector go to work for the firms they previously regulated. In either case, questions exist about whose interests – society's or the industry's – are actually served by the regulatory agency.

Why the DISAGREEMENT?

What You See May Not Be What You Get

In 1984 the Congress passed the *Cable Communications Policy Act*, which reduced the regulation of the cable television industry. In addition, during the 1970s and early 1980s, the Federal Communications Commission passed a number of rulings that greatly reduced programming and other restrictions on cable broadcast companies. As a result of these actions, firms were allowed to set rates for subscribers on the basis of market demand. In effect, because most localities are served by a single provider of cable, cable companies were allowed to act as unregulated monopolists.

Subsequent to deregulation, rates for cable TV increased dramat-

ically in many areas of the country. According to one study, the average monthly basic rate rose approximately 80 percent between 1984 and 1990, with rate increases in excess of 115 percent in some areas of the country.[11] In addition, a growing percentage of subscribers expressed dissatisfaction with the service provided by their cable company. In light of these facts, many members of Congress began proposing legislation that would reregulate the cable TV industry. These efforts culminated in the passage of legislation in 1992 that required the FCC to regulate the rates for certain services offered by cable companies. However, industry representatives and a number of industry analysts and cable customers opposed this move and continue to question it. In

light of the broad range of individuals opposed to reregulation, it is worth asking the question, Why the disagreement?

The answer to this question requires consideration of a number of factors. Clearly, those in favor of reregulation saw such a move as the most direct means of controlling the rates that are charged to cable customers and the level of service that is offered. Opponents argued that the regulation of rates would impede the efficiency of the system and, in particular, its ability to adjust to new developments such as programming alternatives. Many cable customers opposed direct regulation of rates for fear of the adverse effect that it might have on the variety of programs offered by the cable company. It is also

2. The information problem: Because regulators must often rely on the regulated firm for most of their information, the reliability of such information is often questioned. Recall from our discussion in Chapter 13 that, in most cases, prices are established on the basis of the costs of production.

3. Empirical studies: A study by Stigler and Friedland[9] examined the rates charged by regulated and unregulated electric utilities from 1912 to 1937. The study indicated that there was no statistically significant difference in the rates charged by the two types of firms, suggesting that regulation does not significantly alter the market–determined outcome. More recent studies tend to support this finding.[10]

4. The true degree of monopoly power: In some cases, economists have questioned the assertion that a monopoly actually exists. To the extent that viable substitutes are available for a good or service, the monopolist might be forced to behave in a much more competitive manner than would otherwise be expected. The Du Pont case referred to earlier is an excellent example of this issue.

5. Legal cartel theory of regulation: Some observers have argued that some industries prefer the certainty provided by regulation relative to the uncertainties associated

possible that cable companies would withdraw service from localities where the regulated rate was considered too low to allow the company to earn a reasonable profit, thus restricting the television viewer's options.

Another factor in the debate over reregulation concerns the potential for competition within the television industry to hold down rates. For example, a technology known as direct digital satellite, or DDS, allows communications companies to use satellites to broadcast signals directly to homes equipped with receiving dishes. Unlike existing satellite systems, which require large receiver dishes many feet in diameter, a DDS receiver dish is only eighteen inches in diameter. In addition, DDS systems are capable of broadcasting more than 150 different channels, compared to thirty to sixty channels for the average cable company. In addition to DDS, many local phone companies are preparing to enter the cable TV market.

To the extent that DDS and the local phone companies are able to compete on the basis of price with cable companies, it is reasonable to expect that this will create incentives for cable companies to hold down their rates to the lowest level possible. However, industry analysts have pointed out that DDS faces a number of technological hurdles that may reduce its advantages relative to cable TV. For example, in its current form DDS does not carry locally broadcast signals. Thus, depending on the circumstances, consumers may need to install a separate antenna to receive broadcasts from local stations. In addition, many cable companies are considering becoming providers of DDS. This could also blunt the effects of competition if DDS and cable are packaged in such a way that they become complements, rather than substitutes.

Since rates were reregulated, the evidence suggests that initial efforts may have missed the mark. A survey of the 25 largest cable companies, conducted by the FCC in 1993, indicates that in many cases, rates actually increased following implementation of the new regulations. This is especially true in the case of rates for what is often described as "basic service." In fact, most of the reductions in rates appear to have occurred in those cases in which the customer buys the largest (and most expensive) package consisting of both basic service and premium channels such as HBO and Cinemax.

Whether Congress should have reregulated cable television is clearly a matter for debate. Studies of the effects of regulation, such as those cited elsewhere in this chapter, suggest that in many cases, direct regulation has no appreciable effect on the rates ultimately charged to customers. On the other hand, experience since 1984 suggests that the customers of cable TV paid a considerable price as a result of deregulation. The only thing that appears to be certain is that the cable television industry will be experiencing additional changes.

with operating in a competitive environment. We noted in Chapter 12 that many otherwise competitive industries have been regulated in an effort to protect the interests of consumers and the general public. However, this regulation has also resulted in barriers to entry, creating a form of *legal cartel*. As we will see in our discussion of the recent move toward deregulation, certain industries, such as the trucking industry, worked hard to maintain a regulated environment.

Direct regulation has been used to influence the pricing and output decisions of certain firms and, in other cases, limit the amount of competition in certain markets. The actual effects of direct regulation on the efficiency of markets is subject to considerable debate.

Section Recap

The Deregulation of Business Behavior

Regulation has traditionally been viewed as a means to increase the level of efficiency in specific markets and otherwise promote the interests of consumers. However, since the late 1970s we have witnessed a growing trend toward the **deregulation** of previously regulated industries. Examples of recently deregulated industries include airlines, banking, trucking, railroads, buses, natural gas, and telecommunications. The trend toward deregulation,

Deregulation:
The removal of specific regulations that govern the economic activity of the firms in a particular market or industry.

which began during the Ford and Carter Administrations, was intensified by the Reagan Administration. Activity leveled off during the Bush Administration. However, the Clinton Administration's initiative to "reinvent" government, the Republican party's ascent to power in 1994, and subsequent efforts to reduce the size of the federal government generated a new series of deregulatory initiatives.

It is important to note that the term *deregulation* is not meant to imply that all regulations governing the firms in a particular industry are eliminated. Instead, deregulation refers to any situation in which at least part of the regulations governing a particular production activity are removed or relaxed. All of the industries that have been deregulated in the last decade are still subject to some degree of regulation. However, firms in those industries are now more responsive to changes in market forces than they were before deregulation.

A Brief Review of Significant Deregulation Developments

Table 14.1 summarizes the major pieces of legislation passed since 1978 directed at deregulation of specific markets. As the table indicates, deregulation has not been limited to any one sector of the economy. Its effects have been felt in such diverse areas as the transportation, finance, and energy sectors.

Table 14.1

Major Deregulation Legislation Since 1978

Date:	Act: Major Provisions
1978	*Airline Deregulation Act*: Allowed increased freedom of entry and exit in markets and price competition. Provided for phase-out of the Civil Aeronautics Board.
1978	*Natural Gas Policy Act*: Provided for gradual decontrol of wellhead prices of natural gas.
1980	*Motor Carrier Act*: Provided individual trucking firms more control over rates. Eased restrictions on entry into new markets by new and existing firms and abandonment of unprofitable routes.
980	*Staggers Rail Act*: Granted railroads more control over rates charged. Also provided easier methods for abandoning unprofitable routes.
1980	*DIDMCA*: Equalized regulations governing all depository institutions. Began phase out of Regulation Q (deposit rate ceilings). Authorized expansion of specific services offered by depository institutions.
1982	*Bus Regulatory Reform Act*: Eased conditions to be met by new firms entering the market. Superseded many state regulations that restricted operation of buses between states.
1982	*Garn-St. Germain Depository Institutions Act*: Allowed depository institutions to offer money market deposit accounts. Accelerated the phase out of Regulation Q.

One of Congress's first major moves in the direction of deregulation was passage of the *Airline Deregulation Act* in 1978. This law reflected a growing awareness of the potential for workable competition in the airline industry. Its purpose was to facilitate increased competition, which was, in turn, expected to result in more efficient production, lower fares, improved service options, and, in general, prices that more closely match the costs of production. The law also provided for the elimination of public subsidies to the airline industry. As is shown below, deregulation of the airline industry appears to have resulted in many of the predicted outcomes. However, it is still too early to assess all the long-run effects, positive and negative, of airline deregulation.

Ground transportation was also deregulated. The *Motor Carrier Act* of 1980 gave individual trucking firms more control over rates and increased the ability of new and existing firms to enter and compete in new markets and abandon unprofitable routes. The *Staggers Rail Act*, passed in the same year, gave railroads more control over the rates they could charge and established easier methods for abandoning service routes that were unprofitable. In 1982, the Congress passed the *Bus Regulatory Reform Act*, which eased the conditions that must be met by new firms entering the market. This act also removed many state regulations that had restricted the operation of buses between states.

The banking sector has felt the effects of deregulation as well. In 1978, the Federal Reserve began to loosen its control on the interest rates that banks can pay on savings deposits. This move came in response to increased competition for savings through the development by investment firms of money market mutual funds[12] and other interest-bearing assets that were not subject to the same restrictions as depository institution savings accounts.

In 1980, after earlier failed attempts, Congress passed a sweeping reform bill entitled the *Depository Institutions Deregulation and Monetary Control Act* (DIDMCA). The DIDMCA was designed to improve the competitive position of depository institutions relative to other financial institutions. As a follow-up to DIDMCA, in 1982 Congress passed the *Garn-St. Germain Depository Institutions Act*, which was directed primarily at ailing savings and loan institutions. A major effect of this law was to allow depository institutions to develop accounts, called money market deposit accounts, that could compete directly with money market mutual funds by offering comparable rates of return and conditions for participation in the fund. In addition, the DIDMCA had already set in motion the process of phasing out the difference in interest rates on savings accounts paid by savings and loan institutions and commercial banks. The Garn-St. Germain Depository Institutions Act also reduced the amount of time over which this phase-out would occur.

More recently, Congress has been working to further deregulate the banking industry. A number of bills were considered in the late 1980s and 1990s. However, at the time this book was being written no new sweeping legislation had been passed.

Deregulation first came to the natural gas industry with the passage of the *Natural Gas Policy Act* (NGPA) in 1978. The major thrust of the NGPA was to allow a gradual decontrol of the wellhead price of natural gas. (The wellhead price refers to the price of a unit of natural gas as it is extracted from the ground.) This decontrol was to be phased in over a period of time, depending on the specific source of the gas in question. The purpose of the NGPA was to improve the supply of natural gas by allowing market forces to send the appropriate price signals to producers of natural gas.

Policymakers have also initiated a number of failed attempts to pass legislation that would significantly deregulate the telecommunications market. In particular, repeated efforts have been made to allow increased competition in the markets for local telephone service and cable TV services. However, as in the case of banking deregulation efforts, no new legislation had been passed at the time this was being written.

As the next section indicates, deregulation can, in fact, result in more efficient levels of output and prices. This is not meant to imply that deregulation is necessarily appropriate for all currently regulated industries. Rather, it suggests that policymakers must keep abreast of ever-changing market conditions to ensure that regulation continues to promote, rather than limit, market competition.

Section Recap

Over the last twenty-five years, a number of industries including airlines, banking, trucking, railroads, buses, natural gas, and telecommunications have been deregulated. The purpose of deregulation is to allow firms to respond more directly to market forces that affect pricing and output decisions.

The Case for Deregulation

Regulation Influences the Form of Competition

Regulation of a particular industry is seldom complete. That is, the restrictions placed on firms in a regulated industry are not designed to control all the different aspects of firm behavior. Instead, regulation usually focuses on the price charged by each firm in an effort to ensure that consumers pay a price for the good that reflects the costs of production. This price also enables producers to earn a normal return on their investment. In such cases, the usual response of regulated firms is to find some other way of competing with each other.

Airlines: Nonprice (Service) Competition Prior to 1978, the Civil Aeronautics Board (CAB) exerted considerable influence over the structure and pricing policies of the airline industry. In particular, the CAB controlled the number of major interstate airlines (formerly referred to as *trunk* airlines) that were allowed to operate, the number of airlines operating between any two cities (called *city-pairs*), and the fares that could be charged for specific flights. Consequently, airlines were unable to compete on the basis of these characteristics.

As a result of such restrictions, airlines tended to compete instead on the basis of quality of service. Service includes such characteristics as the number of flights between city-pairs, on-time performance, seating comfort, meals, drinks, and availability of seating. This tendency illustrates the powerful incentive to earn economic profits and the degree to which firms respond to this incentive.

Many analysts argued that the rates airlines were permitted to charge induced them to offer a higher level of service than they would have under competitive conditions. It was argued that competition would result in a reduction not only in fares, but in the quality of service offered as well. The regulated fares airlines were allowed to charge (set by the CAB) exceeded the costs of production (including a normal profit). Airlines then used this difference between price and cost to finance an increase in service above the level associated with the competitively determined price. In support of this view, Alfred Kahn, a noted economist and one-time chairman of the CAB, has argued that "essentially unregulated competition among the certificated carriers in scheduling and in the quality of service airlines offered generally brought costs into line with CAB-determined fares on all types of routes – upward toward the prescribed fare levels in the markets where those fares were set above standard costs, downward, with skimpy services, where the fares would otherwise have been unremunerative." [13]

Regulation Redistributes Income Deliberately or Arbitrarily

The usual intent of regulation is to ensure that consumers receive the product they want at a price that reflects the costs of production. However, it is often the case that regulation also results, either intentionally or unintentionally, in the redistribution of income.

Separation of Price and Cost When the price charged for a product exceeds the marginal cost of production, the results are an inefficient level of output and the potential for the creation of economic profits. (Recall that firms earn economic profits when the price of the product sold exceeds the average total cost of production.) In effect, economic profits constitute a redistribution of income from consumers to producers; consumers end up paying a per-unit price that is higher than the price that would be charged under competitive conditions.

This type of redistribution of income is illustrated in Figure 14.1. The market demand for and supply of a good are illustrated by the curves labeled D and S. In the case of competition, the equilibrium market price and output would be P_C and Q_C. Consumer surplus would therefore equal the area $P_C AB$. However, if the price were instead set at P_R, which is greater than P_C, output would fall to Q_R. As a result, consumer surplus is reduced by the shaded region $P_C P_R CB$. This loss is composed of two parts. The triangle ECB is a deadweight loss. The rectangle $P_C P_R CE$ would now constitute income to the producer. Consequently, income has been redistributed from consumers to producers.

A logical question at this point is, Why would regulators set a price that is above the competitively determined price? One possible answer is that because the industry is regulated, some of the benefits of competition are forgone. In particular, the costs faced by firms may not reflect the costs that would result if firms were forced to compete more actively. (Recall that competition encourages firms to constantly seek out less costly methods of production in their efforts to maximize profits.)

Another possible answer is that price is purposely set above cost to create profits that can then be used to *subsidize* the purchases consumers make in other markets. This approach is known as cross subsidization.

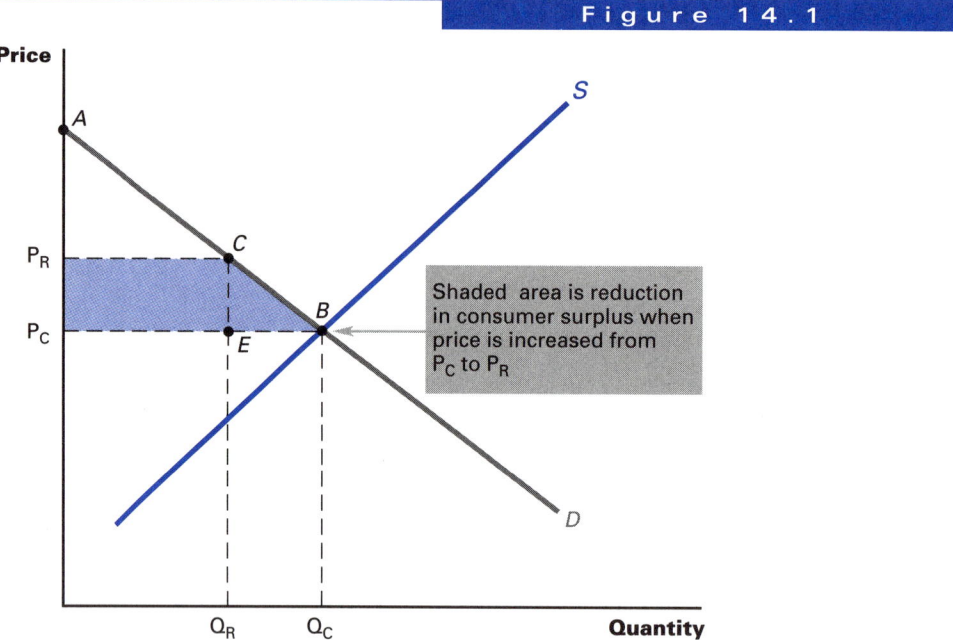

Figure 14.1

Regulated Pricing and the Redistribution of Income

Under competitive conditions, the equilibrium price and output would be P_C and Q_C. Consumer surplus would be equal to the area P_CAB. However, if the price is instead set at P_R, Q_R units will be sold. Consumer surplus is thus reduced by the area P_CP_RCB. Of this amount, the area ECB represents a deadweight loss to society. The remaining area, P_CP_RCE, is redistributed to producers.

Cross subsidization: The practice of charging different prices to different groups of customers and using profits from one group to cover the losses generated by another group.

Cross Subsidies Another means by which regulation can result in a redistribution of income is through the effects of **cross subsidization**. Cross subsidizations occur in a variety of situations. Consider, for example, the situation in which there are two (or more) groups of purchasers of the same product. It is often the case that the costs of producing the product for each group will differ. A good example is the provision of airline service. Per-unit costs of production are lower for heavily traveled routes of a given distance than they are for lightly traveled routes covering the same distance (because fixed costs are spread over more passengers). If each group were charged according to the costs of production, they would pay different prices for the service.

However, as a result of regulation, one of the groups (for example, passengers on heavily traveled routes) often ends up paying a price that is higher than that which would be determined in a competitive market. The other group (for example, passengers on less heavily traveled routes), on the other hand, pays a price that is actually below cost. Consequently, the excess profits earned from one group can be used to pay part of the other group's costs. One group subsidizes the purchases of the other group.

The regulation of air fares prior to 1978 resulted in cross subsidies of the type described above. The CAB set fares on longer, more heavily traveled routes above cost and fares on shorter, less heavily traveled routes below cost. It justified this approach as a means of facilitating the continued development of the air transportation system by encouraging air travel on shorter and less heavily traveled flights. The profits resulting from the regulated fares charged to customers on the major routes were used to cover part of the costs of providing service on shorter and less popular routes.

As a result of this approach, customers on the heavily traveled routes paid a higher price than they would in a competitive situation. Customers on less heavily traveled routes paid less than they would in a competitive situation. From an economic perspective, the result of the regulated air fares and cross subsidization was a redistribution of income from customers on heavily traveled routes to customers on less heavily traveled routes.

The effect of this cross subsidization is shown graphically in Figure 14.2. Figure 14.2 (a) illustrates the demand and cost conditions for flights on usually longer-distance and heavily traveled routes. Figure 14.2 (b) illustrates the demand and cost conditions for flights on shorter-distance and less heavily traveled routes. P_R represents the regulated price in each market. With the price set at P_R (not necessarily the same in each market) it is clear from Figure 14.2 (a) that firms in this market will earn an economic profit. The amount of profit is indicated by the shaded rectangle. With price set at P_R in Figure 14.2 (b), Q_R units of output will be produced. However, this will result in an economic loss equal to the shaded area. As a result of cross subsidization, however, the profits earned in the market illustrated in Figure 14.2 (a) can be used to offset the losses incurred in the market depicted in Figure 14.2 (b). An additional result is that the optimal, or efficient, quantity of the good is not produced in either market. Instead, the quantity produced is either less than or greater than the efficient level, depending on the market in question.

Regulation Can Reduce Competition and Efficiency: The Establishment of Cartel-Like Conditions

In some instances policymakers have concluded that too much competition is, in fact, undesirable from the consumer's point of view. This conclusion was one of the principal motivations for regulation of the airline industry. However, the effort to limit competition as a means of improving product quality may lead to the creation of cartel-like conditions as entry into the market is restricted. The cartel-like conditions reduce the competitive pressures that firms might otherwise face in their day-to-day operations. A major result is that there is less incentive for firms to reduce costs or pursue research and development intended to provide consumers with a better product or service. As we have already noted, the CAB's pricing and entry policies had essentially this effect on the airline industry.

If restrictions on entry are removed and the firms in the industry are forced to compete, one possible result is a reduction in costs. The potential for economic profits – which will accrue to firms that reduce costs below those of existing firms – creates an incentive for the entry of additional firms into the market. As firms enter, existing firms reduce costs and product prices in response to the increased competition. The result of freedom of entry into the market is that firms now produce a larger amount of output than before and sell it at a lower price.

Studies of the effects of deregulation of the airline industry suggest that airlines have responded to increased competition in the manner just described. In particular, there is strong evidence to suggest that during the 1980s fares were lower than they would have

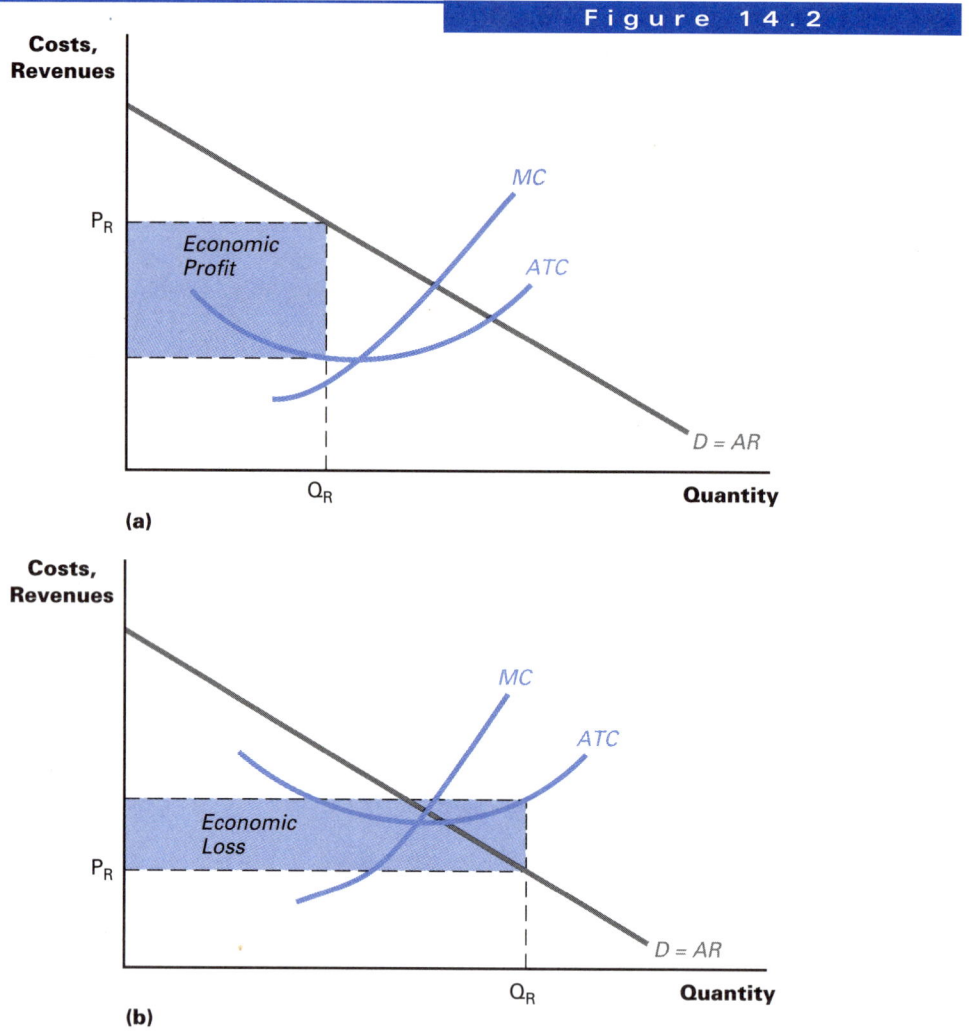

Figure 14.2

Economic Effects of Cross Subsidization

In Figure 14.2 (a) the regulated price is set at a level that allows firms to earn an economic profit, indicated by the shaded region. The regulated price in Figure 14.2 (b) is set at a level that causes firms to incur an economic loss. However, the profits earned in the market in Figure 14.2 (a) can be used to offset the losses incurred in the market in Figure 14.2 (b). This effect is referred to as cross subsidization.

been under the pre–1978 regulatory scheme. In addition, the empirical evidence indicates that the average number of carriers that serve a particular route increased by approximately 25 percent during the period from 1978 to 1988.[14]

Before deregulation, cartel-like conditions existed in the trucking industry as well. It is not surprising that among the strongest opponents of deregulation of the trucking industry were the trucking firms themselves. It was clear to existing firms that deregulation would force an increase in the already growing level of competition as new firms entered existing markets. Consequently, when Congress began to consider deregulation of the trucking industry, existing firms vehemently opposed such action. Increased competition was expected to reduce profitability and induce efforts to increase productivity. However, despite the well-organized opposition of the trucking industry, the *Motor Carrier Act* of 1980 was passed and observers have argued that society has benefited considerably.[15]

Proponents of deregulation argue that regulation can have a number of undesirable effects, including an emphasis on costly nonprice competition, redistribution of income, and a reduction in the efficiency of regulated markets.

Airline Deregulation: A Case Study

In the early 1930s, many airlines were experiencing financial difficulties, and the number of airline accidents was increasing. Many observers blamed these conditions on the high degree of competition in the airline industry. It was argued that the increase in accidents was the result of a lack of attention to safety-related measures in an effort to hold down costs. Consequently, Congress passed the *Civil Aeronautics Act* of 1938, which established the Civil Aeronautics Board (CAB) and empowered it to set fares and limit the amount of competition on individual routes. The theory behind this action was that with decreased competition firms would be more financially stable and could therefore devote more attention to factors such as safety and service.

However, the policies of the CAB resulted in what amounted to a cartel in the interstate flights market. Before the passage of the *Airline Deregulation Act* of 1978, eleven airlines (the trunk airlines) dominated the routes between major cities and controlled almost 90 percent of the total market revenue and traffic. The CAB maintained this oligopolistic market structure by rejecting all of the seventy-nine applications for new major airlines filed between 1938 and 1978. The CAB's reasoning was that reduced competition would encourage airlines to focus more of their attention on safety and service.

During the time that the airlines were regulated, the average level of service offered by airlines did improve. The financial stability of the major airlines licensed to operate in the interstate market also steadily improved, and airline safety increased. However, fares tended to exceed competitively determined levels, and consumer choice among airlines on a given route was restricted. Moreover, because fares were set by the CAB and requests for increases or decreases in fares could be matched by competitors, there was little incentive for firms to invest in strategies designed to reduce costs. Consequently, some would argue that the increased service and improved financial stability of the industry would have occurred even in the *absence* of regulation.

Analyses of the effects of deregulation on prices and service indicate that in the years following the passage of the Airline Deregulation Act average real fares decreased. A study by the U.S. General Accounting Office found that between 1978 and 1984, while nominal fares increased, the real average fare (the nominal fare adjusted for the effects of inflation) per revenue passenger mile (a measure of output for airlines) fell by approximately 6 percent. The study also concluded that fares appeared to be more closely related to costs than was the case prior to 1978.[16]

Many analysts had argued that the average level of service would decline after deregulation as competition brought fares and service in line with each other. However, the data indicate that the average level of service, in fact, increased between 1978 and 1984. It has been suggested that this improvement may have been the result of an increase in the number of shorter, less heavily traveled routes offered by the airlines. This, in turn, resulted in a greater total availability of flights and departure times, thus benefiting the air-traveling public.

These results – lower fares and improved service – suggest that, at least through 1984, society benefited from deregulation of the airline industry. This does not imply, however, that at least some groups did not lose as a result of deregulation. A large number of markets lost through-plane service (when passengers do not have to change planes on stopovers) as a result of deregulation. However, the total number of markets receiving through-plane service increased between 1978 and 1984.

More recent developments in the airline industry have led some observers to question the benefits of deregulation indicated in the GAO study. First, full fares have increased. Thus, certain groups are now paying an increased price for air travel. The increase in full fares, however, has been more than offset by even lower discount fares (fares offered subject to specific restrictions on travel times, length of stay, and other factors). Consequently, average real fares have continued to decline. In addition, consumers now enjoy a wider range of fares than ever before. The greater number of fares reflects an increase in price discrimination designed to boost profits, but it also reflects the effects of increased competition for customers. Customers benefit from this competition in the form of a greater number of fares to choose from.

Second, there has been a decline in the number of airlines operating in the United States. A number of medium and small carriers have gone out of business in recent years. Between 1984 and 1986, eighty-two certificated carriers and commuter airlines declared bankruptcy or ceased operations. In addition, a number of mergers, such as the purchase of Ozark Airlines by TWA, have reduced the number of competing firms. Table 14.2 presents data on four-firm and eight-firm concentration ratios and the Herfindahl–Hirschman Index for the years indicated. As the table illustrates, the degree of concentration in the domestic airline industry has increased since the advent of deregulation. Table 14.3 indicates that in the case of direct flights between city-pairs, measures of concentration exhibit a similar pattern. However, in the case of all trips involving city-pairs – the usual measure of the competitiveness of the airline industry – concentration has steadily decreased in the period following deregulation of the industry, suggesting an increase in the level of competition. In addition, the data in Table 14.3 indicate that competition tends to increase with the distance traveled.

Third, a number of serious accidents have led to questions about the safety associated with air travel. Some observers have linked this apparent decrease in safety to deregulation. The argument has been made that increased competition has led some airlines to reduce safety-related expenditures to hold down production costs. However, statistics for the period January 1983 to March 1990 indicate that the total number of accidents, as well as

Table 14.2

Concentration Measures in the Domestic Airline Industry

Year	4-firm Concentration Ratio	8-firm Concentration Ratio	Herfindahl-Hirschman Index[a]
1977	56.2%	81.1%	0.106
1982	54.2%	80.4%	0.093
1987	64.8%	86.5%	0.123
1990	61.5%	90.5%	0.121

[a] In this case, the HHI is calculated as the sum of squared market shares (where each share is a number between 0 and 1). As such, the index ranges between 0 and 1, with concentration increasing as the value of the index approaches 1.

Source: Severin Borenstein, 1992, "The Evolution of U.S. Airline Competition," *The Journal of Economic Perspectives*, Vol. 6(2): 45-73.

Table 14.3

Average City-Pair Herfindahl-Hirschman Indexes[a]

ALL TRIPS

	Market Distance in Miles			
Year	0–200	501–1000	1500+	All
1984	0.600	0.537	0.415	0.531
1987	0.689	0.498	0.363	0.512
1990	0.618	0.518	0.357	0.506

DIRECT TRIPS ONLY

	Market Distance in Miles			
Year	0–200	501–1000	1500+	All
1984	0.601	0.601	0.536	0.590
1987	0.691	0.612	0.532	0.620
1990	0.612	0.672	0.536	0.632

[a] In this case, the HHI is calculated as the sum of squared market shares (where each share is a number between 0 and 1). As such, the index ranges between 0 and 1, with concentration increasing as the value of the index approaches 1.

Source: Severin Borenstein, 1992, "The Evolution of U.S. Airline Competition," *The Journal of Economic Perspectives*, Vol. 6(2): 45-73.

fatal accidents, actually declined.[17] In addition, safety regulations were *not* affected by the Airline Deregulation Act and continue to be enforced by the Federal Aviation Administration.

While the foregoing arguments deserve serious consideration, the available evidence does not appear to support the contention that, overall, deregulation has had an adverse effect on the service or efficiency aspects of air travel. On the contrary, it appears that deregulation has resulted in considerable benefits to air travelers as a group.

In the airline industry, customers have witnessed a dramatic increase in the number of available fare-service options. Depending on a customer's needs, substantial savings in air travel can be realized. For example, many airlines regularly offer reduced fares on selected flights subject to specific restrictions. These restrictions usually involve days and times when tickets are valid, required length of stay, and refund limitations. While such offerings obviously are not appropriate for everyone (business travelers, for example), they nonetheless constitute an increase in the amount of choice available to consumers. In addition, the proportion of trips involving a change of airlines (as opposed to simply a change of planes flown by the same airline) has steadily declined, from 11.2 percent in 1978 to 1.2 percent in 1990.[18] This is especially noteworthy given that changing planes is considered costly by passengers, since there is an increased likelihood of missed connections and lost baggage.

Section Recap

Recent evidence indicates that as a result of deregulation in the airline industry, full fares have increased, but average real fares have declined. Also, although the number of airlines has declined, competition per route increased through 1990. The level of safety also appears to be increasing.

The Market Mechanism in Action

Deregulation Spurs the Market On

The foregoing discussion suggests that where the potential for competition exists, deregulation can encourage product development and hence expand the set of choices available to consumers. Competition constantly forces firms to attempt to minimize costs (to maximize profits) and to upgrade and improve products in the effort to maintain or increase their share of the market. From the consumers' standpoint, where the potential for workable competition exists, deregulation constitutes a preferred policy option.

The experiences of the airline and trucking industries tend to support the argument that deregulation can be beneficial from society's point of view. As we have seen, after deregulation of the airline industry, average fares decreased and the average level of service actually improved. In a similar fashion, rates in the trucking industry tended to decline while the level of productivity increased. However, it is still too early to assess the overall impacts, positive and negative, of deregulation in either of these industries.

Conditions within the economy and particular markets or industries are constantly changing. Consequently, what may have been appropriate policy at one time may become inappropriate over time. Moreover, it is quite possible that policies originally designed to improve the efficiency of a particular market may in time lead to increased inefficiencies. When these results arise it is important for policymakers to step back and reevaluate the policies that have been put in place. Just as the economy is constantly changing, so should government policy be ready to change to achieve the greatest amount of social welfare possible.

Summary

Government has several alternatives in the event of market failure that results from a lack of competition. The alternatives include government ownership of business, antitrust legislation, and the direct regulation of business.

Government ownership (**public enterprise**) is used much less extensively in the United States than it is in other countries. The objectives of government ownership are essentially the same as those of direct regulation: to provide an adequate supply of the good or service at a fair price. However, depending on the objectives of the firm's managers, efficiency in production may not be realized.

Antitrust legislation is designed to control business behavior ranging from pricing policies to mergers to false or deceptive advertising. The enforcement of antitrust policy has varied along the lines of bigness versus behavior.

Direct regulation has been used extensively in the United States. Regulation has been aimed primarily at two different situations: (1) industries that are characterized as natural monopolies, and (2) situations in which it is felt that competition is excessive and that allowing it to persist without regulation would result in a monopoly or some other socially undesirable outcome.

An examination of the broad body of regulation and legislation that has been developed over time suggests that, in many cases, the restrictions imposed on a particular industry have served more to protect existing firms than to benefit consumers. This emerging awareness has resulted in a trend toward **deregulation** in many sectors of the economy.

One of the underlying themes in the deregulation movement has been the emphasis on competition. Arguments for deregulation have centered on the effects of regulation on the competitiveness of the industry in question. In many cases (for example, the airline, trucking, and telecommunications industries) it has been argued that regulation limited competition and led to industry cartels. This resulted in excess costs and, consequently, prices in excess of those that would result in a more competitive environment.

Consumers appear to have generally benefited from the effects of deregulation. These benefits have accrued in the form of lower prices as costs have declined in the face of increased competition. Gains have also been realized in the form of increased consumer choice as firms develop new and different products in an effort to maintain and increase market share.

There have also been losers as a result of deregulation. As is always the case when choices must be made, opportunity costs will be incurred. The decision by airlines to increase the number of flights in some markets has led to declines in the number of flights in other markets. Similarly, deregulation in the trucking industry has resulted in reduced service options on some routes.

Questions for Thought

Knowledge Questions

1. List and discuss the three basic approaches to market failure that are employed in the United States. In your discussion of each alternative be sure to list the basic features of each approach.

2. How has the interpretation and application of antitrust policy evolved over time? What is the *rule of reason*? Cite influential cases in your answer.

3. List the major pieces of deregulation legislation that have been passed since 1978, and discuss the major features of each piece of legislation. In general, what has prompted the move toward deregulation?

4. What is meant by the term *cross subsidization*? What is its purpose in a regulatory setting? Give an example of the use of cross subsidization in regulation and how it worked.

Application Questions

5. Government ownership of business has been employed in a number of instances in the United States as a means of dealing with the problem of market failure. What businesses do you think are best suited to this type of approach? Why? In your opinion, are there any businesses for which this approach is not suitable? List them.

6. It was noted that the airline industry has experienced an increase in the number of mergers and failures in recent years. What factors would you consider in determining whether this is leading to a decrease in competitive pressures in the industry? Why, and how, are the factors you have listed important?

7. Regulation Q, which limited the rate of interest that banks could pay to depositors, was originally intended to protect smaller banks from the effects of competition by larger banks for savings deposits. Do you think that this regulation was justified on the basis of competition? Why or why not?

8. Explain how price discrimination could be used to eliminate the inefficiencies associated with a monopoly. Could price discrimination serve as a substitute for the regulation of monopolies? What problems do you perceive with price discrimination?

Synthesis Questions

9. On the question of bigness versus behavior, the courts have tended to focus on the behavior of a firm in determining whether the firm is in violation of antitrust laws. Do you agree with this approach? Why or why not? (State specific reasons.)

10. Assume that industry X is currently regulated on the basis of the number of firms that can enter into and compete for customers in its market. Many analysts have

begun to argue, however, that industry X should be deregulated to promote increased competition and the resulting benefits that competition can bring to consumers. What questions would you consider important in determining whether industry X should, in fact, be deregulated?

11. Many analysts are predicting that the financial sector of the economy is destined for more changes in the near future as competition between depository and nondepository institutions increases. In fact, it is argued that some day such a distinction will not exist. What would be the likely result if the government continued to regulate depository institutions while nondepository institutions were left basically free of regulation? Would this be good for consumers? Explain.

End Notes

[1] Other sources of market failure also exist. The most important of these – public goods, externalities, and common property resources – are discussed in Chapter 20. Unless otherwise indicated, in this chapter market failure is used to refer to the case in which, due to a lack of competition, firms produce an inefficient level of output.

[2] Jared Sandberg, "Regulators Try to Tame the Untamable On-Line World," *The Wall Street Journal*, July 5, 1995, p. B1.

[3] See S. Breyer, *Regulation and Its Reform* (Cambridge, MA: Harvard University Press, 1982), p. 182 and the references cited therein.

[4] Breyer, p. 182.

[5] Price discrimination, which was discussed in Chapter 6, refers to the practice of charging different customers different prices for the same good or service in an effort to increase revenues and profits.

[6] S. C. Salop, 1987, "Symposium on Mergers and Antitrust," *Journal of Economic Perspectives*, Vol. 1, No. 2, pp. 3-12.

[7] S. Lipin, "Mergers, Acquisitions Rose 20% in the 1st Half to Record," *The Wall Street Journal*, July 3, 1995, p. A12.

[8] For a review of the mechanics of the HHI, see Chapter 13.

[9] George Stigler and Claire Friedland, "What Can Regulators Regulate? The Case of Electricity," in Paul MacAvoy, ed., *The Crisis of the Regulatory Commissions* (New York: W.W. Norton, 1970), pp. 39–52.

[10] See for example, William G. Shepard, "Causes of Increased Competition in the U.S. Economy," *Review of Economics and Statistics*, November 1982, pp. 613–26.

[11] "Untangling the Debate Over Cable Television," *The Wall Street Journal*, March 19, 1990, p. B1.

[12] A money market mutual fund pools the contributions of a large number of investors and buys high-quality, short-term, highly liquid assets including commercial paper (the short-term bonds of large corporations) and Treasury bills.

[13] Alfred Kahn, "Deregulation and Vested Interests: The Case of Airlines," in R.G. Noll and B.M. Owen, eds., *The Political Economy of Deregulation* (American Enterprise Institute for Public Policy Research, 1983), p. 135.

[14] S. A. Morrison and C. Winston, "The Dynamics of Airline Pricing and Competition," *American Economic Review*, 1990, Vol. 80, pp. 389-93.

[15] Marcus Alexis, "The Political Economy of Federal Regulation of Surface Transportation," in R.G. Noll and B.M. Owen, eds., *The Political Economy of Deregulation* (American Enterprise Institute for Public Policy Research, 1983), p. 129.

[16] Report of the U.S. General Accounting Office, "Deregulation: Increased Competition Is Making Airlines More Efficient and Responsive to Consumers." GAO/RCED-86-26. November 6, 1985.

[17] Nancy L. Rose, 1992, "Fear of Flying? Economic Analyses of Airline Safety," *Journal of Economic Perspectives*, Vol. 6(2):75-94.

[18] Severin Borenstein, 1992, "The Evolution of U.S. Airline Competition," *The Journal of Economic Perspectives*, Vol. 6(2): 45-73.

Part III: Factor Markets

The Theory of Resource Markets

Overview

We have focused thus far on product markets. The analysis of how prices and levels of output of final goods and services are determined is based on a few simple yet powerful ideas. The most important principle is that economic decisions are based on marginal costs and benefits. Rational choices by consumers yield downward-sloping demand curves for goods and services. In a similar manner, supply schedules are derived from application of the marginal benefit-marginal cost rule to profit-maximizing firms.

Your investment of time and mental energy in the preceding chapters now pays off in two ways. First, we have gained important insights into how product markets and the price system work to allocate goods and services efficiently. Second, and perhaps more importantly, the same principles can be applied to other types of markets where individuals face choices involving costs and benefits.

In this section we apply the demand and supply model to resource markets. To produce finished goods and services, firms must employ resources such as labor, capital goods, raw materials, and energy. These resources are supplied by other firms or individuals. In the resource markets the roles of firms and households are reversed from those of product markets – firms comprise the demand side of the market, and individuals are the suppliers.

Just as the interaction of supply and demand determines equilibrium price in product markets, resource prices are set by supply and demand. Under competitive conditions, these prices result in an efficient allocation of resources to firms. Each resource is attracted to the firm where the value of the output produced by the resource is highest.

This chapter provides a general introduction to the functioning of resource markets and the decision making of firms and resource owners in these markets. Subsequent chapters apply the concepts developed here to the labor and capital markets.

Learning Objectives

After reading and studying this chapter, you will be able to:

1. Explain the concept of *derived demand*

2. Define and calculate marginal revenue product and marginal resource cost

CHAPTER 15

3. Derive the firm's resource demand schedule and identify the three major factors affecting short-run resource demand

4. Calculate the price elasticity of resource demand and identify the major determinants of resource demand elasticity

5. Identify the major determinants of supply elasticity

6. Summarize the efficiency properties of competitive resource market outcomes

Determinants of Resource Prices

Our focus is still on the decision making of households and firms. However, these economic agents assume roles in the resource markets that are the reverse of their roles in the product markets. In the product markets, households are on the demand side. In the resource markets, households are suppliers. They own the available resources – labor, capital, land, and entrepreneurial skill – and seek to maximize the per-unit price they receive from the sale of their resources. They use the resulting income to purchase goods and services in the product market. In resource markets, firms are on the demand side – they demand resources to produce and supply goods and services that consumers wish to buy in the product markets.

The decisions that households and firms make in the resource markets are just as important to their economic well-being as the decisions they make in the product market. Because household income and costs incurred by firms are determined in resource markets, the product and resource markets are linked. Changing conditions in resource markets affect resource prices. As resource prices change, the cost of supplying output changes and the product market equilibrium is altered. Consequently, *an understanding of resource markets is necessary for a complete understanding of a market economy.*

The income of an individual in a market economy depends on the quantity of economic resources he or she supplies to the market and the prices paid for these resources. Suppose Smith is a professor of law. His income depends on the going salaries of law school lecturers. This price is determined by conditions of supply and demand in a resource market – in this case, the market for law school lecturers. If the supply of qualified legal scholars doubles (holding all other factors constant), we can predict that Smith's income will decline.

Most individuals possess property rights to significant amounts of only one economic resource – their own labor. Compensation for labor services (wages, salaries, and benefits) has always accounted for most of our national income. During 1994, an estimated 74 percent of annual national income was earned by households as employee compensation. The remaining quarter of the national income included payments for land (rent), financial capital (interest), buildings (rent), and entrepreneurship (profit). Labor market outcomes, therefore, have very significant implications for the distribution of income in the United States. Because of their importance in the determination of income distribution, labor markets are the focus of a significant amount of public policymaking. As we shall see in later chapters, a great deal of legislation is aimed at affecting the distribution of income by altering the outcomes of labor markets.

The Firm's Demand for Resources

Resource demand schedule:

The quantity of a resource demanded at each price.

The price of a resource affects the amount of the resource that a firm wishes to employ in the production of goods and services. The relationship between price and quantity demanded is captured in the firm's **resource demand schedule**. The first step in analyzing resource demand is to ask, Why do firms employ resources (labor, capital, or land)? A little reflection yields the obvious answer. Firms employ resources to produce a product that the firm expects to sell at a profit. That is, the demand for a resource is a **derived demand**. A firm's resource demands are derived from (depend on) the demand for its final product. This simple yet crucial idea links the product market with the resource market. If the demand for the firm's product falls to zero, so too will the firm's demands for resources.

The concept of derived demand explains why firms employ resources, but not why they employ particular quantities of resources. Assuming that the firm's goal is to maximize profits, the employment decision boils down to the question, What level of resource utilization generates the greatest profit for the firm? Applying the general rule for profit maximization, profits are maximized when resources are employed such that the marginal revenue attributable to the *last* unit of each resource equals its marginal cost. This marginal revenue is a function of both the additional output produced by the last unit of the input employed and the price at which the additional output is sold.

Expanding employment of a resource increases the firm's output and revenues, but it also increases costs. If the increase in revenues associated with one more unit of a resource exceeds the increase in costs incurred by hiring another unit of the resource, profits will increase. *So long as the increase in revenues resulting from the employment of an additional unit of a resource is greater than the increase in costs, the firm adds to its profits by employing more of the resource.* Expansion stops when employment reaches the level at which marginal revenue product equals marginal resource cost. The marginal revenue–marginal cost rule means that the employer must weigh three pieces of information when making a hiring decision: (1) the productivity of the resource, (2) the marginal revenue of the output, and (3) the cost of the resource.

Derived demand: The demand for a resource is derived from the demand for the product the resource is used to produce.

The demand for a resource is derived from the demand for the product it is used to produce. Additional units of a resource are hired up to the point at which the addition to profit of the marginal unit is zero.

Section Recap

Marginal Physical Product

The demand for a resource is derived from its value in producing a final product. The greater the productivity of the resource, the more valuable it is as an input to the firm. To make our discussion less abstract we will consider the case of a particular input, labor. However, you should keep in mind that the basic principles developed below apply equally to other resources.

The productivity of labor depends on a number of factors, including the technology used by the firm, the amount of other resources (such as capital goods) that are employed, and the efficiency of management (that is, how skilled management is at combining various resources in the most efficient manner). These variables are all captured in the firm's *production function*, which characterizes the relationship between the quantity of inputs employed and the quantity of output produced.[1] Table 15.1 presents the production function for a typical firm. It is a short-run production function, showing only how output responds to changes in the amount of labor employed. The other inputs in the production process are assumed to be fixed in amount.

Table 15.1

The Short-Run Production Function and Marginal
Revenue Product Schedule for a Firm with One Variable Input

(1) Number of Workers	(2) Total Physical Product (TPP) (lbs./hour)	(3) Marginal Physical Product (MP) (lbs./hour)	(4) Marginal Revenue Product (MRP) ($/hour)
1	10	10	$20
2	22	12	24
3	36	14	28
4	48	12	24
5	58	10	20
6	66	8	16
7	70	4	8
8	72	2	4
9	70	−2	−4

Product price and marginal revenue are assumed to be $2.00

Marginal physical product:

The change in total output that results from employing an additional unit of a resource.

In this example, as additional units of labor are combined with the fixed capital input, output increases.[2] The change in the firm's total physical product (TP) caused by a change in employment (by one worker in this case) is called the **marginal physical product** of labor (MPL). As shown in column 2 of Table 15.1, adding the second worker causes total output to increase from ten pounds to twenty-two pounds – thus the marginal physical product of the second worker is twelve pounds (as shown in column 3). The marginal physical product of the third worker is fourteen pounds of output.

Calculating the change in total physical product attributable to each additional worker yields the marginal physical product schedule, which is illustrated in Figure 15.1 (a). The important feature of this schedule is how, beginning with the fourth worker, marginal physical product declines continuously. As more workers are added, the addition to output becomes smaller and smaller. In our example, marginal physical product actually turns negative with the ninth worker. This production function thus conforms to the law of diminishing returns. As more of the variable resource, labor, is combined with the fixed inputs, the marginal physical product of labor ultimately declines. This technological law is responsible for the downward-sloping portion of the marginal physical product schedule shown in Figure 15.1 (a).

Product Price and Marginal Revenue Product

The marginal physical product of an input is essential information for a firm. However, additional information is required to determine resource demand. The rational firm employs additional units of an input up to the point at which the *revenue* attributable to the marginal unit of the input is equal to its cost. Consequently, marginal physical product

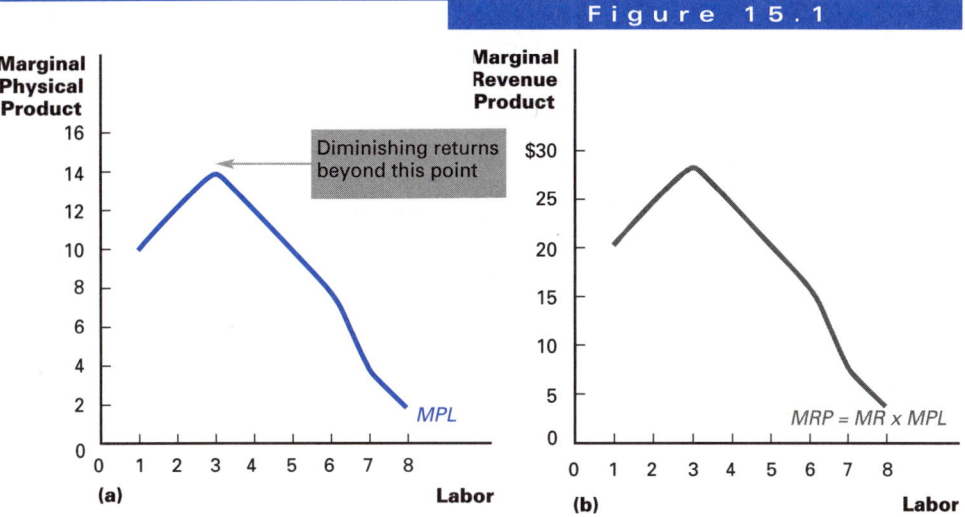

Figure 15.1

Marginal Physical Product and Marginal Revenue Product of Labor

The information from Table 15.1 has been plotted in Figure 15.1 (a). The important feature of the MPL schedule is that, as a result of the law of diminishing marginal returns, at some point (in this case beginning with the fourth worker) MPL begins to decline. The MRP schedule in Figure 15.1 (b) indicates the contribution of each additional worker to the firm's total revenue and is calculated as MR × MPL.

must be transformed into its dollar value to the firm. Even if an input, like labor, is very productive, the dollar value of additional workers to the firm will be relatively low if the market price of the product is low. Again, the demand for a resource is derived from conditions in the product market.

The dollar value to the firm of each additional unit of an input, measured as the change in total revenue, is equal to the marginal physical product (MP) of the marginal unit of the input times the marginal revenue (MR) of each unit of output. This measure of marginal productivity is called **marginal revenue product** (MRP). In mathematical notation:

$$MRP = MP \times MR$$

Marginal revenue product is the change in total revenue that results from employing an additional unit of an input.

If the firm sells its output in a perfectly competitive product market, the firm is a price taker. For the price-taking firm, marginal revenue is constant and equal to the per-unit price of output (price equals marginal revenue). In our example, a perfectly competitive firm sells the marginal output of the first worker and the eighth worker for the same price. This means that marginal revenue product for the competitive firm is equal to marginal physical product multiplied by the price of the product:

$$MRP = MP \times P$$

for a perfectly competitive firm.

Marginal revenue product:

The change in total revenue resulting from the employment of an additional unit of a resource.

Column 4 of Table 15.1 is created by multiplying column 3 by $2, the market price of each pound of output. The marginal revenue product of the fourth worker is $24 per hour – this worker brings in $24 per hour to the firm by producing an extra twelve pounds per hour, which can be sold for $2 each. The marginal revenue product of the fifth worker is $20 per hour, and so forth.

The marginal revenue product schedule is shown in Figure 15.1 (b). It indicates the contribution of each additional worker to the firm's total revenues. Note that it takes the same shape as the marginal physical product schedule. The value of the marginal worker to the firm declines as more units of labor are employed, reflecting diminishing marginal returns.

In the case of the price-searching firm, MR is less than P at each level of output. In addition, MR declines as output increases and the firm moves down its demand curve. Consequently, the MRP curve for a price-searching firm is steeper than the MRP curve for a competitive firm, *ceteris paribus*.

Section Recap

For a perfectly competitive firm, the marginal revenue product (MRP) of a resource is calculated as MP times the market price of output. MRP is the addition to total revenue gained by employing the marginal unit of the resource.

Marginal Resource Cost and the Demand Schedule for Labor

The marginal productivity of an input and the price of the product combine to determine marginal revenue product, which, in the case of the perfectly competitive firm, is the value of the marginal worker to the firm. The final ingredient in the hiring decision is the **marginal resource cost** (MRC). Marginal resource cost is the change in total resource costs to the firm when it changes the level of employment of a resource by one unit. The profit-maximizing firm compares marginal revenue product with marginal resource cost in determining how much of each resource to employ.

Marginal resource cost: The change in total cost resulting from the employment of an additional unit of a resource.

We already have assumed that our firm sells its output in a perfectly competitive product market. Assume also that the firm hires labor in a perfectly competitive resource market. Perfect competition in a resource market means that each firm is a price taker – it is such a small part of the overall market that its decision about how much to employ cannot affect the market price of the resource. For example, a business firm in New York City does not set the wage it pays its secretaries. Rather, it must pay the going wage that is determined by the interaction of market demand and supply in the New York market for secretarial workers.

In effect, from the firm's perspective the supply curve for secretaries is perfectly elastic (horizontal) at the current market-determined wage. In addition, since the wages of all previously hired workers are unaffected when an additional worker is hired, the increase in total labor cost is simply the wage paid to the marginal worker. *For the competitive employer of labor, the marginal resource cost of an extra worker is equal to the wage (W) paid to the extra worker (MRC = W).*

Knowing the marginal revenue product and the marginal resource cost of each worker, the firm has all the information it needs to determine the profit-maximizing number of workers. All workers for which marginal revenue product is greater than marginal resource cost (or equivalently, marginal revenue product is greater than W) will be hired.

Referring to Figure 15.1 (b) again, suppose the wage for this type of worker is $19 per hour. How many workers will be employed? As indicated in the figure, the marginal revenue product is greater than marginal resource cost for each unit of labor up to and including the fifth worker. The fifth worker adds $20 to revenues but only $19 to costs. Consequently, the firm increases its profits by $1 by hiring the fifth worker. However, the firm will not expand to six employees because marginal revenue product ($16) is less than marginal resource cost for the sixth worker ($19), and the firm would lose $3 by hiring the sixth worker at $19 per hour. At a wage of $19 per hour, the profit-maximizing firm hires five workers.

Now suppose the wage drops to $15 per hour. Employment will expand to six workers. At the lower wage the sixth worker, whose MRP is $16 per hour, adds $1 to profits. By the same reasoning, if the wage were to increase to $21 per hour the firm would cut back to four workers.

The marginal revenue product schedule determines the amount of labor the firm will demand at different wage rates. *The marginal revenue product schedule is the firm's demand schedule for labor.* Given any wage rate, the competitive firm employs labor up to the point at which marginal revenue product equals marginal resource cost (which is, in turn, equal to the market wage). As the wage rises or falls, the firm moves up or down the marginal revenue product schedule, decreasing or increasing the quantity of the resource it employs.

Assuming the firm is a price taker in the input market, for any given wage rate the level of employment can be read off the marginal revenue product schedule. The marginal revenue product schedule and the firm's resource demand schedule are synonymous.[3] The firm's demand schedule for labor, or any other resource, is downward sloping. This is a consequence of two factors: diminishing marginal productivity of the resource and the profit-maximizing behavior of firms.

Section Recap

The amount of a resource that will be employed is determined by equating its MRC and MRP. As MRC changes, we move along the MRP schedule. Hence, the MRP schedule is the firm's resource demand curve.

Market Demand for Resources

The market price of the resource was taken as a given in deriving the firm's resource demand schedule. The next logical step is to consider how these resource prices are determined. The

Is It Efficient to Overpay Workers?

According to the theory we have developed in this chapter, efficiency requires that resources be hired up to the point at which marginal revenue product and marginal resource cost are equal. In the case of labor, this means that a firm should continue to hire additional workers until the added cost incurred just equals the last worker's net contribution to the firm's total revenue. Under competitive conditions, the wage paid to the last worker and all previously hired workers will be equal to the last worker's marginal revenue product. In addition, assuming that all firms in the economy make their hiring decisions on this same basis, there will be no involuntary unemployment. So long as the labor supply curve is upward sloping (that is, more workers can be hired only by offering a higher wage), all of the workers that are willing to work at the going wage will be able to find work.

Although theory suggests that involuntary unemployment is not possible under competitive conditions, reality tells us a different story. Everyday we hear reports about people who are out of work and looking for but unable to find a job. While some of these individuals are no doubt simply waiting for the "right" job to come along, many others who would take a job at the prevailing wage simply cannot find work. Such individuals are referred to as involuntarily unemployed. A number of theories have been developed over time to explain the existence of involuntary unemployment. One explanation holds that the failure of wages to adjust to changing market conditions (for example, wages do not fall when labor demand decreases) results in periods of involuntary unemployment. Another explanation, referred to as "efficiency wage" theory, contends that firms purposely set wages above the equilibrium level, that is, in excess of the marginal revenue product of the last worker. Because wages are set above the equilibrium level, the quantity of labor supplied exceeds the quantity demanded; involuntary unemployment is the result. In light of the

answer requires an analysis of total market demand and supply. We begin by deriving the market demand curve for a resource.

Market demand for a resource is obtained in a familiar fashion. Continuing with our labor market example, we begin by horizontally summing the labor demand schedules of the individual firms. This aggregation is illustrated in Figure 15.2. Suppose there are n firms. (In Figure 15.2 it is assumed, for simplicity, that n = 2.) At each wage rate, total labor demanded is the sum of the quantity of labor demanded by each firm. At any given wage rate we obtain the quantity of labor demanded from each of the *n* firms' demand schedules, and then we sum these quantities across all n firms. At W_1 total demand for labor is $L_1^1 + L_1^2 + ... + L_1^n = L_1^M$ (subscripts refer to the wage level, superscripts refer to each firm.) At W_2 each firm demands more labor, so that $L_2^1 + L_2^2 .... + L_2^n = L_2^M > L_1^M$. Since the quantity of labor demanded by each firm increases as the wage falls, the market demand schedule is also downward sloping. One reason is diminishing marginal productivity, which determines the slope of individual firms' demand schedules.

However, another factor explains why the market resource demand curve is downward sloping. In analyzing the individual firm's resource demand curve, product price was assumed constant as the firm expanded output and employment. This assumption must be dropped when deriving the market demand schedule. Suppose the wage falls to W_2 and all firms expand employment. The resulting increase in total output drives down the product price as well. (As supply increases, the product supply curve shifts to the right, causing the

apparent implications of such behavior for the firm's profits, does such a theory make sense?[4]

Economists have a developed a number of rationales to explain the type of behavior suggested by efficiency wage models. One explanation has to do with the problem of *shirking*. In this context, shirking refers to the situation in which an employees avoid doing part of their duties or otherwise performing up to their ability. Put differently, an employee who shirks is someone who occasionally goofs off on the job. So long as someone who shirks and gets fired can readily find another job, the possibility of being fired is not a credible threat as a punishment for shirking. However, if the firm were to pay a wage in excess of the equilibrium, the costs of getting fired would increase. Thus, the employee who receives an efficiency wage has an incentive not to shirk (and therefore be more productive than he or she otherwise might), and the firm has an incentive to pay the efficiency wage.

A second explanation for an efficiency wage is that employers who wish to avoid costly labor turnover can do so by offering a wage that exceeds the market equilibrium. When a worker quits her job the firm must go out and find someone to replace the former employee. This search process and any training that the firm must provide the new employee are costly. In addition, if the former employee had a number of years of on-the-job experience, it may require a considerable amount of time for a new employee to become as productive. Thus, the firm has an incentive to offer wages in excess of the current equilibrium in order to retain its workers. This higher-than-equilibrium wage is an incentive for the employees to stay on rather than quit in search of a better-paying job.

A third explanation for efficiency wages concerns the firm's hiring practices. This explanation, which is related to the concept of *adverse selection*, is based on the assumption that better, more pro-ductive workers demand higher wages, *ceteris paribus*. Thus, by offering higher wages, the firm will attract those individuals that are best qualified for the job. Anyone who is willing to work for less than the efficiency wage can be assumed to be less productive than those who demand at least the efficiency wage as a condition for employment. Firms that are adverse to selecting inferior employees can minimize the chances of doing so by offering wages in excess of the current equilibrium.

The concept of an efficiency wage would appear to contradict the basic theory of how to determine the efficient level of resource use. However, further consideration suggests that the firm's decisions of how much labor to employ, and how much it should pay labor, depend on more than simply the amount of additional revenue an employee can deliver. The amount of wages paid to a worker can have an effect on productivity just as worker training and skill do.

---

equilibrium price to decline.) This, in turn, causes each firm's marginal revenue product schedule (P × MPL) to shift to the left. That is, there is a decrease in demand for the resource. This is shown in the graph for the market by a leftward shift of the curve labeled $\sum MRP_1^{Fi}$ to $\sum MRP_2^{Fi}$. The net result is that total market employment expands by less than that given by the horizontal sum of the marginal revenue product curves of the individual firms. The fall in product price tempers the incentive for firms to expand employment when the wage falls. Likewise, the fall in employment that is caused by rising wages is offset by rising product prices.

Remember that the product and resource markets are linked. In Figure 15.2, when product price falls, each firm's marginal revenue product schedule shifts to the left. The market demand curve for labor is steeper than the horizontal sum of the individual firms' labor demand curves because of the feedback from the product market to the resource market through changes in market price.

The shape of the market resource demand curve has extremely important implications for society, and especially for labor. Negatively sloped resource demand curves imply that employment opportunities are negatively related to input prices. Higher input prices imply fewer employment opportunities and vice versa. In the labor market, attempts to raise wage rates through legislation or collective bargaining will result in fewer jobs and consequently lower employment (unless there are offsetting increases in labor productivity).

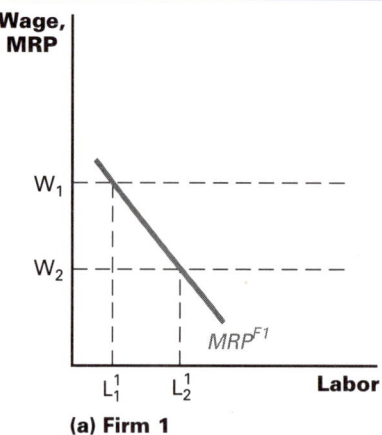

(a) Firm 1

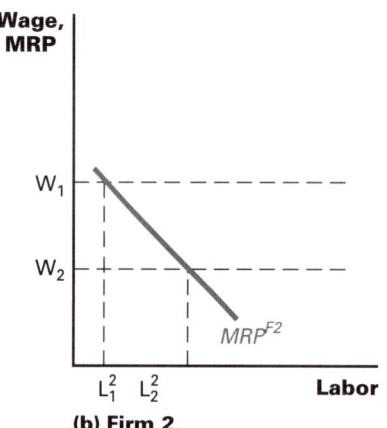

(b) Firm 2

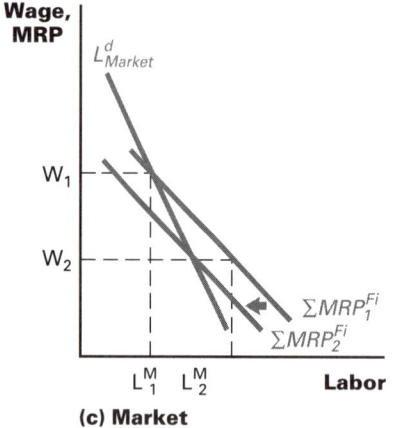

(c) Market

Figure 15.2

Deriving the Market Demand Curve for a Resource (a) *Firm* **(b)** *Firm* **(c)** *Market*

At each wage rate, total labor demanded is the sum of the quantity demanded by each firm. At W_1 total demand is $L_1^1 + L_1^2 = L_1^M$. Diminishing marginal returns is one reason for the negative slope of the market demand curve for labor. However, suppose the wage falls to W_2 and all firms expand employment. The resulting increase in total output must drive down the product price as well. When product price falls, each firm's MRP schedule shifts back to the left. The market demand curve, L_{Market}^d, for labor is steeper than the horizontal sum of the individual firms' labor demand curves because of the feedback from the product market.

Section Recap

The market demand curve for a resource is downward sloping. It is steeper than the firm's demand curve due to the feedback effects of changes in market output and price on MRP.

Price Elasticity of Demand for Resources

Frequently, we need to know not only the relationship between the quantity of a resource demanded and its price, but also by how much quantity demanded changes when the price changes. For example, unions need to know by how much employment will fall if higher wages are negotiated. Congress must estimate how much additional employment will result if wages are subsidized through tax credits. OPEC would like to know how much the quantity of oil demanded will change if OPEC raises the price of oil by a certain percentage. Many decisions depend on the sensitivity of resource users to changes in resource prices. This sensitivity is called the **price elasticity of resource demand**. It is a measure of how responsive demanders of resources are to changes in resource prices.

Price elasticity of resource demand is based on the same general concept as the price elasticity of product demand introduced in Chapter 6. In that situation, we used the notion of price elasticity to measure the sensitivity of consumers to changes in the prices of consumer goods and services. This concept can also be applied to firms' demands for resources.

The **coefficient of elasticity** is the ratio of the percentage change in quantity demanded to the percentage change in price, or:

$$e_r = \frac{\% \text{ change in quantity of resource demanded}}{\% \text{ change in price}}$$

where e_r is the elasticity coefficient.[5] (The subscript r indicates that the elasticity coefficient is for resource demand.) *The value of the elasticity coefficient allows us to calculate the amount by which quantity demanded changes in response to a given price change.* As in the case of consumer goods, resource price elasticities vary across markets. For example, suppose employment of labor falls by 2 percent when the wage rate rises 1 percent. The elasticity coefficient would be 2.0, indicating a relatively elastic market demand for labor. In another labor market, a 1 percent wage increase may reduce employment by only 0.5 percent. The elasticity coefficient would be equal to 0.5, revealing demand to be relatively inelastic.

The elasticity coefficient of 1.0 is an important benchmark. When the absolute value of the elasticity coefficient is greater than 1.0 (2.0, for example) and resource demand is therefore relatively elastic, a change in the resource price causes total income received by the resource owners to move in the opposite direction. Resource price and income move in the same direction when the absolute value of e_r is less than 1.0, for example, 0.5. If the elasticity of resource demand is less than 1.0, a rise in the resource price is not fully offset by the drop in employment. While fewer units of the resource are employed when price rises, the higher price each unit receives leads to an increase in total income paid to the resource. However, if the elasticity coefficient is 2.0, a 1 percent rise in the resource price will be more than offset by a 2 percent decline in employment. While each employed unit of the resource earns more, the large loss in employment means lower total income.[6]

Price elasticity of resource demand:
A measure of how responsive the quantity demanded of a resource is to a change in its price.

Coefficient of elasticity:
The ratio of the percentage change in quantity demanded to the percentage change in price.

The price elasticity of resource demand measures the sensitivity of quantity demanded to a change in the price of a resource.

Section Recap

Determinants of Resource Price Elasticity

This section considers factors that influence the elasticity of resource demand. As in the case of consumer goods, the availability of substitutes is an important factor affecting resource price elasticity. Elasticity of resource demand is greater in the long run than in the short run; over a longer period of time firms are able to make more adjustments to price changes. Stated differently, firms have more alternatives available to them over a longer period of time.

Price Elasticity in the Short Run

Four factors influence short-run resource demand elasticity. First, the slower the rate at which marginal productivity declines, the more elastic is resource demand. As the price of a resource – marginal resource cost – declines, the quantity demanded of the resource increases to maintain equality of marginal revenue product and marginal resource cost. If the marginal physical product, and hence marginal revenue product, of additional units of the resource decrease slowly, the firm will expand its employment of the resource by more than it would if marginal physical product fell rapidly. The percentage by which the quantity demanded of a resource responds to a percentage change in price is greater, the slower the decline in the marginal physical product of the resource.

Second, the greater the price elasticity of demand for the industry's product, the more elastic is resource demand. Recall that changes in the employment of a factor of production are dampened by changes in the price of the industry's product. For example, as wage rates rise, firms economize on labor and reduce employment. Layoffs are partially offset by the decline in industry output, which increases product price. The greater the elasticity of demand for the product, however, the less product price rises when output declines. This means that the dampening effect of changes in product price is smaller and employment changes in response to changed resource prices are greater when product demand is elastic.

This particular adjustment process is called *substitution in consumption*. When consumers are relatively insensitive to product price changes (product demand is inelastic), an increase in an input price causes a smaller decrease in employment of the resource (resource demand is more inelastic). A timely example illustrates this point. American automobile manufacturers are more responsive today to changes in auto workers' earnings than in the 1960s. A major reason is that the price elasticity of demand for American cars is higher today, as a result of increased competition from Europe and Japan. Being less able to pass along higher labor costs by raising prices, domestic auto makers are more likely to reduce employment when wages rise.

Third, the greater the share of total costs represented by the resource, the more elastic is resource demand. Suppose wage costs are 80 percent of total production costs in industry X but just 10 percent of total costs in industry Y. An increase in wages of 10 percent for workers in both industries will raise total costs by 8 percent for industry X, but only by 1 percent in industry Y. If product price elasticities are the same for both industries, profit-maximizing output and employment fall by more in industry X.

Fourth, the greater the availability of substitutes for a resource, the more elastic is resource demand. Recall that the elasticity of demand for a good or service increases with the availability of good substitutes; buyers have a larger number of alternatives to choose from in the event of a price increase. The same logic applies to the elasticity of resource demand. As the number of available substitutes for a resource increases, a firm's ability to alter the combination of resources it uses in its production process increases as well. In this case, the quantity demanded of a resource is relatively sensitive to a change in its price. Just the opposite is true in the case in which there are few or no good substitutes for a resource.

The short-run price elasticity of resource demand increases (1) the slower the rate of decline of MP, (2) the greater the price elasticity of the firm's output, (3) the greater the share of total costs accounted for by the resource, and (4) the greater the availability of good substitutes for the resource.

Section Recap

Price Elasticity in the Long Run

Resource demand elasticity is greater in the long run than it is in the short run. In the short run, a firm may be unable to substitute a cheaper input when the price of a particular resource rises. However, given enough time such substitution possibilities arise. The primary long-run determinant of resource demand elasticity is the relative ease of substitution of other inputs in production. This avenue of adjustment by the firm is called *substitution in production*.

In general, it is technically possible to produce products using different combinations of inputs. A canal can be dug using 500 workers with hand shovels, or one worker with a steam shovel. The choice of inputs depends on the relative costs of labor and capital. If labor is relatively cheap, the canal will be dug using a labor-intensive technique. When the wage rate rises, the firm will want to substitute relatively cheaper capital for labor, but it is unable to do so in the short run. The decrease in labor employment depends solely on the short-run elasticity determinants discussed above. Over the long run, however, capital can be substituted for labor and the employment of labor will decline further. *The extent to which capital can be substituted for labor depends on the technology employed, and varies across industries. As the technical feasibility of input substitution increases, so does the long-run demand elasticity of each input.*

Often, we understate the ability of firms to substitute inputs in production, and thereby understate the elasticity of resource demand. For example, consider the airline industry. Most passenger jets flown in the 1970s required three pilots. Throughout this period, pilots' earnings escalated rapidly. In the short run, the airlines were technically unable to respond to these higher wage costs. The 1980s, however, brought the introduction of Boeing 757s and 767s, which require only two pilots. The airlines, given enough time, were eventually able to substitute capital for the more expensive labor. Similarly, most

414

observers were surprised by how much industry in the United States was able to reduce its petroleum usage by substituting other inputs for energy when energy prices rose sharply in the 1970s.

Supply of Resources

In analyzing the relationship between market price and quantities of a resource willingly supplied to the market, we assume that resource owners seek to maximize the income derived from employment of their resources (subject to constraints). The sale of their resources determines the income with which resource owners purchase consumption goods and services. Thus, resource owners supply their resources to those employment opportunities offering the highest price. The owners of capital equipment seek to rent or sell the equipment to the highest bidder. Land owners rent their land to those who offer the highest rent. From the jobs available to workers, they select those jobs offering the highest rate of pay. (Other conditions of employment may be as important as the wage. These will be discussed in the next chapter. For now we assume that only the rate of pay matters to workers.)

The income-seeking behavior of resource owners suggests that resource supply functions are positively sloped – market price and quantities willingly supplied to the market are positively related. Higher resource prices attract more resources. However, the mobility of resources and the time available for response to price changes exert a strong influence on the precise relationship between market price and quantities supplied. **Price elasticity of supply** is the percentage change in the quantity supplied that is caused by a percentage change in market price. This supply elasticity measure is used to consider further the determinants of the shape of resource supply curves.

Price elasticity of supply:

A measure of the responsiveness of quantity supplied to a change in market price.

Resource Supply in the Short Run

When discussing resource supply, care must be taken to identify the use of or the market for the resource. The resource supply curve depends on how broadly defined that use or market is.[7] The range of alternative uses is determined by our definition of a market. The more broadly the market is defined, the less elastic the resource supply schedule tends to be.

Consider the supply of land. For practical purposes, the total supply of land to the entire U.S. economy is fixed in the short run. When the supply of a resource is fixed, the supply curve is perfectly inelastic, as in Figure 15.3 (a). In the short run, the supply of land is inelastic because owners will not withdraw land from production should land rents fall. Land cannot be used for purposes other than U.S. production. In other words, the opportunity cost of its use in the United States is zero. Similarly, if rents should increase, no additional land can be brought into use. In the short run, there are no alternatives for users of U.S. land.

The economy-wide short-run supply curve of other resources is also very inelastic, although not necessarily perfectly inelastic. The quantities of labor or equipment supplied to the economy in the short run are relatively unresponsive to price changes, but if price movements are sufficiently large, some supply response may occur. These resources are

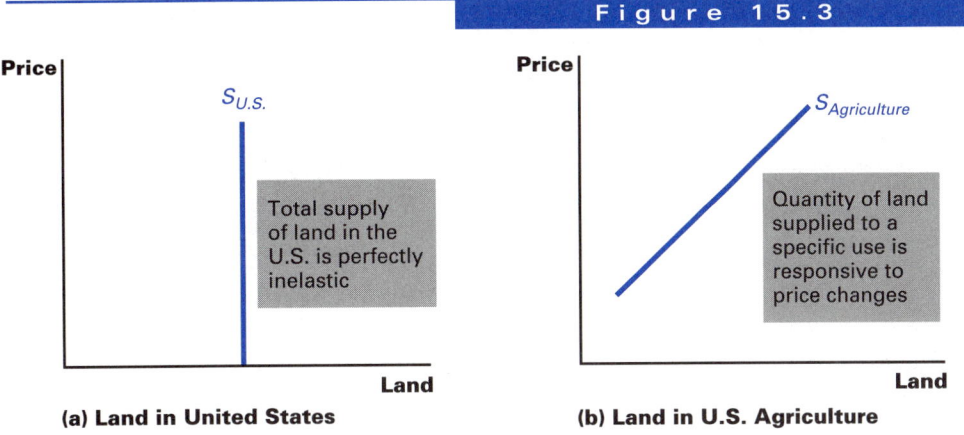

Figure 15.3

(a) Land in United States

(b) Land in U.S. Agriculture

The Supply of a Resource (a) *Land in the United States*
(b) *Land in U.S. Agriculture*

When supply is fixed, the supply curve is perfectly inelastic, as in Figure 15.3 (a). The supply of resources to specific uses, or more narrowly defined markets, is positively sloped, as shown in Figure 15.3 (b).

more mobile than land in the short run. The supply of resources to specific uses, or more narrowly defined markets, is positively sloped.

Resources generally have a variety of uses. Resource owners seeking to maximize their income employ their resources in the most profitable opportunities available and are therefore sensitive to price changes. If the price paid for resources in one market rises, resource owners respond by moving their resources from other employment opportunities to the new, more rewarding use. To hire additional resources firms must bid them away from other employment opportunities.

The elasticity of supply depends on the mobility of resources. **Resource mobility** refers to the ability of resources to move among alternative uses. Resources that move easily and inexpensively between uses are said to be highly mobile. Resources that are difficult and costly to move between uses are said to be highly immobile. *The more mobile a resource is, the more sensitive its supply is to price changes, and the more elastic is the resource supply function.*

It may sound strange to say that land is mobile, but land is quite mobile between many uses. The supply of land to different markets is positively sloped. Land can be used for growing crops, housing families, or building golf courses. A positively sloped supply curve for agricultural land implies that land rents must rise to draw additional acres into agriculture [Figure 15.3 (b)]. This follows from the imperfect substitutability of different types of land. At low agricultural prices, land best suited for agriculture is used first. The pay-

Resource mobility:
The ability of resources to move among alternative uses.

Why the DISAGREEMENT?

Are We Running Out of Resources?

From time to time, various experts predict that the world will run out of some important natural resource within the foreseeable future. During the 1970s the most often mentioned resource destined for rapid depletion was oil. Farmland also has been high on the list in recent years. Yet, even after the rise in oil prices caused by the Iraqi invasion of Kuwait in August 1990, the real price of oil (adjusted for inflation) was still lower than it was in the early 1980s, and farm prices fell during much of the 1980s. Experts in the area of natural resource scarcity hold widely differing views on the subject. Why the disagreement?

The position of many experts, whom we will call the "pessimists," is that resource depletion is inevitable. In his book, *The Population Time Bomb*, Paul Ehrlich argues that the existence of all life forms on earth is threatened by population growth which, ultimately, will exhaust the world's stock of natural resources. This viewpoint is consistent with an earlier study, *The Limits to Growth*, published in 1972, which concluded that, absent any changes in the economic, social, and physical relationships that govern world development, the world would run out of nonrenewable resources within 100 years. In general, the pessimists maintain that in the face of the rapid growth rate of the world's population, it will be impossible for a finite resource base to meet the world's expanding needs in the future.

In contrast, "optimists," including Herman Kahn and Julian Simon, argue that resource scarcity is not the inevitable conundrum that the pessimists make it out to be. For example, in *The Next 200 Years: A Scenario for America and the World*, Kahn and his co-authors predict that a combination of technological progress and an eventual decline of the population growth rate to zero will result in an improved standard of living for the world's population. In his book, *The Ultimate Resource*, Simon argues that rather than threatening the world's resource base, population growth enhances the prospects for a brighter future. By adding to the stock of human intelligence, the increase in the world's population enables humankind to discover new ways to meet its material needs through ingenuity and technological development.

The notion that the world is running out of valuable resources at a

ments made to its owners do not need to be high, as this land has a low value in alternative production. As agriculture expands, land more suitable for other activities must be brought into production. To expand farming, additional land must be bid away from alternative uses. The rents paid to land more suitable for housing or shopping malls must be higher because the opportunity cost is greater.

The supply of land to a particular agricultural market, say sunflowers, is even more elastic because there are even more land alternatives available. Sunflower production is such a small portion of the agricultural market that it could expand greatly without firms in the sunflower industry having to pay substantially higher rents. On the other hand, if sunflower prices fell, and the returns to land used for this purpose declined even slightly, the land could easily be used to produce a different crop.

Of course, land does not physically move between locations. If land becomes very valuable in the center of downtown Los Angeles, the rising land prices do not attract more land to downtown LA. The supply of land at a particular location is perfectly inelastic. The fixed amount of land at a desirable location simply earns greater rent to reflect its value and inelastic supply.

rapid rate is not new. The basic idea has been around for centuries. It received its most famous expression in the writings of Thomas Malthus, who was convinced that the natural physical limitations on the amount of land available to be farmed would eventually result in widespread food shortages as population growth outstripped growth of the food supply. Although it is true that starvation exists in the world today, people are not starving in the heavily populated nations, which Malthusian theory would have predicted, but in sparsely populated countries whose economies have broken down for one reason or another.

In 1865, famed British economist William Stanley Jevons predicted that long-term progress was impossible because the world would soon run out of coal. In 1970, over a century later, it was estimated that enough fossil fuels existed to last 520 years at the 1970 usage rate.[8] Similar predictions could be cited for any number of other important mineral resources that now have known geological reserves sufficient to last for centuries.[9] How could so many predictions (and there are literally hundreds, if not thousands, of them) be so wrong?

The main reason so many predictions have been so far off base is that they concentrate on the technological aspects of resource acquisition and ignore the economic aspects. It is true that the earth contains a finite amount of resources. However, the amount of resources contained in the earth's crust is so great that millions of years of consumption would hardly make a dent in the supplies of most major minerals. If the reserves in the top kilometer of the earth's crust are considered, resource shortages of any major minerals still appear to be over a century away. Furthermore, geologically proven reserves of mineral resources have increased over time.

The economic aspects of resource availability are extremely important. A resource in plentiful supply carries a low price. Little economic incentive exists to spend funds searching for more of the resource or developing substitutes for it. As the demand for a resource rises relative to its supply, the price begins to rise. It becomes profitable to search for more of the resource or to undertake research to develop substitutes for it. This process results in an increase in the proven reserves of the resource or a decline in the demand for it.

Thus it would appear that, for the time being, the evidence favors the optimists. As a footnote to this discussion it is interesting to note that in 1980 Julian Simon and Paul Ehrlich made a $1,000 bet regarding the prices of five metals: chrome, copper, nickel, tin, and tungsten. Simon maintained that over the period from 1980 to 1990 the prices in question would decrease, reflecting a decline in their relative scarcity, while Ehrlich bet that the prices would increase, reflecting increased scarcity. Simon won the bet.

The mobility and elasticity of labor vary. Geographic moves are costly. Labor of a given quality is highly mobile within a geographic area, such as a city or metropolitan area, but much less mobile when alternative employment opportunities are some distance away. In addition, the skill level of labor affects the elasticity of supply. The supply of higher-skilled workers is less elastic in the short run because of the costly training that is required to develop the skill. In the short run, the supply of machine operators is more elastic than the supply of cardiovascular surgeons.

The supply elasticity of machinery, equipment, and buildings also varies, depending on the nature of the resource. The more general the purpose of the resource, the more mobile it is and the more elastic is its short-run supply. Fork lifts, desks, lathes, and drills are fairly mobile. Special-purpose equipment and buildings are very immobile. It is probably fair to say that most physical capital is relatively immobile. Steel-making machines cannot be used to make computer cabinets. An old downtown warehouse is not suitable for housing an auto assembly plant.

Generally, short-run resource supply curves are positively sloped. The price elasticity of supply depends on how mobile the resource is.

Section Recap

Resource Supply in the Long Run

The long-run supply curve for all resources is positively sloped. Over time, resources may be depleted or deteriorate, but we can also add to our stock of resources through investment. The amounts of available resources typically grow over time; investment adds resources at a rate that exceeds the rate of depreciation.

The quantity of resources supplied to the market in the long run depends on resource prices. Resource prices influence the profitability of investments, and therefore the amount of investment and the rate at which it is undertaken. If the price of oil rises relative to the price of other resources, the relative profitability of investment in the search for and development of new oil supplies increases. These profit opportunities attract investors who finance the search for new oil. The resources committed to the development of new oil are drawn from other investment opportunities. As a result of these investments, the future supply of oil increases.

Time is a key factor affecting the elasticity of supply. Investments require considerable amounts of time to increase resource supplies. Figure 15.4 shows three supply curves for oil, S_{SR}, S_{MR}, and S_{LR} (where the subscripts refer to the short run, intermediate run, and

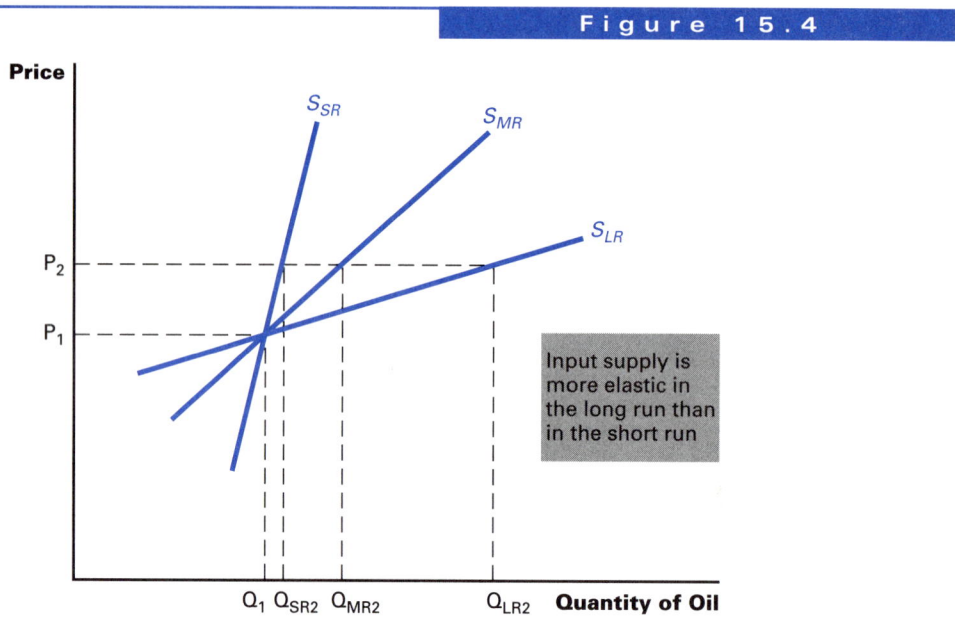

Figure 15.4

The Elasticity of Resource Supply Over Time: The Oil Market

In this figure, three supply curves for oil, S_{SR}, S_{MR}, and S_{LR}, have been constructed where each reflects the supply over a different period of time – one, two, and three years, respectively. The longer the period of time available, the more elastic is the supply curve. Note the effect of a price increase from P_1 to P_2. At P_1, quantity supplied, Q_1, is the same in all three cases. However, when price increases to P_2, the longer the time period being considered, the greater the response of quantity supplied will be, that is, $Q_{SR2} < Q_{MR2} < Q_{LR2}$.

long run). Each curve reflects the supply over a different period of time – one, two, and three years. The longer the period of time available, the more elastic is the supply curve. The effect of the varying elasticities is illustrated by observing the effect of a price increase from P_1 to P_2. At the original price, P_1, quantity supplied, Q_1, is the same in all three cases. However, when price increases to P_2, *the response of quantity supplied is greater the longer the time period being considered.* That is, $Q_{SR2} < Q_{MR2} < Q_{LR2}$.

In the long run, even the total supply of land is not fixed. If land prices were to rise high enough, it might become profitable to use other resources to expand the supply of productive land. We could drain lakes and wetlands, fertilize deserts, or reclaim seashores. These measures may sound outlandish at present land values, but they might be reasonable projects if land prices were much higher than current levels. The higher prices would make these costly investments profitable. Japan is a country with a land problem. It is an island country whose population size is very large relative to its land area. As a consequence, land values are high compared to land values in the United States; the Japanese take steps to use their land more efficiently than we do in the United States. They have built facilities on land created by filling in the shores around parts of the islands. This additional land was added by long-run investment projects. In one case, a new airport, Kansai Airport, was constructed in Osaka Bay and began operation in 1994. The airport was built on a man-made island at an estimated cost of $11 – $14 billion dollars.

Human capital refers to the productivity-determining skills and abilities embodied in labor. We make investments in human capital in much the same way as we do physical capital. We acquire additional education and training to increase our productivity and our earnings. We make such human capital investments on the basis of profitability. We acquire costly training when we believe that the benefits in terms of higher earnings will exceed the training costs. There is considerable evidence that the long-run supply of college- and graduate school-educated workers responds to relative earnings.

Human capital:
The productivity-determining skills and abilities embodied in labor.

Growing college enrollments in the late 1960s and early 1970s caused the demand for graduate-educated faculty to rise. The increase in demand bid faculty salaries up, attracting many students into Ph.D. programs and then into college teaching. However, as enrollment growth slowed and then ended in the 1980s, the demand for college and university faculty fell sharply, and faculty salaries fell relative to other occupational groups. The poor prospects in higher education reduced the number of people seeking these positions.

Note again the importance of the time dimension. Training takes time. It may take a matter of weeks or months to train people as carpenters, mechanics, machine operators, secretaries, and data entry operators. It takes years to train people for other occupations – attorneys, actuaries, scientists, physicians. The investments necessary for any of these occupations slow the response to higher pay in such jobs. *The short-run supply elasticity is much lower than the long-run elasticity.*

In the long run, the supply curve for all resources is positively sloped. Also, the price elasticity of supply is greater in the long run than in the short run.

Section Recap

The Labor Supply Schedule: Costs and Benefits ... Again

The supply of labor to the American economy is a matter of much practical interest. Since World War II, the percentage of the potential labor force that has actually entered the labor market has increased steadily. In 1948 the **labor force participation rate**, the percentage of the noninstitutionalized, nonmilitary population 16 and over who were employed or who were without a job but looking for work was 58.8 percent. In 1994, this percentage was up to 66.6 percent. This overall trend masks very different underlying trends. The participation rate of older males has fallen, while that for women has nearly doubled, from 32.7 percent to 58.8 percent over the same period.

Labor force participation rate: The percentage of the noninstitutionalized, nonmilitary population between ages 16 and 70 who are employed or without a job but looking for work.

What determines the aggregate supply of labor? How responsive is total labor supply to changes in average wage rates? Why has the labor supply of older men and married women moved in opposite directions?

Each individual weighs the costs and benefits of time spent at work. Each person has limited time to devote to working for pay, working at home (housekeeping or do-it-yourself tasks), or pure leisure. The opportunity cost of an hour spent at leisure or working at home is simply the market wage – what the person gives up by not working at a job. The person who is deciding if and how much to work in the market must weigh the benefits of leisure or work at home against the cost of forgone wages.

When the wage rises, the opportunity cost of not working in the market goes up. Economic theory suggests that as the cost of nonmarket time rises, rational individuals demand less of it. There is a substitution of work time for home time. This adjustment to a wage change is called the *substitution effect*. Perhaps you may have heard very highly paid professionals claim that they "can't afford to take a vacation." What they often mean is that the opportunity cost of not working is too high to take time off. For example, available data indicates that surgeons take shorter vacations than general practitioners, reflecting the higher opportunity costs incurred by the relatively higher-priced surgeons. The substitution effect suggests that the individual's supply of labor curve will be positively sloped, as higher wages attract the worker from the home into market work.

At the same time, higher wages raise a worker's income. If leisure time is a normal good, the demand for leisure increases as wages and income rise. The increased consumption of leisure implies less work time. This tendency to consume more leisure is called the *income effect* of a wage change. The income effect tends to offset the substitution effect. What happens to hours of labor supplied to the market as wages rise depends on which effect is stronger. If the substitution effect outweighs the income effect, the labor supply schedule has the familiar positive slope. However, a negative slope is possible if the income effect becomes stronger with higher wages and dominates the substitution effect. In this case, we see a backward-bending labor supply curve, which is illustrated in Figure 15.5. At lower wage rates the labor supply curve is upward sloping. However, above the wage rate at which the income effect begins to dominate the substitution effect, W*, the labor supply curve bends backward, and successively higher wage rates are associated with successively lower levels of employment.

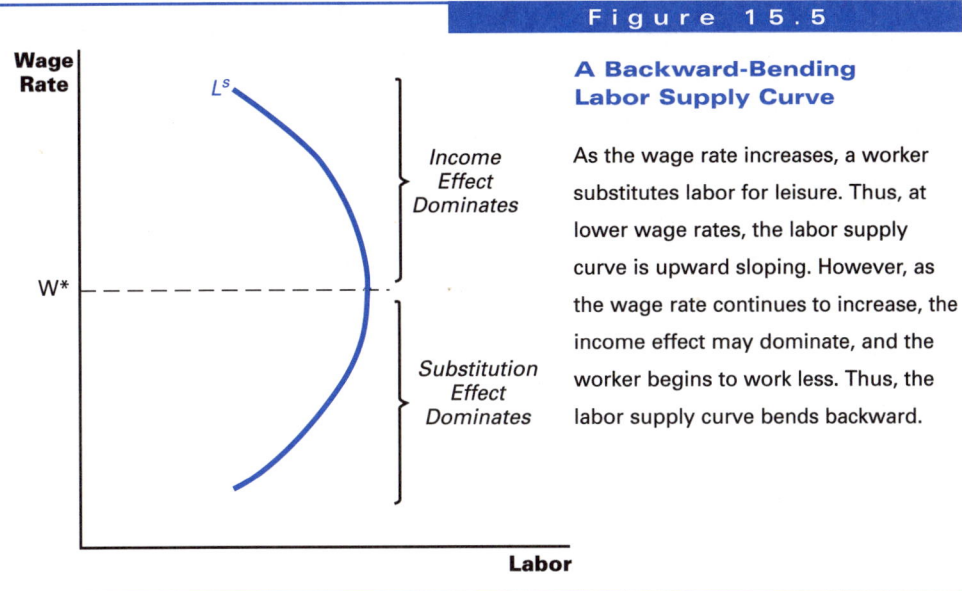

Figure 15.5

A Backward-Bending Labor Supply Curve

As the wage rate increases, a worker substitutes labor for leisure. Thus, at lower wage rates, the labor supply curve is upward sloping. However, as the wage rate continues to increase, the income effect may dominate, and the worker begins to work less. Thus, the labor supply curve bends backward.

Statistical studies have indicated that the total supply of labor is rather inelastic, imply-ing income and substitution effects that are offsetting. However, the labor supply schedule of married women is quite elastic. Apparently, rising real wages since World War II have attracted women into the labor force. On the other hand, the decline of labor supply by older men suggests a strong income effect, as wealthier workers now take earlier retirement.

The long-run supply of labor appears to be rather inelastic, suggesting that the income effect and substitution effect offset each other.

Section Recap

Equilibrium in the Resource Market

The competition of firms for resources – the demand for resources – and the competition of resource owners for available employment – the supply of resources – combine to deter-mine market equilibrium in resource markets. The interaction of demand and supply in the resource market is, in general, just like the interaction in product markets. Equilibrium is reached when the price is such that the quantity of the resource demanded by firms equals the quantity resource owners are willing to supply. At the equilibrium price, nei-ther buyer nor seller has an incentive to bid the price up or down. All parties are satisfied, in the sense that they are able to buy or sell as much as they desire at the equilibrium price.

In resource markets, just as in product markets, the equilibrium adjustment process takes time. A change in the demand for a resource causes a short–run change in the mar-ket outcome, which then sets in motion a long-run change. Ultimately, a new long-run equilibrium is established. Suppose the OPEC nations doubled the price of oil. Firms would look for alternatives to oil, such as coal, thus causing the demand for coal to increase. Figure 15.6 illustrates the changes in the coal market.

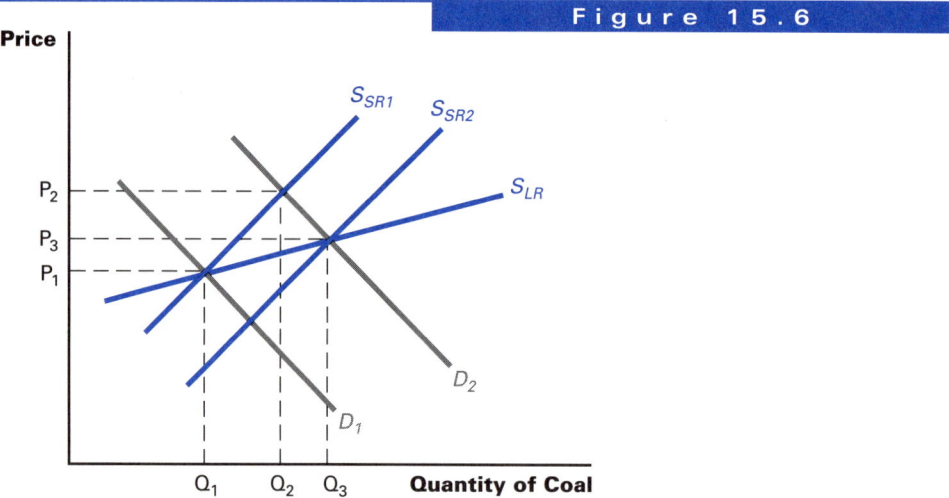

Figure 15.6

Long-Run Supply in the Coal Market

This figure illustrates the effects in the coal market of an increase in the price of oil. The increase in demand for coal from D_1 to D_2 drives the market price up from P_1 to P_2. Because there are now more profitable opportunities in coal, more resources are attracted into the industry over time, causing the short-run supply curve to shift to S_{SR2}. The market price for coal is driven down, and a new long-run equilibrium will be established at a price of P_3, where the new short-run supply curve, S_{SR2}, and the demand curve, D_2, intersect. The long-run supply curve for coal is found by drawing a straight line through the original short-run price-quantity combination and the new short-run equilibrium.

In the short run, the increase in demand for coal from D_1 to D_2 creates excess demand at the initial price, P_1. As a result, the market price is driven up to P_2 from P_1. This new price is determined by the intersection of the short-run supply of coal, S_{SR1}, and D_2. The movement along S_{SR1} occurs because existing coal producers react to the shortage by expanding production. However, the higher coal price attracts more attention. There are now more profitable opportunities in coal. More resources are attracted into the industry over time. Existing firms expand their mines. New firms open new mines. These new investments take time to implement, but after a period of time the supply of coal at the new price rises.

As new supplies come to market, the short-run supply curve shifts to S_{SR2} and the market price for coal is driven down. A new long-run equilibrium is established at a price of P_3. At this new equilibrium the new short-run supply curve, S_{SR2}, and the demand curve, D_2, intersect. The long-run supply curve for coal is found by drawing a straight line through the original short-run price-quantity combination and the new short-run equilibrium, as shown in Figure 15.6. The long-run equilibrium price is lower than the short-run price, while output has increased even more.

As in the case of product markets, long-run equilibrium in competitive resource markets has several properties that are desirable from an efficiency perspective:

1. There is no surplus or shortage of the resource. Price adjustments guarantee that quantity demanded equals quantity supplied. This takes on special significance in the labor market, where excess supply is another term for unemployment.

2. Resources are allocated to their most valuable use. Industries that experience an increased demand for their final product, or that experience productivity gains, expand. Suppose the demand for an industry's product rises. Its product price rises and so does its demand for resources. Similarly, an increase in resource productivity shifts each firm's marginal revenue product schedule to the right, raising total market demand for the resource. Declining industries reduce their resource demands, causing resources to be reallocated to other industries that are expanding.

3. The value of the marginal resource in production equals its opportunity cost. In a competitive market, all resources whose marginal revenue product exceeds their price are employed. Remember that, for perfectly competitive firms, marginal revenue product equals product price times marginal physical product. The resource price is a measure of the opportunity cost of the resource, or its value in the next-best alternative use. All resources are employed in the market in which they are most productive. If a resource is more productive in another industry, its marginal revenue product will be less than its opportunity cost. Stated differently, the resource would be paid a higher price in the industry where it is more productive. Thus, the market allocation of resources is efficient.

4. All resources are paid a price equal to the value of their marginal product. This is a requirement for an efficient allocation of resources, but it also has important implications for income distribution. In a perfectly competitive market economy, each individual receives an income equal to the contribution of his resources to national output.

Assuming competitive markets, in long-run equilibrium, resources are allocated efficiently, that is, to their most highly valued uses.

Section Recap

Summary

The demand for a resource is a **derived demand**. A firm's resource demands are derived from (depend on) the demand for its final product. The firm's resource demand curve is its **marginal revenue product** curve. It is downward sloping because of diminishing marginal productivity. The firm maximizes profits by hiring resources up to the point at which marginal revenue product is just equal to **marginal resource cost**. Industry resource demand is less elastic than firm demand because increases in industry output (and employment) reduce market price. Thus, declining marginal physical product and market price cause marginal revenue product to fall.

The short-run **elasticity of resource demand** is greater the slower the decline in marginal physical product, the greater the elasticity of demand for the industry product, the greater the share of total firm costs accounted for by a resource, and the greater the availability of good substitutes for a resource. It is through the second factor that consumer behavior influences resource demand.

In the long run, firms are able to substitute among inputs. The greater the relative ease of substituting one input for another, the greater the long-run elasticity of resource demand. Because there are more substitution possibilities in the long run, the long-run resource elasticity of demand is greater than the short-run elasticity of demand.

The quantity of resources willingly supplied to the market is generally directly related to market price. Resource owners seek to employ their resources in the most profitable employment alternatives to maximize their incomes. The **price elasticity of resource supply** is determined primarily by resource mobility, the relative ease with which resources move between alternatives.

Long-run supply is also positively related to price. Investment adds to our stock of resources, while depreciation reduces the stock of capital. Resource prices influence the relative profitability of investments. Higher relative prices make investment more attractive and thereby expand the long-run supply of the resource.

Resource market equilibrium is achieved by the interaction of supply and demand. An equilibrium price that equates quantity supplied and demanded is established by market forces. The allocation of resources achieved by this equilibrium is efficient. Each resource is employed in the activity for which its marginal revenue product (P × MP) is highest. No other allocation of resources could result in a higher value of output for consumers.

One of the most important applications of this resource market analysis is to the labor market. The shape of the labor supply curve depends on two opposing forces: the substitution effect (higher wages make leisure more costly) and the income effect (higher wages increase the demand for leisure).

On the demand side of the labor market, the negatively sloped resource demand curve yields an inverse relationship between resource price (the wage) and employment. This tradeoff is a crucial aspect of analysis of the labor market. The next two chapters demonstrate how the demand schedule for labor and its elasticity determine the success of government or trade union policies to raise wage rates.

Questions for Thought

Knowledge Questions

1. The marginal revenue product of a worker is the contribution of that worker to the firm's revenue. Explain how the worker's marginal revenue product is determined.

2. Calculate the price elasticity of the demand for oil if a 10 percent oil price increase causes the quantity of oil demanded to fall by 4 percent. Is demand elastic or inelastic?

3. List four factors that influence the elasticity of demand for a resource.

4. Explain how the income effect and the substitution effect work together to generate a backward-bending labor supply curve.

Application Questions

5. Calculate the marginal physical product of labor from the following short–run production function (assume other inputs fixed):

Units of Labor	Total Daily Output
2	100
3	150
4	195
5	232
6	262
7	285
8	300
9	308
10	308

Graph the marginal physical product schedule. Assume this firm is a perfectly competitive firm in both the input and output markets and market price is $2 per unit of output. Calculate and graph the marginal revenue product schedule. To maximize profits, how much output would the firm produce if the daily wage rate were $30? What would happen to output if the wage rose to $46 a day?

6. Do you think organized labor would support or oppose legislation that restricted immigration into the United States? Explain.

7. Suppose that the oil and coal markets are initially in long-run equilibrium and then the price of oil falls relative to the price of coal. What happens to coal price and output in the short run? Long run?

8. What happens to the demand for labor in question 5 above when the product market price rises to $2.50 per unit? What happens to the profit-maximizing level of employment?

Synthesis Questions

9. Long–run price elasticity is greater than short–run price elasticity on both the demand and supply sides of resource markets. Account for this pattern on both sides of the market using the concept of alternatives.

10. We have used an abstract model of production to derive the firm's short-run demand function for labor. We observe some workers being paid by the hour and others being paid by the piece (the units of output actually produced). What factors would influence the manner in which a worker was paid?

11. Use the resource market equilibrium analysis to explain the impact of an effective price ceiling in the gasoline market on the long-run supply of oil.

12. Assume that the total supply of land in the United States is fixed. What is the price elasticity of supply? What determines the equilibrium price of land? What impact would a land tax have on the price of land?

End Notes

[1] The production function was introduced and discussed in detail in Chapter 9.

[2] Note, however, that the MP of the ninth worker is negative and therefore total output begins to decline beyond the eighth unit of labor.

[3] For reasons we need not enter into here, only the downward-sloping portion of the MRP schedule represents the firm's resource demand curve. We ignore the upward-sloping portion.

[4] This discussion is adapted from Chapter 1 of *Efficiency Wage Models of the Labor Market*, George A. Akerlof and Janet L. Yellen, eds., Cambridge University Press, Cambridge, 1986.

[5] As in the case of the price elasticity of a good, the elasticity coefficient has a negative sign as a result of the inverse relationship between price and quantity demanded. However, we once again drop the negative sign for convenience.

[6] Note that the relationship between elasticity of resource demand and the impact of a price change on the income of resource owners is the same as the relationship between elasticity of product demand and the income of suppliers. This relationship was discussed at length in Chapter 6.

[7] Remember that the availability of substitutes or alternatives plays an important role in determining the sensitivity of decision makers to price changes.

[8] William D. Nordhaus, 1974, "Resources as a Constraint on Growth," *American Economic Review*, Vol. 64:24.

[9] An interesting summary of many of the predictions made over the years – and why they were wrong – is given by David Osterfeld in "Resources, People, and the Neomalthusian Fallacy," *The Cato Journal 5* (Spring/Summer 1985), pp. 67–102.

The Labor Market

Overview

In the preceding chapter we presented a general theory of how the prices and levels of employment of resources are determined. In this chapter we apply that theory to a specific resource – labor. The practical issues that can be analyzed by applying market analysis to labor questions are among the most important in economics. Why do some workers earn more than others? For example, why do physicians make more than janitors? Is an economy where basketball players' salaries are twenty times that of teachers' rational? Why do some individuals go to college, while others drop out of high school? Are workers in risky jobs exploited? Why do women and blacks earn less than males and whites?

Political scientists, sociologists, and industrial psychologists have written volumes about these and other labor market problems. The economist's approach to the same issues is distinguished by its use of market analysis and its emphasis on the efficiency aspects of these issues. The principles of supply and demand are applied to the determination of wages and employment. In effect, labor is treated as any other product or resource. The application of one set of economic principles to all types of markets sets economists apart from other social scientists. Our understanding of economic principles and market behavior is used to address a number of important economic and social issues.

In this chapter we focus on a number of issues concerning the labor market. We begin by considering possible sources of variations in wages across jobs, focusing on *equalizing* and *nonequalizing wage differences*. We then go on to consider wage differences that result from disequilibrium in specific labor markets. We then turn our attention to the effects of discrimination in the labor market. Next, we examine the effects on wages and employment levels when there is only one employer in a particular market. We conclude the chapter with a discussion of possible explanations of the observed long-term stability in the labor market.

Learning Objectives

After reading and studying this chapter, you will be able to:

1. Explain why labor is such an important resource in the economy

2. Identify the determinants of equalizing wage differences and explain the causes of nonequalizing wage differences

CHAPTER 16

3. Distinguish between equilibrium and disequilibrium wage differences

4. Identify the factors that influence the profitability of human capital investments

5. Compare the wage and employment outcomes of a monopsonistic and a competitive labor market

Significance of Labor in the Economy

Many individuals object to a market analysis of labor on the grounds that it is dehumanizing to speak of labor as a commodity, traded as if it were bushels of corn or bars of gold. However, such an objection misses the fundamental point of market analysis: We apply economic principles to labor issues because we believe that wages and the level of employment are determined by the same economic forces that determine the prices and outputs of other goods and resources. Whether labor is more important than, say, capital is a *normative* question. What happens to wage rates when worker productivity rises is a *positive* question that can be answered by economic theory and scientific inquiry, regardless of subjective feelings about how wages and productivity should be related.

If the labor market operates fundamentally just as any other market does, why single it out for special attention? In fact, the labor market has several unique aspects that set it apart from other markets.

Labor cannot be divorced from its owner. Excuse the expression, but "Labor is us!" Since the abolition of slavery, the owner and the supplier of labor are the same person. The owner must be present when labor is employed. This one seemingly trivial difference between labor and other resources is extremely important because it means that nonwage factors are important in labor markets. Employees may be willing to sacrifice higher wages to have jobs that are safer, less boring, or more prestigious. The owner of capital is concerned only with the price that will be paid for the capital, not the conditions under which it will be used.

Functional distribution of income:

The distribution of earnings among the factors of production.

The distribution of income is largely determined by the outcomes in the labor market. Approximately 74 percent of national income was paid out in wages and salaries in 1994. The distribution of earnings among labor, capital, and land, called the **functional distribution of income**, reflects the workings of the labor market and other resource markets. The large share of national income that accrues to labor suggests that labor also accounts for a large share of production costs. The share of total costs attributable to labor varies across industries, but in general the labor share is large. (Therefore, economizing on labor can substantially reduce costs.) In addition, labor market outcomes determine how total labor income is distributed among various types of workers – physicians, teachers, grape pickers, miners, and so forth. Income differences by occupation, industry, and so on largely determine the **personal distribution of income** – how income is distributed among individuals and households in the economy.

Personal distribution of income:

The distribution of income among individuals and households in the economy.

The labor market is probably the focus of more government regulation than any other market in the economy. Employment and wages are affected by the Thirteenth Amendment (which outlawed slavery), Social Security, minimum wage laws, affirmative action regulations, occupational licensing, workers' compensation, occupational safety and health regulations, unemployment insurance, and collective bargaining legislation, as well as other regulations. However, this does not mean that the forces of supply and demand do not affect labor market outcomes. The regulator who ignores the economic behavior of workers and firms may be surprised when the impact of regulations turns out to be different than expected or desired.

Labor market disequilibrium has implications for the unemployment rate. If wages are too high for equilibrium, a surplus, or excess supply, results. Excess supply, which is inefficient in any market, is another name for labor market unemployment, with all of its attendant social consequences.

Labor costs account for over 70 percent of national income. Outcomes in specific labor markets determine how income is distributed among workers.

The Labor Market as an Abstraction

This book is organized around markets. A market is often thought of as a place where trading occurs, such as a livestock auction pen, an open-air farmer's market, or the trading floor of the New York Stock Exchange. However, in the case of labor, it is clear that the market refers to an abstract, rather than a physical, concept. "The San Francisco labor market" refers to general wage and employment conditions in the San Francisco area, not one location in the city where labor is traded.

The **labor market** is the interplay of buyers and sellers of labor services. There are few markets today in which workers and firms come together in a single place to set wages and employment. Undergraduate business majors wonder, for example, what the market for accountants will be like when they graduate, even though there is no one place where accountants' services are auctioned. *Equilibrium wage and employment levels are established by competition among employers for workers and competition among workers for jobs.*

Labor market:
The interplay of buyers and sellers of labor services.

A Labor Market for Each Skill

Workers, of course, differ. Some are unskilled; others are highly trained. In a similar manner, some firms use unskilled labor while others utilize production processes requiring a highly trained work force. These two types of labor obviously are not traded in the same market. In general, there is a different labor market for each skill.

Labor markets may also be regionally segmented. Consequently, it may not be accurate to conclude that an increase in the demand for teachers in Florida will raise teachers' salaries in South Dakota. Imperfect information about employment opportunities elsewhere and the costs of moving may create geographically distinct markets, particularly for less-skilled workers.

One can push the separation of labor markets by skill and space too far, however. If wages for skilled employees rise high enough, unskilled workers will try to obtain the training that will allow them to compete in this market. If teachers' wages in Florida are high enough relative to wages paid to teachers in South Dakota, at least some of the teachers in South Dakota will migrate to Florida. In a broad, long-run sense, all labor is traded in the same market.

The Aggregate Labor Market: Wage and Employment Determination

As a starting point, it is useful to think of all labor as being traded in the same market. If we assume that all workers have the same skills, job information is costlessly obtained, and moving has zero cost, we can aggregate all labor demand and supply schedules into one labor market for the U.S. economy. Figure 16.1 (a) illustrates equilibrium in the aggregate labor market. L^d represents the aggregation of all firms' demand schedules for labor into economy-wide demand. If all firms are competitive, L^d approximates an aggregate marginal revenue product schedule.

The equilibrium wage in the economy is W_e, and the equilibrium level of employment is L_e. Wage flexibility ensures the realization of this equilibrium. At any wage above W_e, such as W_1, the number of individuals seeking work is greater than the number of jobs: An excess supply of labor exists. Competition among individuals seeking employment will bid the wage down. As the wage falls to W_e, firms increase hiring and some workers drop out of the labor market. The number of jobs and workers is equal when W_e is reached. The aggregate labor market equilibrium has several desirable properties:

1. There is no involuntary unemployment. Wage flexibility guarantees that the number of workers firms wish to hire equals the number of workers who are willing to work at the going wage. Those who are not hired – those on the supply schedule above W_e – are not seeking work because W_e is too low to compensate them for sacrificing nonmarket work activities or leisure time. They are considered to be out of the labor force. They are *not* considered unemployed. To be unemployed, a worker must be actively seeking, but unable to find, work at the current wage.

2. The wage equals the marginal revenue product for the last worker hired. Assuming that all firms and industries are perfectly competitive, marginal revenue product is equal to product price times marginal physical product. As is illustrated in Figure 16.1 (a), the marginal revenue product of the last worker hired is exactly equal to what she is paid, W_e. (Recall that the demand curve for labor is the marginal revenue product curve: It shows the value of the last unit of output generated by each additional worker.)

3. The marginal worker's productivity in the labor market equals the opportunity cost of time. Recall from the previous chapter that the resource price is a measure of the opportunity cost of obtaining a unit of a resource. In the case of the aggregate labor market, the alternatives to market work are leisure or work at home. A labor market equilibrium ensures that workers whose market productivity is greater than the value of their time at home are, indeed, working.

The aggregate labor market illustrated in Figure 16.1 (a) is, of course, an abstraction. However, it is a useful model for evaluating broad labor market issues. Consider the relationship between labor productivity and real wages – the nominal wage divided by the price level. Suppose the United States devotes more of its resources to the education and training of its workforce. Average worker productivity should rise as a result, shifting the

Figure 16.1

Supply and Demand for Labor and the Equilibrium Wage

The curve labeled L^d in Figure 16.1 (a) represents the total demand for labor. S is the aggregate supply of labor. The equilibrium wage and level of employment are W_e and L_e. At any wage above W_e, such as W_1, there is an excess supply of labor – competition will bid the wage down. In Figure 16.1 (b), an increase in labor productivity shifts labor demand right to $L^{d'}$, causing the equilibrium nominal wage and level of employment to increase to W_e' and L_e'. Since $W_e'/P_1 > W_e/P_1$, the real wage is now higher.

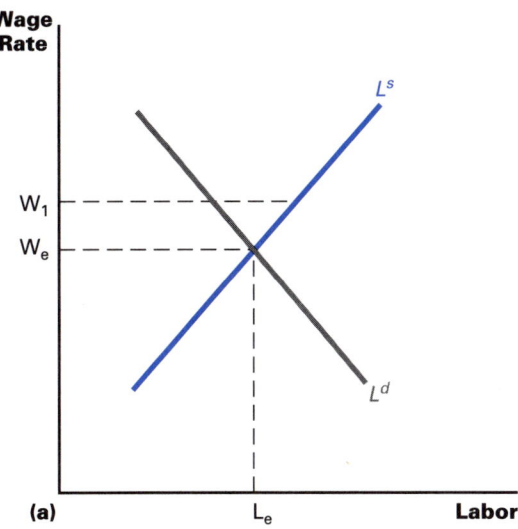

(a)

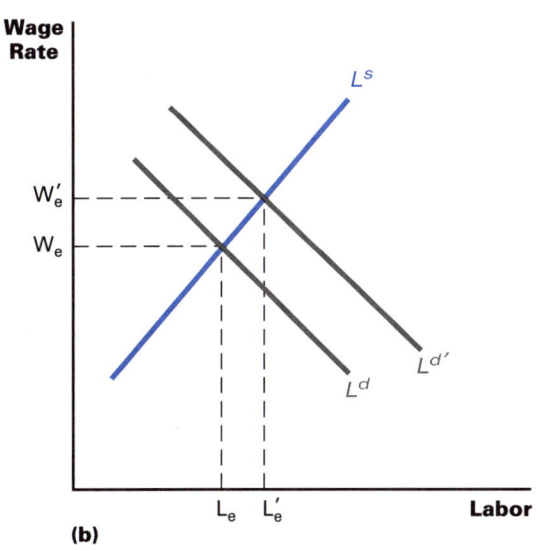

(b)

aggregate demand schedule for labor to the right. Given the relative inelasticity of aggregate labor supply, and assuming the price level does not change, the result will be higher real wages and a modest increase in employment.

The link between aggregate productivity and the general level of real wages is illustrated in Figure 16.1 (b). An increase in labor productivity causes labor demand to shift right to $L^{d'}$. This causes the equilibrium nominal wage to increase to W_e' and the equilibrium level of employment increases to L_e'. For a given level of prices, P_1, the real wage is now higher since $W_e'/P_1 > W_e/P_1$.

The simple model of one labor market in the economy also serves as a useful benchmark. We know how such a market would function if it existed. The conditions necessary for an economy to have one aggregate labor market with one equilibrium wage are equivalent to those required for any perfectly competitive product or factor market. In the labor market these conditions take the following form:

1. Workers must be identical. All units of labor must be homogeneous with respect to tastes and productivity characteristics.

2. Jobs must be identical. Since nonwage aspects of employment matter, all jobs must be the same in all dimensions.

3. Labor must be perfectly mobile. Resource mobility allows prices to move to equilibrium levels when market equilibrium is disturbed.

These assumptions imply that labor is truly just a commodity. However, labor services are provided by human beings with diverse skills, preferences, and attitudes. Thus, the first of these three assumptions does not hold. In addition, we know that assumptions 2 and 3 do not hold in the real world – jobs are not all identical, and labor is not perfectly mobile. The result is a distribution of wages across a set of labor markets. These three criteria can, however, be used to explain the observed differences in wages.

Section Recap

The fact that workers and jobs are not identical and that labor is not perfectly mobile can be used to explain differences in wages across labor markets.

Explaining Observed Wage Differences

Contrary to the implications of Figure 16.1, we know from personal experience and observation that not all workers are paid the same wage. In fact, wages vary widely. Table 16.1 lists the average yearly earnings for males and females in several different occupations. The disparities are striking. Why does a physician earn more than an engineer? A cashier less than a computer operator? A lawyer more than a school teacher? Why do men earn more than women in the same occupation?

The answers to these questions are important. If wage differences are due to luck or discrimination, a strong case can be made for legislation that seeks to alter the distribution of earnings to suit society's notions of efficiency and equity. However, if wages vary according to ability, or the costs of education and training, or other systematic differences in workers or jobs, government policies designed to alter or equalize wages may have adverse consequences in the labor market. In general, wage differences can be classified into two broad categories: equalizing and nonequalizing.

Equalizing Wage Differences

Equalizing wage differences:

Differences in wages that are based on nonwage job characteristics and that tend to equalize the total benefits offered by different jobs.

Equalizing wage differences exist to compensate workers for nonwage job attributes. Jobs differ in many respects, and these differences matter to workers. Certain jobs require extensive education and training, are unpleasant, involve seasonal unemployment, or impose high levels of physical risk on workers. A wage premium must be paid to attract

Table 16.1

**Annual Earnings by Selected Occupations
For Males and Females in 1992**

Median Income

Occupation	Males	Females
Cashiers	$14,230	$12,686
Farm operators and managers	15,294	12,801
Construction laborers	19,196	NA
Auto mechanics	20,933	NA
Carpenters	21,338	NA
Motor vehicle operators	25,566	17,436
Computer equipment operators	28,491	21,098
Primary and secondary school teachers	34,301	28,491
Accountants and auditors	40,565	27,291
Engineers	47,765	41,955
Lawyers and judges	78,052	57,855
Health-diagnosing occupations	87,224	52,233

NA: Not Available

Source: U.S. Bureau of the Census, Current Population Reports, Series P-60, No. 184, *Money Income of Households, Families, and Persons in the United States: 1992*. U.S. Government Printing Office, Washington, DC, 1989, Table 32.

workers into these jobs. Otherwise, all workers would choose pleasant and safe occupations with steady employment. Similarly, workers in jobs that have desirable nonwage attributes – prestige, interesting work, beautiful scenery – earn less, *ceteris paribus. Wage differences based on nonwage job characteristics tend to equalize the total benefits offered by different jobs.*

So long as labor markets are competitive, equalizing wage differences will result. Figure 16.2 makes this result clear. L_A^s is the supply curve for job A, for which nonwage job characteristics are favorable: The work is in an air-conditioned office, with low noise levels, and little risk of injury or death. Occupation A is assumed to be such a small part of the total labor market that the supply curve faced by each employer is perfectly elastic. Firms can hire all the workers they require at W_A.

However, what about the supply of workers to occupation B, where the boss is subject to periodic fits of rage and machinery produces both loud noise and noxious fumes? If job B paid W_A, no one would want the work. They could earn the same wage under the more pleasant working conditions in job A. To entice workers into job B, a higher wage must be offered. This wage must be high enough to compensate for the unpleasant characteristics of the job. The amount $W_B - W_A$ is such an equalizing wage difference. It is just sufficient to make workers indifferent between jobs A and B. At any wage less than W_B, job A is preferred and the supply of labor to job B is zero.

So long as workers are free to choose whichever job they prefer, equalizing wage differences must be paid. Jobs that are unpleasant will carry a higher wage. By the same reasoning,

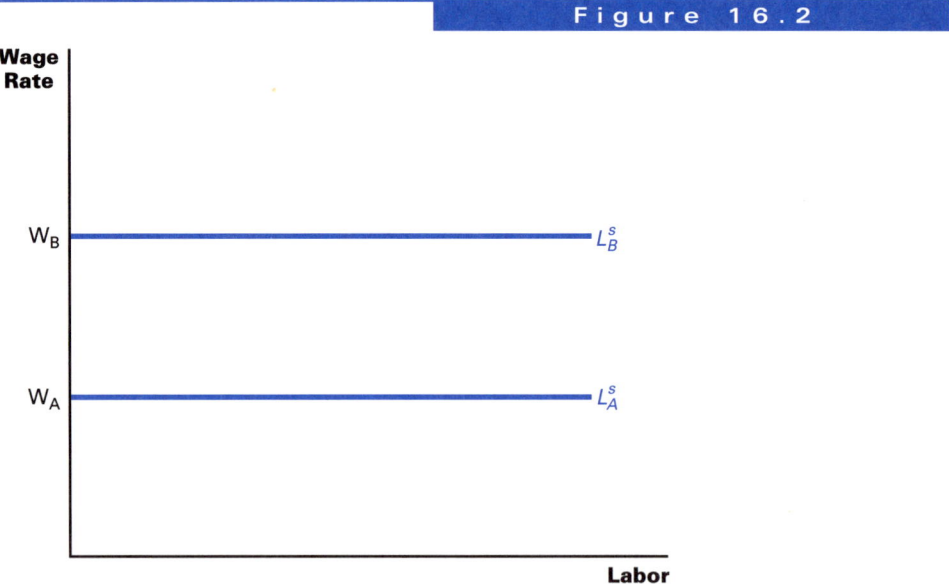

Figure 16.2

Variations in Job Quality and Equalizing Differences

In this figure, L_A^s is the supply schedule to job A, for which nonwage job characteristics are favorable. Occupation A is assumed to be such a small part of the total labor market that the supply schedule is perfectly elastic. Firms can hire all the workers they require at W_A. L_B^s is the supply curve for job B, which has a number of undesirable characteristics. If job B paid W_A, no one would want the work. To entice workers into job B, the wage must be high enough to compensate for the unpleasant job characteristics. The amount $W_B - W_A$ is an *equalizing wage difference*. It is sufficient to make workers indifferent between job A and B. At any wage less than W_B, job A is preferred and the supply of labor to job B is zero.

an occupation that requires a costly training or apprenticeship period must pay a higher wage to compensate for the extra costs of entering that labor market. Physicians must be paid more than unskilled labor, or else few will incur the considerable costs of college and medical school.

This reasoning can be reversed to show that jobs with very favorable job characteristics will pay a lower wage. Workers will crowd into these jobs until the wage has fallen low enough to equalize the total benefits of favorable and unfavorable jobs.

Worker Preferences Affect Relative Wages An equalizing wage difference is a wage premium that must be paid to attract labor to less desirable jobs. Figure 16.2 illustrated such a premium – a wage premium equal to $W_B - W_A$ had to be paid to workers in job B to attract any workers to job B. Worker perceptions about the value of the differences in job traits determine the size of the wage differential. In Figure 16.2, it was implicitly assumed that all workers had the same perceptions. As such, the wage difference was the same for each level of employment.

Because worker preferences vary, however, the premium necessary to attract workers into less preferred jobs also varies. In fact, what one person considers to be an attractive work environment might be the very same environment that someone else finds quite unattractive. Some of the observed differences in wages are attributable to these differences in preferences.

Figure 16.3 illustrates the impact of worker preferences on observed wage differences. Consider once again jobs A and B, where job B is generally less preferred than job A. Because worker tastes with respect to job attributes vary, the supply of labor to job B is no longer perfectly elastic at the exactly equalizing wage difference in Figure 16.2. When worker tastes vary, different workers are willing to go to job B at different wage differences and, hence, L_B^s is now upward sloping.

In Figure 16.3, the wage difference, D ($D = W_B - W_A$) between job A and B, and not the absolute wage, is measured on the vertical axis. A few workers might actually prefer job B to job A – they would be willing to work in B at a wage lower than the wage in job A. The availability of such people is shown by a supply curve that intersects the vertical axis at a value of D that is less than 0. When $W_B - W_A < 0$, $D < 0$. Employers offering job B hire those workers who dislike job B least because it minimizes labor costs.

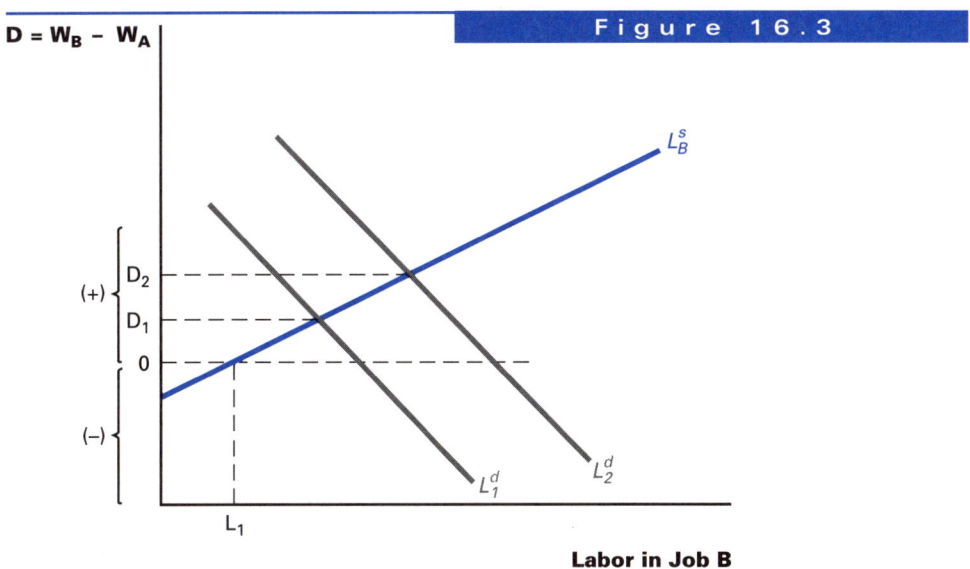

Equalizing Wage Differences and the Level of Labor Demand

When worker tastes vary, different workers are willing to go to job B at different wage differences. Hence, L_B^s is upward sloping. The wage difference, D, between job A and B, is measured on the vertical axis. A few workers, L_1, might in fact prefer job B to job A, *ceteris paribus*. The availability of these people is illustrated by a supply curve that intersects the vertical axis at a value of d that is less than 0. When demand is equal to L_1^d, the equalizing wage difference is D_1. However, if demand increases to L_2^d, the equilibrium wage difference will increase to D_2.

438

The wage difference is determined by supply and demand. When demand is equal to L_1^d, the equalizing wage difference is D_1. However, as demand for job B workers rises, employers must bid away more and more job A workers by offering larger and larger wage premiums. As illustrated in Figure 16.3, if demand increases to L_2^d, the equilibrium wage difference will increase to D_2. Thus, the observed difference in wages between A and B depends not only on the differences in the two jobs, but also the distribution of worker preferences for the attributes of A and B and the demand for workers in each job.

Equalizing wage differences compensate workers for differences in nonwage job attributes. In general, less attractive jobs command a higher wage premium.

Nonequalizing Wage Differences

Nonequalizing wage differences: Differences in wages that cause the total benefits of working in different jobs to vary.

As the term implies, **nonequalizing wage differences** are not necessary to attract and retain workers in given occupations. Nonequalizing wage differences cause the total benefits of working in different jobs to vary, with the result that some occupations are, all things considered, preferred to others. We would expect nonequalizing differences to be competed away if workers are free to enter any occupation they wish. Workers would crowd into the preferred jobs until the nonequalizing wage difference is eliminated. *For nonequalizing wage differences to persist, there must be a barrier to the entry of new workers, which limits the degree of competition among workers for the better jobs.* Resource immobility arises for a variety of reasons; we mention three important ones.

Special Skills When a few individuals (maybe only one person) possess a special, unique skill, in effect they have monopoly power conferred upon them. Dr. Robert Kerlan, the famed sports surgeon, earns much more than other orthopedic specialists. His earnings premium is based on a rare ability. It cannot be competed away because other surgeons, lacking his skill, are not really competitors. Similarly, an individual may be willing to play basketball for the Chicago Bulls for much less than Michael Jordan is paid. The fact that the owners of the Bulls don't take the individual up on his offer suggests that he is not competing in the same labor market as Jordan.

Figure 16.4 illustrates the manner in which prices are determined for such rare skills. This figure represents the market for Michael Jordan's basketball skills. There are few other players who possess the basketball talents that Jordan does. Thus, the supply of those talents is perfectly inelastic – the supply curve is vertical. In this situation, the wage paid to Jordan or other such talented players is determined by demand. Jordan receives W_1 if demand is L_1^d. If demand rises, the wage rises. There is no change in quantity supplied in the short run. Nor is there an increase in supply over the long run. Jordan has a monopoly on those rare, special skills in demand for basketball.

Reservation wage: The minimum amount of money that would attract a worker into a particular line of employment.

In this situation, Jordan, or whoever has the special skills in demand, earns a wage that is far in excess of the minimum amount that would just make him willing to play basketball. The wage at which he would be attracted into basketball is called the **reservation wage.** The amount he earns above and beyond his reservation wage is called

Figure 16.4

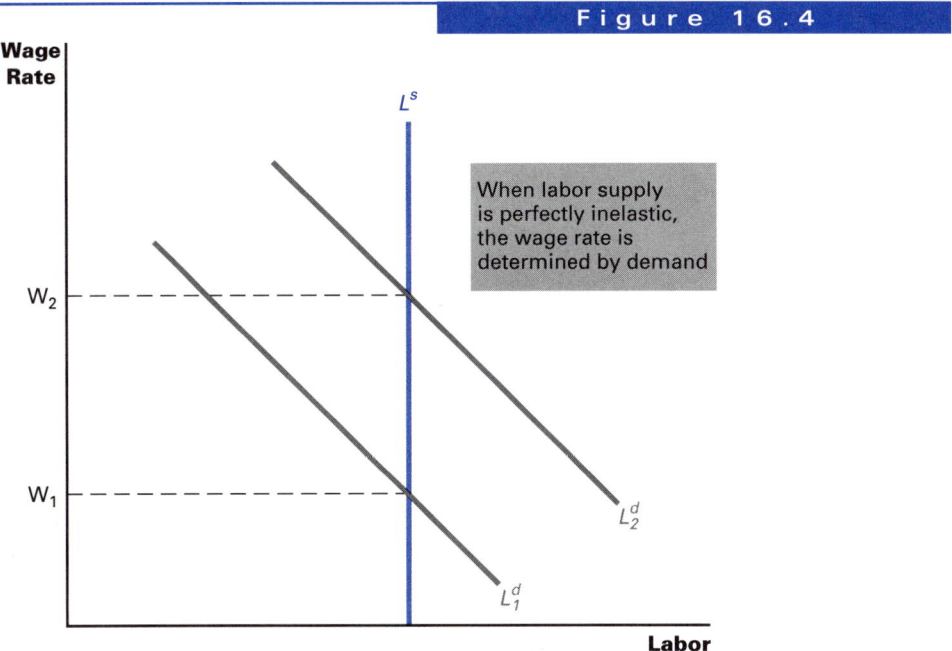

Supply of and Demand for Specialized Skills

This figure illustrates the manner in which prices are determined for rare labor skills. There are few, and some would say no, other players who possess the basketball talents that Michael Jordan does. Thus, the supply of those talents is perfectly inelastic – the supply curve, L^s, is vertical. In this situation, the wage paid to Jordan or other such talented players is determined by demand. Jordan receives W_1 if demand is L_1^d. If demand rises to L_2^d, the wage rises to W_2. There is no change in quantity supplied in the short run or the long run. Jordan has a monopoly on those rare, special skills in demand for basketball.

economic rent. Most of Michael Jordan's salary, and that of others with special skills, is economic rent.

Trade Union Restrictions   Trade union actions can create nonequalizing wage differences. Labor unions may restrict entry into an occupation or trade or convince workers not to work for a lower wage. If union efforts are successful, supply may actually fall, pushing up wages. Alternatively, unions may simply bargain for a higher-than-equilibrium wage and then ration entrance into the occupation. In both cases their actions restrict entry and prevent the higher wage levels from attracting additional workers into the jobs.

Government Restrictions   Occupational licensing laws also may prevent free entry and cause wages for licensed workers to be higher than they otherwise would be. Entry into certain occupations, such as medicine, hair styling, and nursing, is regulated through licensing and training requirements. These regulations are established to ensure a minimum level of competency for all those individuals who practice in one of

Economic rent:

The amount of income in excess of a worker's reservation wage.

440

Market Wages: Professional Sports Versus Education

Since the late 1980s, many of the top players in professional sports have been able to negotiate multi-year contracts worth millions of dollars per year. In 1990, Jose Canseco, then of the Oakland Athletics, became baseball's highest-paid player when he signed a contract worth more than $5 million per year over a five-year period. In 1992, Barry Bonds signed a contract with the San Francisco Giants that amounted to approximately $42 million over a seven-year period. And in 1993, Larry Johnson signed a twelve-year contract with the Charlotte Hornets of the National Basketball Association worth a reported $84 million.

In contrast to the salaries in professional sports, starting salaries for elementary school teachers averaged less than $20,000 per year during the same time period, and average teacher salaries were around $30,000. In addition, many teachers across the country have received raises in recent years that fell short of the rate of inflation, resulting in a loss in real buying power. This disparity in outcomes in the sports and teaching labor markets clearly does not make sense to most Americans. For many, this is evidence of the irrationality of American society — that we pay individuals who play catch or jump around in shorts so much more than those who largely shape the abilities and attitudes of our children. Does this make economic sense? Possibly.

To understand how such seemingly illogical differences exist, we must consider the characteristics of supply and demand in each of these two markets. The forces of supply and demand set wages based on the value of the marginal worker, not the average. The fact that a professional athlete earns more than a teacher cannot be taken as evidence that society values professional sports more than educating its young. Consider Figure 16.5, which illustrates the supply and demand for teachers and professional major league baseball players.

The demand for major league baseball players is less than the demand for teachers because society places a higher total value on education. In addition, demand for professional baseball players is restricted by the number of teams that are allowed to compete and the number of players that a team can have on its roster. However, the supply of teachers is much greater than the supply of professional baseball players. A limited number of baseball players possess the skills required to enable them to compete effectively in the market for major league players. In relative terms, a much larger number of individuals possess the skills necessary to compete in the market for teachers.

Price elasticity of demand also plays a role in the differences between the two markets. In baseball, a certain number of players are required to compete in a game. In addition, it is important to maintain a number of reserves in the event of injury to a starter. Quantity demanded is relatively fixed, regardless of price. In contrast, it is possible to alter the number of teachers needed to educate a fixed number of students by altering the number of classes an instructor must teach, the number of students per instructor (class size), and so forth. These differences imply that the demand for professional base-

these occupations. However, these regulations have supply-side effects as well. They are much like union effects to the extent that they restrict entry into the occupation, causing wages to be higher than they would be in the absence of restrictions on entry. The federal government enforces laws that prevent some wages from falling. An example is the *Davis-Bacon Act*, which requires that federal construction projects pay the going wage in the area, prohibiting contractors from hiring construction workers at a lower wage.

Section Recap

Nonequalizing wage differences cause some occupations to be preferred to others. They reflect resource immobility that can be the result of special skills and trade union or government restrictions.

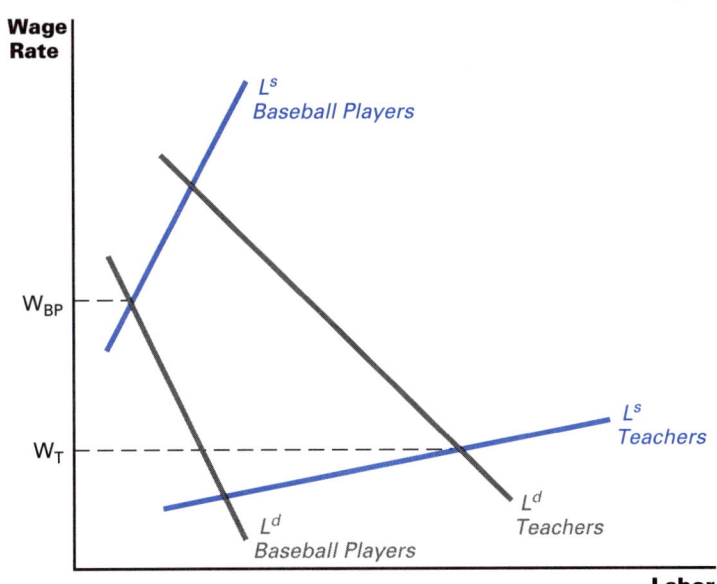

Comparing the Salaries of Teachers and Professional Baseball Players

The demand for baseball players is less than the demand for teachers because society places a higher total value on education. However, salaries for teachers, W_T, are well below those paid to baseball players, W_{BP}, because the supply of teachers is much greater. Baseball players earn more because so few have the required skill, relative to demand.

ball players is inelastic relative to the demand for teachers.

As a result of the differences in supply and demand in the two markets, salaries for teachers, W_T, are well below those paid to baseball players, W_{BP}. While the total value to society of teachers is much

higher, the marginal value of one more or one less teacher is small. Just the opposite is true with respect to the marginal baseball player.

To demonstrate that society is irrational, one would have to show that teachers would earn less if

they were as rare as athletes – a doubtful proposition. Society's valuation of the two occupations is reflected in the demand curve. But it is the interaction of demand and supply that determines wage rates.

Disequilibrium Wage Differences

Whether equalizing or not, wage differences caused by differences in working conditions, special skills, or competitive restrictions are equilibrium wage differences. That is, they will continue to exist over the long run until fundamental demand and supply conditions change.

Ours is a dynamic economy, however. Constantly changing technology and changing demands for products mean that labor markets are always adjusting to a new equilibrium.

Disequilibrium wage differences:
Differences in wages that are caused by a short-run disequilibrium in one or more labor markets.

Disequilibrium wage differences, or *transitional wage differences*, are commonly observed. These wage differences are eliminated in the long run.

Consider, for example, the earnings of newly graduated economics and finance majors. In long-run equilibrium, these occupations should have roughly similar starting salaries because both require a similar level of education. If the demand for finance majors dramatically increases, the starting salary of finance majors initially rises, and there is a transitory disequilibrium wage difference between finance majors and economics majors. This wage difference is competed away in the long run, however, as college students switch their majors from economics to finance. The increased supply of finance majors pushes their starting salaries back down, while the relative scarcity of economics majors drives up their starting salaries. Long-run equilibrium is reestablished when economics and finance majors again have the same starting salaries, and the transitory wage difference is eliminated.

You might well ask, How long is the long run? Transitory wage differences might last for a few weeks or years, depending on how quickly workers can change occupations. In the case of temporary, unskilled jobs in the same geographic area, wage differences are eliminated very quickly. However, an increased demand for brain surgeons produces a disequilibrium wage difference of much longer duration. The supply of brain surgeons cannot increase overnight. It takes years for new individuals to acquire the necessary education and training to enter this market.

Similarly, wage differences for the same skill across different regions may persist for a long time. These transitory wage differences are eliminated by workers moving from low to high demand areas. However, moving is costly, particularly for older workers. It may take the next generation to move to where employment opportunities are more attractive before long-run labor market equilibrium is reached.

Section Recap

Disequilibrium wage differences are the result of short-run changes in the supply of or demand for a resource. Over the long run, these differences tend to disappear.

Investment in Education: Costs and Benefits...Again

Human capital:
The productivity-determining skills and abilities embodied in labor.

The way economists explain education decisions is a good example of how economists view the world differently than other social scientists do. Sociologists emphasize the roles of culture, family background, and social expectations in the decision to attend college. Although not dismissing these as unimportant, economists focus on education as an economic choice, with rational individuals once again comparing costs and benefits. Economists consider an investment in education a **human capital** investment. Education choices are similar to firms' decisions to purchase physical capital. Both types of investment require large initial cash outlays, but yield a continuing stream of benefits into the future. For the individual considering college, the costs are both explicit (tuition, books, fees, and so on) and implicit (the loss of full-time earnings for four years, or longer). After these costs are incurred, the investment is expected to yield returns in the form of higher earnings throughout the college graduate's working career. The increase in earnings associated with the additional education represents the benefits of the investment.

The benefit-cost comparison is illustrated in Figure 16.6, where two *age-earnings profiles* are depicted. The curve labeled "high school" measures the annual earnings over a lifetime for those with a high school education. The curve labeled "college" measures the annual earnings for those with a college degree. The profiles have markedly different shapes. The high school graduate goes to work at age 18 and works to age 65. Annual earnings rise gradually over the work life. On the other hand, the person who goes to college forgoes market work for four years, until graduation at age 22. The implicit cost of the education is the market earnings forgone because of the four-year education: the difference between high-school graduate and college graduate earnings until the two become equal. Moreover, the college student incurs explicit education costs such as tuition and fees. Total cost of the education is the sum of implicit and explicit costs, or the area between the high school and college earnings profiles between age 18 and the age at which earnings for the two groups are equal.

The benefit of the investment in college is the anticipated earnings increase associated with college that accrues over a substantial portion of a lifetime. When should a person undertake such a human capital investment? Whenever the expected benefits are greater

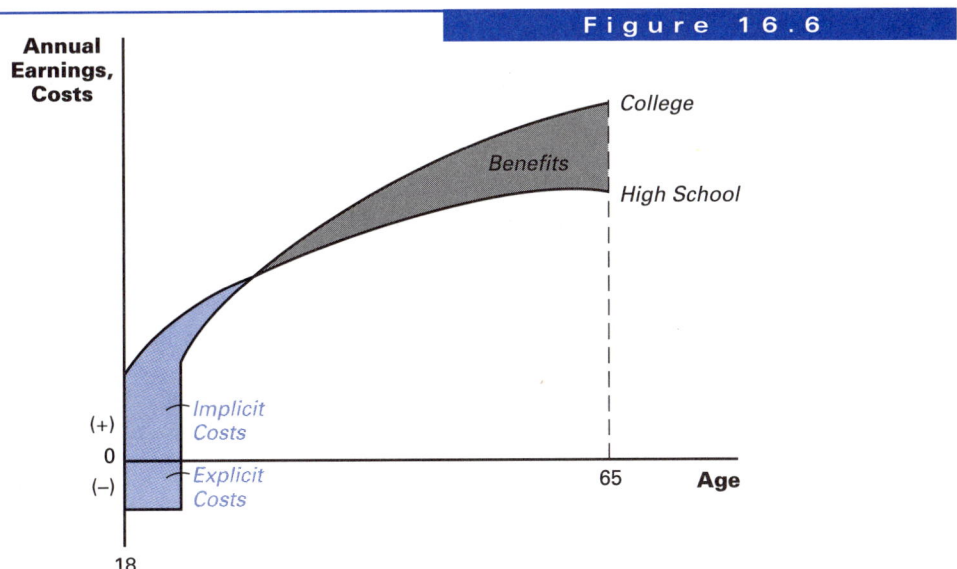

Figure 16.6

Age-Earnings Profiles for High School Versus College Graduates

This figure illustrates two "age-earnings profiles." The curve labeled "high school" measures the annual earnings over a lifetime for those with a high school education. The curve labeled "college" measures the annual earnings for those with a college degree. It is assumed that the high school graduate goes to work at age 18 and works to age 65. For the college student, the implicit cost of education is the market earnings forgone during the four years of school; explicit costs include tuition and fees. Total cost of the education is the sum of implicit and explicit costs, or the area between the high school and college earnings profiles between age 18 and the year that earnings for the two groups are equal.

than the expected costs. Because the costs and benefits of this choice problem occur over a long period of time, however, the decision-making process should take account of the fact that a given amount of benefits received in the future is less valuable than the same amount of benefits received today. To adjust for this difference, we calculate the value today, or the *present value*, of expected costs and benefits over the individual's lifetime.[1] If the present value of the increased earnings exceeds the present value of implicit plus explicit costs, a rational individual will choose to attend college.

A recent study investigated the effects of education on income by examining data on a large sample of twins in Australia.[2] According to the study's results, returns to education range between 7.8 percent and 8.3 percent depending on the specific form of the model used in the analysis. A similar study of returns to education using data on twins in the United States estimated returns to education ranging between 11.6 percent and 16.7 percent.[3] Both of these studies as well as numerous other studies suggest that education is an important determinant of an individual's total income.

The studies referred to above are another illustration of the equalizing wage difference for occupations requiring schooling or other kinds of training. Because a college education is costly, the wage in occupations requiring a college education must exceed the wage in alternative occupations that require no degree by enough to compensate workers for the cost of the training. Otherwise, workers will not be attracted into occupations that require a college education.

This wage differential serves as the mechanism for adjusting relative supplies of college-educated and high-school-educated workers. If the wage of college-educated workers rises, it makes a college education look more profitable. Enrollments increase as people are attracted by the now more-profitable investment. After a few years, this change in the profitability of college will increase the supply of college-educated workers and reduce the supply of high-school-educated workers. These supply shifts decrease wages for college-educated workers and increase wages for high-school-educated workers. These shifts reduce the benefits of a college education, causing the number of individuals seeking college training to fall and relative wages to return toward an equilibrium level.

The analysis of a college education as a human capital investment is not meant to suggest that economists deny noneconomic motives for attending college. College can be viewed as a consumption good as well. However, the investment motive is an important one, and we expect the general predictions of the human capital model to be correct. For example, a reduction in federal subsidies for higher education would reduce enrollments. On the other hand, a widening of the earnings differential between high school and college graduates is predicted to increase college attendance. Although it is not the full story, the theory of human capital has proven enormously valuable in understanding a wide range of labor issues.

Section Recap

From an economic perspective, the decision to invest in education is an investment in human capital. It requires a comparison of the benefits and costs of additional education.

Discrimination in the Labor Market

So far we have considered how wages vary by occupation or educational attainment. Another very important policy issue is how and why wages vary across other groupings of individuals. There is strong evidence that, on average, blacks are paid less than whites, and females earn less than males. In 1992, the average full-time level of earnings of black males was 70 percent that of white males, and black females earned about 86 percent of what white females earned. Overall, females employed full-time earned about 68 percent of what males earned, on average. This evidence suggests, at first glance, that widespread discrimination against blacks and women exists in labor markets. Yet one cannot simply attribute observed earnings differences to a single factor like labor market discrimination. Measuring labor market discrimination is a difficult task. Explaining its origins is even more complex.

Labor market discrimination is said to exist if equally productive workers are paid less because of race or gender. Obtaining a measure of average discrimination requires that the observed earnings differences for blacks and females be adjusted for average differences in their productive abilities.

Labor market discrimination:
Equally productive workers are paid less because of race or gender.

Blacks have significantly lower average education levels than whites. Various studies have indicated that between 50 and 80 percent of black-white earnings differences are due to measurable differences in productivity characteristics. This implies that if a black male worker and a white male worker have equal levels of education and training, that is, they are equally productive, the black will earn 85 to 94 percent of what the white worker is paid.[4] The remaining 6 to 15 percent gap may be due to labor market discrimination, or it may be that there is some unmeasured productivity difference between blacks and whites. We simply do not know how much to attribute to discrimination.

On the other hand, many would argue that observed differences in productivity characteristics, like levels of educational attainment, may be due to more complex patterns of discrimination in society. For instance, we would expect a smaller percentage of blacks to acquire a college education if the wages of black college graduates were not as high relative to the wages of high-school-educated blacks as were the relative wages of these two schooling groups for whites. The payoff for a college education may be less for blacks than for whites. Discrimination in access to education may also account for differences in educational attainment.

Estimating the extent of discrimination by gender also requires an accounting for differences in productive characteristics between men and women. The most important of these appear to be job training and experience. For several reasons, women are likely to have less job experience at any given age and to work in occupations where less training is provided. The primary cause of these differences is that women are more likely to work in the home, particularly when small children are present. If a woman expects to be dropping out of the labor market intermittently during child-rearing years, her incentive to choose a job that requires much training and an uninterrupted career to recoup the costs of that training is diluted. At the same time, firms may be reluctant to invest in training women, given their greater likelihood of quitting. It might be less risky to hire men for jobs that involve training costs for the firm.

One result of such differences is occupational segregation, a primary factor in female-male earnings differentials. Women tend to crowd (or be crowded) into lower-paying jobs with less opportunity for advancement, such as clerical and retail sales. Occupational segregation may be due to the reluctance of firms to train females for more responsible, higher-paying positions. However, it is also possible that some females prefer more casual employment. Clerical and retail jobs do not require a high level of training – they can be easily entered and exited. Further, many of these jobs have flexible hours, which is important for women who, for whatever reasons, have the primary responsibility for homemaking.

Approximately half of the male-female earnings gap can be attributed to differences in training and experience. Again, the remainder of the gap is the result of a combination of discrimination and unmeasured productivity differences between men and women.

Section Recap

Labor market discrimination exists when equally productive workers are paid different wage rates. Empirical evidence suggests that minorities and women may be victims of labor market discrimination.

Noncompetitive Labor Markets

An important assumption of this chapter is that workers are paid a wage equal to the value of their marginal product, that is, their marginal revenue product, when the labor and product markets are perfectly competitive. It is important to understand the reasoning behind this result. If a worker's marginal revenue product exceeds his wage, another employer has a profit incentive to hire away that worker because he adds more to the employer's revenue than to cost.

However, in some situations the additional cost of hiring the worker is greater than the wage. Such a condition arises in the case of a **monopsony**. Monopsonistic firms may not have an incentive to expand employment until marginal revenue product equals the wage.

Monopsony:

Only one buyer of a good or resource; for example, only one employer of labor in a particular location.

A monopsony is said to exist when there is only one employer in a labor market. For example, the school board in an isolated small town may be the only employer of local teachers. The National Football League is said to be a monopsonist since it is the sole employer of professional football players in the United States. *The crucial difference between a monopsonist and a perfectly competitive employer is the monopsonist's incentive to restrict employment to hold down wages. Unlike a competitive employer who faces a perfectly elastic supply schedule for labor, a monopsonist confronts the entire market supply schedule.*

In Figure 16.7 (a), the market supply curve is upward sloping. This means that the monopsonist must pay a higher wage to attract more workers. Contrast this situation with the competitive employer in Figure 16.7 (b). The competitive employer's demand for labor is such a small portion of the total market that it can hire all it requires at the going wage. Supply and marginal resource cost (MRC) are identical for the competitive employer; both equal W_C.

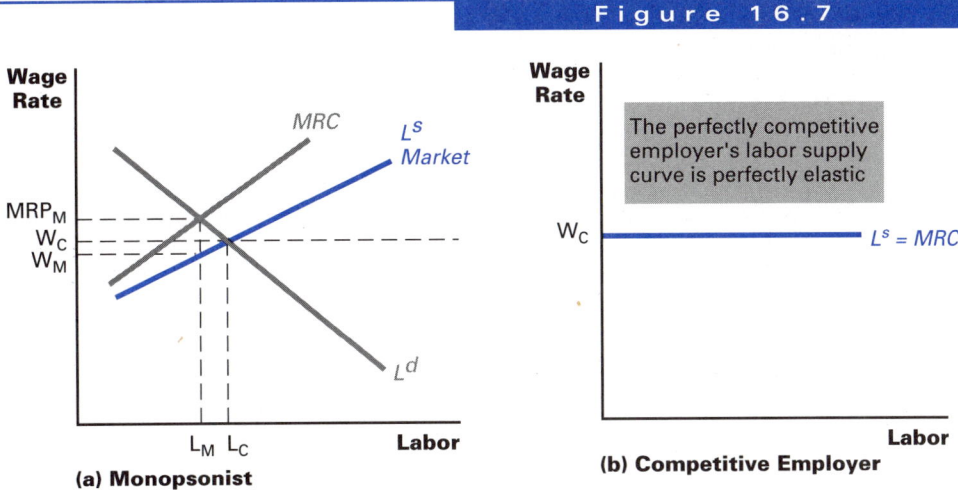

Figure 16.7

(a) Monopsonist

(b) Competitive Employer

Equilibrium in Monopsony Versus a Competitive Market

Figure 16.7 (a) illustrates the situation faced by a monopsonist. As Figure 16.7 (b) illustrates, supply and marginal resource cost (MRC) are identical for the competitive employer – both equal W_C. However, because the market supply schedule is upward sloping, marginal resource cost is greater than the wage for the monopsonist. It not only must pay a higher wage to attract the new employee, but also must increase the wage of all employees who were previously hired at a lower wage. Given its MRP schedule, the monopsonist will hire L_M workers at a wage of W_M. Note that the wage and employment would be W_C and L_C if the labor market in Figure 16.7 (a) were competitive. Monopsony results in lower wages ($W_M < W_C$) and employment ($L_M < L_C$) because, unlike the competitive employer, a monopsonist can reduce wages by restricting employment.

However, marginal resource cost is greater than the wage for a monopsonist. It not only must pay a higher wage to attract new employees, but it also must increase the wage of all employees who were previously hired at a lower wage. Suppose a monopsonist can employ ten workers at $5 per hour, but the eleventh worker requires $6 per hour. The marginal cost of the eleventh employee is $16 the wage, $6, plus the additional $1 per hour that must be paid to the other ten employees to bring them up to $6 per hour. The monopsonist's MRC curve lies above the supply curve, as shown in Figure 16.7 (a).

Fewer workers are employed in a monopsony situation than when the labor market is perfectly competitive. Given its marginal revenue product schedule in Figure 16.7 (a), the monopsonist hires workers up to the point at which marginal revenue product equals marginal resource cost. Thus, L_M workers will be hired. The supply curve in turn tells us that the monopsonist must offer a wage of W_M. Note that the wage and employment would be W_C and L_C if the labor market of Figure 16.7 (a) were competitive. Each competitive firm, such as the one shown in Figure 16.7 (b), would continue to hire workers until marginal revenue product equals the wage. *Monopsony results in lower wages ($W_M < W_C$) and* *employment ($L_M < L_C$) because, unlike the competitive employer, a monopsonist can reduce wages by restricting employment.*

Note also that monopsony breaks the equality of the wage and marginal revenue product. If the monopsonist sells its output in a competitive product market, marginal revenue product is equal to marginal resource cost. However, in Figure 16.7 (a), the L_Mth worker is paid W_M, which is less than his marginal revenue product. This gap creates an incentive for another employer to hire the L_Mth worker. However, by definition, there is no other employer. Competition is needed to ensure that workers are paid the value of their productivity.

Section Recap

In a monopsony, workers are paid a wage that is less than their MRP. Monopsonies result in lower employment and lower wages than perfectly competitive labor markets.

The Minimum Wage Controversy

In early 1995, President Bill Clinton proposed that the minimum wage be increased to $5.15 per hour. The last time the minimum wage was raised was in 1989, when the Congress and President George Bush agreed on legislation that increased the minimum wage from its previous level of $3.35 per hour to $3.80 per hour on April 1, 1990 and $4.25 per hour on April 1, 1991. (In addition, the new law contained a provision that allows employers to pay a lower training wage to teenaged employees.) In total, the minimum wage has been increased sixteen times since it was first established as part of the Fair Labor Standards Act in 1938. (The first minimum wage was 25¢ an hour.)

Viewed from the perspective of economic efficiency, the minimum wage law has certain undesirable characteristics. Experienced and educated workers are not directly affected by the law, since they earn wages in excess of the proposed minimum. However, in the market for relatively unskilled workers the minimum wage is a price floor established above the equilibrium wage. As we discussed in Chapter 4, the result of an effective price floor is the creation of a surplus (excess supply) in the affected market.

Figure 16.8 illustrates the impact of an increase in the minimum wage law in this less-skilled market. Assuming that the market for unskilled workers is initially in equilibrium at the old minimum wage level, an increase in the minimum wage creates excess supply. The new minimum wage decreases the quantity of labor demanded by $L_e - L_d$ and increases the quantity of labor supplied by $L_s - L_e$. Some workers previously employed lose their jobs, and some individuals previously out of the labor force are now attracted into the market to look for work. Reduced employment occurs because of the negatively sloped demand curve. Labor is now more expensive to employers. In the short run, employers reduce output because of the higher costs. In the long run they attempt to minimize the cost increase by adopting production techniques that rely on less of the now more expensive labor.

The minimum wage law has both supporters and detractors. Firms that rely to a large extent on unskilled labor, such as restaurants and many retail merchandise outlets, are

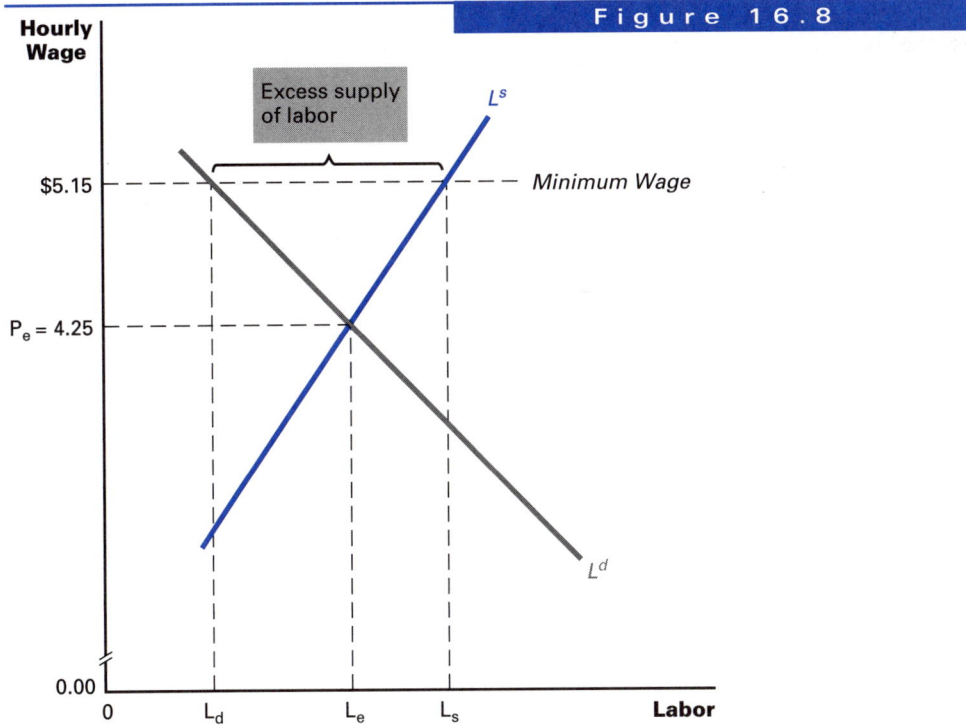

Figure 16.8

The Economic Effect of an Increase in the Minimum Wage Law

This figure illustrates the impact of an increase in the minimum wage law. Assuming that the market is in equilibrium at the old minimum wage level $P_e = \$4.25$, the new minimum wage, $\$5.15$, would decrease the quantity of labor demanded by $L_e - L_d$ and increase the quantity of labor supplied by $L_s - L_e$. Some workers previously employed would lose their jobs, and some individuals previously out of the labor force would now be attracted into the market to look for work. Reduced employment occurs because of the negatively sloped demand curve. Labor is now more expensive to employers.

opposed to the minimum wage law. For example, the U.S. Chamber of Commerce and the National Restaurant Association took a strong stand against the increase in the minimum wage law in 1991 and the increase that was proposed in 1995. They argued that an increase would cause more unemployment among the least–skilled workers and that a higher minimum wage would deny more young people the opportunity for the on-the-job training that is important to get them started on careers of productive employment.

Advocates of a higher minimum wage law point out that full-time work at the prevailing minimum wage yields an annual income that is insufficient for a minimum standard of living. Such an income would be, in fact, just above the official poverty line for a single person. Organized labor is an especially strong proponent of increases in the minimum wage. They argue that increases are needed to ensure that everyone who works earns a decent wage. Organized labor's position is that although an increase in the minimum

450

DISAGREEMENT?

Will the Real Minimum Wage Impacts Please Stand Up?

According to the simple economic analysis of the effects of an effective minimum wage presented in this chapter, increasing the minimum wage causes employment of low-wage workers to decrease. The increase in the minimum wage causes employers to move up their demand curve for labor, leading to a reduction in quantity demanded. Numerous studies of the impacts of changes in the minimum wage law on the employment of low-wage workers have supported the model's predictions. However, recent studies have produced results that contradict the findings of earlier studies. At the same time, a number of new studies have produced results consistent with the earlier findings. Why the disagreement?

To understand why the disagreement exists we need to consider the studies at the heart of the debate. Two economists, David Card and Alan Krueger, have produced a number of studies and a book that provide evidence that contradicts the model's predictions. The most noteworthy example of their work is a study of the impacts of the minimum wage on employment in the fast-food industry in New Jersey and Pennsylvania.[6] In the study, Card and Krueger examined the effects of an increase in New Jersey's minimum wage law that went into effect in April 1992. Based on telephone survey data collected from 410 fast-food restaurants in the two states before and after the wage increase took place, Card and Krueger determined that employment actually increased in New Jersey after the increase and fell in some establishments in Pennsylvania (where the minimum wage did not change). These results are the direct opposite of what would be predicted on the basis of standard theory and previous studies.

Card and Krueger's results stand in stark contrast to the results of two other studies of the effects of the minimum wage increases that occurred on April 1, 1990 and April 1, 1991.[7] According to a study by Deere, Murphy, and Welch, the

wage may cause some unskilled workers to become unemployed, those who keep their jobs have a higher income.[5]

The important question for society is the net effect of the law. There are gainers and losers in many parts of the economy. However, is the net effect of a higher minimum wage beneficial? If the law causes unemployment, it reduces economic efficiency in society. As a policy to reduce poverty, the law's impact is questionable. It reduces employment opportunities for low-wage workers. Those workers who maintain employment at the higher wage might not be members of low-income families. Many beneficiaries are young people, some of whom are from poor families but many of whom are from middle-income or even upper-income families.

Long-Term Employment Contracts

An important feature of labor markets in the United States is the long-term nature of much employment. Professor Robert Hall of Stanford University has estimated that 40 percent of men above the age of 30 hold jobs that they will stay in for at least twenty years.[8] The simple competitive labor market model does not reveal why workers and employers should form such strong attachments. Instead, it implies that workers will quit their jobs whenever another firm offers even a temporarily higher wage, or that firms will

employment/population ratio for teenage men and women dropped by 15.4 percent and 12.9 percent, respectively, after the second increase. In addition, the study considered subgroups within the population formed on the basis of race, education, and marital status. In each case, the group with the highest percentage of low-wage workers showed the greatest drop in employment after the minimum wage was raised. A study by Neumark and Wascher concluded that increases in the minimum wage increase the probability that teenagers will leave school to become employed or work more hours. The study also found that an increase in the minimum wage increases the probability that teenagers employed in low-wage jobs will drop out of school and eventually end up unemployed. Thus, there are serious incentive effects that policymakers need to consider when debating whether to increase the minimum wage.

The results of these three studies provide an ample basis for the disagreement over the effects of the minimum wage law. However, the disagreement extends to the methods that have been used to produce the results in question. In the case of the study by Card and Krueger, follow-up research funded by the Employment Policies Institute (a research organization funded by manufacturers, restaurants, and retailers) raises many serious questions about the research methods used and, more importantly, the quality of the data collected. The EPI study collected data on a subsample of the restaurants included in the Card and Krueger study and found large discrepancies between data collected in their survey and data that came from the firms' payroll records. Further analysis of the subsample of data from the payroll records produced results consistent with those of previous studies; for every 10 percent increase in the minimum

wage in New Jersey, employment decreased by 2.7 percent.

Card and Krueger have responded by suggesting that many of the studies that have reported results consistent with the simple model we have considered are biased. They contend that pressure to produce statistical results that are consistent with the underlying economic theory and statistically significant (that is, that suggest that increases in the minimum wage cause employment to fall) has resulted in a distorted picture of the overall effects of the minimum wage.

Clearly, the debate over the effects of the minimum wage is far from being resolved. However, it would appear that, for now, the majority of the evidence supports the long-held view that increasing the minimum wage causes employment in low-wage jobs to decline. Whether this result will continue to stand remains to be seen.

---

always lay off workers whenever their marginal revenue product declines below their current wage.

In fact, the labor market appears to be much less responsive to short-term fluctuations in demand and supply than other markets are. Unlike the wheat market, for example, where prices and quantities fluctuate widely, wages and employment are more rigid. Some economists believe that the relative rigidity of labor markets suggests that supply and demand conditions are relatively unimportant in determining wages and employment. However, there are good reasons why, even in very competitive labor markets, workers and firms make long-term employment commitments and ignore temporary fluctuations in market conditions.

There are at least three reasons why workers and firms can benefit from continuous employment:

1. Many jobs require some initial training. The time and cost of training a new employee in the firm's particular production, management, or marketing techniques constitute investments that make workers more productive. The sooner workers quit, the lower the return on this investment. Firms pay trained workers higher-than-market wages to establish an incentive for long job tenure. Alternatively, firms may offer employees deferred compensation in the form of bonuses or pensions as a means of

retaining trained employees. The result of such incentives is that both the firm and the worker share in the returns. Both will want to continue the employment relationship unless marginal revenue product drops substantially or another firm offers a very large wage increase.

2. Work incentives increase longevity. The productivity of a worker depends on her effort. Employees may be able to shirk, or work less productively than expected, if firms are unable to monitor a worker's effort. Without a long-term employment agreement, shirking is riskless: If the worker is caught and fired, she can move to another employer at the same wage. Many firms, however, promise workers a bonus if they remain with the firm for a long duration. The bonus may be in the form of a high wage paid to senior employees or a pension. Either way, the worker who is dismissed for shirking loses the bonus. The delayed-payment incentive reduces shirking and increases career worker productivity, benefiting both the worker and the firm.

3. Employees prefer stable wages (and incomes). Some economists argue that stable wages reflect workers' dislike for risk. If so, workers and firms may form long-term employment agreements in which firms agree to pay stable wages, even though product demand fluctuations shift the marginal revenue product schedule. Firms in effect insure workers against temporarily adverse demand conditions. Workers, for their part, agree not to leave the firm when labor demand is temporarily high and other firms are offering higher wages.

Whenever there are long-term labor commitments, the wage might be different from the worker's marginal revenue product in any given period. For example, the firm may pay a bonus to a worker, pushing the wage above the worker's marginal revenue product late in his career. Normally, we would expect that firms would lay off workers whenever the wage exceeds marginal revenue product, but in this case the firm has promised the bonus as part of the contract. The profit-maximizing condition for hiring workers when long-term contracts are present is that the total marginal revenue product, summed over the worker's career with the firm, equals the total value of wages paid.

Section Recap

Long-term employment contracts benefit both workers and firms by lowering training costs, creating incentives for increased productivity, and providing workers with a stable income.

Summary

We observe a distribution of wages in the labor market. Equilibrium wage differences exist that are equalizing and nonequalizing. There are also disequilibrium wage differences.

Equalizing wage differences exist to compensate workers for differences in non-wage job attributes. When preferred employment opportunities are available, workers must be attracted into less-preferred jobs by wage premiums that equalize the overall attractiveness of different jobs.

Nonequalizing wage differences arise when labor mobility is restricted. Competition on the supply side is reduced and wage levels above competitive long-run equilibrium levels persist. These wage differences arise when special skills become valuable in the market and when unions or government policies restrict entry into certain occupations or jobs.

Both equalizing and nonequalizing wage differences are equilibrium differences. **Disequilibrium wage differences** occur due to shifts in supply or demand in the market. An increase in demand for one occupation causes wages to rise, but only in the short run. As workers are attracted to the occupation, supply shifts and a new equilibrium is established. These disequilibrium differences are important allocation and rationing functions of the labor market.

The acquisition of education or other skills that improve productivity is a **human capital** investment. An individual undertakes the costs of the investment only if the expected benefits are at least as great as expected costs. The benefits of human capital investments usually accrue in the form of increased earnings. Changes in relative wages of workers with different skills change the profitability of these investments and prompt adjustments in the supply of workers with these skills.

Labor market discrimination exists when groups of equally productive workers are paid different wages. There is substantial evidence of labor market discrimination by race and gender. Blacks and women earn less than whites and men, even after accounting for differences in productivity characteristics such as educational attainment.

When there is only one employer in a labor market a **monopsony** exists. The monopsonist faces a positively sloped labor supply curve and must pay all workers higher wages when each additional worker is hired. The result is that the marginal resource cost of a worker exceeds his wage. The monopsonist has an incentive to reduce employment to save on labor costs. A monopsonist's wage and employment levels are less than those for an employer in a competitive labor market.

Finally, there is considerable employment stability in the United States. Workers tend to remain employed by one firm for relatively long periods of time. These longer-term employment relationships make labor markets less responsive to market changes. Labor market rigidity is beneficial to firms and workers in a number of ways. Long-term relationships make human capital investments more profitable. Longer-term payment schemes may improve worker productivity. Because workers prefer wage stability, employers keep wages constant while product demand fluctuates and equate worker costs and productivity over a longer period of time.

Questions for Thought

Knowledge Questions

1. What is the difference between a disequilibrium wage difference and a nonequalizing wage difference?

2. Define labor market discrimination.

3. Define human capital investment.

4. What role does resource mobility play in the determination of equilibrium wage rates?

Application Questions

5. Why are nonprice (wage) working conditions important in the labor market but not in other resource markets?

6. Suppose there are only two occupations, X and Y, and that workers are employed in the labor force for only two years. Occupation X is unskilled work, but occupation Y requires a year of training. If the annual salary in X is $10,000, what will the annual salary be for Y? Explain.

7. Use the aggregate labor market model to explore the wage and employment consequences of immigration restrictions that prevent families from migrating to the United States from other countries. What happens to equilibrium wages and employment?

8. In what sense is a wage premium for noisy, dusty work equalizing?

Synthesis Questions

9. According to the definition of unemployment used in the United States, a person is considered unemployed if he or she is currently not working, is available for work, and is actively seeking a job. Can this definition lead to an underestimate of the number of people without jobs who would like to be working at current wage rates? Explain.

10. A biotechnology company expending millions of dollars on research for a new drug is much like a talented high school baseball player training and working to develop into the best baseball player he can be. In what way are these two situations similar? (Hint: Compare economic rent to monopoly profit.)

11. Currently, many college students are eligible for low-cost (low-interest) college loans. In addition, in many situations, students do not have to pay any interest or principal on these loans until after they finish school. However, in 1995 Congress proposed changes that would require students to begin making interest payments on the federally sponsored loans as soon as the loans are received. How would this proposed change affect the relative benefits and costs of investments in higher education?

End Notes

[1] The present value of a future amount, say $100 in the year 2000, is simply the amount that, if invested today, with the effects of compounded interest, would be worth $100 in the year 2000. Chapter 18 contains a more technical discussion of how the present value of a stream of benefits is calculated.

[2] Miller, Paul, Charles Mulvey, and Nick Martin. 1995. "What Do Twins Studies Reveal About the Economic Returns to Education? A Comparison of Australian and U.S. Findings," *American Economic Review*, Vol. 85(3):586-99.

[3] Ashenfelter, Orley, and Alan Krueger. 1994. "Estimates of the Economic Return to Schooling from a New Sample of Twins," *American Economic Review*, Vol. 84(5):1157-73.

[4] This range is calculated as follows: According to the statistics cited, blacks are paid an average of 30 percent less than whites, and 50 to 80 percent of this difference is due to productivity differences. In other words, 15 (.5 × 30) to 24 (.8 × 30) percent of the difference in wages is accounted for by productivity differences. Eliminating productivity differences would increase the salaries of blacks to 85 (70 + 15) to 94 (70 + 24) percent of what whites earn.

[5] Another impact of the legislation is generally beneficial to unions. Because unions are always attempting to increase wages and improve working conditions for their members, they must face up to the adverse employment consequences of higher labor costs. Unions attempt to minimize management's opportunities to substitute other inputs for unionized labor. Unskilled minimum-wage labor is one kind of substitute for union labor. When the price of this substitute rises because the minimum wage rises, the gains to the employer from using this substitute are reduced. In a relative sense, union labor is less costly. A higher minimum wage makes the demand for union labor less elastic.

[6] David Card and Alan Krueger, 1994, "Minimum Wages and Employment: A Case Study of the Fast-Food Industry in New Jersey and Pennsylvania," *American Economic Review*, Vol. 84(4):772-93.

[7] Donald Deere, Kevin Murphy, and Finis Welch, 1995, "Reexamining Methods of Estimating Minimum-Wage Effects," *American Economic Review*, Vol. 85(2):232-37; and David Neumark and William Wascher, 1995, "Minimum-Wage Effects on School and Work Transitions of Teen-agers," *American Economic Review*, Vol. 85(2):244-9.

[8] Robert E. Hall, 1982, "The Importance of Lifetime Jobs in the U.S. Economy," *American Economic Review*, Vol. 72(4):716-24.

Trade Unions and Collective Bargaining

Overview

In the preceding chapter, we stressed the unique characteristic of labor markets: Owners of labor services accompany their delivery to the workplace. Therefore, both monetary and non-monetary conditions of employment are important to workers. The bulk of most people's incomes is determined in the workplace, and workers spend a large portion of their time in their places of employment. We also showed how monopoly power on the buyer's side – labor market monopsony – can lower wages and employment. Throughout modern economic history, workers have sought to achieve more favorable employment conditions for themselves by generating their own monopoly power on the sellers' side of the labor market. They have tried to develop this market power through the organization of workers into labor unions.

Some of the most important issues in labor economics concern unions. In this chapter we examine a number of these issues. One might imagine that the introduction of such a major noncompetitive element as a labor union would cause us to abandon the supply and demand model of wages and employment. Such is not the case. In fact, we will rely heavily on the analysis of the two preceding chapters in evaluating the impact of unions. The underlying competitive supply and demand conditions in labor markets have a substantial effect on how successfully unions meet their goals. Unions, contrary to popular thinking, cannot set wages independently of market conditions. In this respect, unions are like monopolies. We have seen that monopoly power in the product market does not give a firm unlimited power to raise prices and profits. Like monopolists, unions are constrained by the level and elasticity of market demand.

Learning Objectives

After reading and studying this chapter, you will be able to:

1. Define labor unions and distinguish between craft and industrial unions

2. Summarize briefly the history and development of organized labor in the United States

CHAPTER 17

3. Identify factors contributing to the decline of labor unions in recent years

4. Identify the factors that limit the ability of unions to increase the wages of their members

5. Describe the objectives and economic impacts of labor unions

The Purpose of Labor Unions

Labor union:

A group of employees who band together to improve their terms of employment.

A **labor union** is an organization whose goal is to improve the terms of employment – both wages and working conditions – for its employee members, primarily by controlling the supply of labor to an industry. Sometimes these organizations are called *trade unions* because the early labor unions were organizations of skilled tradespeople such as carpenters, electricians, and cigar makers. Professional organizations like the National Education Association, the National Football League Players Association, and the Airline Pilots Association are also labor unions in the sense that they devote considerable resources to furthering the economic well-being of their members by using traditional labor union methods.

Unions seek to establish more favorable work rules surrounding the exchange of labor between a firm and its employees. Many aspects of the labor exchange have a public goods rather than private goods character to them. Recall from Chapter 5 that public goods are economic goods consumed jointly; the consumption of the good by one person does not reduce the quantity available for other consumers. In addition, it is difficult, if not impossible, to exclude specific individuals from consuming the public good. Workplace rules governing such things as safety procedures or conditions, established procedures for layoffs or overtime work, expected production per hour, and the responsibility assigned to supervisors have a public-goods dimension. Once established, they tend to benefit all employees at no additional cost. Like other public goods, however, they are underproduced if they are generated by individual action. Workers tend to free-ride. Why should I risk my job to complain about workplace hazards if Joe will complain? The problem is that individuals do not have an incentive to convey the true value of workplace rules to their employers. An organization representing the preferences of all workers can improve upon this free rider situation.

Craft union:

An organization that represents a particular type of skilled workers such as electricians, pipe fitters, or carpenters.

There are two main types of trade unions. The first employee organizations were **craft unions** (earlier called *guilds*), which sought to organize members of a particular skilled occupation. Today craft unions represent such skilled workers as electricians, pipe fitters, plumbers, boilermakers, and carpenters. *Craft unions attempt to raise wages by restricting entry into the union and occupation, frequently by controlling access to training opportunities for the craft.* Today much craft training occurs through union apprenticeship programs. When craft unions are able to reduce the supply of labor, as shown in Figure 17.1, wages rise while employment falls. Because the equilibrium wage with the union, W_U, is higher than the equilibrium wage without the union, W_1, those workers who are fortunate enough to be admitted and obtain employment will benefit. However, the higher-than-equilibrium wage creates an excess supply of workers. The union is forced to ration training opportunities as a result.

Industrial union:

An organization of workers in an entire industry; membership is not determined on the basis of a particular skill.

Industrial unions seek to organize all workers – regardless of skill – in an entire industry. This type of union developed much later than craft unions. The most commonly recognized examples of this type of union include the United Auto Workers (UAW) and the Teamsters Union. Because industrial unions represent less-skilled workers, they must try to organize *all* potential employees. If industrial unions restricted membership, firms

Figure 17.1

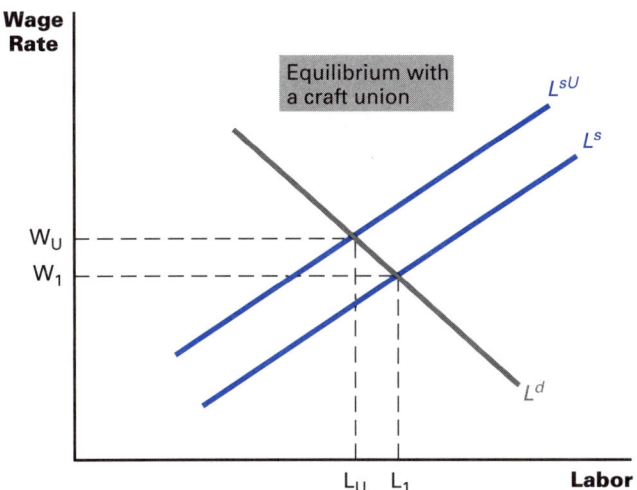

Craft Unions and the Supply of Labor

When craft unions are able to reduce the supply of labor, shown by the shift of the labor supply curve from L^S to L^{SU}, the equilibrium wage rises – $W_U > W_1$ – and the equilibrium level of employment falls – $L_U < L_1$. Those workers who are fortunate enough to be admitted and obtain employment benefit. However, the higher-than-equilibrium wage creates an excess supply of workers.

could simply ignore the union and hire from the pool of excluded workers. *Industrial unions attempt to improve wages and working conditions by direct negotiation with employers.* The primary source of an industrial union's bargaining power is its ability to withhold labor from the industry. If employment terms are unacceptable to the union, it attempts to obtain more favorable conditions by preventing the firm from producing output. The union attempts to persuade all employees to refuse to work and to prevent the firm from hiring replacement workers. The refusal to work is called a **strike**.

In Figure 17.2, all workers agree not to work for less than W_U, altering the effective labor supply schedule to $W_U a L^s$. Even though $L_1 - L_U$ workers are unemployed at this above–equilibrium wage, they have agreed not to work for less. *Taking wages out of competition* is an important union goal. There is evidence that unions have been successful in raising the wages of their members relative to nonunion labor.

In the United States, both craft and industrial unions seek to negotiate with the employer a written contract that governs the terms of employment. These contracts are very comprehensive, covering a wide array of workplace issues: wages, hours of work, vacations, pensions, length of work breaks, which job classes do which assignments, how worker grievances are handled, and much more. Because the union represents a group of employees in its negotiations with the employer, this process is called **collective bargaining**. For that segment of the U.S. workforce – approximately 13 percent in 1994 – that belongs to a

Strike:

An organized refusal by employees to work that is designed to obtain more favorable working conditions by preventing the firm from producing output.

Collective bargaining:

A union represents a group of employees in their negotiations with the employer.

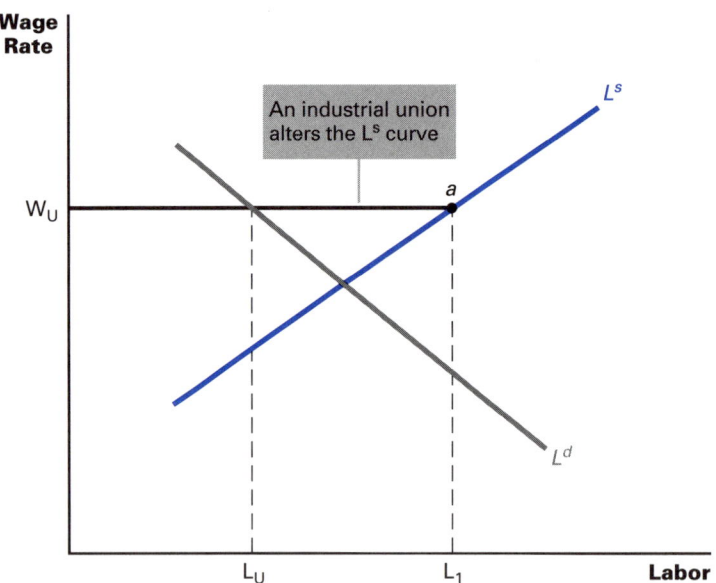

Figure 17.2

An industrial union alters the L^s curve

Industrial Unions and the Level of Wages

The primary source of an industrial union's bargaining power is its ability to withhold labor from the industry. In this way, the wage can be driven above the competitively determined equilibrium. As illustrated in this figure, if all workers agree not to work for less than W_U, this will alter the effective labor supply schedule to $W_U a L^s$, as shown by the heavy black line. Even though $L_1 - L_U$ workers are unemployed at this above-equilibrium wage, they have agreed not to work for less.

union, collective bargaining constitutes a significant departure from the perfectly competitive labor market model. Under competition, workers compete against each other for jobs by bidding down the wage rate. The essence of collective bargaining is that workers agree not to compete with one another, even if some workers become unemployed.

In the United States, there are over 200,000 collective bargaining contracts in existence. These contracts, typically two or three years in length, are usually renewed through union and management negotiations as the contract term expires. Most strikes occur during this period of negotiations. Strikes receive considerable attention. Firms shut down and workers go without pay. Strikes may even be accompanied by violence; they always produce frustration and anger for both sides. However, it is important to note that most contracts – more than 95 percent on average – are renegotiated without incident.

Section Recap

Labor unions work to improve wages and working conditions by using a variety of methods including restrictions on labor supply and direct negotiation with employers.

American Unionism: Structure and Membership

In 1994, 12.8 percent of the American workforce belonged to a labor union. Most of these approximately 16.7 million workers are members of the American Federation of Labor-Congress of Industrial Organizations (AFL-CIO). The AFL-CIO is a federation of approximately 95 independent national unions including such diverse industries and occupations as musicians, college teachers, autoworkers, and machinists. The AFL-CIO is an umbrella organization. It does not engage in collective bargaining; rather, it supports the entire trade union movement by focusing on the broader issues of organized labor's membership and influence. Perhaps the most important function of the AFL-CIO is to represent organized labor in political affairs. The AFL-CIO formulates positions on public policy issues and seeks to achieve favorable state and federal legislation through lobbying and support for pro-union political candidates.

Section Recap

The true power of organized labor in the United States resides with the national unions and their local union affiliates. There are about 195 national unions. As we noted above, approximately one half are affiliated with the AFL-CIO; the others are independents. Each national union represents workers in the same industry or occupation, depending on whether it is an industrial or craft union. Most of the 41,100 local unions are affiliated with a national union. Whether part of the AFL-CIO structure or not, much of the power of organized labor is focused in the national unions' offices. Generally, contract negotiations are conducted by the national unions, with ratification by local unions. The national unions exercise strong control over the locals. For example, frequently only the national union can authorize a strike.

Local unions represent grass-roots unionization. They administer the contract, perform the important function of overseeing the grievance machinery, and communicate the concerns of union members to the national office.

The characteristics of the 16.7 million union members reveal much about the past growth and future prospects of the trade union movement in the United States. Table 17.1 shows that union membership among employed workers is highest in the public sector. Unionism is also strong in the transportation and public utilities sector and manufacturing industries. Blue-collar workers are more likely to be union members than are white-collar employees, and males are more likely than females to belong to unions. Finally, unions organize a greater share of nonwhites than whites.

These patterns should be interpreted with caution. The differences do not necessarily reflect a greater preference for unions among males or nonwhites. They may merely reflect the occupational and industrial patterns of unionization. For example, females are more likely than males to hold white-collar service jobs, which traditionally have had low rates of unionization.

Currently, approximately 13 percent of the workforce is unionized. The majority of union members are public service employees and blue-collar workers in the utility and manufacturing sectors of the economy.

Are Strikes Logical?

Why do strikes occur? Management would prefer that they never did. Firms may find it less costly to raise wages and benefits than to incur the costs of being shut down. For the union, the right to strike is an important source of bargaining power. Unions feel that the strike threat is effective only if the strike weapon is used every so often. Nonetheless, strikes are costly to both sides: Firms lose production and profits, and workers forfeit wages. Moreover, any final contract agreement could have been reached without a strike. Do strikes make economic sense?

One theory is that strikes are a result of imperfect information; they occur when one side underestimates the bargaining strength and resolve of the other. The process of collective bargaining begins with both sides making offers that are far apart. In Figure 17.3, the union's initial demand is W_U, while the firm offers W_C. That the two sides are initially far apart reflects optimal bargaining strategy. The costs of making an offer are low because there is plenty of time before the strike deadline (T_S) to make concessions. At the same time there is always the possibility that the other side will accept or be so impressed that it revises downward its expectations of what it can get and begins to make concessions faster. In the early stages of bargaining, you should expect to hear union leaders complaining that "management is trying to take away everything we have achieved over the last twenty-five years." Management pleads that unions are out to "bankrupt" the firm.

As the strike deadline approaches, each side begins to

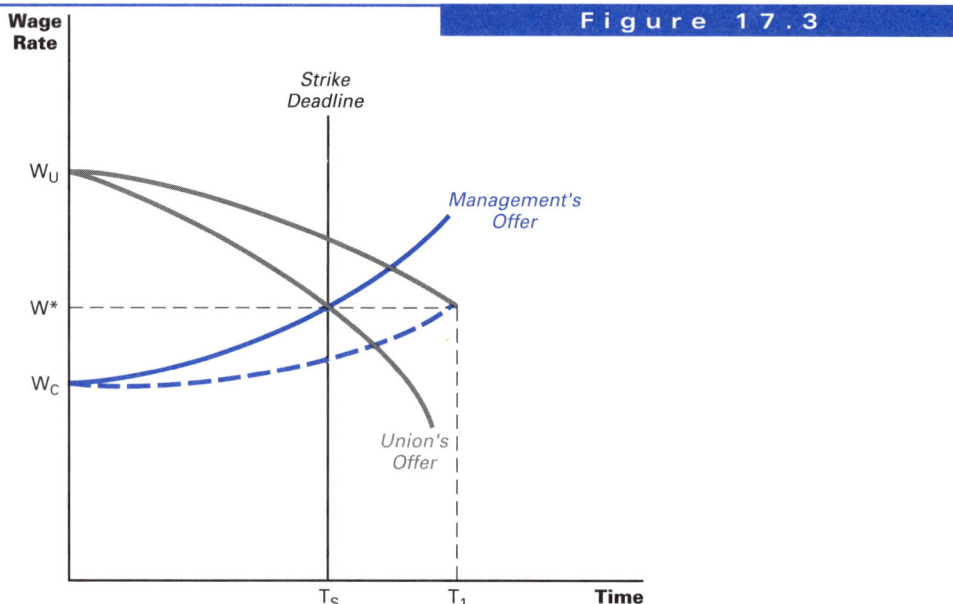

Figure 17.3

Wage Bargaining in the Face of a Strike Deadline

One theory of strikes is that they occur when one side underestimates the bargaining strength and resolve of the other. In this figure, the union's initial demand is W_U, while the firm offers W_C. However, as the strike deadline approaches, each side will begin to make concessions. An agreement is reached when the union and firm offer curves intersect, and both sides agree to W^*. However, suppose the two sides remain far apart at the strike deadline, as depicted by the dashed offer curves. A strike results when bargainers believe that the benefits of a better contract (resulting from a strike) will outweigh the costs of the strike. Negotiations continue during the strike and eventually W^* is reached after a strike of $T_1 - T_S$ days.

make concessions for two reasons: (1) the probability of a strike increases and (2) each side learns more about the other's bargaining strength. An agreement is reached when the union and firm offer curves intersect, and both sides agree to W*, as shown in Figure 17.3. As depicted, both sides make concessions near the deadline, and a strike is averted.

Why do the bargainers waste time early with unrealistic bargaining positions, only to have marathon round-the-clock sessions up to the strike deadline? Again, optimal bargaining strategy requires each side to withhold major concessions until the last minute, hoping that the other side will compromise more. The last-minute rush is a feature of any bargaining situation, whether it be trade talks between the United States and Japan, salary negotiations between a professional athlete and a sports team, or legislative negotiations between the House and Senate.

However, suppose the two sides remain far apart at the strike deadline, as depicted by the dashed offer curves. A strike results when bargainers believe that the benefits of a better contract (resulting from a strike) outweigh the costs of the strike. Each side believes it can do better by refusing the other's last offer and continuing to negotiate during the strike. Negotiations continue and eventually W* is reached after a strike of $T_1 - T_S$ days. In hindsight, both sides realize that W* could have been agreed to without a costly strike. A strike has occurred because one side was mistaken about the concessions the other side would make.

Note that strikes do not occur if one party is in a much stronger position than the other. If the industry faces a high demand for its product and low inventories, and if the union has a rich strike fund to pay benefits to its members, management knows that the union is in a strong position. It is better for management to yield quickly to the inevitable higher wage than to suffer a strike and still end up paying more.

The *mistake theory* suggests that strikes do not make economic sense, and thus they should be fairly rare. The tremendous media attention that surrounds a strike may give the impression that collective bargaining frequently breaks down without agreement. Such is not the case. U.S. Department of Labor statistics indicate that from 1980 to 1993 the United States lost less than one-tenth of 1 percent of work time to strikes in each of those years.

Union Membership in the United States: Growth and Decline

Table 17.2 reveals that the extent of unionization in the United States has been far from constant. Through 1930, unions represented a very small portion of the workforce. However, the Great Depression saw a spurt in union membership that continued through World War II and peaked in the mid–1950s at about 25 percent. Since then, union membership has steadily declined as a percentage of the workforce. What explains this pattern of growth and decline?

Labor Unions Prior to the 1930s

Trade unions were formed in the United States shortly after the birth of the republic. However, as Table 17.2 shows, they really did not gain a significant foothold until 150 years later. This is explained, in part, by the fact that before 1935, there was no federal legislation that guaranteed the right of workers to organize and bargain collectively. Instead, the courts were left to rule over disputes between a union and a firm's management, and the legal system was generally hostile toward unions.

In these early cases, courts applied the common law doctrine of criminal conspiracy to union organizing. They held that a union was, by definition, an organization that sought to artificially raise the price of labor and thus was illegal, just as a cartel of businesses that engaged in price fixing would be illegal. Later decisions relaxed the position that unions were per se illegal, but the courts still allowed management an arsenal of powerful union-

Table 17.1	

Union Membership in 1994

Category	Percent of Employed*
Total:	15.5%
Industry:	
Government	38.7%
Transportation and public utilities	28.4%
Manufacturing	18.2%
Wholesale and retail trade	6.2%
Occupation:	
Operators, fabricators, and laborers	24.1%
Managerial and professional specialty	14.4%
Technical, sales, and administrative support	10.3%
Service occupations	14.3%
Sex:	
Male	17.9%
Female	12.9%
Race:	
Black	20.6%
White	14.8%
Hispanic	14.2%

* Data are for 1994.

Source: U.S. Department of Labor, Bureau of Labor Statistics, *Employment and Earnings,* Vol. 42, No. 1, January 1995, Tables 40 and 42.

busting tools. Among these were (1) court injunctions against striking, (2) *yellow dog contracts*, through which a worker agreed not to join the union as a condition of employment, and (3) the right to refuse to bargain if a union were formed.

Organized Labor's Golden Years: 1935 to 1955

The 1930s brought both the Great Depression and the New Deal. The Roosevelt administration actively encouraged the growth of trade unions and delivered two favorable pieces of legislation that kicked off twenty years of union growth. The *Norris-La Guardia Act* of 1932 effectively eliminated two of management's strongest anti-union weapons. It declared the yellow dog contract to be unenforceable in federal courts and severely restricted the ability of employers to gain federal court injunctions.

The *Wagner Act (National Labor Relations Act of 1935)* was even more favorable to unions. Essentially, its provisions sought to enforce the idea that the decision of whether to join a union was the worker's alone. The Wagner Act established legal procedures for conducting unionization elections as well as sanctions against employers who attempted to interfere with union organizing efforts. Perhaps more importantly, it established that management had a legal obligation to bargain in good faith once workers established a union. Failure to do so was an unfair labor practice punishable under federal law. The Wagner Act

Table 17.2

Union Membership, Selected Years

Year	Membership (millions)	Percentage of Labor Force	Percentage of Nonagricultural Employment
1880	0.2	n.a.	2.3
1890	0.4	n.a.	2.7
1900	0.8	n.a.	5.2
1910	2.1	n.a.	9.8
1920	5.0	n.a.	18.3
1930	3.4	6.8	11.6
1940	8.7	15.5	26.9
1950	14.3	22.3	31.5
1955	16.8	24.7	33.2
1960	17.0	23.6	31.4
1965	17.3	22.4	28.5
1970	19.4	22.6	27.4
1975	19.6	20.3	25.5
1980	20.0	18.8	22.1
1985	17.0	14.4	16.3
1990	16.7	13.2	14.6
1992	16.4	12.8	14.3
1993	16.6	13.0	14.3
1994	16.7	12.8	14.0

*These figures include membership in professional associations.

Source: U.S. Department of Labor, *Handbook of Labor Statistics*, 1980; U.S. Department of Labor, Bureau of Labor Statistics, *Employment and Earnings*, January 1987, 1991, 1993, 1995.

established an independent regulatory authority, the National Labor Relations Board, to implement provisions of the legislation.

By the 1930s the character of America's modern industrial relations system was taking shape. The legislation in this period embodied its most important feature: free collective bargaining. From this period to the present, the government has attempted to establish the rules of the game for labor-management relations, while leaving both parties alone to settle the specific terms of their relationship. Often it is a delicate balancing act. Government control of labor-management relationships is intended to be objective, not giving an advantage to labor or management. The legislation attempts to protect the rights of individual workers to free choice in their relationship with their employers, but it also recognizes the rights of groups – unions – that do succeed in improving the terms of employment for all employees.

Assisted by this legislation, industrial unionism grew rapidly. The Congress of Industrial Organizations (then separate from the American Federation of Labor) quickly organized many major industries, including meat packing, rubber, and steel.

Stagnation and Decline: 1955 to the Present

Since reaching its peak in 1955, the union sector has slowly but steadily declined as a percentage of the total workforce. The obvious question is whether this trend will continue or whether a reversal of union fortunes can be expected in the coming decades. The answer depends on what caused the decline. While there is much disagreement about the relevant factors, several possible explanations have been offered:

1. Unfavorable legislation. In 1947, a more conservative Congress enacted the *Taft-Hartley Act*. This legislation significantly reduced the power of organized labor and was designed to balance the power of labor and management. The new law altered the union security provision that defines the relationship between the firm's employees and the union. It outlawed the **closed shop** provision, which had required employers to hire only union members, in favor of the **union shop**, which allowed employers to hire anyone they wished, but required the new employees to join the union after they had been hired. The union shop is a compromise between the closed shop and an **open shop**, an arrangement whereby employees do not have to belong to a union if they choose not to.

   The Taft-Hartley Act also established more stringent unfair labor practices for unions. The act's most controversial provision allowed individual states to pass *right-to-work* legislation, which allows a worker the option of not joining a union even if the workplace is organized. States can essentially establish the open shop rule by enacting right-to-work legislation. At present, twenty-one states have adopted right-to-work statutes. Organized labor has sought unsuccessfully to repeal or modify the Taft-Hartley Act since its inception.

2. Structural changes in the economy. This hypothesis recognizes that certain sectors of the economy are more conducive to unionization. The data cited earlier suggest that goods-producing industries are more receptive to unionization than service industries. Also, blue-collar and male workers seem more likely to join unions than female and white-collar employees. Over the period that the union sector has been in decline, growth in total employment in the United States has favored the nonunion sector. In the post-war period, goods-producing employment has fallen relative to that in the service sector, and white-collar employment has grown faster than blue-collar employment. This period also has seen a dramatic increase in the number of women entering the labor force. Another factor is the expansion of employment in traditionally nonunion southern and southwestern states. These structural changes suggest that union membership would have declined even if basic attitudes toward unionization were unchanged.

3. Substitution of government for unions. Many of the social services now provided by state and federal government had their roots in early union contracts. Programs such as Social Security, workers' compensation, unemployment insurance, and occupational safety and health regulations have roots in collective bargaining. Gradually, government has replaced the trade union as the supplier of these services. One view

Closed shop:

Employers are able to hire only union members.

Union shop:

Employers can hire anyone they wish; however, new employees must join the union after they have been hired.

Open shop:

Employees are not required to belong to a union if they choose not to.

of union decline is that, with the government so heavily involved in providing benefits and employment security, workers no longer feel it is necessary to belong to a union. In essence, government substitutes for unions.

There are two problems with this theory, however. Expansion of government services does not reduce union bargaining strength. If unions have the power to compel employers to provide costly fringe benefits or improved job safety, why don't they bargain for higher wages or other benefits when the government takes over the former? Second, there is the intriguing question of why the AFL–CIO has strongly supported the expanded role of government if the effect is to diminish its own influence. Currently, organized labor endorses national health care. Are they aware that this would diminish the value of union contracts, which generally provide very generous health care benefits, or are they confident that, with the federal government guaranteeing health care, they could bargain instead for higher wages?

4. Active management opposition. There is evidence that employers are becoming more aggressive in opposing the introduction of unions and in decertifying unions that are already in place. (Just as workers have a legal right to vote to establish a union, they also have the same right to vote to throw out an existing union. The latter process is accomplished through a **decertification election**.) At the national level, conservatives have begun to press their views that federal labor legislation is unbalanced and bestows too much power on organized labor.

Decertification election: Workers vote on whether to remove an existing union from their workplace.

In the case of Eastern Airlines in the late 1980s, for example, management was unsuccessful in getting labor to agree to a wage cut that management maintained was necessary for Eastern to remain competitive. Subsequently, Texas Air, which controlled both Eastern and Continental (which was nonunion) began selling part of Eastern's operations to Continental. However, a federal judge ruled that this was a violation of federal labor law and ordered Texas Air to stop. Eastern's mechanics went on strike when management refused to settle on a new contract.

More recently, Caterpillar, Inc. was struck by the United Auto Workers (UAW) in June 1994 (the strike was still ongoing 15 months later when this book was being written). Among a number of issues over which the union and company management disagreed, one of the union's major complaints was that the company was trying to break the union. Management responded that the union was imposing unrealistic demands on the company.

As a percentage of the workforce, membership in unions peaked in the 1950s and has steadily declined since then. Possible explanations for this decline include unfavorable legislation, structural changes in the economy, substitution of government provision of certain services, and active management opposition to unions.

Section Recap

The Days of Wine and Unions

In June 1995, the farm workers employed by Chateau Ste. Michelle, the largest winery in Washington state, voted to be represented by the United Farm Workers union. The fact that the workers were even able to vote on the proposal was noteworthy, not only because the company did not oppose the move, but because "outside California, 'this is the first time a mechanism [was]...found to let farm workers decide on union representation'."[1] One of the unique features of the process that led up to the workers' vote on whether to unionize was an agreement between the company and the workers guaranteeing that the company would submit to arbitration if the union were approved and a contract settlement could not be reached. Not surprisingly, many of the growers in the region opposed the agreement, as well as the more general movement in the direction of increased labor rights. However, other growers viewed the agreement as a step in the right direction. Why the disagreement?

Those in favor of the approach, including the United Farm Workers union and some of the potentially affected growers in Washington and other states, emphasized, among other things, their preference for voluntary arrangements over direct government intervention. At the present time there is no federal law that guarantees the rights of farm workers to organize. Among the various states, only California has passed such legislation. Chateau Ste. Michelle supported similar legislation in Washington for six years, but no bill was passed. Thus, for farm workers to organize requires the cooperation of the employers in question. However, increased efforts by workers could result in the passage of such legislation. Support for voluntary arrangements such as the one between Chateau Ste. Michelle and its workers could forestall the impetus for pursuing legislated remedies.

One of the advantages of voluntary arrangements relative to legislated labor rights is the increased

The Goals of Labor Unions

The impact of trade unions cannot be evaluated until we have a theory of what unions try to do. When we assumed single-minded objectives for consumers and producers, namely utility and profit maximization, we were able to derive fairly specific predictions about their behavior in markets. Unfortunately, identifying a similarly single-minded labor union goal appears to be impossible. Samuel Gompers, a cigar maker and the first president of the AFL, was once asked just exactly what trade unions wanted from employers. His response was straightforward: "More, more, and more." While Gompers's opinion on union goals may be accurate, it misses an important point. Clearly, unions would prefer to maximize both employment and wage rates. However, the downward-sloping demand curve for labor implies a tradeoff between these goals.

The weakness of always pursuing only a higher-wages objective is apparent from Figure 17.4. Given downward-sloping labor demand, the wage rate is maximized when only one worker is employed. Of course, no rational union leader would pursue a strategy that causes all members but one to lose their jobs. This patently absurd result suggests that, in general, unions do not always demand more and more, even if they are powerful enough to impose their demands on the industry.

flexibility associated with the former. Under a voluntary arrangement, workers and the company are able to forge agreements that might not be possible in the case where such arrangements are governed by law. In particular, under a voluntary system it is possible for one side or the other to make concessions based on unique characteristics of the employer or employees in question. Such concessions might be precluded by legislation that spells out, point by point, a worker's rights and corresponding limitations on what the employer can and cannot stipulate in a labor contract. Thus, an argument could be made that voluntary arrangements encourage a greater degree of efficiency than legislated workers' rights.

Those opposed to the voluntary arrangement between Chateau Ste. Michelle and its workers included many of the growers in the region. Their opposition was no doubt motivated, in part, by general opposition to unions and the bargaining clout they impart to their members. Many farm workers are migrants, moving from one location to another as demand for their labor increases and decreases with the seasons in different parts of the country. Given the relatively large pool of unskilled workers who are able to do this type of work, there is a high degree of competition among workers for jobs. The competition acts to hold down wages. Being able to organize into a union would provide farm workers with additional bargaining power, not only with respect to wages, but also with respect to such benefits as health insurance. Thus, it is likely that employers' labor costs could increase substantially.

Opposing both voluntary agreements and labor rights legislation is therefore consistent with a desire to maintain an advantage in bargaining situations. This raises the question, Why would some growers appear to be willing to give up this advantage? One possible answer is that by allowing workers to organize and bargain for an improved level of compensation, employers might see an increase in the workers' productivity. Increased productivity could spring from an improvement in worker morale, which results from allowing workers to have a greater say in the terms of their employment.

Clearly, it is difficult, if not impossible, to say, before the fact, which approach would benefit employers more. Opposing voluntary agreements could enable employers to maintain the status quo indefinitely. However, it is also possible that labor rights legislation could be passed, making the organization of additional workers more likely. On the other hand, entering into voluntary agreements may or may not enhance labor productivity. In any event, there is likely to be considerably more activity in the area of farm labor's rights in the years to come.

The union must be prepared to trade off higher wages against employment losses. Readers who think this is just a sterile theoretical point – that unions, practically speaking, never are able to push wages high enough to worry about excessive employment losses – should review the collective bargaining experiences of the 1980s, when the economy went through the worst recession since World War II. To save jobs, many unions actually agreed to accept reduced compensation. Frequently the alternative to such givebacks was a plant closing.

A Public Choice Model of Union Decision Making

The emphasis thus far has been on unions as organizations whose aim is higher wages. However, for understanding union objectives and behavior, probably the most useful way to view unions is as political organizations. Unions are organizations of workers who represent the collective preferences of their members. The aims of labor unions reflect the aims of their members. Union leaders and members face a situation very similar to that faced by voters and politicians. Union leaders are elected by the membership. Their job is to achieve the goals of the membership. Thus, we can better understand union behavior by applying the simple principles of the economics of public choice that we first introduced in Chapter 5.

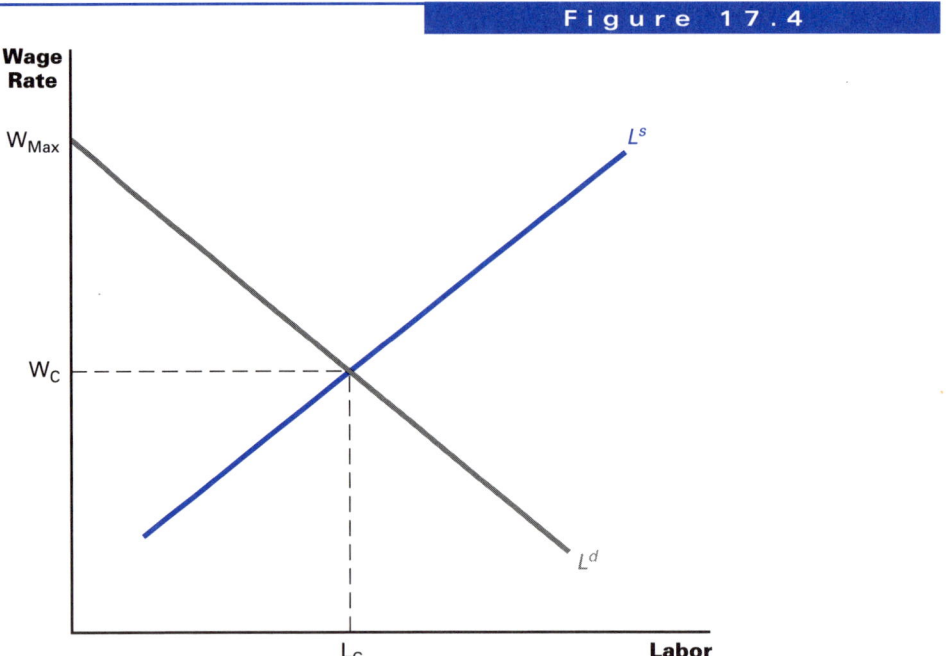

Figure 17.4

Higher Wages as a Union Objective

This figure illustrates the weakness of always pursuing only a higher-wages objective. Given downward-sloping industry demand, the wage rate is maximized (at W_{max}) when only one worker is employed. Of course, no rational union leader would pursue a strategy that causes all members but one to lose their jobs. This patently absurd result suggests that, in general, unions will not always demand more and more, even if they are powerful enough to impose their demands on the industry.

The goals of the membership are determined by the preferences of the union members, their heterogeneity, and the economic environment of the firm and the economy. (The price elasticity of demand for labor is an important determinant of union goals and strategy.) The objective of union leaders is to be reelected by delivering those benefits that the membership wants. Failure to do so can cost the leader his job.

Workers are motivated by better pay and working conditions. We expect these to be general union goals. More specific objectives vary by union, industry, and period of time. Within the same company, at a given point in time some workers would rather have higher wages, while others would rather have lower wages but a better pension plan. Others want more paid time off instead of higher wages. Since members essentially vote to determine the union's specific objectives in a given bargaining year, the size and heterogeneity of the union influence the extent of consensus within the union on its objectives. Smaller craft unions have an easier time establishing priorities because the members are very similar. Larger industrial unions have a much more difficult time agreeing on specific objectives. Worker groups with different skills want different benefits; different age groups have different needs. The size and political power of these groups determine their relative influence in the union's decision making. If the union votes by majority rule, a significant number of members are always at least somewhat dissatisfied with the leadership. This factor explains some of the observed internal dissension in unions.

A union's bargaining goals vary with economic conditions. When employment is strong and growing, workers tend to want to push for better pay, more time off, and so forth. For example, in inflationary periods many unions negotiated automatic wage increases tied to increases in the cost of living, so-called **cost of living adjustment** clauses, or COLAs. During periods of substantial inflation union members wanted this type of inflation protection. At the same time a strong demand for labor eased the employment consequences of wage increases.

Cost of living adjustment:
A negotiated automatic wage increase that is tied to increases in the cost of living.

However, during recessions the environment is much different, and union objectives change. With slow growth or no growth in output, unemployment becomes a concern. Wage demands are moderated because the employment consequences are more severe. In fact, if unemployment is rising, unions may make job security one of their top demands. Unions seek to negotiate contracts that protect union members from layoffs and spread available work to more workers. In recessions union members are less concerned about inflation, and they are more willing to give up COLAs in exchange for other benefits.

Only one thing is clear: *No one goal can adequately describe the actions of all labor unions.* Unions are organizations whose purpose is to improve the collective welfare of their membership. While they seek generally better terms of employment, they are constrained by market forces to a greater or lesser degree. Their structure is designed to ensure (ignoring corruption) that their leaders will attempt to achieve whatever gains most members want under prevailing economic conditions.

Section Recap

According to the public choice theory of union behavior, unions' objectives vary with economic conditions. The goal of a union's leadership is to satisfy the majority of the union's members.

A Model of Unions' Impact on Wages and Employment

This section examines the economic impact of successful union efforts to obtain above-equilibrium wages for their members. A reasonable assumption is that a union will strive to negotiate wages that are somewhat higher than the prevailing level in the absence of the union. To simplify the analysis, assume that all labor in the United States is demanded by the two competitive industries shown in Figure 17.5. Assume also that all workers have the same skills and that jobs in the two industries have identical nonwage characteristics. Under these assumptions, workers receive the same wage in either industry, W_C. Now assume that workers in industry A [Figure 17.5 (a)] are organized into a trade union that immediately negotiates a wage of W_U. The effective supply schedule to industry A becomes $W_U a L^s$, as union workers agree not to undercut the *union scale* of W_U. The result is a higher wage but lower employment; $L_C - L_U$ workers lose their jobs in industry A.

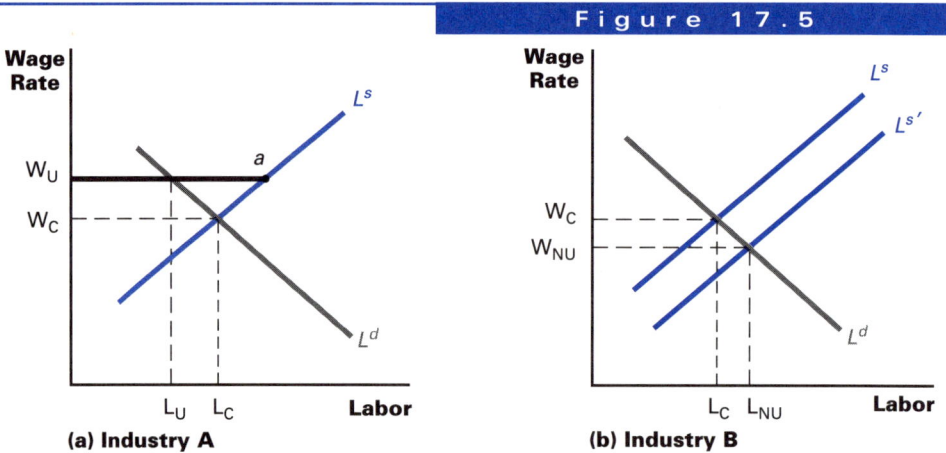

Figure 17.5

The Effect of a Union on Union and Nonunion Wages (a) *Industry A* (b) *Industry B*

This figure illustrates the economic impact of successful union efforts to obtain above-equilibrium wages for their members. Assuming that all labor is demanded by the two competitive industries A and B, that all workers have the same skills, and that jobs in the two industries have identical nonwage characteristics, all workers receive the same wage, W_C. Now assume that workers in industry A [Figure 17.4 (a)] are organized into a trade union that immediately negotiates a wage of W_U. The effective supply schedule to industry A becomes $W_U a L^S$. The result is a higher wage but lower employment. Those who have lost jobs may be expected to spill over into nonunion industry B [Figure 17.4 (b)], raising employment and lowering wages in industry B.

Unless there is some mechanism to spread the unemployment across all L_C workers evenly (such as *work sharing* in the form of a shorter work week for everyone), those who have lost jobs may be expected to spill over into nonunion industry B [Figure 17.5 (b)]. The increased supply of labor raises employment and lowers wages in industry B. This spillover effect means that unionizing industry A has had adverse consequences on workers in industry B.

The impact of the union in competitive labor markets can be summarized as follows: (1) a union-nonunion wage differential of $W_U - W_{NU}$ appears, and (2) employment declines in the union sector, but increases in the nonunion sector. The reallocation of labor lowers economic efficiency and welfare. Workers who were more productive in industry A are now employed in industry B, where their marginal revenue product is lower. Not surprisingly, if labor is efficiently allocated by competitive labor markets, anything that disturbs this equilibrium reduces economic welfare.

Also note that the union causes no involuntary unemployment. All workers who become unemployed by the higher wage in industry A and are willing to work at the lower wage of W_{NU} find work in industry B. However, there is another possibility that could lead to unemployment. Suppose firms in industry B fear that their workers also will organize a union and therefore counter this threat by raising wages above W_C. They hope that workers will be satisfied with a wage close to W_U and will not undergo the expense of an organization drive and union dues. Wages rise in industry B due to a **threat effect**. If wages are higher in both industries, employment must fall and some workers become unemployed.

Unemployment also results if workers decide not to spill over into industry B. Workers who lose their jobs in industry A may feel they are better off waiting for a vacancy to open as a result of a quit, layoff, or retirement. (In addition, unemployment compensation may make it easier for workers to resist moving to industry B.) If the chance of a higher union wage is preferred to the certainty of a lower nonunion wage, workers will not spill over and unemployment will occur in industry A. Note, however, that this is voluntary unemployment – workers are willing to remain unemployed in hopes of earning higher wages in industry A.

Although unions can raise the wages of their members, this may lead to lower wages in nonunionized industries. The latter effect depends on how displaced workers in the unionized industry and management in the nonunionized industry react to the increase in wages.

Section Recap

Policies to Increase Union Power

Unacceptable job losses constrain the union from seeking a wage higher than W_U. For any given wage increase, employment loss is greater the more elastic the labor demand schedule. Thus, unions press harder to raise wages when demand elasticity is low. Recalling the determinants of resource demand elasticity, unions are in a stronger position when (1) the available substitutes for union labor are fewer, (2) demand for the product is less elastic, and (3) the ratio of labor costs to total costs is lower.

It should come as no surprise that unions have been unwilling to passively accept restrictions on their ability to raise wages. Instead, organized labor strives to improve the tradeoff between wages and employment. Much of the behavior of unions can be understood as an attempt to shift the labor demand curve outward and reduce its elasticity. Unions also support policies that reduce the likelihood that workers will undercut the union wage.

Policies to Alter the Demand Curve

Union organizations are aware of the consequences of obtaining above-equilibrium wage rates, although individual union members may not be. Union organizations are also aware of the factors that influence these consequences. Wage increases motivate employers to look for substitutes – either cheaper labor or other inputs to substitute for labor, or both. Unions try to offset these forces. They advertise the union label and encourage consumers to buy union-made products in an effort to increase demand for goods that become more costly with union success. (It is not clear that this campaign has much impact.) Unions also negotiate restrictive work rules to limit employers' opportunities to reduce employment. These work rules are known as *featherbedding* practices. When railroads switched from steam to diesel locomotives, they continued to employ the fireman, a third crew member who was really not needed on the new diesels. When technology reduced the need to employ linotypists to set some kinds of print for newspapers, the union negotiated contracts requiring that the type be set by linotypists anyway – and then destroyed.

We already know that unions support trade barriers to increase the demand for union members and reduce its elasticity. Limiting foreign competition means that U.S. industry faces a less elastic product demand. Union efforts to organize the many nonunion workers in the south can also be viewed as a policy to reduce the elasticity of union labor demand. While unions argue that they are organizing the south to bring the benefits of organized labor to these less fortunate workers, we know that organizing southern workers also increases the power of unions to raise the wages of their northern counterparts. If southern labor is unionized, the ability of firms to use a nonunion substitute by relocating in the south is eliminated.

Similar reasoning suggests why unions must organize a significant share of an entire industry. The more nonunion firms and workers, the greater the number of substitutes for union labor and the greater the elasticity of demand for the unionized firm's product. Unionized mines in West Virginia must take a very tough bargaining stance because they compete with nonunion western coal.

As another example, nonunion supermarket chains have provided an increasing amount of competition for unionized chains in local markets. In many areas of the country, local chains that utilize nonunion labor have been able to gain control of a growing share of the market. This increased market share has come at the expense of unionized national chains such as A&P, Kroger, Safeway, and Eagle supermarkets.

Section Recap

Unions attempt to improve their bargaining position by increasing the demand for labor and reducing the supply of available substitutes.

Policies to Prevent Undercutting the Union Wage

An important concern of unions is what happens to the workers who lose their jobs. A large number of unemployed workers is a potential threat to a union. If the unemployed are willing to work for less than the union wage, nonunion firms will hire them and produce at lower cost. This would force the union to lower its wage demands to allow organized firms to compete. Union leaders worry that the unemployed will become a nonunion substitute, or more colorfully, will *scab*.

Unions have supported a number of public policies to reduce this threat. Unemployment insurance provides income support to the unemployed, reducing the likelihood that workers, desperate for income, will undercut the union wage. Unions strongly support the concept of work sharing, which spreads the costs of unemployment. Instead of a minority of workers totally unemployed, work sharing means that all workers are prevented from working as many hours as they would like. The requirement that any work above forty hours per week be paid at time-and-one-half encourages firms to employ more workers rather than fewer workers more intensively. In certain situations firms find it less costly to add another shift than to use overtime. Union support for the four-day workweek also is consistent with work sharing.

Unions and Wages: The Evidence

Unions are able to raise wages because they control the supply of labor to an industry. If the union can effectively threaten to withhold all labor – to strike – management must weigh the costs of higher wages against the lost sales from being shut down. Thus, unions' bargaining strength varies across industries as the costs of a strike to management are different. How high unions desire to push wages depends on the elasticity of labor demand, which varies by industry. Not surprisingly, unions have had varying degrees of success at raising wages relative to nonunion members.

Ideally, we would like to measure the size of $W_U - W_C$ in Figure 17.5, which represents the increase in wages due to unionization. However, we only observe $W_U - W_{NU}$, the difference between equally productive union and nonunion workers. The wage of nonunion workers may be either higher or lower due to the union, depending on whether the threat effect or spillover effect is greater.

Surveys of statistical evidence[2] reveal that union workers earn from zero to 50 percent more than their nonunion counterparts, depending on occupation and industry. Unions appear to be more effective at raising wages in the construction industry and for blue-collar workers. The average wage gain across all industries and jobs has been estimated to fall in the range of 15 to 25 percent. In addition, there is evidence that the average union-nonunion gap varies countercyclically, rising in a recession (unemployment in the economy is rising) and falling during an expansion (unemployment in the economy is falling).

Other studies point to a spillover effect that is larger than the threat effect. Unions, on average, lower the wages of nonunion workers. Finally, Richard Freeman[3] of Harvard University has shown that earnings dispersion is narrower among union members. Wage differences among union members in similar occupations are less than the variation in the same jobs held by nonunion workers. Thus, unions appear to have made progress toward their goal of equalizing, as well as raising, members' wages.

The evidence concerning the success of unions at raising the wages of their members suggests another question: Who pays for these union gains? We have already indicated that the wages of nonunion workers can be reduced by union actions. There is strong evidence to support this hypothesis. It was noted in the preceding chapter that a large share (approximately two thirds) of national income accrues to labor. This share has remained virtually constant over the past fifty years, a period when union influence expanded greatly. *If unions have achieved wage gains, they have come from other workers. To the extent that unions raise production costs, consumers also pay for union gains.* Higher production costs tend to raise consumer prices.

Evidence suggests that unions have been able to raise the wages of their members by an average of 15 to 25 percent. However, these gains have come at the expense of other workers.

Section Recap

The Effects of Unions: Monopsony

It comes as no surprise that if labor markets are otherwise competitive, unions have a negative effect on economic efficiency. However, what if employers have monopsony power?

Figure 17.6 shows that unions may be able to offset an employer's monopsony power and simultaneously raise wages and employment.

In the absence of a union, the monopsonist employs L_M workers, where MRP = MRC, and pays a wage of W_M. Now suppose a union is organized to counter the firm's monopsony power. It bargains for a wage of W_U. The union wage floor changes the labor supply schedule to $W_U aL^s$, as before. Importantly, the new MRC schedule is equal to W_U up to L_U workers. The monopsonist is forced to pay the same constant wage whether one or L_U workers is hired. As a result it employs L_U workers, where the new MRC equals MRP. The union has increased wages and employment.

The reason the union can do both is that the wage floor removes the monopsonist's incentive to restrict hiring. No longer can the monopsonist reduce the wage by hiring fewer workers. The union counteracts monopsony power. Consequently, the potential for economic efficiency is enhanced. So long as the union does not raise the wage above W', employment and efficiency rise.

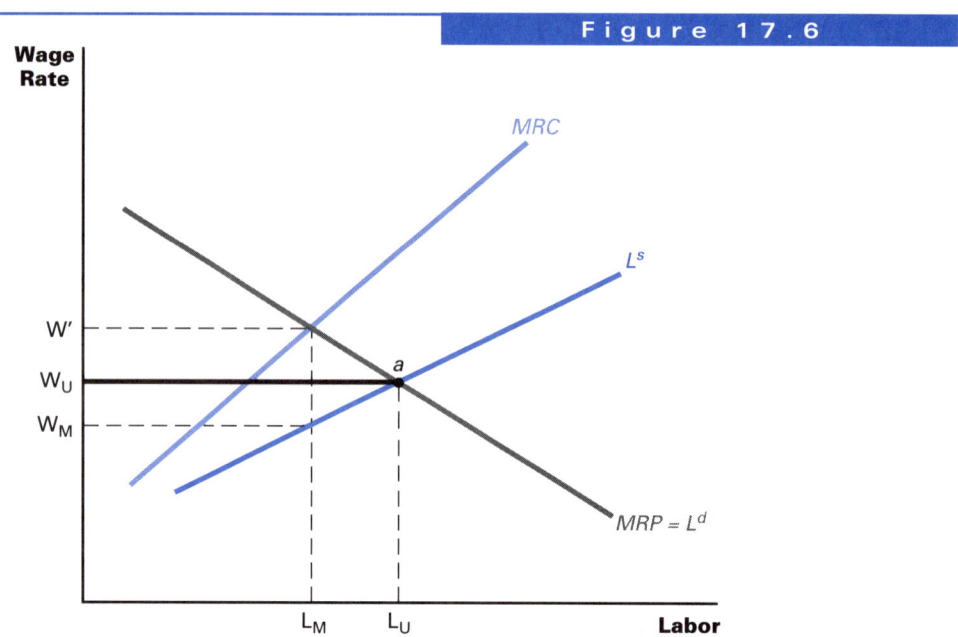

Figure 17.6

The Effect of a Union in a Monopsony Situation

Unions may be able to offset an employer's monopsony power and raise wages and employment. In the absence of a union, the monopsonist employs L_M workers, the employment level at which MRP = MRC, and pays a wage of W_M. Assuming a union is organized, it could bargain for a wage of W_U. The union wage floor changes the labor supply schedule to $W_U aL^S$. Importantly, the new MRC schedule is equal to W_U up to L_U workers. The monopsonist is forced to pay the same constant wage whether one or L_U workers is hired. As a result it employs L_U workers, because MRC equals MRP. So long as the union does not raise the wage above W', employment and efficiency rise.

In the case of a monopsony, a union can increase the level of wages and employment, as well as the level of efficiency, in the labor market.

Unions and Economic Welfare: A Broader View

The similarity between a trade union and a monopolist in a product market is striking. Unions raise wages and reduce employment. The reallocation of labor reduces total economic welfare. This economic analysis of union effects is a positive one; the normative judgment that is difficult to avoid based on the above analysis is that unions, like other forms of monopoly power, should be discouraged.

The reader should keep in mind, however, that we have focused on only one function of the union. Professors Richard Freeman and James Medoff[4] of Harvard University have forcefully advocated their view that unions, on net, are good for the economy. They argue that unions play a much broader role than simply bargaining for higher wages, and that the other union functions raise worker morale, job satisfaction, and productivity. Freeman and Medoff cite the grievance machinery, which reduces the likelihood that workers will be fired without cause; the reduction in compensation disparities; the seniority system; administration of the pension fund; and many other important union roles.

One major difference between the monopoly view of unions and the broader perspective of Freeman and Medoff is the effect of unions on productivity. The former suggests that unions lower productivity. If their main goal is to raise wages while protecting against job loss, unions will pursue contract provisions that establish minimum staffing requirements and restrict management's ability to adjust the production process. The union goal of wage equalization also may reduce productivity: If more productive employees are not paid more, there is little incentive to work harder.

Freeman and Medoff suggest that a more inclusive evaluation raises the possibility that unions may enhance worker productivity by improving worker morale and job satisfaction. In addition, the union provides a formal mechanism for transmitting production process improvements from the shop floor to the boardroom.

A weakness of the Freeman and Medoff hypothesis is that it conflicts with historic opposition to unions by management. If unions raise productivity, why doesn't management invite them in? There is evidence that, in fact, unions lower profitability and stock prices. Whether unions, on average, raise or lower worker productivity, Freeman and Medoff remind us that the role of unions is not confined to simply monopolizing the supply of labor. Economists increasingly are investigating the broader impacts of unions on productivity, on the allocation of capital through their control of pension funds, and on the political process.

Summary

Labor unions organize workers to improve the terms of employment for the membership. Unions represent a significant departure from the competitive labor markets described in the previous chapter. Yet it is easy to overstate the power of organized labor. Unions represent fewer than one in six American workers. In addition, unions do not have unlimited power to raise wages. Like the monopolist, a union is constrained by a downward-sloping demand schedule. Estimates are that unions raise wages on the average of 15 to 25 percent.

Unions also may have a negative effect on nonunion wages. One measure of the welfare of all workers is the share of national income received by labor. This ratio has remained virtually constant over the past fifty years, a period when union influence has expanded greatly, suggesting that union gains come at the expense of nonunion workers.

Legislation has played an important role in shaping the character and size of the labor movement in the United States. The government has attempted to establish the rules of the game and leave management and labor free to determine their own particular economic relationship. This system of **collective bargaining** involves the negotiation of written contracts between labor and management; these contracts cover virtually every facet of the labor exchange. This free industrial relations system is structured through two key pieces of legislation, the National Labor Relations Act of 1935 and the Taft-Hartley Act of 1947.

The negatively sloped demand for labor function is an important constraint on union efforts to improve wages and working conditions. Thus, unions have pursued an array of economic and political strategies to (1) shift the labor demand curve to the right and (2) decrease the price elasticity of demand for labor. In general, unions attempt to reduce the range of substitutes for union labor available to the firm, increase their cost to the firm, or do both.

Evaluating a union in its role as an agent of monopoly leads to the conclusion that unionization makes some workers better off, makes others worse off, and lowers net economic welfare. However, a more complete analysis requires recognizing the trade union's broader functions – as the arbiter of workplace disputes, communicator of employee concerns, fiduciary of union pension funds, lobbyist for pro-union legislation, and numerous others. Not all of these are necessarily beneficial for society in general, but they must be addressed before one comes to a judgment as to the net effect of unionization in the workplace and in society.

Questions for Thought

Knowledge Questions

1. In what years was the unionized share of the labor force the largest? How would you describe the pattern in this variable since World War II?

2. What piece of legislation is associated with the first real period of union growth? Why was this legislation a factor in union growth?

3. What is the average wage effect of unions?

4. Do unions increase or decrease the wages of nonunion workers? Explain.

Application Questions

5. Industrial unions pioneered the use of the *sit-down strike* in the 1930s. In this situation the striking workers just sit down and refuse to leave the plant. Why would this technique be adopted by industrial unions? Why is it effective?

6. Explain why the incidence of strikes tends to fall during recessions.

7. Management prefers an open shop; labor wants a union shop. Why?

Synthesis Questions

8. Occupations and industries in which women account for a large share of employment have usually had low rates of unionization. In recent years more women have been spending a larger fraction of their adult lifetimes in the labor market. Do you think this increased commitment to labor market participation will alter women's traditional lack of interest in unions? Explain.

9. The chapter discussion of unions makes clear the potential benefits to union membership. What are the costs of being a union member? Explain, considering true opportunity costs and the way a union might alter worker behavior in the work place.

10. In recent years, workers in some new firms have voted against unionization. Can you think of economic arguments for why labor may behave in this fashion?

End Notes

[1] G. Pascal Zachary, "Winery's Field Workers Break New Ground in Union Election," *The Wall Street Journal*, June 7, 1995, p. B1.

[2] H. Gregg Lewis, *Union Relative Wage Effects* (Chicago: University of Chicago Press, 1986), and Barry T. Hirsch and John T. Addison, *The Economic Analysis of Unions: New Approaches and Evidence* (Boston: Allen and Unwin, 1986).

[3] Richard B. Freeman, "Union Wage Practices and Wage Dispersion Within Establishments," *Industrial and Labor Relations Review* (1982), Vol. 36, No. 1.

[4] Richard B. Freeman and James L. Medoff, *What Do Unions Do?* (New York: Basic Books, 1982).

The Capital Market

Overview

In the preceding two chapters we examined the labor market, labor unions, and labor legislation in some detail. Now we turn our attention to another important resource market: the capital market. In Chapter 1 we defined capital as any man-made aid to production. It refers to any good produced for use in producing other goods or services – assembly lines, drill presses, earth movers, computers, electric generators, and so forth.

A country's real wealth is its ability to produce goods and services, and that depends to a large extent on the stock of real physical capital. Technological advancement and subsequent growth in the capital stock is the basis for the amazing rise in the standard of living among developed countries in the last 150 years. The large stock of capital per worker in the United States accounts for much of its high level of productivity and real income.

Note that the concern of this chapter is the creation of *physical* capital. In everyday parlance, the term *capital* is often used to denote financial capital-money assets. However, money only facilitates investment in real capital by providing a convenient way to transfer funds from savers to investors through financial markets.

The capital market is similar to the labor market. Capital is a productive input, and the general principles of supply and demand that determine the price and employment of any resource apply to capital as well. The level of capital investment and its allocation among competing uses is determined by the interaction of suppliers of investment funds (savers) with demanders of those funds (investors) in credit markets.

This chapter formally considers the definition of capital, examines the determinants of capital investment, and looks at the relationship between capital investment and savings. The role of financial markets and the rate of interest in the creation of capital are also considered.

Learning Objectives

After reading and studying this chapter, you will be able to:

1. Define the term *capital* and distinguish between a consumption good and an investment good

2. Define the present value of a future sum and calculate the profitability of an investment using the present value technique.

C H A P T E R   1 8

3. Define rate of return to capital

4. Define a firm's demand function for capital

5. Explain the relationship between saving and investment

Consumption or Investment: Costs and Benefits ... Again

One of the first economic choices that confronted human beings was whether to consume or to save and invest. People noticed that, if they were patient, they could increase their ability to produce and consume goods and services in the future by consuming less now and producing capital goods instead. Consider a community of early cave dwellers, which supported itself completely by scavenging for dead beasts. Initially, cave dwellers were scavengers – their bounty was limited to what they could find that had been killed by animals. Then someone realized that they could bring home more meat and hides if they killed their own beasts using spears. The problem was that someone would have to stay home and make the spears, which would mean less manpower available to scavenge for dead beasts and, temporarily, less current consumption of meat and hides. This was the opportunity cost of building spears (investing in capital).

If the cave dwellers were rational, they invested in spears up to the point at which the marginal benefits equaled the marginal opportunity costs. In other words, if the value of reduced current consumption of beasts was less than the value of increased future meat and hides, the spears were made. Clearly, the level of investment depended on two factors: how many beasts would be killed by the spears (the productivity of the capital) and how willing the community was to postpone consumption.

This is a simplistic illustration, but the main ingredients in the investment decision are the same for today's modern economies. Investment in capital can only be achieved by curtailing current consumption of final goods and services. The opportunity cost of producing capital is the value of reduced current consumption.

You may recall that the consumption-investment decision was one of the first economic decisions that we discussed in the book. Figure 18.1 illustrates the basic decision. Society can choose between two uses of its resources: consumption (C) or investment (I). If its production possibilities frontier (PPF) is F_{96} it can choose any combination of C and I so long as it is on or within its PPF, F_{96}. The investment option adds to the capital stock, generating increased quantities of goods and services in the future. The investment payoff is additional future resources and greater future output. If, in 1996, we choose combination B rather than combination A, we forgo more current consumption for greater investment. Our gain is an increased future stock of resources, yielding PPF F_{97B} instead of PPF F_{97A}.

Investment decisions must balance the cost – forgone consumption – against the benefits – an increased ability to consume in the future. The fundamental determinants of investment are (1) the productivity of capital goods and (2) the willingness of households to save a portion of their incomes, in other words, to forgo current consumption.

Section Recap

The decision to invest in capital goods involves a tradeoff between current and future consumption. An increase in investment requires a decrease in current consumption.

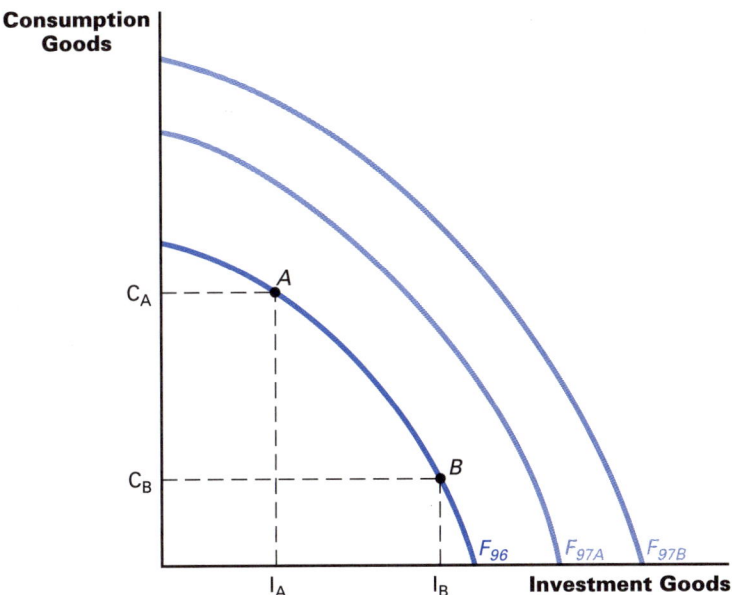

Figure 18.1

Consumption Versus Investment: Shifts in the PPF

This figure illustrates the effects when society chooses between two uses of its resources: consumption (C) or investment (I). Beginning with the production possibility frontier (PPF) labeled F_{96}, society can choose any combination of C and I as long as it is on or within the PPF. If, in 1996, society chose combination B rather than combination A, it would forgo more current consumption for greater investment. The gain is an increased future stock of resources, yielding PPF F_{97B} instead of PPF F_{97A}.

The Investment Decision

An important characteristic of investment, which you have probably already noticed, is that it takes time. We take resources out of consumption today, use them to produce additions to the capital stock, and then later employ the new capital stock to produce more output. *Investment is a long-run decision.* The costs and benefits accrue over a period of time, and often the benefits accrue over a much longer period of time than do the costs. The long-run nature of investment decisions has two important implications.

First, the costs of the investment must be weighed against its benefits. However, to determine the optimal level of investment and the equilibrium price for investment, we must compare benefits and costs through time. Because a dollar received or spent today has a value different from one received or spent next year, we must develop a way to make these comparisons through time.

484

Second, an investment decision is based on *anticipated* costs and benefits. We have acted as if the benefits and costs of investment are known with certainty, but they are not. Because costs and benefits are spread out into the future, they can only be anticipated or predicted. Investment decisions, therefore, are made with an element of uncertainty. This uncertainty can make investment activity more volatile than consumption. Investment is very sensitive to expectations and changes in expectations.

Demand for Capital

Like the demand for labor, the demand for capital is a *derived demand*. Firms invest in capital if it adds more to revenues than to costs. Just as with other productive inputs, *the amount of capital a firm employs depends on the physical productivity of capital, the price of the product, and the cost of capital*. However, there is one major difference between employment of capital and employment of other inputs. Employment of labor can be adjusted with relative ease. If the price of a firm's product declines, the firm can quickly lay off workers whose marginal revenue product has fallen below the wage. However, the firm cannot adjust its capital input so readily. A decision to purchase capital is a long-run commitment. If product demand declines unexpectedly, the firm may be stuck with a capital stock that is too large (unless it is able to sell off part of the capital stock). It cannot lay off plant and equipment. The firm must estimate the productivity of capital and product price for the length of the useful life of the capital. Comparing future benefits with current costs requires calculating the **rate of return** to dollars spent on capital.

Rate of return:
Calculated as the amount of profit attributable to a productive input expressed as a percentage of its cost.

Consider a manufacturing company that is planning to purchase a computer to improve inventory control. The computer has a cost of $1,000 and is expected to lower costs and therefore raise profits by $400 in each of the next three years before becoming obsolete. The computer will be purchased if it adds more to future profits than its initial cost. However, we cannot simply sum up future increases in profits and compare this sum with current costs. A dollar of profit to be received in the future is worth less than a dollar that is spent on the computer today; a dollar spent on the computer could have been earning the market rate of interest. The **time value of money** must be incorporated into our investment decisions. We illustrate how this is done with a simple example before we solve the computer investment problem.

Time value of money:
The amount of interest that a sum of money could earn over a fixed period of time.

Present value:
The amount of money that would have to be invested today at the market rate of interest to yield a future sum.

Present Value of a Future Sum

To understand how to compare dollar benefits or costs that accrue over time, we need to begin by discussing the compound interest problem. Suppose that you invest $100 for one year at a 7 percent market rate of interest. The **present value**, or *PV*, is the $100 you hold at present. The value of the $100 in one year, its **future value** (*FV*), when invested at 7 percent, is calculated as follows:

$$FV = PV(1 + 0.07) = \$100(1.07) = \$107$$

The investment problem requires a calculation that is the reverse of the compound interest problem. That problem involves determining the value today, *PV*, of a sum available in

Future value:
An amount of money held today plus the amount of interest that would accrue over the time period in question.

the future, *FV*. For the example above, the present value of $107 available in one year if the interest rate is 7 percent is calculated as:

$$FV = PV(1 + 0.07)$$
$$\$107 = PV(1.07)$$
$$\$107/1.07 = PV = \$100$$

The present value of $107 to be received in one year is that amount which, invested at 7 percent, yields $107 in one year. Similarly, the present value of $107 to be received in two years is:

$$PV = \$107/[(1 + .07)(1 + .07)]$$
$$= \$107/(1.07)^2$$
$$= \$93.46$$

The future value of $93.46 invested for two years at 7 percent is $107. In general, the present value of any sum, $X, to be received n years into the future is equal to:

$$PV_x = \$X/(1 + r)^n,$$

where *r* is the market rate of interest, and *n* is the number of time periods.

The process by which present value is calculated is called **discounting**, which is an abbreviated expression for *discounting to present value. Amounts to be received in the future are discounted more (1) the further into the future they are to be received, and (2) the greater the interest rate.*

Discounting:
The technique used to calculate the present value of a future sum.

The Computer Investment

Using the formula derived above, and assuming the interest rate is 7 percent, the present value of the benefits from the computer purchase is:

$$PV = \$400/(1 + .07) + \$400/(1 + .07)^2 + \$400/(1 + .07)^3$$
$$= \$373.83 + 349.38 + 326.52$$
$$= \$1,049.73$$

Because the $1,000 cost of the computer is incurred in the current period, it is not discounted. At a rate of interest of 7 percent, the present value of the benefits of the computer exceeds its cost, and the profit-maximizing firm will make the investment. The interest rate is a measure of the opportunity cost of investing the funds in the piece of capital. The higher the interest rate, the more costly it is to tie funds up in an investment. If the interest rate were 12 percent, the present value of the future profits would be only $960.73. In this case, the gain from the purchase is less than its cost. The computer would not be purchased.

In the computer example, the critical interest rate, denoted r^*, is 9.7 percent. At any rate above 9.7 percent the company will not make the investment because the present value of the investment would be less than $1,000. At an interest rate of 9.7 percent:

$$PV = \$400/(1.097) + \$400/(1.097)^2 + \$400/(1.097)^3 = \$1,000.$$

The critical rate of interest, 9.7 percent, is the **internal rate of return** earned by the $1,000 investment. The internal rate of return of an investment is defined as the interest rate that makes the present value of the stream of profits accruing from this piece of capital

Internal rate of return:
The interest rate that makes the present value of the stream of profits accruing from a piece of capital exactly equal to the present value of its costs.

exactly equal to the present value of its costs. Of course, the greater the dollar returns from an investment, the greater its internal rate of return. If the computer yielded $500 per period in increased profits, the critical interest rate would be greater than 9.7 percent.

Because the decision to invest in capital is a long-run decision, it is necessary to calculate the net present value of the stream of benefits from a capital purchase to determine whether it will be profitable.

Demand Curve for Capital

Ranking all possible capital investment projects by their internal rates of return, from highest to lowest, yields a demand curve for capital. Figure 18.2 is such a demand curve. It indicates that investment in capital for this firm yields internal rates of return ranging from 20 percent to zero. The declining internal rate of return to successive investments reflects the assumption that capital, like other inputs, is subject to declining marginal productivity.

We already know that a firm will employ any input up to the quantity at which marginal revenue product equals its marginal cost. Because the return to capital is computed

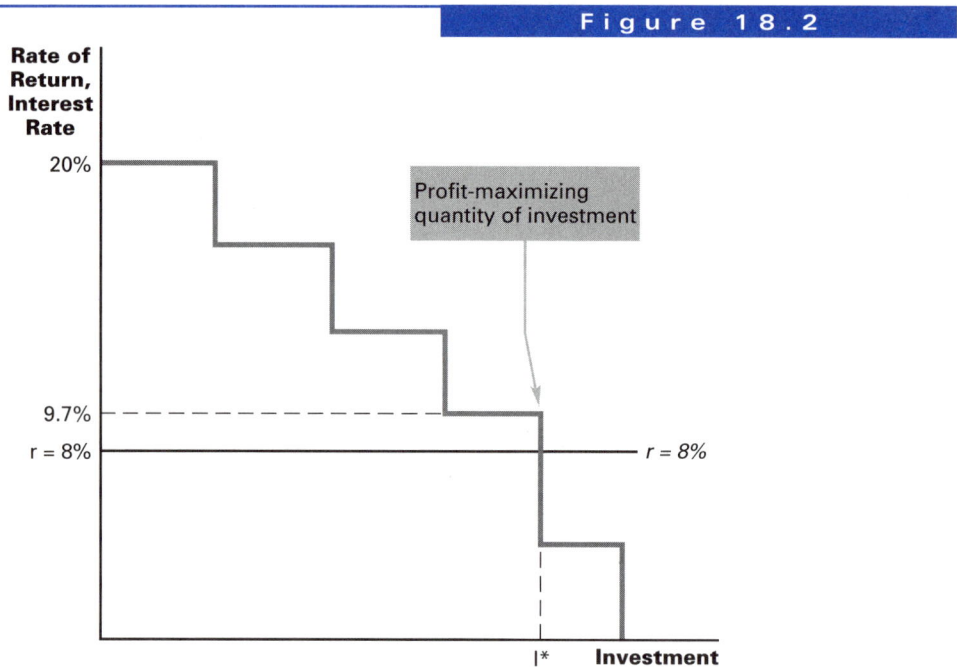

Figure 18.2

The Demand for Capital

Ranking all possible capital investment projects by their rates of return, from highest to lowest, yields a demand curve for capital such as the one shown here. The annual cost of the investment is equal to the market rate of interest. The profit-maximizing firm invests in all capital projects whose rates of return exceed the market rate of interest. For example, if the market interest rate is 8 percent, a firm increases its profits by investing in all capital that yields an annual return higher than 8 percent.

as an annual rate, we must compute the annual cost of capital. Whether the firm borrows the funds to purchase the capital or uses its own funds, the annual cost of the investment is equal to the market rate of interest. If funds are borrowed, the cost is explicit. If the firm uses its own funds, buying the capital good imposes an opportunity cost – the interest that could have been earned if the funds had been invested elsewhere.

In a world of certainty, the profit-maximizing firm invests in all capital projects whose rates of return exceed the market rate of interest. If the market interest rate is 8 percent, a firm increases its profits by investing in all capital that yields an annual return higher than 8 percent. Therefore, the ranking of investment projects in Figure 18.2 is a demand schedule for capital. Given a market rate of 8 percent, the firm invests in the computer and all other capital whose rate of return is greater than 8 percent. A proposed plant expansion that earns 7 percent will not be undertaken, however, unless the market rate falls to 7 percent or below. According to Figure 18.2, the desired stock of capital depends on the productivity of capital, the product price, and the market rate of interest. The first two factors determine the rate of return to capital investments, while the latter is the marginal cost of capital.

Capacity Utilization Rate When we think of unemployment, we usually think of unemployed labor. However, we do have a rough measure of capital employment, and therefore unemployment, as well. It is called the **capacity utilization rate** and is defined as the current output of goods and services as a share of total output that could be produced with existing plant and equipment. This measure is calculated for the manufacturing sector of the economy. Rates for the recent past are summarized in Table 18.1.

The capacity utilization rate is a measure of the share of existing capital equipment being used for current production. It is similar to labor unemployment in two ways. First, it fluctuates over the business cycle, rising as economy-wide output increases and falling during recessions as output is cut back. In the recession of the early 1980s, capacity utilization dropped as low as 73 percent from a peak value of 85 percent at the end of the long expansion that occurred during 1975-1979. Labor unemployment followed a similar pattern but simply moved in the opposite direction.

Second, just as labor unemployment seldom approaches zero percent, the capacity utilization rate seldom approaches 100 percent. In a large, dynamic, and growing market economy, resources constantly are moving around or are being switched from one use to another. These changes keep some of both capital and labor unemployed at all times. Furthermore, as the economy approaches its potential level of output, inflationary pressures build, prompting government measures to slow the growth rate. Output is seldom allowed to reach its potential.

Capacity utilization also affects investment decisions. If existing plant and equipment are underutilized, output can be increased without new investment. The gains from capital investment depend on the extent to which the capital is employed to produce output. When the capital utilization rate is low, expected profitability of new business investment is probably low also.

Capacity utilization rate:
The current output of goods and services as a share of total output that could be produced with existing plant and equipment.

488

Table 18.1	

Capacity Utilization Rates in Manufacturing, 1980-1994

Year	Utilization Rate
1980	80.2
1981	78.8
1982	72.8
1983	74.9
1984	80.4
1985	79.5
1986	79.1
1987	81.6
1988	83.6
1989	83.2
1990	81.3
1991	78.0
1992	79.2
1993	80.9
1994[a]	83.4

[a] Data for 1994 is average of monthly estimates through September and projections for October - December.

Source: Economic Report of the President: 1995, U.S. Government Printing Office, Table B-52.

Section Recap

A firm will find it profitable to invest in capital projects so long as the internal rate of return exceeds the market rate of interest. The capacity utilization rate also affects the expected profitability of new capital projects.

Investment Benefits

The computer example illustrated how to calculate the gain from an investment in a new computer. The gain came in the form of reduced production costs and increased profits. It is also useful to consider the gains from investment activity in a broader framework. The social gains from investment activity include reduced production costs, new goods and services of value to consumers, and increased productivity.

Reduced Costs

Additions to society's capital stock through investment activity can reduce costs in two ways — by taking advantage of economies of scale and technological innovation that results in lower average total costs of production at all output levels. Any time a firm adjusts its capital stock, that is, makes an investment decision, it is making a long-run resource allocation decision. When demand for a product increases, firms respond to the increased profit opportunities by expanding output. This long-run process involves the firm's adoption of a new cost-minimizing production function for the expected higher level of output. In Figure 18.3, such investment activity is represented by a shift from one short–run cost function, $SRATC_1$, to a new cost function at a higher output level, $SRATC_2$. The investment in new plant and equipment is profitable because it allows the firm to produce the greater output at a lower unit cost than it would have experienced employing the old production process. Compare, for example, the average cost of producing Q_1 units of output with $SRATC_1$ and with $SRATC_2$.

When economies of scale exist,[1] the average costs of production vary with the expected level of output: The larger the expected level of output, the lower are average costs. When economies of scale exist, the firms' investment for expansion results in even greater cost savings.

The long-run average cost function, $LRAC_1$ in Figure 18.3, represents the *cost frontier* for society. Given existing technology, costs cannot be reduced below that frontier. However, the devotion of time, effort, and money to research and development (R&D) can generate new, even more efficient production techniques. Note that R&D constitutes a specialized form of investment. The purpose of R&D is to create a more efficient, productive capital stock. Expenditures on R&D can result in increased production – which is generally associated with increased investment.

Figure 18.3

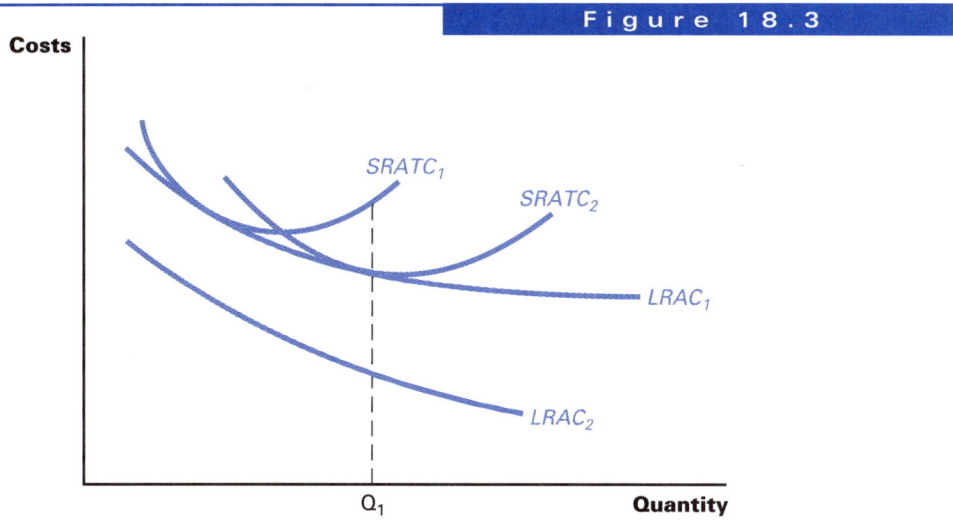

Improvements in Technology and Long-Run Average Total Costs

Additions to society's capital stock through investment activity can reduce costs in two ways. First, investment activity represented by a shift from $SRATC_1$ to $SRATC_2$ is profitable because the firm can produce greater output at a lower average total cost. Second, the long-run average total cost curve, $LRAC_1$, represents the cost frontier for society. Investment in research and development can generate new, even more efficient production techniques, resulting in an overall decrease in production costs as shown by the downward shift of the long-run minimum cost frontier, to something like $LRAC_2$.

In the case of R&D, the investment payoff is an overall decrease in production costs. This decrease means that society can have more output with the same quantity of inputs. The investment payoff is the reduced cost. Such technological progress, requiring lengthy investment periods, can shift the long-run minimum cost frontier down, to something like $LRAC_2$ in Figure 18.3.

Two recent examples of such developments illustrate the concepts just discussed. One advance involves a new process for making paper that may reduce energy costs by 50 percent. Another is the discovery of materials to achieve superconductivity at much higher temperatures than were previously believed possible. Although neither one has yet been adopted for commercial production, these developments hold out the promise for reduced costs of production and even greater computing power in smaller machines, as well as numerous other advances.

New Products

Investments in research and development also produce new final products, some of which are improvements on old products and some of which are completely new products or ideas. These products make consumers better off in some way. They may reduce work effort around the house, save consumers' time, or simply satisfy consumers' tastes in a better way. Here the payoff for the investment is in the form of profits to the firm whose investment has resulted in new products. Consumer electronics is a good example. New ideas and technologies in electronics, for example, the semiconductor and the microchip, have produced a host of new products for use as inputs as well as consumer products.

The investment process is driven by potential profitability. The examples above demonstrate this important force. Firms cannot control market prices. However, they can control costs within limits. Because the difference in revenue and costs is their motivation for being in business, there is a relentless effort to keep costs to a minimum and to develop new products expected to be of value to consumers. Investment in new capital and technology is an important path to lower costs and greater profit for business firms.

Productivity Growth

Productivity:
The amount of output produced per unit of input per time period.

Investment in improved capital can also result in increased **productivity** and, therefore, increase the overall level of output. When we speak of the economy's rate of productivity or changes in the rate, we usually refer to a measure of output per employee hour. Table 18.2 contains annual rates of change in output per hour in the United States for selected years. Just exactly what kind of productivity measure is this? The best way to explain the concept is to note what it is not. Output per (employee) hour is not a pure measure of the productivity of labor. This is because output per employee hour also reflects spillover effects of improvement in capital and technology that increase labor's ability to produce output.[2]

Table 18.2

Productivity: Annual Rates of Change in Output per Hour in the Business Sector

Period	Average Annual Rate of Change
1960–1969	2.4%
1970–1979	1.5%
1980–1989	1.0%
1990–1994[a]	1.6%
1990	0.7%
1991	1.3%
1992	3.0%
1993	1.5%
1994a	1.4%
1960–1994[a]	1.6%

[a] Figures for 1994 are average through third quarter, 1994

Source: Economic Report of the President: 1995, U.S. Government Printing Office, Table B-48.

Technically, output per hour is a ratio of an index of the output of goods and services to an index of hours of labor employed. It tells us output produced per hour of labor employed. If the output per hour index rises by 3 percent in a year, we would read in the local newspaper that productivity increased 3 percent last year. On average we were able to produce 3 percent more output with a given amount of labor.

Noting that productivity has increased leads to the question, To what is the increased productivity attributable? The answer to this question depends on all the factors of production and the extent of their utilization. For example, workers could be more productive, holding constant other inputs. Alternatively, additions to the capital stock – new equipment or improved technologies – could have accounted for the increased output. In addition, it could simply be greater utilization of existing plant and equipment. The increase could have resulted from better management techniques. Finally, it could be a combination of all these factors. This measure of productivity is a general one; it tells us only that we have been able to produce more – or less – output per hour worked than in previous periods.

We can see from Table 18.2 that overall productivity growth slowed in the 1970s and 1980s. In 1990, productivity growth was a meager seven tenths of one percent. However, in 1992 productivity growth increased significantly, to 3 percent, before dropping to 1.5 percent in 1993 and 1.4 percent in 1994 (measured through the third quarter of 1994). Changes in the growth rate of productivity have important implications for both the growth rate of output and the level of real income in the economy. In particular, increases in productivity, *ceteris paribus*, increase the economy's capacity to produce. In addition, as productivity increases, so does the level of real income earned by labor.

Does It Make ECONOMIC SENSE?

Labor Opposition to Technological Change

Investment in plant and equipment reduces costs by making workers more productive. The same output can be produced with fewer workers. For instance, new auto manufacturing plants built in the last few years can produce the same annual volume of cars produced by the older plants, but with 25 to 50 percent fewer workers. Organized labor has often vigorously opposed productivity advances through robots and other automated equipment. They claim that new capital equipment and technological change are causing unemployment. Does this opposition make economic sense?

There are two parts to this problem; one is transitory, the other long term. We tackle the latter one first. Additional capital investment is undertaken when it is profitable to do so. The new auto plants are more efficient in a productive sense: Production costs are lower. These lower costs result in short-run profits that are competed away through lower auto prices. Increased profitability ultimately causes output to expand. The increase in supply (a rightward shift in the supply curve) causes equilibrium price to fall, increasing the equilibrium quantity of cars produced and sold. Increased sales lead to increases in production and the demand for labor. Thus, some of the workers displaced by the more productive capital stay employed because of increased production.

There are long-term effects that extend beyond the auto market as well. In particular, if cars cost less, consumers have more income to spend on other goods and services. The additional spending elsewhere increases the demand for other

Section Recap

Investment in capital goods can benefit society in a number of ways, including reductions in production costs through the development of more efficient capital, the development of new or improved products, and increases in labor productivity.

Investment Costs: The Interest Rate

The *real* rate of interest (as opposed to the nominal rate of interest, which may include an expected inflation component) is the price of investment funds. Each individual firm takes the interest rate as given when it chooses its optimal level of capital stock. But what determines the interest rate? To answer this question, note that the interest rate is the cost of borrowing money and the return to saving. As such, it is the real rate of exchange between current and future goods. Thus, the interaction of the supply of savings and the demand for investment funds determines the equilibrium interest rate.

Suppose all borrowers are equally creditworthy and all loans are for the same length of time. Further assume that investment funds are easily transferred to where they earn their highest return and that there is good information about relative interest rates across different credit markets. (Resources are mobile.) If so, all borrowing and lending can be treated as if it occurred in one credit market. Only one interest rate could exist because any differences would be quickly eliminated by the flow of funds away from low-interest to high-interest markets.

goods and services, causing the demand for labor to increase in the affected industries. Hence, although increased productivity in the auto industry may reduce the number of workers employed by auto makers, it can indirectly cause employment to expand in other industries. In short, because production of cars now requires fewer scarce resources, we can spend more on other goods, causing employment to be reallocated from autos to other industries.

However, this long-run economy-wide adjustment to a productivity change in one market does overlook a transitory development caused by costly mobility and information. The autoworkers who lose their jobs experience some unemployment, if only because they have to acquire information on other employment opportunities, search these opportunities out, and possibly move to a new location. Furthermore, some of the autoworkers who become unemployed may be unemployed for a long time – several years – or they simply may not seek another job. Workers who are in their fifties and who have been employed in the industry for many years may have great difficulty making the transition to new jobs.

In summary, technological change such as the development of productivity-enhancing capital in the auto industry makes society better off – we have more output as a result. However, the temporary unemployment associated with this market reallocation of resources may be especially burdensome to one relatively small group of workers (relative to the total labor force). If these workers are members of a union, it is understandable that the union would protest such developments. Viewed from the perspective of the individual, labor opposition to technological change can, in fact, make economic sense.

In general, jobs lost to improved capital and technological change are made up elsewhere in the economy because the increased productivity generates savings that can be spent in other parts of the economy. However, it is nonetheless true that technological change can also cause considerable hardships in affected labor markets. As such, for both equity and efficiency considerations, it may be reasonable for society to assist these individuals through subsidies for unemployment, training, or relocation.

Figure 18.4 depicts such an aggregate credit market. Demand for investment funds is negatively sloped. A decline in the interest rate increases firms' desired employment of capital, raising the quantity of funds demanded to finance the expansion. This increase is temporary for individual firms. Once the increased capital stock is reached, the firm no longer requires more investment funds. However, new firms are continually being organized, and at the lower interest rate each of these will demand greater investment funds to begin operations with a greater level of capital. Thus, a lower interest rate should lead to a permanently higher level of borrowing.

The rate of interest also is the payment for saving. Therefore, as the interest rate rises, households reduce current consumption because its opportunity cost has risen. An increase in the interest rate means that households will be able to earn a larger dollar return on their savings. In comparing the benefits and costs of consumption, formerly marginally profitable consumption expenditures now generate costs, equal to the dollar expenditure plus the interest forgone on savings, that exceed the benefits realized. Assuming that income is fixed, lower consumption means higher saving. Thus the supply of saving is upward sloping.

The equilibrium rate of interest is r_1, with investment and saving equal to I_1. Only at r_1 does the available quantity of investment funds (savings) equal the desired level of investment spending.

In the cave dweller community that was discussed at the beginning of this chapter, the amount of investment depended on the cave dwellers' willingness to save. Investors and

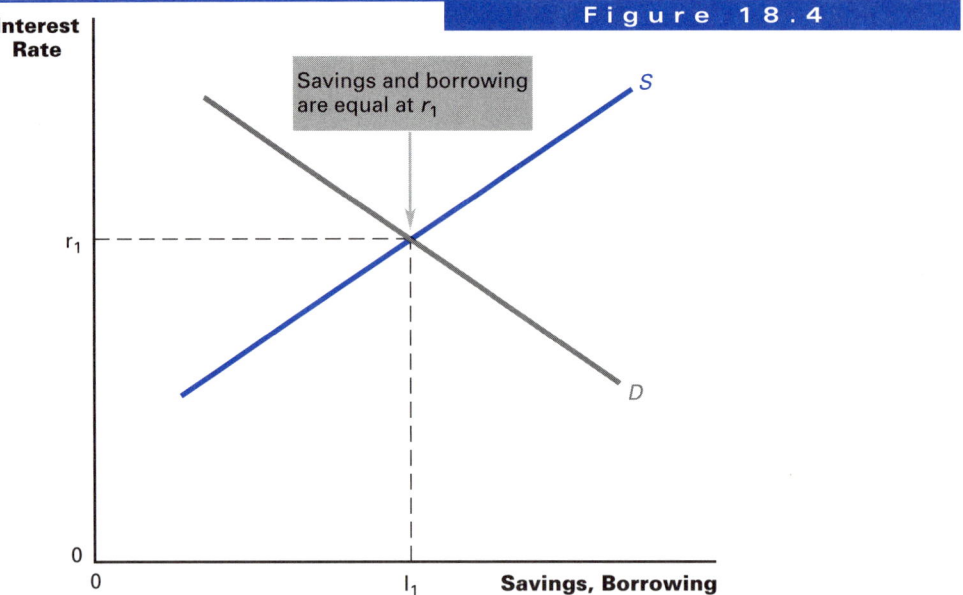

Figure 18.4

Interest Rate

Savings and borrowing are equal at r_1

S

r_1

D

0

0   I_1 Savings, Borrowing

Savings, Borrowing, and the Interest Rate

This figure depicts an aggregate credit market. Demand for investment funds is downward sloping: a decline in the interest rate increases firms' desired employment of capital. The rate of interest also is the payment for saving. Therefore, as the interest rate rises, households reduce current consumption. Thus, the supply of saving is upward sloping. At the equilibrium rate of interest, r_1, borrowing and saving equal I_1.

savers in a real–world economy are likely to be different people, but the basic principle that investment in capital requires reduced current consumption still holds true. The credit market reconciles the willingness of households to save and the desire of businesses to borrow and invest. Flexible interest rates ensure that, when the economy is in equilibrium, the level of saving matches desired investment spending.

We earlier stated that the basic determinants of investment spending in an economy are the productivity of capital and the willingness of individuals to save. Figure 18.5 shows why. Suppose capital becomes more productive. Each firm's marginal revenue product schedule for capital shifts to the right, causing its desired capital stock to increase. Total demand for investment funds shifts to the right, to D', pushing up equilibrium borrowing, saving, and the interest rate. The interest rate increases from r_1 to r_2, and borrowing and savings increase from I_1 to I_2.

Alternatively, an increase in the thriftiness of an economy raises the level of saving at all interest rates, shifting the supply of savings curve rightward to S'. The resulting decline in the equilibrium interest rate to r_3 induces more spending for investment – borrowing and saving increase from I_1 to I_3.

For the past two decades many respected economists, business leaders, and government officials have been concerned that the level of saving and investment has been too low in

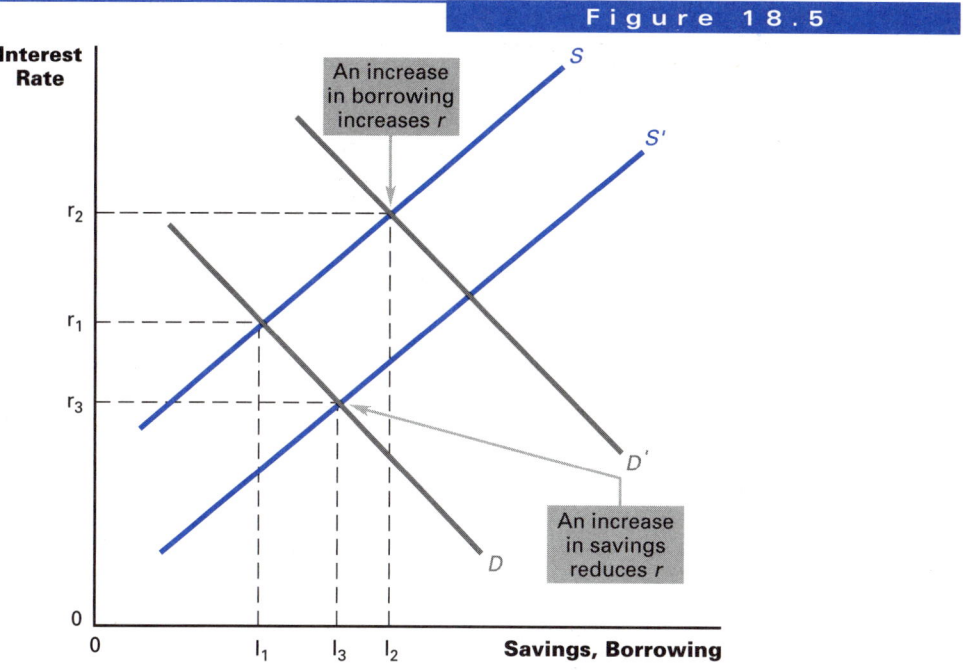

Figure 18.5

Shifting the Supply and Demand Curves for Savings

The basic determinants of investment spending are the productivity of capital and the willingness of individuals to save. Starting at a rate of interest equal to r_1, if capital becomes more productive, total demand for investment funds will shift from D to D', pushing up equilibrium borrowing, saving, and the interest rate to I_2 and r_2. Alternatively, an increase in the thriftiness of an economy would raise the level of saving at all interest rates, shifting the supply of savings curve rightward from S to S'. The resulting decline in the equilibrium interest rate to r_3 would induce more spending for investment.

the United States. They have argued that greater investment is necessary to increase our rate of economic growth and allow American business to become more competitive in world markets. Since 1981, many changes in the federal tax code have been enacted that affect, directly or indirectly, savings and investment. Two of the chief measures contained in the *Economic Recovery Tax Act* of 1981 – the accelerated depreciation provision and the investment tax credit – were designed to stimulate the demand for capital. (Essentially, accelerated depreciation reduced taxes on profits generated by increased investment in capital, raising its after-tax return.) Both of these measures were sharply curtailed in the 1986 tax reform act. This change came about, in part, as a result of arguments that the previous tax breaks had failed to generate productive investment and were therefore too costly in terms of the tax revenues forgone. These arguments were, however, countered by equally compelling arguments that the tax breaks enacted in 1981 helped to spur on the economic recovery that followed the recession in 1981–1982.

More recently, the Clinton Administration proposed a new package of tax changes including new investment tax credits. However, during budget negotiations in 1993, the investment tax credit proposal was dropped. Following the Republican party's victory in the 1994 elections, renewed attention was focused on tax cuts, including a reduction in the capital gains tax (which had long been sought by the Republicans).

Congress has also sought to stimulate investment indirectly, by raising the after-tax returns to saving. The most significant changes reduced the top marginal income tax rate from 70 percent in 1981 to 33 percent and established special tax-deferred savings funds, such as Individual Retirement Accounts (IRAs). The goal was to increase the supply of savings. The combination of increased demand and supply should lead to increased investment spending. However, IRAs were sharply curtailed in the 1986 tax reform act and changes in the tax laws in 1993 resulted in, among other things, an increase in the top marginal tax rate to 39.6 percent for certain income groups. However, following the Republican victory in 1994, there was talk of increasing incentives for individuals to save income by increasing the deductibility of IRA contributions. Proposals have also been floated that would replace the income tax with a federal consumption tax. One of the intents of this change would be to encourage additional savings by the private sector. However, at the time this book was being written, no agreements had been reached regarding any of the proposed changes mentioned here.

Whether the policies directed at stimulating savings and investment have worked is difficult to tell. During the mid to late 1980s business fixed investment rose substantially. This partially reflected the recovery from the 1981-1982 recession. However, the federal government has taken an increasing share of private savings to finance its own budget deficit since 1981. Increased federal borrowing may have offset new saving and investment incentives. While it is difficult to evaluate the net effects of these policies on capital formation, real gross investment was very strong in the 1980s and early 1990s.

Section Recap

The interest rate equilibrates investment spending and savings (the source of investment funds). Efforts to increase savings, investment or both (that is, to shift each schedule to the right) can result in increased investment and therefore an increase in economic growth.

The Rate of Interest and the Return to Capital

The rate of interest is both the cost of borrowing and the payment to savers. However, we can also think of interest as the return to capital as a factor of production. Over the long run, the marginal productivity of capital tends to equal the market rate of interest. Each firm maximizes profit by investing in additional units of capital up to the point at which the rate of return to the marginal unit equals the market rate of interest. In equilibrium, the rate of interest must equal the marginal revenue product of capital (expressed as a percentage rate), just as the wage equals the marginal revenue product of labor.

Why Do Interest Rates Differ?

In reality, the interest rate of Figures 18.4 and 18.5 is a set of rates: the *prime* rate, 90-day Treasury bill rate, AAA corporate bond rates, home mortgage rates, and credit card interest rates, to name a few. Why is the rate on credit card balances higher than the prime rate? Why does the rate on ten-year corporate bonds differ from bonds of shorter maturity? The answer to these and similar questions is that borrowers and loan conditions are different. We arrived at one equilibrium interest rate based on the assumption of equal risk and loan length. In reality, differences in at least four major loan characteristics result in different interest rates.

1. Differences in risk. The lender assumes a risk that the borrower will default – not repay the principal and interest. Default risk is higher for consumer loans than for business loans, so lending institutions charge higher rates to consumers to compensate for this higher risk. For similar reasons, the low default risk of U.S. Treasury bonds makes individuals willing to lend to the federal government at rates below those paid by corporate borrowers.

2. Differences in loan length. In general, lenders prefer not to tie up their savings for long periods. This is called a preference for liquidity. Long-term borrowing generally requires a higher rate of interest to compensate lenders for reduced liquidity. In addition, and possibly more importantly, conventional loans made for a long period of time lock the lender in at a fixed rate of interest. Higher interest rates may therefore be charged on long-term loans as a form of insurance against subsequent increases in the interest rate.

   One of the primary causes of rising interest rates is an increase in the inflation rate. During the 1970s, increases in the rate of inflation drove market interest rates to very high levels. Interest rates on certificates of deposit rose to 18 percent and more. As lenders pay higher interest rates for loanable funds (money deposited by savers) the return on existing loans decreases. Thus, lenders attempt to set interest rates on loans at a level that accounts for this possibility.

3. Economies of scale in service costs. Large loans have lower costs of administration per dollar loaned. A loan of $5,000 may entail the same amount of clerical, credit investigation, and administrative time as one of $50,000. The fixed administrative costs are spread thinner in the larger loan, making rates on larger loans lower. This, is one reason why credit cards, which usually involve loans of relatively small amounts, carry interest charges that are relatively high.

4. Differences in tax treatment. The federal government provides tax incentives to encourage borrowing and lending for certain purposes. To the extent that federal tax treatment differs, favored borrowers are able to pay lower interest rates. For example, interest earned on bonds issued by state and local governments is not subject to federal income tax. Thus, savers are willing to hold such bonds at interest rates below those paid on corporate bonds (which pay a taxable yield).

Each of the factors listed above gives rise to a compensating interest rate premium or discount. In equilibrium, the spread of rates must exactly offset the differences in risk, maturity, service cost, and tax treatment.

Why the DISAGREEMENT?

Discounting the Importance of Future Generations

Investment in capital stock — regardless of whether it is undertaken by a private firm or the public sector — entails the use of scarce resources. As such, before undertaking a particular investment, it is important to compare the expected benefits and costs to better ensure that resources are used efficiently. However, many investment projects yield a stream of benefits over a number of years. For instance, in the computer example in this chapter (a private investment decision) the firm expected to earn profits over a four-year period. In a similar manner, the decision to use tax dollars to construct a dam on a river to create a reservoir (a public investment decision) would provide benefits to both current and future generations. Because of the time dimension in these situations, it is necessary to discount all benefits and costs to their present value.[3]

Discounting enables decision makers to compare benefits and costs that accrue over time. However, depending on the value of the interest rate that is used, the relationship between benefits and costs can vary widely, and even be reversed. The discount rate used in private investment decisions is determined in the market: It is a private discount rate. However, there is disagreement over what discount rate should be used in public investment decisions. Many individuals maintain that, just as in the case of private investment decisions, the private rate of interest should be used. Other individuals have argued that a social discount rate — which is lower than the private interest rate — is appropriate. In view of the ramifications of this controversy, it is worth asking, Why the disagreement?

Section Recap

A range of interest rates exists in the economy. Differences in interest rates reflect differences in the degree of risk, length, cost of providing credit, and tax treatment associated with different loans.

Financial Markets and Intermediaries

Financial intermediary:

An institution, such as a bank or savings and loan association, that facilitates the interaction between lenders and borrowers.

The highly simplified credit market of Figure 18.4 showed that investment decisions must be financed by savings of equal amount. In the United States the transfer of funds from saver to investor is facilitated by a highly developed system of **financial intermediaries**. Commercial banks, savings and loan associations, credit unions, and mutual savings banks accept the deposits of small savers and make these available to firms for capital investment. The financial middlemen play a valuable role. They encourage saving and investment by reducing the risk of saving. Without financial intermediaries, investors would have to borrow directly from savers. If a corporation wanted to build a new plant, it would have to sell bonds directly to individuals. But most savers could only afford to purchase the bonds of a few corporations and would be subject to the considerable risk that one of the corporations would default. The high risk would discourage saving.

A financial intermediary, however, can make large loans with little risk. Because it has pooled the savings of many individuals, it can lend to a diversified group of enterprises, reducing the risk that a default will inflict major losses. In addition, it is able to gather information on borrowers at less cost than would many different lenders who are provid-

Individuals who support the use of the private interest rate argue that the use of a common interest rate to discount all costs and benefits, regardless of whether they are associated with private or public investment, increases efficiency. Resources are scarce and the use of resources for public investment is not different from the use of resources for private investment in terms of the opportunity cost incurred. The use of a social discount rate for public investment decisions and a (higher) private discount rate for private investment decisions would skew the relative opportunity costs and benefits of the investments being considered.

Individuals who support the use of a social discount rate in public investment decisions argue that decisions regarding private consumption alternatives are myopic. In other words, a disproportionate weight is attached to present consumption alternatives relative to future options. This myopia, in turn, results in private discount rates that are too high; therefore, the present value of future benefits is understated. As such, the social discount rate should be set lower than the private rate to correct this imbalance and facilitate a more accurate assessment of the present value of benefits and costs.

It is also argued that, in many cases, greed leads individuals to give inadequate consideration to the welfare of future generations in the course of making decisions. Consequently, the level of private investment is too low. Government can help remedy this situation by applying a lower social discount rate to public investment decisions, thereby increasing the overall level of investment. However, critics point out that government is subject to many of the same problems – myopia and greed – as private individuals. Thus, it is unreasonable to expect that the social discount rate will be any more accurate than the private rate.

The use of a higher or lower discount rate could have a major impact on the relative benefits and costs of many public investment projects. In fact, it could be the deciding factor in many cases. Given the range of issues – both positive and normative – involved in this debate, there does not appear to be a solution to this problem that is both efficient and fair and that will be agreed upon by all parties. There also is little doubt that this disagreement will persist into the foreseeable future.

ing funds to a single borrower. Since the intermediary can lend with little risk, it is able to offer small savers a less risky and more liquid way to save – the passbook savings account, for example. The opportunity to save at low risk allows corporations to tap the savings of people with moderate to low incomes indirectly. By increasing the yields to small savers and decreasing costs to big borrowers, financial intermediaries increase the supply of and demand for borrowed funds, increasing the amount of capital investment.

Summary

Capital is a productive input. When choosing the optimal quantity of capital, the firm considers the same criteria that apply to any other input: productivity of the input, product price, and marginal resource cost. The major analytical difference between capital and labor is that investment in capital yields productive returns well into future periods.

To properly compare benefits and costs through time we must take account of the time value of money. Income and expenses in the future are valued less than income or expenses today because of the forgone opportunities between now and the future. The market interest rate is a good measure of forgone opportunities. A dollar received next year is worth less than one today because I can invest the one I have today for a year and earn interest.

The **present value** of a sum available in the future is the amount of money that would yield the future sum if invested until then at the market interest rate. In investment decisions, we compare the present value of costs to the present value of the benefits; an investment is profitable if benefits exceed costs.

The rate of interest that equates the benefits and costs of an investment is called the **internal rate of return** for the investment. The firm's demand for capital is its ranking of investment projects according to their rates of return. The condition for optimal employment of capital is to invest in all projects that yield a rate of return above the market interest rate.

Production of capital goods requires the sacrifice of current consumption, or saving. The mechanism for ensuring that the sum of investment and saving decisions match in a market economy is the interest rate. The interest rate measures both the cost of borrowing and the return to saving. Flexibility of the interest rate ensures that the quantity of investment funds supplied (savings) equals the quantity of funds demanded.

Ultimately, the level of capital investment in an economy depends on the productivity of capital and willingness of consumers to save.

We have more than one interest rate in the economy because of differences in borrowers, loans, and resource mobility. Capital markets are made more efficient by the presence of financial intermediaries who serve as middlemen for savers and investors.

Questions for Thought

Knowledge Questions

1. Why is investment a long-run decision?

2. Define present value. Explain why an increase in the interest rate reduces present value.

3. Why is there more than one equilibrium market interest rate?

4. What is the difference between financial and physical capital?

Application Questions

5. Suppose households decide to increase their rate of savings. What happens to the market equilibrium rate of interest and quantity of investment? Explain using a graphical analysis.

6. What impact does the tax deductibility of home-mortgage interest payments have on the demand for mortgages (loans for homes)? Explain.

7. Will the following developments increase or decrease the profitability of an investment in a college education? Explain each.

   a. An increase in the interest rate.

   b. An increase in the cost of housing.

c. A decrease in earnings of college graduates relative to high school graduates.

d. A decrease in tuition costs.

8. If a building contractor buys a truck for $15,000 with operating expenses of $1,500 a year, he will save $7,500 a year in other expenses. He plans to keep the truck for three years, after which it will have no market value. Should he buy the truck if the rate of interest is 5 percent? Ten percent?

Synthesis Questions

9. Why have electric power companies opted to build nuclear-powered rather than coal-fired electricity generating plants? Are they more profitable? Why have these decisions caused so much controversy?

10. We noted that increases in productivity can have a positive effect on the level of real income earned by labor. Explain how this can occur.

11. Consumers are often faced with a choice between purchasing a big-ticket item such as a new car today and putting the purchase off to the future. What factors should enter the consumer's decision of whether to buy today?

12. Discuss the issues that must be considered by a developing country when it decides how much to invest in its capital stock versus production that would raise the current standard of living.

End Notes

[1] Economies of scale were defined and discussed in Chapter 9.

[2] Output per employee hour may be a better measure of the productivity of capital, although it is really not clear exactly what it measures, other than changes in total output relative to total employee hours.

[3] Much of this discussion is drawn from R.A. Musgrave and P.B. Musgrave, *Public Finance in Theory and Practice* (New York: McGraw-Hill, 1980).

Part IV: Applications of the Microeconomic Model

Income Inequality and Poverty

Overview

In recent years, the plight of the homeless has received an increasing amount of attention. Efforts to provide temporary shelters, especially in the winter, and food drives to feed the hungry have become routine. However, while almost everyone agrees that homelessness and malnutrition are serious problems in the United States, there is considerably less agreement regarding what should be done to address them. Much of the debate has focused on the extent to which income should be redistributed from higher income groups to the needy versus developing programs that would enable people to earn enough income on their own to meet their basic needs.

Few among us are in favor of allowing income to be distributed wholly by the marketplace. However, although a consensus exists that some income redistribution by government is appropriate, there is substantial disagreement over how income should be redistributed, and to what extent. The notion of a fair income distribution is a normative one; no generally accepted definition of what is fair exists. Nor is there any obvious way to determine what individuals are willing to pay for a more equal income distribution.

Although economic analysis alone cannot settle these issues, it can provide important information to enlighten judgment on this crucial social choice. This chapter provides such information. We define ways to measure the distribution of income and then use these measures to describe the current distribution of income and its trend over time. The causes of unequal income distribution are also important. Policies adopted to alter the distribution of income, as well as the costs of reduced inequality, depend on whether income differences are due primarily to differences in ability and productivity or, for example, simply luck.

An important part of our concern about income distribution is our concern for the members of society with low incomes. With respect to the poverty problem in the United States, we explore the difficulties encountered in defining poverty and the extent of so-called official poverty in the United States. Evidence is presented on the characteristics of the poor and the causes of poverty, and federal antipoverty programs are described and evaluated.

Learning Objectives

After reading and studying this chapter, you will be able to:

1. Characterize the degree of income inequality in the United States

2. Use a Lorenz curve to describe income inequality

CHAPTER 19

3. Explain the reasons for observed income inequality and assess the shortcomings of annual income as a measure of income inequality

4. Explain why there is a tradeoff between efficiency and equity in income redistribution policies

5. Describe the incidence of poverty in the United States and identify the major causes of poverty

6. Summarize the characteristics of antipoverty programs in the United States

The Distribution of Income in the United States

Most of the economic decisions we have analyzed thus far have involved individual choices. Yet one of the most fundamental economic decisions must be made through a collective process. In the course of deciding how, what, and for whom society's goods and services are to be produced, we decide how income should be distributed. Questions of income distribution and redistribution involve both equity and efficiency considerations.

Income differences are a fact of life in the United States. From our own personal experiences we are familiar with variations in income even among our own families and friends. We are also accustomed to changes in income. We regularly observe individual and family incomes rising and falling. Before attempting to evaluate society's efforts to redistribute income, we must summarize the pattern of observed income differences in society. We begin with a very aggregated look at the distribution of income in the United States.

Personal distribution of income:

The share of all personal income received by families at different income levels.

The **personal distribution of income** can be described by calculating the share of all personal income received by families at different income levels. Income data are collected by the U.S. Bureau of the Census each year. The Census Bureau's income measure focuses on family income, which represents the total income received from all members of a family. The Census Bureau includes as family members only those members residing in the same house. In addition to income received as wages, salaries, royalties, interest payments, stock dividends, and rent from real property, the income measure includes all money income received as transfer payments from governments. Thus, it includes income from such sources as Social Security payments, unemployment compensation, and disability payments. Family income measures gross income received by families from the employment of their resources and assets. Excluded from this income measure are capital gains income and the value of nonmoney transfer payments, such as food stamps or medical care.

Table 19.1 presents the personal distribution of family income for selected years. The table shows the share of income received by families grouped by income level. For instance, the first row of the table shows the share of income received by the 20 percent of families with the lowest incomes, and the fifth row of the table shows the share of income received by the 20 percent of families with the highest incomes. A perfectly equal distribution of income would yield equal shares of income for the five fifths of families: Each 20 percent of families would receive 20 percent of income.

Table 19.1 reveals substantial income inequality in any year. In 1992, the 20 percent of families with the lowest incomes received just 4.4 percent of total income, while those families in the top quintile (the top 20 percent) received 44.6 percent. The top 5 percent of families accounted for 17.6 percent of income in 1992.

Between 1929 and 1950, income inequality was substantially reduced. This change was probably not the result of deliberate government policy, but more likely reflected developments such as the loss of great fortunes during the Depression and rising real wages and farm incomes during World War II. Since 1950 the distribution of income has been

Table 19.1

The Distribution of Family Income in United States, Selected Years

Families by Income Quintile	1929	1947	1960	1970	1980	1990	1992	Cumulative Distribution for 1992
Lowest fifth	3.5%	5.0%	4.8%	5.5%	5.2%	4.6%	4.4%	4.4%
Second fifth	9.0	11.9	12.2	12.2	11.5	10.8	10.5	14.9
Third fifth	13.8	17.0	17.8	17.6	17.5	16.6	16.5	31.4
Fourth fifth	19.3	23.1	24.0	23.8	24.3	23.8	24.0	55.4
Top fifth	54.4	43.0	41.3	40.9	41.5	44.3	44.6	100.0
Top 5%	30.0	17.5	15.9	15.6	15.3	17.4	17.6	

Source: U.S. Bureau of the Census, Current Population Reports, series P60-184, *Money Income Households, Families and Persons in the United States: 1992,* U.S. Government Printing Office, Washington, DC, 1993, and earlier issues.

relatively stable. However, it appears that in the late 1980s and early 1990s the share of income going to the richest 20 percent of the population has increased relative to the share received by this group in the 1960s and 1970s. The amount of income accruing to the poorest 20 percent of the population has dropped slightly over the same period.

The personal distribution of income for a given year can be illustrated graphically by plotting the relationship between the percent of families who receive income and the cumulative share of total income received. This functional relationship is called a **Lorenz curve** after M.O. Lorenz, who developed the measure in the early twentieth century. The Lorenz curve for the 1992 income distribution in the United States is plotted in Figure 19.1. The 45-degree line represents perfect income equality – each quintile receives 20 percent of income. When the Lorenz curve is bowed down and away from the 45-degree line, income is unequally distributed. Point A on the curve shows that the poorest 20 percent of families received less than 5 percent of total income. The income of the lowest quintile was just over one tenth of the income of the wealthiest quintile. At point B, we see that the bottom 60 percent of families received approximately 32 percent of total income.

The divergence of the Lorenz curve from the 45-degree line measures the extent of income inequality (the area between the 45-degree line and the Lorenz curve serves as a quantitative indicator of inequality). The less equal is the income distribution, the more bow-shaped the Lorenz curve appears. If 1 percent of the population received 99 percent of the income, the curve would approximate a backward L. Between 1929 and 1970 the income distribution shifted toward more equality; thus, the Lorenz curve shifted toward the 45-degree line.

How does income inequality in the United States compare with that of other economies? Answering this question quantitatively is difficult because of differences in the

Lorenz curve:
A functional relationship that indicates the percentage of the population that receives a given percentage of the total income in the economy.

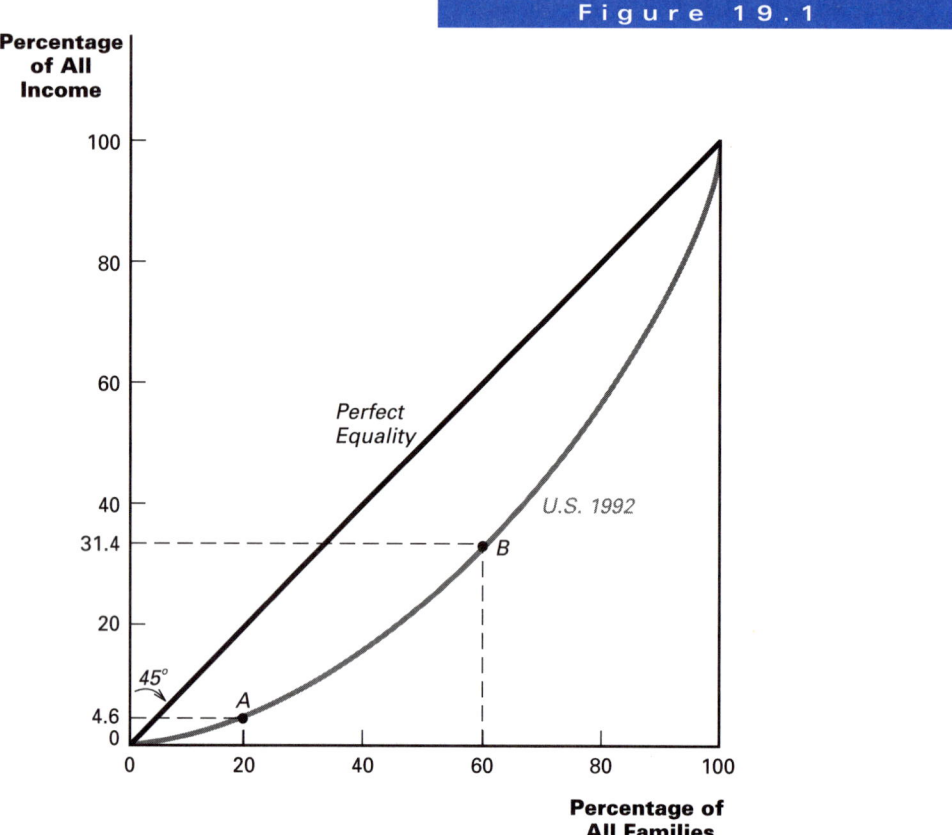

Figure 19.1

Lorenz Curve for the United States

This figure depicts the Lorenz curve for the 1992 income distribution in the United States. The 45-degree line represents perfect income equality. When the Lorenz curve is bowed – as it is in this figure – income is unequally distributed. Point A on the curve shows that the poorest 20 percent of families received less than 5 percent of total income. Point B indicates that the bottom 60 percent of families received approximately 31 percent of total income.

way countries collect economic data and define economic variables. However, the International Labour Organization has calculated income distributions for a number of countries after adjusting each country's income data to make it comparable with that of other countries. Based on their study, the income distribution in the United States can be considered middle of the road compared to income distributions of other countries.

Lorenz curves for three representative countries are provided in Figure 19.2. Denmark's Lorenz curve shows that it has an income distribution more equal than that of the United States. The income distributions of Sweden and Great Britain are quite similar to Denmark's. These countries engage in extensive income redistribution through very progressive tax structures[1] and social programs that provide generous benefits such as medical services, unemployment compensation, and relocation assistance. The income distribution in France, on the other hand, is very similar to that of the United States.

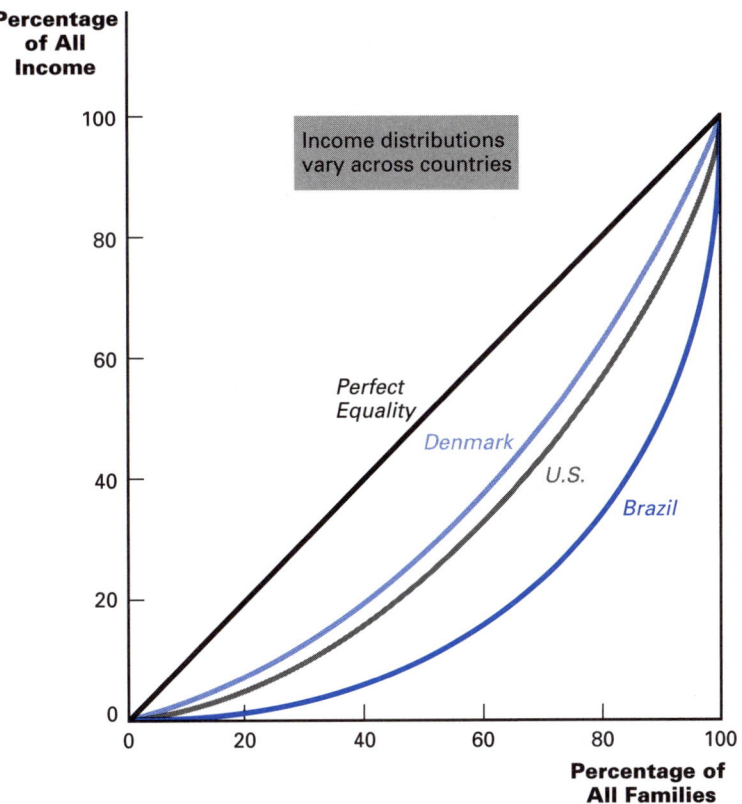

Lorenz Curves for Selected Countries

This figure depicts Lorenz curves for three representative countries. Denmark's Lorenz curve shows that it has an income distribution more equal than that of the United States. This situation is representative of countries that engage in extensive income redistribution through very progressive tax structures and social programs. Developing countries tend to have more unequal income distributions. Brazil's Lorenz curve demonstrates relatively extreme income inequality.

Developing countries tend to have more unequal income distributions. Brazil's Lorenz curve demonstrates relatively extreme income inequality. For instance, 80 percent of families receive just 35 percent of total income, while the top 20 percent of families receive about 65 percent of income. This kind of income distribution is representative of many developing countries, such as Mexico, Zambia, and Honduras.

The personal distribution of income, as represented by the Lorenz curve, provides a very aggregated picture of the extent of income inequality in an economy. Since our primary interest is (a) whether the observed income distribution is somehow satisfactory to society and, if not, (b) what kind of income redistribution should be undertaken, we must dig deeper. Is the Lorenz curve measure of income inequality an accurate and useful measure of inequality? What causes the kind of inequality we observe by whatever measure?

Given our understanding of the extent and causes of inequality, what policies, if any, are appropriate for the redistribution of income?

Section Recap

Over the period 1929–1980, income distribution in the United States moved toward equality. However, there is still a fairly unequal distribution of income. Countries with extensive social programs tend to have a more equal distribution of income while developing countries tend to have a more unequal distribution.

Family Income as a Measure of Well-Being

The data in Table 19.1 suggest substantial inequality in personal income in the United States. However, these figures probably overstate income inequality for several reasons. First, income is measured before personal taxes are paid. Personal taxes include federal, state, and local income taxes, sales taxes, payroll taxes, and property taxes. If the overall personal tax system is *progressive* – that is, if families with higher incomes pay a higher percentage of income in taxes – the after-tax distribution of income will be more equal.

Family income data also exclude nonmonetary government transfers. Many government transfer programs provide economic goods to families, either in kind or through subsidies for the purchase of goods and services. Lower- and middle-income families receive subsidized meals, medical care, housing, and education. The benefits of these programs have a cash value to the recipients. Since most of the beneficiaries are low-income families, counting noncash benefits will raise their share of real income.

Table 19.2 shows the effects of the personal tax system and the inclusion of nonmonetary government transfers on the distribution of income. While the data do not suggest a large shift in the overall pattern of income distribution when these factors are accounted for, they do indicate that people in the lower income quintiles do benefit from such programs.

Table 19.2

The Impact of Personal Taxes on the Distribution of Income, 1992

Income Quintile	Change in Percentage Income Share after Taxes
Lowest fifth	+1.1
Second fifth	+1.6
Third fifth	+0.8
Fourth fifth	−0.1
Top fifth	−3.5

Source: U.S. Bureau of the Census, Current Population Reports, Series P60-186-RD, *Measuring the Effects of Benefits and Taxes on Income and Poverty: 1992*, U.S. Government Printing Office, Washington, DC, 1993. Table B.

Family income measures also omit the value of services produced and consumed in the household. The work done in the household by both spouses – such as cooking, cleaning, child care, and maintenance of home and autos – is valuable to the family and improves real economic well-being. When these services are purchased in the market by families, they are included in income. The omission of home production may alter the distribution of income.

The effects of progressive taxation and government transfer programs tend to reduce the actual inequality of the distribution of income in the economy.

Section Recap

Distribution of Lifetime Incomes

Another important reason why the personal income distribution overstates inequality is that it gives us a picture of family incomes at one point in time. Thus, it ignores **income mobility**, or what we might call the Horatio Alger effect. Some families and individuals who are in the poorest quintile in one year move into a higher income group in a later year. Consider a common case. Bill Hansen, just married, enrolls in medical school, while his wife Kris enters graduate school. Their low combined money income while in school lands them in the poorest 20 percent of families. After Bill receives his M.D. and Kris her master's degree, their combined incomes move them into the top 20 percent. Later, Kris leaves her job to have children, and they drop back to the fourth quintile. When the kids enter school, it's back to the job for Kris and back to the top quintile for the Hansen family. In retirement, Bill's and Kris's pensions, Social Security, and interest and dividend earnings are only enough to place them in the third quintile, but because the Hansen children are gone and the mortgage is paid, their real standard of living does not decline.

Income mobility: The tendency of individuals and families to move among income groups over time.

Clearly, it would be wrong to consider the young Hansen couple poor, given their considerable lifetime income. Differences in lifetime incomes across families are a much better measure of inequality. Yet, even if all families had identical lifetime incomes, the Lorenz curve for any one year would show substantial inequality as families' incomes vary from year to year based on age, child rearing, and just plain luck. For the figures in Table 19.1 to show perfect equality, not only would lifetime incomes have to be equal for all, but income would have to be identical in every year.

So long as there is mobility across income groups over time, the Lorenz curve will overstate income inequality. Several studies have demonstrated substantial mobility among income classes in the United States. In one study, a large number of families was followed for several years, allowing social scientists to monitor changes in their economic status over time. Table 19.3 contains information on the extent of movement by these families among income quintiles during a seven-year period, 1971–1978. The income changes are striking. About half of families in the highest and lowest income quintiles had moved to other quintiles after seven years. Some families from the highest (lowest) income quintile had actually moved to the lowest (highest) quintile, and about two-thirds of all families in the middle quintiles (the second through the fourth) in 1971 changed quintiles within the seven-year period.

Table 19.3

Changes in Family Income, 1971-78

(Percentage of individuals in 1971 family income quintile)

Family Income Quintile, 1978

Family Income

Quintile,1971	Highest	Second	Third	Fourth	Lowest	Total
Highest	**48.5%**	29.5%	14.0%	4.5%	3.5%	100%
Second	22.0	**31.5**	25.5	15.0	6.0	100
Third	14.0	18.5	**30.5**	23.5	13.5	100
Fourth	9.0	13.5	21.5	**34.5**	21.5	100
Lowest	6.0	7.0	9.5	22.0	**55.5**	100

Source: Mark Lilla, "Why the 'Income Distribution' Is So Misleading," *The Public Interest,* No. 77, Fall 1984, p. 70. Adapted from Table 1.1 in Greg J. Duncan, et al., *Years of Poverty, Years of Plenty: The Changing Fortunes of American Workers and Families* (Ann Arbor: Institute for Social Research, University of Michigan, 1984).

Section Recap

The Lorenz curve overstates income inequality to the extent that there is mobility across income groups. Most families move across income quintiles over time.

Income Differences by Family Characteristics

Having established that income is unequally distributed in the United States, it is natural to inquire about the causes of income differences. If income inequality results primarily from differences in individuals' abilities and productivity, we are more likely to view the income distribution as fair, especially if individuals have equal opportunities to acquire productivity-enhancing skills. On the other hand, if income differences are based on discrimination or privilege, or if there is not equal opportunity to climb the economic ladder, society is more likely to choose redistributionist policies.

A review of more specific income patterns by a variety of family characteristics suggests that a mix of factors influences the distribution of income. These differences are summarized in Table 19.4. **Median family income** is reported for each category in this table. The income measure used in this table is the same one used in the Lorenz curves – before-tax income. Median family income is a measure of the average income for families in a particular category.[2]

Median family income:

A measure of the average income for families in a particular category.

Age, Sex, and Race Income differences within these three categories are clearly defined. Income rises with age until about age 45 to 54 and then declines. The age-income relationship reflects, among other things, differences in labor supply: Younger people work less because many are acquiring education and training into their late twenties. Older workers reduce their work hours, ultimately retiring to live off their savings, Social Security, and other retirement income. Table 19.4 also shows significant income differences between different race and sex groups. In every category the income of whites exceeds the income of blacks. In addition, households headed by a male have a higher median income

Table 19.4

Household Income by Household Characteristics, 1992

| Characteristic | All Races | | Whites | | Blacks | |
	Number of Families (1000)	Median Income (dollars)	Number of Families (1000)	Median Income (dollars)	Number of Families (1000)	Median Income (dollars)
All Households	96,391	30,786	82,083	32,368	11,190	18,660
Region						
Northeast	19,437	33,194	17,046	34,789	1,865	19,683
Midwest	23,307	30,911	20,638	32,440	2,320	18,126
South	33,392	27,741	26,696	30,388	6,045	18,108
West	20,255	33,621	17,703	34,119	960	22,595
Type of Household						
Married-couple families	53,171	42,140	47,601	42,820	3,748	34,290
Male householder, no						
wife present	3,026	30,492	2,409	32,412	460	23,439
Female householder, no						
husband present	11,947	18,587	7,848	21,970	3,680	12,606
Nonfamily households	28,247	17,711	24,225	18,479	3,302	12,062
Age of Householder						
15 – 24 years	5,022	17,777	4,079	19,653	718	8,705
25 – 34 years	19,741	31,434	16,256	33,570	2,715	17,894
35 – 44 years	21,717	40,090	18,183	42,182	2,657	24,928
45 – 54 years	16,576	44,540	14,240	46,600	1,777	28,342

Continued on next page.

Table 19.4 Continued

Household Income by Household Characteristics, 1992

Characteristic	All Races		Whites		Blacks	
	Number of Families (1000)	Median Income (dollars)	Number of Families (1000)	Median Income (dollars)	Number of Families (1000)	Median Income (dollars)
55 – 64 years	12,438	34,062	10,675	35,883	1,416	19,118
65 years and over	20,896	17,160	18,651	17,886	1,908	10,396
Size of Household						
One person	23,642	15,423	20,211	15,978	2,892	10,933
Two persons	31,175	31,951	27,478	33,517	2,895	18,638
Three persons	16,895	38,937	14,105	41,429	2,155	21,952
Four persons	14,926	44,392	12,598	46,546	1,721	26,432
Five persons	6,357	42,471	5,194	45,305	863	24,744
Six persons	2,180	37,455	1,616	40,117	418	24,443
Seven or more	1,215	33,634	882	37,895	246	14,249
Work Experience of Householder						
Worked	69,000	38,488	59,406	40,031	7,226	26,500
year-round, full-time	49,923	43,937	43,340	45,405	4,912	31,974
Did not work	27,391	14,283	22,677	15,688	3,964	7,464

Source: U.S. Bureau of the Census, Current Population Reports, Series P60-184, *Money Income of Households, Families and Persons in the United States: 1992*, U.S. Government Printing Office, Washington, DC, 1993. Table 1.

than households headed by a female. Although a portion of these differences can be attributed to differences in education and training, part of the gap between white and black and male and female earnings appears to be attributable to discrimination.

Other Reasons for Income Inequality In addition to the factors noted above, several other factors generate income inequality:

1. Education. Median income varies positively with level of education. White-collar workers have higher incomes than blue-collar workers, blue-collar workers have higher incomes than service workers, and farm workers have the lowest incomes. Differences in education and training (work experience) account for a large part of these income differences. The more education and training one has, generally the higher one's earnings will be.

2. Differences in individual ability and preferences. One of the wonderful characteristics of human beings is their individuality. People have different innate abilities and widely varying preferences. These differences cause differences in earnings, reflecting voluntary differences in behavior, about which policymakers need not worry. Differences in intelligence, physical dexterity, visual acuity, motivation, willingness to work, and thrift can all have an impact on the opportunities available to people and the extent to which people take advantage of those opportunities. Some observed income differences are attributable to these sometimes subtle individual differences. Of course, income differences attributable to physical or mental handicaps are another matter; providing for the handicapped has long been recognized as an appropriate role for the government.

3. Risk taking. We might consider the willingness to take risks as one of the individual differences described in the preceding section. However, since the willingness to take risks can cause large income differences in a market economy, we have separated it out into its own category. The willingness to gamble one's wealth on a single venture or idea can make a person exceedingly rich – or exceedingly poor. Because many business decisions are made in situations of uncertainty, the willingness to assume risks is well rewarded in a market economy. Sam Walton believed that he could develop a discount retailing business that would improve on the existing approaches, and he became the richest man in America because of Wal-Mart. Steven Jobs and Stephen Wozniak believed they could build a small home computer and sell it at a low enough price that families would buy it; thus, Apple Computer and the microcomputer industry were born.

4. Transfers of wealth. The incomes of some fortunate people are altered by the industriousness, thrift, and generosity of others. Individuals inherit or are given wealth acquired by others. When we think of inherited wealth, we usually think of the extreme cases in which an exceedingly wealthy family passes on its assets to members of the next generation. However, the process is much more common than that. Many families pass on some wealth to the next generation. Middle-income parents purchase cars, pay for or heavily subsidize college educations, and make the down payments on first homes for their children. Parents use their resources to improve the

earnings opportunities of their children and give their children assets that generate income streams.

5. **Luck.** A factor in determining income differences in one year and often over a number of years is plain old luck. Sometimes it is difficult to separate luck from other factors, such as the willingness to take risks or to work hard. However, luck does play a role in altering incomes. One person wins a million-dollar lottery. Another person's father invested in an obscure business machine company years ago (International Business Machines). Yet another's brother becomes president of the United States. Some people marry into wealth. Others choose low-paying occupations and then their incomes rise unexpectedly. It is easy to think of other examples in which luck changes someone's income or income prospects. The outcome of many decisions is affected by chance happenings.

Section Recap

There are a number of factors that influence income inequality including age, education, occupation, sex, race, differences in abilities and preferences, willingness to take risks, transfers of wealth, and luck.

Marginal Productivity Theory and Income Distribution

How does the observed distribution of income fit with the model of resource price determination developed in Chapter 15? A fundamental result of competitive resource market theory is that the payment paid each resource equals its marginal revenue product. Thus, each individual's income is equal to the marginal revenue product of the resources he or she supplies. For most individuals, income is determined by wage payments equal to the marginal revenue product of their labor. Workers who are more productive receive higher wages and incomes.

One implication of marginal productivity theory is that income differences reflect different contributions to total output. Those who supply a greater amount of more productive resources are rewarded with higher incomes. Note that this is not a theory of what the income distribution should be; rather, it merely seeks to describe how the income distribution would be determined in a competitive market economy. Nevertheless, the theory is the basis for a case against income redistribution. For some, an income distribution based on each individual's contribution to national output has a ring of fairness to it. Further, if marginal productivity theory is correct, attempts to redistribute income will reduce the efficiency of the economy.

A fundamental criticism of marginal productivity theory and the income distribution it implies is that resource markets are not competitive. Under this view, labor markets are characterized by monopsony, trade unions, and discrimination. We have seen how each of these factors can cause wages to vary. As a result, wages are determined not only by relative marginal productivities but also by race and sex, the degree of exploitation by monopsonies, or the ability to gain admittance to a trade union.

While there is evidence in the existing distribution of income that individual ability and effort (productivity) influence income determination, factors such as inherited wealth and luck also matter. In addition, mean income data by race and sex indicate that discrimination may be an important factor in determining income differences. These facts support a policy of redistribution. Few are likely to believe that income determined by discrimination, luck, or accident of birth is fair. Further, if factor payments do not reflect marginal contributions to output, there may be little efficiency loss from redistribution.

Income Redistribution

We have seen that substantial income inequality exists in the United States. We have also noted some of the reasons for the inequality. Our theory of resource price determination does not provide any normative support for the fairness of the observed income distribution, and we know from earlier discussion that economic efficiency is not tied to a particular distribution of income. Our analysis of markets does, however, demonstrate the importance of some inequality in the economy. Opportunities for gain are what cause markets to function as well as they do.

The question, "What distribution of income is consistent with our concerns for economic efficiency and social equity?" is normative. Its answer requires that value judgments be made. We generally recognize the value of some inequality in society. On the other hand, we generally agree that some income redistribution is appropriate. A broad consensus exists on these matters. The controversy centers on how much income redistribution to undertake and by what methods. We can only note some important guidelines in making these important social decisions.

The Equity-Efficiency Tradeoff Economics teaches us a very important principle of human behavior: Incentives matter. People sell their inputs because they aim to make themselves better off. This desire for individual gain is the driving force in an economy. Income redistribution can weaken this incentive. By taking from those with high incomes and giving to those with low incomes, we run the risk of reducing rewards to those who have been successful as well as those who have been unsuccessful in contributing to society's output. In the extreme, the incentive to work and to produce is removed; each individual gets the same share of output regardless of effort. The result is less output and smaller shares for everyone. Therefore, redistribution policies that preserve individual incentives are preferable to those that destroy incentives.

Equality of Opportunity Income redistribution policies that provide for equality of opportunity rather than equality of results seem generally consistent with our desire to preserve incentives and to make the notion of redistribution more acceptable to society, at least in the United States. Americans appear to tolerate, even cheer, disparities in income, so long as there appears to be a fighting chance that a poor person, through hard work and sacrifice, can pull himself up by the bootstraps and become prosperous. The opportunity, not just the result, is crucial in American capitalism. Our policies to combat discrimination attempt to provide equal opportunity and thereby alter the differences in income between whites and blacks, men and women. Of course, the controversy that has surrounded these policies is often centered on the question of whether such laws provide more than equal opportunity.

Some of our tax laws dealing with inheritances attempt to provide equality of opportunity across generations. In this society we accept – sometimes grudgingly – the notion that the wealth earned by one generation need not – perhaps should not – be fully passed on to the next generation. Some of it can be taxed away and used to provide benefits to other members of society. Inheritance taxes make it more difficult for families to amass more and more wealth over a number of generations, thus helping to preserve the notion of equality of opportunity and sufficient incentives.

A Minimum Standard of Living In the United States, concern with policies that redistribute income and preserve incentives to contribute is balanced by a desire to establish programs and policies that ensure a minimum standard of living for the least fortunate in society. The objective is to reduce the incidence of poverty. These policies are among the most controversial income redistribution policies in existence. The next section analyzes these policies, defining the notion of poverty, examining the extent of poverty in the United States, and explaining the kinds of programs that have been established to fight poverty.

Section Recap

On efficiency grounds, income redistribution policies that favor equality of opportunity rather than equality of income are preferable because of the incentives they create. In the United States, such policies are balanced by the desire to provide a minimum standard of living for the least fortunate.

Poverty in the United States

Poverty:

The result of a level of income that is insufficient to ensure some predetermined minimum standard of living.

Poverty is a close relative of the income distribution issue. Antipoverty policy is one of the most controversial, demanding, and important issues in the United States today. Fundamental disagreement exists over the extent of poverty, its causes, and what, if anything, can be done to reduce poverty and dependency.

Consider first the problem of measuring how many people are poor. It is relatively easy to describe income inequality objectively – one can measure income and construct a Lorenz curve as we did in Figure 19.1. However, defining which families at the lowest relative income levels are poor requires a subjective judgment. Is poverty a low income relative to the rest of the population, regardless of the absolute level of income? If so, we would define those with the lowest x percent of incomes as poor. A problem with such a relative definition is that it equates poverty with income inequality. Poverty could never decline unless income inequality diminished, regardless of how much the real incomes of the poor increased. Comparison of the percentage distribution of income in 1947 and 1992 would suggest that no reduction in poverty has occurred, despite the fact that the real incomes of the poorest quintile are substantially higher today.

Another approach is to determine minimum needs of a typical family and count as poor those families who have insufficient income to purchase these necessities. Under such an absolute standard, poverty is unrelated to income distribution and, at least theoretically, poverty could be eradicated. The difficulty of this approach lies in reaching agreement on what constitutes the bare necessities of life. Should we define a poverty level income as that which provides just enough food and shelter to keep the poor alive? Or should provision be made to allow an occasional steak or even a movie? Today ownership of an automobile is considered a necessity, and yet in the United States sixty-five years ago an auto was a luxury. The point is that even an absolute definition of poverty involves a relative comparison of the poor with the standard of living of the nonpoor.[3]

In the United States, the official measurement of poverty is based on a minimum needs definition. The government's definition of poverty was first developed by the Social Security Administration (in 1965). It is an income measure. A *poverty income* is an income less than the income level defined as sufficient to provide a minimally adequate standard of living. This standard of living is best described as one whose diet is just nutritionally sound. The poverty level of income is adjusted to account for factors such as size of family, number of children in the family, age and sex of household head, and inflation. In 1992, a family of four was considered to be in poverty if its before-tax money income was below $14,335; for a single person the poverty threshold was $7,143. In 1993 these figures increased to $14,763 and $7,363.[4]

Table 19.5 summarizes the incidence of poverty (that is, poverty rates) for different groups in the United States over the last thirty years. In 1993, 15.1 percent of all individuals in the United States lived in families with incomes below the official poverty level, up 0.6 percent from the previous year. It is evident from Table 19.5 that poverty rates differ by characteristics and circumstances. The poverty rates for blacks and families headed by females are over twice that of the national average. The poverty rate for the elderly is slightly *below* the average.

Table 19.5

Percent of Population in Families with Poverty Incomes, 1959-1993

Family Group	Year								
	1959	1969	1979	1984	1989	1990	1991	1992	1993
Total persons	22.4%	12.1%	11.7%	14.4%	12.8%	13.5%	14.2%	14.8%	15.1
Blacks	55.1	32.2	31.0	33.8	30.7	31.9	32.7	33.4	33.1
Whites	18.1	9.5	9.0	11.5	10.0	10.7	11.3	11.9	12.2
Age 65 and over	35.2	25.3	15.2	12.4	11.4	12.2	12.4	12.9	12.2
Families with female householder: no husband present	49.4	38.2	34.9	38.4	35.9	37.2	39.7	39.0	38.7

Source: U.S. Department of Commerce, Current Population Reports, *Income, Poverty, and Valuation of Noncash Benefits: 1993*, Series P60-188, U.S. Government Printing Office, Washington, DC, 1995. Table D-4.

The time trend reveals that poverty declined significantly for all groups between 1959 and 1969. The incidence of poverty stabilized somewhat in the 1970s, rose in the early 1980s, and then fell somewhat in the late 1980s. The data indicate that since 1990, the incidence of poverty has been slightly but steadily increasing. A probable explanation for these trends is that the strength of the economic expansion in the last half of the 1960s reduced unemployment and pulled many of the poor out of poverty. However, economic growth slowed in the early 1970s and unemployment rates increased. The expansion in the last half of the 1970s raised the incomes of many poor. In the early 1980s the Reagan administration reduced funding for many cash-transfer programs serving the poor (funding for in-kind transfers, such as food stamps, increased), and at the same time the United States experienced another recession. The downturn in the incidence of poverty in the late 1980s and the subsequent increase in the early 1990s coincide with yet another economic expansion and subsequent downturn.

The poverty rate for those 65 years old and older is the exception to these broad trends: It steadily and strongly declined between 1959 and the early 1980s. It has, however, increased slightly in the 1990s. Because most people in this group are retired, the performance of the economy is not a major factor affecting their incomes. The more likely explanation for the overall trend is the rapid expansion of cash benefits under the Social Security, Medicare, and Supplemental Security Income programs that took place throughout the 1970s. The wealth of the elderly has also increased dramatically relative to earlier decades, and many elderly have substantial incomes from interest and dividend payments.

Section Recap

In the United States, poverty is based on a *minimum needs* definition. Approximately 15 percent of the population lives below the poverty level. Poverty fell slightly in the 1970s but rose again in the 1990s.

Is the Incidence of Poverty Overstated?

The statistics in Table 19.5 indicate that a significant portion of the population remains in poverty. However, these figures may overstate the extent of officially defined poverty. First, only cash income is counted, yet low-income families receive substantial noncash benefits. The in-kind income of the poor includes food stamps, subsidized housing, and federal medical insurance. These benefits have a monetary value – their provision preserves the cash income of the recipient. The Census Bureau has estimated that including these benefits in measured income would reduce the poverty rate by about 2 to 4 percentage points, depending on how such benefits are valued.

Another shortcoming in the official poverty statistics is that they are *static*. We have previously discussed mobility across income categories over individuals' lifetimes. At any given time families whose total lifetime income is above the poverty level may have, for a variety of reasons, current incomes below the poverty line. For example, a family headed by a middle-income wage earner may fall into poverty one year due to a lengthy strike. Yet the family's prospects for recovering the next year are excellent. For policy purposes we would be less concerned about this family than about another that was perpetually in poverty. Studies suggest that about 45 percent of poverty spells end within one year and 70 percent end within three years. Only 13 percent of poverty spells last more than eight years.[5]

Finally, our understanding of the extent of poverty is only as good as our data and definitions of income. Many economists agree that the Consumer Price Index (which is used to measure the rate of change in the prices of consumer goods) is upward biased as a measure of the true change in the cost of living because it overemphasizes the value of housing as a share of the goods and services purchased by consumers. If the poverty level of income is adjusted each year based on changes in the Consumer Price Index, the poverty income level will rise faster than average price increases. One reason for the increase in the share of the population below the poverty line between 1979 and the early 1980s is the rapid increase in prices experienced from 1979 to 1981. Part of the apparent increase in the number of families in poverty was simply due to errors in the measurement of the *actual* rise in the cost of living.

Statistics may overstate the actual extent of poverty because they do not take account of in-kind transfers, income mobility, or the actual change in the cost of living for specific individuals.

Section Recap

Causes of Poverty

Formulating effective antipoverty policies requires an understanding of the causes of poverty. It is convenient to assume that poverty has one or two causes. Some people believe poverty arises from a basic unwillingness to work; we might label this argument the some-people-are-lazy theory. Others argue that poverty arises because people lack skills to be productive or society simply does not generate enough jobs to employ all those who wish to work. Actually, people have low incomes for a variety of reasons.

A more detailed look at who the poor are gives us more clues about the causes of poverty. Table 19.6 provides information on the number of poor people and the incidence of poverty among various groups for the years 1992 and 1993. Whites, who comprise about 83 percent of the population, account for two thirds of the poverty population. However, the percentage of blacks living in poverty is much higher than the percentage of whites. One third of the black population lived below the poverty level in 1992 and 1993. (Only about 12 percent of whites lived in poverty during the same period.) The number of poor families headed by women is almost 10 times larger than the number of poor families headed by men. In addition, a much larger percentage of the population in families headed by women is in poverty – 35 percent for families headed by women versus 16 percent for families headed by men.

These patterns provide some hints about the causes of poverty. The incidence of poverty is high among black families and families headed by women. Low incomes in these groups can be attributed to a lack of skills, education, and experience relative to white males, reduced amounts of labor supplied to the market, and race and sex discrimination in employment. Young people, especially black youths, experience relatively high rates of

Table 19.6

The Incidence of Poverty, 1992 and 1993

| | All Races | | Whites | | Blacks | |
	Number[a]	Poverty Rate	Number	Poverty Rate	Number	Poverty Rate
Individuals						
1992	38,014	14.8	25,259	11.9	10,827	33.4
1993	39,265	15.1	26,226	12.2	10,877	33.1
Families						
Total						
1992	8,144	11.9	5,255	9.1	2484	31.1
1993	8,393	12.3	5,452	9.4	2,499	31.3
Married-couple						
families						
1992	3,385	6.4	2,677	5.6	490	13.0
1993	3,481	6.5	2,757	5.8	458	12.3
Male householder,						
no wife present						
1992	484	15.8	333	13.8	116	24.8
1993	488	16.8	319	13.9	133	29.6
Female householder,						
no husband present						
1992	4,275	35.4	2,245	28.5	1,878	50.2
1993	4,424	35.6	2,376	29.2	1,908	49.9

[a] Numbers in 1,000s

Source: U.S. Department of Commerce, Current Population Reports, *Income, Poverty, and Valuation of Noncash Benefits: 1993*, Series P60-188, U.S. Government Printing Office, Washington, DC, 1995. Tables C and D-6.

unemployment. Women who are single parents must balance the need for income against the needs of their children. Even though over half of all women with children – even young children – now work, many work only part time or part of the year. In addition, changes in family structure seem to have a disproportionately adverse effect on women's income. When families break up because of death or divorce, women who have not been in the labor market face limited employment opportunities.

Since family income, especially at low-income levels, is comprised primarily of wage earnings, poverty income can be attributed to low wage earnings. Thus poverty, in an accounting sense, is caused by (1) labor force nonparticipation, (2) unemployment, and (3) employment at low wages. Poverty that is associated with nonparticipation – individuals neither working nor seeking work – could be caused by a disability or, in the case of a family headed by the mother, child-care responsibilities. Appropriate policies would include income transfers or provision of child-care subsidies to allow the parent to work. If the major cause is unemployment or low earnings, however, policies should focus on increasing the demand for and skills of low-income workers or promoting high-employment macroeconomic conditions.

Table 19.7 shows that there were 7,070,000 heads of families in poverty in 1992.[6] Slightly less than half did no work in 1992 for a variety of reasons. Foremost among these were home duties and illness or disability. Six percent of all heads of families were unable to find work. Of those who did work in 1992, 17 percent were employed full time. For this group poverty is a result of low wages. The remainder of the working poor did not work full time, due to unemployment or nonparticipation. While we do not know how many of this latter group would have remained in poverty had they been employed full time, lack of full-time employment, rather than low wages, is the immediate cause of most poverty in the United States.

The data in Table 19.7 also highlight the difference in labor force activity between single female household heads and other household heads. Although about 44 percent of these women worked, only about 10 percent worked full time. Among those who did not work, almost one third were involved in home duties or child care. By contrast, almost two thirds of other household heads worked, and approximately 26 percent of them worked full time. The majority of those who did not work were sick or disabled, or so-called discouraged workers.

This picture of the poor suggests that the causes of poverty are varied but that we can group most of the poor into one of a few categories. We have the *working poor* – those poor who are employed or would like to work but cannot find a job. Some working poor work less than year round or only part time. Improved skills, equal opportunity, and economic growth would help this poverty population. The *nonworking poor* include the sick and disabled, some retirees, and single mothers. We do not expect the sick and disabled and the retired to work. To reduce poverty among this group, the government must provide them with transfer income.

Society's attitudes toward the labor market participation of female household heads with children, especially those who are single (divorced, widowed, or never married), have been quite ambiguous over the past twenty-five years or so. Before World War II, single mothers were not expected to work. However, as the role of women in U.S. society has changed, societal views about the labor market participation of single mothers have changed, too. Many people now believe single mothers should be encouraged to work. The appropriate nature of programs targeted at this population is, as a result of this ambiguity, also unclear.

The incidence of poverty is high among black families, young families, and families headed by women. In an accounting sense, poverty is caused by labor force nonparticipation, unemployment, and employment at low wages.

Section Recap

Table 19.7

Work Experience of Heads of Poverty Families, 1992

Work Experience	Number[a]	Percent of total
All Poverty Householders		
Total	7,070	100.0%
Worked	3,799	53.7
Worked year round	1,204	17.0
Worked 1-49 weeks	2,595	36.7
Did Not Work	3,271	46.3
Ill or disabled	809	11.4
Retired	132	1.9
Home or family reasons	1,578	22.3
Unable to find work	426	6.0
School or other	327	4.6
Female Householder, No Husband Present		
Total	3,913	100.0%
Worked	1,737	44.4
Worked year round	373	9.5
Worked 1-49 weeks	1,364	34.9
Did Not Work	2,176	55.6
Ill or disabled	345	8.8
Retired	24	0.6
Home or family reasons	1,387	35.4
Unable to find work	196	5.0
School or other	223	5.7
All Other Families		
Total	3,157	100.0%
Worked	2,062	65.3
Worked year round	831	26.3
Worked 1-49 weeks	1,231	39.0
Did Not Work	1,095	34.7
Ill or disabled	464	14.7
Retired	108	3.4
Home or family reasons	191	6.1
Unable to find work	230	7.3
School or other	104	3.3

[a] Number of householders in 1,000s

Source: U.S. Bureau of the Census, Current Population Reports, *Poverty in the United States: 1992*, Series P60-185, U.S. Government Printing Office, Washington, DC, 1993. Tables 14 and 15.

ECONOMIC SENSE?

Taxing the Working Poor

Politicians have traditionally disagreed over how to address the problem of poverty in the United States. Much of the debate has focused on the relative merits of direct aid to the poor, with no strings attached, versus aid tied to some form of work requirement ("workfare"). Generally remaining outside this debate has been the earned income tax credit (EITC). The EITC, which is directed at the working poor, grants a refundable tax credit for every dollar earned up to a certain limit (in 1994 the limit was $27,000). In effect, the EITC can increase the overall income of working families by providing them with a tax refund, even if they owe no taxes. Since it was first passed into law in the 1970s, politicians of all stripes have supported the EITC. Thus, it came as a great surprise when Republicans announced in 1995 that they wanted to substantially cut the EITC.[7] Does it make economic sense?

Supporters of the EITC, including most economists, would answer with an emphatic no! The most attractive feature of the EITC is that it creates an incentive for people to work for a living. Through the EITC, eligible individuals can increase their spendable income relative to what they would receive by relying solely on government aid. In addition, these people gain the self-respect that comes from contributing to one's own well-being by working. Also, by having an increased incentive to work, even at a low-paying job, people are able to develop work skills that eventually may enable them to move to higher paying jobs. Thus, the EITC enhances the prospects that individuals will be able to pull themselves out of poverty and no longer require the assistance the program provides. Finally, by encouraging people to work, as opposed to simply relying on government handouts, the EITC contributes to overall economic well-being. *Ceteris paribus*, the total amount of output in the economy is greater than it would be in the absence of such an incentive.

Those who are in favor of cutting the EITC cite two main reasons

Income Redistribution and Antipoverty Policy

Economists emphasize the importance of economic efficiency in formulating public policy. On the other hand, government policy decisions generally place more weight on the income distributional consequences of a decision than on efficiency concerns. In such areas as tax reform, health care, deregulation, industrial and trade policy, and Social Security the most decisive arguments concern the impacts on the poor and middle class. While the Congress seldom explicitly debates what the optimal distribution of income should be, distribution is implicit in most of its policy debates.

Consider recent proposals to increase insurance deductibles and limit the growth of spending in the Medicare program. Economic efficiency argues for requiring the patient to bear a share of any medical costs. This provides both the doctor and the patient with an incentive to use the most cost-effective treatment consistent with sound medical practice. It is widely recognized that full medical insurance has led to significant health-care cost inflation and misallocation of resources by removing financial incentives to hold down costs. However, the opposition to proposals to increase patient fees, based on income distribution grounds, has been fierce: Raising the costs of medical care would reduce the welfare of the elderly. (An implicit assumption, contrary to fact, in the debate over Medicare and Social Security is that the elderly are more likely than younger people to be poor.)

for their position: the rapidly growing cost of the program and the estimated level of abuse (i.e., cheating) that occurs. The cost of the program grew by 300 percent between 1990 and 1995. It is projected that the EITC will cost an estimated $25 billion in 1996 and will continue to grow in subsequent years. Given the Republicans' goal of balancing the federal budget by the year 2002, the EITC is a prime candidate for spending reductions. (One Republican proposed cutting the EITC by $120 billion between 1995 and 2005.) Because the Republicans also want to reduce taxes, spending cuts are a primary means to achieving a balanced budget.

The second reason for the proposed cuts is the estimated level of abuse of the program. In 1994, the Internal Revenue Service concluded that approximately 26 percent of all claims were in error. However, the IRS also estimated that approximately one half of the errors were mistakes, as opposed to deliberate abuse. Consequently, the IRS has undertaken steps to reduce the error rate to a level that is less than the error rate associated with the capital gains tax (a tax that falls primarily on the wealthier segment of society).

It is important to note that during the time that the EITC has been in effect, the percentage of families with children living in poverty has increased. At the same time, the purchasing power of the average income of a single mother with two children has fallen relative to what it was in 1972, before the EITC went into effect. Thus, it is quite apparent that reducing the EITC would only worsen the conditions faced by the working poor. In addition, many states rely on the effects of the EITC in developing their welfare programs. At a time when the federal government wants to shift more of the responsibility for welfare to the individual states, cutting the EITC would only make their job that much harder.

Thus, we would argue that cutting the EITC makes absolutely no economic sense. No program is perfect. However, it is important to compare benefits and costs when assessing the overall worth of a program. Cutting the EITC would reduce incentives to work and, at the same time, contribute to a widening of the gap between the haves and the have-nots. While the latter outcome is not necessarily economically inefficient, it has important implications for the long-term stability of society, as well as the potential need for expanded programs to help the poor sometime down the road.

And so it goes on, issue after issue. Should economic policy promote a high-growth, efficient economy? Or should we be more concerned with equality? This philosophical question is at the heart of the income distribution issue. The cost of increased equality is a decreased reliance on market forces and reduced individual incentives.

Antipoverty Policies

We have seen that approximately one in seven Americans is in poverty, as it is officially defined. The figure is substantially higher for blacks. This continuing level of poverty, more than twenty-five years after President Johnson confidently declared a war on poverty, is a major disappointment to policymakers. Antipoverty policy first became a top national priority in the Kennedy and Johnson administrations (1960-1968). President Johnson launched a series of so-called Great Society programs that, it was hoped, would eradicate poverty. Most of the programs initiated during this era still exist today and receive much higher funding levels.

Federal Antipoverty Programs Federal antipoverty programs have had two main thrusts. One is to strike at the root of poverty – poor employment prospects. The Job Corps and *Comprehensive Employment and Training Act* (CETA) sought to provide training in job skills. CETA also employed workers in public sector jobs. CETA has since been replaced by a much less costly *Jobs Training Partnership Act* (JTPA), which shifts much of the responsibility for training to private employers. While the JTPA seeks to augment the supply of skills, another program, the Targeted Jobs Tax Credit, seeks to raise the demand for disadvantaged workers. Employers who hire workers from welfare-eligible families may take a portion of their wages as a credit against federal income taxes.

The second thrust is to provide income support to the poor who are unable to work or whose earnings are not sufficient to pull them out of poverty. Some programs, such as Social Security, unemployment insurance, Social Security disability payments, and Medicare are not conditional upon income. While they undoubtedly do have an impact on the poor, they are not targeted for the poor only. The wealthy, along with the poor, may benefit from these programs. A number of other programs are targeted specifically at poor families. To be eligible for benefits, a person's or family's income or assets cannot exceed a predetermined level.

The most widely known example of the latter type of program is Aid to Families with Dependent Children (AFDC). AFDC is a joint federal-state program providing cash payments to needy families in which at least one parent is deceased, disabled, absent from home, or unemployed. Benefits vary from state to state, depending on the definition of need. As income rises, benefits are reduced, and benefits end when family income rises above 150 percent of the state's definition of need. AFDC families automatically qualify for medical assistance under the Medicaid program.

Food and nutrition assistance to low-income families is provided by a number of federal programs. Food stamps, which reduce the cost of food purchases, are provided based on income and family size. Child nutrition programs subsidize meals for children in schools and day-care programs. Housing assistance is provided by rent subsidies. The Supplemental Security Income program (SSI) provides cash support for the low-income aged, blind, and disabled. SSI recipients also are eligible for Medicaid benefits.

The Welfare Dilemma Perhaps you have heard someone say, in jest or frustration, "I'm tired of working. I'm going to quit my job and go on welfare." While such threats are rarely carried out, programs such as AFDC, food stamps, and housing assistance do pose a major dilemma for policymakers. Scarcity of government resources requires that benefits be targeted to the truly needy. However, if a dollar of benefits is lost when earned income goes up by a dollar, the incentive for the poor to work at low-wage jobs is weakened. Thus, two important goals — targeting benefits to the poor and establishing work incentives — are in conflict.

Why would the AFDC program establish such a work disincentive? If benefits are not reduced, more families with higher incomes will be eligible for benefits, leaving less for the truly needy. Thus, the fundamental welfare dilemma: Targeting benefits to those truly in need creates stiff disincentives for work.

How Effective Have Antipoverty Programs Been? The trend of the data in Table 19.5 reveals that poverty decreased substantially through 1970. Since then, however, there appears to have been little or no progress. Ironically, the rate of poverty stabilized at about the same time the Great Society poverty programs were fully implemented (that is, before effects attributable to the programs themselves could be felt

Why the DISAGREEMENT?

Should Welfare Be Workfare?

The most controversial antipoverty programs are those designed for the working poor. The largest, most visible such program is Aid to Families with Dependent Children (AFDC). This program provides a minimum cash income to single-parent families (and sometimes to families with two parents, at least one of whom is unemployed). Program benefits are reduced dollar for dollar as the recipient earns income. Critics of AFDC argue that recipients can become dependent on it instead of attempting to find employment that pays an income sufficient to allow the recipient to leave the program.

These long-standing criticisms have been translated into actual and proposed changes in the program in the last few years. Most of the changes involve a work requirement. Eligibility for the program would require the recipient's willingness to work, usually for some government agency or office. Experimental programs with work requirements are being, or have been, conducted in California, Illinois, and Massachusetts. A federal law passed in 1988 (the *Family Support Act of 1988*) requires all states to develop and begin to implement workfare programs by 1994. The concept of workfare has a long history. The poor were required to work to obtain state assistance as early as the sixteenth century in England. Yet the opponents of workfare are numerous and vociferous. Why the disagreement over work requirements for welfare recipients?[8]

Proponents of a work requirement say that it is a good indicator of need. One's willingness to work for aid is a good test of how badly one needs help. In addition, a work requirement contributes to future employability by keeping people in the labor market, where they have a chance to improve their skills or at least prevent them from deteriorating, as can happen during unemployment. Requiring work also reduces welfare costs. The cost of welfare payments is offset by the value of the goods or services produced by welfare recipients.

---

in the economy). This lack of progress has led some social critics to question the effectiveness of federal antipoverty programs.

The strongest challenge to the Great Society approach comes from Charles Murray in his 1984 book, *Losing Ground*. Murray contends that (1) poverty has increased since the inception of the War on Poverty and (2) rising federal welfare expenditures are the main culprit. Specifically, Murray is critical of the incentives conveyed by income transfer programs. We have already seen how such targeted programs diminish the incentives of the poor to work. In addition, Murray and others charge that AFDC destabilizes the family and encourages a cycle of poverty by encouraging fathers to leave home and teenagers to become pregnant out of wedlock.

Murray uses the hypothetical Pennsylvania couple, Harold and Phyllis, to press his points. If Phyllis became pregnant in 1960, the couple would have been better off if they had married and Harold had taken a low-wage job. However, by 1970, more generous AFDC benefits and the requirement that Harold be absent would have raised the income of Phyllis and her baby if she remained single.

More generally, Murray criticizes a fundamental change in policy and attitudes toward the poor: a change from assisting the poor to improve their own economic well-being to

Moreover, if the work requirement is really a good indicator of need, the number of people on welfare may be reduced by the requirement, further reducing program costs. Finally, a work requirement helps satisfy an equity concern. Families who are poor but employed and not in a welfare program have a low income and also work, while families in AFDC have a low income but do not have to work. (They may also be eligible for nonmonetary benefits unavailable to the working poor.) A work requirement would make the economic circumstances of the two groups more equitable.

Critics of workfare proposals offer a number of arguments to counter the case made by proponents. An important argument is that workfare stigmatizes welfare recipients even more. Welfare reformers have attempted to develop programs that provide income to poor people, regardless of circumstances. This principle greatly mitigates the stigma associated with seeking assistance through an antipoverty program; workfare proposals are a move in the opposite direction.

Critics also believe that dependency is not an issue. Most program recipients are in the program for short periods of time because low incomes are often due to temporary problems such as unemployment or divorce. In a sense, welfare is an insurance scheme rather than a long-term care program.

Workfare opponents also argue that an additional needs test is unnecessary. Eligibility is now limited to those with very low incomes and few assets. Thus, workfare would not reduce welfare caseloads much at all. A final argument concerns the viability of a successful workfare program. For workfare to be successful – as defined by its proponents – it must provide jobs that deliver skill training and produce socially valuable output. In addition, there must be enough jobs for all program participants, and they must be organized to be effective in the context of short employ-

ment tenure and high turnover. Finally, if these public sector jobs compete with established job opportunities, public-sector employees will claim that they are being displaced by free labor.

The disagreement over the merits of workfare has both positive and normative elements. Although the results of experimental programs have resolved some questions, many of these programs have yielded inconclusive results thus far. Other arguments involve value judgments about the generosity of benefits, the element of compulsion in the programs, and how to help the poor while allowing them to maintain their dignity and self-respect. Despite the continuing disagreements over the merits of workfare, the Family Support Act of 1988 requires states to implement workfare programs. The benefits and costs of workfare will surely be clearer in the wake of widespread experience with it.

---

providing a guaranteed minimum income for them; a change from providing equal opportunity to establishing equal outcomes.

Losing Ground is a very controversial book and was met with vigorous rebuttal. Glen Cain of the University of Wisconsin disputes Murray's claim that poverty programs have led to increased poverty. Cain believes that a sluggish economy was responsible for the failure of poverty rates to decline in the 1970s. Along with the sharp drop in poverty during the high-growth 1960s, this suggests that a strong economy is perhaps the most potent antipoverty weapon.

In her survey of poverty studies, Isabel Sawhill also concludes that high unemployment in the 1970s and early 1980s was the major factor increasing poverty rates. Others have noted that Murray's critique is leveled at only a small percentage of welfare recipients. The SSI program, for example, benefits the aged, blind, and disabled poor, and its work disincentives would seem to be irrelevant. Indeed, the poverty rate for the elderly fell continuously through the 1970s. Still others argue that the AFDC program grew because of a greater incidence of divorce in society, not because it encouraged marital instability itself. However, the existence of AFDC does encourage young single mothers to establish independent households, rather than live with relatives. Such female-headed households add to the poverty rate, as Sawhill notes.

Despite the disagreement over the effectiveness of existing antipoverty programs, there is a consensus emerging among policy experts that new policies and revisions in the existing programs in the 1980s should emphasize work opportunities and strengthened family responsibilities. The *Family Support Act* of 1988 represents a major philosophical change in direction because it requires many recipients of public aid to work part time in government jobs. In addition, families with unemployed fathers residing in the household will be eligible for program benefits.

Additional proposals for welfare reform that have been gaining widespread support include a limit, for example, two years, on the amount of time that an individual can remain eligible for many welfare benefits. The purpose of such a restriction is to prevent people from becoming dependent on welfare for so long that they are unable to compete effectively in the job market. Support has also grown for proposals that would shift many of the programs that are currently administered by the federal government to the individual states. In this case, states would be given block grants by the federal government that they could then allocate in the manner they consider to be most appropriate given their unique circumstances. When this book was being written, final action had not yet been taken on these and other proposals for welfare reform.

Section Recap

The government has developed a number of programs to eliminate poverty in the United States. However, many of these programs pose a dilemma because it is difficult to provide both benefits and an incentive to work. In addition, there is considerable debate over the effectiveness of existing antipoverty programs.

Summary

Income distribution and antipoverty policy choices involve a tradeoff between equity and efficiency. Inequality of income in the United States has remained approximately stable since World War II. Countries with more progressive tax structures and more generous social programs have more equal income distributions than the United States does. Incomes in developing countries tend to be much more unequal relative to U.S. income.

Income inequality can be measured in a number of ways. A **Lorenz curve** is used to make comparisons through time and across countries. The use of annual income to measure income inequality has its shortcomings. Income measures omit the value of nonmarket goods and services, and concentration on annual income fails to capture the income mobility that most families experience.

Observed variations in income occur for many reasons, including differences in education, jobs, individual abilities and preferences, and the amount of labor supplied to the market. Discrimination, intergenerational transfers of wealth, and luck also affect the income distribution. Some income differences arise because of differences in productivity and work effort. In a market economy some inequality is necessary to provide incentives for productive activity.

Poverty is measured by counting all families with incomes below the amount necessary to provide a minimally adequate standard of living. In 1993, this poverty income level for a family of four was about $14,763, and about 15.1 percent of all U.S. families had incomes below the poverty level. The incidence of poverty is greatest among black families and those households headed by single women.

An array of programs addressing the poverty problem exists. Such programs as Social Security, unemployment compensation, and Medicare raise the incomes of both poor and nonpoor. Programs targeted specifically at the poor include Job Corps, food stamps, Medicare and Medicaid, and Aid to Families with Dependent Children. Spending on these social programs has increased dramatically in the past twenty-five years, while the incidence of poverty has changed little, except for the greatly reduced poverty rate among people over the age of 65.

Critics of poverty programs maintain that poverty has not been reduced over time because the programs themselves encourage participants to work less and become more dependent on government assistance. Proponents of the poverty programs argue that recessions are primarily responsible for the continued incidence of poverty and that basic demographic trends have contributed to the poverty problem.

Questions for Thought

Knowledge Questions

1. Explain the equity-efficiency tradeoff associated with income redistribution.

2. Although whites constitute two thirds of the poverty population, the incidence of poverty is greatest among blacks. How can both statements be true?

3. The distribution of income in the United States should be more equal! It should be less equal! Choose one side of this debate and construct a good defense of your position. (You might try it out on a friend.)

4. What is the current poverty income for a family of four in the United States?

Application Questions

5. Suppose adjustments in family income data for noncash government transfers and the value of household services yield an income distribution as follows:

Quintile	Percent of Income
Lowest fifth	8.0
Second fifth	14.0
Third fifth	18.0
Fourth fifth	22.0
Top fifth	38.0

Construct a Lorenz curve for the 1992 data in Table 19.1 and for the income distribution above. Which is more equal?

6. In designing income transfer programs to help the poor, why is it important to distinguish between the poor we expect to work and the poor who are not expected to work? In which category do single female household heads belong? Explain.

7. What is the justification for increasing the poverty income level when consumer prices rise? For example, the poverty income level for a family of four was $4,275 in 1972, but $14,335 in 1992.

Synthesis Questions

8. What do you consider a minimally acceptable standard of living? Do you think the official poverty income level is sufficient to support this standard of living?

9. The minimum wage law is touted as an antipoverty program. In terms of the provision of new jobs and additional training opportunities, how does it compare to a program like the Comprehensive Employment and Training Act? Explain.

10. Referring to Table 19.4, what is the relationship between median household income and the size of the household? Can you develop an explanation for the pattern that you observe?

End Notes

[1] In a progressive tax structure, the percentage of income paid out in taxes is an increasing function of the amount of income earned.

[2] The median of a distribution is the middle observation when the observations in the distribution are ordered from lowest to highest.

[3] Studies have indicated that the self-avowed happiness of people depends rather heavily on their perceived *relative* situation. This has important implications for social policy, since raising the absolute standard of living to very high levels might not increase the happiness of those at the bottom of the income distribution. For an interesting discussion of the conditions necessary for happiness and their impact on social policy, see Charles Murray, *In Pursuit: Of Happiness and Good Government* (New York: Simon and Schuster, 1988).

[4] Note that the increase in each case is approximately 3 percent – the rate of inflation for 1992.

[5] Isabel V. Sawhill, "Poverty in the U.S.: Why Is It So Persistent?" *Journal of Economic Literature* 26 (September 1988), p. 1081.

[6] 1992 is the most recent year for which data were available when this book was being written.

[7] "A Slap in the Face for the Working Poor," *The Economist*, July 8, 1995, p. 23.

[8] The arguments for and against workfare discussed here are based on a comprehensive paper by Michael Wiseman about workfare, the experimental welfare programs, and evaluations of these programs that appeared in *Focus*, University of Wisconsin Institute for Research on Poverty, Fall and Winter 1986.

Externalities, Public Goods, and Common – Property Resources: Problems for the Market Mechanism

Overview

In Chapter 1 we noted that the issue of environmental quality has received a great deal of attention in the United States over the last three decades. The debate over survival of the spotted owl versus logging jobs in the Northwest spurred a great deal of controversy that is sure to continue into the foreseeable future. The debate over the effects of acid rain and what to do about it continues to rage. Among the many issues involved is the adverse effects of acid rain on aquatic life versus the jobs of coal miners in the East and Midwest. Concerns about ozone depletion and global warming have also spurred many groups to demand actions by the federal and state governments. Ever since the Love Canal incident, people have become increasingly concerned about the problems of waste management.

In previous chapters we identified the conditions necessary for markets to efficiently allocate scarce resources to satisfy competing wants. In many situations, however, the market allocation of resources is not efficient and market failure is said to occur. In Chapter 5 we briefly considered some of the causes of market failure and the effects of market failure on the efficiency of resulting outcomes. This chapter considers in greater detail three specific sources of market failure – externalities, public goods, and common-property resources – and describes policies designed to correct each type of failure.

In addition, this chapter explores the causes and consequences of a classic outcome of market failure: environmental pollution. We will examine the sources of pollution – where it comes from and where it goes – and discuss the important role played by property rights in creating or limiting the extent of this externality. A number of pollution control policy options are also identified and analyzed.

In the course of considering the policy prescriptions for each of the different types of market failure analyzed, we will discuss the difficulties involved in determining the best course of action to take to cope with market failure. We will show that the way in which property rights are assigned has an important effect on the extent to which market failure occurs.

Learning Objectives

After reading and studying this chapter, you will be able to:

1. Explain how poorly defined property rights can be a source of externalities

2. Explain how external costs and benefits affect the efficiency of a market equilibrium

CHAPTER 20

3. Describe various approaches that can be used to reduce the level of pollution to the socially efficient level

4. Derive the market demand curve for a public good

5. Explain the problems associated with common-property resources

6. Discuss the steps that must be taken in a cost-benefit study

Conditions That Lead to Inefficient Market Outcomes

According to economic theory, rational choice requires that consumers and producers consider all the marginal benefits and marginal costs of their choices. In each of the situations we have considered thus far, the additional, or marginal, benefits and costs have been *private*, or internal, to the individual. All resources have been assumed to be privately owned, and markets control the allocation of each resource. If the production process requires labor, land, and capital, the producer pays for all the labor, land, and capital used. We have also assumed that when a consumer buys a good, all the benefits of consumption are enjoyed by the consumer.

However, many consumption and production decisions confer benefits or costs on individuals who are not involved in the original market transaction. For example, assume a steel mill uses a river as the dumping ground for its effluent (wastes). If this action forces a nearby city to build additional water treatment facilities, the city is, in effect, bearing the cost of properly disposing of the effluent. Next, assume that a neighborhood is considering the purchase of land to create a park. The purchase will be financed by voluntary donations, but everyone will be allowed to use the park. This act would automatically contribute to the increased well-being of everyone in the neighborhood, even if some of them do not donate funds. In this case, there is a clear disincentive to donate and instead to rely on the other guy to foot the bill. And, finally, when someone allows his cattle to graze on public land, he does so for the benefits he realizes. However, this action may, at the same time, impose costs on other people who would like to let their cattle graze there as well.

In all of the examples listed above, third parties (individuals not directly involved in the transaction) bear part of the costs or benefits associated with the action in question. Such examples illustrate the problems of external costs, public goods, and common-property resources, respectively. Before examining each of these sources of market failure in detail it is necessary to examine the problems that impede the proper functioning of the market mechanism.

Property Rights Revisited

One of the major characteristics of market economies is the existence of **property rights**. Private market transactions are exchanges of property rights. For example, you may exchange something you have the right to (money income) for something a store owner has a right to (a pound of coffee beans). After the exchange, the store owner has the property right to the money and you have the property right to the coffee.

Property rights:
The legally sanctioned control that an individual exercises over a collection of goods, resources, and services.

For some goods, however, the question of who actually owns the property right to the good in question is unclear. For example, with whom would you exchange your income (profits) if your company wanted to buy the right to use a river to dispose of its effluents? Using a river as a dumping ground causes market failure because no one has clear property rights to the river. The cost of disposing of the effluent in the river becomes an external one – no exchange of property rights can take place. The river is treated as being costless for the firm to use.

A system of well-defined property rights goes a long way toward alleviating such problems. If clearly established property rights were assigned to the air and water, one would not be able to emit pollution unless the owner of the affected resource was compensated for its use. However, establishing property rights in such cases is not easy. This is especially true given the lack of information on the value different individuals attach to such property rights. The following example illustrates the role of poorly defined property rights as a source of external costs.

Suppose you walk into your dorm room only to find that your new roommate smokes. Because you dislike cigarette smoke, you start considering what you can do about the external cost your roommate is imposing on you. So long as the university does not define who has the property right to the clean air in dorm rooms, the first one to the room has, in effect, the opportunity to seize the property right. If one or the other of you were given clear property rights, the two of you could negotiate an exchange of rights; you might be willing to exchange your rights to clean air for the right to use your roomie's personal computer a certain amount of time. However, without clearly defined property rights, the most likely solution to the external cost problem is arbitration by the dorm staff or some other authority. Furthermore, there is no guarantee that the ruling will distribute the property right optimally. That is, the property right might not go to the individual who values it most.

When property rights are poorly defined, there is an increased potential for external costs that are borne by third parties.

Section Recap

The Coase Theorem

In 1960, Ronald Coase addressed the notion that intervention is always required in the case of market failure.[1] When a small number of people are involved, and when transaction costs are low, he argued, private negotiation can result in an optimum allocation of resources. The only things needed for private negotiation to work are a clear assignment of transferable property rights and the ability to identify and bring together all the affected parties. This argument is known as the **Coase Theorem**. According to the Coase Theorem, if individuals stand to gain from a transaction (that is, if the marginal benefits exceed the marginal costs), they will undertake it.

Coase Theorem: So long as all affected parties stand to gain from a transaction (an exchange of property rights), and transactions costs are low, the transaction will take place.

The Coase Theorem is illustrated in Figure 20.1, which depicts the situation faced by you and your chain-smoking roommate. The curve labeled MPB indicates the marginal private benefits your roommate receives from each additional unit of smoking. The curve labeled MEC shows the marginal external cost you incur breathing the smoke-filled air. (The cost is external in the sense that your roommate generates it but you bear it.)

In the absence of property rights to clean air (and assuming that you do not throttle her), your roommate will generate Q_{Max} units of smoking. This is because the marginal

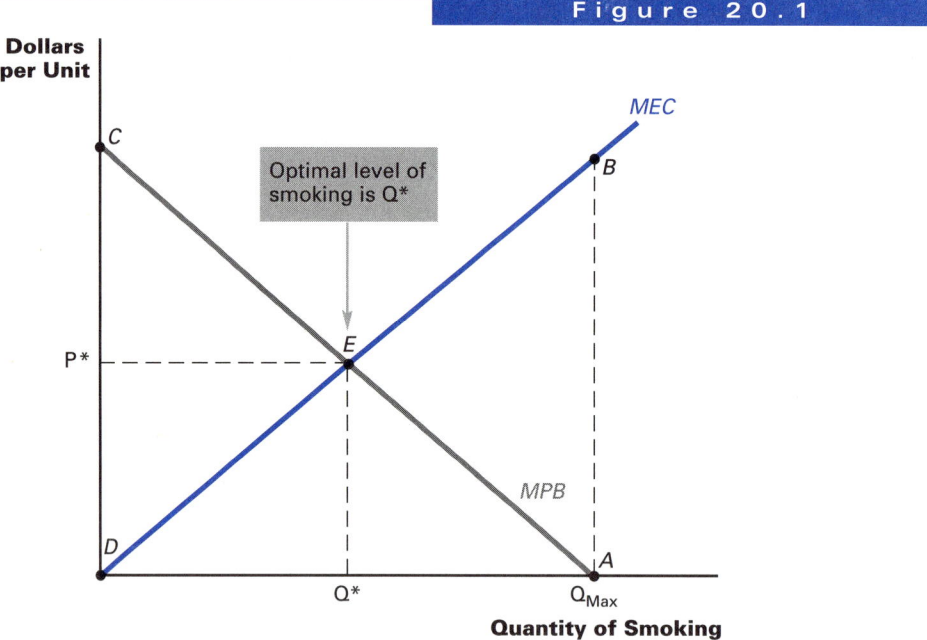

Figure 20.1

The Coase Theorem

The curves labeled MPB and MEC show the marginal private benefits and the marginal external cost of smoking. The optimum level of smoking is Q*. If you have the property right to clean air, you can restrict your roommate's smoking to Q = 0. However, so long as she is willing to pay you an amount sufficient to cover the external cost of her smoking, it is in your best interest to accept the payment. The amount of the bribe paid will lie between DEQ* and DCEQ*. If, instead, your roommate has the property right, it is in your best interest to bribe her not to smoke as much. In this case the total amount of the bribe will lie between Q*EA and Q*EBA.

---

cost to her of each additional unit of smoking is zero. Thus, for your roommate, marginal private benefits equal marginal private costs at Q_{Max}. (Note that beyond Q_{Max} marginal benefits are negative.) You, on the other hand, are left to endure marginal external costs of AB dollars (and hence total costs of DBA dollars). Clearly this is inefficient. The efficient level of smoking is at Q*. At Q* the additional benefits of smoking to your roommate (MPB) equal the additional cost of the smoke to you (MEC).

Assume the university assigns the property right to you, giving you the exclusive right to clean air in the room. Now you have the right to restrict your roommate's smoking to Q = 0. However, suppose she offers you a bribe to endure some amount of her smoking. So long as she is willing to pay you an amount sufficient to cover the external cost of her smoking, it is in your best interest to accept. MPB shows your roommate's maximum willingness to pay to be allowed to smoke. MEC shows your minimum willingness to accept compensation to endure each unit of smoking. So long as she offers you more than the minimum amount you are willing to accept, you will be better off accepting the bribe. The additional benefit of the bribe exceeds the additional cost of the smoking. This implies that when negotiations are finished you would be willing to allow your roommate the pleasure of Q* units of smoking. The amount of the total bribe paid will lie between the amounts

DEQ* – the minimum bribe you would be willing to accept – and DCEQ* – the maximum amount your roommate would be willing to pay.

Suppose instead that the university gives the property right to your roommate. In this case, you can bribe her not to smoke as much. So long as the additional benefit you receive from a reduction in smoking exceeds the additional cost to you, it is in your best interest to offer a bribe. When negotiations are complete, you will offer a bribe to your roommate sufficient to induce her to reduce her smoking to Q* units per day. The total amount of the bribe will lie between Q*EA – the minimum bribe your roommate would be willing to accept – and Q*EBA – the maximum bribe you would be willing to pay.

When the number of affected parties is small, assigning clear property rights facilitates private negotiation toward the optimal amount of pollution. It does not matter who is initially given the property right. So long as both parties stand to gain from an exchange of property rights, private negotiation will produce a socially efficient outcome.

However, merely assigning property rights is not a panacea. Suppose the number of parties affected by smoking is large, for example, passengers on a flight from Honolulu to St. Louis, and that the property rights to clean air have been given to nonsmokers on all flights. In theory, the smokers could get together and offer a bribe to the nonsmokers to allow them to smoke. However, as a practical matter it would be much more difficult to negotiate an efficient solution now that such a large number of people is involved. Also, there is an incentive for individuals to understate their willingness to pay to smoke. This point is made by Coase – in many cases transactions costs will be so large as to preclude negotiations. Instead, resolution of the dispute will have to be handled by a third party such as the courts.

The preceding discussion serves to illustrate the importance of a lack of clearly defined property rights as a source of market failure. To the extent that property rights are poorly defined and transactions costs are high, it often is likely that in the absence of intervention, the market will not generate a socially efficient level of output. This important point is considered in more detail below.

Section Recap

When transactions costs are low, private negotiation will produce an optimal allocation of property rights. However, in many cases transactions costs are such that property rights disputes must be arbitrated by a third party such as the courts.

Externalities

Economists refer to costs and benefits that spill over into other people's lives as spillovers, or more commonly, *externalities*. Externalities that have a negative effect on the well-being of third parties are referred to as **external costs**. Alternatively, externalities can be positive or beneficial, in which case they are referred to as **external benefits**.

In the presence of externalities we need to change our requirement for rational choice. Knowing only the marginal *private* costs and benefits is no longer sufficient to determine the optimal level of output. We must now broaden our perspective to consider the marginal *social* costs and benefits, that is, the costs and benefits borne by society as a

External cost:
Cost of a market transaction imposed on someone other than the parties to the transaction.

External benefit:
Gain from a market transaction going to someone other than the parties to the transaction.

whole. The **social costs** and **social benefits** of production and consumption activities are determined by adding the external costs and benefits to the private costs and benefits.

External Costs

Social costs:

The sum of the private and external costs of a production or consumption activity.

Social benefits:

The sum of the private and external benefits of a production or consumption activity.

Consider once again the example of the steel mill located next to a river. The steel mill, which is situated upstream from a city that draws its drinking water from the same river, dumps a large amount of waste from its production processes into the river. However, before the city can use the river water for drinking, the water must pass through a special treatment process to remove the wastes from the steel mill.

In this situation the steel mill has imposed an external cost on the city in the form of increased water treatment costs. As this example illustrates, an external cost is a cost of production (or consumption) that is imposed on some third party, for which the generator of the cost is not charged. In our example, the steel mill has imposed the cost of waste water treatment on the city rather than bearing the costs itself through the purchase of waste water treatment equipment. This contrasts with the internal costs of production, which the steel mill does pay. The internal costs consist of the fixed and variable costs of production – the cost of the physical capital, workers' salaries, raw materials, utility bills.

From a social point of view the marginal social cost (MSC) of producing steel is equal to the marginal private (or internal) cost (MPC) plus the marginal external cost. Figure 20.2 depicts the market for steel. The curve labeled MSB shows the marginal social benefits of additional steel, assuming no external benefits are generated by its production. The curve labeled MPC shows the marginal private cost of producing steel.

In the situation in which the steel mill does not install waste water treatment equipment, profits are maximized by producing Q_p units of steel, at a price of P_p dollars per unit. This output-price combination is determined by equating the marginal social benefits and the marginal *private* cost of producing the steel. However, due to the external costs, output level Q_p is inefficient.

If we add the marginal external cost to the marginal private costs, the marginal social cost curve (MSC) lies above the marginal private cost curve, as shown in Figure 20.2. The efficient level of output is the quantity at which marginal social benefit equals marginal social cost. Thus, output falls to Q_s and price rises to P_s. Clearly, *failure to consider the external costs of production results in overproduction of the good (and hence an overallocation of resources to production of the good) and too low a market price.*

The actual efficiency (or welfare) loss associated with producing Q_p units of output is measured as follows. Producing units beyond Q_s adds more to costs than to benefits – MSC exceeds MSB. Thus, each unit of output from Q_s to Q_p involves an efficiency loss. The shaded triangle in Figure 20.2 measures the total efficiency loss associated with overproduction of steel at Q_p.

Section Recap

In the absence of market intervention, external costs will result in an overallocation of resources to the production of goods and services.

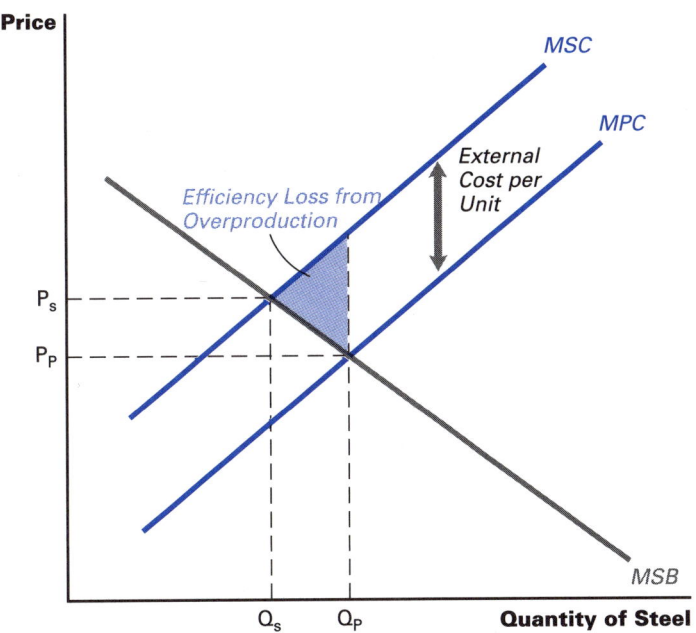

Figure 20.2

Efficiency and the Effects of External Costs

The curve labeled MSB measures the marginal social benefits of each unit of steel produced. The curves labeled MPC and MSC measure the marginal private and marginal social costs per unit produced. The vertical difference between MPC and MSC measures the external cost per unit. The market solution would be Q_p units at a price of P_p per unit. However, the inclusion of external costs reduces output to Q_s and price rises to P_s – the efficient equilibrium. The shaded area is the welfare loss associated with the overproduction of steel when only private costs are considered. A tax equal to the vertical distance between MPC and MSC would induce firms to produce the efficient level of output.

External Benefits

Not all externalities need impose a cost on others. For example, suppose that you decide to pay the required fee and get a flu vaccination. As a result, you incur all the costs of receiving the vaccination. However, not all of the benefits of getting the shot are enjoyed by you alone. Your busy roommate, who cannot find the time to get the (much–feared) shot, your family, and your friends also benefit because you do not expose them to the virus.

In this situation all those getting flu vaccinations confer external benefits on their neighbors in the form of reduced chances of contracting the flu virus. As this example illustrates, an external benefit is an unintended benefit of consumption (or production) enjoyed by some third party, for which the generator of the benefit is not compensated. This contrasts with the internal benefits of consumption that are enjoyed solely by the consumer.

From society's point of view the marginal social benefit (MSB) of being vaccinated is equal to the marginal private benefit (MPB) plus the marginal external benefit. Figure 20.3 depicts the market for flu vaccinations. The curve labeled MSC measures the marginal

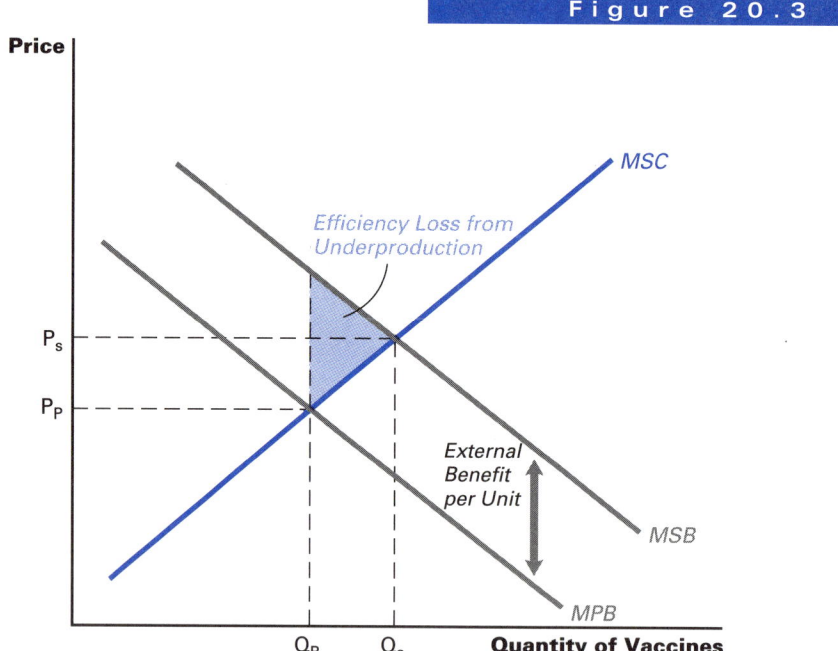

Figure 20.3

Efficiency and the Effects of External Benefits

The curve labeled MSC measures the marginal social cost of vaccines produced. The curves labeled MPB and MSB measure the marginal private and marginal social benefits per unit of vaccines produced. The vertical difference between MPB and MSB measures the external benefit per unit. The market solution is Q_p units produced at a price of P_p per unit. However, the inclusion of external benefits increases output to Q_s and price rises to P_s – the socially efficient equilibrium. The shaded area is the welfare loss resulting from the underproduction of flu vaccines when only private benefits are considered. A subsidy to consumers equal to the vertical distance between MPB and MSB would induce the market to produce the socially efficient level of output.

social cost of flu shots, assuming no external costs are generated. The curve labeled MPB is the marginal private benefit derived from flu shots (reduced chance of illness).

Ignoring external benefits, the equilibrium level of vaccinations is Q_p vaccinations, at a price of P_p dollars per vaccination. However, this number of vaccinations is too low. When the marginal external benefits are added to the marginal private benefits the MSB curve lies above the MPB curve. The efficient price and number of vaccinations are found by equating marginal social benefit and marginal social cost. Thus, the efficient number of vaccinations is Q_s and the efficient price is P_s. *Failure to consider the external benefits of consumption results in the underproduction of the good (and hence an underallocation of resources to production of the good) and too low a market price.*

The MSC curve shows the additional cost to society of producing one more vaccination, and the MSB curve shows the additional social benefit of producing one more vaccination. So long as MSB exceeds MSC, producing that unit is efficient – it adds more to benefits than to costs. Thus, failure to produce each unit of output from Q_p to Q_s involves some efficiency loss. The shaded triangle measures the total efficiency loss resulting from the underproduction of vaccinations at Q_p.

In the absence of market intervention, external benefits will result in an underallocation of resources to the production of goods and services.

Policy Prescriptions

Because markets fail to account for externalities, they result in an inefficient allocation of resources. However, the market has no choice but to fail. When one does not have to pay to use a productive input, or when one does not have to pay to consume a good, the market will necessarily overproduce (in the case of external costs) or underproduce (in the case of external benefits) the good or service in question. Consequently, this is one area where intervening in the market can increase efficiency.

In the case of external costs, the objective of intervention in the market is to *internalize* the external costs. That is, we attempt to create the conditions necessary to ensure that the individual or firm responsible for the external costs pays for all the costs incurred. There are a number of ways to accomplish this.

One obvious way to control negative externalities is to charge those responsible for the costs imposed on others. For example, if the steel mill were taxed an amount equal to the marginal external cost imposed on the city, the costs of steel production would rise. This would, in turn, alter the steel mill's profit-maximizing level of output. Specifically, the steel mill would have an incentive (higher profits) to reduce output.

The imposition of a tax raises the cost of producing each unit of a good and shifts the marginal private cost curve upward by the amount of the tax. In the steel mill example, if the tax were set exactly equal to the marginal external cost of production, marginal private costs would increase to MSC in Figure 20.2. As a result of the tax, the steel mill would reduce output to Q_s and the market price would rise to P_s. Production would occur at the output level at which MSC equals MSB and would be economically efficient.

Although straightforward in principle, setting a tax at the correct level is difficult in practice because many external costs are difficult to measure accurately. In the case of the city and the steel mill it was relatively simple – external costs could be measured as the additional treatment costs incurred by the city. However, how does one measure the cost of health problems or death caused by toxic pollutants? Incomplete knowledge of external costs can lead to the imposition of a tax that is either too high or too low. A tax that is too high causes the MPC curve to shift to a level higher than MSC, resulting in too low a level of output. A tax that is too low shifts the MPC curve to a level lower than MSC, resulting in an output level that is still too high.

External benefits also require intervention in the market. To internalize an external benefit, we could *subsidize* the consumers of the good. In the flu vaccine example, we saw that those who buy the vaccine pass on an external benefit to others. If a per-unit subsidy were offered to those who buy the vaccination, it would raise the marginal private benefit of getting a vaccination at each quantity of vaccinations. (The buyers now get a shot *and* cash in their pockets.) A subsidy exactly equal to the marginal external benefit would shift the MPB curve up to MSB in Figure 20.3. The producers of the flu shots would have an incentive to increase the quantity of vaccines supplied (as a result of the higher price), and consumers would pay less than before. Once again, as a result of the subsidy marginal social benefit equals marginal social cost, and an efficient level of output results.

However, just as it is difficult to set a tax exactly equal to marginal external cost, it is also difficult to set a subsidy so that it is exactly equal to the marginal external benefit. In particular, how does one determine the dollar value of the reduction in health risk associated with the flu vaccination? If the subsidy is overestimated, too many vaccinations will be given. If it is underestimated, too few will be given.

Section Recap

In theory, external costs can be internalized by imposing a tax equal to the marginal external cost on the generator of the externality. In a similar manner, positive externalities can be internalized by subsidizing the consumers of the good in question.

External Costs and Environmental Pollution

When one considers the concept of negative externalities, the first example that usually comes to mind is pollution. The tradeoffs involved in using air, water, and land as a waste dump have drawn increased attention in the last thirty years. Initially, research and legislation focused on the health effects of so-called classical air and water pollutants such as carbon monoxide, sulfur dioxide, lead, volatile organic compounds, industrial waste water, and sewage treatment residues. More recently, attention has been focused on how to control the disposal of the enormous quantities of toxic wastes that are produced annually by U.S. industries, hazardous air pollutants, and the potential threat of global warming.

When Is Pollution a Social Problem?

It is important to understand that not all air or water pollution is caused by production and consumption activities, and not all pollution endangers public welfare. Natural degradation of organic material in water can lead to foul-smelling streams and ponds. Lightning-induced forest fires and volcanic eruptions have contributed greatly to local and global air pollution. In turn, environmental media (such as the air and waterways) have a natural ability to absorb, or assimilate, some pollutants. In other words, the environment has some **assimilative capacity**. For example, some effluents dumped into a stream can be consumed by stream biota and rendered harmless. In a similar manner, air pollutants can be diluted as a result of the mixing and dispersion caused by air currents.

Assimilative capacity:

The environment's natural ability to absorb or assimilate some pollutants.

However, *when the discharge of a pollutant is so great that it exceeds the assimilative capacity of the environment, the pollutant becomes a social problem.* That is when we notice the impact of a production or consumption activity on social welfare.

Opportunity Cost of Improved Environmental Quality

One of the first points we made in Chapter 1 of this book is that choices always involve tradeoffs. Yet when the question "What is the optimal amount of pollution?" is raised, the answer many people give is "Zero." We need to bear in mind, however, that the reduction of pollution often requires investment in pollution-control capital (such as smokestack scrubbers for coal-fired electric utilities) and the use of additional resources that could have been used to produce other goods and services. *The opportunity cost of improved environmental quality is the amount of other goods forgone.* Again, we are faced with choices. In most cases we cannot have both an increase in the output of goods and services and an increase in environmental quality without a change in technology or a change in the stock of resources.

Many people object to this seemingly cavalier acceptance of the consequences of pollution. However, so long as we continue to consume goods whose production generates at least some pollution, there *will* be some damage to vegetation, materials, and human health. The relevant question is not whether to eliminate pollution but whether the additional benefits of pollution control outweigh the additional costs incurred.

Individuals argue, nonetheless, that there is no way one could put a finite value on an increase in the chance of becoming ill, let alone on an increase in the chance of dying. This argument implies that human health and life have an infinite value. However, individuals' daily actions indicate otherwise. If you drive a car without wearing a seat belt, you increase the chance that you will suffer head injuries in the event of a head-on collision. If you eat foods that are not good for you, you increase the chance that you will die of heart disease, obesity, or cancer.

Almost everyone makes choices involving tradeoffs between enjoyment from consumption of goods and an increase in the chance he will become ill or die. This reveals that people do place a value that is considerably less than infinite on human health and life. The trouble is, we often deny that the choices we make convey any risk at all. However, denial does not make it so. Thus, it is important to recognize the implicit tradeoffs we make in our daily actions. Efficient decisions on the optimal level of environmental quality require a recognition of the tradeoffs involved.

Optimal Amount of Environmental Quality: Balancing Benefits and Costs

Figure 20.4 depicts the market for environmental quality (EQ). The quantity (level) of environmental quality is measured on the horizontal axis. The market price per unit of environmental quality is measured on the vertical axis. An individual's marginal benefit from environmental quality is measured by his or her willingness to pay for each additional unit. The demand curve, D, is the vertical sum of each individual's marginal benefits and represents the society's willingness to pay for additional units of environmental quality. It is, in fact, the marginal social benefits of pollution control. The horizontal sum of each firm's marginal private costs of producing environmental quality (that is, reducing pollution) is shown by the supply curve S and represents the marginal social costs of pollution control. The question we want to answer is, What is the optimal amount of environmental quality? Put another way, What is the optimal amount of pollution?

The belief that the optimal level of pollution is zero ignores two very important lessons about consumption. First, as you consume more of a good in a given time period, your willingness to pay for additional units of the good declines. In Figure 20.4, as environmental quality increases (that is, as pollution is reduced) each additional unit of environmental quality is valued less. At low levels of environmental quality, for example, Q_0, consumers are willing to pay P_0 for an additional unit of improvement. However, when the environment is less polluted, for example at Q_1, consumers are only willing to pay P_1 for an additional unit of improvement. Second, there are always tradeoffs. To have more environmental quality, resources must be diverted from the production and consumption of other goods. It is a technical fact that the marginal cost of controlling the emission of additional units of a given source of pollution usually increases. This is reflected in the upward slope of the supply curve of environmental quality.

For levels of environmental quality between 0 and Q^*, the additional benefits of increasing environmental quality exceed the additional costs of doing so. At levels of environmental quality greater than Q^*, the additional costs of increasing environmental quality (that is, further reductions in pollution) exceed the additional benefits of doing so. Hence, *the optimal amount of environmental quality is Q^*, the quantity at which the marginal benefits equal the marginal costs*, which is, in this case, not at zero pollution.

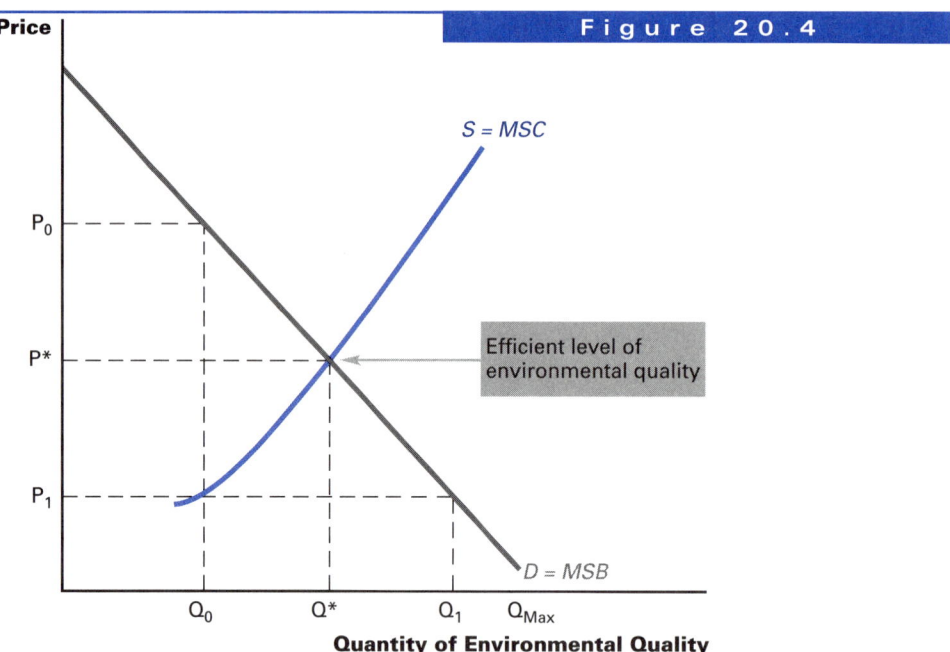

Figure 20.4

The Socially Efficient Level of Pollution Control

This figure depicts the market for environmental quality (EQ), where EQ is measured as a *decrease* in pollution. The demand curve, D, represents society's willingness to pay for additional units of EQ – the marginal social benefits (MSB) of pollution control. The supply curve, S, represents the marginal social costs of pollution control (or increased EQ). The efficient level of pollution control occurs where MSB equals marginal cost, at Q^* units of EQ.

Pollutants are a problem when they are discharged at a rate that exceeds the assimilative capacity of the environment. The economically efficient level of pollution control occurs at the point at which the marginal benefits and marginal costs of pollution control are equal.

Pollution-Control Policies

It is now time to take a look at how policies designed to internalize pollution externalities are formulated. Two different types of control policies are considered. The first approach is to use government regulation directly, through the setting of emission standards. The second approach is to establish the conditions under which the market may work toward the socially optimal equilibrium. This approach also uses government intervention, but indirectly, in the form of emission charges, transferable discharge permits, and specific property rights.

Direct Regulation   The most direct way to reduce the incentive firms have to pollute is to forbid it outright through the use of an **emission (or effluent) standard.** Often referred to as the command and control approach, an emission standard constitutes a legal limit on the amount of a pollutant an individual source is allowed to emit. Such a standard could, for example, require that a source emit, on average, no more than 2.5 pounds of sulfur dioxide per unit of output into the atmosphere.

Emission standard: A legal limit on the amount of a pollutant an individual source is allowed to emit.

Ideally a standard is set such that the resulting market equilibrium is the efficient equilibrium. This case is illustrated in Figure 20.5, which depicts the market for electricity produced by coal-fired plants. Assuming that there are no external benefits from the consumption of electricity, the demand curve, D, represents marginal social benefits (MSB). The sum of the individual producers' marginal private costs (MPC) is shown by the supply curve, S. However, the production of electricity from coal-fired plants generates a number of air pollutants, most notably sulfur dioxide (SO_2). This results in external costs that cause marginal social costs (MSC) to exceed the marginal private costs of production by the amount C.

In the absence of intervention in the market, the electricity industry will produce Q_p units of electricity per year, to be sold at a market price of P_p dollars per unit. However, this solution is inefficient, since the production of Q_p units results in a marginal external cost of C dollars from the sulfur dioxide emissions. The efficient level of output and price are found by equating marginal social benefits and marginal social costs, Q_s units and a price of P_s dollars per unit in Figure 20.5. Once again, the privately determined output is greater than the efficient output, and the privately determined price is lower than the efficient price.

Suppose the government decides to impose an emission standard. The optimal standard should be set such that the industry's output of electricity is Q_s units per year. To meet a given standard, each firm in the industry must install pollution-control equipment. Assuming this raises the marginal private cost of production, the market supply curve will shift to the left. If the standard increases marginal costs by the amount C, the industry's private optimum will be identical to the efficient level of output, Q_s, and will be sold at a price of P_s. Thus, the emission standard eliminates the inefficiency associated with the production of electricity.

It is easy to see the potential for the standard to be inefficient. If the emissions standard is set too low (is too restrictive) and results in marginal compliance costs greater than C, the supply curve will shift too far to the left, and output will be inefficient (too low). If the standard is set too high (is not restrictive enough), the supply curve will not shift far enough to the left, and output will again be inefficient (too high).

Another source of inefficiency with the standards approach stems from the fact that emission standards are usually uniform across firms. However, individual firms are not likely to face the same pollution control costs, and the external costs of pollution are not likely to be as high in rural areas as they are in urban areas. This implies that the marginal social benefits and the marginal costs of pollution control vary across firms. For efficiency, emission standards should be stricter for firms that can reduce pollution at lower cost or are located in heavily populated areas than for firms with higher control costs or sparse surrounding populations.

However, setting different standards for different size firms and firms in different areas is an administrative nightmare that would greatly increase the already high cost of setting and enforcing emission standards. In response, economists have developed alternative approaches the government can use to promote an efficient level of pollution, approaches that recognize differences in individual firms' cost of control and differences in the social cost of pollution.

Incentives-Based Mechanisms As an alternative to direct regulation, the government can obtain the same result at a lower cost by creating financial disincentives to pollute. It can also create property rights where none existed previously. If these property rights are well specified, the generators of an externality will have an incentive to reduce pollution to the efficient level, again at a lower cost.

Emission charge:
A tax imposed on each unit of pollution emitted by a firm.

When producers are charged an amount equal to the external cost their production imposes on others, they have an incentive to reduce their output to a more efficient level. Thus, the government can use **emission charges** to reduce pollution. Emission charges consist of taxes on the pollution emitted by a firm. The tax can be set as a per-unit tax, in which case each firm's marginal private cost rises by the amount of the tax or the per-unit cost of pollution abatement – whichever is less. Referring to Figure 20.5, a tax equal to the marginal external cost, C, would raise the marginal private costs of production and cause a leftward shift in the industry supply curve from S to S'. As a result of the tax, the industry would reduce output to Q_s.

One of the problems with emission charges is knowing at exactly which level to set the tax. In practice, the information needed to determine the marginal external cost of production is extremely difficult to obtain. In the absence of knowledge of the exact increase in each firm's marginal private cost that would be necessary to drive output (and, hence, pollution) to the efficient level, the control agency must take a hit-and-miss approach. It must set a tax, monitor the resulting level of pollution, and compare that level with the efficient one. If the new output is still too high, the tax must be increased. If the new output is too low, the tax must be lowered.

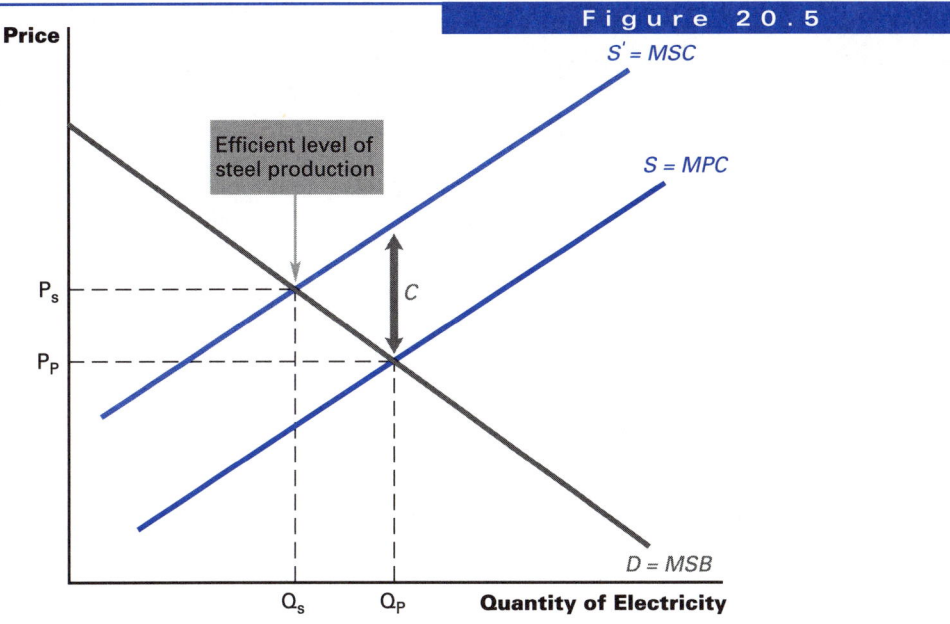

Figure 20.5

External Costs and the Efficient Level of Output

This figure depicts the market for electricity produced by coal-fired plants. Marginal private costs are shown by the supply curve, S. Electricity production generates sulfur dioxide, resulting in external costs. In the absence of market intervention, the industry will produce Q_p units at a market price of P_p dollars per unit. However, this solution is inefficient. Assuming that marginal external cost is equal to the distance C, marginal social costs are shown by the curve S'. To reduce sulfur dioxide emissions, the government could impose an emission standard. As firms install pollution control equipment, the marginal private cost of production increases and the market supply curve shifts to the left.

As an alternative to emissions charges, the government can establish a program of **transferable pollution permits**. A permits program creates a market for pollution rights. If a firm wants to dump effluent into a stream or emit carbon monoxide into the air, it must now pay for the right to do so. The government essentially has created a property right to a good for which property rights had not been established previously.

A permits program works as follows: First, the control agency must set a limit on the total amount of the pollutant that can be generated and released into the environment. Second, the control agency must issue permits to affected firms. These permits entitle the bearer to emit a specified amount of pollution per period. For example, each permit might allow the holder to dump one pound of effluent per day into a nearby river. Without a permit, a firm may not discharge any effluent into the river.

Permits can be issued by the pollution-control agency in a number of ways. They can be sold to the highest bidder, given away on a first-come-first-served basis, or divided evenly among existing firms. *With respect to efficiency, it does not matter how the permits are*

Transferable pollution permit:
A property right to discharge a specified quantity of a particular pollutant; it can be traded among affected parties.

Wood Is Growing as a Source Of Electricity[2]

Electricity is produced using a number of different fuels. Nuclear power accounts for about 22 percent of the electric power produced in the United States. Coal and oil account for over half. However, safety concerns and the problem of what to do with spent nuclear fuel have seriously diminished the demand for new nuclear power plants. In addition, concerns over acidic deposition and the potential threat of global warming have cast a bad light on coal and oil as sources of electric power. The combustion of both coal and oil result in sulfur and carbon dioxide emissions that, in turn, have been linked to acid rain and global warming. Thus, it is not surprising that a large amount of money has been spent on research on alternative energy sources for producing electricity such as solar and wind power. What is surprising is the increasing amount of attention being directed at one of the oldest sources of energy – wood. In light of the fact that wood's share of the energy market has been so small for so long – wood was displaced by coal and oil around the turn of the century – and its image as a source of pollution it is worth asking: Does this make economic sense?

Consider first the fact that during and following the energy crisis of the 1970s many people decided to convert, at least partially, to reliance on wood for heating needs. However, the problems with pollution from wood burning stoves and fireplaces resulted in numerous new regulations and restrictions on wood burning in many areas of the country. A second factor to consider is the backlash against wood as a fuel that grew out of concern about the rate at which the nation's forests were disappearing. Such factors would seem to suggest that replacing coal and nuclear fuel with wood simply amounts to a case of trading one bad situation for

issued. What does matter is that the permit owners must have the right to transfer their ownership of the permit to someone else. (Note, however, that the way in which the permits are initially distributed will affect the distribution of income.)

Figure 20.6 illustrates the effect of a permits program. Assume the control agency sets the pollution limit at Q^* units per year. It will then create only enough permits to allow Q^* units to be emitted. Therefore, the supply of permits is a vertical line at Q^*. The MB curve is the affected firms' demand curve for permits. The market–clearing price for permits is found where the supply of permits (S_P) and the demand for permits (D_P) intersect, at P^* dollars. If a firm's marginal pollution control cost is greater than P^*, it would be cheaper to buy the necessary permits at the market price of P^* dollars each than to pay the additional control costs. If a firm's marginal pollution control cost is less than P^*, it would be cheaper to pay the additional control costs rather than buy the permits at the market price of P^* dollars each.

The Clean Air Act Amendments of 1990 (CAAA) contain specific provisions for the use of a permits program. Title IV of the CAAA calls for the creation of permits, or allowances, for SO_2 emissions in the electric utility industry. SO_2, which is emitted by coal-fired electric generators, results in acid deposition (often referred to as acid rain). In order to reduce the amount of SO_2 emitted into the atmosphere, the CAAA require a gradual decrease in SO_2 emissions by electric utilities. To facilitate this process, firms will be issued allowances that

another. But such a view fails to account for advances in the science of wood as an energy source that have occurred in recent years.

To begin, the wood that is being used in combination with coal or by itself in electric generating plants is coming more and more not from existing forests but rather from plantations that grow special hybrids, or "super trees." Some of these trees can grow as much as 15 feet in a single year. In addition, whereas mother nature can produce wood at a rate of about one ton per acre per year, these special hybrids can produce as much as nine tons per acre annually. As a result, the amount of forested land stands to increase in coming years as more plantations are developed. An added benefit of such plantations is that in addition to providing fuel for the production of electricity, they also provide jobs.

Another important feature of wood as a fuel concerns the amount of pollution it produces. Although the combustion of wood does release some amount of carbon (which is linked to global warming) into the atmosphere, the amount released is less than the amount released by burning coal. In addition, while trees are growing, they are net absorbers of carbon in the atmosphere. Because burning wood does not result in sulfur emissions, wood has another leg up on coal. For example, by mixing wood with coal, a power plant in New York has been able to cut its sulfur emissions in half. Such a strategy enables utilities to avoid more costly alternatives such as the installation of flue gas scrubbers and reliance on more costly, low-sulfur coal. Technological advances in the combustion of wood and methods to clean emissions before they are released to the atmo sphere have contributed greatly to cleaning up wood's act as a fuel.

At the current time wood accounts for about 1 percent of the electricity market. However, experts in the energy field are predicting that share could increase to as much as 15 percent over the next twenty years. To that end, electric utilities, the U.S. Department of Energy, and other federal and state agencies are stepping up funding directed at the development of wood as a renewable energy source. Farmers in Minnesota are getting involved, planting more than a thousand acres of hybrid poplars in 1994 as part of a program funded by the utilities and the Agriculture Department.

The extent to which wood actually becomes a major source of electric power remains to be seen. However, the current signs suggest that the future for wood is growing bright.

permit the holder to emit a specified amount of SO_2 per time period. The allowances can be used to offset current emissions, sold to other entities, or saved for use at a later date.

Emissions charges and permits programs constitute two alternatives to the standards approach to pollution control. In addition, the U.S. Environmental Protection Agency has reformed its air pollution control program over time in a number of innovative ways. Three innovations that reflect a move toward greater use of economic incentives include the off-set program, the bubble policy, and emission banking.

The **offset program** allows new air pollution sources in a particular geographic region to pay existing sources to reduce their emissions below that required by the standard in lieu of installing control technology at the new plant, so long as the total level of the pollutant does not increase. This program enables new sources to find the least expensive way to reduce pollution in the geographic region. So long as the air quality in the region is better after the new plant moves in, the offset is allowed.

The **bubble policy** attempts to treat a number of closely situated sources, usually within a given production facility, as if they were encased in a giant bubble. The standard then applies to emissions coming out of the bubble. This allows a firm to reduce emissions from those sources within the production facility that are the cheapest to control and to relax controls on the more costly sources. The firm can thus attain the standard at a reduced cost. The only restriction is that tradeoffs may only be made between sources emitting the same pollutant.

Offset program:
Allows a new pollution source in a particular geographic region to pay existing sources to reduce their emissions below that required by the existing standard, in lieu of installing control technology at the new plant.

Bubble policy:
Treats a group of closely situated pollution sources as if they were encased in a giant bubble; the pollution standard then applies to emissions coming out of the bubble.

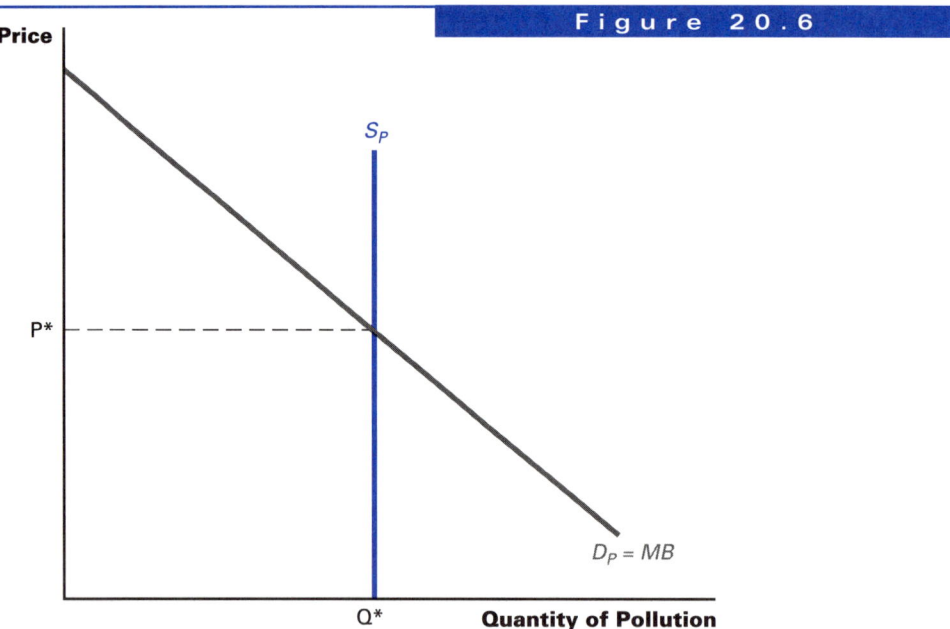

Figure 20.6

The Equilibrium Price of TDPs

Suppose the control agency sets the pollution limit at Q* units per year. It will then create only enough permits to allow Q* units to be emitted. Therefore, the supply of permits is a vertical line at Q*. The MB curve is the firm's demand curve for permits. The market clearing price occurs where the supply of permits (S_p) and the demand for permits (D_p) intersect, at P* dollars.

Emission banking:
A program that grants a firm credit for reducing emissions below the existing standard; the credit can be saved for later use or for sale to another firm.

The **emission banking** program gives firms credit for reducing emissions below the emissions level allowed by the standard. This credit is then deposited in an emissions bank for later use or for sale to another firm. This approach gives existing firms an incentive to adopt new, cost-saving pollution-control technologies. The resulting emissions reduction can be banked and used on days when the control technology is not functioning properly, used to temporarily expand the plant's operations, or sold to a new firm wishing to locate in the area.

Section Recap

Government can use direct regulation or incentives-based mechanisms, such as taxes or transferable pollution permits, to control pollution. The latter approach achieves the same level of control at lower cost and is more efficient.

Public Goods

Public good:
A good whose consumption is nonrival and nonexcludable; markets will not produce the efficient level of public goods.

Most of the goods we buy are produced by private firms and are referred to as *private goods*. However, a number of goods we consume are not produced by private firms but instead by public agencies. Examples include national defense, parks, pollution control, and police and fire protection. These are examples of **public goods**. A number of other goods have characteristics of both public and private goods and are often referred to as *quasi-public goods*. Public roads, education, and libraries are all examples of quasi-public goods.

Public goods differ from private goods in two important ways. First, public goods are *nonrival*. Rivalry does not exist among consumers of public goods because one person's consumption of the good does not diminish the amount available for anyone else. National defense and police protection are good examples of public goods. The benefits I receive from these services do not reduce the benefits you receive. In fact, we are consuming the same good at the same time.

A second difference between public goods and private goods is that public goods are *nonexcludable*. This means that the benefits from consumption of public goods are available to all regardless of whether they pay for the good. If the government builds a dam to reduce the chance of flooding in a particular area, everyone who lives downstream from the dam is protected. In addition, the level of benefits each individual receives does not depend on the amount he or she contributes to any taxes raised to construct the dam. Nonexcludability is present whenever it is prohibitively expensive (if not impossible) to exclude individuals from enjoying the benefits of the good or service once it has been made available for consumption.

Determining the Optimal Quantity of Public Goods

The production of public goods clearly generates external benefits. Consequently, as we have already seen, the market will not provide the optimal amount of the public good. In fact, it is often the case that the market would not provide the public good *at all*. This is the rationale behind government provision of public goods. As with any good that produces external benefits, the optimum level of output is the quantity at which MSB equals MSC. Determining the MSB of public goods, however, requires taking a different approach to aggregating, or adding together, individual demand curves. This difference is illustrated in Figures 20.7 and 20.8.

Individual demand curves are summed horizontally to determine the market demand curve for a private good. Figures 20.7 (a) and 20.7 (b) show the marginal benefit two individuals each derive from consumption of increasing amounts of a private good. Market demand is the horizontal sum of the individuals' demand curves, as shown in Figure 20.7 (c).

An important distinction between private goods and public goods concerns the effects of one individual's consumption on the consumption of another individual. A private good can be consumed by only one person. If I buy a shirt, you and I cannot consume it (wear it) at the same time. This is the logic behind horizontal summation. At a given price, the marginal private benefit received by each individual is summed to obtain the marginal social benefit of the good for the market as a whole.

In contrast, a public good can be consumed by more than one individual simultaneously. As we noted above, my consumption of national defense does not reduce the amount available for you to consume. As a result, *the marginal social benefit of a unit of a public good equals the vertical sum of the marginal private benefits of the individual consumers*. That is, it is

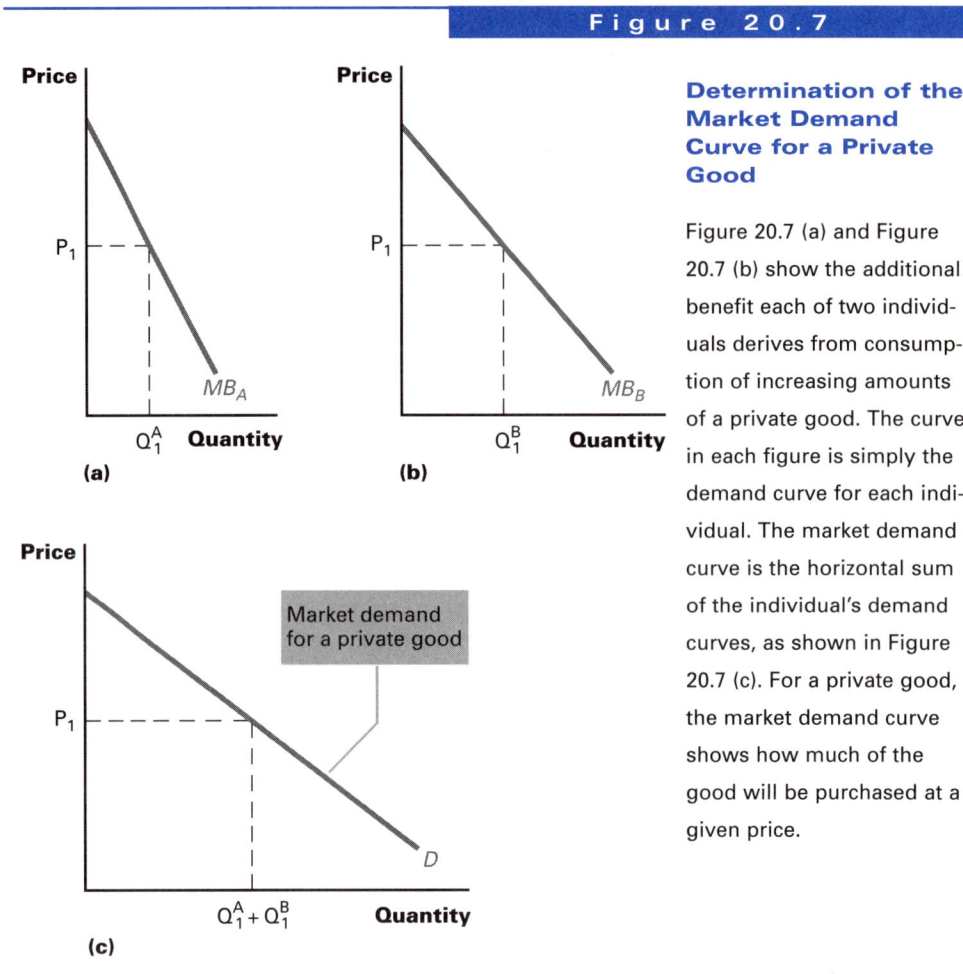

Figure 20.7

Determination of the Market Demand Curve for a Private Good

Figure 20.7 (a) and Figure 20.7 (b) show the additional benefit each of two individuals derives from consumption of increasing amounts of a private good. The curve in each figure is simply the demand curve for each individual. The market demand curve is the horizontal sum of the individual's demand curves, as shown in Figure 20.7 (c). For a private good, the market demand curve shows how much of the good will be purchased at a given price.

equal to the total amount that all the individuals involved are willing to pay to consume the *same* unit of the public good.

Figures 20.8 (a) and 20.8 (b) show the marginal private benefits two individuals receive from consuming a public good. The marginal social benefit of any given amount of the public good is determined by adding up the marginal private benefits enjoyed by each of the consumers. As shown in Figures 20.8 (a) and 20.8 (b), for Q_1 units of the public good, individuals A and B derive marginal benefits of $4 and $6. Thus the marginal social benefit of Q_1 units of the public good is the vertical summation of the individual marginal benefits, or $10, as shown in Figure 20.8 (c).

It is important to understand that the marginal social benefit curve for a public good is *not* a demand curve in the usual sense. Individuals 1 and 2 would not be willing to pay $10 each to consume the first unit of the public good. However, because the sum of their willingness to pay totals $10, if the good can be provided at a marginal cost of $10 or less, the combined payments of both individuals would be enough to cover the additional cost of providing it.

Figure 20.8

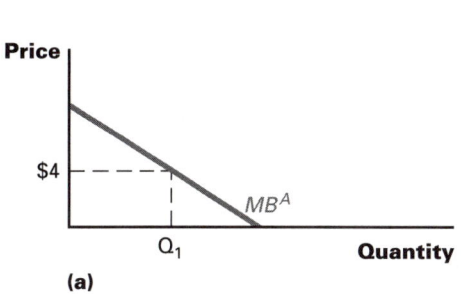

(a)

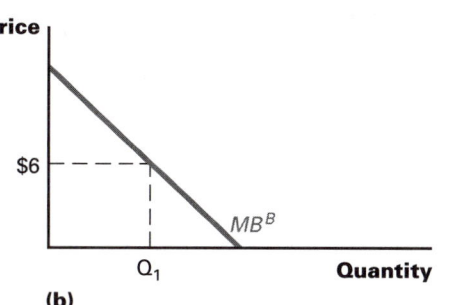

(b)

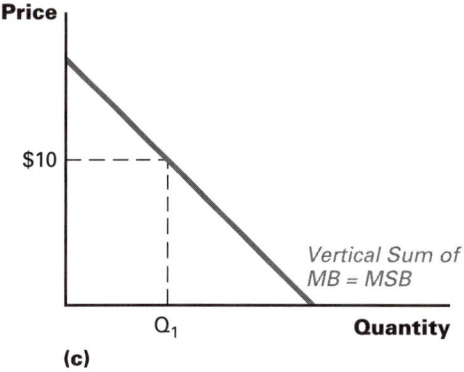

(c)

Determination of the Market Demand Curve for a Public Good

Determining the market demand for a public good is illustrated in this figure. Figure 20.8 (a) and Figure 20.8 (b) show the marginal private benefits two individuals receive from consuming a public good. The marginal social benefit of any given amount (unit) of the public good is found by adding up the marginal private benefits enjoyed by each of the consumers. Thus, Figure 20.8 (c) indicates the marginal social benefits for each unit of the public good. This is the amount that society would be willing to pay, as a whole, for that unit of the public good.

Section Recap

Due to nonrivalry and nonexcludability, the private sector cannot be relied on to produce public goods. Consequently, the government must intervene. The optimal quantity of a public good is determined by equating marginal cost with aggregate marginal willingness to pay.

The Problem of Free Riders

In the old west, when a rancher's livestock was threatened by rustlers the other ranchers would band together and ride the fences to discourage thieves. Everyone contributed to this public good (increased security). However, over time, individual ranchers began to realize that they would get the same protection regardless of the number of hours spent with the posse. As a result, they began spending less time riding, or they dropped out of the group altogether. These ranchers became known as **free riders** for their failure to con-

Free rider:
An individual who receives benefits from a public good but does not pay for those benefits.

Why the DISAGREEMENT?

Reauthorization
of the Clean Air Act[3]

When the Congress amended the Clean Air Act in 1977, it was intended that this legislation would result in a significant improvement in the level of air quality in the United States. However, as time passed it became clear that additional legislation was needed to generate the degree of reductions in air emissions that had been sought previously. By 1990, the air emissions of only seven toxic chemicals, of which there are hundreds, had been regulated. In addition, acid deposition, chlorofluorocarbons, and particulates emissions continue to pose a significant threat to human health and environmental quality.

Most individuals agree that additional steps must be taken to clean up the atmosphere and reduce the amount of air emissions that are generated annually. While the U.S. public expresses a wide range of divergent opinions regarding issues such as national defense and aid to the poor, there is a broad consensus that improvement of environmental quality – including air quality – should be a major priority for policymakers. However, despite this widespread agreement, there has been continuing disagreement over who should be responsible for cleanup and to what extent. This disagreement was most evident in the debate over reauthorization of the Clean Air Act. Why the disagreement?

Clearly, industry will be required to bear the initial burden of reducing the amount of air pollution that is generated. Analysts have put the cost of the new Clean Air Act legislation that was passed in late 1990 at $25 billion annually by the year 2005. While agreeing that improvements in air quality will be costly, however, specific industries disagree over who should do the most to reduce air emissions. For example, when the new legislation was being debated, the steel industry argued that under most proposals it would be forced to bear a disproportionate share of the burden of cleanup. Industry representatives estimated that proposed legislation would cost the industry in excess of $5 billion by 1995. This, they argue, would hurt their competi-

tribute to the safety provided for them by others. The behavior of the free riders led eventually to the dissolution of the group and an increase in the amount of cattle rustling.

Note that each individual rancher who dropped out of the posse was behaving rationally. If one individual failed to contribute to the provision of the good, he would still be able to enjoy the benefits. However, what is rational behavior for the individual turns out to be disastrous if followed by all. As another example of free riders, consider individuals who watch public television shows regularly (or listen to public radio shows regularly) but never contribute during the station's fund-raising drives.

Policy Prescriptions

Because public goods are nonexcludable, individuals cannot be prevented from consuming them, even if they are free riders. However, if everyone acts as a free rider, the public good will not be produced. Thus, the role of a fully informed government is to recognize the social benefits of public goods and establish policies that set marginal social benefits equal to marginal social costs so that the efficient level of the public good will be provided.

One approach the government can use to encourage the efficient level of output of public goods is to subsidize the producers of the public good. A subsidy to producers serves to reduce the marginal cost of producing the public good. If an omniscient government offered the correct subsidy, the optimum number of programs would be produced.

tiveness by taking money away from efforts at modernization.

The coal industry argued that certain provisions of proposed legislation would result in substantial unemployment of coal miners. It has been estimated that the legislation that was finally passed could result in the loss of as many as 15,000 coal mining jobs by the year 2000. These job losses are a result of the effort to reduce acid deposition by limiting the amount of sulfur dioxide emitted into the atmosphere by electric utility plants fueled by high-sulfur coal. Along these same lines, many midwest electric utilities, which are the major users of high-sulfur coal, argued that they will bear a disproportionate share of the burden associated with efforts to reduce acid rain.

Automobile manufacturers also disagreed with the types of steps that were proposed to reduce auto emissions. Many proposals contained provisions that would require a certain percentage of new cars to use alternative fuels, such as natural gas, by specified dates. Automobile manufacturers lobbied instead for a program that would rely on reformulated gasoline. Note that this would minimize the amount of work that must be done to modify engines to run on the new fuels. However, oil companies countered that it would be extremely difficult, if not impossible, to reformulate gas and cut emissions significantly in a relatively short period of time. The final legislation requires both development of vehicles that run on alternative fuels and reformulation of gasoline to reduce emissions of hydrocarbons and toxic pollutants.

The disagreement among industry representatives was exacerbated by calls from environmental group lobbyists for stricter measures than those that had been proposed. In many cases, environmentalists argued, the proposed restrictions did not go far enough to provide an adequate margin of safety for the environment and human health. For many individuals, cost should not be an issue. They point out that, in many cases, once a certain level of damage is incurred, no amount of expenditure will be capable of restoring environmental quality to its previous level. This is especially true in cases where pollution results in the extinction of a particular plant or animal species.

It is still too soon to consider here the actual effects that the requirements of the new Clean Air Act will have on the economy, human health, and the environment. However, it is certain that the new law will impose substantial costs on U.S. industry. It is also clear, given the forces of supply and demand, that although some industries will incur greater costs than others, ultimately many of these costs will be borne by U.S. consumers.

However, determining the correct subsidy is extremely difficult in actual practice – government is not omniscient. A second approach is for the government to produce the good. Production is financed by tax revenues. Indeed, this is how many of the public goods we consume – national defense, public roads, and national parks, to name a few – are produced.

Common-Property Resources

Just as public goods generate positive externalities, another class of goods generates negative externalities when consumed. These goods are referred to as **common-property resources**. Property rights to common-property resources are not clearly specified, or they do not exist at all. Examples include the air, oceans, common grazing land (commons), and fisheries. Because no one has property rights to these resources, they tend to be overexploited.

Garrett Hardin[4] used the example of open grazing areas, or commons, to illustrate the tendency of producers to overexploit common-property resources. The commons was usually an open field near a town where livestock owners were allowed to graze their animals without charge. Each individual had an incentive to consider only the additional benefits and costs to him of feeding another animal on the commons before letting the animal graze there. Because the additional cost to the individual was virtually zero, grazing increased until the commons was denuded of grass and was of no benefit to anyone. Thus, the increased grazing imposed an external cost on other users of the commons.

Common-property resource: A resource for which property rights are poorly defined or nonexistent and whose consumption results in a negative externality.

The "tragedy of the commons," as Hardin labeled it, is that the failure to limit the use of common-property resources will result in their overuse or destruction. Thus, the problem of overgrazing is another example of external costs of production. Because the private cost of using common-property resources is lower than the social cost, the amount of the resource used is too high. Figure 20.9 shows this result for the market for another common-property resource, lobsters. The horizontal axis measures the number of lobsters caught per year. The vertical axis measures the dollar value of the additional benefits and costs of harvesting lobsters.

Assuming no external benefits from the harvesting of lobsters, MSB shows the marginal social benefits of harvesting. The marginal private cost of harvesting the lobsters is shown by the curve labeled MPC. Left alone, the market will generate an equilibrium harvest of Q_p. The marginal external cost of harvesting a lobster today is equal to the losses suffered by future fishermen who will have fewer lobsters to harvest. (As additional lobsters are harvested today, the number of lobsters that can procreate is reduced. Future pop-

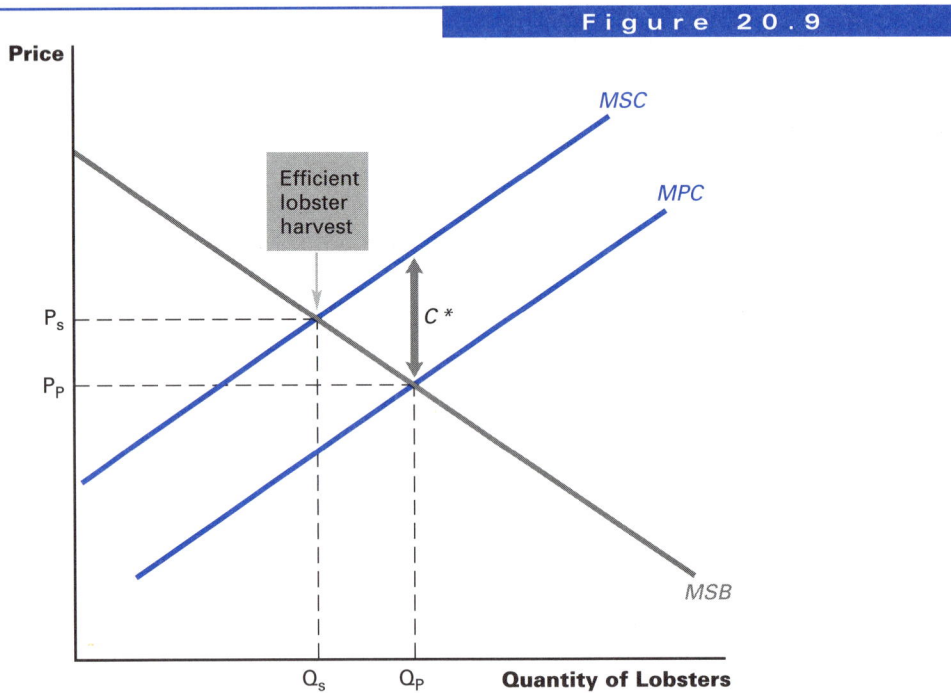

Figure 20.9

MEC in the Case of a Common-Property Resource

This figure depicts the market for lobsters. The curve labeled MSB shows the marginal social benefits of harvesting lobsters. The marginal private cost of harvesting the lobsters is shown by MPC. In the absence of intervention in the market, the equilibrium quantity Q_P will be harvested. The marginal external cost of harvesting a lobster today, which is equal to the losses suffered by future fishermen who will have fewer lobsters to harvest, is equal to C* as indicated in the graph. Hence, the socially efficient harvest occurs where MSB equals MSC, at Q_S lobsters per year.

ulations will therefore be smaller, *ceteris paribus*.) This marginal external cost is equal to C* as indicated in Figure 20.9. When this external cost is added to the private costs, the socially efficient harvest occurs where marginal social benefit equals marginal social cost, at Q_s lobsters per year.

Policy Prescription

One approach to generating a market solution is to tax the fisherman an amount equal to C*, the external cost of harvesting. In this way the producer has an incentive to reduce harvests to the efficient level Q_s. However, the problem that once again arises is trying to determine the correct value of C*. Without this information it is likely that the tax ultimately imposed will result in a level of harvests that is either greater or less than the efficient level.

Because of the potential for overexploitation of common-property resources, it is often necessary for the government to intervene in the market to encourage efficient use of such resources.

Section Recap

Cost of Information

Decisions Made in Ignorance

The primary sources of market failure in each of the examples discussed above are the absence of a clearly defined set of property rights and a lack of information. In those situations in which there are no clearly defined property rights to the air, for example, producers make a decision to compensate no one for any of the air pollution they generate. In other cases, the property right in question may not be assigned initially to the party who values it most. In either of these cases, an inefficient allocation of resources is the likely outcome – especially where the number of affected parties is large.

Likewise, without knowledge of the extent to which individuals derive benefits from consuming specific public goods the market will not, in all likelihood, generate the efficient level of output of such goods. As we have seen, decisions made without this information result in an inefficient output level and price. A lack of information is also the source of some of the major problems with implementing such policy prescriptions as taxes and subsidies.

Each of the policy actions discussed above assumed perfect information on the part of the government. The dollar value of the external costs of a production or consumption activity, the dollar value of the external benefit associated with a public good, and the future social cost associated with overuse of a common property resource all must be known with certainty so that the government can establish the correct tax, subsidy, or restrictions on use.

Efficiency Considerations

Cost–benefit analysis:

The identification and evaluation of all the costs and benefits associated with a particular public policy alternative.

Decision makers must search for and evaluate the information referred to above. One common technique is called **cost–benefit analysis**. Efficiency requires considering the costs and benefits of policies aimed at eliminating external costs, increasing the provision of public goods, or avoiding overuse of common-property resources.

Cost–benefit analysis is used to provide decision makers with information that will help them make efficient choices regarding the reallocation of resources. It is essentially a sophisticated version of what you do when you decide whether to skip economics to study for your calculus exam. You weigh the costs of skipping – important information missed, ability to get class notes, and so on – against the benefits of spending the additional time studying for the calculus exam. If the estimated benefits outweigh the estimated costs, you skip the class and study calculus.

Cost–benefit analyses start from this point of view and go one step further by attempting to place a dollar value on the costs and benefits of public policies. For example,[5] suppose a local planning board wants to know whether it is worthwhile to build a bridge connecting their small island to the mainland. Travel to and from the island is now completed by ferry. The bridge would be a public good so, to avoid free ridership, a bridge toll or a local tax would have to be imposed to finance the project. To make a rational choice, the planners need to:

1. Identify the effects of the project

2. Value the costs and benefits

3. Adjust the costs and benefits

4. Evaluate alternative projects

First, the board must identify the impacts of the project on the local economy. Who will be affected and in what way? Will the bridge cause additional problems as well as solve the traffic flow problem? The next step is to quantify the costs and benefits to all parties affected by the project. Once the costs and benefits of the proposed project have been determined, the board must compare the gains and losses.

One way to make this comparison is to give the benefits and costs equal weight and approve the project if the benefits of building the bridge exceed the costs. However, giving the benefits and costs equal weight may cause problems. Suppose the benefits accrue to a small group of off-island travelers and tourists and the costs are borne by the citizens of the island. What if the costs accrue right away, but the benefits will not be enjoyed for several years? If the existence of the bridge puts the ferry operators out of business, what would happen if the bridge should one day fail (due to a violent coastal storm)?

In such cases, the costs and benefits must be adjusted for equity considerations, the fact that costs and benefits accrue at different times, and the increased risks involved in relying on the bridge. This adjustment process is accomplished by weighting each of the factors being considered. It is in the attempt to determine these weights that the greatest disagreement over the results of cost-benefit analysis occurs. Those bearing the costs want the costs to be weighted more heavily. Those enjoying the benefits want the benefits to be weighted more heavily. Those fighting against the project want future benefits to be weighted less heavily.

Policy Prescriptions

It is important to identify and, to the extent possible, quantify all the costs and benefits of a proposed policy so that they can be viewed in a common light. Not surprisingly, however, it is often difficult to put a dollar value on some benefits (and costs), even though they are very important. For example, suppose reducing the amount of toxic material dumped in a local landfill would result in a decrease in the number of birth defects experienced near the landfill. What dollar value do we place on the reduction in the number of birth defects? Where such situations arise, even though quantification of all benefits and costs may not be possible, it is nonetheless useful to recognize the additional sources of costs and benefits. It is often conceivable that, depending on the potential magnitude of these unknown values, the conclusions of a cost-benefit analysis could be reversed.

The limitations of cost-benefit analysis do not imply that it is useless. Relative to decisions made in ignorance, or on the basis of emotional feelings toward the situation, or for political favor, cost-benefit analysis is an important source of information for policy makers. It is one way to promote rational choice outside the market mechanism.

Section Recap

Government decision making on programs designed to internalize externalities, to increase the provision of public goods, or to reduce the overexploitation of common-property resources can be improved by cost-benefit analysis. However, determining the costs and benefits of policy options can be very difficult.

Opportunities for Collective Action

The Challenge of Good Public Policy

Good public policy requires evaluating the additional costs and benefits of policy actions. However, as we have seen, this is not always easy. The task of making good policy decisions is made even more difficult when a decision must be made with less-than-adequate information. The alternative to making a decision based on less-than-adequate information is to do nothing at all while new information is gathered.

An excellent example of this type of dilemma is found in the case of toxic substances. With the ever-increasing production, use, and disposal of toxic substances, policymakers must face another tradeoff. While additional information is gathered on the potential costs and benefits of controlling the production, consumption, and disposal of toxic substances, more lives may be threatened. The decision maker must then weigh the perceived costs of waiting for more complete information against the perceived benefits of such information.

The Complications of Political Behavior

The formulation of good public policy can also be hampered by the political climate in which it is engendered. The government often finds it necessary to collect taxes to provide a public good, or to give an individual an incentive to internalize an external cost. However, the response of the majority of those taxed is invariably negative.

For example, suppose the government wants to increase the public accessibility of our national forests. If it wishes to imitate the market's provision of this public good it will set a tax such that the total marginal private benefits enjoyed by the consumers of a given level of the public good equal the marginal social cost of providing it. However, this approach will quickly run into trouble. Because access to a national forest is a public good, everyone will receive the same amount of the good for any given tax. However, although consumers receive the same quantity, they do not all enjoy the same marginal private benefit. (Think of the difference in marginal valuation that would be given by an environmentalist and an anti-environmentalist.)

If the government taxed each individual according to his marginal private benefit, enough money would be raised to provide the optimal amount of the public good. However, this approach is bound to run into the problem of free riders, since individuals have an incentive to understate their marginal private benefit. Hence, any attempt by the government to set a charge equal to each individual's marginal private benefit will most likely result in failure.

The upshot of the above example is that, although the imposition of a single tax on all users will be inefficient from the individual's perspective, it does help to get around the problem of free riders. In addition, it is obviously much easier, and probably fairer given the free rider problem, to charge everyone the same fee.

Summary

Normal market transactions involve an exchange of **property rights**. If property rights, to clean air, for example, are not well defined no such exchange is possible and anyone may use the air as he or she wishes. This is true even if one individual's use of the air reduces another individual's ability to use it as well.

Costs or benefits of a production or consumption activity that affect other people's welfare are called externalities. An **external cost** is an unintended cost imposed on some third party or individual. An **external benefit** is an unintended benefit enjoyed by some third party or individual. In the presence of either of these externalities the result is an inefficient level of output.

Pollution is one example of an external cost that most everyone is familiar with. The optimal level of pollution is not always zero. The optimal level of environmental quality is found by comparing the marginal benefits of controlling pollution to the marginal costs of doing so.

Pollution control policies include direct regulation, such as **emission standards** that place a legal limit on the amount of specific pollutants. Policies are also available that promote an optimal level of environmental quality without sacrificing economic efficiency. These policies include **emission charges** – taxes on the output of firms that pollute excessively, **transferable pollution permits**, which create a market for environmental quality and allow the market to determine each firm's level of pollution control responsibility, or some form of **emissions banking, offset**, or **bubble program**.

Public goods are another source of market failure. Unlike private goods, public goods are *nonexcludable* – you cannot be excluded from consuming a public good if you do not pay for it. They are also *nonrival* – one person's consumption of the good does not diminish the amount available for anyone else to consume. Given the nature of public goods and the problem of **free riders**, private firms cannot be relied on to produce the optimum quantity of public goods.

Just as public goods generate external benefits, the consumption of **common-property resources** generates external costs. Common-property resources do not have clearly specified property rights; hence, they tend to be overexploited, that is, consumed without concern for the availability of future stocks.

Questions for Thought

Knowledge Questions

1. State in your own words what the term *externalities* means.

2. How do public and private goods differ? Illustrate this difference graphically.

3. According to the Coase Theorem, under what conditions is government regulation of externalities unnecessary?

4. In your own words, describe how a program of transferable pollution permits would operate.

Application Questions

5. Until the nineteenth century, a vast herd of bison roamed the Great Plains. Now what few bison are left are in zoos and private reserves. What factor contributed most to their relative extinction?

6. "The optimal level of air pollution is zero. So long as someone is suffering from the effects of air pollution it must be reduced – regardless of the cost." Do you agree or disagree with this statement? Explain why.

7. A new lead smelter opens at the edge of town. It produces 1,000 tons of lead ingots per year, at a cost of $100,000. The smelter also emits lead particles into the air over the town. As a consequence of this air pollution the townspeople find their medical

bills rising by $17,000; their wages fall by $6,000 from lost work due to being ill; and their house-painting expenses rise by $2,000. What are the marginal private, marginal external, and marginal social costs of producing the 1,000 tons of lead ingots? (Let one ton equal one unit of lead ingots.)

8. Suppose the town imposes a per-unit tax of $25 on the pollution of the firm in question 7. (Assume one unit of pollution is defined as the amount of pollution associated with one ton of ingots.) What effect would this have on the firm's output? On the price paid for lead ingots? On the social costs of production of lead?

Synthesis Questions

9. How are the gains and losses from public policy programs designed to internalize external costs shared? (Be careful – this is not as easy as you may think.)

10. Competitive firms earn zero economic profits in the long run. Does this imply that the imposition of an emission charge will result in all of the firms going out of business?

11. In this chapter we have demonstrated that the optimal level of pollution is rarely zero. Do you think this argument also applies to other social ills, such as crime? Could we also argue that the optimal level of risk is also rarely zero? If your answers differ, explain why; if they do not differ, explain why not.

End Notes

[1] Coase, Ronald H. 1960. "The Problem of Social Cost," *Journal of Law and Economics*, Vol. 3: 1-44.

[2] "Electric Utilities Study an Old, New Source of Fuel: Firewood," *Wall Street Journal*, Dec. 2, 1993, p. 1.

[3] R. Gutfeld and B. Rosewicz, "Sky War," *The Wall Street Journal*, April 4, 1990, p. A1, and B. Rosewicz, "Price Tag Is Producing Groans Already," *The Wall Street Journal*, October 9, 1990, p. A7.

[4] Garrett Hardin. "The Tragedy of the Commons," *Science*, Vol. 162, December 13, 1968, pp. 1243-8.

[5] This example is adapted from William C. Apgar and H. James Brown, *Microeconomics and Public Policy* (Glenview, IL: Scott Foresman, 1987), pp. 344-59.

International Trade

Overview

International trade is becoming increasingly important to the U.S. economy. Nearly 11 percent of the goods and services produced by U.S. companies are sold abroad. About 12 percent of the things Americans buy are foreign made. In Chapter 2 we argued that international trade benefits an economy. This chapter reviews and extends the theory of international trade, showing explicitly how trade affects prices and how tampering with free trade reduces the total benefits consumers and producers enjoy.

Trading – either domestically or internationally – does not benefit every member of society, although society as a whole benefits from trade. We discuss both the short-run and long-run gains from trade and the costs of trading. Following that, we examine the effects of devices that artificially restrict trade. In particular we are interested in determining the effects of tariffs and quotas on consumers and producers.

After developing the theory of international trade and trade barriers, we examine the importance of international trade to the U.S. economy. Both exports and imports are huge. In the 1980s, U.S. imports exceeded exports, producing large trade deficits. We discuss the sources of the trade deficits, although no final conclusion can be reached without discussing the international financial system.

Learning Objectives

After reading and studying this chapter, you will be able to

1. Explain why international trade is beneficial to society even if some individuals are harmed by it

2. State the major gains from trade experienced by an economy in the short run and over longer periods of time

CHAPTER 21

3. Describe the effects of tariffs and quotas on trade patterns, and explain who gains and who loses from such trade barriers

4. Describe the major trends in world trading and the types of goods and services traded by the United States

Theory of Trade

The modern theory of international trade originated with the British economist David Ricardo in the 1820s. International trade was a much-discussed topic long before then, but the concept of comparative advantage was not understood until Ricardo and some of his peers developed it. The **principle of comparative advantage** (discussed in Chapter 2) states that two countries (or individuals, for that matter) can benefit by each producing the good for which it has the lowest relative opportunity cost and trading for the good which has a higher relative opportunity cost. The gains from trade that come from comparative advantage are illustrated in the following Ricardian example of trade between England and Portugal.

Comparative Advantage: An Example

England and Portugal are two countries that each produce wine and cloth. In the interest of simplicity, assume that the only input in the production process is homogeneous labor. This assumption means that the total cost of producing cloth and wine is labor cost.[1]

Table 21.1 presents the production data for both countries. Portugal has an **absolute advantage** in the production of both goods. The same amount of labor produces more cloth and more wine in Portugal than in England.

Portugal's absolute cost advantage in both goods does not prevent the Portuguese from gaining from trade with the English, because the comparative opportunity costs differ between countries. Consider the opportunity cost of producing cloth in England. If the labor of one worker for one day is shifted from the production of cloth to the production of wine, the English must give up twenty yards of cloth to acquire ten jugs of wine. The opportunity cost of a jug of wine is two yards of cloth. English consumers would be willing to purchase Portuguese wine if they could give up less than two yards of cloth per jug of wine to acquire it. The opportunity cost of a yard of cloth in England is the inverse of the opportunity cost of a jug of wine. English consumers must give up one-half jug of wine to obtain a yard of cloth.

The opportunity cost of a yard of cloth in Portugal is one jug of wine. When labor is shifted from the production of wine to the production of cloth, one jug of wine is given up for each yard of cloth acquired. The Portuguese would be willing to trade with the English if they could acquire more than one yard of cloth for a jug of wine.

Consider the situation facing the two nations. The English are willing to trade if they can give up less than two yards of cloth for a jug of wine. The Portuguese are willing to

Principle of comparative advantage: Two countries can maximize the joint production of two goods by each producing the good for which it is the relatively low-opportunity-cost producer and trading for the other good.

Absolute advantage: The ability to produce a good with fewer resources than another economy can.

Table 21.1

Cloth and Wine Production in England and Portugal
Output per Person-Day of Labor

	Cloth (Yards)	Wine (Jugs)
England	20	10
Portugal	30	30

trade if they can acquire more than one yard of cloth for a jug of wine. Any ratio between one yard of cloth for a jug of wine and two yards of cloth for a jug of wine is acceptable to both nations. That is, any ratio lying between the two nations' opportunity cost ratios presents an opportunity for mutually beneficial trade.

Suppose that England has enough labor to produce either 2000 yards of cloth per year or 1000 jugs of wine, or any linear combination of the two. We will assume that prior to trading with Portugal, the English choose to produce 1250 yards of cloth and 375 jugs of wine. This combination appears as point C on England's production possibilities frontier in Figure 21.1 (a). Portugal, a smaller nation, can produce either 1000 yards of cloth or 1000 jugs of wine, or any linear combination thereof. Before trade begins, the Portuguese choose to produce and consume 500 yards of cloth and 500 jugs of wine, point C' on the Portuguese PPF in Figure 21.1 (b).

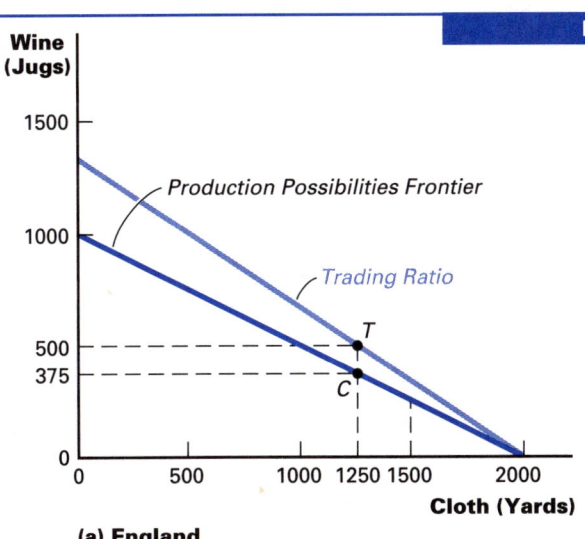

(a) England

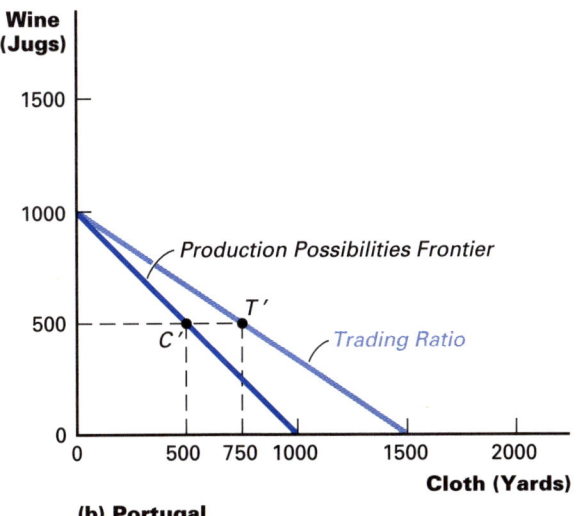

(b) Portugal

Figure 21.1

Comparative Advantage and Trade

By specializing in production and trading, both England and Portugal can increase their consumption. England increases its consumption of wine from 375 jugs to 500 jugs, without consuming less cloth. Portugal increases its consumption of cloth from 500 yards to 750 yards, without consuming less wine.

Assume the two countries trade at a ratio of 1.5 yards of cloth per jug of wine. Because this ratio lies between the two nations' opportunity cost ratios it is acceptable to both countries. Their gains from trade now can be calculated. Instead of producing both cloth and wine, suppose England specializes in the production of cloth. It produces 2000 yards of cloth and trades 750 of them to the Portuguese for 750/1.5 = 500 jugs of wine. The Portuguese specialize in wine production and trade 500 jugs of wine to the English for 500 × 1.5 = 750 yards of cloth. Table 21.2 and Figure 21.1 show that the trade benefits both nations. English consumption of wine rises by one third with no reduction in cloth consumption (a movement from C to T in Figure 21.1 (a)), while Portuguese consumption of cloth rises by one half with no reduction in wine consumption (from C' to T' in Figure 21.1 (b)). The trading ratio lies outside each country's production possibilities frontier.

By specializing in the production of the low-opportunity-cost good and trading for the other good, both England and Portugal were able to expand their consumption beyond the limits permitted by domestic production possibilities. Specialization and trade make both nations better off.

Terms of Trade

In the preceding example both England and Portugal gained by trading cloth for wine at a 1.5-to-1 ratio. This ratio was used because it lies between 2-to-1 (the English opportunity cost ratio) and 1-to-1 (the Portuguese opportunity cost ratio). In fact, *at any ratio between the two opportunity cost ratios both countries would gain from trading.* The 1.5-to-1 ratio was chosen arbitrarily.

How the gains from trade are split between trading countries depends upon the actual trading ratio chosen. In our example both countries gained substantially. English wine consumption rose by 33 percent, while Portuguese cloth consumption increased by 50 percent. At a different trading ratio the relative gains would differ. Suppose, for example, that the two countries traded at a ratio of 1.25 yards of cloth per jug of wine, rather than 1.5-to-1. Then England could have acquired 500 jugs of Portuguese wine for only 500 × 1.25 = 625 yards of cloth. The English could have consumed 1,375 yards of cloth and 500 jugs of wine, increasing their consumption of both goods compared to the no-trade case. However, the Portuguese would not have fared so well at a 1.25-to-1 ratio. They would have 625 yards of cloth and 500 jugs of wine. This is better than they could have done without trading, but inferior to their position at a 1.5-to-1 trading ratio.

Table 21.2

Gains from Trade

	Consumption				
	Before Trade			**After Trade**	
	Cloth	**Wine**		**Cloth**	**Wine**
England	1250	375		1250	500
Portugal	500	500		750	500

In general, a country gains the most from trading when the trading ratio is close to the other country's opportunity cost ratio. This makes sense. If the trading ratio is very close to, say, Portugal's opportunity cost ratio, then the Portuguese will not do much better by trading than by producing their own goods. If the trading ratio is far removed from the opportunity cost ratio, a considerable gain results.

What determines the trading ratio and the relative gains from trade? Within the limits of the two opportunity cost ratios, the strength of demand in each country determines the trading ratio. The more willing England is to give up cloth to obtain wine (the stronger the English demand for wine), the higher the cloth-wine trading ratio becomes. High demand drives up the price of wine (in terms of cloth). Thus, the terms of trade favor the nation with the relatively weaker demand for the other country's product.[2]

A nation can gain by specializing in the production of goods in which it is the relatively low opportunity-cost producer and trading with other nations that are similarly specializing. Any terms of trade lying between the internal opportunity cost ratios of the trading nations benefit both nations.

Section Recap

Price Equalization and Gains from Trade

To this point we have analyzed trade in terms of trade ratios between two goods. In reality the ratio that matters to both consumers and producers is the ratio of units of money per unit of product – the product's money price. International trade affects the money prices of traded goods (and the prices of nontraded substitutes and complements as well). Consumers will not purchase an imported product, identical in its characteristics to a domestically produced good, unless the price of the imported good is as low as the domestic price. Similarly, producers will not export goods unless they can receive a higher price abroad than in the home market.

The price effects of international trade are illustrated in Figures 21.2 and 21.3. Figure 21.2 examines the case of imports. The demand and supply curves depicted in Figure 21.2 (a) are for the domestic market only. If there were no imports the market price would be P_{Dom} (domestic price) and the quantity traded would be Q^*_{Dom}. However, the product is produced more cheaply in other countries; as Figure 21.2 (b) shows, its world market price is below P_{Dom} at P_W. The presence of imports in the domestic market increases the total supply of the good and drives the actual market price down to the world level.

At P_W domestic producers will supply only Q^s_{Dom} units of the good. The difference between Q^* and Q^s_{Dom} is imported. The importation of lower-priced goods enables consumers to pay lower prices for all units of the good, whether produced in foreign countries or domestically. It also causes resources to be reallocated from **import-competing industries** – domestic industries producing goods that can be imported – to other industries.

Some resources will flow into industries that have a comparative advantage in production and can export goods to the rest of the world. In Figure 21.3 we once again see

Import-competing industries:
Domestic industries that produce goods that can be imported or are close substitutes for imported goods.

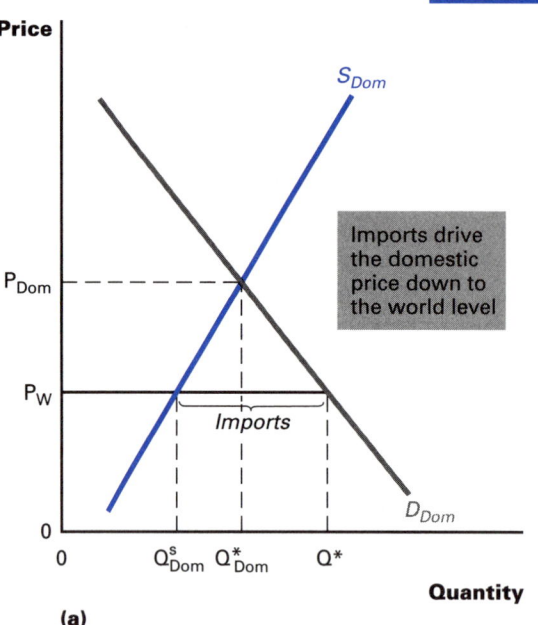

(a)

Figure 21.2

Imports and the Domestic Market

Opening a domestic market to lower-priced imports forces the domestic price down to the world level. Without imports, the domestic price would be P_{Dom} and the quantity traded Q^*_{Dom} **(a)**. Permitting imports drives the price down to P_W, the world price for the good **(b)**. Domestic production falls from Q^*_{Dom} to Q^S_{Dom}, while domestic quantity demanded rises to Q^*.

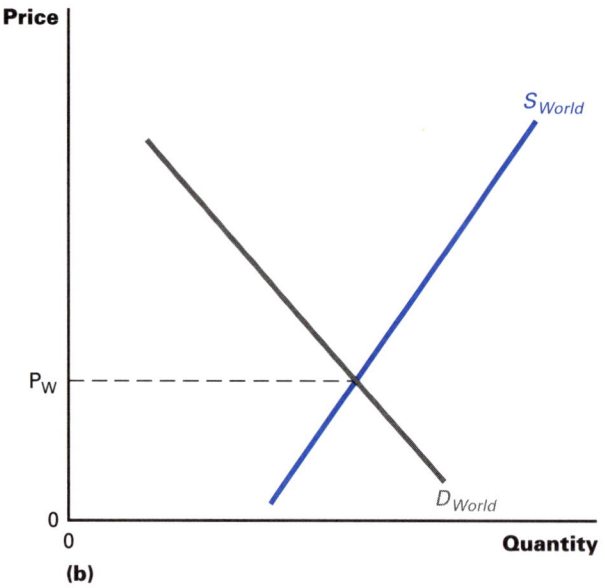

(b)

the domestic demand and supply curves for a product. In this case, however, the domestic price lies below the world price. Domestic producers have a comparative advantage in the production of this good. By selling on the world market, producers can increase their sales and earnings. However, domestic consumers are forced to pay the higher world price for the good; otherwise producers would ship their entire production abroad at prices higher than the domestic price.

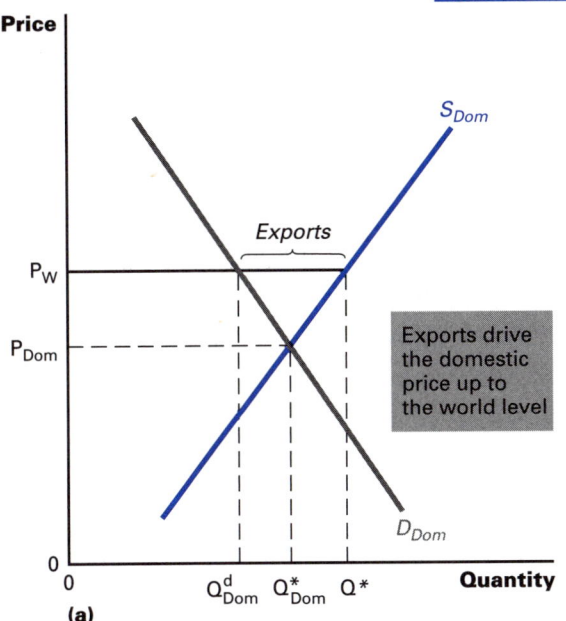

Figure 21.3

Exports and the Domestic Market

Selling goods on the world market pushes the domestic price up to the world level. Firms prefer to export their products, so long as the world price exceeds the domestic price. When the domestic price rises to P_W, domestic quantity demanded falls from Q^*_{Dom} to O^d_{Dom}. Domestic producers produce Q^* units of the good, exporting the difference between Q^* and O^d_{Dom}.

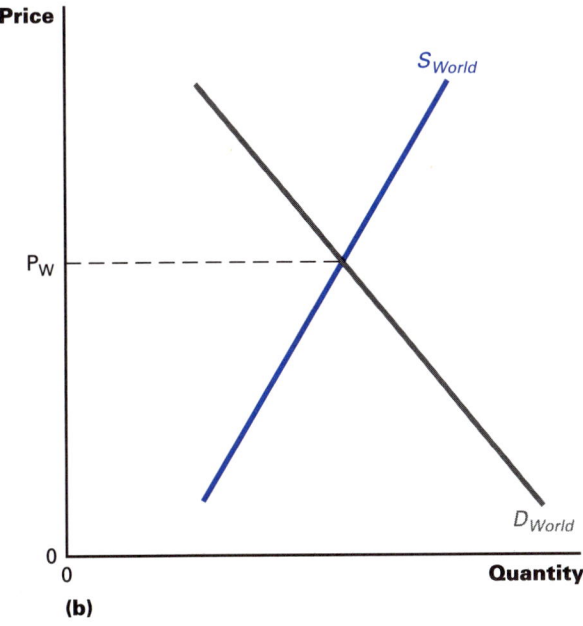

The result of this process — imports driving down prices while exports drive them up in the domestic market — tends to equalize prices across countries. Of course, different nations have different currencies, so the price in one country is quoted in different terms than in another country (U.S. dollars versus Japanese yen, for example), but the relative prices of traded goods within different countries should be driven into equality. Differences in domestic and world market prices induce either imports or exports, and the flow of international trading acts to equalize prices.

Specialization and trade tend to drive the domestic prices of traded goods into equality with the world prices of such goods.

Gains from Trade: A Technical Analysis

The gains to society from international trade can be illustrated with the concepts of consumer and producer surplus developed in Chapter 4. Consider Figure 21.4, which reproduces Figure 21.2 (a) with some additional notation. In the absence of international trade the market price would be P_{Dom} and the quantity exchanged Q^*_{Dom}. Consumer surplus – the difference between what consumers would be willing to pay and what they actually pay – is the triangle $P_{Dom}BC$. Producer surplus – the difference between what producers would be willing to accept for quantity Q^*_{Dom} and what they actually receive – is the triangle $AP_{Dom}C$. Now, compare this situation to the situation with international trade. The price falls to P_W, while the quantity traded rises to Q^*. Consumer surplus now equals the triangle P_WBD. Domestic producer surplus is now the triangle AP_WE.

Obviously consumers have gained and domestic producers have lost. Have the gains of consumers exceeded the losses of producers? The answer is yes. Consumers gain the area $P_WP_{Dom}CD$, while producers lose the area $P_WP_{Dom}CE$. The *net gain* from trading equals the shaded triangle ECD. The gains to consumers exceed the losses of producers by that amount.

Analysis of the case of exports reveals a similar situation. Figure 21.5 reproduces Figure 21.3 (a) with some additional notation. When domestic producers begin to export goods in which they have a comparative advantage, the market price is driven upward from P_{Dom}

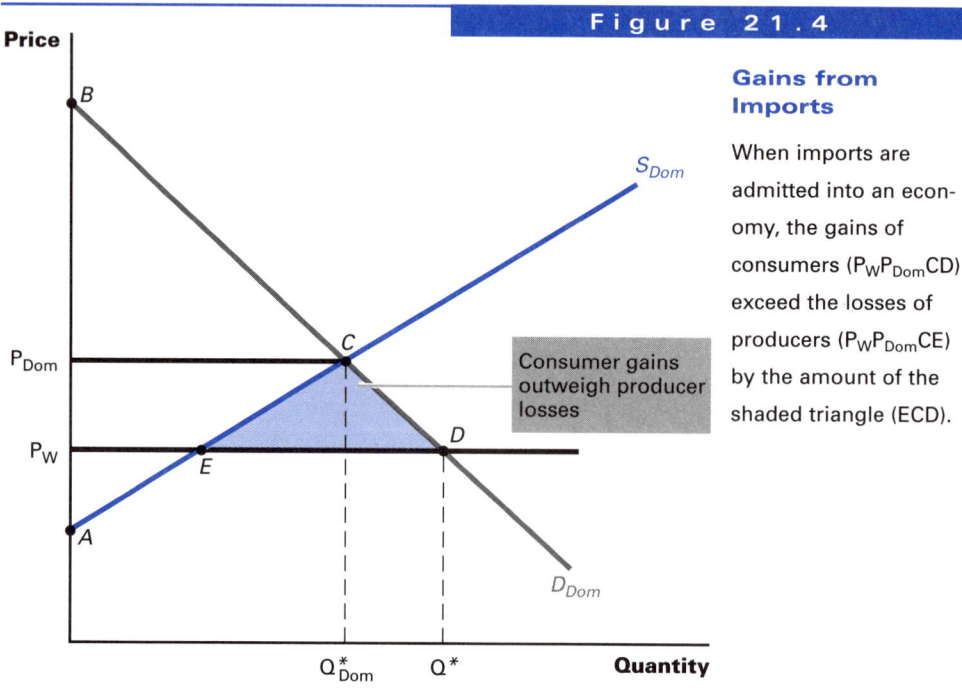

Figure 21.4

Gains from Imports

When imports are admitted into an economy, the gains of consumers ($P_WP_{Dom}CD$) exceed the losses of producers ($P_WP_{Dom}CE$) by the amount of the shaded triangle (ECD).

to P_W. The quantity demanded and consumed by domestic consumers falls from Q^*_{Dom} to Q^*. Before trading, consumer surplus equaled the triangle $P_{Dom}BE$. After trading, consumer surplus declines to the triangle P_WBC, a loss of the area $P_{Dom}P_WCE$ Before trading, producer surplus amounted to the triangle $AP_{Dom}E$. After trading, producer surplus increases to the larger triangle AP_WD. The *net gain* to the economy is the shaded triangle CDE. This area represents the amount by which the gains of producers exceed the losses of consumers. Exports, like imports, benefit the economy.

Costs of Adjusting to International Trade

Free trade benefits the world economy. A nation's consumers gain from importing low-priced goods from countries that have a comparative advantage in their production. Exporters gain by selling on the world market those goods for which they have a comparative advantage. The total world output level rises. However, changing trade patterns usually produce problems for companies that lose their comparative advantage. A firm, or a number of firms in an industry, may fall victim to so-called cheap foreign imports. Workers are laid off and capital goes unused. It can take several years for the workers to find other jobs equivalent in pay and status to their old jobs. Some never locate jobs as good as the ones they lost. This was a major issue in the debate over passage of the North American Free Trade Agreement (NAFTA) in 1993.

Gains from Exports

When an economy exports goods, the gains of producers ($P_{Dom}P_WDE$) exceed the losses of consumers ($P_{Dom}P_WCE$) by the amount of the shaded triangle (CDE).

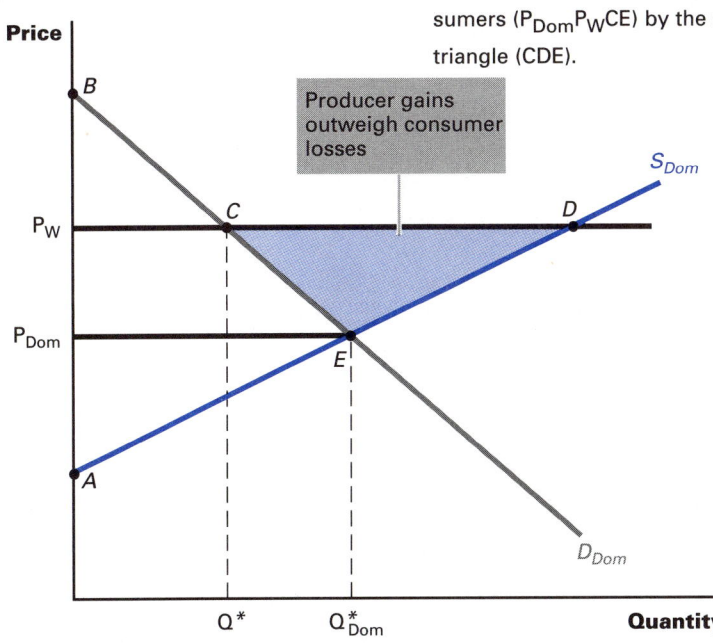

It is important to note that this phenomenon is a feature of the market economy. Shifting trading patterns and changing cost conditions affect firms and workers within a country as well as among countries. In the United States in the 1970s, a large transfer of jobs from the Rust Belt of the northeast and upper midwest to the Sun Belt took place. Many firms found costs of production much lower in the south than in the north and transferred their operations. Northern workers were laid off, southern workers hired. Many of the northern workers had difficulty obtaining new jobs with the same characteristics as their old jobs. A large number of northerners simply moved south in search of work. The adjustment problems caused by shifting demand and cost conditions clearly are not limited to international trade.

A recent study of the international competitiveness of U.S. industry concluded that most industries experiencing job loss during the turbulent 1970s did so because of domestic demand shifts. In thirty-eight of the fifty-two industries studied, international trade contributed to employment growth during the 1973-1980 period. In short, domestic demand shifts caused more problems than did international trade shifts.[3] The situation since 1980 appears not to have changed.[4]

Having said this, it is clear that the perception that jobs are being lost because of imports generates more public and political concern than jobs being transferred from one area of the country to another. Thus, policies to reduce the adjustment costs incurred by workers and firms hurt by import competition are often proposed and sometimes enacted by Congress. The United States has had laws since the early 1960s authorizing payments to workers displaced by foreign competition. While paying workers special adjustment benefits may seem a humane thing to do, it is not necessarily in the best interests of the economy. The incentives created by such payments may not be desirable.

If workers displaced by foreign competition can receive relatively large government payments for an extended period of time (a year or more), they have less incentive to look for other jobs either before or after they are laid off. Workers can usually predict large-scale layoffs before they occur, and they have the incentive to seek more stable employment before they are fired. Generous adjustment benefits reduce this incentive greatly. Such benefits also subsidize unemployment, causing displaced workers to remain unemployed longer than they might otherwise.

If the cost of adjusting to increased trade is to be shared by society (through government payments), a better approach would be to provide wage subsidies for displaced workers who find employment in other industries.[5] Such a subsidy program would encourage firms to hire displaced workers at higher wages than they might otherwise be willing to pay. The program would allow firms to deduct from their income taxes some percentage of their wage payments to newly hired workers. This would reduce the wage cost of hiring these workers. For example, with a subsidy rate of 20 percent, a worker paid $25,000 would cost the firm only $20,000. The firm would be able to save $5000 on its tax bill (20 percent of $25,000) by hiring the displaced worker.

Although a program to ease the cost of adjusting to increased trade may be desirable, constructing a program that does not have negative impacts on the economy is not easy.

Policymakers must realize that the gains generated by a market economy depend upon the principle of comparative advantage being allowed to work, both within an economy and among economies. Policies that prevent the reallocation of resources from less-valued to more-valued uses ultimately reduce the efficiency of the economy and reduce the gains to both consumers and producers that come from an efficiently operating market system.

Adjusting to any shift in demand or cost conditions causes pain for some people. The effects of international demand shifts do not appear to be any worse than the effects of domestic demand shifts.

Changing the Terms of Trade

Various government policies can affect the terms at which goods are traded among countries. Such policies also affect the gains from trade experienced by consumers and producers. The two most frequently used trade policies are tariffs and quotas.

Tariffs and Quotas

A **tariff** is a tax on imported goods. It adds to the price of imports, thus making imported goods less attractive to consumers. A **quota** is a limit on the quantity of a good that may be imported. Limiting the supply of a good also affects its price, as we shall see.

Tariff:
A tax on imported goods.
Quota:
A limit on the quantity of a good that may be imported.

The effect of placing a tariff on an imported good is examined in Figure 21.6. As in Figures 21.2 and 21.4, the world market price lies below what the domestic price of the good would be if there were no international trade. A tariff adds to the price of imported goods, increasing the price that consumers must pay for imported goods from P_W to P_T. The equilibrium quantity demanded declines from Q^* to Q^*_T. The quantity of domestically produced goods rises from Q^s_{Dom} to Q^s_T. The quantity of imports declines from the amount between Q^s_{Dom} and Q^* to the amount between Q^s_T and Q^*_T. The government collects tariff revenue equal to the area of the shaded rectangle (which represents the amount of the per-unit tariff times the number of units imported).

It is clear that domestic producers gain from the imposition of the tariff. Domestic production expands from Q^s_{Dom} to Q^s_T. However, the gains of the domestic producers come at the expense of domestic consumers. Consumer losses exceed producer gains even if tariff revenues are distributed to consumers by the government. Consumers purchase less of the good and pay a higher price.[6]

Imposing a quota on imports has much the same effect, except that the government does not obtain any tariff revenue. Instead, those foreign producers able to continue selling their goods gain from the higher price. Figure 21.7 illustrates the effect of a quota. The quantity of imports permitted by the quota is added to the domestic supply curve to obtain the total supply to the domestic market. The domestic market price rises to P_{Quota}, to clear the market. Domestic production rises from Q^s_{Dom} to Q^s_{Quota}. The higher prices paid by consumers go entirely to domestic and foreign producers; the government obtains no revenue from a quota.

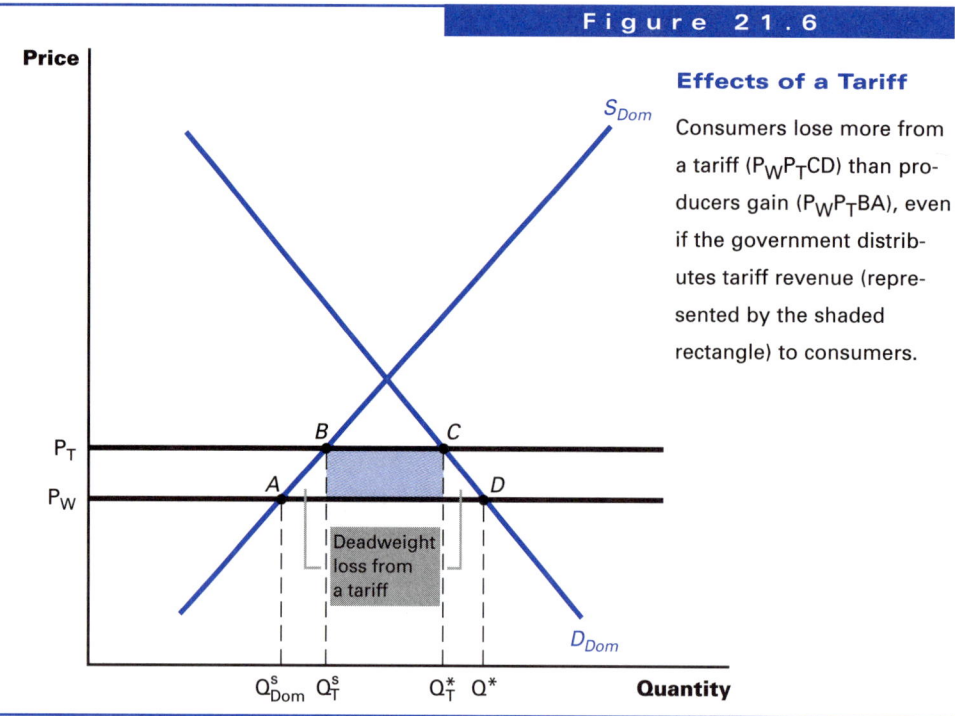

Figure 21.6

Effects of a Tariff

Consumers lose more from a tariff ($P_W P_T CD$) than producers gain ($P_W P_T BA$), even if the government distributes tariff revenue (represented by the shaded rectangle) to consumers.

The same output and price results can be obtained from either a tariff or a quota. A quota of the appropriate size has the same effect as some particular tariff. However, if a restrictive trade policy is to be pursued, tariffs are preferred to quotas for at least two reasons. First, quotas allocate import rights to foreign companies on the basis of some arbitrary rule. Usually future import limits are tied to past import levels. The allocation rule may allow inefficient foreign firms to sell goods, while preventing efficient firms from doing so. Or foreign companies producing relatively inferior goods may have marketing rights, while firms producing relatively superior products are excluded from the market.

The second reason that tariffs are preferable to quotas is that the entire price increase produced by a quota goes to producers. While this may be the desired effect with regard to domestic producers, it merely increases the profits of foreign producers for no good reason. It transfers wealth from domestic consumers to foreign producers. A good example of this was the so-called voluntary import restrictions placed on Japanese automobiles in the early 1980s. U.S. car buyers transferred millions of dollars to Japanese auto companies, whose profits rose considerably after the imposition of the informal quota.

A way to overcome the disadvantages of quotas relative to tariffs has been proposed recently: auctioning quota allotments to foreign producers. The foreign companies willing to pay the largest amount to obtain an import quota would be allowed to import goods into the domestic market. Such a policy would allow the government of the importing country to reclaim a share of the excess earnings of the foreign companies generated by the quota. It would also permit efficient foreign firms to outbid inefficient firms, thus serving domestic customers better.

Figure 21.7

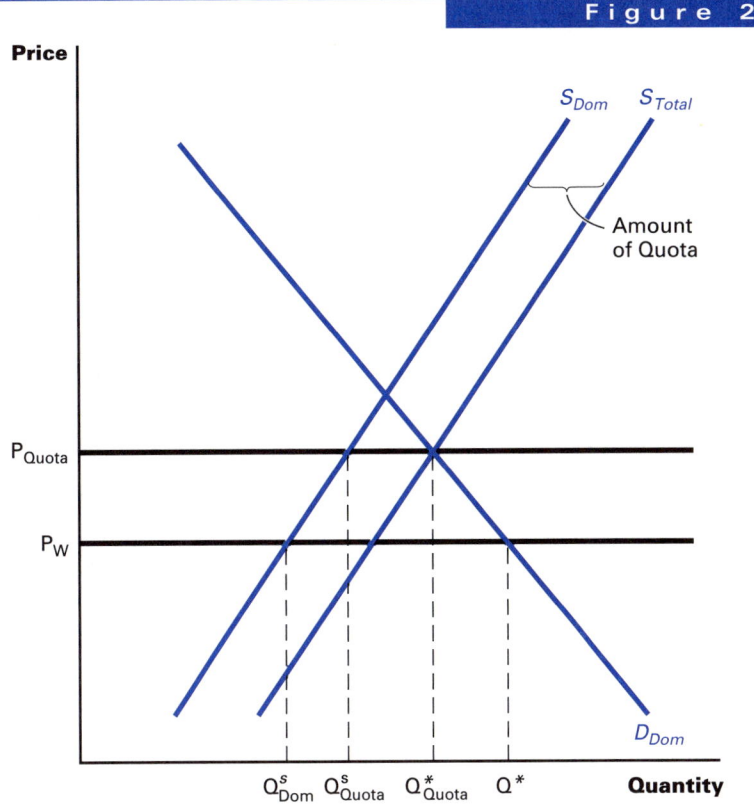

Effects of a Quota

Domestic producers gain less from a quota than domestic consumers lose, and the government obtains no revenues. A quota pushes the domestic price to P_{Quota}, which is higher than the world price (P_W). Domestic production rises from Q_{Dom}^s to Q_{Quota}^s, while consumption falls from Q^* to Q_{Quota}^*.

The terms of trade can be altered by imposing tariffs or quotas. Either trade barrier reduces the gains from trade. Tariffs are preferred to quotas, however, because tariffs allow efficient foreign firms to undersell inefficient firms and because they allow the nation imposing the tariff to capture some of the benefits of higher product prices.

Section Recap

Arguments in Favor of Tariffs

If tariffs reduce the welfare of an economy, why do they seem to be so widely used? In reality, the theory of public choice goes a long way toward explaining why tariffs and quotas are enacted. However, narrow private interest is not often the argument used to defend tariffs. It is hardly an attractive political argument to say, "Everyone should have to pay more so I can increase my profits (or wages)." We will examine several of the more frequently used arguments in favor of tariffs.

Infant-Industry Argument When new firms begin producing a product, they are often relatively inefficient. They have not yet developed the managerial, production, or marketing expertise of an experienced firm. Often they begin production at relatively low output levels, when larger output levels can be produced more efficiently using larger factories and more automation. Given time, these infant firms become more efficient. Their costs of production decline, and they become competitive in the world market.

The infant-industry argument asserts that firms entering a new market should be protected by tariffs until they develop enough to become efficient. The argument is often used by less-developed countries, which claim that protection of industry is a necessary part of their development process. Although this argument has a plausible ring to it, it suffers from several problems. First, if private investors believe a product will eventually be profitable to produce, then they will be willing to absorb losses for some time while the firm establishes itself in the world market. Tariff protection forces consumers to share the risks with the owners of the firm, who stand to benefit anyway once the firm becomes profitable.

Another problem is picking winners. The government cannot protect every new industry that develops. Which of the new industries will prove to be profitable and which will not? There is little evidence that the government can pick winners and losers effectively.

Finally there is the problem of getting rid of a tariff. Once levied on an imported good, a tariff is very difficult to remove. Domestic producers and their workers argue that removal of the tariff will mean real hardship for them. Since the gains to consumers from removing a tariff are spread out over millions of people, while the costs to producers are concentrated on a much smaller number of individuals, politicians are likely to hear much more pro-tariff than anti-tariff sentiment. A tariff, once established, often takes on a life of its own.

A slightly different variant of the infant-industry argument also deserves mention. It might be called the **senile-industry argument:** Industries that employ large numbers of workers, but that can no longer compete in the world market, should be afforded protection in order to save jobs. Anyone who understands the notion of comparative advantage can see immediately that this argument simply calls for abandoning international trade whenever a domestic industry is at a comparative disadvantage. The harmfulness of such a policy should be obvious.

Senile-industry argument:
Industries that are no longer internationally competitive should be protected to save domestic jobs.

Preventing Job Loss to Cheap Foreign Labor

A frequently heard argument for tariff protection is that foreign imports are produced cheaply because foreign workers are paid so little. These workers are exploited, being paid a wage barely sufficient to keep them fed and clothed (so the argument often goes). If such cheap goods are allowed to replace domestically produced goods, domestic workers will eventually be driven into poverty too. This was, in fact, one of Ross Perot's major arguments against NAFTA.

It is true that, other things equal, firms using relatively cheap labor have an advantage over firms using relatively expensive labor. However, other things are seldom equal. Productivity differs greatly from country to country. Productivity depends to a large extent on the amount of capital provided to workers and the technological sophistication of that capital. One worker in an industrial country using sophisticated machinery often can produce as much as several workers in a less-developed country using only rudimentary tools. The high-productivity worker can be paid much more than a low-productivity worker, while still producing a lower-cost product.

The firms being driven out of business in relatively high-wage countries, such as the United States, by firms in low-wage countries are typically low-capital, low technology firms. For example, among the U.S. industries suffering most from foreign competition are shoe and textile manufacturing. Both industries use rather simple, low-cost machinery. Entrepreneurs in Third World nations can afford such machinery, and the equipment is simple enough that even uneducated people can run it efficiently. Foreign firms can undersell U.S. firms paying wages eight or ten times higher.

In industries in which expensive, sophisticated equipment is used, however, firms in poor, relatively undereducated nations cannot compete with U.S. firms. The productivity of U.S. workers is so much higher that U.S. costs of production are lower even though U.S. workers are much better paid. Furthermore, U.S. firms often cannot shift their sophisticated manufacturing facilities to low-wage countries because the workers are too uneducated to operate the equipment properly. Protecting workers from cheap foreign labor really amounts to forgoing the benefits of comparative advantage in those industries that are at a relative disadvantage.

National Defense The tariffs-for-national-defense argument stresses the need to maintain production in key industries in case of armed conflict. In a war, imports of vital products might be cut off. To ensure the ability of the nation to defend itself, industries vital to the defense effort should be protected.

The problems with this argument are twofold. First, how do we define what is vital to national defense? A large number of industries might claim to be important. Where is the line to be drawn? For example, in the mid-1980s the U.S. shoe industry argued for tariff protection because army boots are vital to the nation's defense program. (The argument failed to win them a tariff.) If the shoe industry can argue that it is vital to national defense, what other industries can do so too? (Our argument does not imply that *no* industries are vital to defense, only that the defense argument tends to be overused.)

The second problem with the argument is that only a major war could disrupt supplies of most important imports. (Oil is a major exception. A local war in the Mideast could disrupt the world oil market, which is why the United States went to war when Iraq invaded Kuwait.) However, in the nuclear age the probability of a worldwide conventional war is quite small. The next world war, if it ever occurs, probably will be nuclear and very short. Imports will be the least of our worries.

Tariffs as a Bargaining Chip Though many nations pay lip service to free trade, pressure for protectionism is always great. A country that totally disavows tariffs may be put at a competitive disadvantage when dealing with other less-restrained nations. Even though most major trading nations are members of the General Agreement on Tariffs

Does It Make ECONOMIC SENSE?

Protectionism and Domestic Employment

The proponents of protectionism usually justify their support of tariffs and quotas on the grounds that such barriers to trade increase the number of jobs in the economy. The logic behind this argument is straightforward. Tariffs and quotas make foreign firms less competitive with import-competing firms in the domestic economy. As domestic firms win a larger share of the domestic market, they expand production. Increased production requires more workers. Thus, trade barriers actually increase employment. Since, in a nation as wealthy as the United States, national income is less of a concern to most people than having enough jobs to go around, this benefits society.

Although we know that trade barriers reduce the total consumption level of society, might not trade barriers increase employment? The argument has a certain plausibility. However, a number of studies of trade and employment have indicated that increasing trade barriers would actually *decrease* the number of jobs provided by the U.S. economy. Does this make economic sense?

In his international economics textbook, Peter Lindert reviews the studies showing that protective tariffs cost the U.S economy more jobs than they protect.[7] Net job losses result because (1) exports decline approximately dollar-for-dollar with imports, and (2) more jobs are tied to a billion dollars of exports than to a billion dollars of production of import-competing industries. We will examine these arguments in turn.

When imports are restricted, exports decline for several reasons.

and Trade (GATT) and have pledged themselves to promote free trade, many trade barriers exist, and new ones are popping up all the time.

The best way to promote free trade may be to threaten massive retaliation against any countries that impose tariffs or quotas on an economy's exports. Adam Smith recognized this over two centuries ago, listing it as one of the arguments in favor of tariffs in *The Wealth of Nations*. Threatening retaliation in many cases may be sufficient to persuade trading partners to forgo protectionism. President Reagan used this tactic in late 1986 to gain tariff concessions for U.S. products from the European Economic Community.

As a long-term strategy, using the threat of tariff retaliation works only if a nation is, in fact, willing to retaliate. Sooner or later it will be called upon to back its threats with action. Then what? Adam Smith's suggestion was to back down. While foreign tariffs on our exports are bad, placing tariffs on imported goods just makes things worse. Consumers as well as producers suffer. But a consistent policy of backing away from threats will destroy their usefulness. It is sad but true that the best way to preserve mostly free trade in the long run may be to play tit-for-tat in the short run. Tariff retaliation may have its place in the maintenance of mostly free world trade.

Summing Up the Arguments With the possible exception of the retaliation argument, none of the arguments in favor of tariffs holds up under close scrutiny. The bottom line is simple and familiar: Tariffs restrict trade and reduce the gains from trade experienced by an economy. The majority (consumers) loses, while a protected minority (producers) gains. The losses of consumers outweigh the gains of producers (including workers).

First, many exporters use imported inputs in their production. When imports are restricted, the price of their inputs rises, forcing domestic firms to raise their product prices and making them less competitive in world markets. Export sales decline as a result. Second, when foreigners cannot sell goods to us, they cannot afford to buy products from us. Foreigners must have dollars to buy American products. They earn dollars by selling goods in the United States. When imports are curtailed, foreigners earn fewer dollars and thus can afford fewer U.S. products. U.S. export sales decline. Third, when one nation imposes import restrictions, other nations usually retaliate. Increased trade barriers reduce trade worldwide, including U S. exports.

The total effect on exports of these three factors (and some oth-ers we have ignored) is to decrease exports by approximately the same amount as the trade restrictions decrease imports. The effect on net exports should be close to zero.

If exports and imports fall by about the same amount, shouldn't the net effect on jobs be zero? Not necessarily. The amount of labor used in the production of exports may differ significantly from the amount of labor used by import competing industries, since differ-ent products are being produced by the two groups of industries. Professor Lindert cites eight differ-ent studies conducted in the post World War II period of the number of jobs tied to $1 billion of exports and $1 billion of import-replacing production. All eight studies con-cluded that *more jobs are tied to a billion dollars of exports than are tied to a billion dollars of import-replacing production.* Reducing both exports and imports by $1 billion would cost the U.S. economy jobs, since more workers are required to produce $1 billion of goods for export than are required to produce $l billion of import-replacing goods.

This result adds to the case for international free trade. Trade restrictions reduce both the con-sumption level and the number of jobs in an economy. Trade restric-tions cannot be used as a kind of back door government employment policy, because their effect on employment is negative.

A number of arguments are made to support tariffs. Of these, only the argument that the threat of tariffs serves as an important bargaining chip in the effort to obtain free trade holds up under scrutiny.

Section Recap

NAFTA and the Reduction of Trade Barriers

Following a period of intensive lobbying, President Clinton won congressional approval of the North American Free Trade Agreement with Mexico in November 1993. NAFTA is the first step toward turning North America into a free trade zone. Proponents of the leg-islation envision a common market larger than the European Union, in which producers from any of the three North American nations can freely sell to consumers in Canada, Mexico, and the United States. Many supporters, including former president George Bush, view NAFTA as merely the first step in a process that will create an American free trade zone stretching from Hudson Bay to the Tierra del Fuego.

Economic theory indicates that reducing trade barriers should lead to higher output levels across North America. Trade barriers curtail or eliminate the gains from specializa-tion and trade according to comparative advantage. The evidence bears this out. Mexico had been in the process of reducing trade barriers for some time. The results of Mexican trade liberalization – for both Mexicans and Americans – have been encouraging. U.S. exports to Mexico nearly tripled between 1987 and 1993, while U.S. imports of Mexican goods nearly doubled. Trade grew even faster in 1994 after NAFTA went into effect.

Mexico passed Japan to become the world's second-largest buyer of American-made goods and now trails only Canada.

However, NAFTA did not bring completely free trade to North America. The vote in the House of Representatives was close; NAFTA met strong opposition. Some of the opposition came from free trade advocates who opposed NAFTA because it created a multinational bureaucracy to police the agreement and because it contained too many exceptions to unbridled free trade.

The major opposition to NAFTA, however, came from groups opposed to free trade with Mexico. Their opposition generally was based on two types of issues: concerns about environmental and labor conditions in Mexico; and fear of competition from Mexican producers. Mexican environmental laws are much more lenient than U.S. laws. Some environmentalists feared that, if NAFTA were successful in boosting Mexican production, the environment might suffer greatly. They noted the terrible conditions along the U.S.-Mexican border, where Mexican factories turn out goods for exportation to the United States. Furthermore, American companies feared that Mexican competitors would have a built-in cost advantage, not having to meet stringent U.S. environmental standards.

To meet these objections a "side agreement" on environmental issues was reached by Canada, Mexico, and the United States. It created an agency to investigate environmental abuses and empowered it to levy fines on any nation failing to enforce its own environmental laws.

Economists recognize that as nations become wealthier, they ordinarily spend more on cleaning up the environment. In economic terms, environmental quality is a normal good; as people become wealthier, they demand more of it. If Mexico follows the pattern traced out by other nations, increased wealth should also lead to improved environmental quality.

Concerns about labor conditions were also partly motivated by concern for the health and safety of Mexican workers and partly motivated by the fear that relatively low-paid Mexican labor would take away American jobs. (This was the "giant sucking sound" Ross Perot claimed he kept hearing.) Another side agreement was reached under which an agency headquartered in Washington, D.C. would be empowered to investigate labor abuses. Fines could be imposed if countries failed to enforce their own worker-safety rules, child-labor laws, or minimum-wage standards.

Once again, evidence indicates that free trade itself may be the best way to improve the conditions of Mexican workers. In 1987, when Mexico began liberalizing trade with the United States, real wages in the U.S. chemical, food, and transportation equipment industries were 9.1, 7.1, and 7.6 times as high as real wages in their Mexican counterparts. By 1992, the wage gap had narrowed significantly; U.S. real wages in chemicals, food, and transportation equipment were 6.6, 4.5, and 5.8 times as high as Mexican wages. The gap narrowed by 24 to 37 percent in only five years.[8]

Most economists believe that the United States stands to gain directly from the removal of tariffs between Mexico and the United States. In 1993 Mexican tariffs were, on average, two-and-a-half times as high as U.S. tariffs (10 percent versus 4 percent). However, specific U.S. industries face severe competition from Mexican producers. In his effort to assure the passage of NAFTA, President Clinton traded concessions for votes. Whereas most tariffs and quotas were scheduled to be phased out over a few years, producers of products such as peanuts, sugar, orange juice, and textiles, who were likely to face severe challenges from Mexican producers, were favored with tariff protection for a much longer period (up to 15 years).

The justification of such continued protection is nearly always the desire to prevent massive job losses. Tariffs undoubtedly are responsible for many of the jobs currently existing in industries such as those obtaining extended protection. But the cost of such protection to American consumers is high. A 1993 study by the U.S. International Trade Commission found that trade barriers cost American consumers some $19 billion a year in higher product prices. Most of that – $15.85 billion – comes from protecting one industry, textiles and apparel. Were the protection removed, the Commission estimated that 71,639 textile workers would lose their jobs. In calculating whether the protection is justified, you should note that each textile-worker job protected by tariffs and quotas costs American consumers $221,248. You can be sure that the average textile worker earns nothing close to that![9] It would therefore be possible to compensate the displaced textile workers through government transfers or employment and still reduce the cost to the American public by a large fraction.

NAFTA came to a vote at a time when many Americans were fearful that the United States was losing its international competitiveness. We have argued at various places in this book that such is not the case. However, the increase in trade with Asian economies over the past several decades has forced a major restructuring of markets in the United States. To a lesser extent, so will NAFTA. Despite the pains and displacements of restructuring, the net effect on U.S. employment is likely to be small – no more than a half million jobs gained or lost in the long run. For an economy that destroyed 20 million jobs in the 1980s, while creating nearly 39 million new jobs, the employment effects of NAFTA must be regarded as minor. NAFTA's real importance may lie more in what it signals to the rest of the world than in its direct effects. For NAFTA indicates that the United States remains the world's major advocate of free trade.

Exports, Imports, and the Balance of Trade

Trade theory predicts that in the absence of artificial restrictions, nations will export goods for which they have a comparative advantage and will import goods for which they have a comparative disadvantage. This prediction appears to be borne out by the evidence. If nations are grouped into three classifications – those with abundant capital, those with abundant unskilled labor, and those with abundant skilled labor – the trading patterns that emerge are consistent with the theory of comparative advantage. Less-developed countries with little capital and abundant unskilled labor tend to export raw materials and agricultural products, while importing manufactured goods. Developing nations, such as South Korea or Taiwan, that have large unskilled workforces but also have an abundance of basic capital tend to export basic manufactured items, such as textiles, shoes, and consumer electronics. Developed nations, such as the United States and Japan, have an abundance of skilled labor and tend to export more sophisticated products, such as capital goods, computers, and high-tech services.

Trade balance:
Difference between the money value of a country's exports and the money value of its imports.

Trade surplus:
Positive trade balance; exports exceed imports.

Trade deficit:
Negative trade balance; exports are less than imports.

A nation's **trade balance** is the difference between its exports and its imports. A **trade surplus** indicates a positive trade balance; exports exceed imports. A **trade deficit** indicates that imports exceed exports. There is no reason for a nation's trade balance to be zero in any particular year. When a nation's trade balance is not zero, it must finance the difference by acquiring or issuing financial claims. A country that runs a trade surplus s produces more than it consumes and acquires financial claims against other nations (that is, it acquires financial assets in foreign countries). A country that runs a trade deficit consumes and invests more than it produces and issues financial claims against itself (that is, it borrows from foreigners to finance its spending).

Trends in International Trade

In the years immediately following the end of World War II, the United States dominated the world economy. The United States was the source of manufactured goods of all types. U.S. producers had an artificial comparative advantage in many products, such as textiles, because the manufacturing facilities in much of the rest of the world had been destroyed. As late as 1953, U.S. exports of manufactured goods accounted for nearly 30 percent of the world total of manufacturing exports. This was a much higher percentage than before the war and was not a figure that could be sustained as other nations rebuilt their economies.

The trends in international trade that have occurred in the nearly five decades since the war reflect changes in comparative advantage. Less-developed countries (LDCs) have increased their share of world manufacturing exports only slightly overall but have made significant progress in goods that are relatively simple to manufacture. Such countries as South Korea, Hong Kong, Taiwan, and Singapore have greatly expanded their share of world production of textiles and clothing, shoes, small appliances, and electronic components for stereos, TVs, and computers. These manufactured goods require relatively simple machines that can be operated by unskilled labor.

In the manufacture of goods requiring more sophisticated capital and highly skilled labor, the United States, Japan, and (West) Germany have prospered. For example, in 1953 the three countries accounted for 39.2 percent of world exports of chemicals. In 1976, this figure stood at 36.9 percent. Much the same story appears if exports of machinery and transportation equipment are examined. In 1953, the three nations accounted for 53.8 percent of exports and that figure fell only to 48.6 percent in 1976.[10] A major redistribution of market shares has occurred among the three industrial giants. Germany, and especially Japan, have gained market share at the expense of the United States over the past three decades.

The most important trends in world trade in recent years were the sharp increase in the value of petroleum exports and imports in the 1970s and the collapse of those values in the 1980s. The quadrupling of oil prices in 1973-1974 and a further doubling of prices in 1979 increased the dollar value of petroleum exports and imports immensely. OPEC nations acquired billions of dollars from oil exports, as did non-OPEC, oil-exporting nations such as Great Britain. The oil revenues allowed oil-producing countries to finance all sorts of projects that were previously unaffordable. When oil revenues collapsed along with oil prices in the 1980s, these nations found it very difficult to finance the levels of imports they had been acquiring. The import levels of many oil-producing nations fell dramatically in 1983 and 1984. This affected the export levels of industrial nations, because what one nation imports, another must have exported. If world imports fall, so do world exports.

What Does the United States Trade?

The United States is a major participant in world trade. In 1994, U.S. exports totaled $716.1 billion, equal to 10.6 percent of GDP. Imports were even higher, $818.2 billion, or 12.1 percent of GDP. In other words, more than one tenth of U.S. production was sold to foreigners, and nearly one eighth of U.S. purchases of new goods and services were from foreigners.

What does the United States export and import? The single most important category of merchandise exports is capital goods other than automotive products. U.S. companies produce and export all kinds of capital equipment, from earth movers to computers. In 1993 the value of such exports was $182 billion, comprising over one quarter of U.S. exports. The second most important merchandise export category is industrial supplies and materials. Included in this category are such things as chemicals and intermediate goods that go into the production of other goods.

It may come as a surprise that U.S. exports of services exceed even capital goods exports in value. How is it possible to export services? Insurance and financial and transportation services can be provided to foreigners quite easily, and U.S. producers have a comparative advantage in these skill-intensive areas.

Figure 21.8 shows the behavior of major merchandise export categories since 1970. All categories trended upward in current dollar terms, although the growth was not even across categories or over time. Especially evident is the sharp decline in exports in 1982 and 1983 and the small rebound in 1984. The recession experienced in the United States in 1981 and 1982 was worldwide. Demand for all products, including those made in the United States, fell significantly. This decline in exports had serious implications for the U.S. balance of trade.

The pattern of U.S. merchandise imports is shown in Figure 21.9, which shows that major growth took place in imports of petroleum in the 1970s and in imports of other goods, primarily consumer goods, in both the 1970s and 1980s. Rapid growth also took place in the importation of automotive products and capital goods.

The United States is a major *net* exporter (exports minus imports) of agricultural products and capital goods (other than automobiles) and a major *net* importer of petroleum products, consumer goods (such as textiles and shoes), and automobiles. These trade

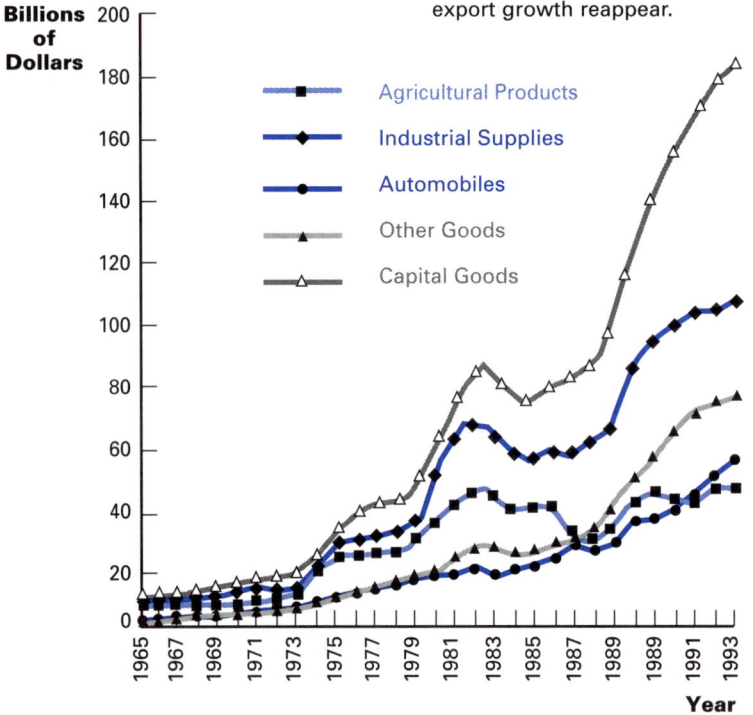

Figure 21.8

U.S. Merchandise Exports, 1965-1993

The dollar value of all major U.S. merchandise exports trended strongly upward until the 1981-1983 world recession. Not until 1987 did strong export growth reappear.

Source: Economic Report of the President, 1995, Table B-106.

patterns reflect a comparative advantage in goods produced by skilled labor working with sophisticated capital and a comparative disadvantage in goods produced with simple capital and unskilled labor. The exception to this in the 1980s was automobiles, where Japanese technology was more advanced than U.S. technology and Japanese autoworkers earned less than U.S. autoworkers, giving Japan a comparative advantage in automobile production, even though it is a sophisticated industry. Both of these Japanese advantages are disappearing in the 1990s – and U.S. automobile imports have stopped growing.

Figure 21.10 shows the U.S. balance of merchandise trade (excluding services) with several countries or groups of countries. A major feature stands out. The U.S. trade balance turned sharply downward against all countries and groups of countries in the 1980s. Why did this occur? One reason has already been mentioned. The worldwide recession of the early 1980s caused many countries to cut back on their imports. The U.S. economy came out of the recession more quickly than did most other economies. When the U.S. economy began expanding, U.S. consumers began buying more goods – some of which were foreign made. Consequently, imports rebounded but exports did not. As other economies began to grow more rapidly, U.S. exports have increased.

Figure 21.9

U.S. Merchandise Imports, 1965-1993

The dollar value of petroleum imports leaped upward in 1974-1977 and again in 1979-1980, before dropping off after 1980. The fastest-growing import categories in the 1980s were "other goods" (a category including consumer goods), capital goods, and automobiles.

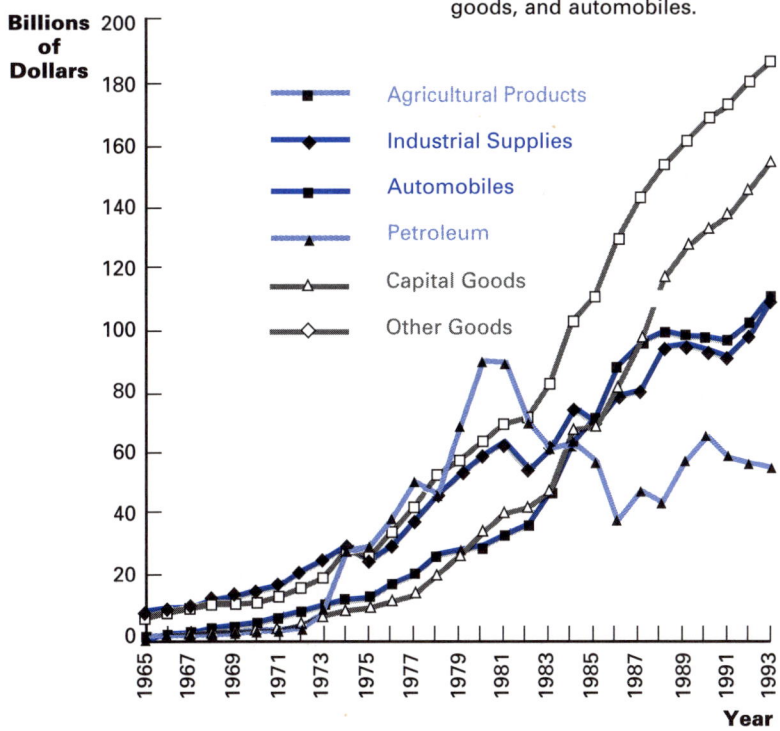

Legend:
- ■ Agricultural Products
- ◆ Industrial Supplies
- ■ Automobiles
- ▲ Petroleum
- △ Capital Goods
- ◇ Other Goods

Source: Economic Report of the President, 1995, Table B-106.

The second reason for the large U.S. trade deficits of the 1980s has to do with the exchange rate – the price of U.S. currency in terms of foreign currencies. The exchange rate rose sharply from 1980 to early 1985. This raised the cost of U.S. products to foreigners and made foreign-produced goods cheaper to Americans. The result was an expansion of imports and a contraction of exports. The exchange rate declined from 1986 to 1994, eventually contributing to the decline in the U.S. trade deficit that began in 1988.

Section Recap

The United States tends to export goods that require sophisticated capital and skilled labor to produce. U.S. imports primarily include goods that can be produced with simple capital and unskilled labor. The worldwide recession of the early 1980s, from which the United States recovered more quickly than other nations, plunged the U.S. balance of trade into a deficit from which it has never fully recovered.

Why the DISAGREEMENT?

No Fair!
Does Japan Play the
Trade Game by Its
Own Set of Rules?

Sony, Toyota, Panasonic, Nikon – all are common names in American homes. The truth is obvious: Americans love Japanese products. Less well known, Japanese love American products too. Japan is the largest importer of U.S. agricultural products and ranks third (behind Canada and Mexico) in total imports of American-made goods.

Persistent, large U.S. trade deficits with Japan, heavy Japanese investment in the United States, and anecdotal accounts of the difficulties faced by U.S. firms trying to break into the Japanese market have combined to produce among Americans widespread antagonism against the Japanese. The suspicion that the Japanese don't play fair appears widespread. Economists have not ignored the question either, yet as many seem willing to defend Japanese practices as to condemn them. Why the disagreement?

At first glance it might seem that the question of whether the Japanese raise unfair barriers to keep out U.S. goods could be answered by looking at the data. Many noneconomists appear to believe that the existence of continued trade deficits with Japan is itself evidence of unfair Japanese behavior. But this is clearly not the case. Japan lacks natural resources, but the Japanese have a disciplined, well-educated labor force and a large and sophisticated capital stock. Any economist immediately recognizes that such a combination of factors gives Japan a comparative advantage in the production of sophisticated manufactured goods relative to the rest of the world. Perhaps that comparative advantage also extends to Japan's relationship with the United States.

A more sophisticated response is to examine the quotas and tariffs Japan places on imported goods. Economists who have done this agree that Japan's tariff and quota barriers are, in general, quite low. (There are some exceptions. Japan protects its farmers with strict

Summary

The principle of **comparative advantage** states that producing low-opportunity-cost goods and trading them for high-opportunity-cost goods increases the amount of goods and services a society can consume. Two nations can benefit from trade by specializing and trading one good for another if the opportunity costs of the goods differ between the countries. The **terms of trade** must lie between the two countries' opportunity cost ratios if both nations are to benefit from trade.

As nations trade, resources flow from high-opportunity-cost industries, which become unprofitable, to low-opportunity-cost industries, which become more profitable. The price of traded goods tends to equalize across different economies, as consumers buy from the cheapest producers and producers sell in the markets with the highest prices. Such trading drives prices toward equality across economies.

Restricting international trade is profitable to producers who do not have a comparative advantage in their product. **Tariffs** (import taxes) and **quotas** (import quantity restrictions) are both used to drive up the price of imports and protect domestic producers. Although such policies help the producers of protected goods (owners of companies and workers), the losses suffered by consumers exceed the gains to producers. The quotas

quotas or high tariffs on rice, fruits, and meat. But then, the United States does the same for producers of sugar, oranges, and peanuts.)

But low tariffs and lenient quotas do not guarantee an open door for imports. Americans who have attempted to sell in Japan often find it difficult to break into the Japanese distribution system. Many Japanese retailers are reluctant to market foreign products. Indeed, economists who believe that Japan restricts imports usually focus on the Japanese industrial structure as the source of trade barriers.

The relationships among companies in Japan are often much closer than the relationships among U.S. firms. Many large Japanese companies belong to *keiretsu* — affiliations of firms. There is no single definition of *keiretsu*. So-called horizontal *keiretsu* link together different types of corporations, generally including manufacturing companies, a major bank, other financial companies, and a trading company. These companies own one another's shares, have common directors and top officers, and engage in joint investment in new industries. Vertical *keiretsu* link together firms in a particular industry: a major company with firms that produce components for that company, important customers, and subcontractors. A third type of *keiretsu* has been created by major manufacturers who have organized their own distribution networks by linking together wholesale and retail outlets.[11]

The close linkages among Japanese manufacturers and distributors may make it more difficult for foreign products to break into the Japanese market. Some evidence indicates that the share of imported goods in industries dominated by *keiretsu* is smaller than the share of imports in other industries. This could indicate that members of *keiretsu* act to keep imports out of Japan. However, this effect shows up clearly only in markets dominated by vertical *keiretsu*. If formal relationships between a manufacturer and its suppliers, distributors, and major customers enhance efficiency (reduce costs), the lower import share in such markets could be a reflection of comparative advantage at work.

Not only is the importance of Japanese industrial structure for imports unclear, economists disagree over just how different Japanese industrial structure really is. Every society differs from others in ways that appear strange to outsiders, but many times the perceived differences have little effect on trading patterns. This may be the case with respect to Japan. [12]

Economists disagree over the importance of trade barriers in Japanese trade performance because no generally agreed-upon estimates of the effects of Japanese trade structure have been derived. Unless and until such measures are developed, the disagreement is likely to continue.

---

and tariffs protecting U.S. textile manufacturers illustrate this point. For every textile-worker job saved, American consumers paid $221,000 in higher prices. The **North American Free Trade Agreement (NAFTA)** seeks to phase out such tariffs and quotas between North American economies.

Tariffs are defended with a number of arguments, including the **infant-industry argument,** the **cheap foreign labor argument,** the **defense argument,** and the **bargaining chip argument.** With the possible exception of the last one, none of these arguments holds up under careful scrutiny. If trade barriers are to be erected, tariffs are preferred to quotas, because tariffs allow consumers to choose the product they wish to purchase and raise revenue for the government, while quotas restrict choice and raise no revenue.

Nations tend to export goods in which they have a comparative advantage in production. Less-developed countries export raw materials and minerals, developing countries export simple manufactured goods, and highly developed economies export sophisticated manufactured goods. The United States is a major net exporter of capital goods and agricultural products and a major net importer of consumer goods, petroleum, and automobiles.

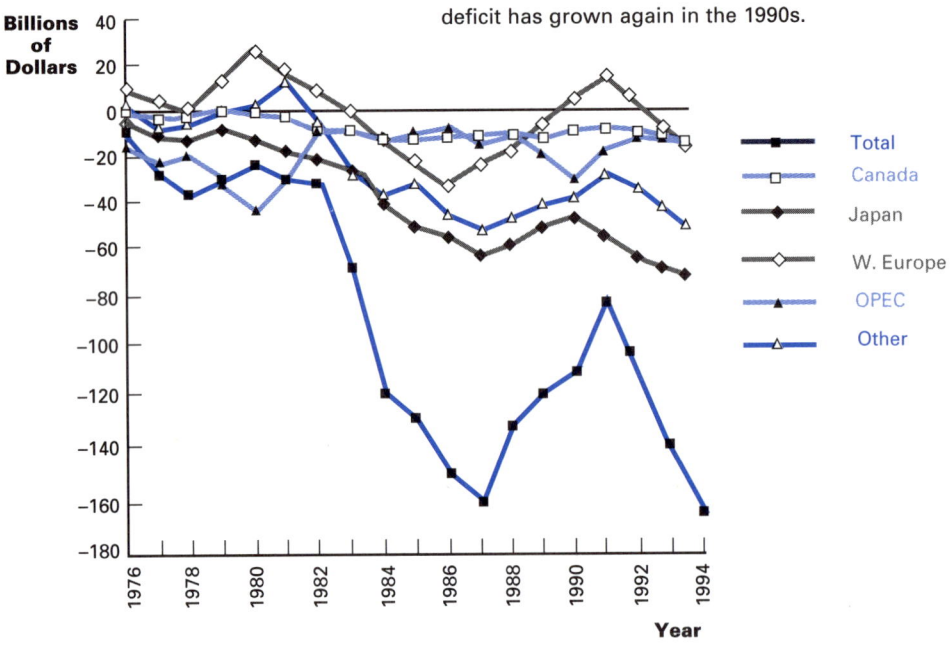

Figure 21.10

**U.S. Trade Balances
with Selected Regions**

The U.S. merchandise trade balance plunged sharply into deficit from 1983 to 1987. The U.S. deficit with most major trading nations and regions grew until 1987, when it began to recover. The deficit has grown again in the 1990s.

Source: Economic Report of the President, 1995, Table B–107. Data for 1994 are for the first three quarters at an annual rate.

Questions for Thought

Knowledge Questions

1. Define what is meant by the terms *tariff* and *quota.*

2. Explain why, if the domestic market is to be protected, tariffs are preferred to quotas.

3. What is the infant-industry argument? What are its shortcomings?

4. What kinds of goods does the United States export? Why?

5. How does international trade affect domestic aggregate supply?

Application Questions

6. Use a demand-supply diagram to explain what happens when a tariff is applied to an imported product.

7. Using the theory of consumer and producer surplus, show how a tariff applied to an imported good affects consumers and producers.

8. Explain why adjustment benefits for workers displaced by foreign competition might not be good for the economy.

9. The production possibilities frontiers for two countries are provided. Determine the following:

    a. If the countries could benefit from trade

    b. Which country should specialize in which good

    c. The limits between which any acceptable trading ratio must lie.

Gondor Steel (tons)	Wheat (tons)	Rohan Steel (tons)	Wheat (tons)
0	100	0	60
20	80	5	48
40	60	10	36
60	40	15	24
80	20	20	12
100	0	25	0

Synthesis Questions

10. Explain why and how the prices of freely traded goods are driven toward equality across nations.

11. It is well known that international trade affects jobs. When a domestic industry loses business to foreign competitors, workers are displaced and incur adjustment costs. Is this problem a uniquely international problem? Explain.

12. Why do you think there is more concern over a job lost to foreign competition than over a job lost to domestic competition?

13. A friend argues that the United States ought to increase tariffs sharply to keep out goods from developing countries. He believes that it is only a matter of time until all U.S. manufacturing jobs are lost and the standard of living in the United States is dragged down to a Third World level. How do you counter his argument?

End Notes

1 This approach is closely related to David Ricardo's original treatment of comparative advantage. See his *Principles of Political Economy and Taxation*, Chapter 7.

2 David Ricardo never figured out what determined the exact terms of trade. Another English economist, John Stuart Mill, is usually given credit for that. However, a recent book by D.P. O'Brien, *Thomas Joplin and Classical Macroeconomics* (Aldershot, Hampshire, England: Edward Elgar, 1993), demonstrates that Thomas Joplin understood the importance of reciprocal demand well before Mill.

[3] Robert Z. Lawrence, *Can America Compete?* (Washington, DC: The Brookings Institution, 1984), Chapter 4.

[4] See Paul Krugrnan and Robert Z. Lawrence, "Trade, Jobs, and Wages," *Scientific American*, April 1994.

[5] Such a program is proposed by George R. Neumann in "Adjustment Assistance for Trade-Displaced Workers," in David B. H. Denoon, ed., *The New International Economic Order* (New York: New York University Press, 1979).

[6] Producer surplus rises by the area P_WP_TBA. Consumer surplus declines by P_WP_TCD. The net loss to consumers is ABCD, which cannot be completely replaced even if government distributes the tariff revenues to consumers.

[7] *International Economics*, 9th ed. (Homewood, IL: Richard D. Irwin, 1991), pp. 86–88.

[8] Fred R. Bleakley, "Mexican Wages Are Seen Rising Under Nafta," *The Wall Street Journal*, October 8, 1993, p. A4.

[9] Figures are from "Trade Barriers Cost U.S. $19 Billion in Higher Prices," *The Pantagraph* (Bloomington-Normal, Ill.), November 27, 1993, pp. C1, C2.

[10] These and other figures in this section are drawn from William H. Branson, "Trends in United States International Trade and Investment since World War II" in M. S. Feldstein, ed., *The American Economy in Transition* (Chicago: University of Chicago Press, 1980), pp. 183-273.

[11] See Robert Z. Lawrence, "Japan's Different Trade Regime: An Analysis with Particular Reference to *Keiretsu*," *Journal of Economic Perspectives* 7, Summer 1993, pp. 3-19.

[12] So argues Gary R. Saxenhouse in "What Does Japanese Trade Structure Tell Us About Japanese Trade Policy?" *Journal of Economic Perspectives* 7, Summer 1993, pp. 21-43.

Index

A

Absolute advantage, 38
   definition, 568
Accounting profit, 263–265
   definition, 263
Acid rain, 5, 40–41, 555
Adjustment benefits, 576
AFC, *see* Average fixed cost
AFDC, *see* Aid to Families with
   Dependent Children
AFL-CIO, *see* American Federation of
   Labor-Congress of Industrial
   Organization
After-tax corporate profits, 218
Age-earnings profiles, 443
Aggregate labor market, 432–434
Aggregate profits, 217–218
Agricultural employment, 112
Agricultural products, 108–111
Aid to Families with Dependent Children
   (AFDC), 527–529
AIDS, 11, 12
Airline deregulation, 391–394
Airline Deregulation Act of 1978, 385, 391,
   393
Airlines, 386–387

Allocation decision, 56
Allocative efficiency, 36
   definition, 299
American business, profitability, 217–220
American Federation of Labor-Congress of
   Industrial Organization (AFL-CIO),
   461, 465, 467, 468
American jobs, quotas, 304–305
American unionism, structure/member-
   ship, 461–463
Antipoverty policy, 521, 525–530
   see Federal antipoverty programs
Antipoverty programs, effectiveness,
   527–530
Antitrust legislation, 381, 395
   definition, 376
   development, 376–377
   impact, 377
AR, *see* Average revenue
Arc elasticity, definition, 154
Assimilative capacity, definition, 544
ATC, *see* Average total cost
AVC, *see* Average variable cost
Average cost, 234, 260
   see Long-run average cost, Marginal
      cost

Average fixed cost (AFC), 237, 238
  definition, 235
Average revenue (AR), 260, 269, 280
  definition, 266
Average total cost (ATC), 237–240, 256, 257, 298,
    300, 302, 326
    see Short-run average total cost
    curve, 273
    definition, 235
Average variable cost (AVC), 237–240, 257,
    277, 289
    definition, 235
Average-marginal relationship, 238–239

B

Bailouts, 296–297
Banking deregulation, 386
Bar chart, 25
Bargaining chip argument, 591
Barriers, *see* Legal barriers
Barriers to entry, *see* Entry barriers
Behavior, *see* Business behavior, Cartel-like
    behavior, Consumer behavior, Entrepreneurial
    behavior, Firm behavior, Large firm behavior,
    Political behavior, Rational behavior, Small
    firm behavior
Benefits, 35, 45–46, 96–101, 307–308, 420–421,
    442–444, 482–483
    see Demand curve, Environmental quality,
        External benefits, Investment benefits
Bigness versus behavior, 377–379
Biogenetic engineering, 12
Block pricing, definition, 351
Bond, definition, 215
Bubble program, 563
Budget constraints, 14–22, 179, 193–195, 197
    definition, 178
Budget-constrained choice, 59
Bus Regulatory Reform Act, 385
Business, government ownership, 373–376
    policy objectives, 374–375
    political issues, 376
Business behavior, deregulation, 383–386
Business behavior, regulation, 370–398
    end notes, 397–398
    learning objectives, 371

overview, 370
questions, 396–397
summary, 395
Business cycles, 132, 487

C

CAAA, *see* Clean Air Act Amendments
    of 1990
CAB, *see* Civil Aeronautics Board
Cable Communications Policy Act, 382, 383
Capacity utilization rate, 487–488
    definition, 487
Capital
    demand, 484–488
    demand curve, 486–488
    return, 496
Capital formation, definition, 20
Capital goods, 482, 492
Capital investment, 480
Capital market, 480–501
    end notes, 501
    learning objectives, 481
    overview, 480
    questions, 500–501
    summary, 499–500
Capital requirements, 339
Capital stock, 68, 230, 482–484, 488, 489, 491,
    494, 498
    see Fixed capital stock
    definition, 20
Capital-intensive production, definition, 250
Cartel-like behavior, 363
Cartel-like conditions, establishment, 389–391
Cartels, 361
    see Legal cartel theory of regulation
    definition, 359
CDs, *see* Certificates of deposit
Celler-Kefauver Act of 1950, 377, 379
Central bank, definition, 131
Centralized decision making, 88, 133
CERCLA, *see* Comprehensive Environmental
    Response, Compensation, and Liability Act
Certificates of deposit (CDs), 497
CETA, *see* Comprehensive Employment and
    Training Act

Ceteris paribus, 61, 62, 68, 77, 82, 83, 165, 176, 177, 182, 184, 186, 187, 191, 244, 435, 491
    definition, 60
Chateau Ste. Michelle, 468, 469
Cheap foreign labor argument, 591
Choice/value, 34–35
    see Individual choice
City-pairs, 386, 392
Civil Aeronautics Board (CAB), 363, 386–391
Clayton Act, 377, 379
Clean Air Act Amendments of 1990 (CAAA), 4, 40, 550
    reauthorization, 554–555
Clean Water Act, 4
Closed shop, definition, 466
Coase Theorem, 537–539
    definition, 537
Coefficient of elasticity, see Elasticity
COLA, see Cost of living adjustment
Collateral, 58
Collective action, opportunities, 133–140, 561–562
Collective bargaining, 456–479
    definition, 459
    end notes, 479
    experiences, 469
    learning objectives, 457
    overview, 456
    questions, 478–479
    summary, 477–478
Collective decision-making options, 373–383
Collusion, 358–364
    definition (collude), 125
    definition (collusion), 358
Command economy, definition, 57
Common law doctrine, 463
Common stock, 215
Common stockholders, 215
Common-property resources, 534, 556–559, 561, 563
    definition, 556
    end notes, 564
    learning objectives, 535
    overview, 534
    policy prescription, 559
    questions, 563–564
    summary, 562–563

Comparative advantage, 37–41, 43–45, 48, 50, 568–570, 574, 575, 585, 590
    see International trade
    principle, 40
        definition, 568
Competition, 72, 356–358
    see Imperfect competition model, Monopolistic competition, Nonprice competition, Perfect competition, Perfect competition model, Service competition
    absence, 125, 372–373
    alternatives, 358–364
    definition, 102
    degree, 216
    escape incentive, 327–328
    reduction, see Regulation
    regulation influences, 386–387
Competitive disadvantage, 581
Competitive environment, rules establishment/enforcement, 376–381
Competitive firms, see Monopolistically competitive firms
Competitive market, 104, 284, 286, 291
    see Monopolistically competitive markets, Perfectly competitive markets
    economy, 307
Competitive pressure, 327–332, 338–342
    absence, 375–376
Competitive resource market theory, 516
Complementary goods, 62
Comprehensive Employment and Training Act (CETA), 526
Comprehensive Environmental Response, Compensation, and Liability Act (CERCLA), 19
Computer investment, 485–486
Concentration ratio, definition, 355
Conglomerate merger, 377
    definition, 363
Constant economies of scale, definition, 249
Constant-cost industries, definition, 295
Consumer behavior, theory, 172–205
    end notes, 205
    learning objectives, 173
    overview, 172
    preferences, 177
    questions, 198–199

rationality, 176–177
  summary, 197–198
  theory, 178
  tradeoffs, 177–178
Consumer choice problem, 174–175
Consumer decision making, 185–190
Consumer equilibrium, 186
Consumer expectations, 61
Consumer goods, 243
  production, 17
Consumer income, 61
Consumer Price Index (CPI), 521
Consumer response, *see* Price
Consumer responsiveness, 147–149
Consumer sovereignty, 296–297
  definition, 296
Consumer surplus, 99–101, 116, 346
  definition, 101
Consumer tastes, 61, 64
  see Heterogeneous consumer tastes
Consumer utility, 175–181
  assumptions, 176–178
Consumers, *see* Voters as consumers
Consumption, 37, 482–483, 541
  see Substitution in consumption
  alternatives, 161
  decisions, 59–65, 174, 187, 188
  expenditure, 493
  opportunity cost, 66
Consumption-investment decision, 482
Contestable markets, 372, 379
  theory, 365–366
    definition, 365
Corporate profits, taxation, 220–221
Corporation, 214–217, 220
  definition, 214
  financial capital, 215–216
Cost conditions, 577
Cost functions, *see* Firm, Short-run cost functions
Cost minimization, *see* Long-run cost
  minimization
Cost of living adjustment (COLA), definition,
  471
Cost-benefit analysis, 561
  definition, 560
Cost-minimizing response, 245

Costs, 35, 45–46, 96–101, 307–308, 420–421,
  442–444, 482–483
Craft union, definition, 458
Credit ratings, 58
Cross subsidies, 388–389
Cross subsidization, 387, 389
  definition, 388
Cross-price elasticity, *see* Demand
Customer classifications, 352

D

Dairy policy, 110–111
Davis-Bacon Act, 440
Deadweight loss, 347
Decentralization, 122
Decentralized economy, 88
Decertification election, definition, 467
Decision, *see* Long-run decision, Short-run
  decision, Short-run/long-run decision
Decision makers, 128, 208
  see Political decision makers, Rational
  decision maker
Decision making, 102, 120–142, 206, 310
  see Centralized decision making, Consumer
    decision making, Government decision
    making, Market decision making,
    Nonmarket decision making, Political
    decision making, Public decision making,
    Union decision
    making
  end notes, 142
  learning objectives, 121
  overview, 120
  questions, 141–142
  social benefits, 102
  social costs, 102
  summary, 140–141
Decision-making costs, 188–190, 198
  definition, 186
Decision-making device, 122–124
Decision-making options, *see* Collective
  decision-making options
Decision-making process, 208, 209, 224, 228
Decline, 466–468
Default risk, 497
Defense argument, 591

Delayed-payment incentive, 452
Demand, 59–66
    see Capital, Derived demand, Elastic demand,
        Inelastic demand, Law of demand, Market
        mechanism, Perfectly elastic demand,
        Perfectly inelastic demand, Quantity
        demand, Resources, Unitary elastic
        demand
    analysis, 99
    changes, 63, 76–77, 83–87
        see Perfectly competitive markets
    conditions, 577
    cross-price elasticity, 167–168
        definition, 167
    decrease, 294–295
    income elasticity, 166–167
        definition, 166
    point elasticity, 154–155
        definition, 154
    price elasticity, 144, 152, 154, 155, 157, 158,
        163, 164, 470
        definition, 147
        determinants, 160–165
    schedule, see Labor
    theory, transactions costs, 185–190
Demand and supply curves, 572
Demand curve, 77, 96, 99, 146, 147, 149, 150,
    152, 153, 182, 274, 291, 321, 324, 326, 341,
    344, 349, 351, 408, 439, 450
    see Capital, Market demand curve, Negatively
        sloped demand curve
    derivation, 181–184, 195–197, 203–205
    factors, 61–64
    inelastic portion, 158–159
    policies, 473–474
    social benefits, 94–96
Demand elasticity, 144–171
    end notes, 171
    learning objectives, 145
    overview, 144
    questions, 169–170
    summary, 168–169
Demand schedule, 64
Depository Institutions Deregulation and
    Monetary Control Act (DIDMCA), 385
Depreciation, 418

Deregulation, 370, 386–391, 394–395, 525
    see Airline deregulation, Business behavior
    definition, 383
    developments, review, 384–386
Derived demand, 423
    definition, 403
DIDMCA, see Depository Institutions
    Deregulation and Monetary Control Act
Differentiated product, 354
Diminishing returns, see Law of diminishing
    returns
Direct ownership, 376
Direct regulation, 383
Disability payments, 506
Discount rate, 498, 499
Discounting, definition, 485
Discrimination, see Labor market
Diseconomies of scale, 257
    definition, 249
Disequilibrium
    definition, 73
    price, 77
    wage differences, 453
        definition, 442
Dividends, definition, 215
Domestic employment, 582–583
Double taxation, 221
Downsizing, 224
Drive, satisfaction, 19–22
Dynamic economy, supply decisions, 279

E

Earned income tax credit (EITC), 525, 526
EC, see European Community
Economic analysis, 4, 30
Economic choices, 6–8
Economic decisions, 35, 307
Economic depreciation, 228
Economic efficiency, 35–37, 44, 48, 50, 92–119,
    124, 290, 297–300, 308–309, 326, 364–366,
    373, 472, 517, 525
    see Market equilibrium
    definition, 35
    end notes, 119
    learning objectives, 93
    overview, 92

questions, 117–118
summary, 116–117
Economic growth, 495
Economic inefficiencies, 106–111, 115, 353
Economic model, 143–398
see Microeconomic model
Economic principles, 1–142
Economic problem, 308–309
Economic profits, 262–265, 275, 280, 286, 287,
293, 322–325, 330, 332, 340, 341, 342,
344–346, 357, 359, 361, 364–366, 387, 389
see Firms, Long-run economic profits, Short-
run economic profits
definition, 262
maximization, *see* Firms
Economic Recovery Tax Act of 1981, 495
Economic rent, definition, 439
Economic stability, absence, 131–133
Economic thinking, 2–31
end notes, 31
graphical analysis, 25–31
introduction, 4–6
learning objectives, 3
overview, 2
questions, 23–24
summary, 22–23
Economic variables, 25
Economic welfare, 472, 477
Economic well-being, 113, 123, 124
see Society
Economics, 14, 308–312
see Public choice
definition, 6
fundamental premise, 8–9, 19, 22, 32, 35, 37,
89, 290
science, 9–13
Economies of scale, 247–250, 257, 339, 340–342,
497
see Constant economies of scale,
Diseconomies of scale
definition, 248
Economy
see Dynamic economy
general equilibrium, 304–307
stability, 102–103
structural changes, 466
Education, investment, 442–444
EEC, *see* European Economic Community

Efficiency
goal, 36–37
implications, *see* Long-run equilibrium position
reduction, *see* Regulation
wage theory, 408, 409
Efficiency-equity tradeoffs, 114–115
Efficient decisions, 545
Efficient market, 94
outcomes, conditions, 101
Effluent standard, definition, 547
EITC, *see* Earned income tax credit
Elastic demand, 159
see Perfectly elastic demand
definition, 151
inelastic demand comparison, 151–154
Elasticity
see Arc elasticity, Demand, Demand elasticity,
Price elasticity, Supply
coefficient, 149, 151, 153
definition, 147, 411
measures, 165–168
Electric utility industry, 244–245
Emission banking, 563
definition, 552
Emission charge, 563
definition, 548
Emission standard, 563
definition, 547
Employment changes, 44
Employment contracts, *see* Long-term
employment contracts
Employment determination, 432–434
Employment impact, *see* Unions
Employment levels, 431
Employment losses, 469
Employment opportunities, 123, 409, 415, 417,
442, 450, 522
Entrepreneurs, 262, 293, 581
definition, 209
Entrepreneurial ability, 226
Entrepreneurial behavior, 206–222
end notes, 222
learning objectives, 207
overview, 206
questions, 221–222
summary, 220–221
Entrepreneurial challenge, 208–210
Entry, ease, 320, 321

Entry barriers, 338–340, 342, 366
    definition, 338
Environmental pollution, external costs, 544–552
Environmental quality, 5
    benefits/costs, balance, 545–547
    opportunity cost, 545
    optimal amount, 545–547
EPA, *see* U.S. Environmental Protection Agency
Equal output curve, 251
Equality of opportunity, 517–518
Equilibrium, 72–88, 104–106
    see Disequilibrium, Market equilibrium,
        Price-output equilibrium
    analysis, *see* General equilibrium analysis,
        Partial equilibrium analysis
    definition, 72
    interest rate, 492
    market outcome, 96
    market price, 87, 101
    output, 327
    price, 83, 86, 87, 107, 295, 311
    quantity, 83, 86, 87
    wage, 431, 448
Equity-efficiency tradeoffs, 517
European Economic Community (EEC), 582
European Community (EC), 110
Excess capacity, 244–245
Excess demand, definition, 73
Excess supply, 82
    definition, 75
Exchange
    costs, 46–50
    gains, 37–46
Exit, ease, 320, 321
Expectations, 64
Explicit costs, 256, 262
    definition, 226
Explicit/implicit costs, comparison, 226
Exports, 585–590
External benefits, 140, 539, 541–544, 559, 562
    definition, 126, 539
External costs, 127, 140, 536, 537, 539–542, 544,
    557, 559, 560, 562
    see Environmental pollution
    definition, 126, 539
Externalities, 126–129, 534, 539–544, 561
    definition, 126

end notes, 564
learning objectives, 535
policy prescriptions, 543–544
overview, 534
questions, 563–564
summary, 562–563

F

FAA, *see* Federal Aviation Administration
Factor markets, 399–501
Factors of production, 6
Family income, 522
    well-being measure, 510–511
Family Support Act of 1988, 528
Farm credit system, 296–297
Farm programs, 114–115
Fast food industry, shakeup, 328–329
FCC, *see* Federal Communications Commission
Federal antipoverty programs, 526–527
Federal Aviation Administration (FAA), 393
Federal Communications Commission (FCC),
    375, 382, 383
Federal Home Loan Bank Board (FHLBB), 139
Federal Reserve, 385
Federal Trade Commission (FTC), 377, 379
    Act, 377
FHLBB, *see* Federal Home Loan Bank Board
Financial capital
    see Corporation
    definition, 212
Financial intermediary, definition, 498
Financial markets, 498–499
Financial resources, 212
Financial transactions, 263
Firm behavior
    see Large firm behavior, Small firm behavior
    regulation, 381–383
Firms, 320
    see Monopolistically competitive firms,
        Noncompetitive firms, Perfectly competi-
        tive firm, Price-searching firms, Price-
        taking firms
    categorization, 210–217
    cost functions, 232–239
    economic profit maximization, 264–265
    objective, 217–220
    output, 265–269

revenue, 265–269
short-run capacity, 240–241
supply, 70–72
Fiscal policy, definition, 132
Fixed capital, 68
Fixed capital stock, 66
Fixed costs, 238, 275, 277, 278
see Average fixed cost, Total fixed costs
definition, 233
Fixed-cost obligations, 279
Food and Agriculture Act of 1977, 110
Food Security Act of 1985, 110
Foreign competition, 49
Foreign labor, 580–581
Foreign-made goods, 82
Free rider, 140, 563
definition, 130, 555
problem, 130, 555
Free-trade agreement, 46–47
Fringe benefits, 48, 68
FTC, see Federal Trade Commission
Full opportunity costs, 224
Future generations, discounting, 498–499
Future sum, present value, 484–485
Future value (FV), 485
definition, 484
FV, see Future value

G

Game Theory, 360
GAO, see U.S. General Accounting Office
Garn-St. Germain Depository Institutions Act, 385
GATT, see General Agreement on Tariffs and Trade
General Agreement on Tariffs and Trade (GATT), 4, 5
General equilibrium, 313
analysis, definition, 306
Genetically engineered corn, 340–341
Goods
cost, 162
prices, 62–64
production, 123
Goods-producing employment, 466
Government decision making, 561

Government economic policies, 104
Government intervention, 116, 134, 373
Government ownership, see Business
Government regulation, 331–332
Government restrictions, see Wages
Government services, 49, 136
Great Depression, 12, 463, 464, 506
Great Society, 526–528
Gross domestic product, 587
Group well-being, see Individual well-being
Guilds, 458

H

Health care, 17, 18
reform, 138–139
Health maintenance organization (HMO), 174
Herfindahl-Hirschman Index (HHI), 356, 380, 392
Heterogeneous consumer tastes, 319
HHI, see Herfindahl-Hirschman Index
Homogeneous labor, 568
Homogeneous product, 319, 320, 354, 359, 361
Horizontal merger, 379
definition, 363
Human capital, 6, 20, 453
definition, 419, 442
investment, 443, 444

I

Illinois Farm Bureau, 81
Illinois Farmers Union, 80, 81
Imagined product differentiation, 333
definition, 329
Imperfect competition model, 316–369
Imperfect information, 310–312
Implicit costs, 256, 264
comparison, see Explicit/implicit costs
definition, 226
Import competition, 576
Import-competing industries, definition, 571
Imports, 585–590
Incentives, 9
Incentives-based mechanisms, 552
Income, 5, 61–62
see Family income, Lifetime incomes, Total income

after-tax distribution, 510
    functional distribution, definition, 430
    personal distribution, definition, 430, 506
    stream, 58
    support, 114
Income differences, 512, 515, 517
    age, 512–515
    race, 512–515
    sex, 512–515
Income distribution, 115, 504, 507–510, 518, 526
    (U.S.), 506–518
Income effects, 182–184, 195–198, 420
    definition, 183
Income elasticity, *see* Demand
Income inequality, 509
Income inequality/poverty, 504–532
    end notes, 532
    learning objectives, 505
    overview, 504
    questions, 531–532
    summary, 530–531
Income mobility, definition, 511
Income redistribution, 113–114, 391, 517,
    525–530
    see Regulation
    policies, 517
Increasing-cost industries, 295–296, 299
    definition, 295
Indifference curves
    analysis, 190–197
    definition, 190
    map, definition, 192
Individual choice, 34–35, 72
Individual Retirement Account (IRA), 496
Individual well-being, group well-being
    comparison, 48–50
Industrial union, 458–459
    definition, 458
Industries, definition, 210
Inefficient markets, 116
    outcomes, conditions, 536–539
Inefficient outcomes, 372–373
Inelastic demand
    see Elastic demand, Perfectly elastic demand
    definition, 151
Infant-industry argument, 579–580, 591

Inferior good, 62
Inflation, 10, 134, 471, 519
    rate, 26
Informal markets, 209
Information
    see Imperfect information
    problem, 382
Information costs, 186–187, 198, 318, 559–561
    decisions, 559
    definition, 186
    efficiency considerations, 560–561
    policy considerations, 561
Inheritance taxes, 518
Initial equilibrium, 291–292
Input prices, 68–69, 250–256, 300–302
    see Relative input prices
Input substitution, 413
Interest rate, 226, 486, 492–499
    see Equilibrium
    differences, reasons, 496–498
Intermediaries, 498–499
    see Financial intermediary
Internal rate of return, 500
    definition, 485–486
International competitiveness, 576
International trade, 41, 45, 566–594
    adjustment costs, 575–577
    comparative advantage, 41–45
    end notes, 593–594
    learning objectives, 567
    overview, 566
    questions, 592–593
    summary, 590–592
    trends, 586–587
Internet, regulation, 374–375
Interstate Commerce Commission, 363
Investment, 482–483
    see Computer investment
    decision, 21, 483–484, 487, 498
    definition, 20
    tax credits, 495, 496
Investment benefits, 488–492
Investment costs, 492–499
Investment funds, 480, 493
Investment payoff, 489, 490
Investment spending, 494, 496

Invisible hand, 123–124, 308
    see Market
IRA, *see* Individual Retirement Account
Isocost line, 252–253
    definition, 252
Isoquants, 250–256
    definition, 251
    map, definition, 252

J

Japan, trade, 590–591
Job loss, 580–581
Jobs, *see* American jobs
Jobs Training Partnership Act (JTPA), 526
JTPA, *see* Jobs Training Partnership Act

L

Labor
    demand schedule, 406–407
    service, 114
    significance, 430–431
Labor costs, 431
Labor force nonparticipation, 522, 523
Labor force participation rate, definition, 420
Labor market, 428–455, 475
    see Aggregate labor market, Noncompetitive
        labor markets
    abstraction, 431
    definition, 431
    discrimination, 445–446, 453
        definition, 445
    disequilibrium, 431
    end notes, 455
    equilibrium, 432
    learning objectives, 429
    monopsony, 456
    overview, 428
    questions, 453–454
    skill, 431
    summary, 452–453
Labor opposition, *see* Technological change
Labor supply schedule, 420–421
Labor unemployment, 487
Labor unions, 458–460, 463–468, 477–478
    definition, 458
    goals, 468–471

Labor-intensive production, definition, 250
Labor-management relationships, 465
Large firm behavior, 336–369
    end notes, 369
    learning objective, 337
    overview, 336
    questions, 367–368
    summary, 366–367
Law of increasing opportunity cost, 18
Law of demand, 88, 184, 186
    definition, 60
Law of diminishing returns, 256
    definition, 230
Law of supply, 88
    definition, 68
LDCs, *see* Less-developed countries
Least-cost producer, 42
Least-cost production, 250–256
Least-opportunity-cost producer, 40
Legal barriers, 339–340
Legal cartel, 383
Legal cartel theory of regulation, 382–383
Legal entity, 214
Legal liability, 13, 213
Legal structure, 210–217
Less-developed countries (LDCs), 585, 586
Lifetime incomes, distribution, 511–512
Limited liability, 214
Limited partnership, 214
Liquidity, 497
Loan defaults, 296
Loan length, 497
Long run, definition, 68
Long-run average cost (LRAC), 246–247, 257,
    292, 298–300, 348, 488, 490
    curve, definition, 246
Long-run cost
    see Production
    minimization, 243–246
Long-run decision, 228, 256, 483
    see Short-run/long-run decision
    definition, 227
Long-run economic profits, 316, 340–342, 380
Long-run elasticity, 419
Long-run equilibrium, 291–297, 301, 307, 324,
    422, 423, 442
    output level, 297

position, 322–327
efficiency implications, 325–327
Long-run inefficiencies, 325
Long-run labor supply, 421
Long-run market adjustment, 293
Long-run market equilibrium, 293–294, 304, 309
quantity, 300
Long-run market prices, 307
Long-run price, 326
Long-run production costs, 242–250
Long-run profit maximization, 343–344
Long-run supply, 295–296
curve, 295, 422
Long-term employment commitments, 451
Long-term employment contracts, 450–452
Lorenz curve, 509, 530
definition, 507
Loss, determination, 272–279
Losses, 280–281
see Short-run losses
Love Canal, 5, 534
Low-opportunity-cost production, 41
Low-tech markets, 209
LRAC, see Long-run average cost
Luck, 516
Luxuries versus necessities, 163–165

M

Macroeconomics, definition, 132
Managers, performance, 248–249
Marginal benefit, 96–98, 111, 310, 400, 536, 554
definition, 60
Marginal cost (MC), 67, 96–99, 111, 234, 237, 241, 242, 257, 260, 270–273, 275, 276, 294, 297–300, 302, 324, 400, 486, 536, 554
see Marginal value, Pollution, Production
average cost relationship, 238–239
definition, 66, 235
Marginal external benefit (MEB), 542
Marginal external cost (MEC), 538, 548, 558
Marginal output, 405
Marginal physical product (MP), 243, 244, 252, 254, 256, 403–405, 413, 423
definition, 230
Marginal physical product of labor (MPL), 404
Marginal private benefit (MPB), 538, 541, 542, 544

Marginal private cost (MPC), 538–540, 543, 547, 548, 558
Marginal productivity, 231, 237, 244, 407, 486
theory, 516–517
Marginal rate, see Substitution, Technical substitution
Marginal resource cost (MRC), 406–407, 412, 423, 446, 447, 476
definition, 406
Marginal revenue (MR), 260, 268, 269, 270–273, 275, 276, 280, 297–300, 322, 343, 403, 405, 406
definition, 266
product (MRP), 404–410, 412, 423, 446, 448, 452, 472, 476, 496, 516
Marginal social benefit (MSB), 540, 541, 543, 544, 547, 553
Marginal social cost (MSC), 540–544, 547, 554, 559
Marginal utility (MU), 191, 192, 194, 195, 202–204
comparison, see Price, Total utility
definition, 190
Marginal value, marginal cost relationship, 98–99
Market
cornering, 340–341
invisible hand, 307–308
Market adjustments, 87–88
Market concentration, 356
Market decision making, 134
Market demand, 64–65, 96
see Resources
curve, 64, 94, 410
Market disequilibrium, 104–106
Market economies, 123
definition, 57
Market equilibrium, 54, 72–76, 88, 106, 294
economic efficiency, 94–104
Market failure, 103–104, 372–373, 534, 537
definition, 372
Market forces, 323–325
Market inefficiency, 104–106
Market intervention, 92, 543
Market mechanism, 58–59, 72–88, 100, 111, 122–124, 127, 295, 304, 309, 394–395, 561
dynamics, 291–297
end notes, 90

learning objective, 55
overview, 54
problems, 534–564
questions, 89–90
summary, 88–89
supply and demand, 54–90
Market outcomes, 76, 82, 96, 102, 114, 125, 127, 297, 309, 354, 355, 402
    see Efficient market outcomes, Equilibrium, Inefficient market outcomes
Market performance, measure, 92–119
Market price, 58, 59, 64, 69, 72, 76, 82, 83, 96, 101, 102, 108, 109, 114, 180, 269, 272, 287, 289, 293, 294, 300–304, 310, 573, 574
    see Equilibrium, Long-run market prices
    definition, 59
    short-run response, 293
Market problems, 124–133
Market productivity, 432
Market structure, 216–217, 220
    definition, 216
Market supply, 70–72, 293, 294, 306
    curve, 70
Market wage, 420, 440–441
Market-determined exchange rate, 179
Maturity, definition, 215
MC, see Marginal cost
MEB, see Marginal external benefit
MEC, see Marginal external cost
Median family income, 512
Medicaid benefits, 527
Medical technology, 4, 12
Medical-care providers, 13
Medicare, 520, 525
Medium of exchange, 103
Mergers, 363–364, 379–381
Microeconomic model, applications, 503–594
Microeconomics, definition, 125
Minimum needs, 520
Minimum standard of living, 518
Minimum wage controversy, 448–450
Minimum wage impacts, 450–451
Mistake theory, 4463
Mixed economy, definition, 57
Mobility, 310–312, 318, 319
    see Income mobility, Resource mobility

Mobility costs, 187–188, 198, 311
    definition, 186
Modeling, introduction, 14–22
Models, see Scientific models
Monetary policy, definition, 131
Monopolist, 345, 346
Monopolistic competition, 267, 319–322, 326, 332, 373
    definition, 320
Monopolistic competitor, 326
Monopolistically competitive firms, 322, 326, 331, 332
Monopolistically competitive markets, 320, 321, 323, 327, 328, 330, 331, 344
Monopoly, 220, 267, 342–353, 366, 372
    see Natural monopoly, Regulated monopolies
    definition, 342
    efficiency implications, 346–347
    market, 343
    power, 382
Monopsony, 448, 453, 475–477
    see Labor market
    definition, 446
Motor Carrier Act of 1980, 385
MP, see Marginal physical product
MPB, see Marginal private benefit
MPC, see Marginal private cost
MPL, see Marginal physical product of labor
MR, see Marginal revenue
MRP, see Marginal revenue
MRS, see Substitution
MRTS, see Technical substitution
MSB, see Marginal social benefit
MSC, see Marginal social cost
MU, see Marginal utility
Mutual interdependence, 357, 358
Mutually beneficial exchange, 32–53, 50, 58–59, 94, 108
    end notes, 53
    learning objectives, 33
    overview, 32
    questions, 51–53
    summary, 50–51
Mutually beneficial trade, 569
Mutually interdepence, definition, 354

N

NAFTA, *see* North American Free Trade Agreement

National defense, 581

National income, 218, 431
  definition, 217

National Labor Relations Act of 1935, 464–465, 478

National Restaurant Association, 449

National security, 112

Natural Gas Policy Act (NGPA), 385–386

Natural monopoly, 347–353, 367
  regulation, 350–353
  rethinking, 352–353

Necessities, *see* Luxuries versus necessities

Negatively sloped demand curve, 60–61, 267, 327

Net gain, 99, 106
  definition, 35

New products, 490

NGPA, *see* Natural Gas Policy Act

Noncompetitive firms, 125

Noncompetitive labor markets, 446–448

Nonequalizing wage differences, 441
  definition, 438

Nonexcludability, 554

Non-health care goods, 18

Nonmarket decision making, 120

Nonprice competition, 386–387, 391
  definition, 327

Nonrivalry, 554

Nonunion labor, 474

Nonunionized industry, 473

Nonworking poor, 523

Normal goods, 62

Normal profit, 256, 279
  definition, 226

Normative issues, 11–13

Normative position, 12

Norris-La Guardia Act of 1932, 464

North American Free Trade Agreement (NAFTA), 4, 5, 46, 47, 80–81, 575, 583–585, 591

O

Offset, 563

Oligopolistic firms, 358, 365

Oligopoly, 267, 353–358, 364–366, 372
  characteristics, 354–356
  definition, 353
  market concentration, 355–356

OPEC, *see* Organization of Petroleum Exporting Countries

Open shop, definition, 466

Operating expenses, 350

Opportunity cost, 8, 14, 18, 22, 44, 48, 50, 59, 123, 228, 307, 329, 423, 482, 493, 545, 568
  see Consumption, Environmental quality, Law of increasing opportunity cost, Output, Production
  definition, 7
  ratios, 570, 571

Opportunity-cost producer, 571

Organization of Petroleum Exporting Countries (OPEC), 359, 362, 411, 421, 587

Organized labor, 464–465

Output, opportunity costs, 67

Output decision, 270, 272, 340

Output level, *see* Long-run equilibrium, Profit-maximizing output level

Output prices, 69–70, 324

Output-cost relationship, 270

Output-revenue relationship, 270

P

Partial equilibrium, 313
  analysis, definition, 306

Partnership, 213–214, 217, 220
  definition, 213

Patent, definition, 338

Payoff matrix, 360

Pension funds, 477

Perfect competition, 309–310, 312, 336
  definition, 286

Perfect competition model, 284–315
  end notes, 315
  learning objectives, 285
  overview, 284
  questions, 313–315
  summary, 312–313

Perfectly competitive firm, 326, 405
  short-run equilibrium, 287–289

Perfectly competitive labor market model, 460

Perfectly competitive markets, 287, 290, 291, 295, 304, 319, 327, 332, 344, 358
    characteristics, 286–287
    cost changes, 300–304
    demand changes, 291
    model, 308–312
    resource allocation, 307
Perfectly competitive resource markets, 406
Perfectly elastic demand, definition, 151
Perfectly inelastic demand, definition, 151
Personal income taxes, 220
Personal taxes, 510
Physical capital, 480
Physical product, 404
Point elasticity, *see* Demand
Political behavior, complications, 562
Political decision makers, 136
Political decision making, 112
Political self-interest, 139–140
Politicians as suppliers, 137–139
Pollution
    see Environmental pollution
    marginal costs, 548
    social problem, 544
Pollution-control policies, 547–552
    direct regulation, 547–548
    incentives-based mechanisms, 548–552
Pollution-control technologies, 552
Positive issues, 11–13
Positively sloped supply curve, 66–68
Poverty, 530
    see Antipoverty policy, Income
    equality/poverty
    causes, 521–524
    definition, 518
    income, 519
    overstatement, 520–521
    rates, 529
    programs controversy, 188–189
    (U.S.), 518–525
PPF, *see* Production possibilities frontier
Present value (PV), 485, 486, 498, 499
    see Future sum
    definition, 484
Price, 186–187
    adjustments, 423
    consumer response, 154–158
    marginal utility comparison, 201–203

Price ceilings, 92, 106, 117
    definition, 104
Price changes, 146–160
Price controls, 106–111
Price and cost, separation, 387–388
Price discrimination, 157–158
    definition, 157, 352
Price elasticity, 154–158, 163, 412–414
    see Demand, Resource price elasticity,
        Resources, Supply, Tax incidence
    coefficient, 149–150
    slope, difference, 151–154
    substitutes availability, 161–162
Price equalization, *see* Trade
Price floors, 92, 106, 117
    definition, 104
Price leadership, 359–361, 367
    definition, 359
Price mechanism, 107
Price reduction, 268
Price searchers, 265, 267, 280
Price support system, 110
Price takers, 265, 269, 280, 287
Price-output equilibrium, 103
Price-quantity change, 148
Price-searching firms, 267–269, 274
    definition, 267
    profit maximization, 271–272
Price-taking firms, 265–267, 269, 272, 276
    definition, 265
    profit maximization, 270–271
    short-run supply curve, 289–290
Price-taking producers, 304
Pricing decisions, 340
Prime rate, 496
Prisoner's dilemma, 360
Private benefits, 124, 126, 128
Private goods, 553
    definition, 129
Process of adjustment, 76
Producer surplus, 116
    definition, 101
Product differentiation, 320, 321, 328–331, 359, 363
    see Imagined product differentiation, Real
        product differentiation
    definition, 319
Product market, 421

Product price, 404–406
Product supply, 305
Production
    see Goods, Least-cost production
    decision, 66–72, 275–277
    efficiency, 297–304
    function, 229–232, 234, 243, 251, 256, 403
        definition, 229
    long-run costs, 339
    marginal costs, 108
    opportunity cost, 307, 338
    process, 309, 338, 414
        see Short-run production process
        control, 338–339
    products, control, 338–339
    total costs, 232–233, 256
        definition, 226
Production costs, 104, 127, 224–259, 297–304,
    339, 364, 392, 430, 475, 488
    see Long-run production costs
    end notes, 259
    learning objectives, 225
    overview, 224
    questions, 257–259
    summary, 256–257
Production possibilities frontier (PPF), 14–22, 23,
    28, 29, 34–37, 43, 44, 482, 483
    social choice, 16–19
Production process, 413
    variable inputs, 234
Productive efficiency, 36
Productivity, 302, 419, 432, 433, 477, 488
    see Marginal productivity, Market
        productivity, Worker productivity
    definition, 490
    growth, 490–492
Productivity-enhancing capital, 493
Products
    see New products, Production
    invention, 208–209
Professional sports, 440–441
Profit, 217–220
    see Aggregate profits, Corporate profits,
        Normal profit
    definition, 66, 217
    determination, 272–279
    levels, variations, 218–220

maximization, 224
seekers, 66
Profit maximization, 260–282
    see Long-run profit maximization, Price-
        searching firms, Price-taking
        firms, Short-run profit
        maximization
    end notes, 282
    learning objectives, 261
    overview, 260
    questions, 281–282
    summary, 279–281
Profit opportunities, 418
Profitability, 419
    see American business
Profit-maximizing decision, 356
Profit-maximizing firm, 279, 485
Profit-maximizing level, 343, 543
Profit-maximizing output level, 273
Progressive taxation, 511
Prohibition, 164–165
Property resources, *see* Common-property
    resources
Property rights, 103, 536–537, 549, 559, 562
    definition, 102, 373, 536
Proprietorship, 217
    see Sole proprietorship
Protectionism, 582–583
Public choice, economics, 134–140
Public decision making, 135
Public enterprises, 395
    definition, 374
Public goods, 131, 534, 536, 552–556, 563
    definition, 130, 552
    end notes, 564
    existence, 129–131
    learning objectives, 535
    optimal quantity, determination, 553–554
    overview, 534
    policy prescriptions, 555–556
    questions, 563–564
    summary, 562–563
Public policy, 525
    challenge, 561
Public smoking, 132–133
Public-goods dimension, 458
PV, *see* Present value

Q

Quantity demand, 146–160
Quotas, 577–579, 590
   see American jobs
   definition, 577

R

Rate of interest, *see* Interest rate
Rate of return, 487
   see Internal rate of return
   definition, 484
Rate-of-return regulation, 367
   definition, 350
Rational behavior, 290–291
Rational decision maker, definition, 8
Rationality, 8
Rationing device, 56–59
Rationing mechanisms/behavior, 54, 57–58
Rationing by queue, 57
Real product differentiation, 333
   definition, 329
Real-world economies, 102
Recession, 589
Redistribution, 36
Redistributionist policies, 512
Reduced costs, 488–490
Regulated monopolies, 216
Regulation
   competition reduction, 389–391
   efficiency reduction, 389–391
   income redistribution, 387–389
Regulatory capture, 381
Relative input prices, change effects, 254–256
Relative wages, 436–438
Relocation services, 508
Rent control, 106
   laws, 111
Rental housing, 106–108
Research & development (R&D), 365, 389, 488, 489
Reservation wage, definition, 438
Resource, definition, 6
Resource allocation, 44
   see Perfectly competitive markets
Resource constraint, 15, 16, 34

Resource demand
   elasticity, 473
   price elasticity, definition, 411
   schedule, definition, 402
   short-run elasticity, 423
Resource immobility, 338–342, 438
Resource market, equilibrium, 421–423
Resource markets, theory, 400–426
   end notes, 426
   learning objectives, 401
   overview, 400
   questions, 424–426
   summary, 423–424
Resource mobility, 312, 325
   definition, 415
Resource price elasticity, determinants, 412–414
Resource prices, determinants, 402
Resource scarcity, 56, 307
Resource supply, 414–419
   function, 415
   price elasticity, 424
Resources, 224
   see Financial resources
   control, 338
   demand, price elasticity, 411
   firm demand, 402–407
   market allocation, 534
   market demand, 407–410
   overallocation, 540
   stock, increasing, 20–21
   supply, 414–421
Retained earnings, definition, 215
Retirement income, 512
Return to capital, *see* Capital
Revenue requirement, definition, 350
Revenues, 219, 260–282
   see Firm, Total revenue
   end notes, 282
   learning objectives, 261
   overview, 260
   questions, 281–282
   summary, 279–281
Risk taking, 515
Riskiness, 208
Robinson–Patman Act of 1936, 377
Rule of reason, definition, 377

S

Savings & loan associations (S&Ls), 139, 498

Scarcity, 14, 16, 172
    see Resource scarcity
    choices, 56–57

Scatter diagram, 26

Science, progress, 11–13

Scientific models, 10–11

Secret agreements, 361, 367

Securities market, definition, 216

Security, definition, 216

Senile-industry argument, definition, 580

Service competition, 386–387

Service costs, 497

Shares of stock, definition, 215

Sherman Antitrust Act, 377, 378

Short run, definition, 68

Shortage, 87, 111
    definition, 73

Short-run average total cost (SRATC), 240–242, 247, 489

Short-run capacity, 240

Short-run cost, 271, 302

Short-run cost functions, 239–242

Short-run costs, determinants, 241–242

Short-run decision, 228, 256
    definition, 227

Short-run economic profits, 293, 310, 327, 345, 346

Short-run equilibrium, *see* Perfectly competitive firm

Short-run losses, 295

Short-run production process, 228–242

Short-run profit maximization, 269–272, 309, 320–322, 343–346, 356–358

Short-run profits, 295, 312

Short-run resource supply curves, 417

Short-run supply, 417
    curve, *see* Price-taking firm
    elasticity, 419

Short-run/long-run decision, comparison, 227–228

Shutdown, 288, 289

Shutdown point, definition, 276

Sin taxes, 158

Skilled labor, 588, 589

S&Ls, *see* Savings & loan associations

Slope, *see* Price elasticity

Small firm behavior, 316–335
    endnotes, 335
    learning objectives, 317
    overview, 316
    questions, 334–335
    summary, 332–334

Smith, Adam, 9, 10, 124, 308

Smoking, *see* Public smoking

Social benefits, 102, 124–126, 128
    see Decision making, Demand curve
    definition, 540

Social choice, 16–19

Social costs, 102
    see Decision making, Supply
    definition, 540

Social goals, 11–13, 111–113

Social Security, 430, 506, 512, 520, 525–526
    Administration, 519
    disability payments, 527

Social perspective, 49

Social welfare, 544

Social well-being, 102

Society
    economic well-being, 139–140
    gain, 96–101
    inefficiency, 111–116

Sole proprietorship, 210–214, 220
    definition, 210

Special-interest group, 138, 140
    definition, 137

Specialization, 22, 103, 574, 583
    potential costs, 47–48

Spillover effects, 475
    definition, 126

SRATC, *see* Short-run average total cost

SSI, *see* Supplemental Security Income

Stagnation, 466–468

Stock, *see* Shares of stock

Stockholders, 215, 218
    see Common stockholders

Strike, 460, 467, 475
    definition, 459
    logicality, 462–463

Substitutes
    see Price elasticity

definition, 62
time/availability, 163
Substitution
   see Input substitution, Technical substitution
   effects, 182–184, 195–198, 420
      definition, 182
   marginal rate (MRS, 178, 187, 190–193, 195, 198
      definition, 177
Substitution in consumption, 412, 413
Sunk costs, 256, 277–279, 366
   definition, 228
Superfund, 19
Supplemental Security Income (SSI), 520, 527, 529
Suppliers, *see* Politicians as suppliers
Supply, 66–72
   see Excess supply, Firm supply, Long-run
      supply, Market supply, Resource supply,
      Resources
   analysis, 99
   changes, 77–87
   curve, 67, 70, 82, 83, 96, 99, 159, 290, 414, 435, 447, 548
      see Long-run supply, Market supply
         curve, Positively sloped supply
         curve, Price-taking firm
     factors, 68–72
      social costs, 96
   decisions, *see* Dynamic economy
   price, 101
   price elasticity, 168
      definition, 414
   schedule, *see* Labor supply schedule
Supply and demand, 86–87, 106, 456
   see Market mechanism
   conditions, 318
Support price, 109
Surplus
   see Consumer surplus, Producer surplus
   definition, 75

T

Taft-Hartley Act, 466, 478
Targeted Jobs Tax Credit, 526
Tariffs, 577–583, 585, 590, 591
   arguments, 579–583

bargaining chip, 581–582
   definition, 577
Tax credits, *see* Investment
Tax incidence, price elasticity, 158–160
Tax revenues, 556
Tax treatment, 497
Taxi decontrol, 332–333
TC, *see* Total cost
Technical substitution, marginal rate (MRTS), 251–253, 255
   definition, 251
Technological change, 21–22, 302–304
   labor opposition, 492–493
Technology, 21, 68, 69, 250, 441, 489, 551
   see Medical technology
Tennes*see* Valley Authority (TVA), 375
Terms of trade, 590
   definition, 44
TFC, *see* Total fixed costs
Thoreau, Henry, 34, 36–41, 45, 46
Threat effect, definition, 473
Thrift institutions, 59
Through-plane service, 392
Time series graphs, 27
Time value of money, definition, 484
Total costs (TC), 220, 228, 253, 254, 264, 273, 322, 344, 412
   see Average total cost, Production
   definition, 232
Total fixed costs (TFC), 233, 234
Total income, 162
Total revenue (TR), 154–158, 217, 224, 262, 264, 268, 273, 277
   definition, 154, 266
Total utility, marginal utility comparison, 200–201
Total variable cost (TVC), 276, 287
TR, *see* Total revenue
Trade, 22, 48
   see International trade, U.S. trade
   balance, 585–590
      definition, 586
   barriers, reduction, 583–585
   deficit, 590
      definition, 586
   gains, 45–46, 94, 571–575
   price equalization, 571–574
   surplus, definition, 586

technical analysis, 574–575
terms, 570–571
    changing, 577–585
theory, 568–577
Trade unions, 456–479
    end notes, 479
    learning objectives, 457
    overview, 456
    questions, 478–479
    restrictions, 439
    summary, 477–478
Training, 451–452
Transaction costs, 46–47, 58, 198, 539
    see Demand
    definition, 46, 185
Transferable pollution permit, 563
    definition, 549
Transitional wage differences, 442
Transportation costs, 67, 311
Trunk airlines, 386
Trusts, 381
    definition, 376
TVA, *see* Tennessee Valley Authority
TVC, *see* Total variable cost
Tying contracts, 377

U

Unemployment, 10, 13, 134, 408, 423, 432, 450, 475, 521–523, 576
    see Labor unemployment
    compensation, 506, 508
    insurance, 430
    rate, 26, 520
Unfair competition, 106
Union decision making, 469–471
Union membership (U.S.), 463–468
Union power, policies, 473–474
Union scale, 471
Union shop, definition, 466
Unions, 475
    effects, 475–477
    employment impact, 471–473
    wages impact, 471–474
Unit cost, 256
Unitary elastic demand, 151
United Auto Workers (UAW), 304, 458, 467
United Farm Workers, 468

Unrestricted monopoly, 347
Unskilled labor, 588
U.S. Bureau of the Census, 506
U.S. Chamber of Commerce, 449
U.S. Environmental Protection Agency (EPA), 551
U.S. General Accounting Office (GAO), 391, 392
U.S. Patent and Trademark Office, 339
U.S. Postal Service, 375
U.S. trade, 587–589
Utility function, 190
    definition, 175
Utility maximization, 194–195, 200
    theory, 180
Utility-maximizing condition, 178–181, 184, 185, 198
    definition, 179

V

Value, 30, 31, 50
    see Choice/value, Future value, Present value
Value of money
    see Time value of money
    definition, 103
Variable cost, 234, 241, 275, 277, 279, 287
    see Average variable cost, Total variable cost
    definition, 233
Variable input, 242, 279
    see Production process
    average product, definition, 231
Vertical merger, 377, 379
    definition, 363
Voters as consumers, 135–137

W

Wage determination, 432–434
Wage differences, 428, 435, 437–439
    see Disequilibrium, Transitional wage
        differences
    disequilibrium, 441–442
    equalization, 434–438, 452
    explanation, 434–442
    nonequalization, 438–441, 452–453
        skills, 438–439
Wage differential, 436, 472
Wage earners, 522
Wage premium, 436

Wages, 48, 106, 408, 430, 475
 see Market wage, Minimum wage controversy,
  Relative wages, Reservation wage
 government restrictions, 440–441
 impact, *see* Unions
Wagner Act, 464–465
Walden Pond, 37–41
Wealth, transfers, 515–516
Welfare
 see Economic welfare
 caseloads, 529
 dilemma, 527
 maximization, 45
 policy, 135

Well-being, *see* Family income, Individual
 well-being, Society
Wheeler-Lea Act of 1938, 377
Wood, electricity source, 550–551
Work incentives, 452
Work sharing, 472
Worker preferences, 436–438
Worker productivity, 477
Workfare programs, 528
Working poor, 523
 taxation, 525–526
World Wide Web, 375